EASTERN EUROPE

EASTERN EUROPE

An Introduction to the People, Lands, and Culture

VOLUME 2

EDITED BY RICHARD FRUCHT

Santa Barbara, California • Denver, Colorado • Oxford, England

Library of Congress Cataloging-in-Publication Data
Eastern Europe : an introduction to the people, lands, and culture / edited by Richard Frucht.
p. cm.
Includes bibliographical references and index.
ISBN 1-57607-800-0 (hardback : alk. paper) — ISBN 1-57607-801-9 (e-book)
1. Europe, Eastern. 2. Europe, Central. 3. Balkan Peninsula.
I. Frucht, Richard C., 1951–

DJK9.E25 2005
940'.09717—dc22

2004022300

This book is also available on the World Wide Web as an eBook. Visit abc-clio.com for details.

ABC-CLIO, Inc.
130 Cremona Drive, P.O. Box 1911
Santa Barbara, California 93116-1911
This book is printed on acid-free paper.

Manufactured in the United States of America

Contents

Eastern Europe

Volume 1: The Northern Tier

Volume 2: Central Europe

Volume 3: Southeastern Europe

PREFACE

In *The Lexus and the Olive Tree* (Farrar, Straus, and Giroux, 1999) and *Longitudes and Attitudes* (Farrar, Straus, and Giroux, 2002), the award-winning reporter for the *New York Times* Thomas L. Friedman observed that the world has made a remarkable transition during the past quarter century from division to integration. What was once a world of separation, symbolized by the Cold War and "the Wall," evolved, especially with the collapse of the Soviet Union, into a world of globalization and global interconnectedness, symbolized by "the Net." That new reality has led to remarkable changes. Moreover, it is not merely a passing trend; it is a reality that affects every facet of human existence.

Regrettably, however, not everyone has become part of what amounts to a revolution; in some cases, an antimodernism has caused a lag in the developments of the critical trends of democratization and economic change. That gap, epitomized by the difference between the world of the Lexus and that of the olive tree, forms the core of Friedman's analysis of the Middle East, for example. As perceptive as he is of this clash in that region, in many ways Friedman's observations regarding the necessity of seeing the world in a more global and integrated manner are prophetic for many in the West as well. Although Friedman's emphasis is on an antimodernism that creates a gap between the world of the olive tree and the world of the Lexus, preventing interconnectedness from being fully realized, there are other barriers, more subtle perhaps, but no less real, that create gaps in the knowledge of so many areas of the world with which we are so closely linked.

Certainly in the United States, knowledge of other parts of the world is at times regrettably and, some might argue, even dangerously lacking. The events of September 2001 and the actions of a handful of al-Qaeda fanatics are but one example of an inattention to the realities of the post–Cold War world. Despite the fact that the organization of Osama Bin-Laden had long been a sworn enemy of the United States (and others) and his followers had already launched attacks on targets around the globe (including an earlier attempt on New York's World Trade Center), many, if not most, Americans knew very little (if anything) about al-Qaeda, its motives, or its objectives. What is troubling about that limited knowledge is the simple fact that if an organization with such hostile designs on those it opposed could be so overlooked or ignored, what does that say about knowledge of other momentous movements that are not so overtly hostile? In a world that is increasingly global and integrated, such a parochialism is a luxury that one cannot afford.

Although educators have at times been unduly criticized for problems and deficiencies that may be beyond their control, it is legitimate to argue that there are occasions when teaching fails to keep pace with new realities. Language training, for example, hasn't changed much in the United States for decades, even though one can argue that languages critical to the future of commerce and society, such as Japanese, Chinese, or Arabic, are less often taught than other "traditional" languages. Thus the force of tradition outweighs new realities and needs. Such myopia is born out of a curricular process that almost views change as an enemy. Similarly, "Western Civilization" courses, on both the high school and college level, for the most part remain rooted in English and French history, a tunnel-vision approach that not only avoids the developments of globalization or even a global outlook, but also ignores key changes in other parts of Europe as well. Provincialism in a rapidly changing world should only be a style of design or furniture; it cannot afford to be an outlook. In a world of rapid change, curriculum cannot afford to be stagnant.

Such a curriculum, however, especially on the high school level, is often the inevitable by-product of the materials available. When I was asked to direct the Public Education Project for the American Association for the Advancement of Slavic Studies in the early 1990s, I had the opportunity to review countless textbooks, and the regional imbalance (overwhelmingly Eurocentric in presentation, with a continued focus on England and France) present in these books was such that it could lead to a global shortsightedness on the part of students. Despite the fall of the Berlin Wall and the collapse of the Soviet Union, the books usually contained more on obscure French kings that on Kosovo. Educators recognized that, and from their input it was clear that they needed, more than anything else, resources to provide background material so that they could bring to their students some knowledge of changes that only a few years earlier had seemed unimaginable.

This need for general resource works led to the publication of *The Encyclopedia of Eastern Europe: From the Congress of Vienna to the Fall of Communism* (Garland, 2000). Its goal was to provide information on the rich histories of Albania, Bulgaria, Czechoslovakia, Hungary, Poland, Romania, and Yugoslavia. The reception the book received was gratifying, and it has led to this work, which is designed to act in tandem with the information in the *Encyclopedia of Eastern Europe* to offer the general reader a broad-based overview of the entire region running from the Baltic to the Mediterranean. In addition, this book expands the coverage to other areas in the region not addressed in the encyclopedia.

The three volumes of this work cover three groups of countries, each marked by geographical proximity and a general commonality in historical development. The first volume covers the northern tier of states, including Poland and the Baltic states of Lithuania, Estonia, and Latvia. The second volume looks at lands that were once part of the Habsburg Empire: Slovakia, the Czech Republic, Hungary, Slovenia, and Croatia. The third volume examines the Balkan states of Serbia and Montenegro, Bulgaria, Albania, Romania, Macedonia, Bosnia-Hercegovina, and Greece, lands all once dominated by the Ottoman Empire. Each chapter looks at a single country in terms of its geography and people, history, political development, economy, and culture, as well as the challenges it now faces; each also contains short vignettes that bring out the uniqueness of each country specifically and of the area in general. This structure will allow the reader not only to look at the rich developments in each individual nation, but also to compare those developments to others in the region.

As technology makes the world smaller, and as globalization brings humankind closer together, it is critical that regions once overlooked be not only seen but viewed in a different light. The nations of East Central and Southeastern Europe, that is, "Eastern" Europe, are increasingly a vital part of a new Europe and a new world. What during the Cold War seemed incomprehensible to many, namely, the collapse of totalitarianism and the rise of democracy in these countries, is now a reality all should cherish and help nurture; first, though, it has to be understood. It is the hope that this series may bring that understanding to the general reader.

Putting together this work would have been impossible without the scholarship, dedication, professionalism, and patience of the authors. The words are theirs, but the gratitude is all mine. In addition, I would like to thank a number of students and staff at Northwest Missouri State University who helped with the mountain of work (often computer-related) that a project of this size entails. Chief among them is Patricia Headley, the department secretary, who was not only my computer guru but also someone whose consistent good cheer always kept me going. I would also like to thank Laura Pearl, a talented graduate student in English who filled the role of the "general reader" by pointing out what might make sense to a historian but would not make sense to someone without some background in the region. Other students, including Precious Sanders, Jeff Easton, Mitchell Kline, and Krista Kupfer, provided the legwork that is essential to all such projects. And finally, I would like to thank the staff at ABC-CLIO, especially Alicia Merritt, for keeping faith in the project even when delivery of the manuscript did not match initial projections; Anna Kaltenbach, the production editor, for navigating the manuscript through the various stages; the copy editors, Silvine Farnell and Chrisona Schmidt, for their thoughtful and often painstaking work; Bill Nelson, the cartographer; and the photo editor, Giulia Rossi, for creating such a diverse yet balanced presentation.

And finally there are Sue, my wife, and Kristin, my daughter. Words can never express how important they are, but they know.

Richard Frucht
September 2004

INTRODUCTION

The use of the term "Eastern Europe" to describe the geographical region covered here is standard, but it is nevertheless something of a misnomer. The problem is that it not only makes a geographical distinction between this area and "Western Europe"; it also implies a distinction in development, one that ignores the similarities between Western and Eastern Europe and instead separates the continent into two distinct entities. It even suggests that Eastern Europe is a monolithic entity, failing to distinguish the states of the Balkans from those of the Baltic region. In short, it is an artificial construct that provides a simplistic division in a continent that is far more diverse, yet at the same time more closely linked together, than such a division implies.

Western Europe evokes images of Big Ben and Parliament in London, the Eiffel Tower and the Louvre in Paris, the Coliseum and the Vatican in Rome, the bulls of Pamplona in Spain. Eastern Europe on the other hand brings to mind little more than the "Iron Curtain," war in Kosovo, ethnic cleansing in Bosnia, orphanages in Romania, and the gray, bleak images of the Cold War and the Soviet Bloc. Just as colors convey certain connotations to people, so too do the concepts of "Western" and "Eastern" Europe convey very different impressions and mental images. The former is viewed as enlightened, cultured, and progressive; the latter is seen as dark, uncivilized, and static. Western Europe is democratic; Eastern Europe is backward and totalitarian, plagued by the kind of lack of fundamental humanity that leads inevitably to the horrors of Srebrenica.

Some of these stereotypes are not without some degree of justification. Foreign domination—whether German, Habsburg, Ottoman, or Russian (later Soviet)—has left parts of the region in an arrested state of development. All the peoples of the region were for much of the last half-millennium the focus and subjects of others rather than masters of their own destinies. Accordingly, trends found in more favored areas were either delayed or stunted. Albanian nationalism, for example, did not take root until a century after the French Revolution. The economic trends of the West as well as the post-1945 democracy movements (notably capitalism and democracy) are still in their infancy.

But labels are often superficial, and they can blind individuals to reality. Certainly, Tirana would never be confused with Paris. Estonia is not England. At the same time, the Polish-Lithuanian state was at its height the largest empire in Europe. Prague stuns visitors with its beauty no less than Paris; in fact, many remark that Prague is their favorite city in Europe. Budapest strikes people in the same way that Vienna does. The Danube may not be blue, but it does run through four European capitals, not just Vienna (Bratislava, Budapest, and Belgrade being the other three). The painted monasteries in Romania are no less intriguing in their design and use of color than some of the grandiose cathedrals in "the West." The Bulgarian Women's Chorus produces a sound no less stunning than that of the Vienna Boys' Choir. In short, to judge by labels and stereotypes in the end produces little more than myopia.

To dismiss Eastern Europe as backward (or worse, barbaric) is to forget that many of the Jews of Europe were saved during the Inquisition by emigrating to Poland or the lands of the Ottoman Empire. To cite the Magna Carta as the foundation of democracy in England, even though in reality it meant little more than protection for the rights of the nobility, is to ignore the fact that first written constitution in Europe was not found in the "West" but rather in the "East" (Poland). And although backwardness and even barbarity certainly can be found in the recent past in the region, no country in Europe is immune from a past that most would rather forget (the Crusades, the Inquisition, religious wars, the gas chambers of World War II, to name but a few). Myths are comfortable, but they can also be destructive. They can ennoble a people to be sure, but they can also blind them to reality and lead to a lack of understanding.

Eastern Europe is not exotic, and an understanding of it is not an exercise in esoterica. Rather the region has been and will continue to be an integral part of Europe. In one sense Europe became a distinct entity when Christianity, the cultural unifier, spread through the last outposts of the continent. In another sense, it has again become a unified continent with the demise of the last great empire that held sway over so many.

When former president Ronald Reagan passed away in June 2004, the media repeatedly recalled perhaps his most memorable line: "Mr. Gorbachev, tear down this wall," a remark made in 1984 as the American president stood in front of the Berlin Wall. In this case the American leader was referring to the concrete and barbed wire barrier behind him erected in the 1960s by the former Soviet Union to seal off its empire from the West. Yet, in many respects, the modern history of Eastern Europe was one of a series of walls, some physical (as in the case of the Iron Curtain), others geographical (all of the nations in the region were under the domination of regional great powers), and, one could argue, even psychological (the at times destructive influence of nationalism that created disruption and violence and has been a plague in the lands of the former Yugoslavia on numerous occasions in the past century). These walls have often determined not only the fate of the nations of the region but the lives of the inhabitants as well.

The past is the DNA that tells us who we are and who we can be. It is the owners' manual for every country and every people. Without that past there would be no nation and no nationalism. It is that past that provides the markers and lessons for nations and peoples. It gives direction to the present. It provides a bedrock upon which we build our societies. Whether it leads to myths that embody virtues or myths that cover up what we don't wish to acknowledge, it is the shadow that we can never lose. Thus, when each of the nations of East Central and Southeastern Europe was reborn in the nineteenth or twentieth centuries (in some cases twice reborn), the past was the compass directing them to the future.

Nations are a modern concept, but peoples are not. Poland, for example, once a great and influential European state in the Middle Ages, was partitioned in the late eighteenth century, only to rise again, like a phoenix, in 1918. And even when it again fell prey to the domination of outside influences following World War II, it was the people, embodied in Solidarity, the workers' union, who toppled the communist regime. Despite the fact that at one time or another all of the peoples and nations addressed in these volumes were under the rule or direction of a neighboring great power, the force of nationalism never abated.

Nothing is more powerful than an idea. It can inspire, unify, give direction and purpose; it can almost take on a life of its own, even though it may lie dormant for centuries. In his *Ideen zur Philosophie der Geschichte der Menschheit* (Ideas on the Philosophy of the History of Mankind), the eighteenth-century German philosopher Johann Herder captured the essence of nationalism in his analysis of the *Volk* (the people). Herder emphasized that a spirit of the nation (which Georg Hegel, the nineteenth-century German philosopher most noted for his development of the concept of the dialectic of history, later termed the *Volkgeist,* or "spirit of the people") existed that transcended politics. From the point of view of Herder and the other German idealist philosophers, peoples developed distinct characteristics based upon time and place (reflecting the *Zeitgeist,* the "spirit of the time"). Societies were therefore organic, and thus each had to be viewed in terms of its own culture and development. Accordingly, each culture not only was distinct but should recognize the distinctiveness of others, as characteristics of one culture would not necessarily be found in another. To ignore that uniqueness, which gives to each Volk a sense of nobility, would be to ignore reality.

For the peoples of Eastern Europe, language, culture, and a shared past (even if that past was mythologized, or in some cases even fabricated), exactly that spirit of the Volk that Herder, Hegel, and others saw as the essence of society, proved to be more powerful and more lasting than any occupying army or dynastic overlordship. And when modern nationalism spread throughout Europe and for that matter the world in the nineteenth and twentieth centuries, culture became the genesis of national revivals.

For centuries, Eastern Europe served as a crossroads, both in terms of trade and in the migrations (and in some cases invasions) of peoples. The former brought prosperity to some parts of the region, notably the northern and central parts of the belt between the Baltic and Mediterranean seas, while the latter left many areas a mosaic of peoples, who in the age of nationalism came to struggle as much with each other for national dominance as they did with their neighbors who dominated them politically. As the great medieval states in the region, from the Serbian Empire of Stefan Dušan to the First and Second Bulgarian Empires, to the Hungarian and Polish-Lithuanian states, fell to stronger neighbors or to internal difficulties, no peoples were left untouched by outsiders. Greece may have been able to remain outside the Soviet orbit in the 1940s, but for centuries it was a key possession of the Ottoman Empire. Poland may have been the largest state of its time, but it fell prey to its avaricious neighbors, the Russians, Prussians, and Austrians. Yet, despite centuries of occupation, in each case the Volk remained.

One of the dominant elements in modernization has been the establishment of modern nations. While the rise of the modern nation-state was late arriving in Eastern Europe, and some in Eastern Europe had failed to experience in the same manner some of the movements, such as the Renaissance or the rise of capitalism, that shaped Western Europe, it was no less affected by the rise of modern nationalism than its Western neighbors. Despite the divergent and, in some cases, the retarded development of the region in regard to many of the trends in the West, the nations of Eastern Europe in the early twenty-first century are again independent members of a suddenly larger Europe.

The story of Eastern Europe, while often written or at least directed by outsiders, is more than a mere tale of struggle. It is also a story of enormous human complexity, one of great achievement as well as great sorrow, one in which the spirit of the Volk has triumphed (even though, admittedly, it has at times, as in the former Yugoslavia, failed to respect the uniqueness of other peoples and cultures). It is a rich story, which will continue to unfold as Eastern Europe becomes more and more an integral part of Europe as a whole (a fact evident in the expansion of the European Union and NATO into areas of the former Soviet Empire). And in order to understand the story of that whole, one must begin with the parts.

Contributors

VOLUME 1

Terry D. Clark is a professor of political science and the director of the graduate program in international relations at Creighton University. He received his Ph.D. from the University of Illinois at Urbana-Champaign in 1992. A specialist in comparative politics and international relations, he was instrumental in developing Creighton University's exchange program with universities in Eastern Europe. He has published three books and numerous articles devoted to the study of postcommunist Europe. His research interests include the development of democratic institutions and the evolution of public opinion supporting such institutions in Lithuania and Russia.

Mel Huang is a freelance analyst on the Baltic states and is also a research associate with the Conflict Studies Research Centre (CSRC) at the Royal Military Academy, Sandhurst. He previously worked as the primary Baltics analyst for the analytical department of Radio Free Europe/Radio Liberty and served as the Baltics editor of the award-winning online journal Central Europe Review.

Aldis Purs received his Ph.D. in history from the University of Toronto in 1998. He has taught at Vidzeme University College, Wayne State University, and Eastern Michigan University. He is a coauthor of *Latvia: The Challenges of Change* (Routledge, 2001) and *The Baltic States: Estonia, Latvia, and Lithuania* (Routledge 2002) and a contributor to the University of Manchester research project "Population Displacement, State Building, and Social Identity in the Lands of the Former Russian Empire, 1917–1930."

Piotr Wróbel holds the Konstanty Reynert Chair of Polish Studies at the University of Toronto. He received his Ph.D. from the University of Warsaw in 1984. He has been a visiting scholar at the Institute of European History in Mainz, at Humboldt University in Berlin, at the Institute of Polish-Jewish Studies at Oxford, and at the United States Holocaust Memorial Museum in Washington, D.C. He has authored or coauthored some fifty articles and nine books, including *The Historical Dictionary of Poland, 1945–1996* (Greenwood, 1998). He currently serves on the advisory board of *Polin: A Journal of Polish-Jewish Studies,* on the board of directors of the Polish-Jewish Heritage Foundation of Canada, and on the governing council of the American Association for Polish-Jewish Studies.

VOLUME 2

June Granatir Alexander is a member of the faculty of the Russian and East European Studies Program at the University of Cincinnati. In addition to numerous scholarly articles, reviews, and encyclopedia entries, she is the author of two books: *The Immigrant Church and Community: Pittsburgh's Slovak Catholics and Lutherans, 1880–1915* (Pittsburgh, 1987) and *Ethnic Pride, American Patriotism: Slovaks and Other New Immigrants in the Interwar Era* (Temple University Press, 2004).

Mark Biondich is an analyst with the Crimes against Humanities and War Crimes Section of the Department of Justice of Canada. He received his Ph.D. in history from the University of Toronto in 1997 and is the author of *Stjepan Radić, the Croat Peasant Party and the Politics of Mass Mobilization, 1904–1928* (Toronto, 2000), as well as a number of articles and reviews concerning Croatian, Yugoslav, and Balkan history.

András A. Boros Kazai was raised in a proletarian district in Budapest before coming to the United States, where he studied at Kent State University and the University of Pittsburgh. He earned his Ph.D. in history from Indiana University in 1982. He is currently a freelance translator, a researcher-consultant, and an adjunct member of the faculty at Beloit College.

Brigit Farley received her Ph.D. from Indiana University. She is an associate professor of history at Washington State University. A specialist on twentieth-century Russian and European cultural history, and the author of a number of articles, reviews, and encyclopedia entries, she is currently working on the life and death of a Moscow church.

Daniel Miller received his Ph.D. from the University of Pittsburgh, and is a professor of history at the University of West Florida in Pensacola. His research involves Czech and Slovak history, especially between the two world wars, and focuses largely on agrarian political history. He is the author of several chapters and articles along with *Forging Political Compromise: Antonín Švehla and the Czechoslovak Republican Party, 1918–1933* (Pittsburgh, 1999), which has been translated into Czech. He is also one of the coauthors of a volume in Czech on the history of the Slovak and Czech agrarian movement. In the preparation of his chapter, he would like to acknowledge the contributions and suggestions of Gregory X. Ference of Salisbury University, Lenka Kocková and Pavel Kocek (on several aspects of Czech culture and history), Alex Švamberk (on Czech popular music), and Ivan Lalák (on modern architecture).

VOLUME 3

Robert Austin is a lecturer and project coordinator with the Centre for Russian and East European Studies at the University of Toronto. He is also a project manager with Intermedia Survey Institute in Washington, D.C. His current research focuses on interwar Albania and media trends in contemporary Albania. He was aided in the preparation of his chapter by Brigitte Le Normand, who received her M.A. from the University of Toronto and is currently pursuing her Ph.D. in history at UCLA.

Richard Frucht is a professor of history and chair of the Department of History, Humanities, Philosophy, and Political Science at Northwest Missouri State University. He received his Ph.D. from Indiana University in 1980. The author of a number of books and articles on Eastern Europe, most recently he was the editor of *The Encyclopedia of Eastern Europe: From the Congress of Vienna to the Fall of Communism* (Garland, 2000).

Alexandros K. Kyrou is an associate professor of History and the director of the Program in East European Studies at Salem State College. He received his Ph.D. from Indiana University and was a Hanaah Seeger Davis Visiting Research Fellow in Hellenic Studies at Princeton University, a senior research fellow of the Kokkalis Program on Southeastern and East Central Europe at the John F. Kennedy School of Government at Harvard University, and a research scholar at the Institute on Religion and World Affairs at Boston University. He is also the associate editor of the *Journal of Modern Hellenism*.

Katherine McCarthy teaches history at Bradley University and is a research associate in the Russian and East European Center at the University of Illinois, Urbana-Champaign. She completed her Ph.D. in East European history at the University of Pittsburgh in 1996 and has written on peasant issues in the former Yugoslavia.

Nicholas Miller is an associate professor at Boise State University. He has written extensively on the Serbian community in Croatia, Serbian nationalism, and Serbia since 1945, including *Between Nation and State: Serbian Politics in Croatia, 1903–1914* (Pittsburgh, 1997). He is currently completing a manuscript on an intellectual circle in Serbia during the communist era.

James P. Niessen is World History Librarian at Rutgers University in New Brunswick, New Jersey, and Vice President for Research and Publications of H-Net: Humanities and Social Sciences OnLine. He earned a Ph.D. in East European history from Indiana University and taught history at several universities before pursuing a library career since 1994. His published works include more than fifteen studies on modern Romanian and Hungarian history, libraries, and archives.

Aleksandar Panev teaches history and philosophy at Appleby College in Oakville, Canada. He received his B.A. and M.A. degrees from the University of Belgrade and his Ph.D. from the University of Toronto. He is also an associate of the Centre for Russian and East European Studies at the Munk Centre for International Studies at the University of Toronto and has served as a faculty research associate at Arizona State University and the University of Skopje.

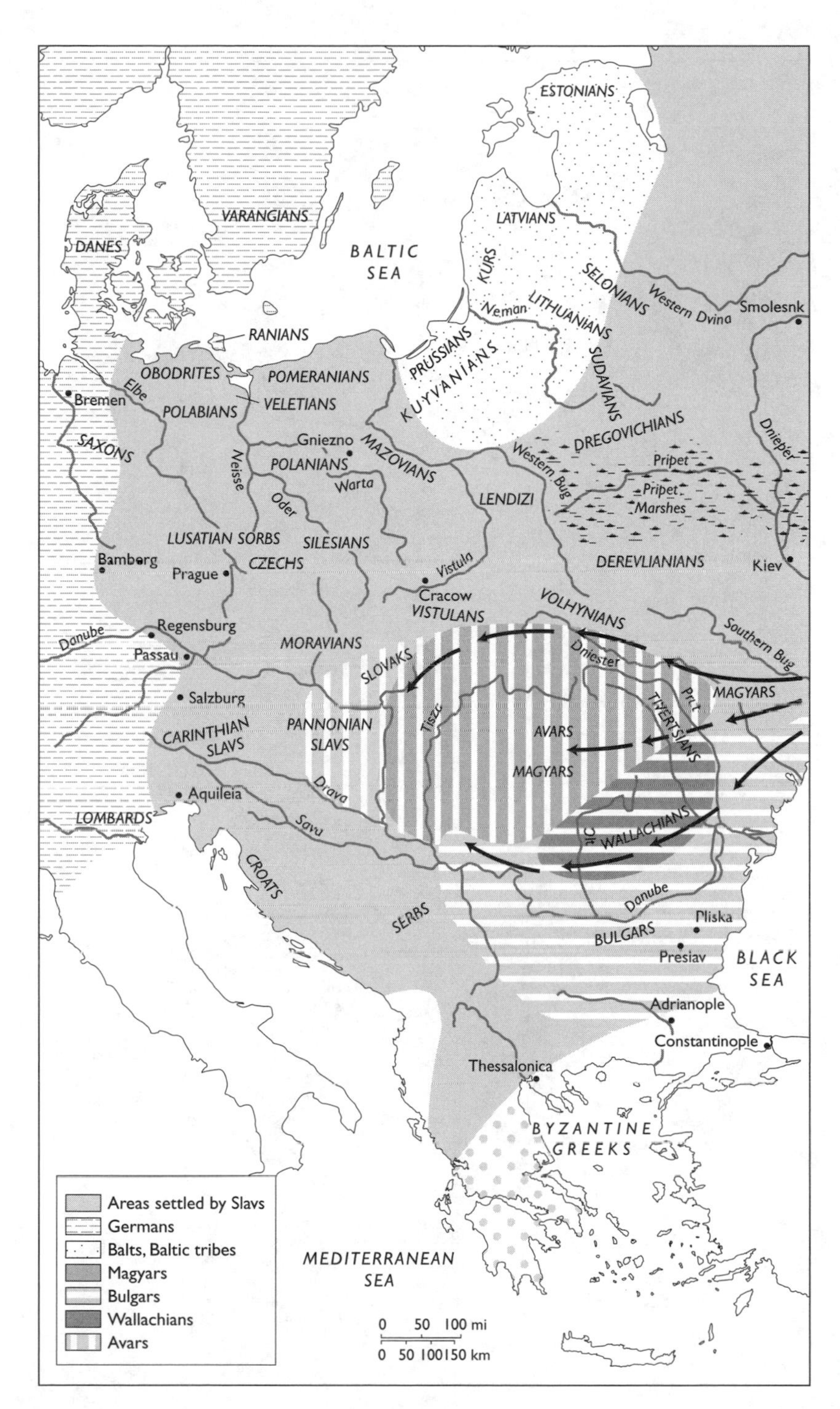

The peoples of Eastern Europe in the ninth century.

Territorial divisions in Eastern Europe in the thirteenth century (at the time of the Mongols).

Eastern Europe in the late sixteenth century.

Eastern Europe after the Congress of Vienna (1815).

Eastern Europe in 1914.

Eastern Europe between the World Wars.

Eastern Europe after World War II

Eastern Europe in 2004.

The Habsburg Monarchy, 1867–1914.

THE CZECH REPUBLIC

DANIEL E. MILLER

LAND AND PEOPLE

Situated in the geographic center of Europe, the Czech Republic encompasses 78,866 square kilometers and is about the size of Vermont, New Hampshire, and Massachusetts combined. The Czech Lands, as historians often term them, consist of three historic provinces: Bohemia (Czech, Čechy) in the west, Moravia (Czech, Morava) in the east, and two small portions of Silesia (Slezsko) in the northern part of the province of Moravia-Silesia. Historically, the state had eight administrative regions: Prague (Czech, Praha; German, Prag), the capital; Central Bohemia; Southern Bohemia; Western Bohemia; Northern Bohemia; Eastern Bohemia; Southern Moravia; and Northern Moravia. The government has recombined the political divisions over the years; in 2000 it created fourteen regions *(kraje),* most named after the cities that serve as administrative centers: Prague, Středočeský (Central Bohemia, with administrative offices in Prague that are distinct from those of the capital city of Prague), Karlovarský (Karlovy Vary; German, Karlsbad), Ústecký (Ústí nad Labem), Liberecký (Liberec; German, Reichenberg), Královéhradecký (Hradec Králové; German, Königgrätz), Pardubický (Pardubice), Plzeňský (Plzeň; German, Pilsen), Jihočeský (Southern Bohemia, with České Budějovice; German, Böhmisch Budweis, as the administrative center), Vysočina (Jihlava), Jihomoravský (Southern Moravia, with Brno as the administrative center), Olomoucký (Olomouc; German, Olmütz), Zlínský (Zlín, known in the communist era as Gottwaldov), and Moravskoslezský (Moravo-Silesia, with Ostrava as the administrative center).

About 10.3 million people inhabit the Czech Republic—Czechs (94.9 percent of the population—Czechs in Bohemia, 81.2 percent; Moravians, 13.2 percent; and Silesians, 0.4 percent), Slovaks (3.1 percent), and the remaining 2 percent Poles (59,400), Germans (48,600), and Roma or Gypsies (32,900, although the actual number may be four times higher). Prague has 1.16 million people and is a typical major European city, with a modern airport and an excellent mass transit system that includes a subway. The second largest city is Brno in Southern Moravia, the capital of Moravia, with nearly 317,000 inhabitants. Other key cities are Ostrava in Northern Moravia (314,000 inhabitants), Plzeň in Western Bohemia (164,000 inhabitants), Olomouc in Northern Moravia (102,000 inhabitants), Liberec in Northern Bohemia (98,000 inhabitants), Hradec Králové in Eastern Bohemia (96,000 inhabitants), České Budějovice in Southern Bohemia (96,000 inhabitants), and Ústí nad Labem in Northern Bohemia (95,000 inhabitants).

The Czechs are historically Roman Catholic but underwent a successful reformation known as the Hussite movement nearly three-quarters of a century before the

The Old Town of Prague. Jan Palach Square and the Philosophical Faculty of Charles University are in the foreground; Týn Church is in the background. (PhotoDisc, Inc.)

birth of Martin Luther, and most Czechs in the fifteenth through the sixteenth centuries were essentially Protestant. In the seventeenth century the Counter-Reformation eradicated Protestantism in the Czech Lands, but it reemerged with religious toleration in the eighteenth century. After World War II, the communists persecuted Protestant and Catholics alike, and church membership dropped precipitously. Jews were present in the Czech Lands from the Middle Ages. In Bohemia they encountered the same blend of toleration and persecution that their coreligionists encountered elsewhere in Central Europe. With the advent of official religious toleration in the eighteenth century and the elimination of restrictions on Jews, some middle-class Jews began to assimilate. Under Nazi occupation, the Jews in the Czech Lands faced renewed persecution, exclusion from society, and extermination, and few remained after the war. According to the latest published statistics (2001), Catholics compose 26.8 percent of the population. There are also small numbers of Orthodox, Byzantine Catholics (also known as Greek Catholics or Roman Catholics, Eastern Rite), and Old Catholics in the republic. Members of churches in the Hussite tradition account for about 4 percent of the population. About 3 percent of the population are adherents of other Protestant sects. There are only 1,300 practicing Jews in the country. A total of 59 percent of the population lacks any religious affiliation, and the religious preference of 8.8 percent of the population is unknown.

The Czech Republic's distinctive diamond-like shape on the map is due to the mountains of the Bohemian Massif, which help form the perimeter of the state. In the northeast, dividing the Czech Republic from Poland are the Sudety (German, Sudeten; English, Sudetes), which consist of the Hrubý Jeseník and Nízký Jeseník Mountains in Moravia and the Krkonoše (German, Riesengebirge; English, Giant Mountains) in Bohemia. In the Krkonoše, close to Trutnov, is the highest peak in the republic, Sněžka (1,602 meters). The Krušné hory (German, Erzgebirge; English, Ore Mountains) in the northwest divide the Czech Republic from the German state of Saxony. The Šumava group, including Český les (German, Böhmerwald; English, Bohemian Forest) and the Šumava Mountains, form the border with the German state of Bavaria and Austria. Between Moravia and Slovakia are the Carpathian Mountains, specifically portions of the Outer Carpathians—from south to north the Biele Karpaty (White Carpathians), Moravskoslezské Beskydy (Moravian-Silesian Beskids), and Javorníky. In the interior are the Bohemian Plateau, the Berounka system of uplands and highlands, which includes the fertile plain of the Labe River, the Central Bohemian

The Czech Language

Czech is a Western Slavic language related to Slovak (its closest linguistic relative), Sorbian (the language of a small Slavic ethnic group scattered in eastern Germany and western Poland), and Polish. It has several dialects, a modern colloquial form, and a modern literary form that dates from the middle of the nineteenth century. Czech uses the Latin alphabet, as does English, with diacritical marks. A haček (as in *č*) has a softening, or palatizing effect on certain letters. With the letters *d* and *t,* sometimes an apostrophe immediately after the letter replaces the haček, strictly for the sake of typographical aesthetics. The *čárka* (acute accent: ´) lengthens vowels. A *kroužek* (°) is used to lengthen a *u (ů)* only when the letter is not in the initial position, when it would receive a čárka (*ú*). The language has a series of dipthongs built with vowels and the letter *j* (e.g., *ej, aj, uj, áj, ůj).* The dipthong *ou* is pronounced like the *ow* in *low;* the dipthong *au,* like the *ou* in *out.* Stress is always on the first syllable, and there is no secondary stress. Czech is essentially phonetic, making pronunciation relatively simple. The language has three genders, each with hard and soft endings. Nouns and pronouns decline in seven cases. Verbs conjugate in five classes and reflect tense, aspect, gender, voice, mood, person, and number. Note that all female last names end in *-ová* (nominative case).

Czech Pronunciation Guide

An asterisk (*) indicates letters only used in foreign words.

á	long *a,* as in *awful*
č	*ch* as, in *champion*
ď	soft *d,* as in *duress*
é	long *e,* as in *edible*
ě	soft *e,* as in *yet*
h	voiced, not merely aspirated
ch	*ch,* as in *Bach*
í	long *e,* as in *eel*
j	*y* as in *yellow*
ň	soft *n,* as in *onion*
ó	long *o,* as in *absorb**
q	*kv**
r	trilled or rolled
ř	simultaneous trilled *r* and *zh,* approximately the *tr* in *tree*
š	*sh,* as in show
ť	soft *t,* as in *tulip*
ú	long *u,* as the *oo* in *brood* (only in initial position)
ů	long *u,* as the *oo* in *brood* (other than initial position)
w	*v**
x	*ks**
ý	long *y,* as the *ee* in *bee*
ž	*zh,* as the *s* in *pleasure*

Upland, the South Bohemian Basins, the Brno system of uplands and valleys, the Bohemian-Moravian Highlands, and the Odra Lowland.

The rivers of the Czech Republic facilitate contacts with its neighbors and place it on the one of the major crossroads between Danubian Europe and the Great Northern European Plain. All the major rivers of Bohemia empty into the Elbe River (Czech, Labe), which flows through Germany to the North Sea. The most important tributary of the Elbe is the Vltava (German, Moldau), which is 433 kilometers long. It begins in the Šumava, supplies the Lipno Reservoir, and turns north toward České Budějovice, where it takes on the Malše River, which begins in Austria and forms part of the border between Austria and the Czech Republic. The Lužnice River flows through Třeboň, a town surrounded with lakes and ponds that have supported a lively fish farming industry since the Middle Ages, passes through the historic city of Tábor, and meets the Vltava at Týn nad Vltavou. The Vltava continues north to Prague, where it gracefully bends around the hills to lend the city a special charm.

Mělník, within view of the legendary dome-shaped Říp Mountain (also visible on clear days from the heights of Prague), is the confluence of the Vltava and the Elbe. Beginning in the Sudety, the Elbe follows a course through the Czech cities of Hradec Králové, Pardubice, Chrudim, Kolín, Poděbrady, Nymburk, Brandýs nad Labem, Mělník (where it meets the Vltava), Roudnice nad Labem, Litoměřice, Ústí nad Labem, and Děčín before heading toward Dresden, the first German city on its way to the North Sea. Moravia's major rivers link it to lands in the south by way of the Danube River. The Morava River begins in the Sudety and flows through Olomouc, Kroměříž (German, Kremsier), Uherské Hradiště, and Hodonín. The Dyje River, which passes through Znojmo, joins the Svratka River, which runs through Brno, at the Nové Mlýny reservoir. The Dyje then progresses toward Břeclav and forms a few miles of border between the Czech Republic and Austria. The confluence of the Dyje and Morava is the intersection of the Czech-Austrian-Slovak border, and the Morava continues, forming the Slovak-Austrian border until it reaches the Danube. The Odra River (German, Oder) begins in the Jeseník Mountains and with its tributary, the Opava, which runs for a few kilometers along the border between the Czech Republic and Poland drains what was once the historic province of Silesia. The major city of this region is Ostrava, which is on the Ostravice, another tributary of the Odra. After flowing through the southern part of Poland, the Odra forms the border between Germany and Poland and empties into the Baltic Sea.

Both maritime and continental effects and elevation influence the climate in the Czech Republic. The low-lying areas, such as Prague, have warm summers and cold winters, while the higher elevations are cooler. Average temperatures in Prague are about -2.7 degrees Celsius in January, generally the coldest month along with February, and around 19.5 degrees Celsius in July, which is the warmest month, along with August. Rainfall is adequate for crops, but Western Bohemia historically receives less rain than do other parts of the country. Most precipitation falls in the winter, although the spring and summer also may be wet. As a result, flooding is a recurrent problem in some areas; the floods that occurred in August 2002 were the worst in recorded history. Climate combines with soils, especially the chernozems (black soils) of the Polabí region, to create favorable conditions for agriculture.

The Czech Republic has a wide range of natural resources. The rich soils support a variety of large-scale agricultural enterprises that grow such crops as wheat, barley, oats, rye, and corn. Also important are root crops, including potatoes and sugar beets; industrial crops, such as rapeseed, sunflower seeds, poppy seed, and flax, along with fodder and vegetables. Livestock farming is focused on pork, cattle, and poultry. Fisheries in Southern Bohemia raise trout and carp, a popular fish and the highlight of the traditional Christmas Eve dinner. The country has a number of mineral resources that support its industrialized economy. There is plenty of coal in the north, which has made the region an important center of manufacturing since the eighteenth century. Other minerals include lead, zinc, tin, copper, peat, graphite, antimony, uranium, manganese, silver, and gold. There is also some natural gas.

The Czech Republic has emerged from the socialist era with a thriving industrialized economy. Its workforce in 2002 was well educated, with 18.6 percent having a basic education, 57.5 percent completing secondary school, and 8 percent having university degrees. In 2002 the unemployment rate was 8.8 percent. The economy had a gross domestic output (GDP) in 2000 of 1,959.5 billion Czech crowns (Kč; the annual average exchange rate for the U.S. dollar in 2000 was 38.59 Kč). The country has a lively import and export business with countries throughout the world, but its most important trading partners are states with developed economies, especially those members of the Organization for Economic Cooperation and Development (OECD) and the European Union (EU). Germany is its single most important trading partner; other countries in order of importance include Slovakia, Austria, Russia, France, Italy, Poland, the United Kingdom, and the United States. In 2000 the Czech Republic imported Kč1,244,243 million while exporting Kč1,121,198 million worth of goods, leaving a negative trade balance of Kč123,045 million.

According to standard international trade classifications (SITC) in 2000, machinery and transportation equipment accounted for the largest amount of imports (40.1 percent), followed by producer goods (20.73 percent), chemicals (11.18 percent), finished goods (10.31 percent), mineral fuels and related products (9.64 percent), food and live animals (4.04 percent), raw materials (3.17 percent), beverages and tobacco (5.94 percent), animal and vegetable oils, fats, and waxes (0.21 percent), and commodities and miscellaneous items (0.03 percent). The value of specific imports in 2002 in order of importance included automatic data processing machines, natural gas, pharmaceuticals, crude oil, automobiles, telecommunication equipment, plastics, rolled stock of iron and steel, fruits and nuts, chip-removing metal-working machines, iron ore, vegetables, television receivers, leather footwear, pig iron, synthetic rubber, cotton, refrigerators and freezers, sheet glass, wool, vegetable fat and oil, washing machines, tobacco, fish, natural rubber, nonalcoholic beverages, cocoa, zinc, and copper.

Exports in order of importance were machinery and transportation equipment (44.46 percent), producer goods (25.43 percent), finished goods (12.53 percent), chemicals (7.1 percent), raw materials (3.53 percent), mineral fuels and related products (3.05 percent), food and live animals (2.94 percent), beverages and tobacco (0.75 percent), animal and vegetable oils, fats, and waxes (0.11 percent), and commodities and miscellaneous items (0.09 percent).

In 2002 specific exports from the Czech Republic in order of importance based on value included automobiles, paper and cardboard, tires, electrical power, rolled stock, coal, pharmaceuticals, tubes and pipes, chip-removing metal-working machines, fabrics of synthetic fibers, timber, artificial casings, iron and steel scrap, coke and semi-coke, beer (mainly from Plzeň, České Budějovice, and Prague),

The Pattern of Interrupted State Building

Similar to other ethnic groups in East Central Europe and the Balkans, the Czechs have experienced a discontinuous state-building process that has resulted in major shifts in the nature of politics that often correlate with significant abrupt social, cultural, or economic transformations. While some of these dramatic changes may have been positive, many have been disastrous. Historic discontinuity has left its mark on the Czech political culture, that is, the way in which Czechs perceive their state. The average Czech is likely to be cynical about governments, leaders, major new state policies, and official ideologies used to justify state actions. Most Czechs accept some form of Christianity, although the Hussite revolution of the fifteenth century, the excesses of the Counter-Reformation in the seventeenth century, and the persecution of religion under the communists from 1948 until 1989 has engendered in Czechs a strong current of ambivalence toward religion. Still, Czechs count on the state to provide an advanced, complex system of social services similar to those found in the EU, expectations rooted in the legacy of the Czechoslovak First Republic and the socialist era. The drama of the twentieth century has left a deep impression on Czechs. They desire stability for their state, but they are skeptical about the permanency of regimes, institutions, and allies. In the international arena, Czechs view their state as a small player at best, or in the worst case a pawn of other powers, particularly strong neighbors.

The Czech mind-set evolved over many centuries. The Kingdom of Bohemia emerged in the early Middle Ages to become a powerful regional player under the rulers of the native Přemyslid and then the Luxemburg dynasty. In the first part of the fifteenth century it suffered from the Hussite Wars. At the end of the conflict, Bohemia became the first European country where those professing variations of Christianity could live side by side. The subjects of the Kingdom of Bohemia did not perceive the accesion of the Habsburgs, who ruled in Austria and added Bohemia and Hungary to their possessions in 1526, as anything more than another change in dynasties. Their perception altered, however, when the Catholic Habsburgs sought to integrate Bohemia into their domains and persecuted Protestants. When the Bohemian estates rebelled in 1618 and lost the Battle of White Mountain in 1620, the Habsburgs treated Bohemia as a conquered territory, eliminated their enemies within the nobility, suppressed all Protestant religions, and ruled the country from Vienna. In the nineteenth century the Czechs, armed with notions of liberalism and nationalism, hoped to restore Bohemia's lost legal status. The failed revolution of 1848 was one manifestation of this hope. After the Austro-Hungarian *Ausgleich* (Compromise) of 1867, when the Austrian political system took on the character of a developing democracy, the Czechs had renewed optimism that the state would better serve their interests, perhaps in a monarchy that placed Bohemia on an equal footing with Hungary and Austria.

In the twentieth century the Czechs faced a number of discontinuities in state building—nearly every generation experienced at least one change in the state's structure. Near the end of World War I, the Czechs abandoned their hopes for a reformed, fully democratic Habsburg monarchy and united with Slovaks and Rusyns to embark on a new experiment—an independent state. The Czechoslovak First Republic was a democracy that treated its minorities well, although the Germans, Hungarians, Poles, and even Slovaks aired valid complaints. The machinations of

(continues)

milk and milk products, tractors, semi-finished iron and steel products, leather footwear, fertilizer, lignite, vegetables, hops, butter, sugar, bicycles, cement, wheat, motorcycles, gravel, and beef. The Czech Republic produces high-quality art glass and stemware, porcelain, pianos, and toys, although they are not significant export factors.

Tourism is an important component of the Czech economy. In 2002 alone, approximately 4.6 million foreign tourists visited the Czech Republic. More than 2.2 million foreigners traveled to Prague to see the imposing Hrad or Prague Castle, wander through its twisting and narrow medieval streets, visit its galleries and museums, attend its many concerts, find repose in its cathedrals and churches, and marvel at its Gothic and baroque architecture. (Prague also has phenomenal examples of Romanesque, classical, art nouveau, cubist, socialist realist, modern, and postmodern structures.) Not just Prague but nearly each city and town can boast of an architectural and historical heritage. Several UNESCO world cultural heritage sites are located in the Czech Republic. All of Prague's major attractions are on the list—the Hrad, Strahov monastery, Old Town and its famed Jewish Quarter, Lesser Town, and New Town. Other sites in Bohemia are the city of Kutná Hora, with its St. Barbara Church and the royal palace and mint in the Italian Court (Vlašský dvůr); Holašovice, where charming "peasant baroque" homes line the village square; and Český Krumlov, a town on the Vltava with Renaissance and baroque architecture. On the register from Moravia are the

(continued)

Adolf Hitler brought an end to the state in 1938, and Czech society developed in the shadow of Nazi Germany. The Czechoslovak Second Republic had a short existence as a German ally from 1938 to 1939, when Germany incorporated the Czech Lands into the German Reich as the Protectorate of Bohemia and Moravia, created an independent Slovakia, and returned Ruthenia to Hungary. During World War II, the future of the Czech nation was precarious, given Hitler's desire for eastward expansion and his policy of subjugation and elimination of Slavs. After the war, Czechoslovakia reemerged with new hopes for permanency and undisturbed development. The state expelled the Germans and many of the Hungarians to ensure that irredentist minorities would never again negatively influence Czechoslovak politics. It also enacted political, social, and economic reforms to correct some of the ills of the First Republic. The Third Republic, however, faced a new threat because of its location in the European "shatter zone" of the Cold War. In 1948 the Czechoslovak Communist Party, with the support of the Soviet Union, came to power in Prague. State ownership of industry and commerce, the development of agricultural collectives, and economic planning combined with the imposition of totalitarian rule under the Communist Party to yield disastrous results. After an attempt at reform in 1968, which the invasion of the Soviet Union and its allies in the Warsaw Pact brought to a halt, Czechoslovakia faced two more decades of political and cultural restrictions along with economic stagnation. The reactionary Communists' adoption of a federal constitution to satisfy Slovaks, a product of the reformist period, was little more than window dressing.

The Velvet Revolution of 1989 that overthrew the Communist Party's monopoly of power was accompanied with unbridled optimism, which soon diminished. The population gained a pluralistic, representative democratic political system but now faced the legacy of communism—ecological damage, outdated industries, and a poor work ethic. The Slovaks alleged continued unfair treatment, and leading politicians demanded independence, achieving it peacefully on 1 January 1993. The majority of Czechs and Slovaks felt betrayed that their leaders had brokered the so-called Velvet Divorce without a referendum, reinforcing cynicism in both countries about government leaders. The independent Czech Republic continued to face new hurdles after 1993. Economic restructuring progressed slowly, and it was fraught with closings of inefficient factories, tunneling schemes, lack of transparency, and other failings. Politicians—those who had not left public service in disgust or as a result of some scandal—lost the confidence of the population. Yet there were some reasons for optimism. The Czech Republic has had a stable political system, and its president until 2003, Václav Havel, achieved worldwide respect and recognition. The Czech Republic has had a relatively low overall unemployment rate and plenty of investment from abroad. Membership in the North Atlantic Treaty Organization (NATO) offers the Czech Republic a reliable network of defense. Its most recent significant step occurred in 2004 with its entry into the European Union.

archbishop's palace and medieval town center of Kroměříž; the Holy Trinity Column in Olomouc; the baroque town of Telč; the baroque-Gothic St. Jan Nepomuk Pilgrimage Church in Zelená Hora, Žďár and Sázavou, by the Bohemian architect Jan Blažej (Giovanni) Santini-Aichel (1677–1723), who came from a family of Italian masons in Prague; the palaces at Valtice and Lednice; and the palace at Litomyšl. The newest UNESCO world cultural heritage site added in 2003 is the centuries-old Jewish ghetto in Třebíč, Moravia. Many tourists gravitate to the more than thirty spas throughout the country, the most famous being in Karlovy Vary, Mariánské Lázně, Františkovy Lázně, and Janské Lázně.

The country has a large number of national parks, protected landscape areas, nature reserves, and nature monuments. It also boasts of several UNESCO biosphere reserves: Krkonoše, Šumava, Bílé Karpaty, Křivoklátsko in Central Bohemia, Pálava in Southern Moravia, and the lakes of Třeboňsko in Southern Bohemia. Considering that a third of the country is covered with largely coniferous forests, stunning vistas and romantic woodland paths abound. The Czech Republic also boasts of many unusual natural features. There are the Soos peat bogs in the Ore Mountains. In the Český ráj (Bohemian Paradise) and elsewhere in Northern Bohemia are sandstone formations, and the Pravčická brána natural bridge is on the Labe River near Hřensko. Volcanic domes grace the forests of Lužické hory, and over a thousand caves are scattered in the Moravský kras area. A steppe lies above a lush valley at Mohelnik. A massive basalt outcropping casts its spell over the landscape at Panská skála just outside Kamenický Šenov. The republic lacks only a desert and a seacoast. In the winter, the main sporting attraction in the countryside is skiing. Though the courses are not as challenging as those in Alpine regions, skiers from all over Europe flock to the Czech Republic to join Czechs on the slopes. No matter what draws them to the Czech Republic, tourists drink Czech beer and sample such traditional dishes as pork,

Hradcany Castle, Prague, Czech Republic, with St. Nicholas in the Lesser Town (foreground, left). (Courtesy of Daniel Miller)

sauerkraut, and the ubiquitous Czech bread dumpling *(vepřoknedlozeli)*. Afterward they enjoy crepes *(palačinky)* or pastries for desert.

HISTORY

SETTLEMENT OF THE SLAVS AND EARLY RECORDED HISTORY

During the great movement of Indo-European people, the Slavs settled in the area around the Pripet Marshes. In the fifth and sixth centuries, the Slavs migrated again. Those who went west became the Poles, Czechs, Slovaks, and Lusatian Sorbs (today in Saxony). Slavs who migrated into the Balkans and around the Danube River became South Slavs—Slovenes, Croats, Serbs, Macedonians, and Bulgarians. Those who remained in the east were the Russians, Belorussians, Ukrainians, and Rusyns. Before the arrival of the Slavs, the Czech Lands hosted other Indo-Europeans. The first were the Celtic tribe of Boii, from which the name Bohemia is derived. Remnants of a few of their hill fortresses, known as *oppida,* are still scattered throughout the republic. Next, a few Germanic tribes inhabited the area. By the seventh century, the Slavs in what was to become the Czech Lands had assimilated all other ethnic groups, aside from parts of Southern Moravia. That area was under the Avars, a Turkic tribe that also settled around the Danube in the sixth century and established a powerful kingdom that subjugated the surrounding Slavs. As the Avars weakened (the remnants of the tribe being assimilated by the turn of the ninth century), the Slavs in the Czech Lands and Slovakia began to unite.

The first Slavic political entity emerged in the seventh century when the Frankish merchant Sámo (who died in 658 or 659) united Slavs in parts of what is now Moravia and Slovakia against the Avars, warred against the Franks, and expanded his kingdom. After Sámo's death, his kingdom vanished from the historical record. The next known Slavic state began between 833 and 836, when Prince Mojmír I of Moravia took the territory around Nitra in Western Slovakia from Prince Pribina and created the Great Moravian Empire. The first known Christian church was in Nitra during the reign of Pribina, and records as early as 852 mention the Great Moravian Empire as Christianized. Prince Rastislav sought to limit the influence of the Franks over his kingdom and invited the Byzantine emperor to send Slavic-speaking missionaries from the Orthodox Christian tradition to Moravia. The task fell on two monks, Cyril and Methodius, whose mother was Slavic. Before departing on their mission, Cyril devised a Slavic alphabet, known as Glagolithic, which eventually evolved into Cyrillic, and translated some church writings into Slavic (other translations came later, including the Old Testament, which Methodius translated in 883).

Cyril and Methodius arrived in Moravia in 863 or early 864, and they made great progress in Christianizing the bulk of the population, partly because the Slavic ceremony and writings were understandable, as opposed to the Latin liturgical language of the church in Rome. The Latin and Slavonic Christian traditions coexisted uneasily in Moravia, even after the pope appointed Methodius bishop in 869, although the Slavonic tradition enjoyed greater prestige. In 870, however, Rastislav lost his throne to the intrigues of his nephew, Svatopluk, who had Frankish backing. After Methodius died in 885, the pope forbade the Slavonic liturgy in Moravia, and Svatopluk upheld the decision. Only at the monastery in Sázava, Bohemia, did the liturgy survive until 1097, although not without interruptions. The disciples of Methodius had to leave Moravia and went to Bulgaria, which had adopted the Slavonic liturgy.

The Moravian Empire was on the eastern fringe of European civilization and eventually succumbed to nomadic hordes. The Magyars (Hungarians) menaced Moravia beginning in 889. Torn by internal strife, weakened by the separation of the Czechs in Bohemia and the Lusatian Sorbs, both of whom came under the protection of the Franks, and plagued with continued skirmishes with the Franks, particularly the Bavarians, Moravia could not withstand the advance of the Magyars. By 908, the Magyars precipitated the collapse of the Great Moravian Empire, seizing control of the Pannonian Plain and Slovakia. The Magyar conquest disrupted the political and cultural links of the West Slavs on either side of the Carpathian Mountains, ensuring the eventual differentiation between Czechs and Slovaks. Moreover, the Magyars joined with the Austrian Germans and Romanians in separating the West Slavs from the South Slavs.

THE PŘEMYSLID DYNASTY OF BOHEMIA

The early history of leaders in Bohemia is enshrouded in legend, some of which may be contained in the chronicle of Kosmas (ca. 1045–1125). Great grandfather Czech was said to have climbed Říp Mountain, proclaiming the land he saw around him to be the home of the Czechs. A battle fought between men and women resulted in a matriarchal government that enslaved men. Equally romantic is the story of how, in the eighth century, Princess Libuše chose as a husband a peasant, Přemysl Oráč (Přemysl the Ploughman), who subsequently established the Přemyslid dynasty, the only native Czech dynasty in Bohemian history. The first historical evidence of the Přemyslids comes from the time of Prince Bořivoj (died c. 894) and his wife, Ludmila. Methodius baptized the couple during a mission to Bohemia in 885, and Bořivoj built the first church at Prague Castle, where he established his capital. In 895 Bořivoj's successor, Spytihněv, took Bohemia out from the suzerainty of Greater Moravia, placing it directly under the Franks.

Prince Vratislav continued to strengthen Přemyslid control over competitors in the Czech Lands and warded off the Magyar threat. Vratislav's two sons, Václav (English, Wenceslas; German, Wenzel) and Boleslav, were young when Vratislav died, and two camps formed around the princes. Václav, who succeeded his father, came under the influence of his grandmother, Ludmila, while Boleslav had the support of his mother, Drahomíra. As the tension between the two camps heightened, Drahomíra had Ludmila murdered, and Ludmila was later proclaimed a saint. Boleslav arranged or actually participated in the assassination of Václav, in 929 or 935, during the baptism of Boleslav's son in the town of Stará Boleslav. As Václav opened the church door to attend morning mass, an assassin stabbed him in the back. The Church quickly canonized Václav, and St. Wenceslas became popular in the West through the nineteenth-century English Christmas carol. Boleslav reversed Václav's preference for weakening Frankish influence in Bohemia, and he undertook an active and expansive foreign policy. Boleslav extended his realm eastward, acquiring Silesia and Cracow, and he married his daughter to the Polish Prince Mieszek, who accepted Christianity from the Czechs.

His son and successor, Boleslav II, further expanded his territories in the east while becoming involved in a conflict between Bavaria and the Roman Empire. He completed the consolidation of the Přemyslids in Bohemia when he murdered the entire Slavníkov family, a clan that competed with the Přemyslids for power. In 973 he acquired for Bohemia an independent bishopric and established the country's first monastery, the Benedictine Convent of St. George at the Prague Castle. The new bishopric removed the Bohemian Church from the control of the German bishopric in Regensburg, although it was still responsible to the archbishop in the German city of Mainz. The first bishop in Prague was a German, but the second, in office from 982 to 997, was St. Vojtěch, a member of the Slavníkov clan who had escaped the fate of his relatives. Vojtěch studied abroad, was an adviser at the Ottonian court of the Roman Empire, and is Bohemia's first internationally recognized intellectual. After Boleslav's death, the Poles, under Bolesław I Chrobry (the Brave), took territory from Bohemia and entered Prague. They captured the Czech prince, Boleslav III, whom they blinded and imprisoned. The Czechs, with German assistance, expelled the Poles, at first from Bohemia and then from Moravia. The era of Bohemian expansion in the direction of Poland came to an end, aside from the later reacquisition of Silesia.

Only a few Czech rulers formally acknowledged their vassalage to the Holy Roman Emperor, yet the Czechs, as part of the empire, were entangled in the political contests among the German rulers, including the emperor. Bohemia, like other political entities within the empire, attempted to improve its status through military alliances when the emperor was weak. Strong emperors, however, frequently intervened in Bohemian affairs, and the Bohemian rulers respected their authority. As a result of shrewd diplomacy, Bohemia won special status within the empire. The emperor made the Bohemian prince Vratislav II a king in 1085, although the title did not apply to his successors. In 1114 the rulers of Bohemia became cupbearers to the emperors, a position that later enabled them to become one of the electors of the emperor. In 1158 Frederick Barbarossa granted a hereditary crown to Vladislav, but owing to dynastic difficulties, the title lapsed after Vladislav's death. Barbarossa then attempted to weaken the position of the Bohemian ruler. He divided Bohemia, creating the margrave of Moravia in 1182 and five years later granting the title of prince to the bishop in Prague, whom he appointed. Later developments in Bohemia reversed the effect of these changes. In 1181 the margrave of Moravia acknowledged the suzerainty of the prince of Bohemia, as did the bishop of Prague in 1197, whom Vladislav Jindřich had installed in defiance of the Roman emperor. Bohemia's rulers continued to install bishops afterward.

Bohemia renewed its strength under Přemysl Otakar I, who came to the throne for a short time in 1192–1193 and then returned in 1197. He exploited disorder in the empire to obtain the title of king in 1198. In 1212 the Imperial Golden Sicilian Bull confirmed the hereditary title of king, made Moravia and the Prague bishopric inseparable from the Bohemian kingdom, and guaranteed the Bohemian king a powerful position in the emperor's court. As the coat of arms of his kingdom, Přemysl Otakar I received the double-tailed lion, the basis of the current state symbol of Bohemia. Přemysl Otakar I regularized the succession to the throne, firmly establishing primogeniture, yet he had the nobles in the Bohemian diet elect his successor, setting a precedent for when the dynasty would become extinct. His son, Václav I (the change in numbers reflected the new kings of Bohemia), attempted to acquire Austria, where the Babenberg dynasty had become extinct in 1246, and fought the advance of the Tatars (Mongols) in Southern Moravia. The daughter of Přemysl OtokarI, Anežka (1211–1282), became a nun and established a Franciscan convent (the Poor Clares) and an associate Franciscan monastery—Prague's first Gothic structure, which is known as Anežka's Monastery. She was canonized in 1989.

Václav's son and successor, Přemysl Otakar II, who came to the throne in 1253, was progressive and ambitious. He chartered towns and attracted German immigrants to improve trade, increase the production of goods, and create a counterweight to the nobility. He strengthened the feudal system in Bohemia with the establishment of the Provincial Court of Justice (Zemský soud), which dealt with such items as the exchange of noble property, debts, privileges, and sentences. Its records are contained within the famous Provincial Record (Zemské desky). Přemysl Otakar II had led the Czechs in occupying Austria before he came to the throne but later had to divide the country with the Hungarian king. He pursued other adventures, such as the acquisition of territory to the Adriatic Sea, the failed attempt to capture today's Slovakia from Hungary, and in 1255 a crusade against the Prussians, a pagan Baltic tribe, during which he established the city of Königsberg (today Kaliningrad). He also sought election to the imperial throne. Many Bohemian nobles grew dissatisfied with Přemysl Otakar's exploits, and they joined with the new emperor, Rudolf of Habsburg, to force Přemysl Otakar to surrender his provinces outside Bohemia and acknowledge Bohemia and Moravia as fiefs of the emperor. Přemysl Otakar attempted to regain his territories and position through force, but the emperor defeated him on 26 August 1278, and Přemysl Otakar died in battle. Rudolf occupied Moravia for five years and appointed a regency under the Brandenburgs for the young Václav II. Once he assumed control of his kingdom, Václav became king of Poland, although not all Polish nobles were satisfied with his reign. Václav attempted to install his son as king of Hungary after the death of the last Árpád ruler, which alienated the pope, emperor, and many Hungarian nobles. After he suddenly died in 1305, his son, Václav III, managed to placate the emperor. He was prepared to invade Poland to keep his title, but he was assassinated in 1306 and had no heir.

With the extinction of the Přemyslid dynasty, Rudolf of Habsburg was strong enough to have his son elected as the king of Bohemia. He died the next year, however, and the Bohemian diet elected Heinrich of Carinthia, who had married into the Přemyslid family. The nobles were still dissatisfied and negotiated with the new Holy Roman Emperor, Heinrich von Luxemburg, to have his son Johann marry into the Přemyslid family and become king of Bohemia. Heinrich of Carinthia fled the country when Johann von Luxemburg arrived in 1310.

The Přemyslids provided Bohemia with roughly 450 years of stability under one family whose legacy was to secure Bohemia an important role in the affairs of East Central Europe. They solidified the country's borders and gave Bohemia several rulers whose capable military and diplomatic skills acquired Polish and Austrian territory. The consolidation of the Roman Catholic Church in Bohemia under the Přemyslids cast aside the Czech flirtation with Orthodoxy and the Cyrillic alphabet. The Přemyslids provided the Czechs with their first saints, Ludmila and Václav, for a total of three Přemyslid saints after Anežka's canonization in 1989. They fostered the creation of an independent Bohemian Church administration with a bishopric in Prague. During the Přemyslid rule, the medieval cultural heritage of the Czechs, like their political, social, and economic development, became bound to the West. The beginnings of feudalism along with Romanesque and Gothic trends in Bohemian art, date from the time of the Přemyslids. The dynasty strengthened the position of Bohemia with respect to the country's neighbors, especially the Roman Empire. The struggle between Prince Václav and his brother Prince Boleslav demonstrates the importance the empire had in Bohemian affairs and illustrates Czechs' persistent efforts to accommodate themselves to their powerful neighbor, benefit from their close association with the German world, and keep the Germans at bay. The Přemyslids' political skill with respect to the empire was shown in their acquisition of a hereditary royal title. The crown also demonstrated Bohemia's independence from the Roman Empire and its strength and importance to the Western world. Finally, during the time of the Přemyslids, the Czechs attracted German colonists to towns and the mountain areas, spurring the economy and laying the foundations of the dual German-Czech ethnic character of the Czech Lands.

THE LUXEMBURG DYNASTY

Jan Lucemburský (Johann von Luxemburg), who reigned in Bohemia from 1310 to 1346, was one of Europe's great medieval knights. He enjoyed tournaments as much as he reveled in the success of his dynasty. His relationship with the Bohemian nobles was often shaky, at first because he appointed Germans to high positions in Prague and intimidated the nobles with his foreign troops. The nobles limited his involvement in Bohemian internal affairs, although not foreign policy, when they forced him to sign the Peace of Domažlice in 1318. Jan acquired Cheb (German, Eger), the ethnically German town on the western fringes of Bohemia at the juncture of the Ore and Bohemian Forest Mountains. By 1335 Jan gained all of Silesia, which Přemysl Otakar II had lost, after Jan renounced his claim to the Polish Crown. He attempted to expand in other directions and even acquired portions of northern Italy, where he positioned his son Václav (who later changed his name to Charles, or Karel in Czech) as ruler. Jan also made Václav margrave of Moravia, and in that position Václav negotiated in 1344 with his former tutor and close friend, Pope Clement VI, to have Prague elevated to an archbishopric, freeing it from the German Catholic hierarchy in Mainz. The new archbishop crowned the kings of Bohemia, and under him came the bishopric of Olomouc and the new bishopric of Litomyšl. Concurrent with the establishment of the archbishopric was the groundbreaking for a new high Gothic St. Vitus Cathedral (Chram sv. Víta) in Prague Castle. Lucemburský was blinded in a crusade in the Baltic but continued his adventures. He fought at the Battle of Crécy to aid his brother-in-law, the king of France, against the invading English at the opening of the Hundred Years War. On 26 August 1346, he fell victim to the English longbowmen; the legend that the blind king died charging the English on his horse, which he had tied between the horses of two noblemen, is incorrect. Thus he died on the anniversary of the day Přemysl Otakar II died on the field in 1278—and Czechs still consider 26 August fateful.

Charles of Luxemburg came to rule in Bohemia in 1346 after ascending to the throne of the Roman Empire as Charles IV just before the Battle of Crécy. He was cosmopolitan, having a German father, a Czech mother, and a French education, but he felt himself to be Czech. He had a string of major political, economic, and cultural accomplishments in Bohemia, ushering in what historians recognize as Bohemia's golden age. He strengthened the succession laws in Bohemia to ensure that the throne would pass to his descendents, and as part of his plan he had his son, Václav IV, elected king of Bohemia in 1363. Charles IV made the king of Bohemia a principal elector of the emperor, and he reaffirmed the independence of the Kingdom of Bohemia within the empire. In 1355 he was crowned in Rome as Holy Roman Emperor. Charles IV added Upper and Lower Lusatia to the Bohemian Crown and secured Bavaria and Oberpfalz for his sons. He accomplished this expansion through diplomacy, using as tools his four marriages (his fourth wife was Alžběta Pomořanská, a Polish noblewoman who reportedly broke swords and horseshoes and bent steel with her bare hands) and the marriages of his many children. One of his children, Anna, became the wife of King Richard II, which facilitated cultural ties between England and Bohemia and promoted the spread of English teachings regarding church reform. Before Charles IV died in 1378, he partitioned his realm among his three sons, and Václav IV came to the throne in Prague. Unlike his father, Václav had little political sense. The German princes deposed him as emperor because he neglected the affairs of empire. At home, he failed to extinguish a pogrom in Prague in 1389 that killed 3,000 Jews. The Bohemian nobles revolted, partly because Václav wished to weaken the nobility and appointed lower nobles and burghers to positions that traditionally were reserved for the upper nobility. He even alienated his half brother, Zikmund, then king of Hungary, who conspired to take the Bohemian throne, capturing Václav and deporting him to Vienna. Václav managed to escape and made peace with the Bohemian nobles.

Václav also had difficulties with the Catholic Church. In an attempt to form another diocese within Bohemia in order to weaken the archbishop, he arrested and tortured several clerics, one of whom died and was canonized in 1729 as St. Jan Nepomuk. During Václav's reign, Rome began to sell indulgences in Bohemia to augment its finances. Many Czech clerics, with the backing of the Czechs at the university, intensified the cry for drastic reform that had inspired earlier clerics, like Milič of Kroměříž. The most vocal was Jan Hus (ca. 1371–1415). Under Václav and his half brother, Zikmund, the last Luxemburg king of Bohemia, religious controversy broke into open schism and civil war.

THE HUSSITE ERA

The Hussite era, a pre–Martin Luther reformation of the Catholic Church in Bohemia, witnessed a complex interaction of religious disputes, Czech and German nationalism, politics between the nobility and the king, and a reaction to certain aspects of feudalism. In 1403 Germans at the Prague University, in an effort to preserve their control over decision making at the university, condemned the writings of the English cleric John Wycliffe as heretical. Czech opponents of the Germans rallied around Jan Hus, who taught at the university and since February 1402 had been preaching at Prague's Bethlehem Chapel (erected in 1391). The controversy continued, and in 1409 Václav IV granted Czechs majority status at the university to gain the support of Czech professors in his struggle against the archbishop of Prague, who had opposed Václav's solution to the Great Schism and the divided papacy in the Roman Catholic Church. In retaliation, several hundred German professors and students left Prague for Leipzig, Saxony, where they participated in the founding of the university there. Hus became the new rector of the university. The archbishop and Václav came to terms in support of the election of Pope Alexander V, but the archbishop continued to condemn the Czech reformers, particularly Hus, and placed Prague under an interdict (i.e., a prohibition of most rites and sacraments, including Communion and Christian burial). The archbishop's death eased the tension, but some reformers, including Hus, began to attack the sale of indulgences, and they had the support of Queen Sophie, who had appointed Hus as her confessor. In another attempt to cool tempers, Václav expelled the anti-indulgence clerics from Prague, prompting Hus and others to carry their teaching to the countryside. When the Council of Constance, which finally solved the Great Schism, decided to have Hus explain his teachings, Zikmund, as emperor, guaranteed Hus safe passage. Nevertheless, Hus was arrested in November 1414, tried as a heretic, and burned at the stake on 6 July 1415 (now a national holiday in the Czech Republic along with the feast of Cyril and Methodius on 5 July, thus satisfying both Hussites and Catholics).

The fate of Hus deepened the schism in the Bohemian Church. Reformers of various stripes set aside their disagreements and united with Bohemian nobles to protest the arrest and execution of Hus, in part because the Czechs felt belittled by foreigners. Czech reformers latched on to the practice of offering their faithful not only the wafer but the wine during Communion under both species (Lat., *sub utraque specie*). Hus approved the practice from prison after an associate, Jakoubek ze Stříbra, resurrected the ancient practice in November 1414. The Council of Constance condemned the Czechs who sided with Hus, and in May the council burned another reformer who had traveled with Hus, Jeronim Pražský (Jerome of Prague). In 1418, with the university now closed, the archbishop refusing to ordain priests, and the queen and nobles dismissing priests who sided with the archbishop, Pope Martin V demanded that Václav enforce the orders of the Catholic Church. Václav, however, had no control over the reformers, who continued to say mass, or the crowds that supported them. In July 1419 a mob of reformers marched on the New Town Hall to demand that several of their adherents be released from prison. When the king's counselors refused, demonstrators broke into the town hall and threw the king's counselors to the crowd below, who killed them. Historians generally accept this act, known as the first defenestration of Prague, as the beginning of the Hussite Wars.

Jan Hus (ca. 1371–1415), the Czech religious reformer. (Library of Congress)

Certain beliefs united all Hussites, such as the right to receive Communion under both species, the validity of transubstantiation (the transformation of bread and wine during the mass into the body and blood of Christ, challenged by other reformers), a married clergy that shunned material luxury, and the belief that statues, vestments, and ornaments were superfluous, although not sinful. Yet there were significant differences between sects of the Hussite reformers. The Utraquists desired moderate church reform, accepted many teachings of the early Christian Church, and were close to the Catholics. The more radical Hussites accepted teachings based only on the Bible, held millennarian beliefs, and advanced social policies that won them the support of the rural and urban underprivileged. Radical Hussites re built the town of Hradiště in Southern Bohemia in 1420 and renamed it Tábor. They came under the leadership of Jan Žižka, who was an experienced military leader, despite being blind in one eye since 1416 and totally blind after a war injury in 1421. Faced with the Catholic threat after the defenestration at the New Town Hall, the two major Hussite groups rallied around Žižka and proclaimed the Four Articles of Prague in June 1420, a crucial document in the history of religious toleration. It called for freedom of religion in Bohemia for both the Hussite and Catholic traditions, the right to receive Communion under both species, the requirement of poverty for the clergy, and the punishment of all mortal sins in order to preserve the reputation and advance the welfare of the country. Hussite unity, however, was superficial. Žižka found the Táborites too radical and in 1423 established another center of Hussites in Hradec Králová, often called the Lesser Tábor. After Žižka's death, the group referred to itself as the Orphans. In addition to the Utraquist, Táborite, and Lesser Táborite groups, many other sects emerged. One group under Jan Želivský took control of Prague in June 1421, with the support of some of its poor inhabitants, and opposed the rich. In March 1422 burghers in the Old Town captured and executed Želivský and several of his associates. Prague essentially remained in moderate hands for the remainder of the Hussite Wars. Táborites expelled a group known as Pikartists, who rejected transubstantiation and even permitted other foods to be used during the mass instead of bread and wine. Another small sect originating from Tábor was the Adamites, who advocated a return to nature, nudity, and sexual openness. To them, God was in the goodness of man, while the devil was in man's evil acts. Žižka eliminated both of these communities.

In March 1420 at a battle outside of the village of Sudoměř, Žižka's forces engaged those of Zikmund and the Hussites won the day. Hussite success in this and other battles was the result of innovations in weapons, capable leadership, and dogged determination and novel means of boosting morale, such as singing hymns and displaying the host in a monstrance above the warriors. The Hussites never lost a campaign, and their self-confidence and reputation for success struck fear in the enemy. In 1420 the pope declared a crusade—the first of five—against the Czechs, and the Catholic forces met their defeat at the hands of the Hussites in July at Vítkov, near the modern-day Czech Republic's military museum and the gigantic equestrian statue of Žižka in Prague. Žižka's forces were victorious over those of Zikmund a second time at Vyšehrad Castle in Prague that October. Now the Hussites drove Catholics from Prague, razed Vyšehrad, took Prague Castle, and in a rage of iconoclasm destroyed church ornaments. Zikmund, who had managed to be crowned king in Prague earlier, fled the capital, attacking the estates of Hussite nobles as he retreated. For the rest of 1420 and into 1421, Hussite forces, which had received enormous popular support in the countryside and towns, secured most of Bohemia in a series of significant battles, with the city of Plzeň being a notable exception. By the end of 1420, Hussitism became associated with Czechs in Bohemia, while Catholicism remained the religion of Germans.

In August 1421 a second crusade of five armies under the leadership of Zikmund approached Bohemia, but its soldiers scattered in fear of Žižka's troops before the armies ever met. The Hussites repelled yet another army of Zikmund in January 1422 at Kutná Hora, and another supporting him fell apart in October 1422. Bohemia was free of foreign interference beginning in the fall of 1422, but sporadic conflict broke out within the country between Hussite and Catholic forces. During this time, the Hussites ventured into Moravia and in June 1424 won the bloody battle of Malešova, near Kutná Hora. Žižka died in October 1424, and according to legend, he commanded that his skin be used to make war drums. The leadership of the Hussite troops passed to the Hussite priest and warrior, Prokop Holý. A third crusade succumbed to the Hussites at the battle of Ústí nad Labem in June 1426. Armies of the fourth crusade in August 1427 broke and ran when they heard the Hussites singing their hymn, "Ye Warriors of God" (Ktož jsú boží bojvoníci). Over the next three years, the Hussites invaded neighboring territories, being most active in 1429, when they advanced into Silesia, Upper Lusatia, Saxony, and Bavaria. The fifth, last, and largest crusade confronted the Hussites near Domažlice in August 1431, and once again the crusaders fled when they heard the Hussite hymn.

From time to time, both sides had made overtures for compromise, but now the Czechs were weary of the hostilities and the Catholics realized they could not defeat the Hussites. Prokop Holý and a delegation of Hussites went to Basel, Switzerland, in January 1433 to negotiate with the Catholics. They demanded that all Christians in Bohemia receive Communion under both species, but the Catholics could not agree. Hoping to force their hand, the radical Hussites decided to eliminate the Catholics in Plzeň. Prokop Holý broke with the moderates and led the Táborites and Orphans in an attack on Plzeň. The Utraquists joined with the Catholics to defeat the extremists, first by taking the New Town in Prague and then by meeting Prokop Holý and his forces on the battlefield. On 30 May 1434, at Lipany, the Utraquists and Catholics defeated the radicals. Prokop Holý died in the battle. Moderate Hussites renewed the negotiations at Basel, where they reached an agreement with the Catholics. In 1436 Jan Rokycana became archbishop of Prague, the Bohemian diet having approved his selection (although not the Catholic Church), and Zikmund officially became king. Finally, on the basis of the Four Articles discussed at Basel in 1433, the Council of Basel reached a compromise between the Catholics and Utraquists (the radical Hussites were not included) known as the Compactata of 1437. It permitted Communion in both kinds in Bohemia and for Utraquists elsewhere, required the punishment of mortal sins, granted priests the freedom to preach their beliefs, and demanded that priests honor the vow of poverty. Catholics and Utraquists were to live side by side in Bohemia without fear of persecution.

Historians long have debated the meaning and significance of the Hussite era of Czech history. Some see it as primarily a progressive movement that paved the way for the Protestant Reformation. Many concentrate on the national aspect of the Hussite Wars, a time when Czechs advanced their political agenda and cultural goals, including the use of Czech as the country's official language as opposed to German. Faults with this interpretation become apparent when one considers that many of the wealthy, moderate Czech Utraquists aligned with Catholic Germans. Still other historians, principally the socialists during the communist era, focus on the triangulated class struggle among the serfs and poor urban dwellers, who wanted relief from feudal oppression, the Catholic Church, which sought to maintain its status and wealth, and the nobles and burghers, who hoped to control the masses and take the wealth of the Catholic Church. One difficulty with the socialist interpretation is that no single class was solidly behind one social and religious program. In the end, moderate voices predominated, and Hussite radicals of all stripes fell in defeat. The Hussite era redefined politics and society in the Kingdom of Bohemia. It strengthened the nobles and towns with respect to what had been a powerful Catholic hierarchy and Crown. The compromise solution to the military struggle left Bohemia a country of religious toleration a century before Luther nailed his ninety-five theses to the church door in Wittenberg. Nevertheless, the fact that Bohemia was both Hussite and Catholic isolated it to some extent in European affairs. Finally, the economic devastation and depopulation from the wars encouraged nobles to find ways to legally tie peasants to the land, which facilitated the process of neoserfdom as a result of further economic dislocation during the Thirty Years' War (1618–1648).

THE HUSSITE KING

In 1437 both the Bohemian and Hungarian diets elected the Habsburg Albert II of Austria to their respective thrones, the first time a Habsburg united Austria, Bohemia, and Hungary. Albert resented the Hussites, causing a great deal of dissension. When he died in 1439, the diet, unable to find a successor, established a regency. In 1444 the regency came under the control of Jiří z Poděbrad, a Utraquist who had defended the Compactata of 1436 and the Utraquist archbishop, Jan Rokycana. The Bohemian diet had recognized Albert's underage son, Ladislav Posthumous, as the heir to the throne in 1444, and he ascended to the throne in 1453. Jiří z Poděbrad remained as the administrator of the realm. When Ladislav Posthumous died two years later, the diet elected Jiří z Poděbrad as king.

Jiří z Poděbrad, known as the "Hussite king" even though he was a moderate Utraquist, had difficulties with Popes Pius II and Paul II, both of whom wanted him to renounce the Compactata and persecute the Utraquists. Jiří z Poděbrad refused to do so, and Paul II excommunicated and deposed him in 1466. Some Catholic nobles, with the aid of the Hungarian king Matthias Corvinus, attempted to remove Jiří z Poděbrad, but their efforts failed (Jiří z Poděbrad even captured Matthias Corvinus at one point). From 1462, the year Pius II renounced the Compactata, until 1464, Jiří z Poděbrad attempted to consolidate his position against the pope by advancing a European-wide union of Christian states to settle disputes, thereby preventing war among them, and to halt the Turkish threat, if necessary through war. The French king was to convene the union, which would reach decisions through a majority vote, with one vote each to the kings of France, Germany, Italy, and Spain. Decisions were to be binding on all members. The envoys of Jiří z Poděbrad unsuccessfully sought to convince Europe's leaders to accept the proposal. Although the proposal for a Christian union aroused a great deal of interest, no ruler subscribed to the plan. An organization with a similar goal of preserving peace did not appear until the twentieth century with the League of Nations and the United Nations. It was also during the reign of Jiří z Poděbrad in the 1450s that a certain Brother Řehoř, the nephew of Rokycana, established the Jednota bratrská, also known as the Unitas Fratrum, Bohemian Brethren, or Moravian Brethren. The Brethren's most noted early thinker and leader was Petr Chelčický, who wrote *Sít' víry* (The Net of Faith) and other works. Chelčický accepted the Hussite reforms but held that believers should return to the teachings and lifestyles of the early Christians and preach strict nonviolence. Eventually the Brethren influenced several Protestant sects, including the Quakers.

Before Jiří z Poděbrad died, he excluded his sons from the throne of Bohemia, realizing that his family's Utraquism had a divisive influence on politics, and successfully encouraged the Bohemian diet to turn to the Jagiellonian dynasty of Poland. In 1471 the Bohemian diet elected Vladislav II Jagiellonian to the throne. Matthias Corvinus of Hungary also wanted the crown, and he managed to place Moravia, Silesia, and Lusatia (as well as part of Austria, including Vienna) under the Hungarian Crown until his death in 1490. At that time, the Hungarian diet too elected Vladislav Jagiellonian as king, which effectively reunited the Kingdom of Bohemia. In 1515 Vladislav concluded a double marriage agreement with Maximilian of Austria that enabled the Habsburgs to come to the thrones of Bohemia and Hungary if the Jagiellonian family died without an heir and stipulated that the Jagiellonian family would inherit Austria should the Habsburg family expire. It was one of the most fateful marriage agreements of history. When Vladislav II Jagiellonian died in 1516, his son, Ludvík Jagiellonian, who had married Maximilian's granddaughter, came to the thrones of Bohemia and Hungary. The Turks, having conquered the entire Balkan Peninsula with the fall of the Byzantine Empire in 1453, now set their sites on Central Europe. They attacked Hungary, and the Hungarian forces, with Ludvík Jagiellonian at the lead, suffered a terrible defeat at Mohács on the Danube River. As he retreated, Ludvík Jagiellonian drowned; after his horse reared, he fell into a swamp, and his heavy armor prevented him from standing. The Turks advanced northward, ravaging nearly all of Hungary.

BOHEMIA IN THE EARLY YEARS OF THE HABSBURG MONARCHY (1516–1618)

With the death of Ludvík, the Jagiellonian-Habsburg marriage agreement was to take effect. Nevertheless, the diets of Bohemia and Hungary each had to accept the Habsburgs, and the accession of Ferdinand I of Habsburg to both thrones paved the way for the Habsburgs to rule in Austria, Bohemia, and Hungary for the next four hundred years.

Whereas Ferdinand had to resort to force to secure the throne in the case of Hungary, diplomacy sufficed in Bohemia. Shortly after Mohács in 1526, the Bohemian diet elected Ferdinand as king of Bohemia based on Ferdinand's acceptance of Bohemia's existing laws, including the Compactata, limits on the Crown's rights to impose taxes, and exempting the nobles from participating in any war outside the Kingdom of Bohemia. In 1541 a fire devastated the Lesser Town of Prague and spread up the hill toward Hradčany and the Hrad. In its path, it consumed the building that housed the archives, including the agreement Ferdinand had made in 1526. Many believed that Ferdinand may have been involved in setting the fire to rid himself of the document. In 1546 German Protestants in the Schmalkaldic League rebelled against the Catholic Holy Roman Emperor, Charles V, Ferdinand's brother. The Bohemian nobles and towns refused to help Ferdinand, and in 1547 they actually assisted the Protestants by preparing to attack him. Ferdinand styled the creation of the army an act of treason, and after defeating the Bohemian estates with an army he borrowed from Charles, Ferdinand tightened his control over Bohemia. He executed four Protestant leaders (although not the most prominent ones), confiscated property, and meted out other punishments. Most of the towns in Bohemia (unlike Moravia) had opposed Ferdinand, and he removed their privileges, most of which were restored over time; Ferdinand placed the towns under royal control and

Members of the Bohemian Estates throw three representatives of the Habsburg emperor from a window of the Prague Castle on 23 May 1618. (North Wind Picture Archives)

taxation. The diet met in August-September 1547 and accepted the Habsburgs' hereditary right to the throne, canceled the right of the estates to form confederations, and recognized the king's prerogative to call the diet and regional assemblies and appoint provincial officials. The dominant theme in the political history of Bohemia from 1547 until 1620 was the effort by the estates to regain their lost privileges and limit the Crown.

Ferdinand divided his realm among his three sons, with Maximilian II receiving Upper and Lower Austria, Bohemia, Hungary, and the empire and holding the strongest position (unity came in 1611). Maximilian was sympathetic to the Protestants, but he had promised his father that he would remain faithful to the Catholic Church, and he feared open religious division should he declare his support for Protestantism. Nevertheless, when some Bohemian nobles agreed on a document to unite Protestants, Utraquists, and Bohemian Brethren to form the Bohemian Confession in 1575, Maximilian refused to approve it. Czech non-Catholics lost their chance for unity. Many of the Utraquists gravitated toward Catholicism, and Maximilian, under pressure from the Catholic princes in Germany, resumed persecution of the Bohemian Brethren.

The next Habsburg ruler, Rudolf II, moved the capital from Vienna to Prague. Rudolf's policies brought the nobility in some areas of his realm to rebel in 1606, forcing him to turn over Moravia, Austria, and Hungary to the control of his brother, Mathias, in 1608. The diets of Bohemia and Silesia remained loyal to Rudolf and used the opportunity to force him into a legal compromise. Despite Rudolf's tolerance for the accepted religions of the Czech Lands, the estates in 1609 persuaded Rudolf to sign the letter of majesty, which guaranteed freedom of religion in Bohemia for Catholics and Protestants, placed control of the Utraquist Consistory in the hands of the diet, created a group of thirty representatives from the diet to ensure freedom of religion, returned control of the University of Prague from the Jesuits to the Utraquists, and enabled the nobility and royal cities to build churches where they saw fit. The religious question in Bohemia seemed solved, and the diet successfully limited the king.

In 1611 Rudolf II faced another enemy, the bishop of Passau, who had invaded Bohemia. Rudolf turned to Mathias for protection, and Mathias forced Rudolf's abdication in Bohemia. Mathias I reunited the monarchy. He moved the capital back to Vienna and left a group of governors, all devout Catholics, in Prague. Mathias, like Rudolf, had no heir, and his successor was his cousin, Ferdinand II. Like his cousin and uncle before him, Ferdinand II accepted the letter of majesty, although he violated it on many occasions.

Within a short time, the tense relations between Ferdinand II and the Bohemian nobility exploded over the destruction of two Protestant churches that had been built on Catholic Church lands. On 23 May 1618, the Protestant nobility met with Habsburg representatives in Prague at the Hrad. After a heated exchange, the nobles seized two governors and a scribe and threw them from the window. All survived, thanks to the presence of a dung heap below, although not without injuries. Reminiscent of the defenestration nearly two hundred years before, the events of 1618 symbolized the estates' defiance of the Habsburgs. The estates formed a directorate of thirty nobles, and in July 1619 they deposed the Habsburgs and elected as king Frederick of the Palatine. The estates hoped that his wife, who was the daughter of England's James I, would help cement diplomatic and military ties with Protestant states throughout Europe.

The subsequent war between Austria and Bohemia was the first round of the Thirty Years' War. Although initially the Bohemian estates successfully defended the kingdom, Bohemia received only minor assistance from its allies. Although the Bohemian army advanced as far as Vienna in June 1619, it had to withdraw because it lacked sufficient forces to lay siege to the city. The Austrians advanced toward Prague and defeated the Bohemian forces at White Mountain outside Prague on 8 November 1620. Instead of regrouping, relying on the defenses of Prague, and accepting the assistance of allies—a Transylvanian army was only a few kilometers from Prague—the Bohemian estates panicked. Thurn and others fled the country, as did King Frederick, whose flight during the coldest season of the year won him the epithet "the Winter King."

Once again in control of Bohemia, Ferdinand made sure that the kingdom would never again rebel. On 21 June 1621, twenty-seven leaders of the rebellion—three nobles, seven knights, and seventeen burghers—were publicly executed. Included among the victims were three men who had been important figures in Prague's intellectual life since the reign of Rudolf II: Kryštof Harant z Polžic a Bezdružic, a nobleman, a composer, and the author of a popular book (1608) about his travels to the Middle East; Jan Jesenský-Jessenius, the personal physician of Rudolf II and Mathias, philosopher, and rector of Prague University who conducted the first public anatomical dissection in 1600 in Prague; and Václav Budovec z Budova, a member of the Bohemian Brethren who was among the members of the Bohemian diet responsible for Rudolf's acceptance of the letter of majesty. The heads of twelve of those executed were displayed in iron cages suspended on the tower of the Old Town side of Charles Bridge for just over a decade, until Protestant forces occupying Prague in 1632 removed them. Today, twenty-seven crosses in the pavement before the Old Town Hall mark the location of the executions.

In May 1627 Ferdinand issued the Renewal Ordinance, in effect a new constitution for Bohemia, an act that Ferdinand claimed was his right because he had suppressed a rebellion (he issued similar ordinances for Moravia and Silesia). To weaken the nobility, Ferdinand II readmitted the Catholic Church to the diet as the first estate, giving it more powers than any other estate. He required towns to pay special taxes for their part in the rebellion, with the exception of the loyal towns of České Budějovice and Plzeň. The diet could not attach conditions to money appropriations and lost the right of legislative initiative. Convoking the diet became the sole responsibility of the king. The king reserved the right to appoint royal officials without the approval of the diet. Bohemia lost its status as a kingdom, its component parts becoming mere provinces of Austria; the Habsburgs became the hereditary dynasty in Bohemia, Moravia, and Silesia following the male and female lines. Ferdinand revoked the letter of majesty and made the Roman Catholic Church the only legal faith. Finally, he made German legally equal to Czech in the courts.

Reprisals, confiscations, and religious persecution caused approximately 36,000 families, including many noble families, to flee from Bohemia to the neighboring countries of Saxony, Poland, and Hungary. Two individuals who went into exile were Augustin Heřman and Frederick Philips (Bedřich Filip). After first going to the Netherlands and later to New Amerstdam (today's New York City), Heřman finally settled in Maryland, where he received a tract of land (Bohemian Manor). There, he produced the first accurate map of Maryland and Virginia. Philips settled in New Amsterdam and became an adviser to the new English governor when the English took control of the colony. Some exiles went to Germany, where they found refuge on the estate of Count Nikolaus Ludwig Zinzendorf. Here they revived the Moravian Church, which spread in 1735 to England and America. The Moravian Church continues to exist, especially in America, Europe, and Africa. Another Czech to leave his country was the educator and cleric of the Bohemian Brethren Jan Amos Komenský (also known as Johann Amos Comenius), who contributed to the development of education in several European states.

Ferdinand's confiscation of three-quarters of all the country's estates not only removed resistance to the Crown but also augmented the coffers of the court in Vienna and strengthened the bureaucracy. The defeat of the Bohemian estates at White Mountain thus helped pave the way for absolutism in the realm of the Habsburgs. Ferdinand guaranteed Bohemia's subjugation by transplanting Catholic nobility from all over Europe to Bohemia to take possession of confiscated landed estates. One of those who acquired property in this manner was Filip Fabricius, the scribe whom representatives of the rebel Bohemian estates had cast from the window in the Hrad in 1618. Ferdinand II had honored him with the title Hohenfall, "high fall," adding to the title that Rudolf II had granted him. He thus became known as Filip Fabricius z Rosenfeldu a Hohenfallu. Another who benefitted from the acquisition of confiscated land was Count Albrecht z Valdštejna (Albrecht von Wallenstein), who led Habsburg troops during the Thirty Years' War and commanded the executions in Prague in 1621. Wallenstein was born to Czech nobility of the Bohemian Brethren; for political reasons he decided to Germanize and convert to Catholicism, although he had more faith in astrology than the mass. Wallenstein made a vast fortune through a strategic marriage and the acquisition of confiscated estates. He eventually purchased the Friedland estate in Northern Bohemia, which brought him great status. His pretentiousness and political ambition are apparent in the scale and grandeur of his baroque palace and gardens in Prague (constructed by Italian architects), now housing the Senate of the Czech Republic.

Although Ferdinand conquered Bohemia, the Thirty Years' War continued. After the Bohemian period came the Danish, the Swedish, and the International or Franco-Habsburg periods. In the Danish period (1625–1629), Wallenstein continued to fight the Protestant Danes, who had given military support to the Bohemians, until he imposed a treaty on Denmark. This marked the apogee of Habsburg strength in the wars. At the conclusion of this period, Ferdinand dismissed Wallenstein for good reason. In 1630 Wallenstein received a letter from the Swedish monarch Gustavus Adolphus, who tempted Wallenstein with a principality in exchange for peace. Meanwhile, exiled Bohemians spoke of giving Wallenstein the crown of Bohemia. Spain, Austria's ally, wanted to continue hostilities, since there had been no clear Catholic victory, and Wallenstein's army objected to peace because it meant fewer estates and spoils. Nonetheless, he continued his contacts with the Swedes and opened discussions with the Saxons, Brandenburgers, and even the French—and alienated all of them. The Swedish period (1630–1635) brought initial success for the Protestants when the Saxons occupied Prague for a few weeks in 1632 and enabled exiled Bohemian Protestants to return to the city. Meanwhile, the Swedes, with Catholic French support, advanced toward Austria. Ferdinand had to reappoint Wallenstein as commander, and within a few weeks he ejected the Saxons from Bohemia. After Gustavus Adolphus died in battle in 1632, Wallenstein was less than indispensable for the Habsburgs. In early 1634 Wallenstein began to plot against Ferdinand, but not all of his generals remained loyal to him. Before he was to meet with the Swedes and Saxons, troops loyal to Ferdinand murdered Wallenstein. The Swedish period of the war ended with the Treaty of Prague in 1635, in which Saxony received Lusatia, which never returned to the Bohemian Crown.

In the International or Franco-Habsburg period (1635–1648), Protestant Sweden became allied with Catholic France, demonstrating that politics motivated rulers more than religion. The Swedes entered Bohemia in 1639, and their engagements with the Habsburg forces ravaged the countryside. In 1648 the Swedes took the Prague Castle and Lesser Town, but they were unable to capture the Old Town because of the resistance from the inhabitants, including the Jews. The Swedes plundered Bohemia, confiscating the bulk of paintings from the Hrad that Rudolf II had acquired, transported the library of the noble Petr Volk from Třeboň to Sweden, and sent to Sweden the statues Wallenstein had commissioned for his palace. It became apparent to all belligerents that neither side could claim ultimate victory. Negotiations began for a general peace, but sporadic conflicts erupted. The Peace of Westphalia (24 October 1648) ended the war and extended to Calvinist princes the religious provisions of *cuius regio eius religio* (whose the region, his or hers the religion; in other words, subjects must accept the religion of their ruler) of the Peace of Augsburg (1555). After thirty years, the Habsburgs had the luxury of peace in Europe to reshape the economy and culture of the devastated Czech Lands.

Charles VI, having no male heirs, strove to secure the throne of Austria for his daughter, Maria Theresa, and the Holy Roman Empire for her husband, Francis Stephen of Lorraine. The Hungarian diet accepted Charles's Pragmatic Sanction with renewed Habsburg recognition of the Hungarian legal system and diet; however, the Bohemian estates approved the Pragmatic Sanction without wresting any concessions from Vienna. Foreign powers also accepted the Pragmatic Sanction, but Frederick the Great, who had come to the Prussian throne in 1740 (the same year Maria Theresa took the Austrian throne), did not honor the agreement his father had made. The ensuing War of Austrian Succession (1740–1748) included two conflicts over Silesia (1740–1742; 1744–1748). In the first, Frederick the Great took Kladsko and most of Silesia (aside from Těšínsko and Opavsko) from Bohemia, losses that Austria recognized with the Treaty of Berlin. In 1741 the Bavarian duke, Charles Albert, invaded Bohemia with the assistance of France and Saxony and took the throne. Charles Albert became Holy Roman Emperor in 1742, but in the same year, Austria occupied Munich and Prague, forcing him into exile. Maria Theresa was crowned in Prague in 1743. She rescinded Charles Albert's patent (decree) that had granted freedom to serfs who had supported him against the Habsburgs. Francis Stephen came to the throne of the Holy Roman Empire in 1745, after Charles Albert's death. In the second Silesian War, the Prussians seized Prague for a short while, and the 1745 Treaty of Dresden between Prussia and Austria acknowledged once again Prussia's hold over most of Silesia. Because they supported the Prussians, Maria Theresa issued a decree expelling the Jews from Prague and the Czech Lands by February 1745. (International pressure along with economic necessity however forced Maria Theresa to permit Jews to resettle in the Czech Lands; the expulsion orders were rescinded in 1755.) The War of Austrian Succession, which continued in Italy and Western Europe with France and Spain as allies against Austria, finally ended in 1748. During the Seven Years' War (1756–1763), the Prussians and Austrians again fought over Silesia. The Prussians invaded Bohemia several times, and in 1757 they bombarded Prague. In February 1763 at the Peace of Hubertsburg near Leipzig (the Seven Years' War had ended a few days earlier with the Treaty of Paris), Austria again recognized Prussia's hold over Silesia.

Maria Theresa's military, fiscal, and administrative reforms were consistent with those of other absolutist monarchs in the eighteenth century who sought to centralize the state and eliminate the last vestiges of feudalism. Maria Theresa dramatically increased the size of the standing army and made it more professional to keep Austria's military readiness on a par with that of other major European states. She also hoped a stronger military would help her regain Silesia, where a nascent textile industry had begun to take on economic significance before she came to the throne. To support the military reform, Maria Theresa's chancellor, Count Friedrich Wilhelm Haugwitz, dramatically increased taxes in Austria and Bohemia, which bore the heaviest burden, through the Decennial Recess, so named because the taxes were payable over a period of ten years. To ensure that the proper amount of revenue reached the state coffers, Maria Theresa ordered the First Theresian Cadaster (1748), which surveyed rustical land (i.e., the land the peasants worked), and the Second Theresian Cadaster (1756), which registered the lands of the estates (dominical lands). The tax rate on rustical land was much higher than on dominical land.

Maria Theresa modernized the state administration and centralized it in Vienna. She abolished the separate Austrian and Bohemian Chancelleries in Vienna and replaced them with a Directory of Public and Financial Affairs, under Haugwitz, and a Supreme Court for both Bohemia and Austria. She later abolished the directory and created the Bohemian and Austrian Court Chancellery, which no longer had fiscal powers, other than collecting taxes, and a Treasury. Previously the diets of Bohemia, Silesia, and Moravia (like those in Austria) had elected governors, but Maria Theresa began appointing governors selected from the local nobility. She abolished the administrations under the diets and replaced them with a bureaucratic hierarchy centered in Vienna. Maria Theresa's other reforms included the transfer of censorship from the church to the state and the elimination of most forms of torture. Because Maria Theresa realized that Hungarian nobles would resist any reforms that centralized power in Vienna, she extended few of her reforms to Hungary.

Maria Theresa realized that augmenting the level of education throughout the monarchy would advance the economy, increase state revenues, and improve military efficiency, so she established a system of primary schools, created a network of schools to train teachers, and transferred the *Gymnasia,* college preparatory high schools that focused on the humanities, from the Jesuits to the Piarists after the pope banned the Jesuits in 1773. She placed the universities under the control of the state, which modernized the curricula, for example, by adding agriculture along with administration and commerce as subjects.

After Francis Stephen died in 1765, Maria Theresa's son, Joseph II, served as coregent and Holy Roman Emperor. After Maria Theresa's death, Joseph began a rapid process of reform that represents the culmination of enlightened absolutism in Austria. He was arguably the most "enlightened" of European monarchs. Shortly after coming to the throne, he issued the toleration patent of 1781, which legalized the Lutheran, Calvinist, and Orthodox faiths but did not grant full equality with Catholics. Toleration had its limits, however, and Joseph persecuted those professing religions not enumerated in his toleration patent, frequently sending their adherents to internal exile in Transylvania. The Jews benefited from decrees that eliminated proscriptions regarding their clothing, permitted them to enter schools and universities, allowed them to engage in agriculture, and enabled them to take up specific trades. Because Jews no longer had to live in ghettos, the Jewish population grew in urban areas, such as Prague. Joseph further restricted the power of the Catholic Church. General seminaries under state auspices, including one in Prague and another in Olomouc, became the only means of training priests. Joseph eliminated the contemplative orders, closed 71 out of 154 monasteries and convents in Bohemia and 41 out of 74 in Moravia, and closed 37 churches and many more church-related buildings in the Czech Lands. Joseph earmarked the financial windfall from these closures to fund poor parishes.

Joseph II (1741–1790); Holy Roman Emperor, 1765–1790; King of Austria, 1780–1790. (Library of Congress)

Joseph continued to centralize administrative power in Vienna, systematically destroying what little control over local affairs remained in the hands of the diets. In 1783 he eliminated the Permanent Committee of the Bohemian Kingdom, which since 1714 had managed the affairs of the estates when they were not in session, and transferred its duties to the provincial governor. In 1788 he announced that he would no longer convene the Bohemian diet on an annual basis. Joseph instituted several legal reforms, including the reorganization of the court system of the Czech Lands, the requirement that judges be trained lawyers, the elimination of all forms of torture, and the restriction of capital punishment. He made commoners and nobles equal before the law. In 1786 he issued a decree with respect to individual rights and responsibilities and family law that included the recognition of marriage as a civil contract and the ability of women and illegitimate children to inherit property. Finally he prepared a complementary reform regarding civil matters that became law in 1811. Centralization and the broadening network of schools under Maria Theresa replaced Latin, which had become increasingly cumbersome, with German as the language of administration and education. Joseph went a step further and decreed in 1784 that German was the official state language, even for Hungary.

Hungarian opposition to Joseph's reforms caused him to eliminate all but the toleration and serfdom patents and his monastic reforms in Hungary in 1790 just before he died. He considered himself a failure, despite the fact that many of his reforms had a lasting impact on the monarchy. Joseph's brother, Leopold II, who succeeded him in 1790, undid more of Joseph's reforms, including the tax and urbarial patent and the general seminaries. He reformed Joseph's penal code and placed limits on Joseph's secret police. Inspiration for Leopold's changes came in part from public opinion and the standpoint of the representatives of the upper classes in the diets.

THE NAPOLEONIC WARS

Joseph II opposed the French Revolution, which began in 1789, but he had no desire to involve Austria in French affairs. Leopold II also hesitated to become embroiled in the revolution. For political reasons, in February 1792, he concluded an agreement with Prussia to attack France, should the proper alliance with Britain come about. Leopold died a month later. His successor was Francis II (I) (Francis II of the Holy Roman Empire, 1792–1806; Francis I of the Austrian Empire, 1804–1835), and just weeks after he came to the throne, France went to war against what became known as the First Coalition, ultimately comprising Austria, Prussia, Britain, Spain, and Holland. Russia and Prussia became preoccupied with the second partition of Poland in 1793, and in 1795 Prussia, Russia, and Austria partitioned Poland into oblivion. The First Coalition gradually disintegrated, ending with the peace of Campo Formio in October 1797 between Austria and France. In 1798–1799 Britain organized the Second Coalition against France, which included Austria, Prussia, and Russia. Prussian and then Russian troops marched through the Czech Lands, evoking in some segments of Czech society a sense of Slav solidarity. The Second Coalition ended with the French defeat of Austria and the 1801 Treaty of Lunéville.

In France, Napoleon rose from the position of a general to become First Counsel and then proclaimed himself emperor in 1804. A few months later, Francis, correctly fearing for the fate of the Holy Roman Empire and the loss of his imperial title, proclaimed Austria an empire. In 1805 the British brought together the Austrians and Russians in the Third Coalition against France, which on the Continent appeared unstoppable. In November Napoleon took Vienna and in December defeated Russian and Austrian troops at Slavkov (Austerlitz), not far from Brno, Moravia. In the Treaty of Pressburg (Hungarian Poszony; Slovak Bratislava), the capital of today's Slovak Republic, Austria lost an extensive amount of territory. In 1806 Francis announced the end of the Holy Roman Empire, and Napoleon combined several German states into the Confederation of the Rhine. The Third Coalition ended with the defeat of Prussia and the Treaty of Tilsit in 1807 between Russia and France. In 1809 the Austrians attempted to fight Napoleon alone. The French again marched into Vienna and defeated the Austrians at the Battle of Wagram in July. During this campaign French troops destroyed the Castle Děvín near Bratislava. In early October Francis called on the German Prince Clemens Wenzel Lothar von Metternich-Winneburg to salvage what he could from Austria's defeat. At the Treaty of Schönbrunn, the summer residence of the emperors in Vienna, Austria lost even more territory.

Metternich's intelligence, strategic thinking, cynicism, and perceptiveness with regard to his enemies (i.e., Napoleon) and his allies aided in the defeat of France and the elevation of Austria to one of the great powers of Europe. Metternich must be counted among the outstanding statesmen of modern Europe. In March 1812 Metternich formally allied Austria with France as Napoleon was about to lead his Grand Army eastward in June to defeat Russia, which in 1810 had ended its involvement in the Continental System, Napoleon's grand scheme to boycott Britain, cutting off all trade.Napoleon took Moscow late in the year but had to retreat in 1813, mainly because of the harsh Russian winter. Metternich, who long had been scheming behind Napoleon's back, devised the Fourth Coalition of Austria, Britain, Prussia, and Russia. In the ensuing conflicts, armies of both sides occupied the northern parts of the Czech Lands. The most important engagement was the Battle of Přestanov and Chlumec on 29–30 August, 1813, which the French forces lost. The Fourth Coalition followed through, overcoming the French and their allies at the Battle of Nations on 16–19 October near Leipzig. Finally, Austria and its allies concluded the defeat of France in May 1814 and secured the abdication and exile of Napoleon. Although Napoleon escaped a year later, his defeat at Waterloo brought the wars to an end. Metternich and British prime minister Viscount Castlereagh were the principal negotiators of the Treaty of Vienna in 1815, which restored dynasties to their thrones and redrew the map of Europe.

THE CZECH RENAISSANCE (1781–1848)

The national awakening, or Czech Renaissance, began during the reign of Joseph II and continued until the revolutions of 1848. The Theresian and even more so the Josephinian reforms encouraged an already bourgeoning interest in Czech language and history. As the nineteenth century progressed, economic and political liberalism, nationalism, and romanticism strengthened throughout Europe, and in the Czech Lands they inspired what became known as the Czech Renaissance.

Much of the interest in the history and culture of Bohemia in the late eighteenth century originated with the nobility, even though many of them did not have Czech roots. The *Landespatriotismus* (national patriotism) of the nobility was not merely a result of curiosity. The nobility sought legal grounds for having the Czech Lands regain their long-lost political rights. With the growth of an educated Czech middle class, Landespatriotismus gave way to nationalism.

In the first half of the nineteenth century Czech nationalism was largely cultural. The literary work of Josef Dobrovský (1753–1829) and Josef Jungmann (1773–1847) inspired increased literary activity among Czechs, as well as a broader interest in history and ethnicity. Next, historian František Palacký (1798–1876) and others blended history with politics to advance the Czech nation. Aiding the Czechs in discovering their past and planning their political, cultural, social, and economic future were a series of new institutions, such as theaters and museums, which received broad popular support.

The shift to political nationalism did not come with the French Revolution and the Napoleonic Wars, when the Czechs were loyal to the Habsburgs, despite some intellectuals' flirtation with the idea of Russian assistance in advancing Czech interests in Austria. Political nationalism came late in the *Vormärz* (pre-March) period—the time before the revolutions of 1848, that began in 1835 with the reign of Ferdinand I, known as Ferdinand the Benign because of his limited mental capacity. In 1842 a change in the bylaws of the Society for the Promotion of Industry in Bohemia (Jednota k povzbuzení průmyslu v Čechách), originally an aristocratic organization, extended membership to Czech and German intellectuals and industrialists. The Czechs soon used the society as a forum for cultural and political demands. The first truly politically oriented organization was a secret group that began in 1844 known as Repeal, named after the Irish society that opposed English rule. In 1845 the Citizens Club (Měšťanská beseda) formed as a social group, but it was a haven for political debates.

Espousing a political stand in the first half of the nineteenth century was dangerous. Managing the affairs for Ferdinand I was a state conference of a half dozen men, including Metternich and the Czech noble Count Franz Anton Kolowrat-Liebsteinsky. Metternich continued to concentrate on foreign affairs while Kolowrat, as minister of state, handled the internal administration. To limit the spread of the political aspects of nationalism and liberalism, Kolowrat relied on the Karlsbad Decrees, which Metternich negotiated at a conference in 1819 of the German Confederation in Karlovy Vary (Karlsbad), Bohemia. The Karlsbad Decrees empowered the states of the German Confederation to control universities, prohibit student organizations, provide for strict censorship, and maintain a blacklist of unreliable individuals. One of the victims of the Metternich-Kolowrat regime was the Prague-born priest, mathematician, and philosopher Bernard Bolzano, the son of an Italian art dealer and German mother (Bolzano wrote in German). In 1819, immediately after the proclamation of the Karlsbad Decrees, Bolzano lost his professorship at the University in Prague, in large part due to his efforts to demystify Catholicism and his criticism of social inequality. He had the good fortune to continue his intellectual pursuits through the generosity of a close friend, but he had difficulty publishing his writings. Bolzano is respected today for his work in mathematics as well as logic, methodology, and epistemology.

Aside from the conference in Karlovy Vary that resulted in the Karlsbad Decrees, the other congresses and less important conferences designed to maintain the post-1815 order took place in other cities in the Czech Lands and Austria. From October to December 1820, Metternich hosted a congress in Opava (Troppau), which decided to suppress liberal and nationalist revolts in Naples, Spain, and Portugal. At the Congress of Ljubjana (Laibach), Slovenia, the participants decided to employ Austrian troops against the Neapolitans. At another conference in Mnichovo Hradiště (Münchengrätz), Bohemia, in September 1833, Austria, Russia, and Prussia agreed that Cracow, a small, neutral, and independent republic under the protection of its neighbors since the Congress of Vienna, would lose its independence should the Cracow government prove incapable of restraining nationalism and liberalism.

THE REVOLUTION OF 1848

The revolution that erupted in Prague in the spring of 1848 was related to the revolutions elsewhere in Europe: liberalism and nationalism were at its core; intellectuals, students, and the middle class were its leaders; moderate and then radical demands were its ideological fuel; and military intervention brought its end and the reimposition of the old regime. When news of the 22 February revolution in Paris reached Prague, Repeal organized the St. Václav Committee to draft a petition to the emperor. Initially radicals dominated the discussions, but the involvement of moderates, such as Palacký and the journalist Karel Havlíček Borovský, increased. The lawyer František A. Brauner drafted the petition and another lawyer, Adolf Maria Pinkas, revised it. The final draft, which the emperor received on 22 March, called for a yearly diet to manage the internal affairs of Czech Lands, the equality of Czechs and Germans, the abolition of the *robota,* the service serfs owed their lords, and freedom of the press, assembly, and religion. Seemingly empty promises of change from Vienna prompted the St. Václav Committee to revise its petition, again the work of Brauner, to demand an elected representative body instead of a diet and the creation of a separate ministry in Vienna for the Bohemian Crown. Vienna's answer on 8 April promised an expanded diet that was to include representatives from urban centers and agricultural landholders. The unity of the Czech Lands was to be the subject of further discussion. On 10 April the Advisory Commission of conservatives, which the governor of Bohemia, Rudolf Stadion, had created on 1 April as a counterweight to the liberals, merged with the moderates of the St. Václav Committee to form the National Committee. Radical voices were weaker still. In debating the political restructuring of Bohemia, moderates prevailed in proposing limited franchise and an upper chamber appointed by the lower chamber. Havlíček opposed these measures, while Palacký and Brauner supported them.

The atmosphere in the Czech Lands was electric. The newly gained freedom of the press brought a plethora of newspapers, including *Národní noviny* (National News), with Havlíček as the editor, and the radical *Pražský večerní list* (Prague Evening Gazette). The newspapers as well as leaflets contained songs, poems, editorials, and cartoons. Political groups abounded, notably the liberal and increasingly radical *Slovanská lípa* (Slavonic Linden). Strikes were frequent. Peasants, in a surprising burst of political consciousness, sent about five hundred petitions to the National Committee that demonstrated their frustration with the robota and aired a number of other political and social grievances. The National Committee urged the petitioners to be patient until a constitution could empower an elected legislature to deal with their complaints. German liberals in the Czech Lands supported the Frankfurt Assembly and sought to include Austria in a politically unified Greater Germany. When invited in April 1848 to travel to Frankfurt as a delegate, Palacký responded with his famous dictum: "Certainly, if the Austrian monarchy had not already existed for a long time, then it would be necessary, for the good of Europe—yes, for the good of humanity—now without delay to bring it into being." The question about Austria's inclusion in a restructured Germany sparked a great debate between Germans and Czechs. At times, it had a nasty tone.

As the debates over reforms in Bohemia continued, intellectuals in Prague organized a Slavic Congress. Initially it was to be an Austro-Slavic affair, with Slavs from outside the Austrian Empire attending as observers, but the delegates gathering in June decided to grant the more than three hundred representatives equal status, transforming the congress into a pan-Slavic affair. The congress issued the Manifesto to the European Nations, which extolled the glorious Slavic past and called for equality among nations and an international body to resolve disputes. The Slavic Congress prepared a petition for the Austrian emperor, but it never had the opportunity to approve the document. The greatest achievement of the Slavic Congress was to bolster the national pride of Slavic ethnic groups both inside and outside the monarchy.

Prague was relatively quiet from March through May, in comparison to Vienna, where protests on 13 March forced Metternich's resignation and continued unrest in May prompted the court's flight to Innsbruck. In Prague, the worst violence during this time was a riot against Jews on 1–2 May that resembled the 1844 strike of the cotton printers against the largely Jewish textile entrepreneurs that had degenerated into an anti-Jewish pogrom. The visibility of the military in Prague under General Alfred Windischgrätz provoked the students in particular, and a confrontation between protesters and the military on 12 June resulted in an uprising that lasted until 17 June. Windischgrätz was determined to end the revolt not only because he opposed liberalism but also because a stray bullet had killed his wife on the first day of the revolt. Moreover, Windischgrätz preferred military solutions to negotiation, an attitude that had contributed to the tense atmosphere in Prague before the uprising. With the violence mounting, on 15–16 June Windischgrätz bombarded the Old Town with cannons he had placed strategically on the hills of the left bank of the Vltava. Mostly workers and students were among the approximately fifty killed on the side of the revolutionaries. Buildings in the Old Town sustained some damage, and the Old Town Mills, in a prominent position next to Charles Bridge, lay in ruins. On 17 June, the moderates abandoned the barricades, and the revolt ended. Windischgrätz imposed martial law and hunted down revolutionaries and perceived conspirators.

Czech liberals were among the delegates to the Imperial Parliament that opened in July 1848 in Vienna. After rioting again occurred in Vienna, the court fled in October to Olomouc, and the Imperial Parliament relocated a short distance away in Kroměříž. The liberals favored ending the robota but demonstrated their moderate tendencies through their advocacy of compensation to the nobles for their economic losses. The most important work of the Imperial Parliament was to abolish the robota in September 1848. Palacký wrote two drafts for a constitution, the first based on administrative divisions existing before 1848 and the second on provinces determined by ethnicity, but he resigned after the committee did not approve his second plan. František Ladislav Rieger was the only Czech member of the constitutional committee to advocate universal male suffrage. Another lively debate centered on the bill of rights, which considered wording by Rieger that would maintain the monarchy but give sovereignty to the people.

The revolution in Vienna was over by the end of October 1848. In December 1848 Emperor Ferdinand abdicated and took up residence in the Prague Castle until his death in 1875. The new emperor was Ferdinand's nephew, Franz, who added Joseph to his name, thus invoking the image of the earlier revolutionary emperor, to become Franz Joseph I. The new emperor disbanded the Imperial Parliament, and on 7 March 1849, he issued a constitution (referred to, since it was "decreed," as an *octroyed* constitution) and a bill of rights, and a decree compensating the nobility for losses they sustained from the elimination of the robota. In the spring of 1849 Prague German and Czech radicals, mainly students, cooperated with the Russian revolutionary Mikhail Alexandrovich Bakunin to plan a revolt in May that was to follow an uprising in Dresden. The action in Dresden began a few days early, catching the Prague revolutionaries unprepared. Police arrests ended the venture in Prague, and the so-called May Conspirators received prision sentences of various lengths. With imperial power secure in Bohemia and Austria, conflict remained only in Hungary; in August 1849, the Habsburg military, with the help of the Russian army, forced the Hungarians to surrender.

A year and a half of turmoil gave way to a decade of absolutism under Alexander Bach, who was justice minister and later interior minister in the government of the Bohemian Count Felix Schwarzenberg. Bach became the prime minister after Schwarzenberg's death. The government restricted personal freedoms and completely suppressed political liberalism. The Catholic Church received increased powers, including censorship. Symbolic of the repression was Havlíček, who spent nearly four years (1851–1855) in internal exile in Brixen (now in Italy) for having criticized the *octroyed* constitution. Palacký was under police surveillance. A popular joke at the time claimed that the Austrian Empire was the bureaucrat sitting, the priest kneeling, the army standing, and the spy rampant.

THE ERA OF CONSTITUTIONAL EXPERIMENTATION

After Austria's embarrassing defeat at the Battle of Solfarino at the hands of Piedmont-Sardinia and France in 1859 and the loss of Lombardy, Franz Joseph endeavored to reform Austria's political system. In March 1860 he enlarged the appointed Reichsrat (Imperial Council) to include representatives from the nobility, clergy, towns, and countryside. It was to have an advisory capacity, particularly in economic matters. In his October Diploma of 1860 he proposed to reorganize the empire using a federal approach. To complement the Reichsrat, Franz Joseph planned to give broad powers over local affairs to the diets. The October Diploma faced opposition from the German liberals, who feared that weakening the central authority would strengthen the position of the non-German nationalities, as well as invite fierce resistance from the Hungarians, who wanted greater autonomy for Hungary and the return of Croatia and Transylvania to Hungarian administration. Franz Joseph's response was to implement a highly centralized system with the February Patent of 1861. The Reichsrat became a bicameral legislature that, unlike its predecessor, had the right of legislative initiative and control over the budget. The Crown appointed the House of Lords, while the local diets, now weaker than they would have been under the October Diploma, appointed the three hundred members of the House of Representatives. In turn, elections to the diets were based on the curial system, which divided the qualified electors, about a quarter of the adult population, into four groups: great estate owners (first curia), members of chambers of commerce (second curia), urban inhabitants (third curia), and rural inhabitants (fourth curia). Once it convened in 1861, the Reichsrat accomplished little. Hungarians, Croats, and Italians refused to participate, and the remaining representatives split among those in favor of centralism, largely the Germans, and those who opposed it. In July 1865, after years of political impasse, the first government of Prime Minister Archduke Ferdinand Rainer and Minister of State Anton von Schmerling resigned. The new prime minister, Count Richard Belcredi, a Moravian, was no more successful than his predecessors, and in September 1865 Franz Joseph dismissed the Reichsrat. Belcredi opened negotiations with the Hungarians, and many Czechs saw the talks as a first step toward the adoption of a truly federated political system. When Prussia defeated Austria in the Seven Weeks' War at the Battle of Sadová (near Hradec Králová, i.e., Königgrätz), Bohemia, in 1866, the stalemated talks between the Crown and the Hungarians resumed. Just as in the aftermath of Solfarino, Franz Joseph sought a quick solution to stabilize the country; this time he and his chief negotiator, Count Friedrich Ferdinand Beust, conceded to the Hungarians.

The 1867 *Ausgleich* (Compromise) between Austria and Hungary formed two separate political entities known jointly as Austria-Hungary, or the Dual Monarchy: the Empire of Austria, consisting of Austria, Bohemia, Galicia, Slovenia, and Bukovina (also informally referred to as Cisleithania, using the Leitha River as a border), and the Kingdom of Hungary, including Hungary, Ruthenia, Slovakia, Transylvania, and Croatia (also referred to as Transleithania). Austria and Hungary shared a common ruler, foreign policy, military, and finances to fund the court, diplomatic corps, and military. Otherwise, each half of the monarchy managed its own affairs. The non-German and non-Magyar ethnic groups viewed the Ausgleich as a model for further reforms that would elevate their ethnic group to equality with Germans and Hungarians. Their aspirations remained unfulfilled.

While the Ausgleich enabled the Hungarians to pursue their assimilationist magyarization policies that favored only Hungarian political and cultural advances, it enabled the Austrian portions of the monarchy to construct a dynamic developing democracy. In this respect, the compromise was arguably the most important positive turning point for state building in the Czech Lands since the Battle of White Mountain. Bohemia, Moravia, and Silesia had their own diets, managed more of their own affairs over time, enjoyed increasing political and cultural freedoms, and hosted complex multiparty political systems. Of course, the gains were painfully slow, and long agendas for reform remained before World War I. The greatest obstacle to genuine, representative, pluralistic, parliamentary democracy was the Reichsrat's inability to appoint or remove the government, whose appointment and dismissal remained the prerogative of the Crown. In short, the Reichsrat had no ministerial or governmental responsibility.

POLITICS IN THE CZECH LANDS (1859–1914)

With the October Diploma of 1860, Czech liberals organized in the National Party, but an ever deepening division plagued their ranks. On the one side were the traditional liberals or Old Czechs, under the leadership of Palacký and Rieger; on the other were the Young Czechs, the new generation of liberals grouped around Emanuel Engel, the brothers Edvard Gréger and Julius Grégr, and František Tilšer. The gulf between the two became public when Palacký criticized the Polish uprising of 1863. More significantly, the Young Czechs grew weary of the older liberals' lack of initiative, their close relationship with the conservative Bohemian nobility, and their abstention from participating in the Reichsrat and frequently in the diets, a policy they initiated in June 1863. Although divergent with respect to strategy, all the liberals found common ground in what they referred to as Bohemian state's rights. Formulated over time in a number of venues, a concise exposition of Bohemian state's rights appeared in a declaration Czech liberals presented in the Bohemian diet in August 1868. The most important aspect of state's rights was the unity of the Czech Lands (before the compromise the Hungarians had sought the same with respect to Croatia and Transylvania). The demand for self-government was a corollary to the notion of unity. The greatest hope for the realization of Bohemian state's rights and a turn from "abstention" to "activism" occurred in 1871, when Prime Minister Count Karl Hohenwart struck a bargain with the Czechs that would have given the Czech Lands a single diet and broad autonomy and would have resulted in the Czech language

Count Eduard Taaffe (1833–1895), prime minister of the Austrian portion of the Habsburg Monarchy from 1878 to 1893. (Hulton Archive/Getty Images)

essentially being equal to German in the Czech Lands. Hohenwart scrapped the plan, however, largely because Hungarians opposed any change to the balance of power the compromise had created.

An open break occurred between the Old Czechs and Young Czechs in 1874 during the elections to the Bohemian diet. After the election, the seventy-seven Old Czech deputies refused to attend the sessions of the diet. Meanwhile, the seven Young Czechs not only participated in the diet's proceedings but formally established themselves as the National Liberal Party. Their newspaper was *Národní listy* (National Gazette), which Julius Grégr had established in 1861. Before the 1878 elections to the Bohemian diet, the Young Czechs and Old Czechs reached an agreement to campaign independently but to enter the diet as a single club, thus ending the Old Czech policy of abstention. The Czech liberals participated in the elections to the Reichsrat in 1879, came to terms with the prime minister, the Bohemian noble Count Eduard Taaffe, and entered the Reichsrat.

Taaffe combined several parties, including the Czech liberals, into what was known as the Iron Ring. His government, with many changes in personnel, lasted from 1879 until 1893. One of his first concrete accomplishments in the direction of satisfying Czech demands was the 1880 order placing the Czech language on an equal footing with German in the administration. In 1882 the government divided Prague University into German and Czech sections. Taaffe's government lowered the requirements for voter qualification for the second, third, and fourth curiae in 1882 and 1884. In the election of 1885, undertaken with the participation of more voters, Taaffe's Iron Ring remained in power. Differences in strategy between the Old Czechs and Young Czechs remained, and in 1887 the unity of the Czech Club appeared threatened. In 1888 Edvard Grégr established a rival club. In early 1890 the Old Czechs participated in a series of talks with the Germans in Bohemia under the auspices of the government and charted several reforms, known as the *punktace,* designed to solve the nationality problem in Bohemia and bring the Germans back to the Bohemian diet, which they had refused to enter since 1886. The Young Czechs charged the Old Czechs with compromising the historic unity of the nation. Only a few aspects of the proposed changes ever came into effect. Some Old Czechs in the Bohemian diet deserted their party and joined the Young Czech Party, which now had the majority of seats in the diet. In the electoral campaign for the Reichsrat in 1891, the Young Czechs waged a successful campaign against the Old Czechs, winning thirty-seven seats as opposed to two for the Old Czechs. Given the progress in the areas of culture and civic freedoms of the late nineteenth century, Bohemian state's rights often seemed to become merely a mandatary slogan for any Czech politician, yet it could be a powerful weapon if it appeared that a politician or party was not serving Czech interests. A number of difficulties combined with opposition from the Young Czechs, now in the majority in the Reichsrat, to bring down the Iron Ring in late 1893. Taaffe, who once said that the goal of politics in Austria was to keep all the ethnic groups "in the same well-tempered dissatisfaction," is a prime example of Austrian *Schlamperei und Gemütlichkeit,* the characteristic of being easy-going and carefree or the act of muddling through (quoted in Jászi 1961, 115–116). In reality, he attempted and often succeeded in enacting positive reform. In many respects, he was a politician who sought to accommodate differences and undertake small steps designed to tackle monumental problems, masking it all with a generous dose of the cynicism for which Central Europe is famous.

After Taaffe came Prince Alfred August Windischgrätz and Count Erich Kielmansegg, neither of whom attempted any major reform. The most noteworthy event of this two-year period was the Omladina conspiracy, which the police concocted. In a trial in 1894, sixty-eight out of seventy-six students and workers received prison sentences up to eight years. Although all were amnestied in 1895, the government's actions further shook the confidence of Czechs. In October 1895 Count Kazimir Badeni became prime minister. The greatest accomplishment of his two-year tenure was the Reform Bill of June 1896, which added to the Reichsrat a fifth curia with seventy-two seats (the other four curie had 353 seats) elected on the basis of universal suffrage for males above the age of twenty-four. At the end of the year, Badeni further broadened the franchise by reducing the tax qualification of voters for the third and fourth curiae. In 1897 Badeni attempted to solve the language conundrum in the Czech Lands by issuing the so-called Badeni Decrees, requiring that civil proceedings be conducted in the language of the applicant and that officials have a command of both Czech and German by 1901. Badeni brought about the end of Czech obstruction in the Reichsrat that had begun in 1891 but replaced it with German obstruction and demonstrations in the streets. Badeni had no choice but to resign in November 1897, and his successor, Paul von Gautsch, attempted to limit the selection of languages to mixed areas. Gautsch's compromise satisfied neither the Czechs nor the Germans, and when he resigned in March 1898, the Bohemian noble Count Franz Thun became prime minister. Thun failed to resolve the debate, and the short-lived government of Count Manfred Clary-Aldringen formally withdrew the Badeni Decrees on coming to office in October 1899. Now the Germans were satisfied, but the Czechs formally went into opposition. The government of Ernst von Koerber, which lasted from January 1900 to December 1904, offered a reprieve from the language issue by focusing on the economy, partly through such initiatives as railway and canal expansion and social reforms, including old age and health insurance. Following Koerber were the short governments of Gautsch from January to May 1906 and Prince Konrad Hohenlohe-Schillingsfürst from 2 May to 28 May 1906. No prime minister ever found a language formula satisfactory to either nationality.

One glimmer of hope in settling the nationality problem in the Czech Lands came from Moravia through the so-called Moravian Pact (also known as the Moravian Compromise). In November 1905, after seven years of negotiations, the Moravian diet approved changes to the administration of Moravia, regulations regarding the official use of German and Czech, new procedures for elections to the Moravian diet, and education reforms. The laws effectively divided the election rolls and schools along nationality lines. The curiae of the Moravian diet remained, but the reform created a fourth, popularly elected curia (similar to the fifth curia in the Reichsrat), expanded the number of seats in each of the other three curiae for a total of 151 seats (including the archbishop of Brno and the bishop of Olomouc as ex officio representatives), and allotted a specific number of seats in the second, third, and fourth curiae to Czechs (73 seats—a few seats shy of a guaranteed majority) and Germans (46 seats). There was no division along ethnic lines for the first curia of great estate representatives and in the second curia for the cities of Brno and Olomouc, each with three seats. In January 1906, although technically not part of the Moravian Pact, the diet adopted measures to limit obstruction in its proceedings. The Moravian Pact stayed in force, despite its shortcomings, throughout the remaining years of the monarchy, and the Moravian diet continued to function, unlike its Bohemian counterpart. The Moravian Pact reduced ethnic tensions and simultaneously thwarted efforts to introduce universal male suffrage in the diet.

After the fall of Taaffe, Franz Joseph hopelessly sought a prime minister who could bring stability to the administration and the government and calm the politicians in the Reichsrat, who subordinated every major issue to the nationality question. The quick succession of prime ministers after Taaffe was linked with the turmoil on the floor of the Reichsrat, but the deputies' preoccupation with nationality issues was in turn connected to tensions rooted in ideology. For Czechs and Germans, the liberalism of the generation of 1848 had lost nearly all of its credibility. Although it had brought economic progress, it was defenseless against the protracted depression that began of 1873. Despite the cultural achievements to its credit, traditional liberalism could not offer Germans in the Czech Lands a secure position for their culture nor could it elevate Czech culture to at least equal status with German culture. The anticlericalism of traditional liberalism alienated the Catholic Church and its lay supporters. Finally, the ideology of the wealthy and established bourgeois had no appeal to the growing number of workers and the many tradesmen, small business owners, and professionals. The heated debates over cultural issues during the period of the Taaffe government and through the early years of the twentieth century were associated with the decline of liberalism and the rise of competing ideologies and, ultimately, political parties.

After Rieger died in 1903, the leadership of the Old Czechs was insufficient for the party to recapture its former strength. The Young Czechs dominated politics in Bohemia in the early and mid-1890s. Their most important politician was Josef Kaizl and then, after Kaizl's death, Karel Kramář. In the Moravian People's Party, an extension of the Young Czechs, Adolf Stránský was the leading figure. The Reichsrat elections of 1891 marked the first of three electoral victories for the Young Czechs. They handily won the elections to the Bohemian diet in November 1895, emerging with eighty-nine seats to the Old Czechs' three. When the elections to the Reichsrat took place in March 1897, the Young Czechs won sixty seats, and the Old Czechs had none. However, after the elections to the Reichsrat in 1900–1901, the Young Czechs had only fifty-three seats, with rival groups gaining ground. After the 1901 elections to the Bohemian diet, the Young Czechs won only sixty-six seats. They still had the largest number of deputies in the diet, but other parties strengthened their appeal to the voters.

Like the Old Czechs before them, the Young Czechs could not maintain their universal appeal in an increasingly diverse society. Generational differences complicated matters, as they did in nearly all the parties, and young politicians in the liberal and socialist movements formed what became known as the progressive movement. Some socialist progressives actually established a short-lived party, but the movement had a greater impact on the Young Czechs. A liberal group of Young Czechs broke from the party in 1897 to form the Radical Progressive Party. Meanwhile, young nationalist and antisocialist activists, including Alois Rašín, Karel Baxa, and Jaroslav Preiss, coalesced among the Young Czechs and established themselves as the State-Rights Radical Party in 1899.

The most powerful political party to emerge from the Young Czechs was the Agrarian Party. In the 1880s most nobles and well-to-do farmers (as opposed to peasants, most of whom could not vote) lent their support to the Young Czechs, despite their party's weak commitment to rural issues. In the elections to the Moravian diet of 1884 two independent politicians successfully ran on the promise of specifically serving their agrarian constituents. The first Agrarian Party in Bohemia emerged from the Young Czechs in 1891 under the leadership of Alfons Šťastný, and it sent two deputies to the Bohemian diet in 1895. In 1899 agriculturalists in the Young Czech Party sponsored Karel Prášek in an election to fill a vacancy in the Bohemian diet; days after he was elected, the group broke with the Young Czechs to create the Agrarian Party. Šťastný's party merged with the Agrarians the next year. In the Reichsrat elections of 1901 the Agrarians sent five deputies to Vienna. In the elections to the Bohemian diet in 1901 the party secured twenty-one seats and was second in strength to the Young Czechs. The Agrarian Party grew in membership, in part through its sponsorship of auxiliary agricultural organizations throughout the Czech Lands. Crucial among them was the Union of Sugar Beet Growers, which came under the leadership of Antonín Švehla, one of the party's most influential young politicians. In 1905 Moravian politicians merged with the Agrarians in Bohemia. The Agrarians had the third strongest party in the Moravian diet in 1906. In late 1905, when Švehla and his allies amended the conservative 1903 party program to support universal male suffrage, the Agrarian Party was poised to become one of the largest mass parties in the Czech Lands.

Tomáš G. Masaryk (1850-1937), who became the first president of Czechoslovakia in 1918. (Bettmann/Corbis)

The Realist Party, which had its roots in the Young Czech Party, was small but influential. Its founder was Tomáš G. Masaryk, a professor at Charles-Ferdinand University. In 1890 he was elected as a Young Czech to the Reichsrat. Three years later, he left the party, and in 1900 he established the Realist Party (technically the Czech People's Party, later the Progressive Party), which had the backing of a number of respected intellectuals. Although it would be several years before the Realists would send a deputy to the Reichsrat, Masaryk strove to build support for his program. Realism, as best understood through Masaryk's works, including *Česká otázka* (Czech Question; 1895) and *Naše nynější krise* (Our Current Crisis; 1895), as well as *Ideály humanitní* (Ideals of Humanity; 1901), advocated a rational, objective approach to all social, political, and national questions of the day grounded in the principle of humanitarianism, which Masaryk believed was a constant thread through Czech history. Masaryk's views and willingness to take unpopular stands for the sake of the moral foundation of the nation can be seen in two cases. The first was a manuscript controversy that occurred in 1886 when he led a small group of scholars in revealing as forgeries two manuscripts allegedly demonstrating that the Czech literary heritage was one of the oldest in Europe. Then in 1899, during the Hilsner trial, he discredited the crime of ritual murder and commuted the death sentence of a Jew convicted of the crime.

The socialist movement in the Czech Lands had a long history separate from other political parties. In a pub in the Prague district of Březno in April 1878, just over a dozen activists established the Social Democratic Workers Party. At first, socialists throughout the monarchy attempted to maintain one party, in accordance with the theory of Karl Marx and Friedrich Engels that workers were to transcend the capitalist-imposed limits of nationality that prevented or deterred the workers from overthrowing the capitalists. In 1896, however, the Czech socialists voted to maintain a separate party. With Badeni's electoral reforms, the workers could vote in the fifth curia, and in 1897 they elected five Social Democrats to the Reichsrat. In 1897 the Czech National Socialist Party (similar to Germany's Nazi Party only in name) emerged from the Social Democratic movement, its adherents setting aside Marxist internationalism in favor of Czech nationalism and, unlike the Social Democrats, supporting Czech state rights. The National Socialist Party also was decidedly reformist rather than revolutionary in character. As a result of the elections of 1900–1901 to the Reichsrat, the National Socialists sent three deputies and the Social Democrats two deputies to Vienna. In the 1901 elections to the Bohemian diet, neither party gained enough votes to enter the diet, but five Social Democrats entered the Moravian diet after the election of 1905.

To counter the anticlericalism of the liberals and the atheism of the socialists, Catholics organized their own political parties. In September 1894 the Christian Socialist Party began in Moravia, whose population historically was more supportive of Catholicism than that of Bohemia. The

Tomáš G. Masaryk (1850–1937)

Several outstanding individuals are in the pantheon of great historical figures in Czech history, including Charles IV, who in the fourteenth century led the Kingdom of Bohemia during its golden age, and Jan Hus, who in the late fourteenth and early fifteenth inspired Bohemia's pre-Lutheran reformation. The most significant personality of the modern age is Tomáš G. Masaryk. Americans and West Europeans know Masaryk as the founder of Czechoslovakia and champion of its democracy, and his image in this regard is exaggerated. It took the effort of many to create Czechoslovakia during World War I. Between the world wars, Masaryk himself could not sustain Czechoslovak democracy. Nevertheless, Masaryk was a major figure in the culmination of the national movement in the early twentieth century and a key player in the Czechoslovak political arena until shortly before his death.

Masaryk was born in March 1850 in Moravia to a Slovak coachman on an imperial estate and his Moravian wife. He studied at the University of Vienna, where he taught from 1878 until 1882. There he completed his dissertation, published in English as *Suicide and the Meaning of Civilization* (published in German as *Der Selbstmord als sociale Massenerscheinung der modernen Civilisation* in 1881 and in English in 1970). In 1882 he relocated to Prague and began teaching at the newly formed Czech branch of Prague University, where he became a professor in 1897. His publications on sociology, then an emerging field, dealt with work ethics, women's rights, and alcoholism. His interest in philosophy led him to examine the tenets of classical liberal thought. Czech affairs and politics occupied most of his efforts. He analyzed the lives of Hus, Havlíček, and Palacký. He addressed political concerns in such works as *Česká otázka* (The Czech Question) and *Naše nynější krise* (Our Current Crisis), both published in 1895. He helped publish three journals, *Athenaeum, Čas* (Time), and *Naše doba* (Our Age).

After joining the Young Czech Party, Masaryk ran for the Reichsrat and served as a deputy from 1891 until he resigned in 1893 over differences with the party's leadership. With several others, he established the Czech Populist (Realist) Party in 1900, which became the Czech Progressive Party in 1906 and was always popularly known as the Realist Party. This political party had limited success, but it put Masaryk in the Reichsrat from 1907 until 1914.

As a professor and politician, Masaryk became involved in several controversies, advancing his reputation of taking the side of the underdog in the interest of truth and fairness. As a professor in 1886, Masaryk exposed the forged medieval Králův Dvůr and Zelená Hora manuscripts that would have assigned Czech a literary heritage equal to that of the Germans. Then in 1899 he came to the defense of Leopold Hilsner, a Jew falsely accused of ritual murder. Masaryk's efforts moved Emperor Franz Joseph to commute Hilsner's death sentence to life imprisonment, and Emperor Karl pardoned him in 1918. Masaryk discredited the legal basis for ritual murder. In 1909 he proved that the government had used forged documents against Serb students being tried for conspiracy, and Masaryk's efforts brought the repeal of their sentences. He also exposed a forgery in 1909–1910 designed to justify the strong anti-Serb policy of Austro-Hungarian foreign minister Count Lexa von Aehrenthal.

In 1878 Masaryk married the American-born Charlotte Garrigue (1850–1923), whose maiden name Masaryk took as his middle name on their marriage. They had four children: Alice, who was prominent in the Red Cross and YWCA in Czechoslovakia; Herbert, an artist; Jan Masaryk, who became an ambassador between the world wars and Czechoslovakia's foreign minister during and after World War II; and Olga, the youngest.

When World War I erupted, Masaryk left Austria-Hungary and traveled to Italy, Switzerland, France, and finally Britain. With Edvard Beneš and Milan Štefánik, Masaryk established the National Council and the Czechoslovak Legions to liberate the Czech Lands and Slovakia from Habsburg rule. Masaryk and his associates worked tirelessly to create the state, with no guarantee of success until late in the war. Masaryk's old contact in America, the industrialist Charles R. Crane, with whom he shared a common interest in Russian affairs, helped Masaryk meet the American President Woodrow Wilson, who at first was not sympathetic to the destruction of Austria-Hungary. Masaryk toured America, meeting with Czech and Slovak groups and signing documents committing his movement to the creation of a democratic state. The most famous was the Pittsburgh Agreement of May 1918. The desire of other nationalities to separate from the monarchy, the popularity of Masaryk in influential Allied circles, the forcefulness of the Czech and Slovak cause, the exploits of the Czechoslovak Legions, and the pressure of émigré communities of Slovaks and Czechs abroad led the Allies in early 1918 to recognize Masaryk's National Council as the legal representative of the new state.

(continues)

(continued)

Masaryk returned to Czechoslovakia in November 1918, after the Revolutionary National Assembly had elected him president in absentia. Masaryk, now sixty-eight years old, had no intention of assuming a role as a symbolic head of state. When the Revolutionary National Assembly drafted a constitution, Masaryk lobbied for a strong president, achieving only partial success. Masaryk ensured the president would play an active role in foreign affairs, in part through his support of Beneš as perennial foreign minister. He assembled a competent staff of advisers in the Hrad, to which gravitated prominent politicians from all the major political parties. Masaryk was involved as a power broker for coalition governments, particularly in cooperation with Antonín Švehla, the Republican leader. When politicians were unable to reach decisions, Masaryk and the Hrad helped broker deals. When Švehla became ill in late 1927, the Hrad and Masaryk's involvement in political affairs increased. Although as president, Masaryk was never a member of any political party, he favored moderate Social Democratic policies.

Slovaks and Czechs hailed Masaryk as the president-liberator and showered him with admiration when he attended functions or toured the countryside. *Hovory s T. G. Masarykem* (Conversations with T. G. Masaryk, 1928; released in English in 1938 as *Masaryk on Thought and Life),* based on interviews Karel Čapek had with Masaryk, became one of the most widely read books among Czechs and Slovaks. Masaryk resigned from the presidency in December 1935 because of ill health, and he died on 14 September 1937. Czechs and Slovaks mourned his passing. A cult of personality surrounded Masaryk when he was alive, and it intensified after his death. Thousands of laudatory speeches, articles, pamphlets, and books appeared about Masaryk in a variety of languages. Only some are truly useful in gaining an understanding of this career.

Masaryk's devotion to democracy, despite the shortcomings of the Czechoslovak First Republic, motivated many Czechs and Slovaks during the dark days of World War II and in their efforts after 1945 to rebuild the state. After the Communist coup d'état in 1948, the Communist authorities criticized Masaryk for having led a regime that had suppressed the workers and peasants. The efforts of historians and journalists to place Masaryk in a more objective light during the Prague Spring of 1968 ended with the Warsaw Pact invasion of August 1968. Masaryk once again fell out of favor. Nevertheless, the Communist government could not eradicate the positive memory of Masaryk, and flowers always adorned his grave in Lány, Bohemia, in the cemetery not far from the president's residential palace. The openness that accompanied the Velvet Revolution of 1989 brought renewed respect for Masaryk. Václav Havel, the president of Czechoslovakia and later the Czech Republic between 1989 and 2003, openly expressed his desire to return to the office of president the respect Masaryk had brought it. Scholars once again attempted to examine his activities. The significance of Masaryk long after his death can be seen in the high regard Czechs and Slovaks have for him, the painstaking efforts of the Communist regime to discredit him, and the revived interest since 1989 in understanding Masaryk and his role in Czech and Slovak politics.

basis of its ideology was the papal encyclical *Rerum Novarum,* issued three years earlier, which condemned capitalism for the poverty it created and called for socialist parties and trade unions based on Catholic, rather than atheistic Marxist, principles. The most important Christian Socialist politician in the Czech Lands, Jan Šrámek, was a Catholic priest, but his party was not subservient to the Vatican or the Catholic hierarchy. Šrámek cooperated with Mořic Hruban, who established the National Catholic Party in Moravia in 1896 that appealed to the upper classes, as opposed to the workers, and was closely tied with the Moravian National Party (i.e., the Old Czechs in Moravia). Other smaller Catholic parties emerged in Bohemia and Moravia. In the Bohemian diet and the Reichsrat, the Catholic parties never gained more than a few seats. The Catholics' greatest strength, however, was in Moravia, and in the 1906 Moravian diet, the Catholic parties had twenty-four seats, the largest bloc in the diet.

Still important in politics at the turn of the twentieth century was the German and Czech alliance of nobles in the Conservative Estate Owners' Party, which in the 1890s cooperated with the Young Czechs. Its prominent members were Karel Buquoy, Alfred August Windischgrätz, Jiří Kristián Lobkovic, Franz Thun, and members of the Belcredi, Clam-Martinic, and Schwarzenberg families.

In the era of the Taaffe government, traditional German liberalism throughout Austria gave way to new forms of politics, as did Czech liberalism. For younger Germans, traditional liberalism had failed to guarantee the superiority of German culture, and the cooperation of the Slavs in the Iron Ring served as proof. The German Liberal Party, which had undergone several name changes, became the German Progressive Party in 1897. It attempted to attract more small business owners and agriculturalists, but it could not hope to unify German politics or regain its popularity. In 1878 it had eighty-three seats and was the strongest party in the

Bohemian diet, but in the election of 1901 it had only twenty-six seats. Challenges to the German Progressives came mainly from two directions. First, going well beyond the Linz Program of 1882, which called for the unity of German lands in Austria, the Austrian politician Georg von Schönerer advanced his concept of a single German state and his intense anti-Semitism. His supporters in the Czech Lands formed the German National Party in 1891, which became the German People's Party (the Populists) in 1895. The party drew from the German Liberals, and in the 1883 election to the Bohemian diet had thirty-six seats. The movement split, and in 1902 Karl Hermann Wolf, a German in Bohemia who had been close to Schönerer, formed the Free Pan-German Party, eventually known as the German Radical Party. Wolf was not as committed to the division of Austria as Schönerer. Second, German Catholics banded together in the German Christian Socialist Party, led by Karl Lueger in Austria. The agriculturalists formed the German Agrarian Party, which had little influence for several years, and there was a small German Social Democratic Party. In Silesia there were some small Polish parties that reflected the political spectrum elsewhere in the Czech Lands.

The successful struggle for universal male franchise in Belgium in 1893, and more importantly, the Russian Revolution of 1905 encouraged younger politicians, including Social Democrats and politicians from several parties eager to expand their constituencies, to demand universal male suffrage in Austria. An earthquake in Austrian politics came in 1907, when Franz Joseph eliminated the five curiae in the Reichsrat and created one body elected through universal male suffrage. In 1907 voters directly elected 516 deputies to the Reichsrat: 233 Germans, 108 Czechs, 81 Poles, 37 South Slavs, 33 Ruthenians, 19 Italians, and 5 Romanians (voting results by nationalities often show slight variations depending on how authors report, for example, Jewish parties, independent deputies, or unoccupied seats). With universal male suffrage, certain social groups, like the great estate owners, lost their guaranteed representation through the curia system, but representation for other groups (e.g., the workers) dramatically expanded, even though the number of votes it took to elect a deputy varied greatly based on location and nationality. Furthermore, smaller parties found it necessary to cooperate in order to compete with larger ones, a process that the gradual restructuring of provincial diets to universal male suffrage encouraged.

The elections to the Reichsrat in 1907 brought stunning changes in the complexion of politics in the Czech Lands. The Agrarians won twenty-eight seats and became the largest Czech party in Vienna. Švehla, who had championed universal male suffrage in the Agrarian Party, became the most respected politician in the party and was elected party chairman in 1909. Prášek, the senior Agrarian politician in Vienna, accepted the Ministry of Czech Affairs in the newly recast government of Max Vladimir von Beck. The Czech Social Democrats, who once had minimal representation in the Reichsrat, now were the second strongest party with 24 deputies. The Young Czechs had 18 deputies, the clerical parties had 17 (including 10 from the People's Party in Moravia), the National Socialists (who ran with the Radical Progressives and the Radical State-Rights Party in the Czech State Rights Democracy electoral bloc) had 9, the Old Czechs had 6, the Realists had 2, including Masaryk; and 2 deputies had no party affiliation. The major winners among the German parties were the German Social Democrats, with 21 deputies; the German Agrarians, with 19; the German Progressive Party, with 14; the German People's Party, with 13; and the German Radicals, with 12. In the following year the elections to the Bohemian diet confirmed what had occurred in the Reichsrat elections. The Agrarians had the strongest party, with 43 seats. The Young Czechs had 38 seats, the electoral bloc of National Socialists, Radical Progressives, and States Rights Radicals received 5 seats (shortly after the election, the Czech Radical Progressive and the Radical States Rights parties merged to form the State-Rights Progressive Party), the Old Czechs won 4 seats, and the Clericals and Realists each received 1 seat. There also were 6 independent deputies. To the Czechs' 98 seats, the Germans had 68; Progressives, 19; Agrarians, 15; Radicals and Pan-Germans, 15 and 4, respectively; Populists, 8; Christian Socialists, 2; and independents, 5. The Social Democrats received nearly 10 percent of the vote, but the curia system prevented them from entering the diet.

Beginning in 1908, ethnic issues strangled politics in the legislatures in Vienna and Prague. The Bohemian diet began discussing administrative reform and the introduction of universal male suffrage in Bohemia when it met in September 1908. The Germans in the Bohemian diet objected to the proposals and began obstructing the sessions, ultimately closing the diet. The Czechs in retaliation obstructed proceedings in the Reichsrat. Further efforts by the government and the parties both in the Reichsrat and the Bohemian diet to solve the deadlocks met with failure. The stalemate caused Franz Joseph to lose confidence in Beck. The new prime minister, Count Richard Bienerth, headed a government that lasted from November 1908 to June 1911, but the Bienerth cabinet's longevity was not linked with its success in lessening Czech-German discord. When the Czechs succeeded in disrupting the Reichsrat in February 1909, Bienerth adjourned it. From that point, Bienerth circumvented the Reichsrat and ruled by decree, as provided in Article 14 of the Austrian constitution. This tactic became a common policy.

The Reichsrat elections of 1911 brought few major changes. The Agrarians strengthened their numbers in Vienna with 38 seats. The Social Democrats had 25 seats (plus 1 Social Democrat–Centralist from Silesia); the Young Czechs, 18; the National Socialists, 14; the National Catholics and Christian Socialists, which ran as an electoral bloc, 7; the Moravian People's party, 4; the States Rights Progressives, 2; the Realists and Old Czechs each had 1; and there was 1 independent. The strongest German parties in the Czech Lands were the German Radical and German Agrarian parties, each with 22 seats, and the German Social Democrats with 18. On the basis of the election, Paul von Gautsch, the new prime minister, formed a government in June 1911. Franz Joseph replaced him in November 1911 with Count Karl Stürgkh, whose cabinet lasted until October 1916, when Stürgkh fell victim to an assassin. Because of further obstruction, Franz Joseph prorogued the Bohemian diet on 26 July 1913 until new elections could be held, but the monarchy ended before they could take place. In retaliation, the Czechs disrupted the Reichsrat in March 1914. It adjourned in March and did not reconvene until the closing stages of World War I. Obstruction became an infamous political tool in the Bohemian diet and the Reichsrat.

The last major political event before World War I in the Czech Republic was the Šviha Affair of 1914. Information had emerged that Karel Šviha, a National Socialist Reichsrat deputy, was spying on his own party for the police. The Czech political parties appointed a panel of judges from among top politicians to examine the matter. Šviha discussed political affairs with the heir to the throne, Franz Ferdinand, but he was not a police informant. Nevertheless, he had to retire from politics. The affair served to bring to the fore a number of issues and demonstrated the tension between Masaryk and Kramář.

WORLD WAR I (1914–1918)

Normal political life in Austria never resumed after the assassination of Franz Ferdinand and his Czech wife, Žofie Chotková, on 28 June 1914. The emperor did not call into session the Reichsrat or Bohemian diet and closed the Moravian and Silesian diets in July. Count Stürgkh continued to rule by decree, and once the war broke out, he used military courts, persecuted ethnic organizations, such as the Czech Sokols, and restricted basic freedoms. The government imposed press censorship, made German the official language, confiscated objectionable books, and rewrote school textbooks. After the assassination of Stürgkh in October 1916, Franz Joseph once again appointed as prime minister the progressive and devoted von Koerber. Franz Joseph died in November 1916, and Koerber resigned over differences with the new emperor, Karl. Four prime ministers followed. All had the best interests of the monarchy and its people at heart, but they faced insurmountable odds when attempting to adjudicate between the wishes of the emperor, the demands of the Hungarians, the difficulties at the front, the skepticism of political leaders at home, the increasing number of strikes and mutinies, the growing inability to feed urban populations, and a host of other wartime concerns. The last minister, Heinrich Lammasch, for all practical purposes presided over a government in a state that already had collapsed.

In November 1914 Masaryk left Austria, having decided that democratic reform would not happen. He worked with his former student, Edvard Beneš, to help construct a close-knit, secret organization in Prague for the creation of an independent Czech state. It was known as the Mafia (Czech: *Maffie*) because it imitated the intrigue, although not the violence, of the Sicilian gangsters. Some in the Mafia were devoted to the ideals of Masaryk, who preferred a democratic republic, while others, such as the Young Czechs Kramář and Rašín, wanted Bohemia to become part of a large Slavic empire under Russia, which they expected to evolve into a constitutional monarchy as a result of the war. Masaryk and Beneš, who eventually settled abroad as well, joined forces with a Slovak astronomer working in France, Milan Rastislav Štefánik, to establish the Czechoslovak National Council. Masaryk, Beneš, and Štefánik carried on a propaganda effort among the Czech and Slovak emigrants and promoted the Czech cause to governments in London, Paris, Rome, St. Petersburg, Washington, and elsewhere.

Edvard Beneš (1884–1948), foreign minister of Czechoslovakia from 1918 to 1935, president of Czechoslovakia from 1935 to 1938, president of the government in exile during World War II, and president of postwar Czechoslovakia from 1945 to 1948. (Library of Congress)

In the Czech Lands, the various Czech political parties looked after the interests of Czechs and prepared for either eventuality—the continuation of Austria-Hungary or its demise. In an atmosphere of solidarity, they formed several associations to represent Czech interests. One of the most important was the Czech Union of Deputies to the Reichsrat, which included the Agrarians and Socialists, although not the Realists and State-Rights Progressives. The Czech Union presented two declarations of loyalty to the Habsburgs in January 1917. Despite their expressions of confidence in the monarchy, the leaders of the major parties kept abreast of the liberation movement abroad, maintained contact with key

Slovak politicians, especially Vavro Šrobár and Milan Hodža, and cooperated with the Mafia. Although the Mafia continued to collect valuable information and recruited a number of supporters in key political and administrative positions, it faced great difficulties at the hands of the Austrian police. Masaryk's wife was under the watchful eye of the police, and one of his daughters, Alice, spent several months in prison for treason in 1915–1916 because of her Mafia links. In 1914 the police arrested Václav Klofáč, the leader of the National Socialist Party, and in 1915 they took Kramář and Rašín into custody. A court tried them for treason and sentenced them to death, but Franz Joseph commuted the sentences to life imprisonment. When he came to the throne, Emperor Karl released the three along with more than seven hundred others as a gesture of goodwill.

Czechs were generally loyal, although not enthusiastic, as Habsburg soldiers. They donned their uniforms and took up their rifles with a measure of good ol' Austrian *Schlamperei und Gemütlichkeit,* so well depicted in the fictional hero in the famous novel *Osudy dobrého vojáka Švejka za světové války* (The Fate of Soldier Švejk During the World War, 1920–1923, published in English as *The Good Soldier Schweik*) by the Czech novelist Jaroslav Hašek. Although most fought dutifully at the front, there were exceptions. Particularly famous, albeit unusual, were the wholesale desertions of the Prague 28th Regiment in April 1915 and the 36th Mladá Boleslav Infantry Regiment in June 1915 to the Russians. It was common, however, for Czech and Slovak prisoners of war to form regiments fighting the Central Powers. In 1916 Štefánik, who had become a French citizen before the war and a French pilot during the war, spearheaded the formation of the legions from among Austro-Hungarian prisoners of war to fight on the Allied side. Eventually there were nearly 65,000 legionaries in Russia (32,000 troops), Italy (22,000 troops), and France (10,000 troops). The most famous legion was in Russia, where the Slovaks and Czechs could not continue fighting the Central Powers after the March 1918 separate peace the Bolsheviks had concluded with the Central Powers at Brest-Litovsk. Masaryk put the disposition of the Czechoslovak Legion in Russia in the hands of the Allied leaders, particularly the American President Woodrow Wilson. The Allies decided that the Czechs and Slovaks were to make their way across Russia on the Trans-Siberian Railroad to Vladivostok, where they would board Allied ships that would transport them to the Western Front. The Bolsheviks attempted to disarm them, partly to fulfill the requirements of the Brest-Litovsk treaty but also because they feared the legionaries, the majority of whom were not sympathetic to the Bolsheviks and might ally themselves with the noncommunist Whites in the Russian civil war. The Czechoslovak Legion held the Bolsheviks at bay and ended up occupying the entire Trans-Siberian railroad, a distance of some 8,000 kilometers, as they headed toward Vladivostok. By the time the Czechoslovak Legion from Russia landed in Western Europe, the war had ended. Nevertheless, they were heroes to the Czechoslovaks and Allies alike.

When the war erupted, Slovak leaders in Europe and America discussed cooperation between Czechs and Slovaks within a reformed empire or union of the two ethnic groups in an independent state. Close ethnic ties between the Czechs and Slovaks formed the basis of such plans, but geo-political, military, and economic reasons also existed. While on a visit to the United States, Masaryk and his Czech associates concluded several agreements with Slovak emigres. The most important was the one signed in 1918 in Pittsburgh, Pennsylvania, after a Memorial Day parade through the city. The so-called Pittsburgh Agreement pledged to join the two nations in one democratic state, giving autonomy to the Slovaks. Gregory I. Zatkovich, a Pittsburgh lawyer who had emigrated to America as a child, made arrangements with Masaryk for the Rusyns, an East Slavic group closely related to but distinct from the Ukrainians, to join the Czechoslovak state. The Rusyns confirmed this agreement with a referendum after the war.

The Allies did not immediately accept the notion of breaking up Austria-Hungary and creating separate states. The Allied leaders listened to Masaryk, Beneš, and Štefánik, but they did not recognize their Czech National Council as an official government of a new state until near the close of the war—France in June 1918, Britain in August, the United States in September, and Italy in October. A major factor contributing to the Allied decision to back Masaryk's National Council was the Czechoslovak Legionaries' commitment to the Allied cause and their remarkable saga in Siberia.

Despite his promises for reform, Emperor Karl was slow to react and quickly lost credibility with the Czechs. Meanwhile, a change in the attitude of the Czechs in the Habsburg Empire came after America entered the war in April 1917. When Karl finally called the Reichsrat into session, the opportunities for negotiating with the ethnic groups of the monarchy had dwindled. The Reichsrat met on 30 May 1917, and the Czech Union demanded autonomy for the Czechs in an association with the Slovaks within a federated monarchy. Nearly a year later, the Central Powers presented harsh terms to the Bolsheviks and forced them to sign the Treaty of Brest-Litovsk in March 1918. Now, the Czech politicians came to believe that victory for the Central Powers, even though it appeared unlikely, would be disadvantageous and perhaps even disastrous for the Czechs. Politicians who had maintained a glimmer of hope for a truly democratic Austria, including Švehla of the Agrarian Party, who had been instrumental with Bohumír Šmeral of the Social Democrats in coordinating the efforts of Czech politicians, now finally supported independence. The first clear statement calling for Czech independence and Slovak self-determination that had the backing of all the major Czech parties was the Epiphany Declaration of 6 January 1918. In July 1918 all the Czech parties joined together for the first time to form the Czechoslovak National Committee (technically the restructuring of an already existing organization) under the leadership of Švehla. It included the clericals, who had supported the Habsburgs and had not been involved in previous groupings of the Czech parties, but it did not contain any Slovaks, for fear that the Hungarians might persecute them. Karl announced a plan for the federation of the Austrian half of the monarchy on 16 October 1918, but it met with little enthusiasm on the part of any ethnic group.

In October 1918 Beneš and others from the National Council met representatives of the National Committee and the Czech Mafia in Geneva, Switzerland, to form a government. On 27 October, as the meeting was about to take place, the Czech politicians in Prague received information about Vienna's peace proposal to Washington. After lengthy debates that lasted into the night, the Prague politicians decided to declare independence the following day. Among the signers was Šrobár, who had just arrived in Prague after recently having been released from a Hungarian prison. The National Committee took power peacefully. One of the most dramatic events in Prague occurred on 3 November, when a crowd toppled the Marian Column in the Old Town Square that Ferdinand III had erected in 1650 to commemorate Prague's victory over the Swedes at the close of the Thirty Years' War in 1648. The monument was based on a similar column erected in 1638 in Munich that celebrated the victory of the Habsburgs over the Bohemian estates at White Mountain.

The peacemakers in Paris established the borders of the newly independent Czechoslovak Republic in the Treaty of St. Germain, signed with Austria in September 1919, and the Treaty of Trianon, signed with Hungary in 1920. The treaties acknowledged the union of the Czech Lands with Slovakia and Ruthenia. Czechoslovakia was to pay a "contribution to liberation," which in 1921 the Allies set at 750 million gold francs or 12,750,000,000 Czechoslovak crowns—nearly the entire state budget for that year.

THE CZECHOSLOVAK FIRST REPUBLIC (1918–1938)

At first glance, the process of state building took an abrupt turn in October 1918 when the Czechs joined with Slovaks and Rusyns in abandoning the Habsburg monarchy, where only the Austrian portion could boast of a developing democracy, and creating a democratic, pluralistic republic. On closer examination, the continuity between the pre-1914 and post-1918 periods is striking, especially for the Czechs. Aside from replacing the emperor with a president, the most significant change in the political system from the perspective of the Czech Lands was the creation of a government responsible to the National Assembly. The developing democracy of the Austrian portion of the monarchy had reached maturity in the new republic. The party system underwent some adjustments, more marked in the former Hungarian areas, but the political leadership of the prewar era remained. The nobility ceased to exist, the constitution enforced a separation between church and state, and the state sold some noble and ecclesiastical land in a land reform, but nobles and clerics kept most of their property and were financially secure. The Czech, German, German-Jewish, and Polish parallel social structures remained intact, now augmented with the incorporation of similar Slovak, Rusyn, and Hungarian social structures.

Focusing on the period after World War II, the political scientist Arend Lijphart identified the political systems of Austria, Belgium, Netherlands, and Switzerland as consociational democracies in which political elites cooperate to overcome the potentially divisive cleavages in each country. The political leaders in consociational democracies recognize the dangers of fragmentation, and in order to preserve the state, they remain open to discussion and create compromise policies that satisfy their constituents. To build consensus, elites use normal parliamentary means along with extraparliamentary arrangements with specific rules and traditions for sharing power. Consociational states have several similar traits in their governing structures. One is a reliance on coalition governments. Another is pillarization, or the construction of parallel social, economic, political, and cultural systems, frequently based on ethnicity, within the polity. Pillars have limited interaction with each other, aside from the elites. Czechoslovakia between 1918 and 1938 is a classic consociational democracy. As such, consociationalism is more than part of the legacy of the Habsburg Empire. It is the strongest continuous thread in the state-building process that runs between the monarchy and postwar Czechoslovakia.

The party system in Czechoslovakia underwent changes immediately after the war. Nevertheless, Czechoslovakia's political parties were deeply rooted in the past, and the political leaders remained virtually unchanged. On the far left of the political spectrum was the Czechoslovak Communist Party, which formed under the leadership of Šmeral in 1921, after radicals split from the Social Democrats in 1920. The Social Democrats had the strongest socialist party, and the moderate leaders of the prewar years retained their prominent role. Major changes in the Czechoslovak National Socialist Party occurred in 1923, when Beneš joined the party, and in 1926, when Beneš and Klofáč expelled Jiří Stříbrný, who then established a small fascist movement. At the center of the political spectrum, the Agrarian Party, renamed the Republican Party in 1919, expanded in 1922 with the addition of Slovak agrarians, namely, Šrobár and Hodža. Its moderate wing was under Švehla, and its conservatives were under Prášek, until 1924, and then František Staněk. On the right, the small but significant Party of Business and Commerce, also known as the Tradesmen's Party, represented the interests of small business owners and professionals and came into existence in 1919 from the union of two Czech parties that had their beginnings in the first decade of the twentieth century. Catholic groups in the Czech Lands formed the Czechoslovak People's Party (Czech Populists) in 1918–1919 under the leadership of Šrámek and Hruban. The Slovak People's Party was the largest group to emerge in Slovakia after the breakup of the National Party, and its leaders were Andrej Hlinka and later Jozef Tiso, both of whom were Catholic clerics. Finally, the States Rights Progressives became the National Democrats in 1919, with Kramář, Preiss, and Rašín still at the helm. Fascist movements existed on the far right, but they had limited appeal in a society with established parties responsive to the needs of citizens.

German parties classified themselves as either negativist, that is, refusing to cooperate with the Czechs and Slovaks, or activists, which not only participated in the National Assembly but even entered the government. The negativist parties were small before the Great Depression, and the activist parties garnered most of the Germans' support. The German Social Democratic Party, under the leadership of Ludwig Czech, was the most important German party. The Union of Agriculturalists (Bund der Landwirte; BdL) of Franz Spina cooperated with the Republican Party. Heading the German Christian Socialist Party was Robert Mayr-Harting. The Rusyns, Hungarians, and Poles also had a number of small political parties, many of which cooperated with Czech and Slovak parties.

As part of the power-sharing arrangement, the parties monopolized certain ministries. The Republicans almost always controlled the ministries of interior, defense, and agriculture in addition to the State Land Office, which carried out the land reform. The socialists dominated the ministries of social care and rails. The National Democrats generally held the portfolios of finance along with industry, trade, and commerce. For most of the interwar years, the foreign ministry was in the hands of Beneš and, as such, was the prerogative of the president's office, also referred to as the Hrad. Ironically, it was Masaryk and Beneš who attempted to break the hold of the parties over certain ministries when Beneš formed a government in 1922, but the effort met with failure. The Hrad learned that political culture resists abrupt change. Complementing the parties' domination of ministries was the remarkable continuity of personnel from one government to another.

The mainstream parties' ability to manipulate the governing apparatus to their liking was only one manifestation of their control over political life. Parties carefully divided their responsibilities in the National Assembly, and the complexion of legislative committees bore a remarkable resemblance to the balance of parties in the governing coalitions. When issues came to a vote, the party chairmen could count on strict party discipline. Because no party ever received a majority in the elections and multiparty coalitions were a necessity, the parties had to find a means to overcome the divisiveness, especially intense during elections, in order to build consensus. A major instrument in accomplishing this goal was the extraparliamentary institution of the Pětka—the Five—named after the five main parties: Social Democrats, National Socialists, Republicans, Catholic People's Party, and National Democrats. At informal meetings, the party leaders would construct the coalitions, distribute the cabinet seats, and determine policy. When the coalition expanded, the Pětka became the Šestka (The Six) and the Osmička (The Eight). The creator of the Pětka was Švehla, and he was the principal engineer of coalitions and governments from 1918 until he withdrew from public life in 1929 because of illness. Afterward, Masaryk increased his activities as an arbiter among the political parties.

Politicians preferred the broad or wide coalition model that included parties from across the political spectrum. The first coalition that backed the Kramář government in power in 1918–1919 included Social Democrats, National Socialists, Republicans, Czech Populists, and National Democrats. An agrarian-socialist Red-Green Coalition served as the basis of two minority governments under Tusar in 1919–1920 that had support in the National Assembly from parties to the right that had been in the Kramář government. After a cabinet of experts under Jan Černý helped the country weather the crisis of the Communist–Social Democratic split, the broad socialist-agrarian-right coalition reappeared in 1921, with the government of Beneš, and lasted through Švehla's second government, which ended in 1926. In forming his cabinet, Beneš, with Masaryk's support, hoped to break the monopolies the political parties had over specific ministries—an overt attempt to destabilize the consociational arrangement with the aim of steering the political system toward the French model. The effort failed, and the Hrad learned that political culture resists abrupt change. The parties renewed their grips on their preferred ministries with the two governments Švehla headed in the All-National Coalition (the parties in the Beneš cabinet and the All-National Coalition were the same). Černý headed another cabinet of experts in 1926. Then, in an unusual situation, the socialists were isolated from politics in 1926–1929, when Švehla and then the Republican František Udržal led a combination of center-right parties, including Germans, in two governments of the Green-Black or Gentlemen's Coalition. Švehla's third cabinet marked the first time that Germans appeared in governing coalitions, and they maintained their presence in the cabinet until the end of the republic. The Slovak People's Party also entered the coalition, its first and only stint in the government, but Slovaks in other parties always had strong representation in the cabinets. Beginning with the Great Depression of 1929 and throughout the Sudeten German crisis, a wide coalition of socialist, agrarian, clerical, conservative, and German parties governed the state. Udržal led the first government of 1929–1932, the Republican Jan Malypetr headed three governments between 1932–1935, and Hodža was twice premier between 1935 and 1938 (Hodža was the only Slovak to become prime minister during the First Republic). At the height of the Munich crisis, General Jan Syrový led a cabinet of experts—the last government of the First Republic.

The consociational arrangement aided politicians and parties in passing crucial legislation and administering the state in a way that satisfied the demands of a broad range of social, cultural, and economic interests and the vast majority of the citizens. As a result, the citizens supported the parties, the state, and the democratic process. The relatively peaceful transition from monarchy to republic was an indicator of the nature of politics in the new state. After the proclamation of Czechoslovak independence, there was little violence, although scores of Germans were killed during riots in areas that tried to join Austria and ultimately a greater Germany, which the Allies forbade in the Paris treaties. The economy faced the same dislocation and postwar inflation that plagued other states, but the wise stewardship of Rašín as finance minister brought Czechoslovakia a degree of stability lacking elsewhere. The constitution passed in February 1920 was a series of compromises to satisfy all the major parties and the Hrad. It created a "Czechoslovak" nation with two branches, Czechs and Slovaks, an arrangement that guaranteed a Slavic majority of about 8.8 million—approximately 6.7 million Czechs and just over 2 million Slovaks—two-thirds of the population of about 13.4 million inhabitants. The constitution also set the tone for tolerance of minorities that was unusual in the successor states. In 1920 the socialists, some of whom wanted to transform the landed estates into collective farms, and the Republicans, including small farmers, who sought more land, and estate owners, who wished to preserve their holdings, arrived at a compromise on a land reform that theoretically limited estates to 250 hectares of land or 150 hectares of arable land and compensated the former owners for their losses. Over the years, increased tariffs on agricultural goods and a Grain Monopoly were concessions agriculturalists received for advanced disability and retirement insurance along with laws regulating hours and working conditions for workers and an increase in the state salary, or *congrua,* for clergy. In 1927 a massive tax reform bill passed the National Assembly.

While Czechoslovakia's democracy thrived, it had faults. Masaryk and Beneš sometimes manipulated policy through their prestige, and other politicians abused their positions. The Czechs dominated the administration in Slovakia and Ruthenia, which made the Slovaks and Rusyns resent the Czechs. More could have been done to endear the Germans to the state, particularly in the early years, such as speeding German entry into the National Assembly and government, providing minorities with better consideration for state employment and advancement, and ensuring the fair treatment of minorities by the bureaucracy.

The foreign policy of Czechoslovakia, as formulated by Beneš, Masaryk, and the Hrad, focused on maintaining the order of Versailles through collective security with France at the core. Beneš made Czechoslovakia an active member of the League of Nations in the hopes of resolving international disputes before they became conflicts. He succeeded in constructing an alliance known as the Little Entente with Romania and Yugoslavia, which were also allies with France. French investments supported the Czechoslovak defense industry, and the Czechoslovak military modeled itself after the French. In the middle of the 1920s all was well. The Soviet Union's impulse to foster world revolution had abated as early as 1921 with Lenin's commitment to "peaceful coexistence" and his New Economic Policy. Germany signed the Locarno Pact in 1925, entered the League of Nations, and became a model citizen of Europe. Czechoslovakia had remarkably good relations with Austria. Hungary, which pursued an irredentist policy with respect to Hungarian minorities in all its neighbor states, including the Hungarians in Slovakia and Ruthenia, was internationally isolated. When Adolf Hitler came to power in Germany, however, the flaws in the cordon sanitaire the French and their allies had constructed between Germany and the Soviet Union became apparent. The implications for Czechoslovakia were disastrous. In the late 1930s Poland remained a French ally, but difficulties between Poland and Czechoslovakia, including the Czechoslovak seizure of Těšínsko immediately after World War I, prevented them from forming an alliance. Poland mistakenly cared little about Czechoslovakia's territorial integrity. The Little Entente seemed effective, but trade policies of Germany in the 1930s strengthened the economic ties between Germany, on the one hand, and Romania and Yugoslavia, on the other, thus undermining their resolve to support Czechoslovakia. Finally, the French themselves were unwilling to back their allies in the East after they had abandoned democracy. Czechoslovak democracy was an exception, but the French viewed supporting a solitary democratic state as too costly.

The collapse of Czechoslovak democracy came from the outside, specifically the Munich Agreement, rather than from internal difficulties. Throughout the 1920s, the German and Hungarian minorities—about 32 percent and 6 percent of the population respectively—had come to accept the existence of Czechoslovakia, in no small part due to the greater degree of political stability and the more vibrant economy in Czechoslovakia than in neighboring countries. Moreover, the minorities had certain guarantees. The Germans had their own schools and universities, were represented in the bureaucracy, had their own cultural institutions, could use their own language, and had political parties that participated in the National Assembly and the coalition governments. Sentiments among the Sudeten Germans changed with the Great Depression and the rise of Hitler. Banking on the economic disaster the depression brought to the Sudeten German areas and the direct support of the Nazis in Germany, Konrad Henlein gradually increased support for his fascist Sudeten German Party.

MUNICH (1938)

Henlein exploited the tensions of the Great Depression to attract the majority of Germans in Czechoslovakia away from activism, the policy of the German Social Democrats, German Christian Socialists, and the BdL, to negativism and irredentism. In the election of 1935, Henlein's party received 15.2 percent of the vote to take a total of forty-four of the two hundred seats in the National Assembly (about 22 percent of the total). Henlein, with Hitler's backing, demanded ever increasing concessions from the Czechoslovak government for the Germans. In his Karlsbad Program of April 1938, Henlein included demands such as equal rights for the Germans, the recognition of the Sudeten Germans as a separate entity in the state, and the creation of German districts with their own government. President Beneš and the government attempted to negotiate with Henlein, who was never satisfied, even when Beneš had indicated that he would accept nearly all the terms in the Karlsbad Program.

When the Soviet Union became an ally of France in 1935, Beneš, who long had advocated drawing the Soviet Union into the collective security alliance structure, negotiated an alliance between Czechoslovakia and the Soviet Union. Josef Stalin was interested in preserving peace, since the Soviet Union was in no condition to enter a military conflict. To neutralize Germany while the French still supported Czechoslovakia, the Little Entente appeared stable, and German public opinion was against war, Stalin became involved in a bit of intrigue to start a conflict that would result in Germany's defeat and the elimination of the Nazi regime without Soviet involvement. In May 1938 the Soviets supplied disinformation to Czechoslovak spies in Germany about German troops massing on the Czechoslovak border. Beneš mobilized the military but rescinded the order when he realized the information was incorrect. Hitler was furious that he had been upstaged, and he now planned to use unrest in Czechoslovakia as a pretext for invasion. On 30 May 1938, he issued an order for Operation Green (the Czechoslovak military uniform was green) to prepare for military action. Tensions mounted in the summer, and at the Nuremburg Nazi Party rally on 12 September, Hitler condemned Beneš and Czechoslovak democracy.

Throughout the crisis, Czechoslovakia attempted to rally the support of its allies. Paris backed British hopes of finding a peaceful solution and avoiding war. Moscow reiterated that should France honor its commitments to Czechoslovakia, the Soviet Union would come to the aid of Czechoslovakia, in accordance with the treaty provisions. Czechoslovakia's allies in the Little Entente were hesitant and likewise based their replies on the position of France. In August and September 1938 the British businessman and politician Walter Runciman attempted to negotiate a settlement and avoid a war, but he was predisposed to favoring the Germans and was unsuccessful at finding common ground between the two sides.

In an effort to avoid war, Neville Chamberlain, the British prime minister, arranged with Hitler to meet with Édouard Daladier, the French prime minister, and Benito Mussolini at the end of September 1938 in Munich to negotiate a settlement. Neither Czechoslovakia nor the Soviet Union was invited. Britain and France acquiesced to Hitler's demands, hoping he would refrain from future claims for border revisions and realizing that their citizens opposed going to war over Czechoslovakia. The Munich Diktat of 29 September required Czechoslovakia to cede to Germany all territories with a population at least 50 percent German. Czechoslovak citizens along with the military demonstrated their support for a war with Germany. Some recommended that Czechoslovakia reject the Munich Agreement and fight Germany alone with the expectation that Czechoslovakia's allies would realize their error and enter the war against Germany. Beneš, however, concluded that the allies would not assist Czechoslovakia. Furthermore, based on Prague's intelligence about the destructiveness of what was to become known as the Blitzkrieg, Beneš feared that Czechoslovakia would sustain insurmountable damage and loss of life in a conflict with Germany. Beneš accepted the settlement, and German troops took over the Sudetenland from 1–10 October 1938. On 1 October, Czechoslovakia agreed to the Polish demand to cede its portion of Těšínsko to Poland. On 5 October, Beneš resigned from the presidency, and a few weeks later went into exile. In November Germany brokered a settlement between Czechoslovakia and Hungary, known as the First Vienna Accord, in which Czechoslovakia ceded portions of southern Slovakia, including Košice, and portions of Ruthenia, including Užhorod, to Hungary.

THE SECOND REPUBLIC

The Czechoslovak Second Republic dates from the Munich Agreement until Germany's annexation of the Czech Lands in March 1939. In October 1938 Slovakia and Ruthenia became autonomous, and in November the name of the country officially became the hyphenated Czecho-Slovakia. Emil Hácha, who had presided over the Supreme Administrative Court, assumed the presidency. The prime minister in the Czech Lands was the Republican Rudolf Beran, who had replaced General Syrový in December, Tiso headed the government in Slovakia, and a government emerged in Ruthenia. In the Czech Lands, the nonsocialist parties formed the National Confederation, which supported the government, while the socialists established the National Labor Party, a weak, permanent opposition. As during World War I, Czech politicians chose to weather the crisis by joining forces.

The collapse of the First Republic and the severe restriction of democracy in the Second Republic were traumatic for both Czechs and Slovaks. Moreover, Czecho-Slovakia, having lost its Western allies and its fortifications in the Munich Agreement, became a satellite of the Third Reich. With Munich, the Czechs and Slovaks entered a third phase of state building in the twentieth century, one that was less democratic, in the shadow of totalitarian Germany, and served as a transition to an even more threatening period.

Hitler was not content with the Munich Agreement and decided to annex the Czech Lands. He persuaded Tiso to declare Slovakia an independent state on 14 March 1939, and one day later, German forces invaded the Czech Lands. Although Hácha remained president and the Czechs had some semblance of autonomy, Hitler annexed the Czech Lands into Germany as the Protectorate of Bohemia and Moravia. Simultaneously, Hungary annexed the remainder of Ruthenia.

WORLD WAR II

When World War II began, Beneš began organizing an effort to recreate Czechoslovakia, and in 1940 he emerged as president of a Czechoslovak government in exile headquartered in London. Beneš's closest ally was Jan Masaryk, the son of Czechoslovakia's first president and former Czechoslovak minister to Britain who became the foreign minister in the government in exile. Jan Masaryk became famous for his encouraging radio broadcasts back home. He was active in the diplomatic effort to re-create Czechoslovakia, to secure Czechoslovakia's role in Europe as a bridge between the Soviet Union and the West (mainly Beneš's concept), and to establish the United Nations. Other Czech and Slovak exiles joined the government, including Šrámek, who served as prime minister.

In the Protectorate of Bohemia and Moravia, the Czechs under President Hácha and the prime minister Alois Eliáš attempted to placate the Germans and protect Czech interests. This policy succeeded to some extent under Reich Protector Konstantin von Neurath and his state secretary, the former Sudeten German politician Karl Hermann Frank. Germany assumed all key administrative functions in the Protectorate, rendering the government nearly powerless. Hácha disbanded parliament, replacing it with the National Assemblage (Národní souručenství), which united all

Jan Masaryk (1886–1948), son of Tomáš G. Masaryk and foreign minister of Czechoslovakia, 1940–1948. His controversial death occurred in the early days of communist rule in Czechoslovakia. (Library of Congress)

legal parties but was without real governing powers. Once the war began, tensions between Germans and Czechs increased. At that time, the Germans sent about 2,000 Czech notables to concentration camps. During a demonstration on 28 October 1939 (Czechoslovak Independence Day), the Germans killed one Czech and mortally wounded a Czech university student, Jan Opletal. Demonstrations occurred during his funeral on 15 November, prompting the Germans to arrest and execute several student detainees. Hitler closed all Czech universities for three years, and they did not reopen during the war. The Germans then turned their attention to eliminating the various Czech underground organizations.

In late September 1942 Hitler appointed Reinhard Heydrich as Deputy Reich Protector under Neurath, who essentially retired and returned to Germany. During this period, the Czech policy of accommodation with the Germans ran aground. Heydrich intensified the Germanization of the Protectorate and the systematic effort to destroy Czech culture, in keeping with the Nazi leadership's vision of ultimately assimilating, expelling, and exterminating all Czechs. He declared martial law and arrested Eliáš for his contact with the Allies and for his toleration of anti-German resistance. Eliáš was sentenced to death, but he remained in prison. Simultaneously, Heydrich ordered the execution of three hundred Czechs and sent about 1,500 Sokol functionaries to concentration camps. Transports of Jews to ghettos and concentration camps began, and the Germans converted the former barracks at Terezín into a concentration camp.

Beneš decided that a dramatic act of resistance would help the Czechoslovak cause abroad, and he planned to assassinate Heydrich. Two assassins parachuted into the Protectorate and attacked Heydrich's vehicle on 27 May 1942 as he drove along his normal route in the morning to Prague. Heydrich died eight days later. When the attack on Heydrich occurred, the Germans immediately arrested 10,000 hostages. They destroyed the village of Lidice in Eastern Bohemia on 9–10 June because of false information that the parachutists had received refuge there. All 192 men were shot, and 196 women and 104 children were sent to concentration camps. Few survived. The Germans carried out the same revenge in Ležáky, where 33 were killed and 21 were exterminated in a concentration camp. Before the war ended, other villages met the same fate as Lidice and Ležáky as retaliation for various reasons. The German authorities finally found Heydrich's assassins in the Sts. Cyril and Methodius Orthodox Church in Prague. In the ensuing gun battle, five died and two committed suicide. The Germans avenged Heydrich's death with more killing during a period the Czechs refer to as the Heydrichiáda. The German authorities detained 3,188 individuals, many well known, and summarily executed 1,585 of them, including Eliáš and the novelist Vladislav Vančura. Hitler eventually installed Wilhelm Frick as the new Reich protector, although Frank remained the actual decision maker. Periodic arrests and executions continued, but the largest single sweep after the Heydrichiáda was in August 1944, when Germans arrested about two hundred socialists and communists.

Once the Germans occupied the Czech Lands, they imposed regulations on the Jews that separated them from society and then interned them. For the most part, Czech Jews went first to Terezín, which was a transit camp. From there, they were deported to extermination camps. The largest single extermination of Czechoslovak Jews occurred in March 1944 at Auschwitz-Birkenau, when 3,792 people of all ages were gassed and cremated. About 85,000 Jews from the Czech Lands died during the Shoah (Holocaust), about 89 percent of the Jewish population. A total of 6,500 Roma, or 50 percent of the population, died in the extermination camps.

Czechs and Slovaks abroad joined the war effort as individuals within the Allied armed forces or as special units attached to Allied forces. The Poles permitted nearly a thousand Czechoslovak soldiers to form a brigade when the war began. After Poland's collapse, some managed to get to France, and they were part of the Polish Carpathian Brigade that helped defend Tobruk, Libya. There were 1,287 Czechoslovak airmen in one bomber and three fighter squadrons attached to the Royal Air Force whose missions included the Battle of Britain. It is not surprising that when Czechoslovak airmen prepared bombs for German cities, they painted "For Lidice" on each one. When Germany invaded the Soviet Union, Gen. Ludvík Svoboda, who had escaped to Poland in 1939, constructed the First Czechoslovak Army Corps and the First Czechoslovak Air Division. Svoboda led his men in such key engagements as the Battle of Kiev, the Carpathian-Dukla Operation (September–November 1944), during which it crossed into Czechoslovak territory, and to a very limited extent in the Slovak National Uprising. Crucial to the Allied cause was intelligence information the Czechoslovak government in exile provided to the British and Soviets that passed through the Czech underground, including details about the V-1 flying bomb.

Czechoslovak territory was not a battlefield until the end of the war. Resistance groups in the Protectorate never launched major operations, and the Germans liquidated the remainder of the organized resistance forces after Heydrich's assassination. Resistance afterward consisted largely of individual and small group operations aimed at various targets in order to impede German operations. A key form of passive resistance was inefficient factory work and direct sabotage of equipment and production, which brought the risk of heavy reprisals, including execution. On 29 August 1944, the Slovak National Uprising began, and its leadership included the former Republican Šrobár. Because the Slovaks misunderstood the position of the Red Army, the uprising began too early to receive proper support. German troops ended the uprising by October, but partisans remained in the countryside throughout the closing days of the war. The Nazis captured and executed General Viest, who had come from London to command the operation. The Allies did not begin bombing industrial targets in the Protectorate, such as the Škoda works, until late in the war. Bombings of economic targets in Prague were intense in February and March 1945, and the attack of 14 February 1945, by bombers en route to Dresden that reached Prague instead due to a navigational error killed 700 inhabitants. In March-April the Red Army entered Eastern Slovakia, and the Czechoslovaks proclaimed a government in the city of Košice. On 18 April 1945, American forces entered Czechoslovak territory and liberated Plzeň on 6 May. On 5 May a spontaneous uprising broke out in Prague, and there were several days of street fighting. As the Germans withdrew from the city, they attempted to destroy the Old Town Hall and its Orloj, the famous astronomical clock. Fire consumed the building, of which only a portion, including the clock tower, stands today. On 9 May the Red Army entered Prague.

After Munich, Beneš lost confidence in the commitment of the Western powers to protect Czechoslovakia, and during the war, he pursued a foreign policy that resulted in a strong alliance with the Soviet Union. One of the early signals of Beneš's sensitivity to Soviet interests became apparent in late 1943 and early 1944 when he and the president of the Polish government in exile, Stanislaw Mikołajczyk, scrapped a plan they had devised in early 1942 for a postwar Czechoslovak-Polish confederation. In December 1943 Beneš signed the Czechoslovak-Soviet Treaty of Friendship. Beneš acquiesced when Stalin demanded that Czechoslovakia cede to the Soviet Union the eastern province of Ruthenia (formally ceded in June 1945), which together with territory from Romania and Poland enabled the Soviet Union to have a common border not only with Poland and Romania, as it did between the world wars, but also Czechoslovakia and Hungary. In March 1945 Beneš visited Moscow, where he coordinated future policy with Czechoslovak Communists under Klement Gottwald, who had spent the war years in Moscow. Beneš then journeyed to Košice and by rail to Prague, where he arrived on 16 May.

THE POSTWAR YEARS (1945–1948)

The government announced on 5 April 1945, in Košice under Zdeněk Fierlinger, a Social Democrat close to the Communists, included Gottwald and Šrámek as two of five vice premiers, Jan Masaryk as foreign minister, Svoboda as defense minister, and Šrobár as minister of finance. Its Košice Program envisioned a democratic Czechoslovakia. As in postwar Britain and France, the government was to nationalize large industry. Disloyal minorities were to be expelled. The Košice Program prohibited parties that Beneš and his associates considered collaborators with the Nazis, including the National Democratic Party, Republican Party, Party of Business and Commerce, and Slovak People's Party. The only legal parties, all represented in the governing coalition known as the National Front, were the Communists (then with separate Slovak and Czech parties), Social Democrats, National Socialists, Czech Populists, and the new Democratic Party of Slovakia, which included many former Republicans and those from other banned parties. An agreement in June 1945 between the government and the Slovak National Council gave the latter body control of the administration in Slovakia—a provision to grant the Slovaks autonomy without federating the state. American and the increasingly unpopular Soviet troops left Czechoslovakia in late 1945. Beneš essentially ruled by decree until February 1946, when the provisional National Assembly met and approved his actions, which included the nationalization of large industry (financial institutions, mills, mines, and businesses with more than five hundred employees) and the expulsion of the German and Hungarian minorities. Free elections took place in May 1946, and the Communists did not do as well as they had expected, winning 40.1 percent of the vote in the Czech Lands and 30.3 percent in Slovakia. The National Socialists in the Czech Lands and the Democratic Party in Slovakia ranked after the Communists. Reflecting the results at the polls, Gottwald became the prime minister of a new government of twenty-five members, seven of which were Czech Communists, two were Slovak Communists, four each were in the hands of the Czech Populists, National Socialists, and Democrats, and three were Social Democrats. Jan Masaryk and Svoboda retained their posts as experts. The government adopted a two-year economic plan

(1947–1948), and it tried and executed Tiso for his wartime activities, action more popular among members of the Communist Party than members of other parties. In mid-1947 the government announced a resumption of the land reform begun in 1919 and strict adherence to the legal limits on land holdings. When the United States announced the Marshall Plan, the Czechoslovak government unanimously decided to accept American funds, but in July 1947, at Stalin's behest, the government declined the invitation.

The confrontation between Czechs and Germans that had begun with the Munich Diktat and the destruction of Czechoslovakia and had escalated through World War II with Nazi genocidal policies scuttled centuries of Czech and German efforts to cohabit in the Czech Lands. Beneš openly considered expelling all Germans from Czechoslovakia after the war as a means of reducing their ability to destabilize politics, particularly in light of the anti-Czech policies of Heydrich. After Lidice, Beneš was determined to bring about a massive population transfer. He received the reluctant support of the Allies for the transfer, and the Košice Program formally announced the plan for the expulsion of minorities. In May and June 1945 Beneš issued decrees confiscating the property of traitors and collaborators and earmarking dwellings and land for resettlement. The legal basis was secure, but procedural matters remained unresolved. Meanwhile, some local authorities were far from fair in their treatment of accused collaborators, and the minorities faced intense discrimination. In July 1945 rumors that a deadly factory explosion in Ústí nad Labem was the work of German saboteurs resulted in a clash between German workers and Czechs in which at least sixty Germans died. Beneš regarded the continued presence of Germans in Czechoslovakia as threatening stability and wanted to conduct the transfers as quickly as possible. He requested that the Allies consider the issue at Potsdam in July-August 1945, and they agreed to a timetable for expulsion. In the train transports of Sudeten and Carpathian Germans throughout 1946, each person could take only about forty kilograms of personal belongs and a small sum of money. During a forced march of Germans from Brno to the Austrian border on 31 May–1 June 1946, between 649 and 1,700 died or were killed. Officially, approximately 2.2 million Germans were transferred, 1,446,059 to the American Zone and 786,482 to the Soviet Zone. In reality, the total number of Germans who left or were expelled from Czechoslovakia may have been 3.5 million. The population transfer with Hungary took place between 1945 and 1948. During that time, more than 50,000 Hungarians were expelled, and about 40,000 emigrated. Approximately 60,000 Slovaks entered Czechoslovakia from Hungary.

The German destruction of Czech independence and efforts to destroy Czech culture during the Protectorate constituted a threat to the very existence of the Czech nation, let alone the state, with consequences that may have been far more grave than the imposition of Habsburg domination in the Kingdom of Bohemia after the Battle of White Mountain in 1620. For Beneš and those who supported him, the only permanent solution to German-Czech competition was to abandon the consociational arrangement that had been built over generations of cohabitation of the two nations in the Czech Lands and expel the Germans. He applied the same rationale to the Hungarians in Slovakia. Beneš took other steps to alter dramatically the nature of consociational democracy in Czechoslovakia. The Košice Program eliminated not only the clerical-fascist Slovak People's Party and the National Assemblage, but it also forbade key traditional moderate and conservative pre-Munich parties from reemerging, essentially holding them responsible for the actions of several of their former members after their parties had been dissolved during the Nazi era. Beneš supported labeling as traitors certain politicians from the banned parties, such as Beran, who had attempted to placate Nazi Germany in order to protect the interests of the nation. Whereas the politicians of the First Republic, principally Švehla, preferred to neutralize strong opposition parties by having them cooperate in governing coalitions, Beneš precluded the formation of any opposition by forcing all parties into the National Front. Beneš guaranteed that in post-1945 Czechoslovakia, an extraparliamentary institution, such as the Pětka, which he disdained, would not reemerge by ensuring the top leader of every party a posi-

Klement Gottwald (1896–1953), communist president of Czechoslovakia, 1948–1953. (Library of Congress)

tion in the government as either premier or vice premier. The structural changes Beneš engineered to rebuild the republic as strictly a Czech and Slovak venture, which institutionalized multiparty cooperation, ultimately failed in the face of a population desperate for social and economic stability that the Communist politicians, with their marginally legal tactics, promised to deliver.

THE COMMUNIST TAKEOVER

Czechoslovakia's road to socialism was entirely parliamentary and resulted, in part, from the Communist Party's popularity because of its association with the Soviet Union, which had liberated Czechoslovakia from the Nazis, and the lack of involvement of the Communist Party in some of the prewar political scandals. Yet the political, social, and economic difficulties of the postwar years took their toll on Communist popularity, especially because the Communists controlled some of the most important political and administrative positions in the country. In February 1948 several noncommunist ministers gave the Communists an opportunity to come to power.

Since 1945, the Communist Party had had control over important ministries, such as interior, agriculture, education, information, and social welfare. Svoboda, the nonpartisan minister of defense, was close to the Communists. Jan Masaryk was not a Communist, but the state secretary for foreign affairs, a cabinet post, was Vladimír Clementis, a Slovak Communist who had spent the war years in France and Britain. The Communists in the Ministry of Interior, which included the police, the Ministry of Justice, and the courts, used intimidation and false accusations to remove opponents. Communists and their supporters assumed key roles in a broad range of political and civic organizations. Tensions mounted in September 1947, when two noncommunist cabinet ministers along with Jan Masaryk received letter bombs that originated with Communists in Olomouc. On 20 February 1948, twelve noncommunist ministers resigned from the Communist-controlled government of Gottwald in protest over the Communists' practice of packing the police force with Communists and their supporters. The ministers expected that Jan Masaryk would join them to provide the sole additional resignation needed to bring down Gottwald's government. Indications were that the Communists had been losing popular support and that the noncommunists likely would be the winners in an early parliamentary election. Beneš was faced with two choices. The first was to tell Jan Masaryk not to resign, accept the twelve resignations, and allow the largest party, the Communists, to form a new government. The second alternative was to have Jan Masaryk submit his resignation, bring down the current government, and call for new elections. The Communists pressured Beneš to do the former, while the noncommunists hoped for the latter. Jan Masaryk, fulfilling a promise he had made to his father, loyally awaited Beneš's decision. Not physically up to the challenge and fearing civil war that would lead to Soviet intervention, Beneš told Masaryk not to resign and accepted the twelve resignations on 25 February.

Gottwald formed a new government of thirteen Communists, three experts, and nine who cooperated with the Communists from other parties. The Slovak Communists under Gustáv Husák similarly took control of the Slovak National Council in Bratislava. The Communists arrested some noncommunist leaders, and others fled the country. On 10 March, Jan Masaryk was found dead in the courtyard of the Czernín Palace, the seat of the Foreign Ministry. He had fallen from a window of his second-story apartment. Speculation was that the Communists had murdered him because they had feared that he would flee abroad and protest the new government. The Communist officials claimed, however, that he had committed suicide. Investigators are now certain that Masaryk was murdered, and the paper trail to determine exactly who committed the deed leads to Russian archives that are still closed. In May 1948 elections took place to the National Assembly that were far from democratic, and the Communist Party received 89.3 percent of the votes. Instead of signing a Soviet-type constitution, Beneš resigned as president on 2 June 1948, and died three months later. Gottwald became president. Purges of noncommunists took place throughout the country. In June the Social Democrats united with the Communists, and in September the Slovak and Czech Communist Parties merged.

STALINISM AND DE-STALINIZATION IN CZECHOSLOVAKIA

After what became known as the February Revolution, reflecting the Communists' desire to emulate Lenin's November revolution of 1917 in Russia, Czechoslovakia entered into yet another experiment with state building. After 1948 the Czechs and Slovaks technically preserved the state and many of its institutions they had built in 1918 and restructured after World War II. Tied to the Soviet behemoth, however, they cast off capitalism in favor of the Leninist-Stalinist interpretation of Marxist socialist economics and society.

Under the leadership of Gottwald, who controlled the Communist Party and was president of the republic, Czechoslovakia assumed all the trappings of Soviet-style, Stalinist socialism. The Communist Party took the "leading role" in society, according to Soviet phraseology. It not only controlled the government but also purged the administration of noncommunists. The Communist Party eliminated opposition in all organizations. Social and civic institutions merged with their Communist counterparts, elected Communist leaders, or disbanded. Many key noncommunists were executed, such as Milada Horáková, the National Socialist who had been interned by the Nazis and after the war served as the chairman of the Council of Czechoslovak Women and the vice chairman of the Union of Liberated Political Prisoners. The regime began persecuting clergy and believers of all faiths, in keeping with Marxist atheistic doctrine. In 1950, for example, the government eliminated the monastic orders, forcing priests, brothers, and nuns to work in factories and farms. Noncommunist educators lost their appointments, and many managed to leave the country and find employment in institutions abroad. Trade unions, organized since 1945 in the Communist-dominated Revolutionary Trade Union Movement (Revoluční odborové hnutí; ROH), aligned themselves with the Communist Party. Communist ideology became the standard by which Party censors evaluated all forms of expression, including literature, art, and music. Information became a propaganda tool of the regime. The Communists purged all unreliable elements from the military and police and used terror and intimidation as means of ensuring mass compliance to the Party's will. In 1948–1949 nearly 11,000 citizens emigrated, largely for political reasons. Finally, the Communist Party instituted the Stalinist command model for the economy, including complete nationalization of firms, collectivization of agriculture, and central planning.

Governments throughout the period of Communist rule were technically coalitions, which the Communist Party dominated with the support of its National Front partners, the National Socialists and Populists. The Communists' maintenance of coalition governments, including their reliance on vice premiers, supported the Party's image of preserving the postwar democratic system. When Gottwald became president, Antonín Zápotocký assumed the post of prime minister. Rudolf Slánský was the chairman of the Communist Party and a vice premier until he was arrested in 1951, at which point Gottwald resumed his previous role of Party leader, now formally known as general secretary. Gottwald attended Stalin's funeral, became ill, and died a few days later. Zápotocký became president, and Novotný rose to the position of general secretary. The Slovak Communist Viliam Široký was prime minister. When Zápotocký died in 1957, Antonín Novotný became president, keeping his position as general secretary. Široký remained as premier, forming three governments until the Slovak Jozef Lenárt became prime minister in 1963, a post he held until 1968.

The ranks of the Communist Party swelled during the postwar years, and immediately after the 1948 takeover, the Party sought to eliminate opportunists and unreliable elements within its membership. In the atmosphere of Stalin's attack on independent thinkers within the Party elite in the Soviet Union and Eastern Europe, especially in the aftermath of Yugoslavia's expulsion from the Cominform, the Czechoslovak Communists initiated a purge. Beginning with the Communist takeover, the authorities began making arrests of Party and non-Party unreliables. Around 16,000, mostly industrial workers and low-level office workers, were in prisons and camps in 1951–1952. Hundreds were executed, and the Central Committee of the Party approved 148 death sentences between 1951 and 1954 alone. Prison conditions were horrid, and those on trial commonly faced intimidation or torture in order to produce confessions. The most dramatic case was the show trial of fourteen high Party officials in November 1952 that included Slánský, Clementis, and Evžen Löbl. Slánský, Clementis, and nine others were hanged, while Löbl and two others were sent to prison for life. Other trials followed. In 1954 Husák received a sentence of life imprisonment for his having once advocated Slovakia's incorporation into the Soviet Union in 1945. A short while later, Josef Smrkovský, a hero of the Prague Uprising, received a prison term. Several sociological factors added to the suspiciousness of the show trial defendants: a Jewish background, like Slánský; time in the West, such as cooperation with the London government during the war, like Clementis; "nationalist" sentiments, particularly among the Slovaks, like Husák; and activity in the resistance during World War II, like Husák and Smrkovský.

In its foreign policy, Czechoslovakia followed the lead of the Soviet Union, as did other states in the Soviet-dominated region of Eastern Europe. Czechoslovakia aligned itself with the Soviet Union in the United Nations and in its dealings with individual states. In 1948 Czechoslovakia followed the Soviet lead and broke with Yugoslavia. In 1949 it aided in the formation of the Council for Mutual Economic Assistance (CMEA, Comecon), which was to oversee trade within the Soviet Bloc. In fact, it was a mechanism for Soviet bilateral trade with member states. In 1955 Czechoslovakia was one of the founding members of the Warsaw Pact, a Soviet-dominated military defense alliance. When the Sino-Soviet split occurred in 1961, Czechoslovakia was solidly on the Soviet side, as it had been when Stalin had expelled Yugoslavia from the Communist Bloc in 1948.

In mid-1953, after the deaths of Stalin and Gottwald, workers in Ostrava, Kladno, and Plzeň rioted, but their frustration was a reaction to economic conditions, particularly the devastating effect the revaluation of currency that year had on the standard of living. In late 1954 Novotný secured the backing of the Soviet leadership for additional reforms and gained more support at home. Although the leadership of the Czechoslovak Communist Party was deeply divided over the economy by 1956, the Soviet leader Nikita S. Khrushchev did not spark in Czechoslovakia the drama of Poland or the violence of Hungary when he gave his "Secret Speech" condemning Stalin at the Twentieth Party Congress of the Soviet Union that year. The Czechoslovak Communist Party preserved its unity in its debates about the fate of Stalinism, even though it had some pressure from the outside, including writers. It initiated gradual reforms, such as the decision to inject into the new Five-Year Plan for 1957 some economic decentralization measures, including steps enabling managers to have more decisionmaking powers. Then in late 1957, Zápotocký died. Novotný became president without relinquishing his hold over the Party. The Grim Reaper provided phased leadership change in Prague—first with Gottwald and then with Zápotocký—that elsewhere took desperate central committees and pressure from the street to bring about. The passing of Czechoslovakia's key Stalinists contributed to the lack of a rift within the Party as it approached de-Stalinization and helps account for the Party's path toward piecemeal reforms.

Once in power, Novotný spearheaded changes that were welcome in the Party and society as a whole. In 1953 he halted the collectivization process, although he resumed it in 1957, in part because of Soviet pressure. He continued efforts to increase the availability of consumer products, and he wrestled with finding a solution to improving economic productivity. After economic decentralization did not bring about the desired results, he experimented with recentralization in the early 1960s. In 1960 he ushered in a new constitution based on the Soviet model, and the Czechoslovak Republic (ČSR) became the Czechoslovak Socialist Republic (ČSSR). The new constitution further limited what little there was of Slovak autonomy. Novotný issued two amnesties, one in 1960 and another in 1963, the latter resulting from demands of delegates at the Twelfth Party Congress in November 1962. The amnesties rehabilitated more than 8,000 people, and the amnesty of 1963 discredited and removed from power the last Stalinists in the top leadership roles, including Široký.

THE PRAGUE SPRING OF 1968

The Prague Spring—the eight months from January to August 1968–was an attempt of the Slovaks and Czechs to tackle poor economic performance and to make the Communist Party and the government more responsive to the citizens. The impetus for the Prague Spring began well before January 1968. The effects of the command economy, with its central planning and lack of incentives, already were apparent by the early 1960s. Shortfalls in production resulted from deep-rooted systemic difficulties. Financial institutions did not provide investments based on the profitability of firms but were only means of dispensing money the central planners had allocated. The factory and collective farm managers, frequently selected for their political reliability rather than their experience, were concerned mainly with fulfilling the plan, not with profitability or efficiency, and they often falsified data to cover shortfalls. Workers in industry and agriculture had little economic incentive to increase production. Shortages existed in all economic sectors, but the Party's conscious decision to provide greater investment for heavy industry adversely affected the availability of consumer goods. In part their decision was a response to the Cold War but also was rooted in the Marxian-based belief that only advanced industrialized economies can approach socialism. Finally, young people in the countryside viewed their future outside the villages and towns, and those in the cities had no desire to spend their years on the factory floor. The second Five-Year Plan of 1954–1958 was relatively successful, but disastrous results forced the government in 1961 to scrap the third plan of 1959–1963 and to rely on yearly targets. The economy experienced a dramatic decline in its national income, industrial and agricultural production, investment, profit from exports, average wage, and personal consumption in the five-year period between 1960 and 1965. Even with the efforts of planners and politicians to

Young Czechs defy Warsaw Pact tanks in Prague in August 1968 in the hopes that the Soviets and other invading countries will accept the reforms spearheaded by Alexander Dubček (1921–1992) during the Prague Spring. (Reg Lancaster/Express/Getty Images)

improve the situation, economic performance by the late 1960s did not reach the level of the late 1950s for most indicators.

In January 1967 the Party adopted an economic reform, the work of the economist Ota Šik. The central planning underwent some decentralization. Enterprise managers received more autonomy and kept more of their profits to use at their discretion. Agricultural cooperatives made contracts for the amount and type of goods they were to deliver to the state, which in turn increased its purchase prices for agricultural goods. The reform introduced market mechanisms into the command economy, for example, by eliminating fixed prices on some goods so that the prices either fluctuated with a ceiling or fluctuated based on supply and demand, as in a market economy. There was widespread discussion inside and outside the Party about reforms. The first demand for more than just economic change came from the Fourth Congress of Czechoslovak Writers in June 1967, at which the novelist Ludvík Vaculík praised the reforms and called for further advances. Hard-liners retaliated by banning the writers' journal, *Literární listy* (Literary Pages). Widespread discussion about further change occurred inside and outside the Party, but those supporting Novotný remained steadfast for several months.

Under mounting pressure and with little support from the Soviet leader Leonid I. Brezhnev, Novotný resigned his position of first secretary. The new Party leader was one of Novotný's opponents, a compromise candidate from the ranks of the Slovak Communists, Alexander Dubček. In March 1968 Novotný stepped down as president in favor of a candidate who had the respect of both Slovaks and Czechs, General Svoboda. Other personnel changes brought in Oldřich Černík as prime minister, Šik and Husák as vice premiers, and Smrkovský as chairman of the National Assembly. In the months that followed, press censorship eased, and *Literární listy* reappeared. Past political prisoners in the newly formed Klub K231 successfully pressed for further rehabilitations. Other noncommunist organizations emerged, including a group largely of intellectuals known as KAN (Klub angažovaných nestraníků, or Club of Active Nonpartisans) that supported the reforms. Other groups banned after the Communists came to power reemerged, such as the Boy Scouts and Sokols. Noncommunist parties in the National Front took on new initiative, and the Social Democrats prepared to renew their independent party. In April 1968 the Communist Party of Czechoslovakia committed itself to further changes with its Action Program (Akční program) that called for a reform of "the whole political system so that it will permit the dynamic development of socialist social relations, combine broad democracy with scientific, highly qualified management, strengthen the social order, stabilize socialist relations, and maintain social discipline." It condemned "the old methods of subjectivism and highhandedness from a position of power" but envisioned a continuation of the Communist Party's leading role in society. Dubček beautifully described the entire package of reforms in the phrase he made famous, "socialism with a human face."

On 27 June, as Warsaw Pact troops were on maneuvers in Czechoslovakia, Vaculík, with the support of several noted individuals, released Two Thousand Words (Dva tisíce slov), a manifesto lambasting the Stalinists for the damage that had been done to the state and the spirit of the people with their "arbitrary rule." Yet Vaculík did not question the legitimacy of the Communist Party; instead, he demanded that those who opposed reforms be removed and that democratic mechanisms be created to more effectively govern the state and still maintain the friendship of Prague's socialist allies.

As the reform movement in Czechoslovakia deepened, the suspicion of Communist leaders in the Soviet Union and other Warsaw Pact states turned to hostility. The Party leaders of the Soviet Union, German Democratic Republic (GDR), Poland, and Bulgaria were most adamant about the need for Czechoslovak Communists to contain the reforms. The Hungarian leader, János Kádár, was sympathetic but feared the political openness in Czechoslovakia could threaten the Party's control over society and discredit the needed economic reforms, which were similar to the new economic mechanism he was instituting in Hungary. Only the Romanians unabashedly advocated noninvolvement in Czechoslovak affairs and did not participate in any of the crucial negotiations. In March Czechoslovak Communist Party leaders met those of Bulgaria, GDR, Hungary, Poland, and the Soviet Union in Dresden, GDR. In May Dubček met with the Soviet premier, Alexei N. Kosygin, in Karlovy Vary, and Warsaw Pact members met in July in Warsaw (the Czechoslovaks refused to attend), where they criticized, among other things, the Two Thousand Words and the Czechoslovak Party's tolerance of such outspokenness. The Soviet and Czechoslovak leadership had difficult discussions in Čierna and Tisou, Slovakia, in late July. Finally, the Warsaw Pact states met again in Bratislava in early August. Czechoslovak efforts to allay the fears of its allies fell on deaf ears, although the participants always presented an atmosphere of solidarity in their statements. In reality, Dubček could no longer stem the tide of reforms, even if he believed such action was desirable.

On the night of 20–21 August 1968, 750,000 Warsaw Pact troops invaded Czechoslovakia from three sides. Hungary participated, but Romania did not. The invasion caught Dubček and the reformers off guard, although conservatives, such as Vasil Bil'ak, Alois Indra, and Drahomír Kolder, had colluded with the invaders. Bil'ak even claimed the Party leaders, Dubček among them, had signed a letter inviting Warsaw Pact troops to end the "counterrevolution." Dubček, Černík, Smrkovský, and three others were arrested and taken to Moscow, where all but one signed the Moscow Protocol, a document committing the Czechoslovak Communist Party to a reversal of the reforms in a process known as normalization. An agreement signed several weeks after the invasion made the occupation force permanent (no foreign troops had been in Czechoslovakia since 1945). After the fact, the Soviets justified the military action against Czechoslovakia in the so-called Brezhnev Doctrine, which held that socialist states might intervene in the internal affairs of another socialist state should the socialist revolution be threatened.

When the invasion occurred, the defense minister instructed the military not to resist, but the popular reaction was to carry on a campaign of passive resistance. Czechs and Slovaks moved street signs, provided incorrect information to the invading troops, and tried to inform them about the true motives behind the Prague Spring. Czechs and Slovaks also taunted the Soviet soldiers, and the "run home Ivan" jeers were particularly popular. One version was: "Run home Ivan! Your Nataša is waiting for you! The girls here don't like you!" Graffiti in support of the reforms and against the invaders appeared everywhere, as did pictures of Dubček and other reformers. Crowds chanted "Dubček, Svoboda." The Party congress that was to deal with additional steps toward democratization met secretly under the noses of the invaders on 22 August at the ČKD factory in Prague-Vysočany. Occasionally, violence erupted. Nearly eighty people died, and many more were wounded. Some of the invading troops conducted themselves poorly, such as those who sprayed the National Museum with machine-gun fire.

NORMALIZATION AND THE HUSÁK REGIME

At first, the reformers stayed at their posts, although the Soviets and the Czechoslovak hard-liners determined policy. The only significant reform to remain was the federation of the country, which became valid on 1 January 1969. The change had little impact, however, since the Communist Party of Czechoslovakia maintained its unity. The population did not accept the invaders' new order, and continued minor displays of resistance. About 170,000 fled the country during the period of "normalization," which lasted about two years after the invasion. Nearly a quarter of a million Slovaks and Czechs fled altogether by the time the Communists lost their grip on power in 1989. Many of those who chose to live abroad after 1968 were highly respected politicians, intellectuals, and artists. On 16 January, Charles University student Jan Palach's self-immolation in front of the National Museum was both a protest of the invasion and a call for resistance. Palach died three days later. In February a high school student, Jan Zajíc, became the second living torch. In March 1969, when the Czechoslovak ice hockey team won two victories in Stockholm over their Soviet opponents to take the world championship, the Czechs and Slovaks considered it a moral victory and took to the streets in celebration and protest.

In the middle of April 1969 Dubček resigned as first secretary and Husák took his place. Dubček subsequently served as ambassador to Turkey in 1969–1970, was expelled from the Communist Party, and became a manual laborer. He protested the restrictions on personal liberties in an open letter to the government in 1975, but Dubček did not join the ranks of the dissidents. Even before Dubček's removal, other reformers had lost their positions and had been expelled from the Party. Many found nonpolitical jobs, frequently as laborers. A few emigrated, such as Šik. In 1970 Lubomír Štrougal replaced Černík as prime minister and headed five governments until 1988. Svoboda remained president until 1975, when the Federal Assembly removed him for health reasons and replaced him with Husák, who retained his leadership of the Party. In 1970 the Party underwent a purge, resulting in the expulsion of nearly 327,000 members, that is, nearly 22 percent of its membership, and 150,000 resigned from the Party. Others who supported the reform process lost their positions, and a critical target was the intelligentsia. Hundreds of teachers and professors lost their positions and had to find manual jobs. A restaurant not far from the main building of Charles University had excellent goulash, the pride of the former academics who prepared it.

A feature of the political and cultural life of post-1968 Czechoslovakia was the dissident movement. For the Czech Lands and the country as a whole, the most visible dissident was the playwright Václav Havel, who had actively supported reform with other writers in June 1967 and had been one of the organizers of the Club for Independent Authors (Klub nezávislých spisovaetlů). His open letter to Husák (1975) and his essay "Power of the Powerless" ("Moc bezmocních," 1978) offered a biting analysis of the ills of Czechoslovakia after "normalization." His other works—both essays and plays—were equally thought-provoking. Havel became one of the first three spokesmen of those who signed the protest document Charta 77, the others being Jiří Hájek, the minister of foreign affairs during the Prague Spring, and Jan Patočka, a philosopher who died of a stroke when in the custody of the police. Original signers of Charta 77 numbered 239 and included František Kriegel, who had refused to sign the Moscow Protocol in 1968, Zdeněk Mlynář, a Communist Party Central Committee member during the Prague Spring and one of the authors of the "Action Program," and Jiří Dienstbier, an editor and commentator for Radio Prague between 1958 and 1969. A total of 1,883 people signed Charta 77 over the years, and the group released 572 various documents. Charta 77 came about because of the trial of several members of the unofficially recognized rock group Plastic People of the Universe. In the mid-1980s the Jazz Section would suffer a similar fate. Dissidents established several other organizations, but the two most important were the Committee for the Defense of the Unjustly Persecuted (Výbor na obranu nespravedlivě stihaných; VONS), which aided those who had been arrested and imprisoned, and the Social Defense Initiative (Iniciativa sociálni obrany; ISO), which helped those who suffered discrimination in the workplace and had other difficulties because of their views. Active in many respects as an organ of dissent was the Roman Catholic Church. In Slovakia an underground church helped meet the needs of the great number of Catholic believers, thus sidestepping the regime's official organization for clergy, Pacem in Terris (Peace on Earth). As in other East European states, Czechoslovakia had an active underground university. Several samizdat (underground) organizations existed, including Petlice (Padlock), from the 1970s, and Havel's Expedice. In 1988 an independent newspaper appeared, *Lidové noviny* (People's Newspaper).

Several factors combined in the middle of the 1980s to spark an increased boldness in Czechoslovak society to demand reform, among them the continued enfeeblement

Václav Havel (b. 1936), dissident between 1968 and 1989; president of Czechoslovakia, 1989–1992; and president of the Czech Republic, 1993–2003. (Embassy of the Czech Republic/Alan Pajer)

and deepening paralyzation of the Husák regime, not unlike what the Soviet Union experienced with the last years of Brezhnev and the quick succession of two more aged leaders, Yuri V. Andropov and Konstantin U. Chernenko. Such boldness prompted skiers on the slopes of the Tatry Mountains in Slovakia to cheer instead of bowing their heads in a moment of silence when the sirens wailed and the announcement came of Chernenko's death. The inspiration of Mikhail S. Gorbachev and his notions of glasnost and perestroika (openness and restructuring) further emboldened Czechoslovaks. When Gorbachev was to visit Czechoslovakia in 1986, Prague made the standard preparations befitting a Soviet leader. On the morning of the scheduled visit, children in Pioneer uniforms crowded the subways. Placards, banners, and pictures of Gorbachev appeared everywhere, aside from the Aeroflot office on Wenceslas Square. Havel may never have noticed, but the fictitious Green Grocer in "Power of the Powerless," who dutifully placed the Communist placards in his window, transformed in real life, at least in one instance, by the middle 1980s. On the middle of Wenceslas Square, a grocery store displayed pictures of Gorbachev and Husák, but under them, filling the entire display window, was an enormous bed of lettuce—lettuce *(salat)* is an analogy in Czech for one with a weak mind. Gorbachev cancelled his visit because of the flu, but everyone in Prague suspected that his illness was political. He came in the spring of 1987, and the fanfare was noticeably absent. It was apparent when Gorbachev greeted the citizens of Prague that he was more popular than their own leaders. The transformation could even be seen with the Czech Philharmonic Orchestra. Its conductor, Václav Neuman, led the orchestra in a performance of Smetana's patriotic *Má vlast* (My Fatherland) on 28 October 1986, the day celebrating the declaration of Czechoslovakia's independence in 1918, which the Communists had long before eliminated as a holiday (they recognized it as such once more in 1988). The concert took place in the Obecní dům cultural center, not the normal venue for the orchestra's concerts but where the Czechoslovak First Republic had been proclaimed. On the same day, in České Budějovice, an explosion occurred at a statue of Gottwald, although the blast could have been staged by the police.

Glasnost and perestroika, in Czech *nahlas* and *přestavba,* had a positive effect on the Czech and Slovak citizenry, but the political leadership rejected it as inappropriate for Czechoslovakia and applicable only to the Soviet Union. Miloš Jakeš replaced Husák as general secretary of the Party, although Husák remained as president. Štrougal, the perennial federal prime minister, began to incline toward supporting Gorbachev-type solutions, and resigned in October 1988. His replacement was Ladislav Adamec, a supporter of reform. Meanwhile, Czechs and Slovaks were inspired in 1988 by the tragedy of Tiananmen Square and Solidarity's daring resumption of activity in Poland. New dissident organizations emerged, such as the Democratic Initiative (Demokratická iniciativa), formed in the autumn of 1988 to promote political pluralism, and the Renewal Club for Democratic Socialism (Klub obroda, za demokratický socialismus, or Obroda), an organization of former Communist Party members who had supported the 1968 reforms. Artists in January 1989 drafted Several Sentences (Několik vět), a short statement demanding democratic reforms that over the next ten months surprisingly attracted 40,000 signatures. In 1989 Neuman and the Czech Philharmonic publicly boycotted television broadcasts as a protest against the harassment of signers of Several Sentences. Demonstrations that dissidents organized began to take on more significance in the Gorbachev era. Numbers of demonstrators grew larger. Dissidents from Poland and Czechoslovakia began to meet openly. The dissidents' successes demonstrated the Communist Party's weakening resolve. One central committee member noted that fewer high Party officials wanted to put anything in writing or sign anything. They even avoided making decisions.

PRAGUE'S CANDLELIGHT REVOLUTION

The successes of Solidarity in Poland and reform communists in Hungary in the spring of 1989 were significant signs that further changes in Eastern Europe were in the offing. In the summer of 1989 thousands of East Germans prolonged their summer vacation by fleeing from the GDR to the Federal Republic of Germany through Hungary, which had opened its borders with Austria. Some East Germans went to Prague, where they encamped in the courtyard of the West German embassy, demanding safe transport to the FRG (Federal Republic of Germany). The regime of Erich Honecker in the GDR was powerless to stop the flood of emigrants. Similarly, Husák had no alternative but to permit thousands of East Germans in Prague to board special trains to West Germany. On 28 October, to celebrate Czechoslovak independence, about 10,000 people unofficially demonstrated on Wenceslas Square. On 9 November, crowds breached the Berlin Wall.

A week later, students at Charles University planned their annual march to commemorate Opletal, who had been killed by the Nazis. The Husák regime attempted to avoid trouble. For example, they brought to the Hrad the chairperson of the Socialist Union of Students (Socialistický svaz mládeže; SSM), Pavlína Kupová, who had assumed her post some months earlier because of her desire to have a positive influence on the lives of students, not because she was a dedicated communist. The authorities intimidated Kupová into informing the students not to deviate from the officially planned path for their demonstration. Her fellow students heckled her when she informed them of her meeting. The students developed their own plans, and on 17 November, when they reached Wenceslas Square, police were waiting for them on an adjoining street. The students indicated that they did not want a confrontation, and on the ground between them and the police, they placed candles—symbolic in every revolution in 1989. The police attacked, wounding about 150. Another demonstration brought more candles and more violence. This time actors, who had seen the crowds sprayed with water cannons on their way to the theater for a performance, joined the demonstrators.

In Prague, Civic Forum (Občanské fórum; OF), composed of Havel and other dissidents and established on 19 November, began to coordinate protests and open channels with the Party and government. In Slovakia, the Public against Violence (Verejnosť proti nasiliu; VPN) took on a similar role. The musician Michael Kocáb and the writer and lyricist Michal Horáček, the originators of MOST (Bridge), a group founded in the early autumn of 1989 designed to facilitate dialogue between various segments of the society, served as liaisons between the dissidents and the government. On 24 November, Dubček, who had addressed a crowd in Bratislava two days earlier, joined Havel and other dissidents to greet the crowds on Wenceslas Square, and Cardinal Tomášek sent a message of support. The crowd, unimpressed with concessions, such as the resignation of Jakeš, rang bells and jingled keys to ring out the old regime. Demonstrations of about 750,000 took place on 25–26 November in Letná Park, not far from where a giant statue of Stalin had stood. Demonstrations also took place in other cities across Czechoslovakia, and students fanned out across the country to generate support. A successful and peaceful general strike for two hours in the afternoon took place on 27 November, with the goal of having the Communist Party relinquish its monopoly on power. Negotiations continued unsuccessfully; demonstrations in the evening continued peacefully. Communists from various quarters—factory workers, employees at the communist newspaper *Rudé Právo* (Red Right), and even police (many of whom ignored orders of their superiors)—joined the call for change. Entertainers appeared on the balcony overlooking Wenceslas Square to lend their support to the demonstrations. On 29 November, the Federal Assembly eliminated the constitutional leading role of the Communist Party and passed other legislation that effectively ended communist rule. That same day, OF released concrete demands. On 4 December the Warsaw Pact states that had invaded Czechoslovakia in 1968 formally denounced the invasion, shattering the last threads of legitimacy for the Husák regime (the Communist Party of Czechoslovakia had condemned the invasion three days before). After having recast his cabinet a few days earlier, Adamec resigned as prime minister on 7 December. Three days later, Husák installed the Government of National Understanding under the Slovak Communist Marián Čalfa, in which the majority of ministers were representatives from OF and VPN. Husák then resigned the presidency. Ján Čarnogurský, a dissident representing Slovak Catholic interests, became one of two first deputy prime ministers. Valtr Komárek, an economist who had joined OF, was the other first deputy prime minister and one of the ministers of internal affairs. Dienstbier became the foreign minister but temporarily returned to his work as a stoker until he could find a replacement. Dubček became chairman of the Federal Assembly on 28 December, which elected Havel president the following day. Frequently, new postage stamps bearing Havel's image appeared on the same envelopes with old stamps showing Husák. The inmate replaced the jailor.

The dissidents and population, most notably during the massive demonstrations, displayed remarkable restraint in their endeavor to remove the Communists from power. The toppling of the old regime thus became known as the Velvet Revolution. The determination of the population, success of the revolution, and peaceful transformation to democracy restored the self-confidence of the Czechs, who had felt powerless for so many years. Frequently, analysts and Czech citizens alike reflected on the rapidity with which Czechs succumbed to threats on their independence—Munich in 1938, the Communist takeover in 1948, and the Warsaw Pact invasion of 1968 and the subsequent period of normalization. Submissiveness as a function of the Czech political culture even received a name—Švejkism. Those who accounted for the actions of Czechs through the Švejkian set of perceptual lenses often lost sight of the militant aspects of Czech history—what might be termed the Žižkian tradition of the Hussite Wars and, in modern times, the struggle to create the state during World War I and the willingness of the vast majority of the population to wage war against Germany in 1938. Similarly, they overlooked efforts of heroic passive resistance, as exemplified by Komenský, the popular opposition to the Warsaw Pact invasion of 1968, and the heroic dissidents between 1968 and 1989. Few cold warriors cared to admit that in 1948, when the communists came to power in Czechoslovakia, they did so with a large segment of popular support. The lameness of the Švejkian argument became apparent when the discussion about it evaporated after the Velvet Revolution.

POLITICAL DEVELOPMENTS

CZECHOSLOVAKIA, 1989–1992: CONSOLIDATING THE REVOLUTION AND DIVIDING THE STATE

Many legislative revisions dismantled the communist regime and consolidated Czechoslovakia's new pluralistic democracy and the market economy. Highly symbolic was the change of the country's name on 20 April 1990 from the Czechoslovak Socialist Republic to the Czech and Slovak Federated Republic (Česká a Slovenská Federativní Republika; ČSFR), an effort to enhance the visibility of Slovaks as equal partners in the state with Czechs. The federal structure of the communist era remained—the Federal Assembly, with its House of People and House of Nations, the federal government, the prime ministers and governments of Slovakia and the Czech Lands, and the National Councils (legislatures) of the Czech Republic and Slovak Republic. Czechoslovakia restructured its foreign policy to improve relations with the West and newly established postcommunist regimes in East Central Europe and the Balkans. Simultaneously, it distanced itself from the Soviet Union, withdrawing from the Warsaw Pact and CMEA. On 21 June 1991, the last Soviet soldier left Czechoslovak territory.

The electorate had to contend with a proliferation of political parties and movements, that is, loosely structured organizations. Parties that had existed during the communist era went through a process of restructuring. The communists in Slovakia formed their own party, and those in the Czech Republic became known as the Communist Party of Bohemia and Moravia (Komunistická strana Čech a Moravy; KSČM). Although the Czech communists retained their name, which was unusual in the region, they condemned the abuses but not the ideology of the pre-1989 days. The National Socialists, Czech Populists, Freedom, and Democratic parties emerged from under the umbrella of the National Front. The former dissidents in Civic Forum and Public against Violence preferred to remain a movement, rather than to create a disciplined political party. Some political parties of the period before and immediately after World War II reemerged. Most were insignificant—few original members survived and, as in the case of the Republican Party that had catered to agrarian interests, their constituents had changed dramatically. The exception was the Czechoslovak Social Democratic Party (Československá strana sociálně demokratická; ČSSD), which became one of the strongest parties in the Czechoslovakia of the 1990s. A series of new parties evolved that represented specific regional, class, ethnic, religious, environmental, or economic interests. On the humorous side were the Party of the Friends of Beer, Independent Erotic Initiative, which was dedicated to sexual freedom, and Party of Moderate Progress within the Limits of the Law, which was inspired by the writer Hašek.

A total of twenty-three parties, movements, and electoral coalitions participated in the June 1990 elections, but only eight obtained the necessary votes to enter the Federal Assembly. OF and VPN received the vast majority of the votes. The communists did not gain enough seats to claim a position in the government, but they had the second strongest party in the state. Many politicians, analysts, and voters were shocked by the communists' success. In the years that followed, the far left along with the far right continued to attract a significant following but did not gain enough votes to form a government. In this sense, politics after 1989 reflected the tradition of the Czechoslovak First Republic. Broad coalitions characterized all of the governments that resulted from the 1990 elections. OF, VPN, and the Christian Democratic Movement formed a federal government under Prime Minister Čalfa. The Czech government was under the former dissident Peter Pithart and was a coalition of OF, the People's Party, and the Movement for Self-Governing Democracy–Society for Moravia and Silesia. The Slovak government was a coalition of VPN, Christian Democratic Movement, and Slovak Democratic Party under the VPN Prime Minister Vladimír Mečiar. During the period from 1990 to 1992, the number of parties and movements in Czechoslovakia mushroomed to approximately 120. Both OF and VPN splintered, and the most important group to emerge from OF was the Civic Democratic Party (Občanská demokratická strana; ODS), founded in February 1991. Its leader was Václav Klaus, finance minister in the federal government from 1989 to 1992 and vice premier from 1991 to 1992. During the Prague Spring, he had been an economist with the Czechoslovak Academy of Sciences and had to take employment in the State Bank as a result of Husák's normalization campaign. He returned to the Academy in 1988 to enter its newly created Institute for Prognosis, where he studied the conservative economic policies of Ronald Reagan in the United States and Margaret Thatcher in the United Kingdom. Klaus's ODS championed rapid dismantling of the socialist economic system, similar to the "shock therapy" in Poland. In Slovakia, Mečiar broke from the VPN and established the Movement for a Democratic Slovakia (Hnutie za demokratické Slovensko; HZDS), which advocated a slow pace of progress toward privatization and stressed the need to strengthen Slovakia's position in the country.

The federative and republic governments had to deal with a series of problems in the transition from communist rule and socialist economics to democracy and capitalism. Economics received the most attention: privatizing industry and trade; restructuring collective farms; determining the appropriate level of state regulation of private enterprise; rising unemployment; restructuring the administration; and repairing the damaged environment. There were also pressing social questions, including that status of Roma in the society and the large number of Vietnamese guest workers who remained in Czechoslovakia after the revolution. A major concern was ferreting out those who had committed crimes during the period of communist rule, a process called *lustrace*. Anyone identified as having abused power was excluded from government and administrative positions for a decade. A particularly controversial portion of the identification process was determining who had cooperated with the secret police, the hated StB, or State Security (Státní bezpečnost). The published lists included not only notorious agents but also citizens who may have provided assistance to the police in some small way many years before and even those who had never worked with the authorities. In some cases, individuals in the gray area who were in the Party and had responsible positions but who did not actively participate in the repressive efforts of communist rule were hounded out of one position after another.

Politicians also had to readdress the Slovak question. In the June 1992 elections, the plurality of votes—better than one-third—in the Czech House of the People and the House of Nations went to the coalition of the ODS and Christian Democratic Party (Křest'ansko-demokratická strana; KDS). In Slovakia, the HZDS-led electoral coalition scored a similar victory, gaining more than a third of the votes. Both of these parties also did well in the elections to their respective National Councils. Since no party had a majority, a coalition was necessary, but it was apparent that any government would have difficulties passing legislation. The Czech groups in parliament favored a stronger central government, while Mečiar's HZDS and the National Slovak Party spoke of either a confederative arrangement between Slovakia and the Czech Republic or complete Slovak independence. Because the separatist Slovak parties had a plurality of votes in the Slovak Chamber of Nations and the structure of the Federal Assembly required that all bills pass both the House of the People and the two chambers of the House of Nations, a constitutional impasse seemed inevitable. Mečiar and Klaus formed coalition governments for the Slovak and the Czech republics, respectively. They agreed to create a weak federal government that included politicians of lesser importance, clearly a caretaker government.

Slovaks, who in 1990 accounted for about one-third of Czechoslovakia's population of 15.6 million, were concerned about their political and economic status in the republic. Many were convinced that the Czechs were getting a better economic deal with the introduction of capitalism. Unemployment in Slovakia—three times higher than that of the Czech Republic and hovering around 12–13 percent—was largely because of layoffs in Slovakia's outdated industries. The Slovaks also preferred a slow privatization process to ease the transition to capitalism, something Klaus refused to do. Both Slovaks and Czechs claimed that the other nation had received economic advantages in the 1970s and 1980s. In reality, at the time of the Velvet Revolution, the Slovaks' contribution to the national income was on a par with the Czechs on a per capita basis, but the Slovaks received a somewhat greater share of investments. Despite Mečiar's popularity, a poll conducted at the time of the election showed only 17 percent of the Slovaks favored independence. Apparently, the Slovaks were convinced on going to the polls that Mečiar would help them vis-à-vis the Czechs, but they were not expecting him to steer a course toward independence. The Slovaks demonstrated once more the tendency inherent in their political culture to support leaders in troubled times whose radical solutions may not reflect the true sentiments of the population but are perceived as strong bargaining tools in the defense of Slovak national interests. The Czechs, meanwhile, grew weary of Mečiar's rhetoric, his intransigence, and his supporters' insults of President Havel. (At one point, a crowd of Slovaks spat on Havel, though it is also true that Havel's wandering into a rally of Mečiar supporters was far from politically astute.) In July 1992 the Federal Assembly failed to reelect Havel as president because the Slovaks refused to support his candidacy. The vote was a sad defeat for the republic's unity, and it became apparent to Slovaks and Czechs that the rift between the two nations had become irreparable. On 17 July the Slovaks passed a declaration of sovereignty.

Havel, refusing to complete his term and participate in the destruction of Czechoslovakia, resigned as president effective 20 July. No candidate in subsequent elections succeeded in winning enough votes to assume the office. The state was moving quickly toward division.

In the third week of July, Mečiar and Klaus agreed on the procedure for dividing the state through legislative action in the Federal Assembly. Both opposed a referendum, which might have reflected the majority of the population's desire to continue Slovak and Czech unity. Tortuous negotiations determined the precise means of dismantling the republic, and a law passed on 25 November 1992 to partition the state. Mečiar and Klaus had already set the date of the division for 1 January 1993.

Television news coverage broadcast to the world one of the ironies of European history that occurred at the stroke of midnight on 31 December 1992, and 1 January 1993. Guards stationed on internal borders of the EU (European Union) raised their gates and retreated to the warmth of their offices as the EU introduced the fully free movement of individuals and goods. Meanwhile, guards stationed between Slovakia and the Czech Lands emerged from their hastily erected offices and lowered gates on the new international border. Regardless of their opinions about the division of the state, Czechs and Slovaks took consolation in the peaceful division of the country—the so-called Velvet Divorce. Most quipped that they dissolved their common state so that they could reunite in a few years within the EU.

THE CZECH REPUBLIC SINCE 1992

The government of Václav Klaus remained in power through the division of Czechoslovakia, and one of the first acts of the new parliament of the Czech Republic, formerly the National Council, was to reelect Havel as head of state in January 1993 (he was reelected to another term in January 1998). The parliament adopted a constitutional amendment creating a Senate in 1995 and scheduled elections to that body in the following year. Parliamentary elections took place in May-June 1996 (elections for the Senate were in November) in which ODS (which had absorbed its coalition partner, KDS) received 29.62 percent of the votes and lost its majority. The Czech Social Democrats (Česká strana sociálně demokratická; ČSSD) came in second with 26.44 percent of the votes. The Communists received 10.33

The Flag and Coat of Arms of the Czech Republic

The historic flag of Bohemia is white (above) and red (below). The colors of Slovakia and Moravia are red, white, and blue, and after the creation of Czechoslovakia at the end of World War I, the National Assembly superimposed a blue triangle on the left portion of the white and red Bohemian flag. After the division of Czechoslovakia in 1992–1993, the Czech Republic retained the flag, and Slovakia adopted a completely different design that incorporates its historic coat of arms on a field of red, white, and blue horizontal bars.

The seal of the Czech Republic is an emblem that contains the two-tailed white Bohemian lion on a red field in the upper-left and lower-right quadrants, the black eagle of Silesia on a gold field in the lower-left, and the red-and-white checkered Moravian eagle, having the same outline as the Silesian eagle, on a blue field in the upper-right. The eagles and the lions wear the same gold crown. The presidential seal includes the seal of the republic flanked by gold branches of the Czech linden tree. Beneath, on a red banner, is written *Pravda vítězí* (Truth prevails; from the Latin, *veritas vincit*), the motto of the republic's first president, Tomáš G. Masaryk. The field is white, and the border of flowing triangles is red, white, and blue.

percent; the Christian and Democratic Union–Czech People's Party (Křest'anské a demokratické unie-Česká strana lidová; KDU-ČSL), 8.07 percent; the radical right Republican Party, 8 percent; and the Civic Democratic Alliance (Občanská demokratická aliance; ODA), another offshoot from OF, 6.36 percent. The chairman of the Social Democrats, Miloš Zeman, agreed to support a minority coalition government of the ODS, KDU-ČSL, and ODA with Klaus as prime minister.

The coalition partners frequently had difficulties. Then the public learned that the ODS received secret financial support, including funds from a Swiss bank account. Much of the money was from kickbacks connected with advantageous privatization deals. The government collapsed in November 1997. In January 1998 Havel appointed a mixed government of politicians from ODS and ODA along with experts under the leadership of the governor of the Czech National Bank, Josef Tošovský.

In the early elections of June 1998, the Social Democrats won a plurality of votes (32.31 percent), while ODS came in second (27.74 percent), the Communists third (11.03 percent), KDU-ČSL fourth (9 percent), and a new party of the right, the Freedom Union (Unie svobody; US) fifth (8.60 percent). ODS returned the favor to the Socialists and in July signed the so-called Opposition Agreement with the ČSSD that committed the ODS to support the Socialist minority government. Zeman became the prime minister, with Socialists filling all the cabinet posts, aside from the Ministry of Justice, which remained in the hands of a non-party expert. As part of the Opposition Agreement, ODS assumed the leadership roles of the Chamber of Deputies and Senate. Klaus and the ODS formed a shadow government, thus starting a new tradition in Czech politics.

As the Zeman government neared the end of its term, Zeman announced his retirement from politics. Elections took place in June 2002, and the Socialists remained the largest party in the parliament with 30.27 percent of the vote. ODS received 24.53 percent of the votes, and the Communists had 18.55 percent of the votes. A coalition of the KDU-ČSL and US received 14.31 percent of the votes. The Socialists formed a coalition government in July with Vladimír Špidla as prime minister that included the KDU-ČSL and US coalition. Špidla set out to tackle budget deficits—the highest among the countries set to enter the EU—through budget cuts, particularly in the areas of welfare and social services. His controversial measures brought about a vote of confidence in September 2003, which his government survived.

The competition among the parties, primarily ČSSD and ODS, added drama to the presidential elections to replace Havel, whose term was to expire in early 2003. Two rounds of voting in parliament brought no result, aside from frustrating the already cynical electorate that increasingly views politics as a power game to ensure financial gain for a corrupt elite. Finally, parliament narrowly elected Klaus as president in February 2003.

A crisis occurred in the Špidla government in June 2004 as a result of the first elections in the Czech Republic to the European Parliament. ODS won the election, with the Communists coming in second. The ČSSD came in fifth, even behind their coalition partners in the cabinet, the KDU-ČSL. The US, also in Špidla's government, did not win any seats. Špidla soon resigned as prime minister and head of the ČSSD, and his replacement in both positions was Stanislav Gross, a young Social Democrat in his mid-thirties (in fact, the youngest Czech prime minister in history). The new government, which took office on 4 August, had the same constellation of parties and contained many of the same faces as its predecessor. In a personnel change characteristic to a consociationalist parliamentary system, Špidla replaced Pavel Telička on the European Commission. In August 2004 the chairman of European Commission named several representatives from states that had recently entered the EU to positions on the Commission, subject to the approval of the European Parliament. Among them was Špidla, who was to become Commissioner for Employment and Social Affairs.

As politicians continued the transition to a capitalist economy and consolidating the state's democratic institutions, the country faced a number of difficulties. Several floods devastated the republic in recent years, but the worst was that of August 2002, which brought the highest water level in Prague in a century. High unemployment remained in certain sections of the country where older industries had been located, and there is little hope of a solution. The economic transition to capitalism resulted in a degree of social stratification that was unknown in the communist era, when Czechoslovakia had one of the most economically level societies in the world. An important segment of the population, therefore, is discontent, insecure about its financial future, and skeptical about some benefits of the post-1989 order. The country's 300,000 Roma, many of whom are unemployed, poorly prepared for anything but manual labor, and have a low standard of living, have become a major social problem. The Roma face de facto discrimination, in part because the Czechs mistakenly associate the Roma with a high crime rate. In 1997 a wave of Roma fled the country, mainly to the United Kingdom and Canada, seeking political asylum. Authorities abroad realized their motive was economic, but the affair tarnished the image of the Czech Republic, despite the country's solid human rights record. Since that time, the government's Council for Roma Affairs combats discrimination, provides training and employment for Roma, and improves Roma communities. A major economic and political problem is corruption, which has resulted in difficulties for several noted politicians and state contractors. Zeman's campaign to limit corruption had little effect, and Špidla redoubled the government's efforts to stem the tide of corruption. In 2003 Freedom House gave the Czech Republic a score of 3.5 on corruption, above the 4.78 average that year for democratizing states in the region but well behind states like Poland, Hungary, and Slovenia. Transparency International registered a precipitous drop in the Czech Republic's corruption perceptions index. Overall, however, the Czech Republic's record on political rights and the freedoms of expression, assembly, religion, and the press is excellent. In 2003 Freedom House gave the Czech Republic a 1 for political rights and 2 for civil liberties on a scale from 1 to 7. The Czech Republic has made dramatic progress since the Velvet Revolution in implanting democratic ideals and institutions in the country and ranks among the most progressive former socialist states.

As the Czechs and Slovaks introduced capitalist markets and a pluralist democracy after 1989, they also pursued a policy of integrating into West European mechanisms for international cooperation. A major foreign policy achievement has been the Czech Republic's entry into NATO. In February 1994 the Czech Republic entered the initiative of the American president Bill Clinton known as Partners for Peace. The parliament approved entry into NATO in April 1998, and the Czech Republic joined Hungary and Poland as NATO members in March 1999. Already in 1995, the Czech Republic participated in the UN peacekeeping force in Bosnia. Then, in 1999, the government supported the bombing of Yugoslavia and provided humanitarian aid in the war zone, despite the popular opposition to the bombing. The Czech Republic actively participated in the KFOR operation to secure Kosovo. Most recently, it has supported the United States in its efforts against terrorism, and it backed the American military mission against Iraq in 2003. Admission to the EU, a key objective, was another foreign policy success for the Czech Republic. EU members are linked together in a series of international organizations, and the Czech Republic gained admission to several key groups. In 1993 the Czech Republic joined the Council of Europe, in 1994 it joined the West European Union, and in 1995 it joined the Organization of Economic Cooperation and Development (OECD). During the early years of the twenty-first century, the government completed the requirements the EU set forth for membership, and the Czech Republic ascended to the EU with a number of other states in 2004—the largest single expansion of the EU in its history.

Although the Czech Republic has excellent relations with its neighbors, there are two nagging difficulties for Czech policymakers. In Germany, those expelled from Czechoslovakia immediately after World War II and their families demand that Prague rescind the Beneš Decrees and restore their property. The former Sudeten Germans, most of whom reside in Bavaria, are solid supporters of the Christian Democratic Union–Christian Socialist Union (KDU-KSU) and pressure their representatives to champion their cause. When the German government of Helmut Kohl signed an agreement with the Klaus government in January 1997 that released their countries from claims, the question of compensation for the Sudeten Germans as well as compensation for the victims of Nazism during the World War II remained open. The Czech government has resolutely refused to revisit the expulsions of the postwar years and is unlikely to change its position. German politicians are in the most difficult position; they must avoid angering both their constituents and their neighbor, who is now their fellow EU member. Difficulties with Austria center on the Temelín power plant in Southern Bohemia. Designed during the communist era, the Temelín power plant has been the subject of heated criticism on both sides of the border. Even though the design of the plant may have taken into account the highest standards for safety, construction in the 1980s was shoddy. In the spring of 1999 the Czech government decided to complete the plant, realizing that it would be impossible to address every shortcoming in past construction. Temelín is now on line and has operated without incidents, but environmentalists and politicians in Austria along with many Czechs still are wary. Neither the former deportees from the Sudeten region who now live in Germany nor the opposition to Temelín in Austria had enough clout to prevent the Czech Republic's entry into the EU, but their campaigns were a frequent distraction to the Czech government's efforts to demonstrate its cooperative spirit in a conflict-free Europe.

An important foreign policy initiative for the Czech Republic has been its participation in the Vysegrád alliance of former East Central European socialist states. In February 1991 the leaders of Czechoslovakia, Poland, and Hungary signed an agreement in Vysegrád, Hungary, to coordinate their efforts at gaining entry into NATO and the EU. Both the Czech Republic and Slovakia retained their membership in the group when Czechoslovakia disintegrated in 1993. Although the commitment of the Vysegrád states to intensifying their contacts subsequently weakened, the member states renewed their interest in cooperation in 1999. The Czech Republic, Hungary, and Poland began actively supporting Slovakia's admission into NATO. The four states have discussed border policies, especially with respect to the eastern borders of Poland, Slovakia, and Hungary. President Klaus, never enthusiastic about Vysegrád in the past, reasoned in November 2003 that the Vysegrád Four might coordinate their efforts to comply with the EU's Schengen Treaty border policies after they enter the EU. The Vysegrád Four also established means to address common social issues, including the Roma minorities.

Although the transition from communist domination brought dramatic political and economic changes, the Czech Republic, like some other former states of the Habsburg monarchy, exhibits a remarkable continuity with the past in the preservation of consociational political arrangements. In the Czech Republic, as in the Czechoslovak First Republic, no party receives a majority of the votes, and coalitions or minority governments are the rule. Extraparliamentary arrangements, which may be informal or contractual, such as the Opposition Agreement, are reminiscent of the First Republic's Pětka. Governments of experts or mixed governments of politicians and experts are an occasional necessity. Unfortunately, many Czech politicians today fail to grasp the true nature of politics and, like Beneš and Masaryk between the world wars, decry the political machinations of Czech politics in comparison to the apparently clear and simple majority parliamentary politics of Western states, such as Germany. Their frustration became apparent during Zeman's tenure as prime minister, when the ČSSD and ODS cooperated to pass an electoral reform to improve the chances of parties securing a majority. Havel and the smaller parties resisted, as did the courts. Subsequent legislation made adjustments in the electoral procedures that favored the larger parties, but the electorate's preference for proportional representation that truly reflects the social, economic, and ideological diversity of the country remains deeply rooted in the political culture. The future success of Czech politics clearly lies with politicians who understand and respect consociational democracy and who master the fine art of compromise and coalition building.

Once out of the orbit of the Soviet Union, Czechoslovakia could have resumed the process of state building that World War II interrupted. Within a short time, however, Mečiar, Klaus, and their supporters determined that it was in the best interest of their respective nations to dissolve the state. After 1993, the Czech Lands embarked on a path of independent development unexplored since the time of the Jagiellonian kings in the first quarter of the sixteenth century, if one excludes the brief disastrous experience between 1618 and 1620. As the Czechs and Slovaks discarded communism in 1989 and then as they accepted the Velvet Divorce three years later to build their separate states, they enthusiastically embraced entry into the EU. The notion that an ethnic group would gain full sovereignty and then strive to voluntarily surrender many aspects of it a few years later through entry into a multinational organization seems unfathomable. Yet the Czech Republic, along with other former Eastern European states, finds the EU attractive, just as Western European states do, because of the ultimate goals that have marked the association's development since the Rome Treaties of 1957–coordination in the areas of economics, defense, domestic policy, and foreign affairs for the sake of peace and prosperity. The Czechs realize that the EU not only offers economic advancement and security against aggression but also a guarantee for ethnic expression. The EU celebrates ethnicity within the context of internationalism in building what might be termed Europe's postnational age. The Czechs' historic evolution, thoroughly embedded in Europe's cultural, social, political, and economic trends, ensures that they will be active and visible participants in building Europe's future.

CULTURAL DEVELOPMENT

ROMANESQUE PRAGUE

The adoption of Christianity from Rome by the early Přemyslids brought to the Czech Lands the cultural trends of the West, such as literature, music, and art. The most apparent relic from a millennium ago is Romanesque architecture. Some of this heritage remains today. At the Prague Castle is St. George Church (Kostel sv. Jiřího), which dates to the tenth century, although its facade is early baroque. Archaeological remnants of other Romanesque structures are scattered throughout the Hrad. Prague still boasts of several Romanesque rotundas, including the Rotunda of St. Martin (Rotunda sv. Martina) in Vyšehrad that dates from the second half of the eleventh century and the Rotunda of the Holy Cross (Rotunda sv. Kříže) in the Old Town that was built in the beginning of the twelfth century.

THE GOTHIC CULTURAL CONTRIBUTION OF CHARLES IV

The cultural achievements of Charles IV are significant, particularly his sponsorship of High Gothic architecture through his various building schemes. To accomplish his most important building projects, he first employed Matthew of Arras, an architect from Flanders once in the service of Pope Clement VI at Avignon, who began building St. Vitus Cathedral and most likely planned the New Town. He then turned to Petr Parléř from Swabia to continue work on the cathedral, to build a new bridge across the Vltava, which became known as Charles Bridge, and to begin reconstructing the Church of St. Barbara in the mining town of Kutná Hora. During the reign of Charles IV, Gothic construction in the Czech Lands flourished, and one of the most famous structures in Prague independent of Charles's efforts is the Týn Church, formally known as the Church of Our Lady before the Týn (Chrám Panny Marie před Týnem). Charles wrote the first autobiography of a medieval ruler, which he had translated from Latin into Czech. He was a devout Christian—he avidly collected relics and reliquaries, including those from Byzantium (Charles collected many things, including manuscripts, books, and jewels) and strictly observed Church precepts. He established the Emmaus Monastery for Benedictine monks, particularly from Croatia and Dalmatia, to preserve

Charles Bridge

Among the best-known architectural features of Prague is Charles Bridge (Karlův most). Known as Prague Bridge until 1870, it spans the Vltava River and the Kampa Island between the Lesser Town and the Old Town. It is one of the oldest stone bridges in Europe and the second oldest in the republic (the oldest in Písek, Bohemia, was built in the thirteenth century). The first bridge crossing the Vltava in Prague was wooden and dated from the tenth century. The Judith stone bridge, built 1158–1160, spanned the river until a disastrous flood washed it away in 1342. Charles IV commissioned Petr Parléř to erect a new bridge; being somewhat superstitious, the king broke ground for the bridge in 1357 on 9 July at 5:31 A.M., thus creating a date and time that, if given completely in numbers, is a perfect palindrome: 1–3–5–7–9–7–5–3–1.

The sandstone bridge, stretching 516 meters with sixteen arches, was completed in 1402. Thirty statues adorn the bridge (the originals for most are in the Lapidarium of the National Museum). In 1683 Charles Bridge received its first baroque sculpture, that of St. John Nepomuk, the work of Matthias Rauchmüller and Jan Brokoff. The bronze relief at the base of the statue depicts the false legend that Jan Nepomuk would not tell Václav IV the secrets of the queen's confession, so Václav IV had him cast into the Vltava from the bridge (a bronze cross in the bridge parapet marks the alleged spot). Other baroque masters who sculpted works for the bridge included Ferdinand Maximilián Brokoff, Michal Josef Brokoff, and Matyáš Bernard Braun. In the classical era, Josef Max, Emanuel Max, and others sculpted several statues. Karel Dvořák completed the most recent statue, that of the missionaries Cyril and Methodius, in 1938.

On the Lesser Town side of the bridge are two towers. The first is a remnant of the Judith Bridge that was rebuilt in 1591. The taller Gothic tower was completed in 1464, and a Gothic gateway links the two towers. On the Old Town side of the bridge stands a single Gothic tower decorated with saints, the builders, and skillfully executed representations of Charles IV and his son, Václav IV. Also embellishing the tower are the coats of arms of the Bohemian kingdom. The roof is the design of Josef Mocker from the late nineteenth century. A portion of the Old Town Tower facade and the bridge was damaged during a Swedish bombardment in 1648.

the Slavonic liturgy and literature (the front of the church was damaged during Allied bombing in World War II and was reconstructed as two intertwining concrete spires). In 1348 he established what is now known as Charles University in Prague, the oldest university north of the Alps and east of the Rhine. Charles used his friendship with Pope Clement VI to have a faculty of theology at Prague. The university was to be an international affair, with the Czech "nation" having only one in four votes in its governing body; the other "nations" being the Poles, Bavarians, and Saxons (each of these "nations" actually represented a conglomerate of ethnic groups—Czechs, for example, included Hungarians and South Slavs as well as Czechs). Latin was the official language of the university, but Charles made Czech the only official language of the state administration.

THE HUSSITE ERA

The Hussite movement brought significant changes to Bohemia's cultural landscape. The Czech domination of the university after 1409 solidified the status of Czech language and culture in the kingdom, but it did not mean that German influence came to an end. Similarly, the victories of the Hussites ended in the domination of moderate voices in the movement who reached an accord with the Catholics at Basel. The extremists among the Hussites, with their radical social and religious measures along with their iconoclasm, had no place in the Czech Lands after the 1434 Battle of Lipany. The Czech Lands by the late fifteenth century, therefore, were remarkable in the perspective of European culture. German and Czech culture coexisted as did Catholic and reformist Utraquist. Moreover, with the Hussite belief in the need for the laity to understand all the tenets of Christian faith, the Hussite movement resulted in dramatic advancements in the Czech language.

THE EARLY HABSBURGS: THE BEARERS OF THE RENAISSANCE AND BAROQUE

Ferdinand of Habsburg, who had come to the Bohemian throne in 1526, took some time to consolidate his political position. Once he succeeded, Ferdinand began an offensive against the non-Catholics, particularly the Bohemian Brethren. In 1547 he renewed a 1508 persecution order against the Bohemian Brethren and forced most of them to leave Bohemia for Moravia. To strengthen Roman Catholicism in Bohemia, he brought Jesuits to Prague in 1556 under the Dutchman St. Peter Canisius. Their school became a university in 1562 and was located in a building known as the Klementinum, which is now the National Library and Charles University Library. In 1566 they started a college, after 1573 a university, in Olomouc, and opened other centers of learning in Brno, Český Krumlov, Chomutov, Jindřichův Hradec, and Kladsko. To better control Catholic affairs in Bohemia, in 1561 Ferdinand reinstated the archbishop of Prague, a position that had been vacant for 130 years.

During Ferdinand's reign, Prague began to experience the new Renaissance architectural style that heretofore had only a minor presence in the city. Many Italian artists moved to Prague, in part because of the initiative of the queen, Anna Jagiellonian, who preferred to live in Prague, rather than at the court in Vienna. She commissioned the Genoese builder Paolo della Stella to construct her Royal Summer House and Royal Garden, Prague's first Renaissance garden, just outside the Hrad. After 1547, the second son of Ferdinand I, Ferdinand II Tyrolean, ruled in Bohemia for seventeen years as a governor. He was devoted to the arts and designed the star-shaped Renaissance summerhouse at Bílá hora (White Mountain) near Prague known as Hvězda (Star). Renaissance construction continued in Bohemia over the following decades. Noteworthy examples of the style appear in the town of Český Krumlov, where buildings and parts of the castle, including the tower, date from the second half of the sixteenth century. The Bohemian economy was strong enough to support such ambitious building plans and other cultural undertakings. It was at this time that the widely accepted silver coinage was minted in Jáchymov, Bohemia, which was first struck in 1519 and was known as the Joachimsthaler in German, from which English derived the word "dollar."

PRAGUE DURING THE REIGN OF RUDOLF II

Prague became a thriving center of Renaissance activity under Rudolf II, in part because in 1583 he moved the entire Habsburg court to the Prague Castle. Rudolf was rather eccentric. He was taken by magic, astrology, and alchemy, and legend has it that he kept alchemists busy at the Hrad, housing them in the small houses along the so-called Golden Lane. In 1599 Rudolf employed the astronomer Tycho Brahe, who had gathered massive amounts of data on the movement of planets and the sun while working for the Danish king. Brahe was a colorful figure. He lost the tip of his nose in a duel, and he wore a prosthesis made of metal. According to the mathematician Johannes Kepler, who also had come to Prague, Brahe refused to excuse himself during a dinner, in order not to insult his host, and the toxins in his blood brought about his death within days. Historians no longer accept this account as credible. To succeed Brahe, Rudolf appointed Kepler. The two had been in Prague at the same time, but they had not cemented a solid working relationship. Kepler used Brahe's material to prove that Nicolaus Copernicus was correct in positing a heliocentric solar system but that the paths of the planets around the sun were not round but elliptical and that planets travel at different speeds.

Prague at the time of Rudolf II was a haven for European artists and architects. Several Italian Renaissance architects worked in Bohemia during Rudolf's time, and a marvelous example of Renaissance architecture during this period is the Kratochvíle Summer Palace in Southern Bohemia by the Italian architect Baldassare Maggi. Giovanni Maria Filippi, who built the Mathias Gate at the Prague Castle and the Church of Our Lady Victorious (Kostel Panny Marie Vítězná) in Prague's Lesser Town, designed in the baroque style. Rudolf was an important patron of the arts. He brought painters and craftsmen to Prague from all over Europe. Well known is the portrait of Rudolf painted as a collage of fruit, vegetables, and flowers, the work of Giuseppe Arcimboldo. Other artists include the painters Hans von Aachen and Bartholomäus Spranger and the sculptor Adrien de Vries. The acquisition and care of Rudolf's rich collection of paintings, which included many from Albrecht Dürer, was in the capable hands of Jacopo Strada and his son, Ottavio Strada. Another individual who frequented the court of Rudolf II was Petr Vok, the last of the noble Rožemberk family. As a young man, he spent five years traveling throughout Europe. He eventually managed several of the Rožmberk estates, and he reconstructed the residence in Třebon in the Renaissance style and assembled there a library of approximately 11,000 volumes, one of the largest in Central Europe at the time. He left the Catholic Church to become Lutheran and then joined the Bohemian Brethren. He was involved in Bohemian politics, and he was one of the members of the diet who was responsible for ensuring the freedom of religion in the Czech Lands. Vok even successfully led Bohemian troops on a campaign against the Turks in 1594. Finally, it was Vok who hosted the dinner in Prague during which Brahe supposedly made the fateful decision that his bladder could withstand more abuse than his pride.

After Ferdinand had expelled the Jews from Bohemia, Maximilian II permitted them to return. Under Rudolf II, the Jewish community experienced financial and cultural prosperity. Mordekhai Maisel was a financier and court Jew who commissioned the High Synagogue, the original Maisel's Synagogue, and the Jewish Town Hall. Jacob Bassevi was another financier of Rudolf II and two succeeding emperors, and he was the first Jew to enter the nobility in 1622 (as Jakub Bassevi z Treuenburku). Crucial to the Jewish history of Prague was Rabbi Löw (also Loew), Jehudah Liva ben Bezalel, who was a chief rabbi in Moravia and Poland before becoming chief rabbi at a elderly age in Prague. Löw was a conservative rabbi who admonished his followers to remain steadfast to their Jewish culture in order to be prepared for the Messiah. In the nineteenth century, a story appeared about how Löw created a monsterlike golem as his servant. Writers ever since have portrayed Löw as magical and mysterious.

In the 1580s the Utraquist faith nearly collapsed when the head of the Utraquist Consistory became Catholic, but the consistory revived in 1594. The Bohemian Brethren remained vibrant, despite the dislike Rudolf II harbored for them. In 1602 Rudolf (like Ferdinand) renewed the 1508 persecution decree against them. Nevertheless, the sect accomplished an important step for the development of the Czech language when Jan Blahoslav wrote a Czech grammar and translated the New Testament, which was included in the so-called Kralicka Bible the Brethren compiled between 1579 and 1594.

CULTURE IN THE CZECH LANDS AFTER 1620

After the defeat of the Bohemian Estates at the Battle of White Mountain, the Czech Lands experienced a dramatic cultural shift. Catholic religious orders had free reign in the conversion of Protestants to Catholicism, and among them the Jesuits had special status. The Jesuits in the Klementinum took control of the Karolinum, that is, the Prague University that Charles IV had established, and they united the two into one university. The Counter-Reformation forcibly Catholicized Protestants using torture and intimidation, but the Catholic Church did not repeat in the Czech Lands the excesses of the Spanish Inquisition against Jews and Muslims in the fifteenth century and later against some Protestants. Symbolic of the dramatic change was the conversion of the Church of the Virgin Mary Victorious from an originally German Lutheran to a Catholic Church. In the process, the apse, once the eastern part of the church, became the western part of the church. Similarly, the main entrance moved from west to east. In 1628 the church received from the Catholic noble Lobkovic family a wax statue of the infant Jesus made in Spain and based on a Spanish original. Occupying a side altar, the Little Infant Jesus of Prague, the Bambino di Praga, garbed in one of its hundreds of finely crafted and often gem-studded robes, still casts its gaze on worshipers and tourists.

In the atmosphere of religious and cultural repression after 1620, many Czechs chose to flee Bohemia, resulting in the first essentially political mass exodus from the Czech Lands. Among these exiles, the last bishop of the Bohemian Brethren, Jan Komenský, is the most famous. Komenský remained in Bohemia until 1627, even though Spanish soldiers burned his home during one of the battles of the Thirty Years' War, and fled to Leszno, Poland, in 1628, after Ferdinand had issued the Renewal Ordinance. It was in Poland in 1632 that he became bishop of the Bohemian Brethren, the last Czech to hold the honor. Komenský traveled to England, where it appears he declined the offer of the son of the governor of Massachusetts to be the first president of Harvard. He later traveled to the Netherlands and then to Sweden, where he undertook a major reform of the country's education system. He journied to Transylvania in the early 1650s to initiate another education reform. In 1656, during a war between Poland and Sweden, his home and library were again destroyed. He went into exile once more, this time to the Netherlands, where in 1670 he died and was buried in Naarden. In addition to being a religious leader, Komenský was well known as an authority on education. He wrote several major works, including *Janua linguarium reserata* (Gate of Languages Unlocked, 1631), a compilation of sentences using basic vocabulary for teaching Latin; *Labyrint světa a ráj srdce* (Labyrinth of the World and the Paradise of the Heart, 1631), which takes a cynical view of authority; and *Orbis sensualium pictus* (Visible World in Pictures, 1658), which combined pictures of everyday life with Latin, German, Hungarian, and Czech captions for use in language instruction. In the realm of philosophy, he believed that all people must work together to realize God's will, and the means of achieving that goal is through education, a universal language, and a common body of knowledge, which he termed *pansophia*. His educational reforms, texts, and ideas influenced the development of kindergarten as a means of preparing children for the formal educational experience that is to follow, female education, and the teaching of history and geography. Finally, Komenský's Czech patriotism is apparent in his testament, titled *Kšaft umírající matky jednoty bratrské* (Bequest of the Dying Mother of the Unity of Brethren, 1650). In it he wrote: "Live, O nation consecrated to God, and die not! May thy men be without number."

THE BAROQUE PERIOD IN THE CZECH LANDS

Baroque began to become popular in Bohemia toward the end of the Thirty Years' War, and it reached its peak in the last decade of the seventeenth century and in the first half of the eighteenth century. Rococo succeeded it in the middle of the eighteenth century and lasted until near the end of the eighteenth century. The Dienzenhofers built many buildings in Prague and in other locations in Bohemia. Kryštof Dienzenhofer, who was born in Bavaria, constructed St. Nicholas's Church (Chram sv. Mikuláše) in Prague's Lesser Town between 1703 and 1711 (facade and nave) and St. Margaret's Church (Kostel sv. Markéta) in the Břevnov section of Prague between 1708 and 1712. His son, Kilián Ignác Dienzenhofer, became more famous as an architect than his father. The younger Dienzenhofer was responsible for building St. Nicholas's Church (Kostel sv. Mikuláše) in the Old Town between 1733 and 1738 and concluded work on the St. Nicholas Church in the Lesser Town that his father had begun. Among the gems of baroque architecture in Bohemia are the buildings of the Italian architect Giovanni Santini, whose works blend elements of the Gothic style with the baroque (the so-called baroque-Gothic style), which is readily apparent in his use of ribbed vaults. His buildings are located in Prague and throughout Bohemia, but his most famous structure is the church in Zelená Hora u Žd'áru and Sázavou, which is a UNESCO cultural site. The Austrian Johann Bernard Fischer von Erlach was responsible for several structures in Bohemia, including St. James's Church (Kostel sv. Jakuba) in the Old Town. His son, Joseph Emmanuel Fischer von Erlach, designed the silver tomb of St. Jan Nepomuk in St. Vitus's Cathedral. Baroque sculptors and carvers who worked in Prague include Jan Jiří Bendl, whose works are in Týn Church, St. Salvador's Church (Kostel sv. Salvátora) at the Klementinum, and St. Ignatius's Church (Kostel sv. Ignáce), and Matyáš Bernard Braun, who originally was from the Tyrol and who sculpted several of the statues on Charles Bridge. Also famous was the Brokoff family: Jan Brokoff, who was of German origin, and his sons, Michal Josef Brokoff and Ferdinand Maximilián Brokoff, who sculpted two of the statues that adorn Charles Bridge and the Moors on the Morzinský Palace on Nerudová Street. Another dynasty of sculptors that lasted until 1907 began with Ignác František Platzer, who executed the statues at the entrance of the Prague Castle. Baroque painters active in Bohemia include Petr Jan Brandl, whose paintings are above the altars at St. Margaret's Church in Břevnov, St.

The eighteenth-century baroque St. Nicholas Church in Prague's Lesser Town. (PhotoDisc, Inc.)

James's Church in the Old Town, and the Church of Our Lady Victorious in the Lesser Town; Jan Krštof Liška, who painted the altars at the Prague Church at Strahov monastery; Václav Vavřinec Reiner, whose paintings adorn the Mirror Chapel (Zrcadlová kaple) in the Klementinum; and Karel Škréta, who painted the Passion in St. Nicholas's Cathedral in Prague's Lesser Town. Norbert Grund painted during the Rococo era. The greatest contribution to baroque music from Bohemia came from Jan Dismas Zelenka, who lived in Dresden after 1710. He wrote a large body of liturgical music, including twenty-two masses and his Te Deum in D.

CULTURE IN THE LATE EIGHTEENTH CENTURY AND EARLY NINETEENTH CENTURY

As baroque culture came to a close during the reign of Maria Theresa, the classical era—technically the neoclassical era—began. Wolfgang Amadeus Mozart made five visits to Prague, often staying at the Bertranka Villa. Mozart dedicated his Symphony no. 38 in D Major, the Prague symphony (Köchel 504) to the city; it premiered in January 1787. In October 1787 *Don Giovanni* premiered in Prague at the Estates Theater (Stavovské divadlo). Finally, *La Clemenza di Tito,* an opera the Bohemian Estates commissioned Mozart to write in honor of the coronation of Leopold II as king of Bohemia, premiered in Prague in September 1791. The early careers of Christoph Willibald Gluck and Josef Haydn are also associated with the Czech Lands. Gluck was born in what is now Germany, but his father worked as a forester in various locations in Northern Bohemia. Gluck began his studies at the Jesuit College at Chomutov and then enrolled in the Philosophical Faculty at the University of Prague. While in Prague, he served as an organist at several churches, including Týn Church in the Old Town Square. He later went to Vienna, Milan, and London before finally settling in Vienna. The Austrian composer Haydn is most famous for his work at the court of the Esterházy family in Hungary, his years in Vienna, and his visits to London, but early in his career, he served as a court composer for the Count Ferdinand Maximilian z Morzina in Dolní Lukavice. It is there that he wrote his first symphony and the Lukavická Mass, sometimes referred to as the Czech Mass. Ludwig van Beethoven made several trips to Prague, where he performed two concerts in 1798, and he visited spas in other parts of Bohemia. Among Czech composers, the most recognized today is Jakub Jan Ryba, whose Czech Christmas Mass (1796) remains popular.

The Enlightenment had a strong influence on intellectual life in the Czech Lands, which were the home of several scientific advancements. In 1741 the Masons, dedicated to spreading the tenets of the Enlightenment, organized their first lodge in the Czech Lands in Prague. In 1754 Prokop Diviš, a Catholic priest, erected the first lightning rod in the Czech Lands, among the first of such devices in the world. The Klementinum in Prague became the first place in the world in 1775 to inaugurate the daily recording of the weather. The meteorological station and an observatory at the Klementinum were the work of Josef Stepling, a Czech Jesuit and professor at Prague University.

THE CZECH RENAISSANCE (1781–1848)

The first step in the national awakening was to build a modern Czech literary language after Czech was absent for over a century from intellectual pursuits and the administration. The impetus came from unusual quarters. The military recognized Czech as a necessary language of command, and the Military Academy, established in 1754 in Wiener Neustadt, taught courses in Czech. In 1775 the University of Vienna inaugurated a chair of Czech language. Czech courses in Vienna stimulated efforts to modernize and codify the language. Ironically, it was not until 1792 that Francis II (I) gave the University in Prague a chair of Czech language and literature. Historians attribute the genesis of modern Czech to the historian and linguist Josef Dobrovský, who was vice rector and then rector of the general seminary that Joseph II had established in Olomouc. In

1791 Dobrovský boldly addressed the Bohemian Society of Sciences in the presence of Leopold II about the positive qualities of Slavs and their languages, especially the Czechs. Despite his commitment to Czech, Dobrovský published his instrumental works, including his *Geschichte der bömischen Sprache und Literatur* (History of Czech Language and Literature, 1792) and *Lehrgebäude der bömischen Sprache* (Detailed Grammar of the Czech Language, 1809), in German because Czech had not reached a literary level.

Dobrovský inspired lively debates among Czech philologists in his day, and the advances they brought about in the language encouraged creative literary works in Czech. In 1811 Josef Jungmann translated *Paradise Lost* by John Milton, thereby demonstrating the poetic abilities of Czech. He later published his *Slovník Česko-německý* (Czech-German Dictionary, 1835–1839) and *Historie literatury České* (The History of Czech Literature, 1825) in Czech. From 1824 to 1832, Jan Kollár, a Slovak poet and Lutheran minister who wrote in Czech, published *Slávy dcera* (The Daughter of Slava), a collection of poems. A younger generation of Czech literary figures emerged, including Karel Hynek Mácha, whose epic poem *Máj* (May) is a masterpiece of romanticism. In 1826 Magdalena Dobromila Rettigová published her cookbook, *Domácí kuchařka,* and she became the first female to become active in the national awakening and the first devoted to women's interests. Also in 1826 the first Czech opera, *Dráteník* (The Tinker), premiered with music by František Škroup and the libretto by Josef Krasoslav Chmelenský. The tinker—whose trade began in Slovakia and spread throughout Europe and beyond, including the United States—was a poor itinerant craftsman who repaired pottery using wire and created various ornamental and functional wire and metal household items. Škroup (who, although not Jewish, for a while was the organist in a reformed synagogue—an example of the extent to which various Prague cultures were intertwined) wrote the music for *Fidlovačka* (Shoemakers Festival), a play by the actor, director, and writer Josef Kajetán Tyl. The song *Kde domov můj* (Where is My Homeland?) from the play was immensely popular and became the national anthem after 1918. Prominent among historians was František Palacký, who examined Bohemian history before 1526 in *Dějiny národu Českého a v Čechách a v Moravě* (A History of the Czech Nation in Bohemia and Moravia), the first volume of which appeared in German in 1836 (the last in 1865) and only in 1848 in Czech. Josef Pavel Šafařík, another cultural figure whom both Czechs and Slovaks claim, wrote several works, including an examination of Slavic history until the tenth century in *Slovanských starožitnostech* (Slavic Antiquities), which he published in 1837. An important development in the popularization of literary Czech was the establishment of a Czech newspaper. Modern newspapers in Czech existed in the early eighteenth century, but they only took hold by the 1780s, especially under the editorship of Václav Matěj Kramerius, who established his own newspaper in July 1789.

Czech scientific and cultural figures established a number of organizations to exchange ideas and promote their interests. Construction began in 1781 on the Estates Theater, which opened in 1783 and began regular performances in Czech in 1824. The Bohemian Society of Sciences, later the Royal Bohemian Society of Sciences, came into existence in December 1784. A music conservatory began functioning in 1811. The Silesian Museum was founded in 1814, the Moravian Museum in 1817, and the National Museum in Prague in 1818. In 1831 several cultural figures, including Jungmann and Palacký, established the Matice Česká (Czech Foundation) to fund the publication of books in Czech.

FROM BIEDERMEIER TO FIN DE SIÉCLE

The period that begins in 1815 and extends until 1890 is known as the Biedermeier period in the Habsburg monarchy and is roughly equivalent to the Victorian age in the United Kingdom. It was a time that the middle class, growing in economic power and influence, steadily augmented their role in setting cultural trends. For the individual ethnic groups of the monarchy, including the Czechs, the period was also a continuation of the national awakening.

Architecture in the Czech Lands reflected all the neo-Gothic, neoclassical, and neo-Renaissance styles common elsewhere in Europe at the time, but architects designed their structures not only as public spaces for the nation but also as edifices to celebrate the Czech national heritage. Josef Zítek and Josef Schulz used neo-Renaissance themes to design the National Theater (Národní divadlo) and the Rudolfinum concert hall, which between the world wars housed the Czechoslovak National Assembly. Schulz constructed the National Museum (Národní muzeum) at the head of Václavské náměstí (Wenceslas Square) in the neo-Renaissance style. Vojtěch Ignác Ullmann favored the neo-Renaissance style in the Prague Finishing School for Girls (Vyšší dívčí škola) and what is now the Academy of Sciences. Orientalism inspired architects in Europe and America and was the theme for Ullmann's design for the Spanish Synagogue (Španělská synagóga). Preeminent among Czech architects toward the end of the period was Josef Mocker, who painstakingly duplicated Gothic styles in his work to complete St. Vitus Cathedral in the Hrad, to reconstruct Karlštejn and Křivoklat Castle along with the Powder Tower (Prašná brana) in Prague, to reconstruct and complete the Church of Sts. Peter and Paul in Prague-Vyšehrad (Kostel sv. Petra a Pavla), and to build the new churches of St. Ludmila in Prague-Vinohrady (Kostel sv. Ludmily) and St. Prokop in Prague-Žižkov (Kostel sv. Prokopa). The Czech architect and builder Josef Hlávka studied and worked in Vienna and played a role in the construction of the Vienna Opera and other structures along the Ring.

Art in the latter half of the nineteenth century also emphasized national themes, using the romantic movement as a backdrop. Josef Mánes set the tone with his landscapes and portraits. Josef Václav Myslbek, a sculptor, is best known for his statue of St. Wenceslas that stands on Wenceslas Square before the National Museum. His sculptures also adorn the National Theater, and he along with others who contributed their talents to provide a home for the Czech stage were known as the generation of the National Theater. The

Václavské náměstí (Wenceslas Square) in the New Town of Prague. In front of the National Museum, constructed 1885–1890 by Josef Schulz (1840–1917), stands the statue of St. Wenceslas (completed in 1924) by Josef Václav Myslbek (1848–1922). Wenceslas Square has been the scene of many key political demonstrations, including those in 1968 and 1989. (Corel Corporation)

painter and illustrator Mikoláš Aleš similarly favored depicting historic Czech personalities and famous scenes. He decorated the ceiling of the main foyer of the National Theater, and he illustrated the works of Alois Jirásek. Jakub Schikaneder, also of the generation of the National Theater, later painted alluring scenes of Prague in the evening and at night under the influence of realism. In 1887 artists established the Mánes Association for the Creative Arts (Spolek výtvarných umělců Mánes; SVU), which functioned over the years as a society in which artists could exchange their views.

As with architecture and art, music combined romanticism and nationalism, and Czechs became famous for their contribution to the vast body of classical music and opera. Bedřich Smetana, who had been involved in the revolution of 1848, became famous for his operas, including *The Bartered Bride (Prodaná nevěsta)* and *Libuše.* He began composing the symphonic tone poem *Má vlast* (My Fatherland) in 1872, became deaf because of syphilis in 1874, but completed the work in 1879. The most famous segment in *Má vlast, Vltava,* traces the path of the Vltava as droplets and streams form the river that majestically flows through the Czech countryside past hunters, a peasant wedding, the night moon, St. John's Rapids, and Vyšehrad Castle. Of all Smetana's works, *Má vlast* and specifically *Vltava* evoke the greatest emotions among Czechs. Antonín Dvořák, like Smetana, attempted to capture the essence of the Czech nation in his symphonies, operas, chamber works, and other music. His *Slovanské tance* (Slavonic Dances) brought Dvořák international fame. He served between 1892 and 1895 as the director of the national Conservatory of Music in New York. In America he composed the Ninth Symphony (1893), subtitled *Z nového světa* (From the New World), with passages that allude to Native American music and spirituals. On returning home, he headed the Prague Conservatory. Zdeněk Fibich was another Czech composer in the romantic era who is known for his symphonic poems and operas. Finally, Czech production of musical instruments became important, and it was Václav František Červený who created the tubas Richard Wagner used in his *Der Ring des Nibelungen* (The Ring of the Nibelungs).

National themes interwoven with realism and romanticism are the main features of Czech literature in decades that followed the revolution of 1848. The early writers of this era, all associates of Havlíček, turned their attention away from politics to literature after the failure of the revolution of 1848. Among those in the romantic stream was Karel Jaromír Erben, who had been a writer in 1848. Afterward, he became an archivist, a career that influenced him to collect thousands of folk songs, rhymes, and folk tales from the countryside. These folk tales inspired Erben's original work, *Kytice* (The Nosegay), written in 1853 and expanded in 1861. Božena Němcová and her husband were involved in the revolutions of 1848, and they organized the funeral of Havlíček. The couple had difficulties with the authorities and separated because of their unhappy marriage. Němcová never remarried but had many dramatic affairs. She, like Erben, collected impressions from the countryside that she included in her stories. In *Babička* (Grandmother), she uses autobiographical glimpses of her own young life and that of her grandmother. The most noted realist was Jan Neruda, who knew Erben and Němcová in his youth, was associated with the journal *Máj* (May, first published in 1858), and attempted to portray an accurate picture of the world in his poetry and prose, particularly his *Povídky malostranské* (Tales from the Lesser Town). Early in his career as a newspaper journalist, Neruda developed the Czech style of the journalistic feuilleton essay. The Chilean poet Pablo Neruda (born Neftalí Ricardo Reyes) so admired the Czech writer that he adopted his name as a pseudonym. The neoromantics include Julius Zeyer, Svatopluk Čech, and Jirásek. Zeyer wrote epic poetry and prose, and his most important novel is *Jan Marija Plojhar,* the story of a Czech patriot who died in Italy, far from his homeland. Čech is noted for his novels based on Palacký's histories, but the author who perfected the historical novel with Palacký's work as a basis was Jirásek. The writers at the time contributed to the literary journal *Ruch* (Activity), which they established in 1868 to support the National Theater. Realism again influenced the Czech literary scene before World War I, in part through the support of Masaryk's journal *Čas* (Time). A famous realist literary critic and poet during this time was František Xaver Šalda, who was one of the founders of the Modernist Manifesto *(Manifest moderna)* of young writers in 1895.

Throughout the period of the national revival, Czechs continued to establish cultural organizations and further strengthen existing groups. In 1862 Vojtěch Náprstek, who had left Europe after the revolution of 1848 and returned to Prague ten years later, established a museum and library, which is today famous for its African, American, and Asian ethnographic collection. Also in 1862, Jindřich Fügner and Miroslav Tyrš established the Czech Sokol (Falcon) gymnastic movement, patterned after the German Turnverein as an apolitical organization to enhance the physical strength of the nation. Fügner, a businessman, served as the Sokol's president, and Tyrš, who also became a noted art critic, was its gymnastic director. In 1869 the Prague Polytechnical Institute was divided into German and Czech sections, forming the Czech Technical University (České vysoké učení technické; ČVUT), today the Czech Republic's premier institute of technology. Similarly, in 1882, Prague University divided along ethnic lines. Another key educational advancement occurred in 1890, when Eliška Krásnohorská (born Alžběta Pechová), a writer, translator, and critic, established the Minerva Gymnasium (high school) for girls in Prague.

By about 1890, the spiritual descendants of those who manned the barricades in 1848 sought to bring new directions to culture, giving birth in the fin de siècle age of 1890–1910 to the secession movement in Austria-Hungary, called art nouveau outside of Central Europe. Then immediately before World War I, artists experimented with new forms of artistic expression.

Like the artists in Vienna who founded the Secession, the Czech artists shunned the classical, Gothic, and Renaissance themes of their immediate predecessors and sought new inspiration. More than their Vienna counterparts, however, the Czech artists, like other non-Germans in the monarchy, incorporated national themes in their works, which broadened their appeal. Most widely known in Western Europe and North America is Alfons Mucha, whose seductive illustrations, especially with the French actress Sarah Bernhardt, still appear internationally in their original form as masterpieces of graphic art and in their modified form as high-class kitsch. Mucha's works include the *Slovanská epopej* (Slavic Épopée, or Epic), twenty paintings completed in 1928 depicting Czech and Slavic history, and one of the stained glass windows in the neo-Gothic part of St. Vitus Cathedral. Max Švabinský, who also later designed windows for St. Vitus Cathedral, was another artist who moved from the late romantic to the secessionist style. Jan Preisler was one of several Czech secessionist artists. Bohumil Kafka was a noted Czech secessionist sculptor, as was Ladislav Šaloun, who sculpted the statue of Jan Hus in the Old Town Square. Before World War I, other artistic trends began in the Czech Lands. The painter František Kupka experimented with abstract images, as did Vojtěch Preissig, who lived in America from 1910 to 1930. Jan Zrzavý was a noted expressionist painter. Bohumil Kubišta and Emil Filla, both leading figures in the Czech-German Osma (Eight) group of artists, drifted from expressionism into cubism beginning in 1910. Josef Čapek, brother of the famous author Karel Čapek, also painted in the cubistic style. The transition Kubišta and Filla made in painting occurred in sculpture with Otto Gutfreund and Otakar Kubín.

Prague is adorned with scores of secession and cubistic buildings placed like jewels amid the Gothic and baroque structures that form Prague's glorious architectural crown. The beginnings of change came in the 1890s. Various architects worked on the new buildings in what is now Pařížská Street to replace those razed in the Jewish Quarter of Josefov. Neobaroque and neo-Renaissance styles predominate. However, some buildings reflect the secessionist style. For the Industrial Exhibition of 1891 in Prague-Bubeneš, Bedřich Münzberger designed the Průmyslový palác (Industrial Palace) that combined exposed structural members of the industrial style with neobaroque. The Hlavní nádraži (Central Railroad Station) by Josef Fanta has bold geometric patterns. Obecní dům (Municipal House), the design of Osvald Polívka and Antonín Balšánek for a multipurpose civic center, mixes neobaroque, secession, and national motifs. Works by Myslbek and secession artists, such as Mucha,

Preisler, Švabinský, adorn its interior. Friedrich Ohnmann and his students Alois Dryak and Bedřich Bendelmayer designed the Hotel Central, Prague's earliest truly secession building still standing, and Dryak and Bendelmayer continued their collaboration in the famous Hotel Evropa on Wenceslas Square. The peak of the secession movement came with Jan Kotěra, who had studied in Vienna under Otto Wagner. One of his key works is the museum in Hradec Hrálově. On Prague's Wenceslas Square, he is responsible for the Peterka House (Peterkův dům), which lacks a great deal of ornamentation. Kotěra, later experimented in the geometric style, which can be seen in his Laichter House (Laichtrův dům). Kotěra's simplicity went a step farther with his pupil, Antonín Pfeiffer, who designed the Koruna Palace (Palác Koruna) at the lower end of Wenceslas Square, and with the Šupich Department Store (Šupichův obcnodní dům) of Matěj Blecha and Petr Kropáček. The sculptor František Bílek used the geometric style accentuated with thin wheatlike columns for his own home and studio, now a museum of his works. Cubism became popular from about 1910 until the middle of the 1920s. The imposing Dům u Černé Matky Boží (House at the Black Madonna) on Celetná Street is the work of Josef Gočár. Other cubist structures in Prague built before the collapse of the monarchy include the work of Josef Chochol, who was another student of Wagner and Emil Králíček.

The most noted Czech composer of the twentieth century, Leoš Janáček, wrote the opera *Jenůfa* (formally *Její pastorkyňa,* that is, "Her Stepdaughter") and several orchestral works around the turn of the century, but his teaching career delayed his efforts to compose. Another critical young composer at the time was Josef Suk, the pupil and son-in-law of Dvořák. Suk's works span the late romantic period and the modern age, and he gained great respect as a violinist. His most noted compositions completed or begun in the prewar era are the Asrael Symphony and the tone poems *A Summer Tale* and *Ripening.* Josef Bohuslav Foerster, who composed a number of works in the romantic tradition, including five symphonies, did much of his work abroad. Other important Czech musicians at the turn of the century include Vitězslav Novák, who composed the "Slovácko Suite" in 1903, and the composer and conductor Otakar Ostrčil. The soprano Emma Destinn (Emilie Kittlová), who was born in Prague, was recognized worldwide and performed for years with Enrico Caruso. The Prague Philharmonic (Česká filharmonie), founded in 1894, continues to operate and is one of the world's greatest orchestras.

Czech speakers outnumbered German speakers in Prague by the 1860s, and the dynamism of the Czech national revival sometimes has the effect of dwarfing German political, economic, and cultural developments. Czech society did not supplant German society in the national revival; the two developed parallel social spheres in the nineteenth century—separate political parties, schools and educational associations, economic institutions, business networks, cultural groups, sport societies, unions, and churches (or at least religious services, in the case of Catholics). Jews were largely German speakers, but they did not find acceptance with ethnic Germans. As a result, they developed yet a third social structure within the Czech Lands. The German-speaking Jewish writers of the Prague Circle left a lasting impact on world literature. Franz Kafka was writing before the world war, and some of his earlier well-known works—*Die Verwandlung* (Metamorphosis) and *Das Urteil* (The Judgment)—appeared during the war. Max Brod, the writer who became the close friend and publisher of Kafka, and Hugo Bergman became Zionists. Others in the Prague Circle included Franz Werfel, who lived in Prague until 1917 and who had a great affinity for Christianity, Paul Kornfeld, Egon Erwin Kisch, Otto Pick, and Rudolf Fuchs. Noted Germans from Germany and Austria were from or spent time in the Czech Lands. Albert Einstein and Ernst Mach taught at the German University in Prague. Egon Schiele, the Austrian painter who moved from the secession to expressionism, lived during 1911 in the Southern Bohemian town of Ceský Krumlov, the birthplace of his mother. Ferdinand Porsche, the automobile manufacturer and the creator of the Volkswagen, along with the writers Gustav Meyrink (born Meyer), the author of *Golem,* and the great German poet Rainer Maria Rilke were born in the Czech Lands.

CZECH CULTURE (1918–1938)

Czech culture between the two world wars was dynamic and celebrated both national independence and the modern age. In classical music, Janáček produced some of his greatest works. He composed the opera *Příhody lišky bystroušky* (The Cunning Little Vixen), and his *Sinfonietta* (1926) now serves as ceremonial music at the Prague Castle. For the tenth anniversary of the Czechoslovak First Republic and for the millennium of the death of St. Wenceslas, he composed the *Glagolská mše* (Glagolithic Mass), which combines melodies inspired by Bohemia's medieval past and Byzantine contacts with the discordant experimentation of the early twentieth century. Suk composed several works between the wars, including *Epilog* (Epilogue). His *Legenda o mrtvých vítězích* (Legend of Dead Victors) and *V nový život* (Toward a New Life) together with one of his earlier compositions *Meditace na staročeský chorál svatý Václave* (Meditation on the Old Czech Chorale of St. Wenceslas), are noted for their reflections of Czech patriotism. The interwar years produced one of the most noted interpreters of Czech music and greatest directors of the Czech Philharmonic Orchestra, Václav Talich, whose career continued into the 1950s.

Famous among popular composers and the Prague cabaret scene was Karel Hašler, whose songs, including *Ta naše písnička Česká* (Our Czech Songs, composed for a 1932 film in which Hašler starred) and *Po starých zámeckých schodech* (On the Old Palace Steps), are old standards in today's repertoire of Czech popular music. Jiří Voskovec and Jan Werich, simply known as V+W, established their Osvobozené divadlo (Liberated Theater), which operated between 1927 and 1938 and became famous for its satirical plays, its humor, and its songs. For many years, their songwriter was Jaroslav Ježek. The Czech film industry, especially the new Barrandov studios, was quite advanced for its day, releasing a full range of films—comedies, drama, historical films, documentaries, and the like. The first "talkie" films were produced in 1930, and among them was *C. a k. polní maršálek* (The Little Imperial and Royal Field Marshal), which starred the stage and film actor Vlasta Burian in the Czech and German versions, filmed simultaneously. Voskovec and Werich also made the transition to the screen. Among the famous film actresses was Lída Baarová (born Ludmila Babková), whose close relationship with the Nazi propaganda minister Joseph Goebbels brought her difficulties during the World War II and led her to emigrate afterward. In 1933 Gustav Machatý, who left Czechoslovakia in 1935, directed *Extáze* (Ecstasy), starring the Austrian Hedy Lamarr in then shocking nude scenes.

Young painters and sculptors from the prewar period, such as Bílek, Josef Čapek, Bohumil Kafka, and Švabinský, continued their creative activity between the wars. The artist and writer Josef Lada illustrated Hašek's *Švejk,* and his juvenile books are still favorites of children learning to read. The sculptor Otakar Španiel, who designed many medals and coins for the new republic, belonged to the secession early in his career, but he then focused on national themes reminiscent of works done in the late nineteenth century. Experiments of the younger generation led them to surrealism, which was the case of the sculptor Vincenc Makovský, who carved a large statue of Masaryk just before World War II that was cast in 1968 and now stands in Washington, DC, at the small T. G. Masaryk Memorial Park on Massachusetts Ave. Other artists attracted to surrealism were František Muzika, Josef Šíma, who lived in Paris after 1921, Jindřich Štýrský, and Toyen (Marie Čermínová). From 1934 until 1938, Oskar Kokoschka lived in Prague, where he painted views of the city and a portrait of Masaryk. In the medium of photography, František Drtikol mastered reproducing the infinite shades of gray in his portraits that similarly distinguishes the work of Ansel Adams.

Of Czech writers between the wars, two are world known: Hašek and Čapek. Hašek never completed his novel about the bumbling soldier Švejk, but it is a classic piece of Czech humor and a commentary both on society and the military. Čapek is noted for his plays, including *R.U.R.,* in which he coined the term *robot* from *robota* to identify machines that worked for humans, and *White Plague.* Čapek, also a journalist, made occasional forays into the fringe of politics through his writings, involvement in the Hrad's attempt to launch a political party, and reporting information to the Hrad. Other noted Czech writers active between the world wars or those who began their careers at that time were Jan Herben, who had worked with Masaryk on the journal *Čas* (Time), the writer, journalist, and politician Viktor Dyk, the poet Fráňa Šrámek, the literary critic Arne Novák, the novelist Vladislav Vančura, the novelist and journalist Karel Poláček, and the poet Jiří Wolker. Jaroslav Durych wrote poetry, stories, and novels, including *Bloudění* (published in English as *The Descent of the Idol*). Milena Jesenská, who had an affair with Kafka and translated some of his works into Czech, was a writer and journalist who courageously edited the news magazine *Přítomnost* (The Present) in its final days after the Germans had arrested its founder and editor, Ferdinand Peroutka. The first poems of Jaroslav Seifert in the 1920s reflected the struggle of the working class. Karel Teige was the founder and inspiration for the long-lived avant-garde group known as Devětsil (the name of a flower and a play on words that could refer to the nine muses), which published the *Revue Devětsilu* or *ReD.* Devětsil was associated loosely with the Communist Party, and its members included the communist journalist Julius Fučik, the Russian-born linguist Roman Jakobson, Milena Jesenská, Kisch, the architect Jaromír Krejcar, Seifert, Toyen, Vančura, Wolker, and many others. Of the German writers in Czechoslovakia, most important is Kafka, who after the war wrote *In der Strafkolonie* (In the Penal Colony), and the posthumously published *Der Prozess* (The Trial), *Das Schloss* (The Castle), and *Amerika.*

Cubist architecture failed to reemerge from World War I in its original form. The few buildings in the cubist style built after the war had more subdued angularity. The last gasp of cubism was the heavily ornate rondocubism of the Banka Československých legií (Bank of the Czechoslovak Legionaires), by Josef Gočár, and the Palác Adria (Adria Palace), the work of Pavel Janák and Josef Zasche. Václav Havel, the grandfather of the future Czech president Václav Havel, was one of the builders of the Adria Palace. Kotěra's plan for the Právnická fakulta (Law Faculty) of Charles University, executed in 1921–1931 after alterations by Ladislav Machoň, demonstrates a transition that combines a degree of starkness to the facade with such traditional elements as an arched portico. Modernism, in particular functionalism, was to become the dominant postwar style. Gočár abandoned cubism to work on a geometric theme with much cleaner lines in his Československá akademie zemědělství (Czechoslovak Academy of Agriculture) and Kostel sv. Václava (St. Wenceslas Church). Functionalism predominates the work of Max Urban, especially in his Restaurace a terasy na Barrandově (Restaurant and Terraces at Barrandov) and the Filmové ateliéry Barrandov (Barrandov Film Studios). Other functionalist architects include Otakar Novotný, who designed Mánes, Dům výtvarných umění (Manes, House of Creative Arts), Bohumír Kozák, who designed the Palác Avion (Avion Palace) and Thomayerova nemocnice (Thomayer Hospital), and Josef Havlíček, who built the Všeobecný penzijní Ústav (General Pension Institute) in Prague-Žižkov. A prime example of the functionalist style is the Veletržní palác (Trade Exhibition Palace) of Oldřich Tyl and Josef Fuchs. The Obchodní dům Bílá labut' (Bílá Labut' Department Store) of Josef Kittrich and Josef Hrubý displays a further advance in that it has a completely glass curtain wall. Visible from the Hrad and other points of the city in Prague-Žižkov is the Národní památník (National Memorial) and below it the Vojenské muzeum (Military Museum) built by Jan Zázvorka and Jan Gillar. All the residential villas in the Vilová kolonie Baba (Baba Villa Colony) in Prague-Device reflect the modern approaches in an overall plan from Janák. Wenceslas Square has several functionalist structures: Hotel Juliš by Janák as well as the Lindtův obchodní dům–Astra

(Lindt Department Store–Astra), Obchodní dům Bat'a (Bat'a Department Store), and Palác Alfa (Alfa Palace) by Ludvík Kysela. Antonín Engel, the student of Otto Wagner who designed the urban plan for Dejvice and the Podolská vodárna (Podolí Water Works), worked with traditional designs for government projects, as did other architects when fulfilling government contracts. Josip Plečnik, the Slovenian architect and another student of Wagner, reconstructed the gardens, presidential apartments, and various sites of the Hrad and built the Kostel Nejsvětějšího Srdce Páně (Sacred Heart Church) in Prague-Vyšehrad in a remarkable blend of modernism with hints of the secession and classicism. Two foreign functionalists contributed to the Czech architectural heritage between the world wars: the Austrian architect Adolf Loss constructed the Vila Müllerova (Müller Villa) in Prague, and the German architect Ludwik Mies van der Rohe designed the Vila Tugendhat (Tugendhat Villa) in Brno.

WORLD WAR II

Despite the establishment of the Protectorate, the Czechs still had a measure of cultural freedom. It was in 1941, for example, that the writer Eduard Bass (born Eduard Schmidt) published *Cirkus Humberto* (Circus Humberto). The Czech photographer Josef Sudek, famous for his photographs in black and white, was a commercial photographer before the war but intensified his creative activities during the war. Far more repressive was the period after the assassination of Reinhard Heydrich in 1942. Immediately after the Munich Diktat, some Czech cultural figures, such as Voskovec, Werich, Ječek, and the novelist Egon Hostovský fled abroad. From the West, they aided on the cultural front in the struggle to recreate Czechoslovakia.

THE POSTWAR ERA

After World War II, art and architecture resumed its links to Western movements. The architect Jaroslav Fragner had been involved in several progressive projects between the world wars, but after 1945 he devoted himself to restoring historic monuments and rebuilding the Bethlehem Chapel, which had been demolished in 1786. Functionalism continued to inspire architects, like Josef Havlíček, one of the architects who collaborated in designing the United Nations Building in New York, and Václav Hilský, who built in Litínov, Bohemia, one of the first apartment complexes in Europe after the war. Muzika continued his work in art, as did the artists in the Skupina 42 (Group 42), which included František Gross. Švabinský, despite his age, continued to sculpt and work in other media, as did Makovský. In postwar literature, the memoirs of the Communist journalist Julius Fučík of his time in prison were important as prose and as communist propaganda. Seifert dominated poetry. Burian resumed his theatrical activities, as did Voskovec and Werich, who had returned from their wartime exile in the United States. The most important critic to emerge immediately after the war was Václav Černý. In 1946 Charles University established its Faculty of Film and Television Arts (Filmová a televizní fakulta Akademie múzických umění; FAMU), only the fourth such institution in the world at the time.

CULTURE IN TOTALITARIAN AND POSTTOTALITARIAN CZECHOSLOVAKIA

Once the Communists came to power in 1948, they introduced the Soviet cultural style of socialist realism, with its reliance on simple classical styles and photographically accurate forms in a modern context, its demand of realism, its glorification of socialist ideals and achievements, and its anticipation of a utopian communist society. Key in setting the cultural tone in Czechoslovakia was Zdeněk Nejedlý, a noted musicologist and historian. Between the world wars, Nejedlý became close to the Communists, and he joined the Party in 1939. He was in the Soviet Union during World War II, and he held several cabinet posts between 1945 and 1953. Socialist realism can be seen in the sculpture of Miloš Axman, the art of Vojtěch Cinybulk, and the paintings of Karel Stehlík. Some older artists, such as the sculptor Jan Lauda, also worked with socialist realism. Artistic themes included the harmony of the city and countryside, the glory and strength of socialist work and family life, and the portrayal of political figures, including Marx, Lenin, Stalin, and domestic leaders, such as Gottwald. Socialist realist architecture not only expressed the principles of socialism in its form but created an atmosphere in which the ideal socialist society could develop. In urban planning, the workers' residential district of Havířov near Ostrava by Vladimír Meduna is a classic example of socialist principles at the time that included a maze of parks and long medium-story buildings with simple facades, aside from corners, public buildings, and gateways, which took on the stark classicism of socialist realism. There are two socialist realist hotels in Prague: Hotel International in Device by František Jeřábek, who designed his building solidly in the Soviet style, and Hotel Yalta on Wenceslas Square by Antonín Tenzer, who combined hints of functionalism with socialist realism. When the Communists came to power, certain authors were banned, including Čapek. Some cultural figures emigrated, such as Voskovec, who returned to America. Censorship and self-censorship heavily influenced literature. Yet it was in this time that the creativity of the writer Arnošt Lustig emerged. Seifert continued with his poetry, as did Vítězslav Nezval, who shifted his poetic style to reflect socialist realism. The puppet films of Jiří Trnka became internationally acclaimed.

With the death of Stalin, the Czechs abandoned socialist realism and returned for the most part to trends popular in the West and throughout the world. In the realm of art, the sculptor Makovský maintained themes that reflected communist ideology but began experimenting with introducing modern themes to socialist realist art, such as his statue, *Atomový věk* (Atomic Age), that stands before the former Federal Assembly by the National Museum. Zdeněk Sýkora and Karel Malich, both sculptors and painters, and Karel Nepraš, a sculptor, broke with the socialist realist mode, and the painter Jaroslav Vožniak flourished in the liberalism of the 1960s. Yet there were limits to what artists and intellectuals

Playwright, poet, and novelist Milan Kundera (b. 1929). (Hulton Archive/Getty Images)

could do. Josef Škvorecký published his novel *Zbabělci* (The Cowards), which included realistic and unfavorable references to the behavior of the Red Army during liberation from Nazi rule, and the novel was soon after banned. Pavel Kohout, who also began publishing plays during this time, became famous for his political activities in 1967–1968. Writers who began their careers in the 1960s were Bohumil Hrabal, Milan Kundera, Ivan Klíma, and Vaculík. In theater, Lanterna Magika performed for the first time at the 1958 Brussels Exposition, combining live performers, music, film, and projected images. In the early 1960s Václav Havel began writing for Divadlo Na zábradlí (Theater on the Balustrades), which also began in 1958 under the direction of Jan Grossman. Also working at Divadlo Na zábradlí at the time was the mime Ladislav Fialka. There were other important theaters. Reduta was established in 1958 for plays and jazz. Semafor was the creation in 1959 of Jiří Suchý, who had helped establish the Divadlo Na zábradlí and Reduta, and Jiří Šlitr, and the pair wrote a large number of theatrical works and songs until Šlitr's death. Many noted Czech performers started at Semafor, including the singer Waldemar Matuska, who first performed there in 1960, and the tenor Karel Gott, who debuted at Semafor in 1963. The Činoherní Klub (Drama Club) was established in 1965. The mid-1960s in film was the era of the so-called Czech New Wave, in which young film makers departed from the traditional postwar examinations of the struggle against fascism. Věra Chytilová directed *Sedmikrásky* (Daisies). Miloš Forman directed *Lasky jedné plavovlásky* (Loves of a Blond) and *Hoří, má panenko* (Firemen's Ball). Jiří Menzel directed the film version of Hrabal's work *Closely Watched Trains,* which won an Oscar in 1968 for the Best Foreign Language Film.

In architecture, functionalism once again became influential after Stalin's death, and Czech architects steadily experimented with other styles over the years. One of the earliest post–socialist realism structures is the semicircular glass-skinned restaurant overlooking Prague built as a collaborative effort of František Cubr, Josef Hrubý, and Zdeněk Pokorny for the 1958 Brussels World Exposition. Karel Hubáček built the internationally acclaimed futuristic television tower and hotel at Ještěd near Liberec, Bohemia, for which he received the Perret Prize. In Prague, Karel Prager constructed the new glass and steel Federální shromáždění (Federal Assembly) near the National Museum and the Nová scéna (New Scene) of the National Theater, a massive elevated cube adjacent to the historic National Theater that is constructed of glass blocks that are the design of the glass artist Stanislav Libenský. Both structures remain controversial. The husband and wife team of Jan Šrámek and Alena Šrámková are noted for their work on ČKD Praha at the lower end of Wenceslas Square that has hints of postmodernism. The Šrámeks cooperated with other architects, including Jan Bočan and Josef Danda, to design a portion of the reconstruction of Prague's Central Train Station to accommodate a new metro line, and Šrámek individually or in collaboration with others designed several Czechoslovak embassies, including the one in London in the brutalist style. Another husband-and-wife team was Věra Machoninová and Vladimír Machonin, who designed Prague's steel and glass Obchodní dům Kotva (Kotva Department Store) with its honeycomb ground plan. Machoninová also built the Obchodní dům Domov (Domov Department Store) in Praha-Pankrác. An important Czech architect abroad is Jan Kaplický, who left Czechoslovakia in 1968 for the United Kingdom and is one of the founding partners of Future Systems. The firm's Floating Bridge in London is simple and elegant, quite the opposite of its most current project, the Selfridges Department Store in Birmingham, with its skin inspired by the eye of a fly.

The Prague Spring of 1968 brought about a burst of creativity. For example, the Slovak director Jaromil Jireš filmed Kundera's *Žert* (The Joke) during this time. Still, many efforts of artists never were realized before the Warsaw Pact invasion. Afterward, many at the forefront of cultural activities were forbidden to work in their normal venues for several years. Those Czechs who had fled abroad continued their creative activities. Škvorecký, who lived in Canada, wrote many works, including *Příběh inženýra lidských duší* (The Engineer of Human Souls). He and his wife, the exiled writer Zdena Salivarová, established Sixty-Eight Publishers in Toronto, Canada, to release works in Czech. Kundera, who wrote *Nesnesitelná lehkost bytí* (The Unbearable Lightness of Being) and other significant novels, lived in France. The director Forman became world-renowned after leaving Czechoslovakia and is best known for his films *One Flew Over the Cuckoo's Nest, Hair, Ragtime, Amadeus* (which he filmed on location in Prague), and *The Unbearable Lightness of Being,* an adaptation of Kundera's book. Other Czechs stayed in the country. Some became dissidents, such as Havel. Others had to withdraw into the background in their professions, such as Šlitr, and some of those managed to regain a place in the main stream of cultural and intellectual activity. Werich, who had signed Two Thousand Words, apologized for his actions and resumed working in 1975. Menzel returned to directing and produced *Vesničko má středisková* (My Sweet Little Village) in 1986. An interesting case in the history of the stage in the Husák era is that of the theater Husa na provázku (Goose on a Leash). It was established in Brno in 1967, but because of the purely coincidental similarity between its name and that of the Communist Party leader during normalization, Husák, the theater had to change its name in 1969 to Na provazek (On the Leash) until after the fall of communism. One of the key actors in the theater was Boleslav Polívka. The painter and costume designer Theodor Pištěk and the photographer Jan Saudek avoided any major shifts in their careers. Some of the older well-known writers and cultural figures, like Hrabal, Seifert, who won the Nobel Prize for Literature in 1984, and Sudek, remained at the forefront of their professions, in part because they did not play prominent roles in the politics of 1967–1968. In the heat of the post-invasion, the painter Mikuláš Medek lost favor with the regime. Meanwhile, Jan Kotík, who had been a member of Skupina 42, fled to the FRG. Throughout the Husák era, young Czechs left the country. In 1985 the young sculptor Magdalena Jetelová emigrated to the FRG. The twin sisters and painters Jitka Válová and Květa Válová both continued their work in Czechoslovakia during the Husák regime. Television began in Czechoslovakia in 1953 and was widespread by the mid-1960s. Both television and radio played an important role in the Prague Spring, resulting in drastic personnel changes afterward. Although a thinly veiled propaganda tool of the Communist Party after 1968, Czechoslovak television produced an array of compelling dramas with excellent acting, documentaries, and a multitude of children's cartoons, many of which appeared on the popular nightly *Večerníček* short cartoon broadcast before bedtime.

There were several Czech scientists and academics who became famous after 1945. One was Jaroslav Heyrovský, who received the 1959 Nobel Prize for chemistry for the work on polarography he did in the 1920s. Otto Wichterle, who had signed Two Thousand Words, was another chemist who invented the contact lenses in 1956 and a means of producing them in 1961. In the social sciences, Bedřich Hrozný decrypted the Hittite language.

Classical music continued to have a rich tradition among Czechs in the second half of the twentieth century. During the Stalinist era, Czech composers and musicians had to avoid so-called degenerate Western music, but it slowly began to filter into Czechoslovakia after Stalin's death. The two most noted Czech classical composers lived in exile. Bohuslav Martinů, who lived in Paris from 1929 to 1940, in America from 1940 to 1953, and then again in Western Europe, was a member of the neoclassical Paris Six with Igor F. Stravinsky and composed six symphonies (the first in America in 1942) along with operas, chamber works, ballets, and other works. The composer and conductor Rafael Jeroným Kubelík conducted the Czech Philharmonic between 1942 and 1948 and emigrated in 1948. He was affiliated as music director with the Chicago Symphony Orchestra in 1950–1953 and the Royal Opera at Covent Garden in 1955–1958. He served as the conductor of the Metropolitan Opera in New York in 1973–1974 and the Bavarian Radio Symphony Orchestra in 1961–1979. He also composed several orchestral works and operas. Václav Neumann conducted the Prague Symphonic Orchestra in 1956–1963, was artistic director of the Gewandhaus Orchestra in Leipzig in 1964–1967, and from 1968 to 1990 was the chief director of the Czech Philharmonic Orchestra. He was noted for his interpretations of Czech composers, Beethoven, Brahms, and Gustav Mahler. As important as the established orchestras and opera companies in Czechoslovakia was the Prague Spring, which drew serious musicians from throughout the world each year since 1946. Legendary among contemporary Czech performers are Josef Suk (the nephew of Josef Suk), a violinist, and Ivan Moravec, a pianist. Among the noted Czech composers of the second half of the twentieth century are Václav Trojan, Miloslav Kabeláč, Klement Slavický, Vladimír Sommer, Svatopluk Havelka, Miloslav Ištvan, Petr Eben, Marek Kopelent, and Luboš Fišer.

Czech popular music, particularly pop and jazz, began to liberalize in the mid-1960s, but it blossomed with the Prague Spring in 1968. Several artists of the liberal period, such as Hana Zagorová and Helena Vondráčková, made their peace with the Husák regime and continued to perform. Others, like Marta Kubišová, who had once publicly embraced Havel, were forbidden to perform. A curious phenomenon in the Czech music world is the tenor Gott, who has a larger following abroad, particularly in Germany, than in the Czech Republic. The normalizers of the Husák regime were suspicious of rock music at best, and they occasionally harassed some groups and managed to intimidate others, like Olympik and Michael Kocáb's group Pražský výběr, into conforming, even if they occasionally transgressed the norm. Plastic People of the Universe went too far, and two members of the group, along with two other rock musicians, were tried and sentenced in 1976 to various terms in prison. Jazz became increasingly unpopular with the regime, and in 1987 it staged a trial of the banned Jazz Section, which had produced jazz concerts. Only a limited number of jazz musicians performed, such as Emil Viklický, and even they had difficulties. As though attempting to compensate the public for musical limitations, the regime had fewer difficulties with folk music, for example the work of Zdeněk Merta, Brontosauři, and the Spiritual Quintet, and the Porta festivals of the 1980s. The regime actually promoted a type of country music, which included the work of Pavel Bobek, who sings many of the songs of Kenny Rogers, and Michal Tučný. Beginning in 1979, punk, new wave, and alternative rock made their way to

Czechoslovakia. Later, metal, industrial, and other experimental music emerged. In the 1980s a revival of music from the 1920s and 1930s occurred, with the Prague Syncopated Orchestra and Ondřej Havelka. On stage (though not on the air), Havelka managed to sing many songs in English. The most important popular musical dissident was Karl Kryl, who had emigrated to West Germany after 1969. The folk musician Jaroslav Hutka emigrated to the West in 1978.

As in every country, sport is popular among Czechs. Soccer is by far the most important spectator sport, with hockey trailing behind. The two most important soccer teams are both in Prague—Sparta and Slavia. The Communists eliminated the Sokol gymnastic societies and replaced the mass calisthenic gathering of the Sokols, known as the *slet,* with their own mass gymnastic-propagandistic show, called the *spartakiáda* (no longer convened after 1989). The Sokols have reemerged, but they no longer have the appeal they once had. Nevertheless, they are popular gymnastic clubs for young children. The field of sport between 1948 and 1989 has several noted Czechs. The runner Emil Zátopek won a Gold Medal at the 1948 Olympics and the triple crown at the 1952 Helsinki Olympics. In 1999 Zátopek was named Olympian of the Century. Věra Čáslavská won two Gold Medals in gymnastics at the 1964 Tokyo Olympics. Two Czech tennis greats, Martina Navrátilová and Ivan Lendl, emigrated to the West well before the end of Communist rule. Some Czechs convincingly argue that mushroom picking in the forest is just as important as any spectator sport.

CZECH CULTURE SINCE 1989

With the shackles of censorship gone as the Christmas holidays approached in 1989, Czechoslovakia experienced an outburst of expression and an influx of ideas from abroad that took on the character of a deluge. Publishers rushed to translate the best of world literature that had been relatively unknown in the country. Czech writers released pieces they had written "for the drawer." Dissidents finally published their works. Of course, new literary talents emerged, such as Michal Viewegh, who wrote *Výchova dívek v Čechách* (Bringing up Girls in Bohemia). In every field, professionals and academics became acquainted with specialized literature to which they had little access before. The Czech language had to confront an onslaught of new foreign phrases, many of which dealt with computers and finance.

In the 1990s artists of the younger generation, some of whom actually began their careers under the old regime, found a new freedom of expression, including the glass artist Ivana Šrámková-Šolcová, the sculptors Jaroslav Róna, Olbran Zoubek, David Černy, and Ivan Kafka, and the painters Jiří David, Otto Placht, and Antonín Střížek.

Musicians no longer felt the constraints of officialdom. Classical composers, orchestras, and others, such as the underground group Tonton Macoutes of Alex Švamberk, experimented with minimalism, which had entered into the mainstream of Western music. Čechomor mixes vocals, symphonic orchestra, and folk instruments and tunes in compelling musical selections. Also appealing to the sophisticated modern listener are the meaningful lyrics, appealing melodies, and unique voice of Jaromír Nohavica. The latest popular music trends also entered the Czech Republic, including music appealing to young skateboarders.

Since 1989, Czech architecture has been free to experiment with the cutting edge of postmodern design, and Prague, once the exclusive construction site of Czech architects, now has buildings from architects throughout the world as well as Czechs. One of the newest structures to grace Prague is located at 62 Wenceslas Square, near the National Museum, and is the work of Czech architects Ladislav Vrbata and Petr Drexler, whose building blends harmoniously with its older neighbors. The same cannot be said for the Palác Euro (Euro Palace) on the lower end of Wenceslas Square, the work of the Czech architects Richard Doležal and Petr Malinský, and Myslbek (Myslbek Building) on Na příkopě by the Czech architects Zdeněk Hölzel and Jan Kerel. Ladislav Lábus renovated Prague's Palác Langhans (Langhans Palace), preserving the character of the facade but reshaping the roofline with glass-enclosed spaces. The American Frank Gehry and the Serb Vlado Milunic built the Tančící dům (Dancing House) on a corner of Rašínovo nábřeži overlooking the Vltava. Its twin towers represent the American dancers Fred Astaire and Ginger Rogers. Although it punctuates two rows of older buildings, the architects succeeded in complementing the surrounding structures, in part by creatively blending their horizontal lines. In contrast, the new Zlatý anděl (Golden Angel) of Jean Nouvell across the river in Praha-Smíchov is imposing but less sympathetic. One of the most imaginative Czech architects with the ability to create highly pleasing internal spaces and external forms is Josef Pleskot, whose works include portions of the Prague Castle.

Hollywood and the film industry of the West have infiltrated popular culture, but the Czech film industry has maintained its creativity. *Kolja* (Kolya) was the winner of both the Academy Award and Golden Globe as Best Foreign Language Film in 1997. Its director, Jan Svěrák, tapped into the creative cinematography of Vladimír Smutný and the many talents of his father, Zdeněk Svěrák, who had been involved in the Czech stage and screen for many years. In 2001 the same team released *Tmavomodrý svět* (Dark Blue World), a stunning film that failed to capture the imagination of Western critics. Fortunately Czech filmmakers still produce films appealing predominantly to Czechs and international film connoisseurs. A remarkable production is the 1997 work of director Miro Gábor and screenwriter Petr Zelenka, *The Buttoners* (*Knoflíkáři*), with a compelling plot and a creative use of time.

In the world of sport, Czechs are known throughout the world because of the hockey players Jaromír Jágr, who became famous in the 1990s, and the goalie Dominik Hašek, who made his career beginning in the 1980s. The Czech ice hockey team won the Gold Medal at the Winter Olympics in Nagano, Japan, in 1998, and the team won the World Championships in 1999 and 2000. More recently, Vítězslav Dostal achieved fame when he rode a bike around the world between 1994 and 1997.

The Czechs enthusiastically embraced the cultural trends of the West after 1989. Nevertheless, to view culture during Communist rule as uncreative is an exaggeration. Even between 1945 and 1989, Czech and Slovak mainstream artists and intellectuals, along with their dissident counterparts, made positive contributions to the development of Czech and Czechoslovak culture within the context of European and Western civilization, even though totalitarian control of expression placed limits on freedoms of expression. In the twentieth century it was the Nazi occupation that posed the greatest threat to Czech culture, and only World War II and the Nazi's priority of exterminating Jews and Roma spared the Czechs and other Slavs from even further cultural erosion. Czech cultural and intellectual interaction with other European countries flourished during the First Republic, and the trends evident at that time were extensions of the Biedermeier and fin de siècle eras of the Habsburg monarchy during the latter half of the nineteenth century and the early part of the twentieth century. Even the dark years immediately following White Mountain in 1620 witnessed the flowering of baroque painting, architecture, and music in the Czech Lands. Before the seventeenth century, Czech cultural links with the rest of Europe were common. The Hussite movement received inspiration from Western thinkers, whose notions Czechs integrated into their own program for religious and social change, and the many Western ideas of Charles IV took on a specific Czech character. In many respects, the pattern of Czech interaction with other parts of Europe can be traced to the arrival of Christianity in the Czech Lands from both the Byzantine East and Latin West. Throughout history, the Czechs and other inhabitants of the Czech Lands have both assimilated European cultural trends and contributed to the development of European civilization. The Czechs, located in the heart of Europe, are sensitive to Europe's cultural pulse.

ECONOMIC DEVELOPMENT

THE FEUDAL ECONOMY OF THE CZECH LANDS

Under the Přemyslids, Bohemia developed a large number of towns to complement the feudal society of the countryside. The towns were centers of administration, handicrafts, and local trade, but some had trade of an international character, like Prague, Olomouc, and Kutná Hora, which were on well-traveled European trade routes. Frequently in the thirteenth century, the Crown designated towns as privileged, that is, having exclusive rights to engage in certain types of trade or manufacturing. Other towns were centers for mining, such as Kutná Hora, where miners extracted vast amounts of silver that made Bohemia wealthy. In 1300 Václav II concentrated the royal mint in Kutná Hora, and the so-called *grossi Pragenses* became the preferred currency of the region. Crucial to the economic well-being of Bohemia during the time of the Přemyslids was the increasing number of Germans who entered the Czech Lands, a feature that was common in other East Central European states at the time. The presence of Germans in the Kingdom of Bohemia is not surprising, given its location, but deliberate actions on behalf of the kings augmented the number of Germans. Because the Czechs found themselves in the sphere of influence of the Roman Empire, the Czech nobility, including the Přemyslids, intermarried with German noble families. Germans advanced into the forested mountain regions along the border between the German states and the Kingdom of Bohemia to acquire new agricultural lands and to mine. Moreover, commerce between Bohemia and the Roman Empire was responsible for the arrival of German merchants in the Czech Lands. Přemysl Otakar I systematically invited Germans into his realm, beginning with the founding of the town of Bruntál in 1210. He started the tradition in Bohemia of allowing the Germans the right to use their own courts under the famous Magdeburg Law. Under Václav I, German settlements appeared in Prague, Brno, and in trading towns, such as Jihlava. Přemysl Otakar II further increased the number of Germans when he invited them to settle the many cities he established, including České Budějovice.

The era of Charles IV, beginning in the middle of the fourteenth century, marks the peak not only of Bohemia's political significance in Europe but also the apex of its economic strength in the Middle Ages. Charles made remarkable advancements in his efforts to spur economic growth. He expanded the city of Prague through the establishment of the New Town, reconstructed Vyšehrad Castle, built the so-called Hunger Wall as a public works project, founded a number of churches, continued to build the Cathedral of St. Vitus, expanded the Hrad, and ordered the construction of a stone bridge across the Vltava, known today as Charles Bridge. To house the crown jewels of Bohemia and the empire and to serve as an archive, Charles built the impressive Karlštejn Castle not far from Prague. He established fruit groves and dramatically expanded vineyards to advance the wine industry. His vineyards, now a section of Prague, are known as Vinohrady.

Although Bohemia was never among the most important economic centers of the Middle Ages, it played an important role in the European economy. Prague was located on an intersection of trade routes that ran from east to west. Thus the development of Prague and other cities and towns in the realm was not merely a function of serving the needs of the rural population or the result of expanding temporal and spiritual administration but also due to international trade. Bohemia was fortunate to have reserves of precious metals, particularly silver, but Bohemia's wealth from silver was a double-edged sword. It helped pay for essential imports, such as salt and spices, which were necessary for preserving food. Silver also paid for textiles, cattle, wine, salt fish, skins, and furs that made their way into Bohemia. Yet silver tended to retard the evolution of domestic manufacturing, which never advanced to the level of becoming export oriented. Bohemia likewise did not export foodstuffs, which were needed to feed the many towns of the realm—those in the newly colonized areas, the large urban administrative, commercial, and manufacturing city of Prague, and Kutná Hora. In the last years of the reign of Charles IV, the economic stagnation prevalent throughout Europe deteriorated, a phenomenon that eventually had an impact on Bohemia. Agricultural goods became less expensive and more abundant, but manufactured goods from the cities along with the cost of labor in urban areas rose. Associated with the economic difficulties was the spread of the plague, which did not devastate Bohemia as it did western parts of Europe.

The economic repercussions of the Hussite Wars in the fifteenth century were extensive. In addition to the devastation from frequent conflicts, particularly with respect to church property, the surrounding Catholic countries boycotted the non-Catholic towns of Bohemia. The silver mines of Kutná Hora did not achieve their prewar production capacity, and the wars exhausted all reserves of precious metals. The lack of precious metals reduced the attractiveness of Bohemia to international trade. Otherwise, internal production of handicrafts quickly increased. All told, nearly complete economic recovery took place in roughly a generation. A major change in landholding as a result of the Hussite Wars occurred when the church lost its estates. The Crown also lost some property. Most of the holdings went to the nobility, but burghers also purchased land. Fewer church and royal properties exchanged hands in Moravia, where the Catholic faith retained greater legitimacy.

THE AFTERMATH OF THE THIRTY YEARS' WAR

The Thirty Years' War reintroduced a trend that had appeared at first in Bohemia after the Hussite Wars of reimposing legal restrictions on the serfs' ability to leave the land and increasing the serfs' dues and *robota,* that is, the amount of labor the serf owed the lord. The result in the seventeenth century was what historians refer to as neoserfdom. In the thirteenth century serfdom was on the decline in Bohemia, as it was in Western Europe, and by the beginning of the Hussite reformation in 1415, only remnants of the institution existed. With the economic devastation and depopulation resulting from the Hussite Wars, lords sought to guarantee their source of labor. As a result, the Bohemian diet in 1487 made it illegal for anyone to assist a fugitive serf. In 1497 Vladislav II forbade serfs to migrate to towns or settle on other estates. Meanwhile, economic recovery after the Hussite Wars brought increased population in the towns and a greater need for food, which in turn necessitated increases in the robota. Nevertheless, the situation for the serf still was quite bearable. The Thirty Years' War brought renewed devastation and depopulation—the population had fallen by about two-thirds, and the cadaster (land survey) of 1653–1656 revealed that approximately one-third of the dwellings had been abandoned. With the shortage of labor, the nobles enforced laws that enabled them to extract the maximum amount of robota from the serfs. Moreover, approximately two-thirds of the population was still Protestant, and the new Catholic nobility, having won their estates in part because of their loyalty to the Catholic faith, treated the non-Catholic serfs with severity. To make matters worse, the Habsburgs imposed crushing taxes on the serfs and on various goods serfs required. The reasons for the existence of neoserfdom in Bohemia, where agricultural production supplied the towns and cities and only to a small extent entered the market for export, therefore, were different from those in the extensive grain producing areas of the export-oriented agricultural systems in Hungary or on the Northern European Plain. In 1679–1680 the Czech Lands faced a devastating plague and an uprising of serfs that began in the north and spread to the west and elsewhere. In June 1680, to ease the lot of the serfs, Leopold I issued the first robota patent, which limited work on the nobles' estates to three days per week, unless circumstances demanded an increase (frequently the case), and it prohibited nobles from collecting illegal taxes, increasing payments in kind, and forcing peasants to purchase artificially inflated goods. Nobles nevertheless increased the robota and otherwise ignored the patent. Periodic rebellions followed, such as the rebellion in Upper Silesia from 1705 to 1707 during the reign of Joseph I. After a rebellion in 1716, Charles VI issued the second robota patent, which essentially reaffirmed Leopold's patent. Charles issued another robota patent in 1738 that limited each robota workday to ten hours and guaranteed serfs a two-hour break. Both of Charles's patents included procedures for serfs to file complaints against their nobles, but they remained on paper.

THE AGE OF MERCANTILISM

Mercantilist doctrine, which promoted protectionism and government sponsorship of manufacturing to serve the needs of the state and to increase revenue, had strong support in Austria. Maria Theresa eliminated monopolistic restrictions on the woolen and cotton industries, enabling the proliferation of textile manufacturing concerns. Bohemia was the major benefactor of this policy. It had been an important producer of linen, but during the reign of Maria Theresa, it replaced the lost province of Silesia as the principal area for textile manufacture in general. The Czech Lands continued to be famous for the production of glass, which was a major export commodity, although the export market declined as Western European countries began their own glass production concerns. Maria Theresa improved the state's infrastructure and standardized weights and measures, thereby encouraging trade. Although she imposed tariffs on external trade, she abolished internal tariffs, aside from the tariff with Hungary.

The condition of the peasantry concerned Maria Theresa, and she laid the groundwork for further reforms and the eventual abolishment of serfdom. She placed a two-day maximum on the amount of work a serf was to perform on a landlord's estate in Silesia and Lower Austria. In January 1775 serfs on an estate in Bohemia began a revolt against the robota that spread throughout Bohemia and lasted through the summer. The army put down the serfs, including those who made their way toward Prague in March. The Bohemian nobility, heavily dependent on serf labor, had resisted reform, but the violence prompted Maria Theresa to issue her robota patent in August (September for Moravia) that set limits on the robota. Maria Theresa also supported the reforms of Franz Anton von Raab, who began in 1775 to convert robota to rent on estates once in the hands of the Jesuits. Maria Theresa approved the reform in 1777 as a voluntary method of eliminating serfdom. She applied the Raab reform to her own estates, and more than a hundred estates in the Czech Lands also adopted the system.

Mercantilism influenced the policies of Joseph II, as it had his mother. Joseph continued to reduce the power of the guilds to encourage growth in manufacturing. He instituted even higher tariffs on imported goods than his mother and banned many items, resulting in a dramatic increase in domestic production and a reduction in imports. While enacting mercantilist policies, Joseph also came under the influence of the physiocrats, who maintained that agriculture was more important than manufacturing because food is what sustains any society. Accordingly, Joseph instituted policies aimed at improving agricultural productivity and increasing the economic contribution of the rural population, the largest social segment of the monarchy. With characteristic swiftness, Joseph announced the abolition of serfdom in the Czech Lands in November 1781. He issued emancipation patents in other portions of the monarchy later, and his hesitation to do so, partly because of the resistance of the nobility, prompted anxious and confused peasants to attempt revolts. Joseph's patent gave serfs (although not orphans) their personal freedom, that is, the ability to marry, leave the estate, learn a trade, and acquire an education. He did not replace immediately the legal jurisdiction the nobles had over peasants because the necessary new bureaucratic and judicial mechanisms were not yet in place. Joseph carefully planned for the abolition of the robota, which remained in force with the patent eliminating serfdom. In 1785 Joseph ordered a new cadastre of rustical and dominical land—the Josephinian Cadastre—that included information on the gross agricultural yields between 1774 and 1782. In 1787 he ordered a new census. On the basis of information garnered from these statistics, Joseph devised a new economic basis for agriculture, which appeared in his tax and urbarial patent of 1789. According to the proposed system, the implementation of which Joseph postponed and his successor never enacted, the peasant was to replace the robota with a maximum tax of 30 percent—just more than 12 percent going to the state and nearly 18 percent set aside for the lord.

THE INDUSTRIAL REVOLUTION

Throughout the nineteenth century, the industrial revolution in the Czech Lands resulted in the growth of new and existing textile, mining, metallurgical, machine, glass, porcelain, and chemical industries. New agricultural industries included sugar refineries and breweries, and agricultural processing facilities became more numerous to accommodate the greater demand for food in the expanding cities and towns. The share of the total population employed in agriculture declined, falling from over three-quarters in 1756 to just over two-thirds by 1900. By the end of the century, a lower percentage of the population in the Czech Lands was engaged in agriculture than in any portion of the Habsburg monarchy.

The textile industry—at first wool and, to a lesser degree, linen—flourished as a result of mercantilism. In the late seventeenth century woolen factories began to appear, and the one near Duchcov, Bohemia, established in 1697, specialized in socks and employed several hundred people in its third decade of existence. As in the West, cotton began to compete with wool. In the eighteenth century the cotton industry, largely concentrated in Moravia and Silesia, grew to such an extent that it employed about 18 percent of the population. In the late eighteenth century and with increasing vigor in the early nineteenth century, mechanization came to textile production and gave rise to the machine building industry. František Josef Gerstner built the first steam engine in the Czech Lands for instructional purposes at the Prague Polytechnic Institute. In 1815 the first steam engine went into use in the Czech Lands; in 1817 the first experimental steamboat appeared on the Vltava; and in 1823 steam was used in the textile industry. In 1824, through knowledge obtained from England and from English and German emigrants, a factory in Brno produced the first commercial steam engine in Austria and began manufacturing other types of machinery. In the early 1840s the Czech Lands had a greater capacity of horsepower produced through steam engines than all the other portions of the monarchy combined. As mechanization increased, machine-building firms came on the scene. Among the most crucial was that of the Czech engineer Čeněk Daněk, who established a firm in Prague in 1854 that became one of the most important producers of sugar beet processing equipment and served as the basis for the Českomoravská Kolben Daněk (ČKD) manufacturing concern. In 1869 Emil Škoda purchased the Valdštejn (Wallenstein) Factory in Plzeň, which, as Škoda Plzeň, developed into the greatest machine manufacturer in the Czech Lands.

With the increase of factories came an ever growing number of workers, and those employed in factories in the Czech Lands faced the same difficult working conditions and poor pay as those in Britain. Even before 1848, textile workers in Prague protested against low wages and the introduction of machinery that eliminated jobs. Discontented workers supported the radicals in the revolution of 1848 and manned the barricades. In the expanding economy of the second half of the nineteenth century, there were several economic downturns. Thousands of textile workers from numerous factories protested against poor wages in 1869 in Brno. The next year, six textile workers were shot in demonstrations in Svárov, Northern Bohemia. With the depression of 1873, the remaining optimism of the workers evaporated, and discontent increased.

Progress during the first industrial revolution in the Czech Lands occurred in areas other than textiles and machinery. In the 1790s porcelain began to complement the glass industry. The Vitkovice Iron Works began operating in 1828, but iron production in Bohemia lagged behind that of Alpine Austria. The first mechanized paper mill opened in Bohemia in 1833, and the Czech Lands were foremost among the monarchy's most important paper producers. The ever greater need for energy brought about a sharp increase in coal and coke production. Throughout the century, the use of wood declined. Improvements in communication paralleled industrial growth. Josef Ressel invented the screw propeller in 1829, but it was not used until later. A horse-drawn railway opened in 1832 between České Budějovice and Linz, Austria—the first railway in the Austrian Empire and the first on the Continent. The first steam railroad in Austria began operating in 1839, linking Vienna and Nový Bohumín, Bohemia, by 1847. By the depression of 1873, the commercial and industrial centers of the Czech Lands were linked with an efficient rail network that in turn transported goods to Vienna, other parts of the monarchy, and to Germany. Railway development in the Czech Lands after 1873 focused on improving existing lines and building secondary lines. In 1841 the first commercial paddle-wheel steamboat traveled the Vltava between Prague and Dresden. The first telegraph in the Czech Lands began functioning in 1850, and the postal service modernized and expanded in the middle of the century.

Industrial advances in the Czech Lands were intertwined with the development of the sciences and education. The Czech physiologist Jan Evangelista Purkyně contributed to cell theory, introducing the term "protoplasm" and identifying certain types of tissue. The Prague Polytechnic Institute opened in 1806, and its professors not only trained students but conducted significant research. Gerstner, noted for his work with steam engines, became its first director. In 1842 the Austrian Christian Doppler, then a professor at the Prague Polytechnic Institute, presented his theory, known as the Doppler Effect, linking change in the color of stars with changes in distance. In 1865 Gregor Johann Mendel, an Augustinian monk born in Silesia, presented his papers on heredity based on his experimentation with peas.

In agriculture, major changes occurred with the introduction of new crops and the abandonment of the three-field system in favor of crop rotation and fertilization. The potato gained wide acceptance during the Napoleonic Wars, and it provided an alternative source of nutrition along with opportunities for new agricultural products. During the Napoleonic Wars, the British used the continental blockade to prevent cane sugar from entering Europe. The French devised a means of manufacturing sugar from sugar beets, and the first sugar beet factory began operating in Bohemia in 1805 (its construction began in 1801). The sugar beet industry in the Czech Lands, with its many developments to improve efficiency, not only dominated sugar production in the Habsburg monarchy but grew to become one of the most important centers of production in Europe and a key exporter of sugar. In the nineteenth century the production of traditional agricultural goods shifted from the home and local tradesmen to large concerns. Small community flour mills, for example, gave way to large concerns. Similarly, large breweries replaced the individual brewers. Notable in the first half of the nineteenth century is the Pilsner Brewery, which began production in 1842.

With the end of serfdom, the reduction of the agricultural labor force, a trend that had begun before 1848, continued throughout the nineteenth century. Although there were peasants in the Czech Lands who essentially consumed almost all of what they produced, the number of farmers, that is, those who sell most of their produce, increased. Landless cottagers who did not leave the countryside to seek employment in the factories remained as laborers on the farms or the great estates of the nobles.

Financial institutions kept pace with expansion in industry and agriculture. In the middle of the nineteenth century the Austrian National Bank and the Kreditanstalt opened branches in Prague. In the 1860s banks started in Prague that serviced the sugar beet industry. In 1868 what was to become the most powerful bank in the Czech Lands, the Živnostenská banka, or Živnobanka, opened in Prague. A stock market opened in Prague in 1871.

THE DEPRESSION OF 1873 AND THE SECOND INDUSTRIAL REVOLUTION

The crash of the stock market in Vienna in May 1873 and the subsequent depression saw declines in prices and industrial production, bankruptcies in a large number of industrial firms and banks, losses of stock values in industry, banking, and construction, decreases of investments, and reductions in growth rates. The depression was essentially over by 1879, although some economic indicators were sluggish until 1896. The economy declined somewhat in the period between 1901 and 1905 and then prospered again before World War I.

Recovery from the depression of 1873 occurred simultaneously with the beginning of the second industrial revolution, which, in the simplest terms, replaced the reliance on iron with steel and the dependency on coal with the use of electricity and the internal combustion engine. Austria-Hungary joined the states adopting protective tariffs, the use of which had declined after mercantilism. Cartels became a regular feature of the economy that enabled manufacturers to protect markets, limit competition, and set prices. In the Czech Lands, the largest metallurgical works was the Witkowitz concern, which in the years after the 1873 crash witnessed a boom in steel production. Electrification and the manufacture of electrical products began in the Czech Lands in the 1880s, the first electric trams appeared in Czech cities in the mid-1890s, and the firm Kolben and Co., which was to become part of the large ČKD manufacturing firm, began building electric motors in 1896. The first telephone line began operating in Prague in 1881. The first commercial Czech automobile was manufactured in 1897, and motorcycles went into production in 1899. The first bus line in the empire started running between Pardubice and Bohdaneč, Bohemia (between Kolín and Hrádec Kralové), in 1908. The first Czech-built airplane flew in 1910. Traditional forms of transportation also expanded, including railroads. The first totally Czech-built locomotive made by a firm that continuously produced locomotives steamed into service in 1900.

The Czech Lands were the major suppliers of the monarchy's industrial and consumer goods. Because Hungary was largely agricultural, most of the economic statistics compare the Czech Lands to the rest of Cisleithania, and the statistics as of 1910 reveal the extent to which industrialization in the Czech Lands had progressed. The Czech Lands produced more than 80 percent of Cisleithania's coal and 33 percent of the iron ore. It produced about 90 percent of the

A group of Czech brewery workers, each with a tankard, pose around a large barrel of beer in 1907. (Scheufler Collection/Corbis)

cast iron (as of 1900), and more than 40 percent of the steel. The Czech Lands provided 75 percent of Cisleithania's chemicals. In terms of consumer goods, the Czech Lands produced 75 percent of the cotton and 80 percent of the wool. A total of 94 percent of the sugar came from the Czech Lands along with more than 58 percent of the beer and nearly 40 percent of the alcohol. By 1910, the industrial workforce in the Czech Lands accounted for 40 percent of the economically active population, and by 1899, the Czech Lands had 68 percent of the Cisleithanian workforce. In 1899 the Czech Lands had 68 percent of the total horsepower in the monarchy. The Czech Lands also became crucial as an exporter. About 50 percent of the soft coal mined in the Czech Lands was exported (the remainder of the soft coal and nearly all of the hard coal went for domestic production), and about 20 percent of the machines produced were exported. Cotton and glass were other major export products. By 1900, 70 percent of the sugar processed in the Czech Lands was destined for foreign markets. Other important traditional exports were wood and wooden products, textiles, glass, leather and leather products, and various agricultural goods. The second industrial revolution brought advances to agriculture, including innovative methods for processing agricultural products. Large landed estates in the hands of the nobility still played a dominant role in agriculture and food processing, including the sugar refining industry. Rivaling the great estates, however, was a growing farming class with medium-size enterprises that were market oriented. Both estate owners and farmers purchased an ever increasing amount of equipment, the sale of which provided an important outlet for Czech manufacturers. To fund agricultural investment, the farmers turned to the cooperative savings banks, known as *kampeličky,* which began multiplying in the 1890s, and the Agrarian Bank, which opened in 1911. The farmers likewise relied on the increasing number of agricultural cooperatives—machine and electric cooperatives along with production cooperatives, such as dairies, distilleries, and granaries. The Central Union of Cooperatives registered more than 200 cooperatives by 1906 and more than 2,000 by 1914. The farmers, infuriated with depressed prices for agricultural goods that persisted after the end of the 1873 depression and the cartels (including that of the sugar refiners), sought the aid of the Agrarian Party.

The depression and then the low wages, long hours, and poor working conditions that existed as the economy of the Czech Lands expanded during the second industrial revolution frustrated workers. Strikes became common in the monarchy beginning with the 1873 depression, and the strikes grew in frequency, size, and even violence. The first large strike in the Czech Lands occurred in the mining industry in April and May 1882, when about 12,000 miners left the pits in Northern Bohemia. In 1899 more than 15,000 textile workers struck in Brno. In 1900 miners in the Czech Lands joined those throughout Cisleithania in a strike over wages and hours. The first general strike with a political character—highlighting the demand for universal male suffrage—occurred in November 1905 and involved more than 100,000 people. The Social Democratic Party championed the workers' cause, and the workers became the backbone of the party's success in the elections at the turn of the century. Thus the depression of 1873 and the second industrial revolution were the foster parents of two powerful mass parties in the Czech Lands in the latter years of the empire that were key players in the Czechoslovak state between the world wars—the Social Democrats and the Agrarians.

Emigration from the Czech Lands dramatically increased after the revolution of 1848 and fluctuated until World War I, depending on largely economic factors. Although Czechs moved to Canada, South America, Australia, and New Zealand, most went to the United States. At first, the new arrivals sought land in the middle of the country from the Dakotas to Texas, but later they settled in the cities of the Midwest and Northeast. Most were skilled workers or farmers, and only a small percentage were unskilled laborers. From 1850 until World War I, around 350,000 Czechs arrived in the United States, the largest single influx of 13,500 arriving in 1907.

THE ECONOMY OF THE CZECHOSLOVAK FIRST REPUBLIC (1918–1938)

Czechoslovakia checked inflation and stabilized its currency immediately after the First World War, and it entered an era of prosperity that lasted until the Great Depression. The major exception was the economic downturn of 1922, largely the result of the government's deflationary financial policies. The economy also slowed briefly in 1926. Czechoslovakia exported a large amount of its production, and exports typically accounted for about a quarter of its gross national product. Between the world wars, Czechoslovakia was among the ten largest industrialized economies, and it was the world's seventh producer of armaments. In Europe in 1935, Czechoslovakia ranked seventh in steel production after Germany, Soviet Union, Britain, France, Belgium, and Luxemburg. In the same year, Czechoslovakia was the world's second largest producer of brown coal, after Germany, and seventh in hard coal. Czechoslovakia's largest single trading partner was Germany, but it also competed with Germany in the world market. It exported to the Balkans and East Central European states, but these traditional outlets, many of which had been in the Habsburg monarchy, began to develop their own industries and purchased goods from other states, especially Germany, which had inaugurated an aggressive clearing agreement program in the 1930s. To accommodate this change, Czechoslovak manufacturers expanded their markets in the West, especially with Britain and France, and the United States. The export market in agricultural goods experienced similar difficulties after the war. The peace treaties disrupted old markets, and domestic production increases in other states further reduced trade. This was especially true with sugar beets. To protect home industry and agriculture, the government relied on tariffs similar to those found in other states at the time. The contraction of world trade with the Great Depression hurt Czechoslovakia, which never fully recovered its lost markets. The country crawled out of the depression by 1937, in large part because of rearmament.

The Czechoslovak economy was well balanced, with roughly a third of the population employed in each of the industrial, agricultural, and service sectors. Nevertheless, regional economic considerations are crucial. The heavily industrialized and urbanized Czech Lands, which had accounted for 38 percent of the former monarchy's industrial workforce, stood in stark contrast to the overwhelmingly agrarian and rural Slovakia and Ruthenia. The government did little to encourage economic development in the East, believing strongly in laissez-faire economics, and Slovaks claimed that stronger Czech firms took over smaller Slovak enterprises that resulted in the deindustrialization of Slovakia. Agriculture in the eastern provinces also lagged behind the Czech Lands in terms of mechanization and employing the latest technology.

Many small industrial firms made Czechoslovakia a diversified producer of goods, but a few firms dominated the economy. After the war, Schneider Creusot from France became the majority shareholder of the Škoda works, which expanded its operations at home and abroad. Škoda began manufacturing automobiles, airplanes, tanks, and armored vehicles, but it continued its traditional production of large guns, locomotives, and machinery. Škoda and the Kolben-Daněk Company formed a cartel in the mid-1930s that dominated the country's mechanical and armament output. The Association for Chemical and Metallurgical Production, another major exporter, was the largest competitor of Germany's IG Farben-Industrie AG in Central Europe and the Balkans, and the two firms established numerous cartels. Tomáš Bat'a, who had been manufacturing shoes since 1894, developed a large-scale manufacturing factory in Zlín, Moravia, using the mass production techniques of the Ford Motor Company and the tenets of Taylorism. His firm became the largest exporter of shoes throughout the world for almost the entire decade before World War II. Bat'a's housing and other programs for workers in Zlín helped guarantee worker loyalty and productivity. Symbolic of Bat'a's innovative management techniques was his office, which he located in a giant elevator that enabled him to supervise production on any floor within seconds.

Czechoslovakia had one of the most efficient European agricultural economies between the world wars with production in key goods, such as grains, potatoes, and certain industrial crops ranking above the European average. In 1934 it was the largest producer of hops on the Continent and third in the world, after the United States and Britain. In the same year, it was sixth in the production of potatoes after the Soviet Union, Germany, Poland, France, and the United States. The production of sugar beets, an important export used in the production of sugar, fell over time, largely because the price for sugar beets declined as other countries increased their output. Before the Great Depression, Czechoslovakia was the third largest producer of sugar beets, after Germany and the Soviet Union. In 1934 it was the sixth largest producer of refined sugar. At the same time, Czechoslovakia was the fourth largest producer of rye in the world, after the Soviet Union, Poland, and Germany. Czechoslovak agriculture was based largely on small- and medium-sized enterprises, many of which had expanded as a result of the land reform. In agriculture, mechanization, electrification, and education made continued progress between the world wars. One of the most decisive features of the structure of agriculture in Czechoslovakia that helped maintain high productivity was the network of finance, production, machine, and electric cooperatives—all the heritage of the old monarchy. In 1938 there were 5,488 cooperatives of all types in the country, and nearly half were electric. There were 524 dairy and 462 distillery cooperatives. As with the political parties and so many other aspects of the Czechoslovak polity, the cooperative movement had its Czech, Slovak, German, and other divisions.

WORLD WAR II AND ITS AFTERMATH

After the Munich Agreement of 1938, the German government subordinated the Czech economy to German interests, a process that intensified when hostilities began with the West in 1940. The Germans seized Czechoslovak armaments, which they either sold abroad or incorporated into the German arsenal. They seized some of Czechoslovakia's gold reserves and benefited from the confiscation of Jewish and exile German business assets. The Czechs managed their own economy and businesses, although German representatives made certain that the Protectorate's economic policies agreed with those of the Reich and Germans sat on the individual boards of directors of key financial, commercial, and industrial enterprises. Germany became the Protectorate's most important trading partner, but Czech firms continued to trade with the Soviet Union during the time when that country was allied with Germany between 1939 and 1941. In the autumn of 1940 German planners and the German military forced Czech firms to fulfill military contracts. Estimates place the contribution of Czech industrial production to the total German output during the war at 9–12 percent. The standard of living during the war declined, and shortages led to the creation of a black market. Nevertheless, the Czechs generally received more rations than the Germans, and the birthrate among Czechs actually increased. With the establishment of the Protectorate, many Czechs served as contract employers in Germany, helping to ease unemployment in the Czech Lands. The Czechs did not see military action alongside the Germans, but in 1941 the Germans began conscripting Czechs for work in the Reich.

After the war, Czechoslovakia had to contend with a number of difficulties that strained the postwar economy. The war cost Czechoslovakia the equivalent of the country's gross national product for the five years between 1932 and 1937. A total of 360,000 citizens lost their lives as a result of the German occupation, and 100,000 survivors were in poor health. War casualties and executions combined with postwar expulsions to reduce the labor force, and resettlements frequently resulted in employers not having the skilled labor force they needed. Thousands of homes and buildings were destroyed, especially in Slovakia. Large factories had been bombed, and the remainder had been neglected, looted, or otherwise damaged. Nationalization of finance and heavy industry meant losses for investors, as did currency reforms and the so-called millionaires' levy of 1947. To aid in recovery, Czechoslovakia inaugurated a two-year plan for 1947–1948. Because it was not as rigid as a Soviet plan and was closer to the French model in that it gave individual firms a good deal of freedom, the plan resulted in little economic dislocation. In 1948, relative to other European states, but excluding the Soviet Union and Germany, most key industrial products, including hard coal, steel, electricity, textiles, and cement, exceeded the output for 1937, the last full year before the dismemberment of Czechoslovakia. Yields of grains, potatoes, and sugar beets in 1948 were just shy of those in 1937. In mining, manufacturing, and transportation, most of the targets of the two-year plan approached fulfillment or exceeded expectations. Livestock's targets approached fulfillment, although crop yields generally were less than two-thirds of the target. By 1948, the Czechoslovak economy had not recovered from the war, but it had made great progress.

THE COMMAND ECONOMY OF COMMUNISM (1948–1968)

On taking power, the Communists replaced the capitalist market with central planning based on the experience of the Soviet Union. The state reduced the limit of employees for private firms, thus furthering the process of nationalization in industry and commerce that had begun in 1945. Within a decade, the state sector employed nearly the entire industrial and commercial workforce. The first Five-Year Plan that began in 1949, along with subsequent plans, was typical of the strict central planning of the Soviet Union that gave priority to heavy industry. To eliminate the exploitation of workers, the planners reduced differentiation in wages and ended the monetary incentives normal to capitalist economies that increase production. Shortly after 1948, the Communist Party reduced the upper limit of agricultural land any individual could own to fifty hectares. At the same time, they began the process of collectivizing agriculture. Organizers persuaded some agriculturalists to join the collectives and forced others into collectives through violence or by demonstrative harsh treatment of kulaks, the term the Czechoslovak Communists adopted from the Soviet terminology for wealthy peasants (most in fact were not). A farmer entering a cooperative, known in Czech by the abbreviation JZD (Jednotné zemědělské družstv [Unified Agricultural Cooperative]) and in Slovak by the abbreviation JRD (Jednotné rol'nícke družstvo), surrendered control of his or her land to the collective farm, the management of which was in the hands of an elected board that met the approval of the Communist Party. The collective farm manager determined work assignments and was responsible for fulfilling government orders. Each collective farmer had a small private plot of a few hectares to work on his or her own time. In the mid-1950s there was a lull in the collectivization drive, but by 1960, when the regime considered the collectivization process complete, 87 percent of Czechoslovakia's agricultural land was collectivized, slightly more in the Czech Lands (92 percent) and slightly less (80 percent) in Slovakia. As in other socialist countries, a small number of state farms came into existence in which all the employees received only wages. The Communist Party considered these enterprises to be an advance toward socialism, but their performance was as poor in Czechoslovakia as it was in other East European states.

NORMALIZATION AND THE STAGE OF ADVANCED SOCIALISM

After the Warsaw Pact invasion of 1968, the Communist Party dismantled the economic reforms. In particular, they eliminated the market (supply and demand) influences on pricing and the workers' management councils in the factories. The economy remained tightly controlled, and the central planners continued to pour investments into outdated heavy industries, including those in Slovakia built after World War II to increase Slovakia's level of industrialization. Despite such efforts, production lagged, deliveries were late, resources were scarce, production equipment became antiquated, and employees shunned hard work. Firms in need of supplies or unable to fill quotas often relied on barter to obtain goods. As in the German Democratic Republic, economic planners in Czechoslovakia merged smaller and less efficient industries with larger ones in an attempt to streamline the planning process and increase productivity. The oil crisis of the 1970s strained the Czechoslovak economy and resulted in increasing prices, declining growth rates, and climbing trade deficits. The Czechoslovak leadership resisted the sort of economic restructuring that Mikhail Gorbachev introduced in the Soviet Union in the 1980s, and resorted to traditional methods of exhorting citizens to fulfill the economic plan and championed the slogan "quality and effectiveness." One of the achievements of the socialist regime was the industrialization of Slovakia, which was on a par with the Czech Lands in industrial output in the late 1980s.

The Husák regime eagerly supported efforts to foster economic integration within the CMEA, the Soviet-led trading bloc. During the course of the 1970s and 1980s, Czechoslovakia increased its foreign trade with the CMEA states. Such trade was mutually beneficial to all of the socialist states, and Czechoslovakia, for example, exported industrial products to the Soviet Union in return for oil and gas through the Friendship Pipeline. Armaments, including quality Semtex plastic explosives (along with tanks and guns that were not on a par with those of Western manufacturers), were one of Czechoslovakia's largest exports to the Third World. The developing countries in turn supplied oil and such consumer goods as bananas and oranges.

The lack of incentives in collectivized agriculture mirrored those in industry, and agricultural outputs were disappointing. An exception was the Slušovice collective farm, which the Party tolerated as an experiment in socialist-inspired agriculture. With branches throughout the republic, Slušovice operated like a capitalist agro-industrial conglomerate, rather than like the typical ill-managed socialist collective. Slušovice managers had a wide range of decision making powers, and they spent government investments at their own discretion. They paid attention to product development and diversified its operations. In the winter, for example, when many agriculturalists were short on work, Slušovice members even assembled Czechoslovakia's brand of personal computers. A small number of agriculturalists were outside the socialist sector, but their number diminished over the years through retirement. Then in the early 1970s, the Party authorized the collectivization of what experts previously had considered marginally productive agricultural land as a means of exploiting every available hectare of land for production and solving an array of social problems, such as the low standard of living of the independent farmers. The process was ongoing even on the eve of the Velvet Revolution of 1989.

Although Czechoslovakia enjoyed the second highest standard of living in the socialist world, after the German Democratic Republic, the planned economy was no more responsive to the needs of consumers than it was to industry. Products frequently were outmoded, poor in quality, and in short supply. In 1987, for example, an unusual unavailability of toilet paper abruptly gave way to a shortage of writing paper (most likely, the writing paper having been used for purposes other than writing). When a disaster struck the country's feminine napkin producer, the regime turned to imports from the West, prompting murmurs from the population that the new factory should produce the variety and quality of feminine napkins from the capitalist world. For the most part, however, basic consumer goods were available in the stores. To satisfy their demand for a greater variety of basic goods, luxury items, and Western styles, Czechs and Slovaks had a number of options. The few with higher incomes could buy fine-quality imported and domestic products in the expensive Tuzex dollar shops. Many purchased items on the lively black market, also known as the second economy. Employees considered occasional pilferage a necessity of life, and they frequently bartered what they stole for items they needed. In the 1980s many Czechs and Slovaks combined a vacation to Hungary with shopping in the well-stocked small private stores of Budapest and other cities. The youth of the country, raised by a generation disillusioned with communism and the government after 1968, was not materialistic, not ambitious, and generally pessimistic about the future. They found pleasure in various leisure activities, among them hiking and camping, and few seemed excited about entering the work force.

REBUILDING CAPITALISM AFTER 1989

After the Velvet Revolution, the Czechoslovak and then the Czech economy underwent a rapid transformation to capitalism, including a campaign to privatize firms. From the outset, those who favored the rapid shift from economic planning to the open market, dominated Czech politics. Pricing became subject to the market in 1991, regular daily trading on the stock market began in 1994, and the Czech crown became free in 1995. The Czechoslovak government provided for restitution to those who lost property after 1948. With the agriculturalists and their descendants seeking their families' land, the religious groups attempting to reclaim churches, monasteries, and estates, the nobles staking their claims on property, the former building owners trying to take possession of their property, and the former business owners expecting to reacquire their assets, restitution was often lengthy and tortuous. In many cases, the process was further complicated because the socialist state had liquidated assets, had merged firms that had existed before 1948, and had built buildings on residential, commercial, or agricultural land. For the most part, agriculturalists transformed their collective farms to cooperatives, although some became independent farmers. Once firms demonstrated that restitution had been completed, they could proceed with privatization. The most common means to deal with the large firms was through waves of large privatization using Klaus's voucher system. Citizens purchased directly or through an investment fund up to a thousand vouchers worth 1 Kčs each toward the acquisition of shares. Nearly three-quarters of all eligible citizens enrolled in the voucher program. Other methods of privatization included direct sale, auctions, public tender, and transfers. Some firms were to remain state-owned. The voucher system began in 1992 and the Ministry of Privatization ceased to exist in 1996, but the Czech Republic still has petrochemical, energy, steel, and telecommunications enterprises that have not been privatized. Banks were not privatized until 1999–2001, after a rash of bankruptcies that prompted the government to assume responsibility for their bad loans. In a separate so-called small privatization campaign, the Czechoslovak government auctioned 25,000 small enterprises, such as restaurants, shops, newsstands, and other small businesses. Not surprisingly, corruption was inherent in the privatization process, and a common feature with respect to the larger firms was asset stripping, which the Czechs refer to as tunneling.

Workers assemble Škoda Fabia cars at the Škoda plant on 4 November 2002, in Mladá Boleslav, Czech Republic. The Czech car maker Škoda, which is mainly owned by Volkswagen of Germany, has been forced to reduce production of some models due to the lagging European auto market. (Getty Images)

The Czech Republic became a haven for foreign investment. It paid off an International Monetary Fund (IMF) loan early, raising the confidence international firms and markets had in the Czech economy. Most of the investment originating with individual firms came from Germany, and a significant acquisition was Volkswagen's purchase of a large portion of the Škoda works. PSA Peugeot-Citroën and Toyota in a joint venture agreed to produce passenger vehicles in a new plant near Kolín. Well over a hundred automobile manufacturers have a presence in the Czech Republic. Other manufacturing sectors—electronics, aerospace, engineering, chemical, foundry, textile, glass, machinery, food processing, telecommunications, wood, glass, paper, construction, pharmaceuticals, computer, environmental, plastics, and services—also attract foreign investors from throughout the world. For some time, the government and popular pressure kept certain well-known firms from becoming the sole property of foreign investors. The state initially maintained the majority shares in the Plsner Urquell brewery, which exports beer throughout the world, but eventually SABMiller purchased it. Pernod-Ricard, originally a French firm, bought the liqueur Becherovka, which never had been exported and is now available in various countries, even outside Europe. The Budvar brewery in České Budějovice had to fend off a takeover attack from Anheuser-Bush, and after several years of negotiations between the two firms, Budweiser-Budvar preserved the rights to export its label under certain conditions. It remained in state hands as Budějovický Budvar, n.p., as of 2004.

Transforming the economy meant more than restitution, privatization, and foreign investment. Industries, especially the larger ones, had to restructure. Nevertheless, many managers continued to preserve old techniques from the socialist period, resisted downsizing, and relied on the government, as they had in the socialist era, for financial support. Czech citizens met the transformation from socialism to capitalism in various ways. Families had to reconsider their budgets because of inflation and because prices for food and basic goods doubled and rents and utilities increased by a quarter. Parents could no longer rely on certain services that the socialist regime provided, such as inexpensive health care and daycare. Many decried the growing income differentiation that began to emerge after 1990. Bankruptcies, crooked deals, and scams fostered skepticism about capitalism, which complemented suspicions about democracy caused by constantly breaking news about corruption in politics. Many Czechs feared for their economic future, their ability to survive once they retired, and the economic well-being of their children. In a country where career changes had been uncommon, many of those who had begun their careers under socialism and had lost their positions in the transition to capitalism had to find work in totally different fields. Similarly, older individuals could not understand that university students might complete a major and take employment in another area. Men and especially women in the middle of their careers feared losing their positions because firms would hesitate to hire them.

A special economic and social concern has been the environment. The command economy continued to rely on brown coal, with its many pollutants, and the government did not require companies to install antipollution devices. Acid rain from the pollution caused widespread deforestation in Northern Bohemia. Other forms of industrial pollution abounded. The paper plant that made newsprint upstream on the Vltava from the UNESCO-protected town of Český Krumlov simply piped its discharge downstream from the picturesque town. Another problem was toxic waste, not only from industry but also from the Russian occupation forces. Finally, vehicles during the socialist regime did not have antipollution devices, which contributed to smog and accompanying health hazards in urban areas. Since the end of Communist rule, Czechoslovakia and afterward the Czech Republic has made great strides in improving the environment, and the effort is ongoing. The EU, for example, noted that the Czech Republic reduced its emissions of nitrogen oxide by 80 percent, sulphur by 88 percent, and particulates by 92 percent.

Despite some difficulties, the overall performance of the Czech economy since the end of communism has been impressive. Inflation soared and the growth rate declined in Czechoslovakia as a whole in the year after the Velvet Revolution, but recovery began in 1992. Immediately after the separation from Slovakia, the Czech Republic experienced a solid growth rate, a steady influx of foreign investment, and an extremely low rate of unemployment, especially in Prague. In 1997, however, the economy entered into a recession that lasted for two years. It was during this time that much of the corruption associated with the transition to a capitalist economy came to light and precipitated a government crisis. Since 2000, the economy has been on an upturn. The real GDP was 2.2 percent in 2001 and 2.7 percent in 2002. During this time there was a low rate of inflation (1.4 percent in 2002, which was below the EU average rate of 2.1 percent), steady consumption, and increases in wages. Nevertheless, unemployment, especially in certain sectors and regions, remained high. In 2002 it was 7.3 percent, on a par with Belgium and just below the EU average of 7.5 percent. The public deficit climbed, which the Špidla government attempted to control with controversial increased taxes and cuts in expenditures. Several economic indicators show that the Czech Republic, aside from Slovenia, in some respects has been the most successful former socialist states to make the transition to capitalism. The outstanding record the Czechs had in managing their economy guaranteed the Czech Republic a high ranking on the list of former socialist countries seeking admission to the EU, which occurred in May 2004.

CONTEMPORARY CHALLENGES

JOINING THE EUROPEAN UNION

The European Union's first step in intensifying relations with the Czech Republic began in 1989, when the Czech Republic joined the EU's program for economic assistance to former East European states known as Phare: Poland and Hungary Assistance for the Restructuring of the Economy. The EU opened the possibility of former East European states joining the EU in 1993, and since that time, the Czech Republic has actively sought accession. The first step was to sign an association agreement, which was concluded in 1991 and had to be renegotiated in 1993 after the division of Czechoslovakia. It took effect in February 1995 and governed Czech Republic–EU commercial, political, and other relations. In 1996, the Czech Republic formally applied for membership. In 1997 the European Commission issued its opinion regarding the applications for membership of several countries, including the Czech Republic, in what is known as Agenda 2000. The next step occurred in 1998, when negotiations between the Czech Republic and the EU began on accession. The resulting accession partnership agreement set out all the requirements the Czech Republic had to meet for membership. Each year, the European Commission issued a regular report to the European Council on the progress of the Czech Republic toward completing all that is necessary to join the EU. In addition to the Czech Republic, the European Council decided to open negotiations with Cyprus, Estonia, Hungary, Poland, and Slovenia. In 1999 the council expanded the list to include Bulgaria, Latvia, Lithuania, Malta, Slovakia, Romania, and Turkey (as a candidate country). With the Commission satisfied that the Czech Republic met the bulk of the requirements for accession, the two signed an accession treaty on 16 April 2003. As part of finalizing the process, the Czech Republic held a referendum on EU on 13–14 June 2003, and with a turnout of 55.21 percent of the eligible voters, 77.33 percent approved of entry, which made the vote binding. After the accession treaty, the Mission of the Czech Republic had two dozen observers in the European Parliament, and it became the permanent representation of the Czech Republic upon accession on 1 May 2004.

The negotiations between the EU and the Czech Republic were complicated. The 1997 opinion of the European Commission contained a long list of changes the Czech government had to undertake. In the realm of politics, the EU found the Czech Republic wanting in the areas of press freedom, discrimination against the Roma, and the exclusion of former Communist functionaries and police from public service. With respect to its economy, the Czech Republic needed to strengthen the corporate governance and the finance system, restructure major business, privatize the banks, and improve the value of its exported goods. The EU determined that the Czech Republic would likely be in a position to assume the *aquis*—the common rights and obligations of member states; in short, all EU laws and regulations—after legal changes in areas related to the Single Market, transportation, environment, agriculture, energy, borders, and Economy and Monetary Union. Finally, the EU called for modifications in the justice system. For many citizens, the mass of legislation seemed like an impossibility, but parliament made rapid progress over the years. By the end of 2000, the Czech Republic had passed most of the hurdles. In 2001–2002, the EU and the Czech Republic agreed to a transitional period of several years to pass further legislation and regulations regarding energy, environment, free movement of capital and persons, taxation, agriculture, and transport.

In its final report, issued on 5 November 2003, the European Commission praised the Czech Republic's preparations for accession. Still, it decried the deterioration of public finances and encouraged further changes in administrative and judicial regulations, including strenghthening the means of fighting corruption. The Czech Republic, according to the report, had reached a "high level of alignment with the *acquis,*" although it outlined many deficits and urged the Czech Republic to enhance its efforts to fulfill all its commitments and requirements before accession. The most important impediments related to free movement of persons, road transport, and agriculture. The Czech Parliament continued to address these legislative shortcomings before the Czech Republic's accession in 2004.

Czechs have been naturally apprehensive about entry into the EU. A long-term concern is the future of their jobs, but with full economic integration into the EU some years off, these fears will likely abate. An immediate concern was a sharp increase in consumer prices. Yet the Czech National Bank in a report to the government in late 2003 claimed reassuringly that neither food nor consumer products would face dramatic increases, especially in the short run; those predictions appear to be holding. In many respects, prices are already in line with EU markets. The Czechs have much to gain from entry and integration into the EU, with respect to both the economy and their personal options, and the vast majority of the population realizes that.

SELECTIVE BIBLIOGRAPHY

Agnew, Hugh LeCaine. *Origins of the Czech National Renascence.* Pitt Series in Russian and East European Studies, no. 18. Pittsburgh: University of Pittsburgh Press, 1993.

Austrian History Yearbook. 1965–present.

Bradley, J. F. N. *Czechoslovakia's Velvet Revolution: A Political Analysis.* East European Monographs, no. 355. Boulder: East European Monographs, 1992.

Bregant, Michal, et al. *Kuvistická Praha: Cubist Prague 1909–1925: Průvodce: A Guidebook.* Foreword by Tomáš Vlček. Prague: Středoevropská galerie a nakladatelství/ODRON, 1995.

Bruegel, Johann Wolfgang. *Czechoslovakia before Munich: The German Minority Problem and British Appeasement Policy.* Cambridge: Cambridge University Press, 1973.

Bušek, Vratislav, ed. *Comenius: A Symposium Held at the 5th Congress of the Czechoslovak Society of Arts and Sciences in America at New York University School of Law, New York City, November 13–15, 1970, to Commemorate the 300th Anniversary of the Death of Jan Amos Comenius (Komenský) on November 15, 1670.* Translated by Káča Poláčková. New York: Czechoslovak Society of Arts and Sciences in America, 1972.

Campbell, F. Gregory. *Confrontation in Central Europe: Weimar Germany and Czechoslovakia.* Chicago: University of Chicago Press, 1975.

Canadian-American Slavic Studies/Revue Canadienne-Americaine d'Etudes Slaves. 1967–present.

Čapek, Karel. *President Masaryk Tells His Story.* New York: Putnam's, 1935.

Český statistický úřad/Czech Statistical Office. *Statistická ročenka České republiky/Statistical Yearbook of the Czech Republic.* Prague: Český statistický úřad, 2003. www.czso.cz.

Cohen, Gary. *The Politics of Ethnic Survival: Germans in Prague, 1861–1914.* Princeton: Princeton University Press, 1981.

Czech National Bank. "The Impact of the Czech Republic's Accession to the European Union on Consumer Prices in the Czech Republic: Information Material for the Government." Report dated 5 June 2003.

Czech Poetry: A Bilingual Anthology. Translated by Alfred French et al. Introduction by René Wellek. Vol. 1. Michigan Slavic Translations. Ann Arbor, MI: Czechoslovak Society of Arts and Sciences/Michigan Slavic Publications, University of Michigan, 1973.

Dawisha, Karen. *The Kremlin and the Prague Spring.* International Crisis Behavior Series. Berkeley: University of California Press, 1984.

Demetz, Peter. *Prague in Black and Gold: Scenes from the Life of a European City.* New York: Hill and Wang, 1997.

Dowling, Maria. *Czechoslovakia.* Brief Histories. Oxford: Oxford University Press, 2002.

Dubček, Alexander. *Dubček's Blueprint for Freedom: His Original Documents Leading to the Invasion of Czechoslovakia.* Profile by Hugh Lunghi. Commentary by Paul Ello. London: William Kumber, 1968.

———. *Hope Dies Last: The Autobiography of Alexander Dubček.* Edited and translated by Jiří Hochman. New York: Kodansha International, 1993.

East-Central Europe/L'Europe du Centre-Est. 1974–present.

East European Politics and Society. 1981–present.

East European Quarterly. 1967–present.

European Commission. *Agenda 2000: Commission Opinion on the Czech Republic's Application for Membership of the European Union.* Bulletin of the European Union, Supplement 14/97. Luxemburg: Office for Official Publications of the European Communities, 1997.

———. "Comprehensive Monitoring Report on the Czech Republic's Preparation for Membership." 5 November 2003.

Fawn, Rick. *The Czech Republic: A Nation of Velvet.* Postcommunist States and Nations. Australia: Harwood Academic, 2000.

Garver, Bruce M. *The Young Czech Party (1874–1901) and the Emergence of a Multi-Party System.* Yale Historical Publications, Miscellany, no. 111. New Haven: Yale University Press, 1978.

Hanak, Harry, ed. *T. G. Masaryk (1850–1937).* Vol. 3, *Statesman and Cultural Force.* Houndmills, UK: Macmillan; London: School of Slavonic and East European Studies, University of London, 1990.

Harkins, William E. *Czech Prose: An Anthology.* Translated by William E. Harkins. Michigan Slavic Translations, no. 6. Ann Arbor: University of Michigan Press, 1983.

Havel, Václav. *Disturbing the Peace: A Conversation with Karel Hvížd'ala.* Translated with an introduction by Paul Wilson. New York: Random House/Vintage, 1991.

———. *Largo Desolado.* Translated by Tom Stoppard. New York: Grove, 1987.

———. *Letters to Olga, June 1979–September 1982.* Translated and introduction by Paul Wilson. New York: Henry Holt/Owl, 1989.

———. *Living in Truth.* Edited by Jan Vladislav. London: Faber and Faber, 1989.

———. *Open Letters: Selected Writings, 1965–1990.* Edited by Paul Wilson. New York: Knopf, 1991.

———. *Summer Meditations.* Translated by Paul Wilson. N.p.: Knopf Canada, 1992.

Havel, Václav, et al. *Power of the Powerless: Citizens against the State in Central-Eastern Europe.* Edited by John Keane. Introduction by Steven Lukes. Armonk, NY: Sharpe, 1985.

Historical Institutes, History Departments, Archives, Museums in the Czech Republic: A Guide. Prague: Czech National Committee of Historians, 1995.

Hoyt, Edwin P. *The Army without a Country.* New York: Macmillan; London: Collier-Macmillan, 1967.

Iggers, Wilma Abeles. *Women of Prague: Ethnic Diversity and Social Change from the Eighteenth Century to the Present.* Providence: Berghahn, 1995.

Innes, Abby. *Czechoslovakia: The Short Goodbye.* New Haven: Yale University Press, 2001.

Jászi, Oscar. *The Dissolution of the Habsburg Monarchy.* Chicago and London: University of Chicago Press, 1961.

Kaplan, Frank L. *Winter into Spring: The Czechoslovak Press and the Reform Movement, 1963–1968.* East European Monographs, no. 29. Boulder: East European Quarterly, 1977.

Karatnycky, Adrian, Alexander Motyl, and Amanda Schnetzer, eds. *Nations in Transit, 2003: Democratization in East Central Europe and Eurasia.* New York: Freedom House; Lanham, MD: Rowman and Littlefield, 2003.

Karatnycky, Adrian, Aili Piano, and Arch Puddingto, eds. *Freedom in the World: The Annual Survey of Political Rights and Civil Liberties, 2003.* New York: Freedom House; Lanham, MD: Rowman and Littlefield, 2003.

Kerner, Robert J. *Bohemia in the Eighteenth Century: A Study in Political, Economic, and Social History with Special Reference to the Reign of Leopold II, 1790–1792.* 2d ed. Introduction by Joseph F. Zacek. Russian Series, vol. 7. Orono, ME: Academic International, 1969.

Kerner, Robert J, ed. *Czechoslovakia: Twenty Years of Independence.* Berkeley: University of California Press, 1940.

Kieval, Hillel J. *The Making of Czech Jewry: National Conflict and Jewish Society in Bohemia, 1870–1918.* New York: Oxford University Press, 1988.

Klaus, Václav. *Renaissance: The Rebirth of Liberty in the Heart of Europe.* Washington, DC: Cato Institute, 1997.

Klíma, Arnošt. *Economy, Industry, and Society in Bohemia in the Seventeenth and Nineteenth Centuries.* Prague: Charles University, 1991.

Kosmas. 1982–present.

Kovtun, George J., ed. *Czech and Slovak History: An American Bibliography.* Introduction by Stanley B. Winters. Washington, DC: Library of Congress, 1996.

———. *Tomáš G. Masaryk, 1850–1937: A Selective List of Reading Materials in English.* Washington, DC: Library of Congress, n.d.

Krejčí, Jaroslav. *Czechoslovakia at the Crossroads of European History.* London: Tarus, 1990.

Krejčí, Jaroslav, and Pavel Machonin. *Czechoslovakia, 1918–1992: A Laboratory for Social Change.* New York: St. Martin's; Oxford: St. Anthony's College, 1996.

Krejčí, Oskar. *History of Elections in Bohemia and Moravia.* East European Monographs, no. 433. Boulder: East European Monographs, 1995.

Kriseová, Eda. *Václav Havel: The Authorized Biography.* Translated by Caleb Crain. New York: St. Martin's, 1993.

Kun, Miklós. *Prague Spring, Prague Fall: Blank Spots of 1968.* Translated by Hajnal Csatorday. Edited by by Péter Tamási. Budapest: Akadémiai kiadó, 1999.

Leff, Carol Skalnik. *The Czech and Slovak Republics: Nation versus State.* Nations of the Modern World: Europe. Boulder: Westview, 1997.

———. *National Conflict in Czechoslovakia: The Making and Remaking of a State, 1918–1987.* Princeton: Princeton University Press, 1988.

Literature and Tolerance: Views from Prague. Translated by Anna Bryson et al. Prague: Readers International (Prague) and Czech Center of International PEN, 1994.

Ludwig, Emil. *Defender of Democracy: Masaryk of Czechoslovakia.* New York: McBride, 1936.

Lukes, Igor. *Czechoslovakia between Stalin and Hitler: The Diplomacy of Edvard Beneš in the 1930s.* New York: Oxford University Press, 1996.

Mamatey, Victor S., and Radomír Luža, eds. *A History of the Czechoslovak Republic, 1918–1948.* Princeton: Princeton University Press, 1973.

Mansbach, Steven A. *Modern Art in Eastern Europe: From the Baltic to the Balkans, c. 1890–1939.* Cambridge: Cambridge University Press, 1999.

Masaryk, Tomáš G. *The Making of a State: Memories and Observations.* Introduction by Henry Wickham Steed. New York: Fertig, 1969.

———. *Masaryk on Thought and Life: Conversations with Karel Čapek*. Translated by M. Weatherall and R. Weatherall. New York: Macmillan, 1938.

———. *Spirit of Russia: Studies in History, Literature, and Philosophy*. 2 vols. Translated by Eden Paul and Cedar Paul. London: George Allen and Unwin, 1919.

———. *The Spirit of Russia*. Vol. 3. Edited by George Gibian. Translated by Robert Bass. London: George Allen and Unwin, 1967.

Michal, Jan M. *Central Planning in Czechoslovakia: Organization for Growth in a Mature Economy*. Stanford: Stanford University Press, 1960.

Miller, Daniel E. *Forging Political Compromise: Antonín Švehla and the Czechoslovak Republican Party, 1918–1933*. Pitt Series on Russia and Eastern Europe. Pittsburgh: University of Pittsburgh Press, 1999.

Mitchell, Ruth Crawford, ed. *Alice Garrigue Masaryk (1879–1966): Her Life as Recorded in Her Own Words and by Her Friends*. Introduction by René Wellek. University Center for International Studies Series in Russian and East European Studies, no. 4. Pittsburgh: University Center for International Studies, University of Pittsburgh, 1980.

Musil, Jiří. *The End of Czechoslovakia*. Budapest: Central European University Press, 1995.

Navrátil, Jaromír, et al., eds. *The Prague Spring, 1968: A National Security Archive Documents Reader*. Translated by Mark Kramer, Joy Moss, and Ruth Tosek. Budapest: Central European University Press, 1998.

Nolte, Claire E. *The Sokol in the Czech Lands to 1914: Training for the Nation*. Houndmills, UK: Palgrave Macmillan, 2003.

Novák, Arne. *Czech Literature*. Edited with a supplement by William E. Harkins. Translated by Peter Kussi. Joint Committee on Eastern Europe Publication Series, no. 4. Ann Arbor, MI: Joint Committee on Eastern Europe, American Council of Learned Societies; Michigan Slavic Publications, University of Michigan, 1976.

Odložilík, Otakar. *The Hussite King: Bohemia in European Affairs, 1440–1471*. New Brunswick, NJ: Rutgers University Press, 1965.

Pech, Stanley Z. *The Czech Revolution of 1848*. Chapel Hill: University of North Carolina Press, 1969.

Pelikán, Jiří. *The Czechoslovak Political Trials, 1950–1954*. Stanford: Stanford University Press, 1971.

Pelikán, Jiří, ed. *The Secret Vysočany Congress: Proceedings and Documents of the Extraordinary Fourteenth Congress of the Communist Party of Czechoslovakia, 22 August 1968*. Translated by George Theiner and Deryck Viney. New York: St. Martin's, 1971.

Pavitt, Jane. *Prague*. The Buildings of Europe. Manchester, UK: Manchester University Press, 2000.

Porter, Robert. *An Introduction to Twentieth-Century Czech Fiction: Comedies of Defiance*. Brighton, UK: Sussex Academic Press, 2001.

Pynsent, Robert B. *Questions of Identity: Czech and Slovak Ideas of Nationality and Personality*. Budapest: Central European Press, 1994.

Pynsent, Robert B., ed. *T. G. Masaryk (1850–1937)*. Vol. 2, *Thinker and Critic*. London: Macmillan/School of Slavonic and East European Studies, University of London, 1989.

Rechcigl, Miloslav, Jr., ed. *The Czechoslovak Contribution to World Culture*. The Hague: Mouton/Czechoslovak Society of Arts and Sciences in America, 1964.

———. *Czechoslovakia: Past and Present*. 2 vols. The Hague: Mouton, 1968.

Remington, Robin Alison, ed. *Winter in Prague: Documents on Czechoslovak Communism in Crisis*. Introduction by William E. Griffith. Cambridge: MIT Press, 1969.

Rice, Condoleezza. *The Soviet Union and the Czechoslovak Army, 1948–1983: Uncertain Allegiance*. Princeton: Princeton University Press, 1984.

Riese, Hans-Peter, ed. *Since the Prague Spring: Charter '77 and the Struggle for Human Rights in Czechoslovakia*. Foreword by Arthur Miller. Translated by Eugen Loebl. New York: Random House, 1979.

Ripka, Hubert. *Munich: Before and After*. Translated by Ida Šindelková and Edgar P. Young. 1939. Reprint, New York: Fertig, 1969.

Sayer, Derek. *The Coasts of Bohemia: A Czech History*. Translated by Alena Sayer. Princeton: Princeton University Press, 1998.

Selver, Paul. *Masaryk*. Introduction by Jan Masaryk. London: Michael Joseph, 1940.

Seton-Watson, R. W. *Documents/Dokumenty, 1906–1951*. 2 vols. Edited by Jan Rychlík, Thomas D. Marzik, Miroslav Bielik. Prague: Ústav T. G. Masaryka and Matica slovenská, 1995–1996.

———. *A History of the Czechs and Slovaks*. 1943. Reprint, Hamden, CT: Archon, 1965.

Seton-Watson, Hugh, and Christopher Seton-Watson. *The Making of a New Europe: R. W. Seton-Watson and the Last Years of Austria-Hungary*. Seattle: University of Washington Press, 1981.

Shawcross, William. *Dubček*. Rev. ed. New York: Simon and Schuster/Touchstone, 1990.

Skilling, H. Gordon. *Charter 77 and Human Rights in Czechoslovakia*. London: George Allen and Unwin, 1981.

———. *Czechoslovakia's Interrupted Revolution*. Princeton: Princeton University Press, 1976.

———. *T. G. Masaryk: Against the Current, 1882–1914*. University Park: Pennsylvania State University Press, 1994.

Skilling, H. Gordon, ed. *Czechoslovakia, 1918–1988: Seventy Years from Independence*. New York: St. Martin's, 1991.

Skilling, H. Gordon, and Paul Wilson, eds. *Civic Freedom in Central Europe: Voices from Czechoslovakia*. New York: St. Martin's, 1991.

Slavic Review. 1961–present.

Slavonic and East European Review. 1922–present.

Součková, Milada. *A Literary Satellite: Czechoslovak-Russian Literary Relations*. Chicago: University of Chicago Press, 1970.

Spector, Scott. *Prague Territories: National Conflict and Cultural Innovation in Franz Kafka's Fin de Siècle*. Weimar and Now: German Cultural Criticism. Berkeley: University of California Press, 2000.

Spinka, Matthew. *Jan Hus: A Biography.* Princeton: Princeton University Press, 1968.

———. *John Amos Comenius: That Incomparable Moravian.* New York: Russel and Russel, 1967.

Stein, Eric. *Czecho/Slovakia: Ethnic Conflict, Constitutional Fissure, Negotiated Breakup.* Foreword by Lloyd Cutler. Ann Arbor: University of Michigan Press, 2000.

Sterling, Claire. *The Masaryk Case.* Afterword by Adam Ulam. Boston: Nonpareil, 1982.

Stone, Norman, and Eduard Strouhal, eds. *Czechoslovakia: Crossroads and Crises, 1918–1988.* London: Macmillan/BBC World Service, 1989.

Street, Cecil J. C. *President Masaryk.* New York: Dodd, Mead, 1930.

Suda, Zdenek. *Zealots and Rebels: A History of the Ruling Communist Party of Czechoslovakia.* Histories of Ruling Communist Parties. Stanford: Hoover Institution Press, 1980.

Švácha, Rostislav. *The Architecture of New Prague, 1895–1945.* Translated by Alexandra Büchler. Foreword by Kenneth Frampton. Cambridge: MIT Press, 1995. Photographs by Jan Malý.

Taborsky, Edward. *President Edvard Beneš between East and West, 1938–1948.* Stanford: Hoover Institution Press, 1981.

Teichova, Alice. *The Czechoslovak Economy, 1918–1980.* Translated by Richard J. Hockaday. Contemporary Economic History of Europe Series. London: Routledge, 1988.

Tucker, Aviezer. *The Philosophy and Politics of Czech Dissidence from Patočka to Havel.* Pitt Series in Russian and East European Studies. Pittsburgh: University of Pittsburgh Press, 2000.

Ulč, Otto. *Politics in Czechoslovakia.* Introduction by Jan F. Triska. San Francisco: Freeman, 1974.

Valenta, Jiri. *Soviet Intervention in Czechoslovakia, 1968: Anatomy of a Decision.* Baltimore: Johns Hopkins University Press, 1981.

Vaněček, Václav. *The Universal Peace Organization of King George of Bohemia: A Fifteenth Century Plan for World Peace.* Translated by Ivo Dvořák et al. 2d ed. Prague: Publishing House of the Czechoslovak Academic of Sciences/ Czechoslovak Commission for UNESCO, 1964.

Vyšný, Paul. *The Runciman Mission to Czechoslovakia, 1938: Prelude to Munich.* Houndmills, UK: Palgrave Macmillan, 2003.

Wandycz, Piotr S. *Czechoslovak-Polish Confederation and the Great Powers, 1940–1943.* Slavic and East European Series, vol. 3. Bloomington: Indiana University Publications, 1956.

Wheaton, Bernard, and Zdeněk Kavan. *The Velvet Revolution: Czechoslovakia, 1988–1991.* Boulder: Westview, 1992.

Whipple, Tim D., ed. *After the Velvet Revolution: Václav Havel and the New Leaders of Czechoslovakia Speak Out.* Focus on Issues, no. 14. New York: Freedom House, 1991.

White, Lewis M., ed. *On All Fronts: Czechoslovaks in World War II.* 3 vols. East European Monographs. Boulder: East European Monographs, 1991–2000.

Williams, Kieran. *The Prague Spring and Its Aftermath: Czechoslovak Politics, 1968–1970.* Cambridge: Cambridge University Press, 1997.

Winters, Stanley B., ed. *T. G. Masaryk (1850–1937).* Vol. 1, *Thinker and Politician.* London: Macmillan/School of Slavonic and East European Studies, University of London, 1990.

Wiskemann, Elizabeth. *Czechs and Germans: A Study of the Struggle in the Historic Provinces of Bohemia and Moravia.* London: Oxford University Press, 1938.

Wolchick, Sharon, L. *Czechoslovakia in Transition: Politics, Economics, and Society.* London: Pinter, 1991.

Wright, William E. *Serf, Seigneur, and Sovereign: Agrarian Reform in Eighteenth-Century Bohemia.* Minneapolis: University of Minnesota Press, 1966.

Zeman, Zbyněk. *The Masaryks: The Making of Czechoslovakia.* New York: Barnes and Noble, 1976.

Zeman, Zbyněk, with Antonín Klimek. *The Life of Edvard Beneš, 1884–1948: Czechoslovakia in Peace and War.* Oxford: Clarendon, 1997.

CHRONOLOGY

4th century B.C.E. to 1st century C.E.	The Celtic Boii inhabit the Czech Lands.
1st to 5th century	Germanic tribes inhabit the Czech Lands.
5th–6th century	The Slavs arrive in the Czech Lands.
7th century	Sámo's empire unites Slavic tribes.
833–836	Prince Mojmír creates the Great Moravian Empire.
863 or 864	Cyril and Methodius from the Byzantine Empire arrive in Moravia (current national holiday, July 5).
885	Bořivoj baptized; moves his capital to Prague.
10th century	The Magyars destroy the Great Moravian Empire.
929 or 935	On September 28, St. Václav is murdered (current national holiday).
973	Prague becomes an independent bishopric and receives its first monastery.
982–997	St. Vojtěk becomes Bohemia's first Czech bishop.
995	Boleslav II kills the entire Slavníkov clan.
1085	Vratislav becomes the first Czech king, but the title applies only during his lifetime.
1158	Vladislav becomes the second Czech king.
1212	Přemysl Otakar I receives a hereditary crown in the Imperial Sicilian Golden Bull.
1278	Přemysl Otakar killed in battle (August 26) against the Roman King Rudolf of Habsburg.
1300	The royal mint that struck the *grossi Pragenses* is established at Kutná Hora.

1306	Heinrich of Carinthia is elected king of Bohemia.
1306–1307	Rudolf of Habsburg rules as king of Bohemia.
1310–1346	Reign of Jan of Luxemburg, who married a Přemyslid.
1344	Prague becomes an archbishopric.
1346–1378	Reign of Charles IV (born in 1316 as Václav).
1348	Charles IV establishes Prague University and the New Town.
1355	Charles becomes Roman Emperor.
1378–1419	Reign of Václav IV.
1415	Jan Hus is burned at the stake in Constance (6 July, current national holiday).
1419–1437	Reign of Zigmund, whose death ended the Luxemburg dynasty in Bohemia.
1420–1434	The Hussite Wars, including the crusades of 1420, 1421, 1426, 1437, and 1431.
1434	At the Battle of Lipany, the Catholics and Utraquists defeat the radical Hussites.
1436	The Compactata of Basel recognizes both the Utraquist and Catholic faiths in Bohemia based on the Four Articles of Basel discussed in 1433.
1458	After the death of Ladislav Posthumous, the Bohemian nobles elect as king one of their own, Jiří z Poděbrad, who ruled until 1471.
1463–1465	Jiří z Poděbrad attempts to form a European-wide association of states.
1471	The Bohemian Diet elects as king Vladislav II, inaugurating the Jagiellonian dynasty in Bohemia. Vladislav II also becomes the king of Hungary in 1490.
1526	Ludvík's death at the Battle of Mohács ends the Jagiellonian dynasty in Bohemia. The diet elects Ferdinand of Austria as the king of Bohemia; Ferdinand also becomes the king of Hungary. The Habsburgs essentially retain the two states until 1918.
1547	The first rebellion of the Bohemian Estates.
1556	The Jesuits arrive in Prague.
1561	The office of archbishop is renewed in Prague.
1579–1594	The Kralicka Bible becomes the first translation of the Bible into Czech.
1583	Rudolf II (1552–1612, reigned 1576–1611) moves the capital from Vienna to Prague.
1609	Rudolf II signs the Letter of Majesty.
1618	The defenestration of Prague (23 May); the start of the Thirty Years' War.
1619	The Bohemian Estates elect King Frederick of the Palatine, the Winter King, who reigns until 1620.
1620	The Battle of White Mountain (16 November).
1621	The leaders of the 1618–1620 rebellion are executed in Old Town Square.
1627	Ferdinand issues the Renewal Ordinance.
1634	Count Albrecht z Valdštejna (Wallenstein) is murdered.
1680	Leopold I issues the first *robota* patent after the 1679–1680 peasant uprising.
1740–1780	Reign of Maria Theresa.
1748	Austria recognizes the loss of Silesia (once a part of Bohemia) to Prussia.
1754	Prokop Diviš erects his first lightning rod.
1773	Maria Theresa bans the Jesuits.
1775	The first meteorological station in Prague at the Klementinum begins the oldest continuous detailed recording of weather in the world.
1780–1790	Reign of Joseph II.
1781	Joseph issues the toleration patent, which gave religious freedom to Orthodox, Calvinists, and Lutherans. In the same month, Joseph ends restrictions on Jews. Finally, he ends serfdom with the serfdom patent (later repealed).
1784	Joseph unites the four sections of Prague to form one urban center.
1789	Joseph issues his tax and urbarial patent (never enacted).
1804	Francis proclaims the Austrian Empire.
1805	The Battle of Slávkov, or the Battle of the Three Emperors.
1813	In August, the Fourth Coalition defeats Napoleon at the Battle of Přestanov and Chlumec.
1814	The first Czech museum opens in Opava, Silesia. The first museum in Moravia opens in 1817, and the National Museum opens in Prague in 1818.
1815	Josef Božek (1782–1835) builds the first steam engine.
1817	Václav Hanka claims to discover the forged manuscripts of Králův Dvůr and Zelená Hora.
1819	Clemens von Metternich presides over the conference of nine German states at Karlovy Vary that issues the Carlsbad Decrees.
1820	Metternich hosts the meeting of European leaders in Opava known as the Congress of Troppau.
1826	The first Czech opera, *Dráteník* (The Tinker), with music by František Škroup and the libretto by Josef Krasoslav Chmelenský, premiers.
1832	The first regular service on the Continent of a horse-drawn railroad

	begins from České Budějovice, Bohemia, to Linz, Austria.
1835–1839	Josef Jungmann publishes his *Czech-German Dictionary.*
1836	Karel Hynek Mácha publishes his epic poem *Máj* in April.
1836	In September Ferdinand (reigned since 1835) is crowned king of Bohemia, the last coronation to occur in Prague.
1836	In November, František Palacký releases the first volume of *A History of the Czech Nation in Bohemia and Moravia*. The last volume appears in 1865.
1837	Jan Evangelista Purkyně presented his cell theory at a conference of scientists.
1848	Beginning with the St. Václav Committee petition to the emperor on March 22, a liberal and national revolution occurs in Prague that was similar to revolutions that year throughout Europe.
1848	In April, Karel Havlíček Borovský begins publishing his newspaper *Národní noviny.*
1848	In Prague, as the Slav Congress is taking place in June, a revolt erupts. General Alfred Windischgrätz restores order after bombarding the city (June 17).
1848	The Imperial Parliament meets at Kroměříž.
1848	Ferdinand abdicates in Olomouc, and Franz Joseph takes the throne.
1849	In March Franz Joseph issues an *octroyed* constitution and abolishes serfdom.
1851–1859	The era of absolutism under interior minister and later prime minister Alexander Bach.
1860	Franz Joseph institutes decentralizing reforms through the October Diploma.
1861	Franz Joseph issues the February Patent, in which he centralizes the administration.
1862	Miroslav Tyrš and Jindřich Fügner establish the Sokol gymnastic movement.
1865	Johann Gregor Mendel publishes his article on genetics.
1866	*The Bartered Bride* of Bedřich Smetana premieres in May.
1866	On 3 July, the Prussians defeat the Austrians at the Battle of Sadová; the warring parties sign the Peace of Prague on 23 August 1866.
1867	The *Ausgleich* (Compromise) between Austria and Hungary creates Austria-Hungary or the Dual Monarchy of the Austrian Empire and the Kingdom of Hungary.
1868	On 16 May, the cornerstone is laid for the National Theater.
1869	Emil Škoda purchases the Wallenstein (Valdštejn) Factory in Plzeň, which becomes known as Škoda Plzeň.
1874	The Old Czechs and Young Czechs split, and the Young Czechs establish the National Liberal Party.
1878	The Social Democratic Party is established.
1879	The Czechs end their passive resistance and enter the Reichsrat to support the "Iron Ring" of Count Eduard Taaffe.
1882	The Prague University, officially the Charles-Ferdinand University (Karlo-Ferdinandova Univerzita), is divided into separate German and Czech universities.
1885	Construction begins on the National Museum, which is completed in 1890.
1887	Artists establish the Mánes Society for the Creative Arts.
1890	Franz Joseph creates the Czech Academy of Sciences.
1891	Prague prepared for the Jubilee Provincial Exhibition with the first electric tram, the opening of the Petřín Tower, and two funiculars (the one to Petřín operates today).
1891	In the July Reichsrat elections, the Young Czechs defeat the Old Czechs.
1894	Tomáš Bat'a opens his shoe manufacturing concern in Zlín.
1894	The Czech Philharmonic is founded and holds its first concert in 1896.
1894	The Christian Socialist Party is established in Moravia.
1897	Prime Minister Kazimir Badeni issues his language decree on April 5.
1898	The first convention of the Czech National Socialist party takes place in April.
1899	The Agrarian Party is established (renamed the Republican Party after World War I).
1900	Tomáš G. Masaryk begins the Realist Party.
1907	Elections to the Reichsrat take place under universal male suffrage.
1914	On 28 June, Gavrilo Princip assassinates Ferdinand d'Este and his wife; Austria-Hungary declares war on Serbia on 28 July.
1914	T. G. Masaryk leaves Austria-Hungary in November to create an independent Czech state.
1915	In March several Czech political leaders establish the Czech Mafia.
1916	Emperor Franz Joseph dies on 21 November. Karl becomes the new emperor.

1918	In the 6 January Epiphany Declaration, the major Czech parties in Austria call for Czech independence and Slovak self-determination.
1918	On 30 May, Czech and Slovak representatives sign the Pittsburgh Pact.
1918	The creation of the Czechoslovak First Republic takes place on 28 October (current national holiday). T. G. Masaryk becomes the first president.
1919	National Assembly approves the land reform.
1920	On 29 February, the National Assembly adopts the constitution.
1920	In May, the main German parties, including the German Social Democrats, German Christian Socialists, and Bund der Landwirte, enter the National Assembly.
1921	Communist Party holds its first convention.
1922	Antonín Švehla becomes the prime minister and holds the post three times, 1922–1925, 1925–1926, and 1926–1929.
1935	T. G. Masaryk resigns as president for health reasons in November, and Edvard Beneš becomes Czechoslovakia's second president (Beneš was officially elected in December).
1937	On 14 September, T. G. Masaryk dies at 87.
1938	In May Czechoslovakia partially mobilizes against Germany based on false news about German troop concentrations.
1938	The leaders of Germany, Italy, Britain, and France meet in Munich on 29 September and agree to give portions of Czechoslovakia to Germany.
1938	On 30 September, the Czechoslovak government accepts the Munich Diktat. The First Republic ceases to exist, and the Czechoslovak Second Republic emerges with Slovakia and Ruthenia as autonomous components.
1938	On 1 October, Czechoslovakia accepts a Polish ultimatum demanding border concessions. On the same day, Germany begins occupying the Sudetenland, a process it completed on 10 October.
1938	Beneš abdicates on 5 October and heads the Czechoslovak liberation movement from London when the war begins. E. Hácha replaces Beneš as president in November.
1939	Nazi Germany occupies the Czech Lands in March and incorporates them into Germany as the Protectorate of Bohemia and Moravia. Slovakia becomes independent. Hungary takes Ruthenia.
1942	Czech agents from Britain assassinate Reinhard Heydrich, the acting Reich protector of Bohemia and Moravia.
1944	The Slovak National Uprising begins on 29 August.
1945	On 2 April, E. Beneš arrives in Košice after having visited Moscow. On 5 April, the new Czechoslovak government announces its Košice Program.
1945	The Prague Uprising occurs on 5–8 May and Beneš returns to Prague on 11 May.
1948	Klement Gottwald leads the Communist Party in legally coming to power on 25 February and begins to establish a Stalinist totalitarian regime.
1948	On 10 March, Jan Masaryk is murdered.
1948	On 2 June, Beneš abdicates and dies in September. Gottwald becomes president.
1953	Antonín Zápotocký becomes president after death of Gottwald.
1957	Antonín Novotný becomes president.
1968	Alexander Dubček replaces Novotný as first secretary of the Communist Party, inaugurating the Prague Spring reform movement. Novotný abdicates in March and General Ludvík Svoboda becomes president.
1968	The Warsaw Pact invades Czechoslovakia on the night of 20–21 August.
1969	Czechoslovakia becomes a federated state on 1 January.
1969	Jan Palach ignites himself in front of the National Museum to protest the Warsaw Pact invasion in January and dies three days later.
1969	Gustav Husák replaces Dubček as the first secretary of the Communist Party.
1975	Husák becomes president after Svoboda abdicates.
1977	The dissident movement Charta 77 forms.
1989	The Velvet Revolution begins on 17 November, and by December it brings an end to Communist rule in Czechoslovakia.
1989	Husák resigns in December, and the dissident Václav Havel becomes president.
1992–1993	At midnight, Czechoslovakia divides peacefully, creating the Czech Republic and the Slovak Republic.
1993	Havel, who had resigned as president in protest of the division of Czechoslovakia,

	becomes president of the Czech Republic in January.
1998	The government of Václav Klaus of the Civic Democratic Party collapses, paving the way for a minority Social Democratic coalition government under Miloš Zeman.
1999	The Czech Republic enters NATO (the North Atlantic Treaty Organization).
2002	After elections in June, Vladimír Špidla leads the Social Democrats in forming a coalition government.
2003	Czech voters approve a referendum to join the European Union (EU).
2004	On 1 May, the Czech Republic enters the EU. In August the Social Democrat Śtanislav Gross replaces Špidla as prime minister.

SLOVAKIA

JUNE GRANATIR ALEXANDER

LAND AND PEOPLE

Slovakia, which is officially called the Slovak Republic, is located in the heartland of Europe. Five countries border this landlocked nation that has an area of 49,005 square kilometers, which is about equal to the combined size of the states of Vermont and New Hampshire. Poland lies to the north, Hungary to the south, Austria to the southwest, the Czech Republic to the west, and Ukraine to the east. Although a small country, Slovakia's topography varies widely. Its territory extends from lowlands in the south that are approximately 95 meters above sea level to a northern mountainous region with elevations reaching 2,655 meters. It is a mountainous country, but, in addition to rugged highlands, the area within Slovakia's boundaries includes valleys, plateaus, rolling hills, and low fertile plains. It also has dense forests and a wide variety of plants and animal life. Slovakia is a land of natural wonders and diverse peoples.

Mountains, which cover more than 40 percent of Slovakia, represent this small republic's most distinguishing physical feature. They run along its northern periphery, stretch into its central midsection, and flank both its eastern and western perimeters. Slovakia's numerous mountain ranges form part of the vast Carpathian Arc that cuts through Eastern Europe. Winding in crescent-shaped style, the Carpathian Mountains extend across northern Slovakia into western Ukraine and bend south into Romania. Slovakia's own mountains begin with the gentle slopes of the Malé Karpaty (Little Carpathians) in the southwest near Bratislava, the country's capital. As they move northeastward these steep hills, which are located completely within Slovakia's boundaries, become higher and merge into the Bielé Karpaty (White Carpathians), which Slovakia shares with the neighboring Czech Republic. This chain meets the Javorínky that, together with the Malá Fatra (Little Fatra) and Vel'ká Fatra (Big Fatra) ranges, start the eastward curve of the Carpathian Arc. The Vysoké Tatry (High Tatras), located in north central Slovakia, continue the arc across the country's northern region. To the south of the High Tatras lay two other parallel chains: the Nízke Tatry (Low Tatras) and the Slovenské Rudohorie (Slovak Ore Mountains). Separated by valleys, these chains take rugged mountain terrain deep into Slovakia's central region.

The country's elaborate network of mountains has endowed Slovakia with a picturesque natural landscape. The Little Carpathians, which have low elevations, are covered by broadleaf forests and, on the eastern side, with vineyards. The higher mountain ranges in northern and central Slovakia have a far more varied topography. The snowcapped High Tatras contain sharply pointed ridges and deep ravines. With altitudes reaching nearly 2,655 meters at Gerlachovský štít, these mountains are the highest in the entire Carpathian Arc. Ten to twelve thousand years ago melting glaciers flooded

The mountains of the High Tatras, Slovakia. (Liba Taylor/Corbis)

hollows and created deep mountain lakes. The individual lakes that resulted from this natural phenomenon merit a separate designation: "pleso." The Tatra's lakes can be as high as 1,346 meters above sea level; at 53 meters, Vel'ké Hincovo is the deepest pleso. Waterfalls, streams, and an abundant array of wildflowers enhance the mountains' natural beauty. Spectacular dense forests cover hills bordering the numerous valleys that carve north-south routes through the High Tatras. The heavily forested inclines, gorges, and meadows, which characterize the High Tatras, also exist in the Low Tatras to the south.

In addition to shaping its geography, Slovakia's mountains contain the headwaters of many rivers. The Danube flows into Slovakia from neighboring Austria, but several tributaries that feed into this important international waterway originate in the mountains. The sources of the numerous small branches that pour into these tributaries are in the highlands. Two rivers merge in the Tatras and form Slovakia's longest river, the Váh. Beginning in central Slovakia, this body of water, which is 403 kilometers long, runs east and then turns in a southwesterly direction. In addition to the Váh, several other rivers empty into the Danube Basin. Important rivers flowing into it include the Morava, Nitra, Hron, and Ipel'. In the east, the Ondava and Laborec rivers stream north to south and feed into the Bordog River, which continues southwest into Hungary; the Hornád also arcs east to south and across the same border. The Poprad River, in north central Slovakia, flows northward into Poland.

Besides major water arteries, tiny rivers and small streams criss-cross the entire country. Altogether, Slovakia has about 8,000 kilometers of waterways. In addition, small lakes, mineral springs, and natural spas dot the country. There are an estimated 1,200 mineral springs, but nearly all are located in mountainous regions. One count places the number of mountain spas in Slovakia at twenty-three. These are considered excellent places for curing ailments or recuperating from sicknesses or injuries. Using mountain spas for curative purposes as well as relaxation is a centuries-old tradition. According to some accounts, the Piešťany spa and its local mud have been restoring people's health for eight hundred years.

Mountains and water have shaped Slovakia's external terrain, but they have also contributed to the geological riches that lay beneath the earth's surface. Usually forged by running waters, the country has more than 2,000 subterranean caves. These underground caverns contain spectacular stalagmites and stalactites, cone-shaped hard-lime formations created by dripping water. The Belianska Cave in the Tatras is one of the most famous, but subsurface caverns are also located in the plateaus of southeastern Slovakia. Domica, which stretches into Hungary, is part of a cave system that is approximately 21,000 meters long. Caves in the region can reach depths of 123 meters. In addition to underground chambers with intricate hard-lime deposits, this area has ice caves where frozen formations are as thick as 26.5 meters.

Slovakia's underground treasures are covered by a botanically rich land. The climate, together with a varied terrain, has allowed a wide variety of plant life to develop. It has a moderate, continental climate with temperatures reaching about 26 Celsius (79 Fahrenheit) in the summer and 0 Celsius (32 Fahrenheit) in the winter. The more elevated mountainous areas are cooler. In the High Tatras winters can last two hundred days while spring is only two weeks long and the rest of the year is summer and autumn. Wildflowers thrive in the mountain regions that cover Slovakia. The High Tatras contain more than 1,300 kinds of flora. Flowers grow in the mountain meadows and marshes, but at least forty varieties of flowers exist in elevations that are thousands of feet above sea level. Berries and other bushes also dot the mountains. Botanists have identified approximately four hundred different plants in just one small basin of the Tatra mountains and more than 555 different flora in a nearby valley. The Tatras are not alone in providing an environment amenable to diverse vegetation. The Vel'ká Fatra chain hosts an array of unique flowers, and vineyards flourish on the eastern slopes of the Small Carpathians. The nonmountainous regions as well as fertile areas in Slovakia's southern lowlands boast the same vegetation and flowering plants, including an array of roses that are typical of nearby countries in East Central Europe.

Although the wildlife does not match the floral diversity of Slovakia, the undulating terrain and remote mountain areas provide suitable habitats for many animals. Brown bears, lynxes, wild cats, and wolves roam the dense mountain forests; marmots, martens, and chamois inhabit the higher elevations. The golden eagle soars above the High Tatras; the spotted eagle, falcon, grouse, and black stork dwell in mountain areas as well. Wild swine and deer rove the lower regions. Buzzards are common in the lowlands, especially in the southwest. Rabbits, squirrels, fox, and small fowl dwell in the land as well. Slovakia also has the typical variety of farm animals and poultry.

The physical features, which make Slovakia so picturesque and geologically rich, have obviously also influenced its economic and cultural development. Besides enhancing the country's scenic beauty, mountains contained raw materials that stimulated mining early in Slovakia's history. By at least the thirteenth century, mines were yielding copper, gold, and silver. In the fourteenth century a mint located in Kremnica was producing gold coins for royal courts in Europe. In the modern day, Slovakia has only small stores of iron ore, copper, and magnesium; as a result, lignite (brown coal) is now the most commonly mined material. In the early twenty-first century the mountains' most significant impact on the economy is to stimulate tourism. The forests in Slovakia's middle and high elevations also continue, as they have historically, to provide timber. Grains and other commodities are grown on the hillsides as well as in the country's fertile low-lying areas.

Despite early mining undertakings, Slovakia remained a rural, agricultural country; nevertheless, mining had a far-reaching demographic impact. Centuries ago, when mining was more varied and robust, most of the profits went to foreign entrepreneurs or bankers, not to the persons who worked the mines. The "industry," though, encouraged a German migration into the region. The immigrants established villages along rivers and streams that trickled through the mountains. Small Slovak settlements also clustered near rivers and waterways in the valleys that separated central Slovakia's three parallel ranges. In addition, mining gave rise to towns that managed to survive well after that industry declined. For Kremnica, it left a lasting legacy. This town maintains one of the oldest mints in Europe, and when Slovakia became independent in 1993, the Kremnica mint produced the new republic's first coins.

Mining, of course, was not the only economic force influencing early demographic patterns. Slovakia is a country with a long rural tradition. In a self-sufficient agricultural economy where most Slovaks tilled the land, villages naturally developed along waterways. Towns subsequently emerged along the river banks. Hungarians established numerous farming villages in the fertile lowlands. As a result of this early pattern, Hungarians in Slovakia to this day have remained in the plains along the country's southern border.

In 1991 official figures placed Slovakia's a population at 5,289,608 people. Since that year, there has been no census but official estimates put the total number of persons at slightly over 5.4 million. Although the country is ethnically diverse, Slovaks make up the overwhelming majority and account for more than 4.5 million (85.6 percent) of the inhabitants. They are the descendants of Slavic peoples who began migrating into the Carpathian Basin probably in the very late fifth century. With a population of approximately 578,500, Hungarians make up the country's largest minority and account for nearly 10.8 percent of the total populace. In the 1991 census, slightly over 80,600 persons (approximately 1.5 percent of the population) described themselves as Roma, a more acceptable English designation than the term "Gypsies." However some estimates place the Romany total as high as 253,000. The remaining population consists of Czechs with approximately 65,200 (1 percent) and Ruthenian-Ukrainians with nearly 39,000 (0.7 percent). Germans, Poles, Jews, and Croats account for the small remaining percentage. The country's ethnic groups are distributed throughout the country. Even Hungarians, who are more concentrated than most, can be found in locales north of the southern border region. The majority of the country's tiny Jewish population resides in two cities, Bratislava and Košice, but some also live in other large and medium-size towns. The official language is Slovak and the second most common language is Hungarian.

Slovakia is also a religiously diverse country. According to official estimates, 60.3 percent of the inhabitants are Roman Catholic and 7.8 percent are Protestant. Accounting for approximately 6.2 percent of the adherents, Lutherans constitute the country's largest Protestant denomination; most ethnic Hungarians belong to the Reformed Church. Other faiths (totaling 4 percent of the population) include Judaism,

The Slovak Language

Although similar to other Slavic languages, especially Czech, Slovak is linguistically distinct, with its own grammar and vocabulary. Spoken Slovak has three dialects (western, central, and eastern) that roughly correspond with large geographical areas in Slovakia. Slovak, like other Slavic languages, has diacritical marks that govern the pronunciation of both consonants and vowels. In Slovak, the accent is on the first syllable. Slovak is a highly inflected language, which means words have different endings. For example, noun and adjective endings change to indicate gender, number, and case; verb endings also reflect gender and number as well as tense and mood.

The roots of the Slovak language predate the introduction of Christianity into the Slavic lands in the ninth century, but for centuries Slovak was not a written language. In the late eighteenth century Anton Bernolák made the first significant attempt to establish a Slovak literary language. By turning the western dialect into a written language, he developed what became known as *bernolákovčina.* Bernolák's codified version of the Slovak language received its most significant support from the Slovak Learned Society. Founded in 1792 in Trnava and consisting primarily of Catholic clergymen, the society printed Catholic literature in bernolákovčina and disseminated it throughout Upper Hungary. Although short-lived, the society was instrumental in spreading bernolákovčina among Upper Hungary's educated Slovak Catholic clergymen. It was also adopted by Catholic primary schools in the region.

Slovak Protestants did not accept bernolákovčina. In 1803 Lutherans founded the Lutheran Lyceum (gymnasium) in Bratislava, which was committed to the study of Bibličtina, the Czech-language translation of the Bible. Bibličtina was the liturgical language of Slovak Lutheranism. The first serious challenge to bernolákočina came in the 1820s when two Lutherans, poet Ján Kollár, supported by scholar Pavol Šafárik, asserted that Slovaks and Czechs belonged to the same nation. In 1825 Kollár published a reader, *Čítanka,* which introduced Czechoslovak: a literary language that combined Slovak and Czech. Initially this blended version of the Czech and Slovak tongues enjoyed the enthusiastic support of the Lutheran clergy. By the late 1830s, however, some Lutherans who had embraced a "Czechoslovak" language developed serious misgivings. Opposed to the Hungarian government's Magyarization policy, which tried to eliminate ethnic groups by assimilating them into Hungarian culture, they decided to undermine the policy by establishing a more distinct Slovak literary language than bernolákovčina. L'udovít Štúr, a Lutheran clergyman and Slovak nationalist, codified the central Slovak dialect. This alternate version, known as *štúrovčina,* was announced in 1846. Five years later, following negotiations between supporters of bernolákovčina and Štúr's alternative, a modified version of štúrovčina was adopted as the Slovak literary language. In 1852 Martin Hattala, a Catholic and former Bernákolite, published this version in *Krátka mluvnica slovenská* (A Concise Slovak Grammar).

The central dialect, as codified by Štúr, remained the standard spoken and written Slovak. In modern-day Slovakia, the central dialect is employed for all literary, commercial, and official purposes. It is also used for public speaking and radio and television. In the twenty-first century, Slovaks continue to speak in their regional dialects, but the rise of mass communications and an educational system that teaches standard Slovak suggest that regional dialects are destined to fade.

Greek Catholic, and Orthodox. More than one-fourth of the population does not have an identifiable religious affiliation (18.2 percent) or is described as not having one (9.7 percent).

During the last part of the twentieth century, Slovakia's inhabitants increasingly gravitated to urban areas. With a population of slightly over 452,000 inhabitants, Bratislava is the largest city. Košice, located in southeastern Slovakia, has about 240,000 residents and ranks as the country's second largest metropolis. Other major cities with populations over 50,000 include Prešov, Banská Bystrica, Žilina, Nitra, Trnava, Martin, Trenčín, and Poprad.

The migration to the cities reflects the varied nature of Slovakia's workforce. According to estimates for the year 2000, about 45.6 percent of the 3.3 million persons in the labor force are employed in "services." The remaining workers are divided into the following categories: 29.3 percent in industries; 8.9 percent in agriculture; 8 percent in construction; and 8.2 percent in transport and communications.

The ethnic diversity of Slovakia is further enhanced by regional variations. The Slovak language has three distinct dialects: western, central, and eastern. These speech differences are indicative of geographic differences that characterize the general Slovak population. Slovaks have traditionally identified themselves by the region where they grew up. Persons living in different areas established their own folk customs. Folk handicrafts, music, and cuisine reflect regional variations characteristic of Slovak culture. The individual regions also developed their own distinct folk costumes. Even as Slovaks assert their distinct national identity, a sense of regional identity persists to this day.

When Slovakia became an independent nation in 1993, it adopted four national symbols. The constitution both mandates and describes the country's coat of arms, national seal, flag, and national anthem. The coat of arms is a red Gothic shield with a silver double-barred cross situated in the center of three blue mountain peaks. Known as the Cross of Lorraine, one of the cross's two horizontal bars is longer than the other. According to tradition, the Cross of Lorraine was used by Cyril and Methodius, the two missionaries who brought Christianity to the Slavic peoples in the mid-ninth century. The hills supposedly represent the three mountain ranges historically identified with the Slovak people: High Tatras, Low Tatras, and the Small Fatra. In the nineteenth century this emblem was the seal of the Matica slovenská, a nationalist institution devoted to promoting Slovak culture and national identity.

The coat of arms composes part of the Slovak flag. On the left side of the flag, this national crest is superimposed on three horizontal white, blue, and red stripes. Neither the colors of the coat of arms nor the three bands have any official symbolism.

The national seal is the coat of arms with the inscription "Slovenská Republika" (Slovak Republic) encircling it. "Slovenská Republika" is on the seal because that is the country's official name in the Slovak language. In Slovakia the country is popularly called "Slovensko." The national anthem, "Nad Tatrou sa blýska" (Lightning Flashes over the Tatra Mountains), was composed in the early nineteenth century. It is a symbolic melody reflecting the hopes of nineteenth-century nationalists that Slovaks would "come alive" as a people. The author, Janko Matúška, set his verses to the melody of an old Slovak folk song. Initially circulated in handwritten form, the hymn was reportedly first printed in 1848. In 1993 the newly independent Slovak Republic adopted the first two stanzas as its anthem.

HISTORY

The history of modern-day Slovakia reaches back to the late fifth century, when Slavic tribes moved into the region south of the Carpathian Mountains. The precise geographic origins of these tribes are uncertain, but archeological evidence indicates that they came from areas northeast of the Carpathian Mountains. During a gradual migration, which lasted into the seventh century, Slavic peoples moved into

Bratislava Castle looms on a hilltop overlooking Slovakia's capital city of Bratislava, situated on the shores of the Danube River. (Adam Woolfitt/Corbis)

the Middle Danube Basin. Although they established villages and developed an agricultural economy, there is no evidence that the tribes created anything that resembled a political state.

In the sixth century the Avars, a nomadic people probably from Central Asia, invaded the Danube region. By the end of the century, they had established a vast dominion that, together with other territory south of the Danube River, included the southern portion of modern-day Slovakia. Besides subjugating peoples in their empire, the Avars looted and terrorized nearby areas. In the 620s, under the leadership of Samo, a Frankish merchant, several Slavic tribes united to resist Avar rule. Samo's empire, which was centered in Moravia and stretched eastward into central Slovakia, quickly disintegrated after his death in 658.

In 796 the Franks—a Germanic people from the west—defeated the Avars and effectively ended their domination of Central Europe. Fearful of the Frankish Empire's eastward expansion, Mojmír, a Moravian chief, had organized a Moravian state by 830. Meanwhile, another Slavic principality, Nitra, had developed in the west. Although its history is shrouded in obscurity, tradition holds that Nitra came into existence in the early ninth century. Prince Pribina built his castle at Nitra where he also erected a church that, when consecrated in 828 by the archbishop of Salzburg, became the first Christian church in the Slavic world. In 833 Mojmír defeated Pribina and annexed his lands. The merger of the Principality of Nitra and the Moravian state created the Great Moravian Empire.

Mojmír was subsequently deposed but, under his successors, Rastislav (846–869) and Svätopluk (870–894), Great Moravia expanded. The precise boundaries of this empire are not known. When it reached its height during the reign of Svätopluk, however, it included Moravia, Bohemia, southern Poland, northwestern Hungary, and most of modern-day Slovakia. Although the boundaries of the Great Moravian Empire fluctuated and the political organization was loose, it was one of history's first stable Slavic states.

The Great Moravian Empire was also important because, during its existence, Slavs were converted to Christianity. In the early ninth century Rastislav appealed to Byzantium's emperor, Michael III, to provide missionaries who could proselytize among the Slavs in their own languages. In 863 the emperor sent two brothers, Constantine and Methodius—known to history as the "apostles of the Slavs." Constantine, who later assumed the name Cyril, formulated an alphabet for the Slavic language. With this alphabet Cyril and Methodius translated Scripture and liturgical books from Greek into Church Slavonic. Preaching in local vernaculars, these missionaries successfully converted Slavs to Byzantine Christianity. In 880 a papal Bull sanctioned the Slavic liturgy and invested Methodius as archbishop of Moravia. After Methodius died in 885, however, Pope Stephen V reversed his predecessor's policy and banned the use of the Slavic liturgy. As a result, during the 890s the Latin liturgy began displacing Church Slavonic in the Great Moravian Empire.

Svätopluk, the powerful ruler of the Great Moravian Empire, died in 894. Squabbles between his sons, Mojmír II and Svätopluk II, subsequently threw the empire into disarray, but it was an outside invasion that finally doomed it. In the early tenth century, Magyars, a seminomadic people from the northeast, began invading the Great Moravian Empire's southern frontier. The incursions continued until 906 when the Magyars—later known as Hungarians—defeated and killed Prince Mojmír II. Following this defeat, the empire ceased to exist and modern-day Slovakia came under Magyar control. For the next thousand years, Slovak and Hungarian history would be intertwined.

Although its Slavic composition meant that the northern region where Slovaks lived was a culturally distinct area, the Magyars did not treat it as a separate political entity. Stephen (997–1038), who was crowned as Hungary's first king in the year 1000, however, instituted an administrative system that had long-term impacts on Slovakia and its inhabitants. To govern his kingdom, Stephen developed a county system that divided the realm into geographical regions, each governed by an *ispán* (administrator) appointed by the king. As the county system subsequently developed, Magyars, appointed by the king, usually administered northern Hungary where Slovaks lived. Lesser county officials and assemblymen were also typically Magyars.

During the first two centuries following the Magyar takeover, it seems that Slovaks remained a settled people, staying in already established communities. New settlements sprang up near existing ones. In the era spanning the twelfth into the fourteenth centuries, however, some Slovaks migrated from the Danube Basin north to the uninhabited mountainous regions of central and eastern Slovakia. Regardless of where they lived, most Slovaks engaged in agriculture. As Hungary developed a feudal system, the majority of Slovaks were reduced to serfs and subjected to the restraints and limited opportunities that characterized feudal societies. Under this system serfs provided compulsory labor, paid taxes, and performed military service but had no political rights. In the thirteenth century only a few serfs were permanently bound to a master. Most were farmers working on settlements, who, once they had satisfied all their obligations, were free to move. After the mid-fifteenth and into the sixteenth century, however, their freedom of movement greatly declined as Hungarian laws expanded the serfs' obligations and restricted their mobility.

Social and economic conditions in Slovakia were further complicated by the arrival of German colonists, a movement that got under way in the thirteenth century. After a brutal, but short, invasion by Mongols in 1241, Hungary's kings welcomed the migration of Germans into its northern district. These immigrant settlements acted as buffers against future aggression into the sparsely inhabited regions of Slovakia. Foreign settlers also helped repopulate areas that had been devastated by the invasions. In addition, Germans brought skills and commercial expertise to the region. Seeking to encourage this migration and also to create a burgher (urban) class beholden to the Crown, Hungary's monarchs granted special privileges to German colonists and exempted them from control by county officials. Germans also moved into Slovakia's mining regions where they settled in towns and developed the mining industry. Concentrated in commercial and mining areas, German towns evolved into enclaves governed by special laws.

The German influx had multiple impacts on Slovaks. Although only Germans could own municipal lands, the rise of commercial towns probably offered opportunities for some Slovak craftsmen. According to some estimates, though, by the fifteenth century perhaps 80 percent of Slovaks were peasants who belonged to the serf class. In the main, therefore, the general Slovak population enjoyed few rights, while Germans had special privileges.

Strife in kingdoms elsewhere brought other peoples, who would have a far-reaching impact on Slovak society, to the region. The religious turmoil that gripped the Kingdom of Bohemia in the fifteenth century spilled over into northern Hungary. The Hussite Wars, which broke out after the execution in 1415 of Jan Hus, the antipapal reformer, spread into Slovakia. In the early 1440s, under the leadership of Jiskra of Brandys, a Czech noble, Hussite armies advanced into the region. For nearly twenty years, Jiskra controlled territory stretching from Nitra in the west to Košice in the east. Also, during the religious wars in Bohemia, Czech Hussite refugees fled to Slovakia where many stayed permanently.

The Protestant Reformation of the sixteenth century had a more profound impact on Slovakia than its Hussite precursor had had. Lutheranism reached Slovakia through its German towns and quickly spread to the Slovak populace. Starting as an urban phenomenon and embraced by the gentry, by midcentury Lutheranism was attracting the Slovak peasantry. At the same time that the Reformation was gaining momentum, the Kingdom of Hungary was facing challenges from the Ottoman Empire located to its south. The Ottoman Turks invaded the kingdom and inflicted a crushing defeat on Hungarian forces at Mohács in 1526. As a result, a large section of the kingdom was lost to the Turks. Hungary's original territory was ultimately divided into three geographic regions with Slovakia comprising most of the western section. In 1547, following a peace settlement with the Turkish sultan, Ferdinand I, who belonged to the Habsburg dynasty, was recognized as king of a northwestern region that included most of modern-day Slovakia. This territory became known as Royal Hungary. From the mid-1540s onward, Slovakia remained part of Hungary but, because it became part of the Habsburg Empire, the region was affected by the policies both of its Magyar overlords and the imperial government in Vienna.

What would become modern-day Slovakia enjoyed an unprecedented importance in Royal Hungary. With the southern half of the ancient Hungarian kingdom under Turkish domination and Royal Hungary pushed north of the Danube River, Slovakia became the economic, political, cultural, and religious center of the state. In 1536 Bratislava, which was called Pozsony in Hungarian, was made Hungary's capital. The principal government offices were transferred to that city, and the Hungarian diet usually met there. Bratislava was designated as the coronation city, meaning the place where Hungary's royal rulers were crowned. Fleeing the Turks, in 1543 the archbishop of Esztergom escaped to Trnava, a town just northwest of Bratislava. Slovakia thus became the kingdom's religious headquarters.

As a result of the Turkish invasion, Slovakia was inundated with nobles seeking refuge. In one respect this migration benefited Slovaks. The influx of lesser nobility into the towns ushered in an attack on the special privileges German inhabitants traditionally possessed. Nobles were also granted permisson to buy property in commercial and mining towns. This chipping away at German advantages continued into the 1600s.

Political gains, which benefited non-German townsmen, did not offset the detrimental effects that the influx of nobles and also constant warfare had on Slovakia's inhabitants. For example, nobles gained control of butchering trades and the sale of alcoholic products, benefits that allowed them to exploit Slovak peasants. Land grants to the displaced nobility, together with the enlargement of existing manors, reduced the available fertile land and thus further squeezed the peasantry. The war had an especially adverse impact on towns. In addition to paying heavy taxes to maintain royal troops, towns bore the burden of their own defense. Inflation caused by war devastated townsmen and especially the miners in central Slovakia. Discontent among miners occasionally flared into rebellion. The economic hardships inflicted on towns and miners were exacerbated by the nobles' demand that the monarchy respect their traditional privileges, including exemption from taxation. So, in a kingdom significantly reduced, after the 1540s much of Royal Hungary's operation and defense costs fell to Slovakia's inhabitants. Proximity to the Turks made life in the border regions even more difficult. Between 1552 and 1575, the Turks made northward advances and seized additional territory near Slovakia's mining region. By threatening to plunder, the Turks also exacted tribute from districts along the frontier that were close to but not within their domain.

The Turkish occupation of Hungary ended in 1699. In the Peace of Karlowitz, which ended the long invasion, the Ottoman sultan ceded nearly all his Hungarian possessions to the Habsburgs. For small segments of the Slovak populace, the era of Royal Hungary had brought an improvement in their situation. Removing the German grip on commercial and mining towns encouraged the emergence of a Slovak burgher class. As a reward for military service against the Turks, some Slovaks also entered the ranks of the lesser nobility. The situation of the peasantry, however, deteriorated during the nearly one hundred fifty year interlude.

The Protestant Reformation, which was getting under way when the Turks invaded Hungary, continued even amid warfare against the Ottoman Empire. As the Reformation spread across the land, Lutheranism attracted scores of Slovaks while Magyars turned to the Reformed Church. By some estimates, in the early 1600s Protestants in Royal Hungary outnumbered Catholics by a ratio of four to one. These spectacular successes roused both the clergy and secular rulers loyal to the pope in Rome to action and sparked the Counter-Reformation. This counteraction, which aimed to halt the Reformation and reverse Protestant gains, started sluggishly and progressed more slowly in Hungary than in western regions under Habsburg control. Attempts at "re-Catholicization" were initiated as early as 1604, but

Bratislava Castle

Magnificent castles dot the landscape throughout Slovakia. Even in ruins, these massive fortifications are evidence of Slovakia's feudal history as well as the fact that warfare was an intrinsic part of the nation's past. Although not as impressive as several of the country's other old fortresses, Bratislava Castle is one of Slovakia's most important historical landmarks. Sitting high above the Danube River and towering over the capital city, this massive structure is known simply as *hrad*—"the castle."

The history of Bratislava Castle stretches back more than a thousand years. The first known reference to a castle in present-day Bratislava was made in a document dated 907 referring to a battle near a castle. It is therefore likely that a structure existed, or was under construction on the site, by the end of the ninth century. The castle was probably one reason why, in the eleventh century, King Stephen designated Bratislava, which was then called Pressburg, as the administrative center for the district. The hrad became the district's chief castle.

In the early thirteenth century major construction turned Bratislava Castle into a well-fortified edifice. In 1427, efforts got under way to fortify it even more. When the Ottoman Turks defeated Hungarian forces in 1526, the government was moved to Bratislava, which became the capital of Royal Hungary. The castle became the royal residence and again underwent renovations, both to strengthen its fortifications and to make it a dwelling suitable for royalty. The formidable hrad kept the Turkish invaders from advancing across the Danube River and into Bratislava. After the Turks were expelled from Hungary and the capital was returned to Budapest, the need for an armed fortress in Bratislava diminished. Empress Maria Theresa, who was especially fond of Bratislava and spent much time in the city, ordered yet another major renovation of the castle in the 1750s. The hrad became a lavish imperial residence. Bratislava did not appeal to Maria Theresa's successors, who thus did not use the hrad as a residence. Neglected, Bratislava Castle deteriorated and in 1811 was severely damaged by fire. The structure was left standing and continued deteriorating until the 1950s, when a major refurbishing was launched. Bratislava Castle was designated a national historical monument and reopened to the public in the late 1960s as a museum.

Although it has changed over time, a castle has existed on the hill overlooking the Danube River for nearly as long as Slovaks have inhabited modern-day Slovakia. Therefore, though the hrad is engraved on Bratislava's city seal, it is more than a local landmark and emblem; it has become a national symbol. Contemporary images and historical sketches of Bratislava Castle are among the most commonly reproduced pictures in items dealing with Slovakia. This massive square structure with a pointed tower on each of its corners has appeared in nearly every possible kind of printed literature. The images can be found in materials produced in Slovakia as well as in those generated outside the country.

zealous efforts to force the population into the church controlled by the papacy did not get under way until after 1616. The Counter-Reformation, which went on throughout the seventeenth century, was not as complete in the Kingdom of Hungary as elsewhere. By the beginning of the eighteenth century, about 20 percent of northern Hungary's population remained Protestant. Lutherans constituted the majority of the Slovak non-Catholics.

Efforts to force allegiance to the papacy met opposition from Magyar nobles who had embraced Protestantism. Consequently, in addition to battling the Turks, during the seventeenth century, religious conflicts, civil wars, and insurrections racked the kingdom. This strife, which often included bloodshed and the ravaging of villages as well as towns, made life miserable for Slovakia's inhabitants. Peasants and townspeople alike suffered. They endured this situation until 1711, when the era of religious and civil wars finally came to an end.

The Reformation and Counter-Reformation had a lasting cultural impact that went beyond making Slovaks a religiously diverse people. Slovak Protestants adopted the Kralická Bible (Kralice Bible) published in Czech (1579–1593), and consequently Czech became their liturgical language. It subsequently became the language of correspondence for an educated Protestant intelligentsia that survived the Counter-Reformation. Efforts to suppress Protestantism also led to the establishment of two universities: Trnava (1635) and Košice (1657). Jesuits controlled both institutions and both aimed to produce an educated Catholic clergy. The Reformation and Counter-Reformation, therefore, stimulated the emergence of a Slovak intelligentsia dominated by Protestants and Catholic clergymen. This intelligentsia led the Slovak national awakening, an attempt launched in the early nineteenth century to create a sense of themselves as a people among Hungary's Slovak subjects.

Although most Slovaks lived in a rather well-defined region, which became known as Upper Hungary, they did not acquire a national consciousness as a distinct people, or "nation." Instead, during the first nine centuries under Magyar

The Jánošík Legend

Often called the "Slovak Robin Hood," Juraj Jánošík is both a historical figure and a folk hero. Jánošík was born in 1688 in Terchová, located in the northwestern county of Trenčin. His parents were peasants, and during his youth Juraj helped work their land, which was part of a feudal estate. In 1711 Jánošík became leader of a band of outlaws who robbed wealthy individuals and distributed loot among the local poor. For slightly more than a year, he and his fellow bandits targeted officials, members of the nobility, landowners, wealthy townspeople, and merchants in the north-central region of Slovakia. The gang also carried out similar activities in southern Poland and Moravia. In 1712 Hungarian authorities captured Jánošík, but he managed to escape from the prison where he was being held. In early 1713 he was caught again. This time, he was tried by a tribunal in Liptovský Svätý Mikuláš and condemned to death. On 18 March 1713, he was executed in a particularly gruesome hanging.

Jánošík quickly became a legend in the regions where his gang had operated. He was the subject of local folk tales and ballads glorifying him as a hero, a defender of the poor and oppressed. The theme—taking from the wealthy to help the poor—appeared in eighteenth-century Slovak poems. During the Slovak national awakening of the early to mid-nineteenth century and the romantic literary era that accompanied it, the Jánošík legend was further developed. Seeking to stir pride in the Slovak people and enhance their identity as a separate people, romantic poets, in particular, made Jánošík a hero of their writings. Drawing on the existing folk literature, poets memorialized Jánošík and clothed both his life and his death with symbolism. They portrayed the eighteenth-century bandit as a defender of freedom, a seeker of social justice, and a hero of oppressed Slovaks. Poems described magical powers and daring exploits. In the face of seemingly insurmountable odds, he outwitted enemies and escaped pursuers. There was a ladylove, as well as a wicked old woman, who contributed to his final capture.

The Jánošík legend persisted into the twentieth century. An opera and four films about this legendary figure were produced. He continued to symbolize what was considered the historical struggle for freedom and social justice by the Slovak people. Because it suited the ideology of class warfare, the Jánošík legend even found favor during the communist era. From this perspective, Jánošík symbolized the historical struggle of the oppressed Slovak working classes.

Over the past three centuries, Jánošík has been the subject of nearly every possible type of Slovak literary and art form, and the Jánošík legend retains vitality in the modern world. In 1996 Slovakia issued a postage stamp commemorating a 1936 film produced in Czechoslovakia about the legendary hero. Scholarly accounts have separated fact from fiction, and critics have even pointed to the adverse effects of lawlessness on eighteenth-century Slovak society, but the facts are unlikely to tarnish the Jánošík legend or debase the heroic image of the Slovak Robin Hood.

control, Slovak inhabitants typically identified themselves as "Slavs" or "Slavs of Hungary." They did develop a folk culture characterized by regional variations, and they spoke dialects of a common language. At the end of the eighteenth century, this common tongue became the basis for generating a Slovak national awakening, at least among the educated segments of the population.

Religious motives actually stimulated a nationalist impulse in the late 1780s. Anton Bernolák, a Jesuit priest with close ties to Trnava, the ecclesiastical center of Roman Catholicism in Upper Hungary, aimed to promote Catholicism by developing a uniform language to advance the religious education of the masses. Named after him, this version of a literary language was called *bernolákovčina*. Although acceptance of bernolákovčina was limited to the Catholic clergy and an intellectual elite, Bernolák paved the way for the emergence of a Slovak national consciousness.

Despite the early efforts by Catholics, the Slovak awakening that gained momentum in the nineteenth century was spirited primarily by Slovak Lutherans. Initially, Slovak Protestants shunned efforts to standardize the Slovak language. They were committed to Bibličtina, which was Czech and the liturgical language of the Lutheran Church. During the early nineteenth century, however, the Hungarian government developed a policy that turned Lutherans into Slovak nationalists and caused them to change their minds about developing a literary language. Known as Magyarization, it had as its objective the assimilation of non-Magyar nationalities, especially by eliminating minority languages. The government's ultimate aim was to transform Hungary into an ethnically homogeneous state. As the government accelerated its Magyarization program, Protestant intelligentsia became increasingly convinced that Slovaks had to choose between assimilating and thus becoming "Magyars" or asserting a separate, clearly distinctive, language and culture. Concerns heightened in 1840 when Magyar linguistic and cultural nationalism directly threatened the integrity of the Lutheran Church. In that year the church's inspector general attempted to make Magyar the denomination's administrative language. Clergymen openly opposed the policy. Ultimately, three nationalist leaders emerged from this resistance to the Magyarization of the Lutheran Church: L'udovít Štúr, a young professor at the Lutheran Lyceum in Bratislava; and two Lutheran pastors, Jozef Hurban and Michal Miloslav Hodža.

L'udovít Štúr's opposition to the Magyarization of the Lutheran Church convinced him that Slovaks needed a unified language to ensure their cultural survival. In 1843 he and a group of clergymen agreed to establish a Slovak literary language based on the central Slovak dialect. In the late 1840s, however, turbulent events in Hungary caused the Slovak awakening to progress from a linguistic to a political movement. Throughout the 1840s, tensions had existed between the imperial government in Vienna and Hungarian nationalists in Budapest. These reached a high point in 1848–1849 when, as Europe was embroiled in revolutions, Hungary declared its independence and the imperial government temporarily lost control of the kingdom. It was finally returned to imperial control in August 1849. During the interim before Hungary was subdued, the Hungarian diet adopted measures designed to turn the Kingdom into a purely Magyar state.

In response to the stepped-up nationalist fervor in Hungary, about thirty Slovaks met at Liptovský Svätý Mikulaš on 11 May 1848 and drafted the Demands of the Slovak Nation. The petition, which contained fourteen specific points, essentially asked that Upper Hungary be allowed to have its own legislative body (diet), language, and educational system. This was the first attempt to have the region inhabited primarily by Slovaks recognized as a separate political unit.

The Hungarian diet rejected the petition and issued warrants for the arrests of Štúr, Hurban, and Hodža. In September 1848 these three men organized the Slovak National Council. This political organization took on a military function on 19 September, when it declared Slovakia independent from the rest of Hungary and launched a military expedition of perhaps six hundred volunteers. They planned to engage Hungarian forces and simultaneously foment a popular revolt. The general Slovak uprising did not materialize. During this minor upheaval, Hungarian officials took swift action against persons suspected of being Slovak nationalists or Panslavs, a term used to describe persons who advocated "Slavic" unity and cooperation among all Europe's Slavic nationalities. To intimidate the people, gibbets were erected in western villages along the Váh River. According to published reports, 168 persons were executed in these "Kossuth gallows," nicknamed for Lajos Kossuth, the Magyar nationalist, who was Hungary's de facto ruler during Hungary's temporary independence.

In their quest to obtain recognition for Upper Hungary, Slovak nationalists turned directly to Emperor Franz Joseph. In March 1849 a delegation gave him a petition requesting that Slovakia be elevated to a separate crown land within the Habsburg Empire and, therefore, be removed from Hungarian dominance. Under this system, the imperial government in Vienna would directly govern Upper Hungary. At the time, the emperor was noncommittal in his response, but subsequent events worked against the Slovak plea. A few weeks later, Hungary formally declared its independence from the empire; the Vienna government launched a massive countereffort and in August 1849 defeated the Hungarians.

L'udovít Štúr, codifier of the Slovak language, politician, and leader of the Slovak national awakening. (Courtesy of June Alexander)

Following the suppression of the Hungarian revolt, Franz Joseph nullified Hungary's constitution and imposed military rule. In this restructured Hungary, Slovakia was divided into two administrative regions and governed by a bureaucracy. In the Slovak counties, the Slovak language could be used for official local business and in primary schools. From the perspective of Slovak nationalists, these were only minor gains. Encountering suspicion and antagonism from the government in Vienna, during the 1850s, the Slovak nationalist movement waned; its disenchanted leader, L'udovít Štúr, died in 1856.

By the early 1860s, the political situation in Hungary was again changing. In the 1860s, as defeats in foreign wars were undermining Emperor Franz Joseph's rule, Magyar leaders had cause to hope that Hungary might achieve equality with Austria. A resurgence of Hungarian nationalism helped inject new life into Slovak nationalist sentiments. This was evident in a Slovak assembly that took place on 6–7 June 1861 in Turcianský Svätý Martin and drew Protestant and Catholic clergy as well as members of Slovakia's professional classes. A crowd of more than 5,000 persons gathered and hammered out the "Memorandum of the Slovak Nation." The document outlined a moderate political program for Slovakia's future in the Habsburg Empire. Clearly not as radical as the 1848 "Demands," the memorandum stated that Slovakia should remain an integral part of Hungary and called for autonomy but without a separate diet. It requested proportional representation for Slovaks and other nationalities in the Hungarian diet. It sought expanded use of the Slovak language in local government and in the region's educational system. In addition, it asked for the creation of a Slovak Academy of Law in Slovakia and the endowment of a Chair of Slovak Language and Literature at the University of Budapest. Finally, it solicited permission to found Slovak literary and cultural associations in Upper Hungary.

The Hungarian diet rejected the "Memorandum," and consequently, in December 1861, a Slovak delegation appealed directly to Emperor Franz Joseph. The emperor was noncommittal in his response. Nevertheless, through a series of actions taken during the next two years, in a limited way, he granted some of their demands. Franz Joseph refused to recognize Slovakia as a separate political entity and did not reorganize the Hungarian diet to give Slovaks proportional representation, but he did appoint several Slovaks to administrative positions in Hungary. He also authorized the founding of gymnasia (secondary schools). As a result, by 1867 Slovakia had three gymnasia: Lutherans founded two in 1862 and Catholics created the third in 1867. Moreover, in the summer 1863 Slovaks received imperial permission and a donation of 1,000 florin from the emperor to establish the Matica slovenská, a cultural-literary society. Located in Turciansk Sv Martin, the Matica, which published folklore, poetry, and historical materials, became not only the literary center but the seat of political education in northern Hungary. The Slovak National Party, which was organized in the early 1870s, maintained its headquarters in Martin.

Soon, however, the situation in Hungary would change. By 1865, Emperor Franz Joseph's weakened political position was forcing him to loosen his control and make concessions to Hungary. Moves toward restoring Hungary's constitution jeopardized Slovak gains. Slovak officials, who had been appointed by the emperor, were dismissed; in 1865 no Slovak candidates won seats in the restored Hungarian diet. The major setback occurred in the Compromise of 1867. Also known as the *Ausgleich,* this agreement created the Dual Monarchy of Austria-Hungary and granted Hungary control over its own domestic affairs. In the newly organized Austro-Hungarian Empire, Slovakia was governed by Hungarians in Budapest without recourse to the Vienna government and the emperor.

Following the Compromise of 1867, Hungary resumed Magyarization. Actually a liberal measure, the Nationality Law of 1868 assured the linguistic rights of Hungary's subject nationalities by permitting the use of local languages in schools, churches, and parochial government. At the same time, the law reaffirmed Magyar as the kingdom's official language. In the early 1870s, however, a renewed assimilation campaign cast aside the law's guarantees for minority tongues. Secondary education in the Slovak language ended in 1874 with the closing of the region's three gymnasia. In 1875, charging the Matica slovenská with disloyalty and promoting Panslavism, the government shut it down and confiscated its assets. Slovak primary schools declined, especially after 1891 when Magyar was made the compulsory language in all primary schools. The number of schools offering instruction in Slovak plummeted from 1,821 in 1869 to 241 in 1905.

This course of events appalled Slovak nationalists, but how ordinary Slovaks reacted to the government's Magyarization program and the accompanying attack on Slovak nationalism remains one of history's unanswered questions. For all the bustle of activity in the nineteenth century, the Slovak awakening and nationalist movement involved only a tiny segment of the population: the educated intelligentsia. Moreover, activities had focused primarily on cultural preservation or political gains. Taken on the whole, neither the literary developments that occurred over sixty years nor the political activities that spanned nearly three decades prior to the Compromise of 1867 significantly affected the lives of the Slovak peasantry. During this time the peasant class was grappling with real-life problems that had little to do with the Slovak national awakening. In the mid-nineteenth century peasants had seen real improvement in their legal status. The abolition of serfdom in 1848–1851 ended a repressive system, but the act did not provide "freed serfs" with land sufficient to improve their circumstances. On the contrary, the size of peasant landholdings declined after 1848. As conditions for the peasantry worsened, demographic and economic pressures combined to stimulate a massive emigration from Upper Hungary that got under way gradually in the late 1870s and continued until halted by the outbreak of World War I.

Migration was a deeply rooted tradition among Slovaks. The restoration of Hungary in 1699 after the Turkish occupation had been followed by a population shift from the mountainous northern regions to Slovakia's more fertile southern plains. In the eighteenth century Slovaks migrated to other sections of Hungary or to Austria and Russia to work. By the mid-nineteenth century migrating temporarily to nearby areas in order to find work and supplement incomes was an entrenched custom among Slovaks. During the latter part of the nineteenth century, however, changing conditions, especially within Hungary, worked against this tradition. As Hungary's population grew, the country's industries could not absorb the labor increase. According to estimates, the Slovak population increased from approximately 1.7 million in the late 1850s to nearly 1.9 million by 1880. Reduced landholdings proved inadequate to support larger families. Insufficient jobs and low pay for those that were available prompted Slovaks to emigrate overseas. This transatlantic movement started in Upper Hungary's eastern sector and progressed westward. During a fifty-year period, approximately a half million Slovaks emigrated to North America, primarily to the United States. This exodus included a significant number of temporary migrants, primarily young men intending to work, save money, and return home. Over time, many of these transients—whom Americans called "birds of passage"—became permanent immigrants.

Emigration had contradictory effects on Slovakia. On one hand it drained the region of able-bodied young men, especially as temporary migrants became permanent immigrants. On the other hand migrants sent money home that helped improve circumstances for some Slovak peasants. With this newfound largesse they purchased land or paid off debts. Some returning migrants built "American" houses modeled after what they saw in the United States. Returned "Amerikany" showing off their American goods, especially clothes, also raised the expectations and excited the imaginations of persons who stayed behind. At the outset, the Hungarian government did not oppose emigration and instead viewed the positive economic effects it could have. As time passed, however, the authorities increasingly feared that the freer political climate in America was nurturing a Slovak nationalism that could undermine their Magyarization objectives.

Meanwhile, as this mass emigration was taking place, the Slovak nationalist movement went into decline. Following their candidates' unsuccessful attempts to get elected to the Hungarian diet and facing an increasingly hostile government, after the 1870s the Slovak National Party adopted a strategy of noninvolvement. It shunned national elections by refusing to field slates of candidates. By the early 1890s, however, a number of factors combined to shake off this inertia. Dismal economic conditions and worker discontent stimulated the formation of the Hungarian Social Democratic Party. The Slovak National Party was spurred to action by fears that its own nationalist agenda might be overshadowed by this new party's emphasis on workers' issues. Cooperation with other suppressed minorities also helped inject life into the Slovak movement. Finally, the activities of emigrants in the United States inspired nationalists in Upper Hungary. The politically free climate of America fostered the development of a zealous, but small, group of Slovak nationalists. They provided moral and some financial support for Slovak nationalists in Hungary.

Contact with Czechs added yet another dimension to Slovak nationalism in the 1890s. During the decade, Slovaks studying in Prague came in contact with Tomáš Masaryk, a professor of philosophy at Charles University. He advocated cooperation between Slovaks and Czechs and championed "Czechoslovak" unity. In 1896 students formed the Czechoslovak Union to foster these ideas. Two of Masaryk's Slovak disciples, Vavro Šrobar and Pavol Blaho, tried to expand this youth movement to Slovakia. In 1898 they founded the journal *Hlas* (The Voice). It advocated language rights, a Slovak educational system, and universal suffrage. While accepting Slovakia as an integral part of the Hungarian state, the editors called for Czech and Slovak cooperation. These Hlasists, as they were called, did not attract a large following. That fact, together with internal disputes, undermined their efforts. *Hlas* ceased publication in 1904. Nevertheless, the idea that Czechs and Slovaks should work together to achieve political aims had been planted in the spectrum of possibilities for Slovakia.

Popular new leaders emerged from the revitalized Slovak nationalism in Upper Hungary. By the early 1900s, Andrej Hlinka, a young priest, had taken up the nationalist cause and was working to broaden its appeal. His support for Slovak political candidates in the 1906 elections outraged Hungarian authorities and, as a result, he was sentenced to two years in prison. Hlinka's term was nearly doubled when officials charged him with incitement for two farewell letters he sent to parishioners before his incarceration. Local devotion to Hlinka ultimately led to a riot in his native village of Černova. Typically called the Černova Massacre, the melee occurred on 27 October 1907, as villagers protested because Hlinka, who was still in jail, was denied permission to attend the dedication of their new church. When the crowd allegedly became unruly, authorities shot into the gathering. Many Slovaks were wounded; fifteen ultimately died. The following March, fifty-nine villagers were imprisoned for participating in the protest. The Černova Massacre had widespread repercussions, especially in the United States where it stimulated the formation of the Slovak League of America, which became a leading advocate of Slovak nationalism. In 1913 Andrej Hlinka became leader of the Slovak People's Party, which had been formed by

Andrej Hlinka (1864–1938), Slovak politician and advocate of Slovak autonomy. (Austrian Archives/Corbis)

Catholic clergymen dissatisfied with a Hungarian Catholic Party.

Despite such reinvigorated efforts, Slovaks nationalists made little headway in Hungary. Their cause did not gain mass support, and restrictive franchise laws denied them meaningful access to the Hungarian diet. Between 1901 and 1910, the number of Slovak deputies ranged from just one to seven. This paltry number could neither effect political reforms nor moderate Magyarization laws.

For Slovaks, World War I abruptly intruded on their lives and reshaped nationalist goals as well. After August 1914, Slovak nationalism was stifled in Hungary. In the tense atmosphere created by the war, the Slovak National Party halted its political activities. Slovakia's future, however, was unavoidably influenced by external events. In November 1915 a group in Paris led by Tomáš Masaryk issued a declaration demanding the creation of an independent Czechoslovak state. In February 1916 Masaryk, together with Edvard Beneš, a Czech professor of sociology, and Milan Rastislav Štefánik, a Slovak astronomer, formed the Czechoslovak National Council. Under the leadership of these men, the council worked to win over the Entente powers—Austria-Hungary's enemies—to the idea of establishing a united Czech and Slovak state.

Meanwhile, claiming to be spokespersons for minorities silenced by the war in Europe, Slovak and Czech ethnic organizations in the United States cooperated to legitimize arguments for establishing an independent nation. In October 1915 the Slovak League and the Bohemian (Czech) National Union jointly issued the Cleveland Agreement. It called for the unification "of the Czech and Slovak nations in a federal state with complete national autonomy for Slovakia, with its own diet [and] state administration and with Slovak as the official language." Besides issuing declarations of support, when Milan Štefánik tried to recruit volunteers in America for the council's army units, known by 1918 as the Czechoslovak Legion, Slovak organizations backed his efforts.

In 1918, when Masaryk came to the United States to garner support for the cause, both Czech and Slovak organizations helped coordinate his visit. In an enormously significant move, leaders of the Slovak League convinced Masaryk to sign the Pittsburgh Agreement, which would become one of the most important and controversial documents in Slovak history. A modification of the 1915 Cleveland document, the Pittsburgh Agreement of 30 May outlined a "political program . . . to unite Czechs and Slovaks in an independent state." The program stated that "Slovakia will have its own administration, its own Diet and its own courts." In addition, Slovak would be the "official language in the schools, in offices and in public life generally." The 1918 Pittsburgh Agreement left the details of establishing the new state up "to the liberated Czechs and Slovaks." Although the agreement contained no specific mention of "autonomy," Masaryk's willingness to sign the document was interpreted as a commitment to an autonomous Slovakia within a new Czech and Slovak state.

As the Austro-Hungarian Empire stumbled toward collapse in 1918, the unification of Czech and Slovak lands into an independent nation progressed steadily toward becoming a reality. In the summer, France and England both recognized the Czechoslovak National Council as the representative of Czech and Slovak interests and as the foundation of a future government. On 3 September the United States went even further and granted the Czechoslovak National Council recognition as a "de facto belligerent government." In mid-October, after the Central Powers had sued for peace and Austria-Hungary was clearly disintegrating, the council declared itself a provisional government. On 28 October 1918, representatives of the Provisional Government proclaimed Czechoslovakia an independent state.

By fall 1918, Slovaks inside Slovakia were also taking action to demonstrate backing for the creation of a joint Czechoslovak state. Unaware that a provisional government had been announced, on 30 October Slovaks met in Turcianský Svätý Martin, announced the formation of the Slovak National Council, and drafted the "Declaration of the Slovak Nation." It proclaimed: "The Slovak Nation is a part of the Czecho-Slovak Nation, united in language and in the history of its culture." "For this Czecho-Slovak Nation" the declaration demanded "complete independence." Unlike the American-generated documents, it did not call for Slovak autonomy but expressed a desire to form a joint state with the Czechs. Two weeks later, on 13 November, the Prague National Committee adopted a provisional constitution, and the next day the National Assembly elected Masaryk as president. Czecho-Slovakia thus began functioning as a united, independent nation.

Although Czecho-Slovakia's boundaries had not yet been determined, Masaryk and his cabinet immediately began administering this new country. The Czech and Moravian borders, which included the German Sudetenland, were settled in June 1919 by the Treaty of Versailles. The Treaty of Saint-Germaine-en-lage (September 1919) allowed Czecho-Slovakia to incorporate Carpatho-Ukraine, the mountainous region east of Slovakia, into its territory. Stabilizing Slovakia's borders with Hungary took longer because Hungary, unwilling to lose its northern territories, occupied Slovakia in May 1919. Hungarian forces were finally expelled, and the Treaty of Trianon (June 1920) established the Danube and Ipel' rivers as the international boundary between Hungary and Czecho-Slovakia.

The Czecho-Slovakia that came into existence in 1918 was a multinational country created out of the ruins of a multinational empire. At the first complete census in 1930, Czechoslovakia's population totaled 14,480,000. The stitching together of historical territories resulted in ethnic groups essentially dominating specific geographic areas of the country: Czechs (7,406,000) inhabited the western region; Slovaks (2,282,000) occupied the eastern section; Germans (3,232,000) were concentrated in the Sudetenland, a crescent-shaped area winding north-south around the western borders of the Czech Lands; Hungarians (692,000) lived along Slovakia's southern border; Carpatho-Rusyns (549,000) dwelled in the region to Slovakia's east. Although Germans outnumbered Slovaks, Czecho-Slovakia was, nevertheless, a Czech-Slovak state.

Despite their linguistic similarities, the Czechs and Slovaks who were joined together in this new country were separate peoples without a shared history. Moreover, their distinct histories—the Czechs under Austrian control and the Slovaks ruled by Hungary—had influenced their development and fashioned profoundly different societies. Compared to the Czech Lands, Slovakia was a substantially underdeveloped, agricultural region. Discriminatory laws had prevented Slovaks from entering politics or holding administrative positions; Slovakia, therefore, did not have an experienced class of civil servants. The region claimed a small professional, educated class but Slovakia's illiteracy rate was 14 percent; it was only 3 percent in the Czech Lands. Disparities between Czechs and Slovaks created antagonisms between the two Slavic groups. In addition, the country's Germans resented being reduced to minority status in a Slavic state.

Ethnic tensions were already evident in 1918 as leaders of the infant state launched a national government. The 256-member Revolutionary National Assembly, which began governing Czechoslovakia on 14 November 1918, included only Czechs and Slovaks. The Czech deputies were representatives who had been elected in 1911, the last national elections in prewar Austria. Hungary's franchise laws had denied similar representation to Slovaks, and no comparable electoral districts existed in Slovakia; therefore, Slovakia was assigned forty deputies and, instead of being popularly elected, all were appointed. In March 1919 the number of representatives for Slovakia was increased to fifty-four. In addition to Tomáš Masaryk, the cabinet included Karel Kramář, prime minister; Edvard Beneš, minister of foreign affairs; Milan Štefánik, minister of war; and Vavro Šrobar, minister of health. Postwar Czecho-Slovakia and Slovaks lost an important leader when Milan Štefánik died in a plane crash in May 1919.

Establishing a stable national government was one priority for the provisional government; securing Slovakia was another. After the war, Slovakia was in political chaos and the new state's territory was being threatened by a Hungarian government that wanted to keep its northern lands. As early as 4 November 1918 a four-person committee, headed by Vavro Šrobar, a Slovak, was charged with administering the region. On 10 December, the Revolutionary National Assembly passed legislation establishing a minister plenipotentiary for Slovakia, who, with assistants, would manage the territory. Šrobar, the first minister, chose Bratislava as Slovakia's administrative capital. A former Catholic, Šrobar selected primarily Lutherans to assist him. Of the fifty-four persons subsequently chosen to represent Slovakia on the Revolutionary National Assembly, thirty-one were Lutheran, ten were Catholic, and thirteen were Czech. Favoring Czechs and Lutherans over Catholics angered the Slovak Catholic clergy and heightened both ethnic and religious animosities in the country.

Czecho-Slovakia's constitution, which was proclaimed on 29 February 1920, instituted a parliamentary democracy. The constitution also set up a centralized state with political power concentrated in the central government in Prague. The National Assembly, the country's legislative body, included a Senate and a Chamber of Deputies. The president, elected by the Assembly, governed with a cabinet. Despite references to the "Czechoslovak" language, Czech and Slovak were both made official languages. Minority rights were protected by legislation that permitted the use of local languages in educational systems and local administration. With the adoption of the 1920 constitution, the hyphenated spelling—Czecho-Slovakia—was abandoned in favor of the single word "Czechoslovakia." This conveyed the idea that the new country was a "Czechoslovak" nation, not a federation uniting two separate peoples.

Even before the 1920 constitution was in place, some Slovaks were challenging the concept of a centralized state. Fr. Andrej Hlinka quickly emerged as the leading spokesperson for Slovak autonomy within the joint Czech-Slovak nation. Hlinka revived the prewar Slovak People's Party in December 1918 and by the spring of 1919 made implementing the Pittsburgh Agreement the fulcrum of its platform. In late summer 1919 he unsuccessfully attempted to address the Paris Peace Conference where he intended to expose the new government's supposed maltreatment of Slovaks and seek the conference's support for Slovak autonomy. When he returned to Czecho-Slovakia, he was briefly imprisoned for his attempt. Hlinka's action helped fuel lingering suspicions about Slovak loyalty to the new state.

The administrative and constitutional decisions of the early 1920s emanated from a desire to unify and stabilize the infant country. They also stemmed from a concern that Slovakia, with its large Magyarized population, could be lost to Hungary as that government continued a campaign to keep its historic lands. In addition, the actions of Czechoslovakia's authorities reflected the belief that Slovaks were not yet capable of governing and that Czechs thus should run the central government and oversee local affairs as well.

Dealing with the political and economic realities in postwar Slovakia created tensions between Slovaks and Czechs. As a result of Hungarian policies, few Slovaks had government, administrative, or business experience. To fill this vacuum, immediately after the war Czechs migrated to Slovakia to take positions as civil servants, teachers, government bureaucrats, and judicial officials. Czechs were initially welcomed by Slovaks. However the superior attitude some Czechs displayed, especially their disdain for the Slovak language, culture, and traditions, together with the privileged positions some held in local governments and educational systems, stirred resentment and prompted charges of Czech dominance.

Divisions among Slovaks made the situation in Slovakia ever worse. Capitalizing on ethnic animosities, during the 1920s, the Slovak People's Party gained some popularity as it continued pushing its platform of Slovak autonomy. The party, which in 1925 was renamed Hlinka's Slovak People's Party, did not adopt a separatist position but, instead, agitated for self-administration within Czechoslovakia. Hlinka's nationalist movement encountered stiff opposition from Slovak centrists who were convinced that Slovak autonomy would be politically disruptive and economically detrimental to the region. Religious differences further aggravated the situation. Slovak Protestants, primarily Lutherans, leaned toward a centralized government, while autonomists tended to be Catholics. Hlinka's party, however, did not enjoy the wholehearted backing even of Catholics. More than three-fourths of the Slovak population was Catholic, yet in the party's best showing—the 1925 elections—it garnered only 32 percent of the vote and won twenty-three seats in the National Assembly.

Despite animosities between Czechs and Slovaks, the most serious challenge to Czechoslovakia came in the 1930s from the large German minority in the Sudetenland. The ultranationalism that Adolf Hitler was stirring up in Germany found fertile ground in the Sudetenland, an area hit hard by the worldwide Great Depression. By the mid-1930s, the immensely popular Sudeten German Homefront, a political organization under the leadership of Konrad Heinlein, was pressing a scheme designed ultimately to let the Sudetenland secede from Czechoslovakia. In 1938, when unrest led to violence in the region, Hitler exploited the situation to demand that the Sudetenland be ceded to Germany. In September, at a meeting in Munich where representatives from Czechoslovakia were excluded, the Führer pressured the French and British governments into allowing Germany to annex the Sudetenland. Both countries appeased Hitler. France appeased him by failing to live up to a treaty obligation to defend Czechoslovakia from outside aggression, and Britain appeased him by agreeing to stand by and do nothing. On 1 October, one day after the Munich Agreement was signed, German troops occupied the Sudetenland.

Five days later, all of Slovakia's political parties, except for the Social Democrats and the Communists, met at Žilina and formulated a program for Slovak autonomy. The agreement was a redraft of proposals drawn up by the People's Party earlier in the summer of 1938. It vested the executive power of an autonomous Slovak state in a cabinet made up of five ministers. Foreign affairs and national defense remained under the control of the central government in Prague. Weakened by the Munich Agreement and fearful of Slovak secession, the Prague government bowed to the demands. On 22 November 1938, the Czechoslovak Parliament implemented the Žilina agreement and recognized Slovak autonomy. With this action the Second Republic, now called "Czecho-Slovakia" spelled with a hyphen, came into existence. The hyphenated spelling symbolized the fact the country was now a federated state.

Slovakia quickly became a single-party state. Some political groups were dissolved while others were forced into the Party of Slovak National Unity, an umbrella organization dominated by the Slovak People's Party. The National Unity Party submitted the lone list of candidates in the December elections and won 97.5 percent of the vote. Monsignor Josef Tiso, a Catholic priest who had assumed leadership of the People's Party after Andrej Hlinka's death in August 1938, became prime minister.

Only a few short months later, outside aggression paved the way for Slovak independence. By early March 1939 Hitler had decided to move forward with what had always been his plan: to gobble up the Czech Lands. He was willing, however, to leave Slovakia free. On 13 March he summoned Tiso whom the Prague government had just dismissed as Slovakia's prime minister—to a meeting in Berlin. Tiso caved into threats that declaring independence was Slovakia's only alternative either to being partitioned or annexed by Hungary. He returned to Bratislava, and on 14 March the Slovak diet followed his advice and proclaimed Slovakia independent. The next day, Hitler recognized Slovakia and German troops occupied the Czech Lands. Hitler reduced the Czech Lands to a protectorate of the Third Reich and Czecho-Slovakia ceased to exist. Slovakia did not escape intact. In the fall of 1938 the Czechoslovak government had been forced to give southern and eastern sections of Slovakia to Hungary while a small northern portion went to Poland. In March 1939, with Hitler's blessing, Hungary occupied the ceded Slovak lands and Carpatho-Ukraine as well.

Josef Tiso became president when the German Reich took Slovakia under its protection in March 1939. (Corbis)

The Slovak Republic (1939–1945) represents the most controversial period in Slovak history. Defenders of Tiso's actions maintain that Slovakia was spared the fate of the Czech Lands and that Slovakia was independent for the first time in its history. Critics counter that from 1939 to 1945 Slovakia was merely a puppet government supporting Hitler's Third Reich and the Holocaust.

On 23 March, just nine days after declaring "sovereignty," the Slovak government signed agreements that placed the country under Germany's "protection." Josef Tiso became president of the Slovak Republic, and powerful cabinet posts fell to supporters of Germany. After some initial shuffling of offices, two extremists emerged as dominant forces in the government: by 1940 Vojtech Tuka simultaneously held the positions of prime minister and minister of foreign affairs, and Alexander Mach became minister of the interior. Slovakia's wartime independence was, at best, nominal. Slovaks administered the country, but government affairs were overseen by the German minister in Bratislava; a host of German advisers were injected into various levels of Slovakia's government, administration, and institutions.

Slovakia also complied with the Third Reich's Jewish policies. Less than a month after the Slovak Republic came into existence it began issuing restrictive regulations for Jews. Their movement was limited and they were excluded from certain professions. In early September 1941 the government enacted a Jewish Code comprising 270 articles that drew together the various measures governing the country's Jewish population. It provided the rationale and legal sanction for appropriating Jewish-owned property and ultimately for internment.

Following a gradual erosion of Jewish civil and political rights, the government acquiesced in a German demand for resettling Slovak Jews outside Slovakia. In March 1942 the Slovak government began deporting Jews; most were sent to Nazi concentration camps. To cover costs, the Slovak government paid Germany 500 marks for each Jew transported out of the country. The mistreatment of Jews did not sit well with the Catholic Church hierarchy in Rome. It informed the Slovak government that it objected to the fact that a country led by a Catholic clergyman was engaging in such activities. Church officials reportedly opposed both the discriminatory laws as well as the deportation of Jews. Responding to Vatican protests, in October 1942 the practice of deporting Jews stopped. However, in the seven months from 25 March to 20 October 1942 the Slovak government had sent about 57,700 Jews to concentration camps. From the time the practice was resumed in September 1944 until the end of the war in April 1945, approximately another 13,500 were deported. Standard estimates are that two-thirds of Slovakia's Jews perished in World War II. As a result of genocide, deportation, and emigration, the Jewish population in Slovakia plummeted from approximately 90,000 in 1939 to an estimated 30,000 by the end of the war. Responsibility for the Holocaust in Slovakia and Tiso's role remain the foci of heated historical debate.

When Slovakia first made its declaration in March 1939, independence apparently enjoyed popular support among Slovaks. There were, however, exceptions. Protestants were almost universally against the Slovak Republic. By 1941, Communists too were opposed, and small blocks of democratic resistance had also sprung up. Opponents resorted to various forms of sabotage. Some soldiers mutinied; others defected, especially when they encountered Soviet forces on the eastern front. By late 1943 opposition to the Tiso government was small but escalating. In the so-called Christmas Agreement of 1943, Communists and the democratic resistance formed the Slovak National Council, an underground group whose aim was to liberate Slovakia from German control. One of the council's first acts was to devise a plot to overthrow the Tiso government. The plan relied on a coordinated effort between the Slovak army and Soviet forces; it also depended on stirring popular resistance within Slovakia. The council recruited Ján Golian, regional chief of staff at the Slovak army headquarters in Banská Bystrica, to command the effort.

The Slovak National Uprising, which broke out in August 1944, was a dismal failure. Operations started prematurely when guerrilla units led by Soviets began destroying roads and blowing up bridges. They also occupied villages. The actual uprising got under way on 29 August, but by then the Germans had been alerted and had moved forces into Slovakia. Two vital Slovak divisions were isolated in the east and quickly disarmed by the Germans. Expected Soviet forces and military assistance did not come. An estimated 50,000 to 60,000 Slovak soldiers and perhaps 18,000 partisans did participate; moreover, the rebellion rallied some popular support, especially in central Slovakia near Banská Bystrica, the heart of the revolt. Nevertheless, by the end of October, German forces had crushed the poorly coordinated uprising. Remnants of the Slovak resisters, however, escaped into the forests and mountain regions and continued to conduct guerrilla warfare against German forces through the war's end.

In the vicious retaliation that followed the attempted revolt, the resistance leaders were executed. More than sixty villages were burned. Reportedly thousands of Roma (Gypsies) were slaughtered. In addition to mass killings, several thousand persons were condemned to concentration camps. As a reaction to the incident, the deportation of Slovak Jews to concentration camps was resumed in the fall of 1944.

While Slovakia's government collaborated with Germany, throughout the war a Czechoslovak government in exile operated in London. Under the leadership of former President Edvard Beneš, its primary objective was to restore prewar Czechoslovakia. In March 1945, as the war was drawing to an end, Beneš and the exiled government traveled to Moscow where they met with leaders of the democratic resistance and the Communist Party to work out a program for Czechoslovakia's reemergence as a nation. The Slovak National Council, the body that had instigated the Slovak Uprising of 1944, represented Slovakia. At the conference, the participants hammered out an agenda for Czechoslovakia's postwar government. They also settled on what positions Czechs and Slovaks would hold in the reconstructed government. The plan outlined general procedures for punishing collaborators with the Nazi occupation: their property would be taken over by the state; government officials were to be prosecuted for treason by a National Court. The program further acknowledged that Czechoslovakia's postwar foreign policy would be based on a close alliance with the Soviet Union.

One of the sharpest disagreements at the Moscow conference centered on Slovakia's future. The Slovak National Council demanded complete autonomy within a reunified country. Czechoslovakia's President Beneš and the other

London exiles rejected this notion. The council finally settled for a somewhat ambiguous statement recognizing Slovaks as a distinct nation and an equally vague statement about the equality of the two regions once Czechoslovakia was restored.

Czechoslovakia came back into existence in early April 1945. On 3 April, Edvard Beneš went to Košice in eastern Slovakia, which had been liberated by the Soviet army. The next day, he installed the National Front, a coalition government of Czech and Slovak political parties. And on 4 April this provisional body announced its program for postwar recovery. The plan, which had been drawn up in Moscow, was subsequently referred to as the "Košice Program." Soviet forces liberated Prague on 9 May; the next day the government returned from exile, and Beneš followed a week later on 16 May. The Slovak National Council continued functioning in Bratislava. For a short time the council held legislative power in Slovakia. An appointed board of commissioners served as the council's executive body. In reality Slovakia was, for the time being at least, a self-governing region.

At the end of World War II, with the exception of Carpatho-Ukraine, which was ceded to the Soviet Union, Czechoslovakia's pre-Munich boundaries were reestablished. Despite the chaos created by the war and by Czechoslovakia's temporary demise, political stability reigned during the early stages of the country's recovery. Beneš, who assumed the presidency, and the National Front ruled by decree until October 1945, when a Provisional National Assembly was installed. Although general elections were delayed until May 1946, the provisional government implemented significant provisions of the Košice Program. Under a ban against political parties that had collaborated with the Nazis, the Slovak People's Party was outlawed. In December 1946 Jozef Tiso, who was charged with treason for his wartime activities, was put on trial. After a lengthy proceeding, he was found guilty and executed on 18 April 1947. The government wreaked vengeance on Czechoslovakia's Germans by expelling them. Between January and the summer of 1947, approximately 3 million citizens of German ancestry were banished from Czechoslovakia.

To the disappointment of Slovak nationalists the restored government did not advance Slovak autonomy. The Košice Program had recognized the Slovak National Council, but the council's powers were quickly reduced in a revived Czechoslovakia. Between April 1945 and June 1946, three "Prague Agreements" chipped away at the council's power, and consequently the prewar centralized system was essentially reestablished.

The government, however, did not ignore Slovakia's special interests. The war had physically damaged Slovakia more than the Czech Lands. The battles between Soviet forces and the retreating German military had ravaged towns, villages, and industrial sites. The region had endured about eight months of actual fighting on its soil. Slovakia, therefore, became a major target of a two-year plan, instituted in 1946, to reconstruct the country. Some factories formerly owned by now expelled Sudetenland Germans were relocated there. During this period, members of the newly created Democratic Party renewed the push for Slovak autonomy.

It was the Communist Party that benefited most in postwar Czechoslovakia. The Party underwent phenomenal growth. By mobilizing trade unions and local organizations, it built a massive national network. Members controlled government agencies charged with land redistribution, especially in the Sudetenland, and hence doled out largesse that helped endear the Party to workers and farmers. The abolition of right-wing parties and a general swing to the political left further escalated the Communist Party's popularity. In the 1946 elections the Communist Party garnered nearly 38 percent of the popular vote and won 114 seats in the National Assembly. The Party's showing enabled Klement Gottwald, a Communist who had spent the war years in the Soviet Union, to become prime minister, while Edvard Beneš retained the more powerful position of president.

The gain that Communists enjoyed in the 1946 national elections did not reflect the situation in Slovakia. While Communists in the Czech Lands had claimed ninety-three seats in the National Assembly, their Slovak counterparts had earned only twenty-one. Since the Democratic Party captured 62 percent of the popular vote to the Communists' 30.4 percent, it dominated the Slovak National Council and the board of commissioners.

As a result of the 1946 victories in national elections, the Communist Party gained control of key government positions in Czechoslovakia, including the Ministry of Interior and the country's police apparatus. Under the pretext of rooting out fascist collaborators and traitors, the Communist-dominated security force aggressively went after the Party's opponents. In February 1948 these repressive activities provoked a political crisis. On 20 February, twelve noncommunist cabinet ministers protested police tactics by resigning. When Beneš did not act quickly to replace them, Prime Minister Gottwald seized the opportunity to engineer a coup by creating his own list of replacements. On 25 February, Beneš acquiesced in Gottwald's decisions. As a result, a Communist-dominated cabinet was installed. The communist regime immediately set out to remold the country's political and economic structure. A new constitution promulgated on 9 May 1948 pushed Czechoslovakia toward becoming a socialist state. Beneš refused to accept the so-called Ninth of May Constitution and resigned.

In Slovakia, an attempt by Slovak Communists to wrest control of the board of commissioners away from the Democratic Party led to a Communist coup in Slovakia that preceded the overthrow of the central government in February 1948. In the fall of 1947 the Slovak Communist Party, well organized despite its losses in 1946, took advantage of discontent in Slovakia to precipitate a political crisis. A disastrous harvest, together with lingering economic dislocation, fomented unrest and increased radical feeling in Slovakia. Trade unions and ex-partisans organized mass meetings and demanded the removal of Democrats from the board of commissioners, which was the council's executive body. The Communist members resigned, and Gustáv Husák, the Communist chairman, dissolved the board. When it was reconstituted, Husák was made chairman, and Communists effectively controlled the reorganized board. After the February 1948 coup that brought the Communists to power in Prague, the Democrat Party ceased to function.

The new Prague government showed little sympathy for Slovak autonomy; nevertheless, rather than destroying Slovakia's local governmental organs, it restricted them. The Ninth of May Constitution further reduced the already weak powers of the Slovak National Council and the board of commissioners. Both bodies came under the close supervision of the central government, and their activities were limited to minor issues. The Slovak Communist Party, which had been an independent entity, also lost its autonomy. Although permitted to keep its name, the Communist Party of Slovakia was incorporated into the Czechoslovak Communist Party and granted only nominal independence.

Within a few years of the 1948 Communist takeover, Stalinization, a ruthless economic and political program, was transforming Czechoslovakia into a country that fully emulated the system in the Soviet Union. The country adopted centralized planning, which meant that the government controlled the economy. The period witnessed the nationalization of companies, industries, and consumer-oriented shops. Owners of small businesses were forced to turn them over to the state. Doctors and other medical persons had to give up private practices and become state employees. The collectivization of farms, an unpopular process that continued through the 1950s, eliminated private ownership of agricultural lands. The government used various forms of intimidation in order to force farmers, who made up nearly half of Slovakia's population, to merge their property into huge cooperatives. Individuals were no longer free to cultivate their land or sell their agricultural products.

Massive purges, capped by spectacular political trials, shook the Communist Party and terrified Czechoslovakia's inhabitants. Designated committees conducted purges of local institutions, including schools, and deprived persons of their jobs. Organized religions were also suppressed. This repression was particularly hard felt by Slovaks, a historically devout people with a religious tradition reaching back to the proselytizing mission of Cyril and Methodius in the ninth century. The government confiscated religious properties and took over church operations, including paying the clergy. Monastic communities were plundered and persons jailed; female religious orders were consolidated. During the 1950s three bishops were tried on trumped-up charges and sentenced to long prison terms. More than three hundred clergymen went to jail.

Czechoslovakia's foreign policy followed the Soviet lead. This pattern was already evident in July 1947, when, under pressure from the Soviet Union, the Prague government quickly reversed an initial decision to participate in the Marshall Plan. Participation in this American-funded program would have provided the country with much needed financial aid. In 1955 Czechoslovakia became a charter member of the Warsaw Pact, the Eastern Bloc's counterpart to the North Atlantic Treaty Organization (NATO).

Following the Communist takeover in 1948, the government, meaning in effect the Communist Party, controlled the everyday life of Czechoslovakia's ordinary citizens. Individual property rights were decimated. Still, when compared to the situation in the mid-1940s, in some ways the economic situation for ordinary persons improved. The rural regions of Slovakia, in particular, benefited. In order to supplement their incomes, farmers, who lost their lands to collectivization and were forced to work in industry, actually experienced a rise in income. In other ways the standard of living in rural areas went up. Government-subsidized modernization programs brought electricity to villages and the number of schools also increased. Health facilities grew, and medical care became more readily available.

The improved living standards that many Slovaks experienced in the 1950s were accompanied by a fundamental loss of political rights. In addition to squelching all political dissent, during the purges that followed the 1948 Communist takeover the Prague government launched a fierce attack on Slovak autonomy and the federalist position. In the 1950s Czechoslovakia's Communist leadership denounced Slovak "patriotism" as "bourgeois nationalism" and designated it a crime against the state. Longtime Slovak Communists who had advocated autonomy became the chief targets of the political witch-hunt. In 1951 Gustáv Husák and Vladimír Clementis, former secretary of state in the Foreign Ministry, were arrested on charges that included bourgeois nationalism. The next year Clementis was executed. In 1953 Husák received a three-year prison sentence, later extended to life. Other Slovaks, especially writers and the intelligentsia, suffered similar fates.

Klement Gottwald, who had engineered the 1948 coup that brought a Communist government to power, died in 1953. He was succeeded by Antonín Novotný, who was elected first secretary of the Communist Party in 1953 and president of Czechoslovakia in 1957. In 1960 Novotný announced a new constitution that officially proclaimed the country a socialist state: the Czechoslovak Socialist Republic.

The 1960 constitution crippled the remnants of self-government in Slovakia. The board of commissioners was abolished and the Slovak National Council was reduced to a "national organ of state . . . administration" and effectively rendered powerless. Slovaks found no comfort in the appointment of the Slovak, Viliam Široký, as Czechoslovakia's prime minister. Široký had first voiced the charge of "bourgeois nationalism" in 1948 and had subsequently benefited from the campaign against Slovak autonomists. The entrenched Novotný regime still regarded Slovak autonomy as a threat to a socialist state. In the early 1960s, however, economic issues, together with a growing intellectual ferment, injected new life into the federalist concept to allow more self-government for Slovakia.

Despite propaganda claiming glowing successes for the socialist state, at the beginning of the 1960s Czechoslovakia was experiencing serious economic decline. Reacting to this situation, several influential economists suggested some retreat from central planning, where the government controlled every aspect of the economy. Demands for change intensified when the country's stagnating economy went into a tailspin in 1963. In 1966, under pressure from reformers, the Communist Party Congress adopted an action program, later called the New Economic Model (NEM).

The program, which advocated more flexibility, would reduce central planning and give more independence to plants and enterprises. Under this new system local managers would make more decisions regarding production.

During the early 1960s writers and journalists, suffocating under repressive constraints, also began pressing for more freedom. Critics of Stalinization, and especially of the ruthless suppression that had accompanied this brutal process, demanded investigations into the political trials and purges of the 1950s. At its 1962 congress, the Communist Party even ordered an investigation of previous political arrests. Although deficient, the report, which appeared in May 1963, led to the rehabilitation of some persons. "Rehabilitation" became a euphemism for exonerating persons who had been incarcerated or executed for alleged political crimes.

The reform impulse took on special features in Slovakia. The region had fared well during the economic expansion of the 1950s, and Slovaks had made progress toward catching up with Czechs in both agricultural and industrial development. Ironically the improved economic situation fostered resentment among Slovaks because they were dissatisfied over the continued socioeconomic differences between Slovakia and the Czech Lands. Between 1948 and 1959, Slovakia's industrial output increased by 347 percent, but economically Slovakia still lagged behind the Czech Lands. Slovak economists blamed persistent inequities on policies that favored the country's western territories. Stressing the unique characteristics of Slovakia, they called for a program that would grant Slovakia more leeway to develop its own economy.

Slovak intellectuals added yet another dimension to ongoing complaints against the central government. When the special commission on political trials issued its findings, Slovaks were disappointed that it excluded several prominent Slovaks. The Congress of Slovak Journalists, which convened in May 1963, took up the cause of Slovaks denied rehabilitation. Speakers criticized the purges and declared that bourgeois nationalism had merely been a government subterfuge to suppress Slovak national aspirations and to deny Slovaks a greater voice in regional development. Following the congress, journalists continued their campaign and boldly articulated their complaints in print. They wanted the government to redress wrongs committed under the guise of bourgeois nationalism. In December 1963 the Novotný government reluctantly yielded to pressure and rehabilitated Gustáv Husák, Ladislav Novomeský, and Vladimír Clementis, three Slovaks who had been found guilty of bourgeois nationalism.

Although there was some improvement in the political climate, Communist Party ideologues blocked attempts to change Czechoslovakia's economic structure. As the country sank further into an economic morass in the 1960s, President Novotný's grip on power weakened. He retained the presidency until late March, but in January 1968 Novotný lost his position as first secretary of the Communist Party to Alexander Dubček, a Slovak. Dubček had earlier irritated the Novotný contingent by advocating general and political reforms as well as a revision of the Party's position on Slovak autonomy.

Portrait of Alexander Dubček, first secretary of the Czechoslovak Communist Party during the Prague Spring of 1968. (Hulton Archive/Getty Images)

Dubček's rise to Party leadership did not precipitate any immediate economic or political changes. The lifting of censorship two months later, however, ushered in reform programs aimed at achieving "socialism with a human face." For a while, the country experienced the Prague Spring, a popular euphemism for the widespread liberalization movement that swept Czechoslovakia during the spring and summer of 1968. Taken over by reform-minded members, the Communist Party began implementing plans to bring about economic improvements. Linking economic progress to political changes, reformers introduced measures for democratizing the Communist Party and encouraging more participation by the masses in the political process. During this relaxed climate, the idea of Slovak autonomy also gained respectability. The reform agenda called for turning Czechoslovakia into a federal state by recognizing Slovakia as a distinct entity within this communist nation.

The Prague Spring came to an abrupt halt on 21 August, when Warsaw Pact forces invaded Czechoslovakia. The domestic reforms being adopted in Czechoslovakia had frightened the leaders of other communist regimes in Eastern Europe, who feared the effects might spill over into their countries. Dubček remained in power until April 1969, when a civil disturbance in Prague provided an excuse to remove him. He was replaced as first secretary by Gustáv Husák, the Slovak nationalist formerly imprisoned for bourgeois nationalism. Husák's political career had actually resumed in January 1968, when he was appointed a deputy premier; in May he headed the committee charged with developing a plan for federalizing Czechoslovakia. In August Husák was selected first secretary of the Communist Party for all Slovakia. Husák's political fortunes continued to rise after the 1968 invasion of Czechoslovakia. Although his exact role remains unclear, when Dubček and other Party officials were arrested and forcibly taken to Moscow, Husák went along. Having sufficiently endeared himself to the Soviet leadership and to the antireform wing of the Party in Czechoslovakia, Husák replaced Dubček in April 1969 and became first secretary of the Czechoslovak Communist Party, the most powerful political position in the country.

After Dubček's fall, the Husák regime instituted a policy of "normalization": a reassertion of the Communist Party's tight control and a return to centralized planning. Normalization entailed cleansing the Party of "counterrevolutionary" elements; more than 470,000 persons lost their Party membership. Because members had enjoyed special privileges, ejection meant more than simply being ousted from a political organization. In Czechoslovakia supervisory positions and the more prestigious, better paying jobs were given to Party members. As a consequence, between 1970 and 1971 the purge went beyond merely "sanitizing" the Community Party. Persons in local bureaucracies, universities, unions, the news media, the judiciary, and the educational system were dismissed from their jobs. They typically were forced to take less distinguished and less desirable positions. Some were downgraded to common laborers. The purges were less devastating in Slovakia, where Party membership was lowered by only 17 percent, as compared to a 42 percent reduction in the Czech Lands. And although Slovak reformers suffered harassment and discrimination, they typically were demoted rather than forced to take menial jobs.

Federalization was the only provision of the 1968 reforms to survive normalization. Made effective on 1 January 1969, the law of 28 October 1968 amended the constitution and transformed Czechoslovakia into a federated state: the Slovak Socialist Republic and the Czech Socialist Republic. Prague was designated the federal and Czech capital; Bratislava was made Slovakia's capital city. The central government retained jurisdiction over defense, currency, foreign policy, and federal administration. The republics were given responsibility for their own area's education, culture, health, construction, and natural resources. In some spheres, the central government and the republics shared authority. The law established a bicameral federal legislature comprising a Chamber of the People, with representation based on population, and a Chamber of Nations where Slovaks and Czechs had equal representation. Each republic had its own elected legislature and a cabinet but no president or prime minister. Executive functions were carried out by national councils.

For Gustáv Husák federalization represented a victory. He had long championed the cause of an autonomous Slovakia. Almost as soon as federalism was established, however, it began withering under the pressure of normalization. Economic independence, originally part of the federalization scheme, was quickly undermined by central planning and by the failure to decentralize the Communist Party, which held the real reins of power in Czechoslovakia. By 1971, constitutional revisions had returned vital economic functions to the central government in Prague and severely undermined the federal system.

During the 1970s Czechoslovakia's Communist leadership combined political constraints and economic concessions to keep its citizenry quiescent. To pacify the people, the government worked to improve the standard of living by increasing the supply of consumer goods. The continued stress on heavy industry, especially armaments, benefited Slovakia, which was targeted in the 1971–1975 Five-Year Plan for economic development. As a result, by the early 1980s, Slovaks were much closer to catching up economically with Czechs even though nests of poverty still existed in the remote regions of Slovakia.

At the same time that the country's communist regime was trying to deal with rising consumer demands in the 1980s, political opposition was resurfacing. Normalization had demolished the reforms of 1968 and effectively quieted dissent in the country; consequently, for a while acts of protest were isolated and often limited to underground publications. The most significant action occurred in 1977 when 240 persons signed Charter 77, a manifesto authored principally by the Czech playwright Václav Havel, that charged the government with violating internationally recognized civil and political rights. Although few Slovaks openly endorsed Charter 77, some covert groups opposed to the government's suppression of human rights did develop in Slovakia. Overall, though, political dissent was far less active in Slovakia than in the Czech Lands.

During the 1980s events outside Slovakia once again influenced the course of its history and finally led to open political dissent. Dependent on the Soviet leadership for its existence, Czechoslovakia's government followed the rigid economic and political policies of the Soviet Union. The situation changed, however, in 1985, when Mikhail Gorbachev, the new general secretary of the Communist Party of the Soviet Union, initiated political and economic reforms designed to restructure his country's economy and permit more political freedom.

The new openness (glasnost) in the Soviet Union, together with increased tensions in Czechoslovak society, encouraged a resurgence of Czech and Slovak dissent. In 1987 and 1988 the number of dissident groups increased in Czechoslovakia, including in Slovakia where open opposition had practically ceased after 1968. Illegal demonstrations were also on the rise. Defying government warnings, thousands of people in Czechoslovakia assembled on the twentieth anniversary to protest the 1968 Warsaw Pact invasion. In Slovakia, youth involvement helped animate dissent. Opposition energies were also funneled into a religious revival and open defiance of the Communist Party's suppression of religion, especially the Catholic Church. In March 1988 thousands of Slovaks gathered in Bratislava to pray for religious freedom; kneeling demonstrators were dispersed by police with billy clubs. Hundreds of thousands participated in pilgrimages to Levoča, Šaštín, and Slovakia's other holy places. By 1989 Alexander Dubček, the leader of the "Prague Spring," was again speaking out; in an April interview on Hungarian television he called on the Communist Party to renew itself. Because the regime was so closely tied to the Soviet government, Gorbachev's new policies unavoidably had a ripple effect on Czechoslovakia. In March 1987 Husák expressed support for the Gorbachev program but, in Czechoslovakia, uncompromising conservatives prevailed. In December Husák resigned as secretary-general of the Communist Party and was replaced by Miloš Jakeš. Husák retained the presidency.

For the next two years, the government's response to swelling dissent fluctuated between tolerance and brutal crackdowns. In an ill-fated move, however, officials took a hard line on 17 November 1989, when a public commemoration of a student who had been killed during the Nazi occupation evolved into an antigovernment event. Fierce suppression of the crowd by the police outraged and mobilized the country. Dissent, which had been spearheaded by elites and students, now developed into a broad-based popular movement. Two days after the demonstration, Civic Forum, an outgrowth of Charter 77, was organized and began coordinating dissent in the Czech Lands. In Slovakia, Public against Violence, founded on 20 November, did the same. During the next three weeks these two coalitions organized massive demonstrations and strikes in their respective regions. The manifestations in Bratislava proportionately equaled those in Prague, although those in Czechoslovakia's capital city were numerically larger.

Forsaken by the Soviet Union and no longer able to control its citizens, who defiantly took to the streets, the government in Czechoslovakia quickly crumbled. On 7 December, Ladislav Adamec stepped down as prime minister and was replaced by Marián Čalfa, a Slovak and former Communist. Husák resigned as president on 10 December and the first cabinet without a Communist majority since 1948 was sworn in. On 29 December 1989, the Federal Assembly elected Václav Havel president; Alexander Dubček became president of the Federal Assembly. The newly liberated government aimed to establish a Western-style democracy and to create a market economy based on capitalist principles. Because Czechoslovakia's Communist government was brought down without gunfire or bloodshed, its downfall and replacement by a democratic system is popularly known as the Velvet Revolution.

In Slovakia, the Communist Party also acted quickly to reform itself. The first secretary was dismissed on 6 December. During district elections for representatives to a Slovak Communist Party congress, other officials were removed. On 17 December, the congress denounced the policies of the former leadership, made "democratic socialism" its objective, and modified its administrative structure. Changes in the government were occurring simultaneously. The Slovak National Council, the region's governing body, underwent a makeover. On 11 December, Milan Čič became prime minister of Slovakia.

Liberation from the communist regime was accompanied by the reemergence of a nagging historical issue: Slovak autonomy and establishing parity between Slovakia and the Czech Lands. As Slovak and Czech leaders took steps to transform the country, ethnic tensions surfaced. In April 1990 crowds of Slovaks assembled at the parliament building in Bratislava to protest the Slovak government's acceptance of the country's new name, the "Czecho-Slovak Federative Republic." After prolonged debate, the name was finally changed to the "Czech and Slovak Federative Republic." Although the overwhelming majority of Slovaks preferred to remain in a common state with the Czechs, polls also showed that a majority wanted real autonomy for Slovakia within a federal republic.

In the June 1990 elections, Civic Forum won the expected majorities in both houses of the Federal Assembly. The Slovak political movement, Public against Violence, garnered slightly less than 33 percent of the vote in the House of the People and 37 percent in the House of Nations

Vladimír Mečiar. (David Brauchli/Corbis Sygma)

(where Slovakia and the Czech Lands had equal representation). The Assembly subsequently elected the immensely popular Václav Havel president of the republic, Marián Čalfa was reappointed prime minister, and Alexander Dubček retained his position as president of the assembly. Under the federal structure, each republic had a separate prime minister and a governing body. For Slovakia, that body was the Slovak National Council, which was made up of 150 elected representatives. The prime minister came from the political party that won the most votes or could put together a coalition government. As a result of the 1990 elections, Vladimír Mečiar, a former Communist who had been expelled from the Party after the Prague Spring of 1968, became prime minister of Slovakia.

These first postrevolution elections offered no strong evidence that Slovaks wanted to secede from their joint state with the Czechs. Slovak autonomy was an issue, but none of the major parties advocated dissolving the joint republic and creating a separate Slovak country. During the campaign, small groups of Slovak nationalists taunted Havel and called for a "free Slovakia," but they represented the minority view. Although separatism did not enjoy widespread support in the June elections, Slovak nationalism was on the rise. In October 1990 crowds gathered in the streets and opposing sides argued as the Slovak Parliament debated whether Slovak should be designated the official language. In December the country faced a constitutional crisis when Prime Minister Mečiar threatened to declare the primacy of Slovak laws over federal legislation. A compromise outlining specific responsibilities for each level of government defused the situation. But, the struggle indicated a determination by Slovak officials to assert the region's separate interests.

Programs for privatizing and overhauling the country's economic system heightened Slovak suspicions about the central government and widened the rift between Slovakia and the Czech Lands. During the communist era, the government's policy for industrializing Slovakia had made the region economically dependent on the Soviet Union and Eastern Bloc nations. The overthrow of communist regimes resulted in the loss of markets for the type of goods manufactured by Slovak industries. The economic restructuring following the revolution was, therefore, felt more acutely by Slovaks than by Czechs. By the fall of 1991, unemployment in Slovakia had reached 12 percent; in the Czech Lands it was only 4 percent. Some Slovaks, and especially nationalists, blamed the disparities on the policies of a Czech-dominated central government. On 14 March 1991, the fifty-second anniversary of the proclamation of the "independent" Slovak Republic (1939–1945), 5,000 nationalists hurled abuses at Havel when he addressed the crowd and urged Slovaks to oppose separatism. The following October, egg-throwing nationalists again jeered Havel, who went to Slovakia to participate in commemorations of the seventy-third anniversary of the creation of Czechoslovakia. The demonstrations, organized by the Slovak National Party, did not reflect universal sentiment in Slovakia; nevertheless, Havel's popularity among Slovaks had plummeted to 43 percent in December 1991. And while only a minority of Slovaks supported the idea of seceding from the federated state, a majority of them wanted more independent power vested in Slovakia's own government.

The June 1992 elections took place amid rising economic discontent and a growing Slovak nationalism. Aware of the popular mood, Slovakia's political parties generally demanded more autonomy for the republic, while the Slovak National Party advocated outright secession. During the campaign, the Movement for a Democratic Slovakia took a fiercely nationalistic but not an avowedly separatist position. This new political body was headed by Vladimír Mečiar, who had been forced to resign as Slovakia's prime minister in 1991 when the Public against Violence coalition disintegrated. Mečiar indicated that he wanted Slovakia and the Czech Lands to remain together in a confederation, but he also wanted international recognition for Slovakia.

Plans to revamp the country's economy dominated the election and divided the leading Czech and Slovak political parties. The Civic Democratic Party (Czech), headed by Finance Minister Václav Klaus, favored continuing a program of rapid economic reform and privatization. Mečiar and his party wanted to slow the rate of economic change and continue government involvement in the economy. In the Czech Lands, the Civic Democratic Party won and Klaus became prime minister. In Slovakia, Mečiar emerged from the elections, once again, as prime minister. The Movement for a Democratic Slovakia won slightly more than 37 percent of the ballots cast for the 150 seats on the Slovak National Council. This meant that Mečiar's party had received enough votes to allow him to put together a coalition and thus control the Slovak National Council. The openly separatist Slovak National Party eked out less than 8 percent of the popular vote.

Although the Slovak separatists had fared poorly in the elections and Mečiar's party had not directly advocated secession, within a week after the June elections the Czech and Slovak prime ministers began discussing the possible breakup of the country. The two sides could not agree on a mutually advantageous plan for transforming the country to a market economy. In July Slovaks annoyed Czechs when the Slovak Chamber of the National Assembly blocked Havel's reelection as president. Rather than finish his term, which was due to expire in October, Havel resigned the presidency on 20 July.

During the summer of 1992, Czech and Slovak officials negotiated the breakup of the country and the division of shared assets. On 17 July, the Slovak National Council issued a declaration of sovereignty for Slovakia, and on 1 September it adopted a constitution for the future independent republic. By the end of October, Czech and Slovak leaders had worked out the technical details, and on 29 October Prime Ministers Mečiar and Klaus signed an agreement mapping out the dissolution process. On 25 November, the Federal Assembly voted to dissolve the federated republic. The decision for Slovak independence, which finally came in the fall of 1992, was the result of government actions; no popular referendum was ever held to authorize the "Velvet Divorce." This became the popular term for the relatively amicable breakup of the Czech and Slovak lands that, ex-

Slovakia becomes independent, 1 January 1993. (David Brauchli/ Corbis Sygma)

cept for a short period during World War II, had been joined together for seventy-four years.

On 1 January 1993, the Czech and Slovak Federative Republic ceased to exist and Slovakia became an independent nation. The government that had been formed following the 1992 elections—the last held before the breakup—continued administering the country. Vladimír Mečiar, leader of the Movement for a Democratic Slovakia, remained Slovakia's prime minister. The Slovak National Council, now called the National Council of the Slovak Republic, became the country's parliament. On 15 February 1993, the National Council elected Michal Kováč as Slovakia's first president.

Except for a six-month period, Vladimír Mečiar remained Slovakia's prime minister until the fall of 1998. Following a no-confidence vote by parliament, in March 1994, he was replaced by a coalition headed by Jozef Moravčík. Moravčík's term proved short-lived because his new government, proclaiming itself temporary, called for elections to be held in September 1994. Winning the largest percentage but not a majority of the votes in the fall contest, Vladimír Mečiar nevertheless was able, once again, to form a government. It took control in December 1994 and remained in power until 29 October 1998.

After Slovakia came into existence in 1993, the country faced several challenges. In addition to establishing an administrative apparatus to govern its people, Slovakia had to move forward with democratization, transforming its economy into one driven by competition and private ownership, and shaping both a domestic as well as foreign policy that would establish Slovakia's respectability among the world's democratic nations. As the country grappled with these tasks, the first half decade of its existence as an independent country was, to a large extent, dominated by Vladimír Mečiar.

When Slovakia became independent, it was immediately recognized as a legitimate nation. On 19 January 1993, the United Nations accepted it as a new member. In July it joined the Council of Europe. The country's position on joining NATO, however, was somewhat more ambiguous. Prior to independence, Mečiar seemed to favor becoming a NATO member, but afterward his government initially seemed to lean toward developing strong ties to Russia. By 1994, though, he had changed his mind and was tilting toward eventually seeking NATO membership. In February 1994 Slovakia joined NATO's Partnership for Peace program. Ultimately becoming a member of the European Union also ranked among independent Slovakia's foreign policy aims.

Slovakia's domestic politics thwarted its foreign policy objectives. Vladimír Mečiar, who disliked criticism and had a reputation for being dictatorial, attempted to institute measures that gave an ever increasing authoritarian cast to his rule. An attempt in 1996 to make "crimes against the state" part of Slovakia's penal code stirred fears that this infant government was reverting to the despotic practices of the communist era. Ethnic minorities, especially Hungarians, also seemed targeted for discrimination. In November 1995 the parliament passed the Slovak Language Law, which made Slovak the only official language. Hungarians, in particular, were adversely affected by the law. While Hungarians were struggling to maintain language rights, the country's Roma were facing prejudice stemming from the Slovak society's generally unfavorable attitude toward them. In the fall of 1993 Mečiar reflected anti-Romany sentiment and gave voice to stereotypes when, in what was clearly a veiled reference to the Roma, he spoke of socially unadaptable persons.

Slovakia's minority problems, together with Mečiar's authoritarian actions, had the overall effect of projecting a negative image of Slovakia to the rest of the world. Other nations feared that democratization was slowing down and that the government lacked a commitment to protecting minority and human rights. Reflecting these concerns, in July 1997 NATO denied Slovakia's application to join; several months later at its December meeting, the European Union also refused acceptance at that time.

In the fall of 1998 Slovakia held regular national elections. Vladimír Mečiar's party won, but the margin of victory was so small that he could not put together a coalition and form a ruling government. He, therefore, announced that he would not attempt to do so. Following this announcement, the leader of the Slovak Democratic Coalition, Mikuláš Dzurinda, successfully built a coalition that assumed power when the newly elected parliament convened on 29 October 1998. Dzurinda became prime minister and began tackling the country's unresolved economic, employment, and social problems. His government also faced the task of repairing Slovakia's damaged international image and verifying that Slovakia was indeed a country that had thrown off the shackles of nearly a half century of communist rule to become a democratic nation.

POLITICAL DEVELOPMENTS

The collapse of communism in 1989 ushered in dramatic changes for the people of Czechoslovakia. In the months following the Velvet Revolution the country remained calm, but there was general euphoria as the citizenry prepared to vote in the country's first free elections in forty-four years. The end of totalitarianism meant that ordinary citizens could now participate in the political process. With censorship lifted, persons openly expressed opinions without fear of government reprisal. The demise of single-party domination by the Communists also allowed other political parties and interest groups to develop. The liberation that freed the country from the grip of authoritarian rule also sparked a resurgence of Slovak nationalism. Less than a year after the revolution, the thorny issue of Slovak self-government had become a powerful issue in Czechoslovakia's politics and one that finally contributed to the breakup of the country. Political developments in the subsequently independent Slovakia created doubts about its commitment to democratic principles.

The emergence of Slovak nationalism following the 1989 revolution was not a sudden turn of events. Since the mid-nineteenth century, achieving recognition as a distinct political entity had been the underlying theme of Slovak politics. The notion of regional autonomy was first articulated in the late 1840s, when Slovaks were under Hungarian control. During the next half century, though, the Slovak political agenda concentrated on gaining representation in Hungary's legislative body, not on gaining self-rule. Only a small segment of the Slovak people actively engaged in political activities, in part because the kingdom's restrictive franchise laws excluded broader participation. When, after World War I, Slovaks joined with Czechs and created a democratic society, the door was opened both for political parties to develop and for greater mass involvement in the political process.

During the entire interwar era following the creation of Czechoslovakia, the question of Slovak autonomy haunted Czech-Slovak politics. Slovak nationalists, opposed to a centralized government, wanted an arrangement that would give Slovakia more control over its own affairs. It is important to recognize, however, that the question of autonomy versus centralism was not an issue affecting only Czech-Slovak relations. Slovaks themselves were divided. Some Slovaks favored a centralized government while others wanted a federation. These differing positions nurtured multiple political parties within Slovakia. The question of Slovak self-government became a constant political theme of the 1920s and 1930s, but gaining independence, which would mean breaking up Czechoslovakia, was not a goal. Even Hlinka's Slovak People's Party, the most strident advocate of Slovak autonomy, did not demand independence.

Although not an objective of interwar politics, on the eve of World War II, Slovakia did proclaim its independence. Despite the unsavory nature of the wartime Slovak Republic, whose "independence" rested on subordination to the Third Reich, the experiment in self-rule raised expectations of greater autonomy after the war. These hopes were ignored after Czechoslovakia was restored. But there was little time for this to affect political developments before 1948, when the Communists took over and shaped the country's political agenda for the next forty years. Designated as a crime against the state, advocacy of Slovak autonomy disappeared as a legitimate political issue. After the 1968 "Prague Spring," the Communist dictatorship reversed its traditional opposition to Slovak autonomy and made Czechoslovakia a federated state. Since real power still rested with the Communist Party and the Prague government, Slovak control of regional affairs was more fiction than reality. Nevertheless, in theory, Czechoslovakia consisted of two republics.

Following the ouster of Czechoslovakia's communist regime in 1989, the federal structure created in 1968 remained basically intact. The Federal Assembly, which was the legislative arm of the government, was composed of two bodies: the House of Nations and the House of the People. Each house had 150 members. In the House of Nations, Slovakia and the Czech Republic had equal representation; so, each republic had 75 representatives. In the House of the People, where representation was based on population, in 1990 Slovakia was allotted 49 members while the Czech Republic was given 101 deputies.

Since the country adopted a federal system, the Slovak and Czech republics were each governed by a separate council that had authority over specified affairs. The governing body for Slovakia was the Slovak National Council, which was composed of 200 representatives. Unlike the Federal Assembly, where there were two houses, the council consisted of just one chamber. Under the federal system, each republic also had a prime minister and a president.

Pledged to reinstituting representative government, Czechoslovakia's new leadership established a parliamentary democracy. Representation in the Federal Assembly was proportional, which meant each party's allotment of seats was based on the percentage of votes it won in the election. This constitutional structure encouraged the development of multiple parties in Czechoslovakia. The parliamentary system also forced parties that won seats to join together in coalitions to form a ruling government.

Following the Velvet Revolution, citizens took advantage of their newly gained political rights. In June 1990 an estimated 95 percent of eligible voters went to the polls to participate in the country's first postcommunist era elections. The results turned out as generally expected. Public against Violence, which had coordinated Slovakia's opposition to the communist regime, received the highest percentage of votes in both the national elections for the Federal Assembly and in republic elections for the Slovak National Council. The Communist Party came in second in both. The nationalistic Slovak National Party, which had been organized a few months before the election, ranked third. A total of seven parties won seats in Slovakia's National Council.

The elections had the anticipated results, but they also reflected what would become characteristic features of poli-

Elections in Slovakia. In the village of Tomášová, ballot boxes are readied for voting on Friday and Saturday, 25 and 26 September 1998. (David Brauchli/Corbis Sygma)

tics in Czechoslovakia. By March 1990, the country had more than sixty official parties or "movements," as some political groups with programs rather than explicit platforms were called. With such a large number, many of these parties could not have seriously expected that they would be able to submit a slate of nominees in the June elections. Twenty-three parties ultimately met the qualifications and fielded candidates; however, less than half of them finally won seats in both the federal and republic elections. Although the elections aimed to establish a legitimate postcommunist government for Czechoslovakia, many of the competing parties were actually republicwide instead of nationwide entities. Six of the parties participating existed only in Slovakia. Following the 1990 elections, politics became regionalized as Slovak and Czech parties developed programs focusing on their individual republics instead of on countrywide interests.

Multiple parties also reflected the increasingly complicated nature of politics in Slovakia. It was telling that a coalition of two Hungarian parties, which represented the concerns of Slovakia's Hungarian minority, came in fourth in the republic elections and earned fourteen seats. In the national elections one of these Hungarian parties won a total of twelve seats in the two houses of the Federal Assembly. The appearance of ethnically based parties dedicated to promoting the interests of specific minorities was an early indication that nationality issues would be an important aspect of Slovak politics.

The 1990 elections did not reveal fundamental animosity between the Slovak and Czech republics. Prior to the elections, however, there was clear indication of a resurgent Slovak nationalism. In the spring of 1990, in what is sometimes dubbed "the hyphen war," Slovaks and Czechs battled over the country's name. This political altercation ended with the country adopting the cumbersome name "Czech and Slovak Federative Republic." The squabble over an issue that was seemingly more symbolic than substantive reflected a determination by Slovaks to ensure that Slovakia would share equal recognition with the Czech Republic.

While the 1990 elections were indicative of the country's smooth transition from a single-party dictatorship to a multiparty democracy, politics in the postelection era followed a bumpy course. Political parties, in particular, were clearly in a state of flux. Between 1990 and 1992, when the next elections were held, some parties disintegrated, others reorganized under different names, and others were formed. Overall the number of parties, especially regional bodies dedicated to republic-level issues, increased. It became clear that the Federative Republic had a stable multiparty structure; it just did not have stable parties.

In Slovakia, the proliferation of parties stemmed, in part, from the differing opinions about issues affecting the region. Questions about Slovakia's future in particular split Public against Violence (PAV). Bitter rifts occurred between leaders willing to accept a strong central government and nationalists who wanted Slovakia to assert its own identity and have more authority over its affairs. The split led to the ouster of Slovakia's prime minister, Vladimír Mečiar, in 1991. He and his supporters left PAV and organized a rival party, Movement for a Democratic Slovakia (MDS). As a result, PAV, the party that had received approximately 30 percent or more of the popular vote in national and republic elections, simply disappeared.

After the 1990 elections, the relationship between Slovakia and the central government became antagonistic. More and more, politics revolved around the proper division of power between the republics and the central government in Prague. The question was: which government should have the most authority, especially over matters affecting Slovakia. In December 1990 an agreement was reached that did grant the republics more power. They were put in charge of economic decisions affecting their regions as well as all matters not specifically reserved for the central government. As Slovaks and Czechs dealt with political and especially economic issues, they focused more explicitly on what benefited their respective regions. Thus, under the federal system, politics were evolving into a situation where each republic looked out for its own particular concerns.

In the years leading up to the 1992 elections, economic issues became increasingly intertwined with the debate over the country's constitutional structure. Czechs wanted a strong central government to oversee a quick transformation to private ownership and a market economy; but Slovaks, who believed privatization would hurt them more, wanted a strong republic government that could oversee and slow down the process. Given the character of Slovakia's industry, the transformation to a competitive market economy was, in fact, adversely affecting Slovakia more than the Czech Republic. The belief that Slovaks had historically suffered mistreatment at the hands of the Czechs—and more specifically of a Czech-dominated central government—nurtured nationalist sentiment in Slovakia.

By the 1992 elections, republic self-interest and economic concerns had dampened the euphoria that had characterized politics in the immediate aftermath of the Velvet Revolution. A growing Slovak nationalism, coupled with concerns that the central government's economic policies were hurting Slovakia, dominated the preelection campaign. The fact that each republic had its own separate parties also shaped election-year politics. In what became regional instead of national campaigns, candidates battled over issues important to their particular republic, not necessarily the country.

The political situation had evolved into one where, in Slovakia, the important election was for seats on the National Council in Bratislava, not in the Federal Assembly in Prague. The campaign in Slovakia centered on matters involving the transformation of the economy and the constitutional question of how extensive Slovak autonomy should be. Politics in Slovakia were also significantly shaped by a growing nationalism among its citizenry. The fiercely nationalistic stance adopted by the Slovak National Party, which actually called for Slovakia to secede from the common state, forced other parties to be nationalistic as well. While wavering on outright Slovak secession, the popular MDS, led by Vladimír Mečiar, linked protecting Slovakia's economic interests to securing extensive autonomy. In essence, it called for the Federative Republic to become a confederation with two self-governing republics. Under this system, the republic-level governments would be more powerful than the central government.

Slovak public opinion, now a factor in the postcommunist era, further complicated the political situation in 1992. Opinion polls revealed that the overwhelming majority of Slovaks wanted to remain in a common state with the Czechs, but they were unhappy with the federation and wanted more self-government. The results of the 1992 election seemed to confirm this position. The MDS, which in addition to a confederation called for slowing down economic changes, got 35 percent of the vote. The openly separatist Slovak National Party eked out 7.9 percent of the vote for the National Council. Nevertheless, taken together these two strongly nationalistic parties garnered more than 45 percent of the vote in the republic election and about 43 percent for houses in the Federal Assembly. The election allowed Vladimír Mečiar, an aggressive, strong-willed personality, to become prime minister of the Slovak Republic.

It was an irony of the 1992 election that, while Slovaks voted for remaining in a joint state with the Czechs, this democratic process paved the way for letting leaders do what the citizens had voted against: breaking up the country. In order to keep its campaign promise, the MDS had to push for a confederation. Czech leaders, meanwhile, felt compelled to press for a strong central government. As leaders adopted inflexible stands, Slovak opinion polls still showed that the vast majority of Slovaks wanted the country to remain intact. Nevertheless, although a democratic society supposedly based on popular rule, no genuine effort was made to conduct a popular referendum and thus involve the people in the most important political decision of the country's postcommunist era. In the end, it was elected leaders who decided that the Czech and Slovak Federative Republic should split into two independent nations.

The constitutional structure of the newly sovereign Slovakia was the same as what had existed in the federated republic. It was a parliamentary democracy with a 150-member legislature, renamed the National Council of the Slovak Republic. In addition to a prime minister, there was also a president, who was elected by the council but had limited, clearly defined powers. In 1999 the constitution was amended to allow the president to be popularly elected in a nationwide election. The country also established a Constitutional Court, charged with hearing appeals in cases where persons alleged their "fundamental rights and freedoms" had been "infringed." Its many powers also included having jurisdiction over contested elections.

Following the breakup, politics in Slovakia were tumultuous. And during the first five years after independence, when Vladimír Mečiar dominated political life, it was not clear what course the country's political evolution would take. His bellicose and often authoritarian style suggested he lacked commitment to democratic procedures and human rights. Mečiar roused both staunch loyalty and fierce opposition among politicians and the citizenry alike. As a result, in the period until 1998 when he lost the position of prime minister, politics in the country were characterized by personal rivalries and fights among political leaders. The fiercest clashes were between Mečiar and the country's president, Michal Kováč. By the fall of 1993 these two leaders were publicly engaged in bitter disputes. A speech by Kováč denouncing Mečiar contributed to a no-confidence vote that forced the prime minister to resign in March 1994. When elections in the fall of 1994 once again made Mečiar prime minister, he returned with a determination to maintain a tight hold on his power. Sensitive to criticism, he tried to quiet his opposition. Although he used legal means, his attempts to control the television and print media were reminiscent of the repressive shenanigans of the old communist era.

Acrimonious battles among political leaders stimulated an increase in political parties. This proliferation was another feature characterizing Slovakia's ongoing political evolution. Between the Velvet Revolution and 1998, Slovakia experienced about forty political parties and movements. All these groups complicated the political situation in Slovakia and fragmented the country's electorate. This was evident in 1994 when only seven parties won seats in the National Council. Yet, because parties had formed alliances during the elections, at least sixteen different political parties gained representation on the council.

Slovakia's parliamentary system encourages citizen involvement in the political process. While, when compared to the United States, the number of Slovak citizens who vote is high, voter turnout in Slovakia declined from approximately 98.9 percent in 1990 to 75 percent in 1994; the number surged again in 1998 when it reached 84.2 percent. Opinion polls reveal that many Slovaks hold cynical views about politicians and political parties. Also, there is still a contingent of Slovaks, especially persons who have been hurt by privatization and those living in rural regions, who believe that Slovakia was better off before the Velvet Revolution. This attitude is evident in the ability of the successor to the Communist Party consistently to garner more than 10 percent—and up to nearly 15 percent—of the vote and come in second or a close third in elections.

Citizens' attitudes toward democratization have also been part of the country's political evolution. Research conducted in the mid-1990s revealed that Slovaks supported democratization in principle, but the level of this support varied among the country's social classes. Young, more educated Slovaks who lived in urban areas tended to favor democratization more than older persons who resided in the country's conservative rural regions did. In addition, differing degrees of commitment to democratic principles have influenced the treatment of the country's ethnic groups. In general, popular values do not uniformly embrace the idea of protecting the rights of minorities. As a consequence, dealing with minorities was one of the most important issues shaping Slovak politics in the 1990s.

Even before the Velvet Divorce, Slovakia was confronting the especially prickly question of language rights. An unsuccessful attempt by the Slovak National Council in the fall of 1990 to enact legislation designating Slovak as the only language permissible for official business exacerbated an already vexed relationship between Slovaks and the country's Hungarians. The law finally passed on 25 October 1990 stipulated that, in communities where a single ethnic group made up more than 20 percent of the population, official business could be conducted in the minority language. The new law sparked demonstrations by some Slovaks. About eighty Slovak opponents even went on a hunger strike to protest the legislation.

Slovakia's constitution addressed the status of minorities by including clauses in Article 34 affirming minority and ethnic rights. This affirmation guaranteed language rights. Revisiting the language issue in November 1995, the parliament passed the Slovak Language Law, which proclaimed that Slovak was an expression of the nation's sovereignty and made it the only official language. Among other ramifications, the law meant that official documents such as birth certificates had to be rendered in Slovak. This intolerance toward minorities is indicative of the nationalist sentiment among Slovaks. One factor contributing to Mečiar's resilient popularity was his ability to exploit a rather pervasive Slovak nationalism. He framed his actions in ways that stirred national pride. At the same time, popular prejudices combined with nationalism to sanction discrimination against ethnic minorities.

By 1998, although Slovakia had seventeen political parties and movements, the more than half decade of Mečiar's authoritarian rule had divided Slovaks into basically two factions. There were the pro-Mečiar forces and those who opposed him. These conflicting positions created strange alliances as parties with different ideologies found themselves temporarily united either to oppose or support Mečiar. These expedient alliances had a significant impact on national elections in September 1998. The MDS garnered 27 percent, but its nearest opponent, the Slovak Democratic Coalition, claimed 26.33 percent of the vote. This razor-slim victory meant that Mečiar could not put together a coalition. Three days after the election, he announced he would not attempt to form a government. Mečiar's opponent Mikuláš Dzurinda, leader of the Slovak Democratic Coalition, was able to draw parties together and organize a government.

The first direct election of the president demonstrated how politically fragmented and simultaneously polarized Slovaks still were. Ten persons ran for the office. Since no candidate won 50 percent in the first round of voting on 15 May 1999, a runoff election was held on 29 May. It pitted the two top vote getters—Rudolf Schuster and Vladimír Mečiar—against one another. Schuster got slightly more than 57 percent of the vote and won. However, the fact that more than 43 percent of the voters chose Mečiar revealed that, despite his authoritarian policies, he enjoyed a persistent popularity. The country remained divided along the same lines evident in the fall 1998 elections.

In form Slovakia has evolved into a democratic state. Its political institutions resemble those that function in democratic countries. Since 1993, it has had five governments and each change has been characterized by a peaceful, orderly transfer of power. The losing party has voluntarily relinquished its authority. Despite his anti-democratic bent, Mečiar tried mostly to use legal means to squelch his opposition and curtail minority rights. The 1998 and 2002 elections installed a reform-minded leader, Mikuláš Dzurinda, as prime minister. Still, politics remain fragmented and the country's political evolution as a democratic nation is not yet complete.

CULTURAL DEVELOPMENT

Because Slovakia was an integral part of multiethnic nations for more than a millennium, the country does not have a national history peppered with royalty or august personages. Indeed, in the past, the achievements of Slovak military heroes, scientists, inventors, athletes, and creative as well as performing artists were typically subsumed within the accomplishments of multinational states. As a result of its unique past, Slovakia's historically significant personalities are individuals who contributed to the Slovak quest to assert an identity as a distinct "people." These individuals fall into two general categories. One group consists of intellectuals who engaged in the literary and political efforts that fueled the nineteenth-century Slovak national awakening. Writers who subsequently continued nurturing a distinct Slovak identity also belong in this class. In the main, these were persons who challenged Hungary's Magyarization policy of forced assimilation. The second category of significant persons includes twentieth-century political activists. In particular, these were individuals associated with efforts to gain independence from Hungary or promote Slovak autonomy within the subsequently created Czechoslovakia.

The nineteenth-century national awakening stands out as the cultural high point of Slovak history. For many countries, establishing a written language might not be underscored as a significant part of their history, but for Slovakia this development was crucial. Slovak culture derives much of its distinctiveness from its religious heritage and, especially, its folk traditions. Folk literature and peasant life have historically inspired Slovakia's creative artists, including many of the national activists and writers spawned by the national awakening. And in the twenty-first century, its folk heritage is still being recognized as a unique characteristic of Slovak culture.

A description of significant people and the highlights of Slovak culture must begin with Cyril and Methodius, the two missionaries credited with bringing Christianity to the Slavic peoples. Although they actually spent relatively little time in what is modern-day Slovakia, it would be difficult to overemphasize their cultural or historical importance. Rastislav, the ruler of the Great Moravian Empire, initiated the move that brought these two brothers to Slovakia in the mid-ninth century. He wanted Slavic languages used to Christianize the Slavs, and he requested the help of Byzantium's emperor to achieve that goal. In 863 the emperor responded by dispatching the two brothers on a mission to convert Slavs to Christianity. Using an alphabet formulated by Constantine, who later assumed the name Cyril, they translated the Holy Scripture and liturgical works from Greek into Old Church Slavonic. By preaching in Slavic languages, these missionaries successfully won over the so-called pagan Slavs to Byzantine Christianity. While on a visit to Rome, Cyril died in 869; on his trip back to the Great Moravian Empire, Methodius was captured by enemies and imprisoned for probably three years. After his release, he returned to the empire where the ruler, Svätopluk, put him in charge of the empire's Christian churches. In 880 the pope made Methodius archbishop of Great Moravia, and he remained in the empire until his death five years later. After Methodius died in 885, Pope Stephen V banned the use of the Slavic liturgy. As a result, the Latin rite ultimately became the dominant liturgy in the territory inhabited by Slovaks. Nevertheless, the Cyril and Methodius mission endowed Slovakia with a Christian tradition that subsequently permeated Slovak culture. When Slovakia became independent in 1993, the attachment to the "Cyril and Methodius" tradition was evident in the Preamble of the Slovak constitution, which openly invoked "the spiritual heritage of Cyril and Methodius."

Although Cyril and Methodius used Slavic vernaculars to convert inhabitants of the Great Moravian Empire, they did not leave Slovaks with a written language. Into the late eighteenth century, Slovaks did not have a separate literary tongue; instead, educated Slovaks wrote in Czech. Slovaks, however, did speak dialects of a common tongue. At the turn of the eighteenth century, this common language became the basis for generating the Slovak national awakening. This movement, or what some observers label the national revival, is considered a pinnacle of Slovak cultural and national history. It was an epoch dominated by intellectuals whose linguistic and literary achievements, together with their political activism, cultivated a distinct Slovak cultural identity. Although the era witnessed the blossoming of Slovak literature, the codification of the Slovak language marked its greatest achievement.

Roots of the Slovak national awakening can be traced to the late eighteenth-century activities of Anton Bernolák. Although it evolved into a cultural and to some extent a political movement, religious goals initially sparked the Slovak enlightenment. Bernolák, who was a Jesuit priest, wanted to advance the religious education of the Slovak Catholic population. He decided that he could best achieve this goal by developing a written language.

Bernolák came to his conclusion about the importance of a standard literary language relatively early in his life. In

1787, at the age of twenty-five, while studying at the Bratislava seminary, he anonymously printed a justification for a Slovak literary language and a Slovak orthography. In 1790 he published *Grammatica Slavica* (Slovak Grammar). Bernolák's six-volume dictionary, *Slowár slowenski, česko-latinsko-ňemecko-uherskí* (1825–1827), appeared more than a decade after his death. *Bernolákovčina,* the literary Slovak developed by Bernolák, was a codification of the western dialect spoken by educated persons of the Trnava region.

Bernolák was motivated by religious not political or nationalistic objectives. Indeed, he never intended to encourage Slovak nationalism, and he did not engage in political activities. Nevertheless, by treating Slovak as a unique language, Bernolák set Slovaks apart from Czechs, and the Bernolák movement is credited with helping inspire the Slovak national awakening. Bernolák died in 1813, about three decades before the Slovak national awakening would get into full swing. Even though his version of literary Slovak was ultimately rejected, modern-day Slovaks, especially Catholics, still laud him as the first codifier of literary Slovak. The real credit for codifying the modern Slovak language belongs to L'udovít Štúr, a Lutheran minister. His efforts to promote a distinct Slovak national identity in the wake of Hungary's Magyarization program helped fuel the nineteenth-century Slovak national awakening. During the 1840s, Štúr's nationalist convictions prompted him to engage in diverse literary activities and finally to become an ardent political activist as well.

Born in 1815, L'udovít Štúr was relatively young when he became embroiled in cultural activities that nurtured the Slovak national awakening. It was the Hungarian government's Magyarization policy that moved him to action. Realizing that Magyarization would result in the cultural annihilation of the Slovak people, Štúr became convinced that Slovaks needed to create their own written language to ensure their survival as a distinct "nation." Unlike Bernolák, Štúr's objectives were nationalistic, not religious. In 1843 Štúr and a group of clergymen agreed to establish a Slovak literary language. Rejecting *bernolákovčina,* they based their codification on the central Slovak dialect. In 1846 Štúr introduced his version, *štúrovčina*. After compromises with the Bernolákites in 1851, a modified version of štúrovčina became the accepted literary language. It is the foundation of modern-day Slovak.

Štúr's convictions about establishing a Slovak cultural identity made him a leader among intellectuals seeking to counter a rising Hungarian nationalism and took him beyond literary activities to political action. Thus due in great measure to Štúr's influence, the Slovak awakening, which started as a literary movement, took on political overtones. As early as 1842, he was dispatching petitions trying to halt Hungary's Magyarization program. In the mid-1840s, as editor of a newspaper, he combined literary activities and political activism. When he became a representative for the town of Zvolen in the Hungarian Assembly in 1847, his energies were directed into traditional political channels. A year later, however, his political activities took on a more aggressive character when he chaired the conference that drew up the "Demands of the Slovak Nation." It asked for administrative autonomy for Upper Hungary. This was the first public call to make Upper Hungary (Slovakia) a separate political entity.

Štúr's activities became out-and-out militant when, in 1848, he helped organize a guerrilla unit and made an unsuccessful attempt to initiate a popular uprising against the Hungarian government. Following this futile attempt, he again resorted to legal measures to try to obtain autonomy for Upper Hungary. He petitioned the emperor to grant the region self-government. This effort failed. Under surveillance for his radical activities and made despondent by political failures, in the early 1850s Štúr turned his attention almost solely to writing. He died in 1856. By combining wide-ranging literary endeavors with political activities fighting Magyarization, Štúr secured a place of nearly unqualified reverence in Slovakia's national history. He is generally considered the greatest figure of nineteenth-century Slovak history and the person commonly associated with the Slovak national awakening.

Codifying the Slovak language, which was the most important achievement of the national awakening, sparked a vibrant literary movement as well. Indeed, the period saw the flowering of Slovak literature and marked its golden age. Creative works of varying quality, including poems, epics, prose, ballads, treatises on wide-ranging topics, biographies, travelogues, and pamphlets appeared. While some Slovak writers produced prose, it was poetry that dominated the national awakening and the half century following it. Slovak poems of the era emphasized love but especially heroic, nationalistic, and historical themes. Among the most important poets were Janko Kráľ (1822–1876), Samo Chalúpka (1812–1883), Andrej Sládkovič (1820–1872), and Ján Botto (1829–1881). Two other literary masters, Ján Kalinčiak (1822–1871) and Jozef Miloslav Hurban (1817–1888), are better known for their historical prose.

Literature growing out of the Slovak awakening dealt with national themes, but writers of the era, especially poets, were inspired by Slovakia's folk culture. Heroes, heroines, and villains had their roots in folk songs, stories, and fairy tales. Peasant themes flowed through literary works. Thus the literature not only asserted Slovak distinctiveness, it helped perpetuate the rich and varied folk traditions inherent to Slovak culture. The poetry, but more particularly the prose of the era, also drew from Slovakia's historical roots. Themes glorifying Slovakia's history before the Magyar invasion filtered through the literature. Events and personages of the ninth century—Cyril and Methodius and their Christianization of the Slavs, the Great Moravian Empire and its last ruler Svätopluk—were introduced both as Slovak history and as symbols of a Slovak cultural identity.

As a chronological period, the Slovak awakening extended into the 1850s, but its cultural and historical impact carried well into Slovakia's future. The man often recognized as the greatest Slovak poet, Pavol Országh (1849–1921), began producing his important works during the last decades of the nineteenth century. Writing under the pen name, Hviezdoslav, he too highlighted rural themes and the common people. At the same time, Svetozár Hurban-Vajanský (1847–1916) represented both the combined ideological and political spirit of the earlier Slovak national awakening. He wrote poetry but is recognized for elevating prose, especially novels, to a respectable status in Slovak literature. A nationalist fiercely critical of Hungary's Magyarization policies, Vajanský incorporated social and political criticism into his works. His activities as a journalist, writer, and critic angered Hungarian officials and, as a result, he was imprisoned three times. Vajanský's political activism put him squarely in the tradition of L'udovít Štúr and other literary figures of the Slovak national awakening.

During the national awakening and the half century that followed, the Slovak writers who drew on peasant themes and the persons actually involved in the movement belonged to an educated elite. This was not a movement that touched the masses. Few ordinary Slovaks knew about L'udovít Štúr, much less read the literature drawn from folk traditions or glorifying the Slovak past. In order to promote Slovak culture and education, in 1863, with the help of Emperor Franz Joseph, Slovak intellectuals did found the Matica slovenská. Its diverse activities included publishing folklore, poetry, and historical works in Slovak. Creating the Matica marked yet another achievement in an era identified with Slovak cultural advancements. The Matica, however, lasted only a few short years. In 1875, under a reinvigorated Magyarization program, the Hungarian government closed down its operations.

Into the early decades of the twentieth century, Slovaks remained a people poorly educated in their own language. Moreover, when Slovakia separated from Hungary and became part of the newly created Czechoslovakia, Slovaks had not developed a culture steeped in the fine, performing, or creative arts. Instead their culture was characterized by a nationalist literature, religious works, and folk traditions.

Luminaries of nineteenth- and early twentieth-century Slovak history were writers and national activists engaged in a nationalistic mission against Hungarian cultural domination. Prominent figures of the twentieth century included persons associated with Slovak independence from Hungary and then autonomy within the common Czech-Slovak state.

Milan Rastislav Štefánik is the most famous Slovak to emerge from the struggle for Slovak independence from Hungary. Born in Slovakia in 1880, at the age of eighteen Štefánik went to Prague to study and in 1904 earned a doctorate in astronomy. Although he immigrated to France in 1908 and became a French citizen in 1912, his activities during World War I made him an integral part of Slovakia's national history. After war broke out in 1914, Štefánik joined the French army and by 1918 had become a general in the air force. During the war, however, he spent much of his time engaged in political and diplomatic activities designed to bring about the postwar dismemberment of the Austro-Hungarian Empire. In 1915 he joined Tomáš Masaryk and Edvard Beneš to work on behalf of uniting Czechs and Slovaks in a joint state after the war. He was the only Slovak member of this powerful political trio that headed the Czechoslovak National Council, an organization committed to creating Czecho-Slovakia. He also helped organize and seek recruits for the Czechoslovak Legion, a volunteer army that fought with the Allies and thus helped advance the cause of Czech and Slovak independence. When Czechoslovakia's new government was formed, he was appointed defense minister. On his way to assume this post, in May 1919, however, Štefánik died in a plane crash.

Although Štefánik left Slovakia as a young adult, his efforts to liberate Slovakia from Hungary have elevated him to a place of historical and cultural significance. His premature death added a valorous dimension to his life that has embellished his heroic stature. Like other fallen heroes of history, his tragic, early demise stirs speculation about what might have happened *if* he had lived. The image of Štefánik as an ardent Slovak nationalist who would have promoted Slovak autonomy and opposed a centralized Czech-dominated government cannot be effectively challenged. Without future actions to disprove it, his nationalistic image stands firm. The magnificent monument erected at his grave site in Bradlo, Slovakia, both enhances and attests to Štefánik's historical as well as cultural significance.

During the 1920s and until his death in 1938, Fr. Andrej Hlinka was Czechoslovakia's most prominent Slovak political figure. He also belongs to that group of historical luminaries credited with advancing a distinct Slovak national identity. As leader of the Slovak People's Party, Hlinka opposed a centralized government and consistently demanded Slovak autonomy within the common Czech-Slovak state. Among Slovak contemporaries, Hlinka elicited praise and condemnation; moreover, he was not popular with Protestants or Slovak Catholics who believed a central government was in Slovakia's best interest. Still, his advocacy of autonomy makes him part of what many Slovaks have come to see as their historical struggle for a national self-identity. In terms of Slovakia's modern history, Hlinka was unquestionably an important figure. In a country that is predominantly Roman Catholic, the fact that Hlinka was a Roman Catholic priest adds to his historical luster.

The most august modern Slovak figure was Alexander Dubček. His significance stems from his actions as head of Czechoslovakia's communists, especially the reform effort popularly known as the Prague Spring of 1968. The fact that Dubček was a "Slovak," however, stirs national pride among the Slovaks.

Slovakia's "significant people" are not persons of international renown. Slovaks of the nineteenth century whose political activities or literary contributions justify ranking them as "significant" are persons generally unknown to the outside world. For example, with the exception of Svetozár Hurban-Vajanský, most literary works by famous Slovak writers have not been extensively translated into other languages, and thus they do not have global reputations. Dubček is the only political figure who enjoys substantial international recognition.

The historical and cultural significance enjoyed by individuals identified with forging a Slovak national identity has become even more apparent since 1993, when Slovakia became independent. Following independence, the country used its currency to honor important historical figures. It did the same when it subsequently designed postage stamps.

Slovakia's paper bills depict the missionaries Cyril and Methodius. They also honor latter-day figures who belong to the growing national lore emphasizing the Slovaks' historical quest for freedom: Anton Bernolák, L'udovít Štúr, Milan Rastislav Štefánik, and Andrej Hlinka. Postage stamps and cards pay homage to these persons as well. Alexander Dubček's image does not appear on Slovak currency but he is memorialized on stamps and cards. Major as well as several minor literary figures associated with the Slovak national awakening and the later nineteenth-century writings also have stamps dedicated to them.

With the notable exception of Alexander Dubček, who is universally admired, it is important to note that Slovakia's minorities do not embrace nationally significant historical personalities in the same way Slovaks do. Indeed, for Hungarians, the country's largest ethnic minority, the roster of noteworthy figures would actually include the Hungarian nationalists whom nineteenth-century Slovak nationalists defied and whom Slovak history vilifies.

Independent Slovakia has made little attempt to accommodate the sentiments of either its ethnic or religious minorities. In 1995, as part of the celebrated-persons series, the Hungarian composer Béla Bartók, who was famous for collecting folk songs, was featured on a postage stamp. The explanatory literature about his stamp praises Bartók for his contributions toward preserving Slovak folk songs and for the influence these melodies had on his compositions. And in 1994, the government accorded recognition to an important Jewish figure by issuing a postage stamp carrying the image of Chatam Sofer, an early nineteenth-century rabbi. He headed the Bratislava rabbinical school and was an acknowledged authority on the Talmud. Slovakia is clearly intent on stressing Slovak accomplishments and, understandably, achievements that reflect well on its history and society.

Although the nineteenth-century national awakening and the ongoing effort to promote a national identity provided Slovakia with a roster of significant political and literary figures, what influenced Slovak cultural development changed over time. From the mid-nineteenth century through World War I, Slovaks struggled to stave off Magyar nationalism and preserve their language. Following the creation of Czechoslovakia, politically and religiously motivated persons kept up the quest to assert Slovak individuality against what they feared was a rising "Czechoslovakism." Although politicians such as Andrej Hlinka complained about the failure to grant Slovakia more political autonomy, the birth of Czechoslovakia in 1918 did give rise to an environment more favorable to promoting Slovak culture. In 1919 the Matica slovenská, shut down by the Hungarians in 1875, was revived. It organized local branches and resumed its cultural activities. In 1920 Comenius University was opened in Bratislava. Although the faculty was made up primarily of Czech professors, the university, together with the Matica, formed an institutional framework for advancing Slovak education and culture. During the interwar era, unsettling social, political, and economic situations drew attention away from cultural pursuits. Still, the 1920s and 1930s saw the Slovak novel surpass poetry as the most popular form of literary expression. Outstanding novelists of the period included Ladislav Jégé (1866–1940), Milo Urban (1904–1982), and Jozef C. Hronský (1896–1960).

The interim stretching from the onset of World War II until the collapse of communism in 1989 did not provide fertile soil for literary creativity. Indeed, communist ideology had a stifling effect on cultural development in general. Nevertheless, during this repressive era a few writers managed to author creative and even, occasionally, dissident works. These texts were typically not translated into other languages and consequently, in the twentieth century, important Slovak writers did not enjoy widespread recognition. Dominik Tatarka (1913–1989), Vincent Šikula (1936–), Ladislav Ballek (1941–), and Ján Johanides (1934–) rank among the important literary figures of the communist era.

Both historically and in the modern day, Slovakia's list of significant people does not include performing and creative artists of international renown. During the seventy-four years following the creation of Czechoslovakia, Slovak performers and athletes were identified with Czechoslovakia, the country, instead of with the Slovak people. Stressing country over ethnic identity was not something that occurred only in Czechoslovakia; it typically happened in all multiethnic countries and still does. This was particularly true during the communist era. Totalitarian regimes viewed excelling in sports as a way to demonstrate that socialist countries were superior to capitalist nations. As a result of emphasizing citizenship, Slovaks who participated in international sports or achieved recognition typically fell under the "Czechoslovak" nomenclature. Commentators often shortened "Czechoslovak" merely to "Czech." In 1972, when Slovak figure skater Ondrej Nepela won the Gold Medal at the winter Olympics, his achievement was thus recorded as a win for Czechoslovakia; his ethnic identity was irrelevant. In Bratislava, though, a winter sports stadium is named for this Olympic gold medalist.

Slovakia is still dealing with the aftereffects of its long history as an integrated part of multiethnic nations. Asserting its own national identity, independent Slovakia has used postage stamps to distinguish individuals as "Slovaks," highlight their historical, cultural, or scientific significance, and honor their achievements. As a result, since 1993 a wide array of Slovak writers, composers, painters, sculptors, scientists, and inventors have been publicly commemorated through this means.

Slovak culture cannot be viewed only within the confines of important historical figures, literary masters, and artists who have contributed to the development of a national identity or to a body of creative works. Slovak culture owes much to the country's folk heritage and rural past. Since the national awakening of the nineteenth century, literature and music have drawn inspiration from folk traditions. Classical composers adapted folk melodies or incorporated folk motifs into their arrangements. Mikuláš Schneider-Trnavský (1881–1958) and Ján Levoslav Bella (1843–1936) were two of the more well-known composers

Easter and Christmas in Slovakia

Traditional Slovak Easter and Christmas celebrations blend folk traditions and religious beliefs. For Slovak Christians, Easter is the holiest day of the year, and the celebrations associated with it are steeped in symbolism. The symbolism is expressed in traditional foods, usually eaten for breakfast. Typically the fare consists of hard-boiled eggs, a rich yeast bread made with butter and eggs *(paska),* ham, special sausage *(klobása),* a bland, custard-style imitation cheese (*hrudka* or *syrek*), butter, and horseradish. Each item has special meaning, signifying life, Christ, the Resurrection, or other biblical event. Elaborately decorating eggs *(kraslice)* is also an essential part of observing Easter. The contents of the eggs are removed, leaving the shells intact and as fragile as fine porcelain. Intricate designs are then created on the empty shells. Depending on geographic region, patterns on the eggs may include intricate geometric figures, plants, flowers, or religious motifs.

During the two days after Easter, young Slovak villagers traditionally indulged in their own custom. On Monday, boys sprinkled scented water on girls and "whipped" them with boughs made of willow branches and colored ribbon; on Tuesday, young girls threw water on the boys. Villages developed their own versions of these "sprinkling days," and who was involved could differ. There are different explanations of the origins and purpose of this popular tradition.

Slovak Christmas celebrations were influenced by both religious and folk traditions. Christmas Eve was the most important day of this holiday season. For the evening dinner, straw, which symbolized the Christ child's manger, was placed either under the tablecloth or strewn on the floor. Traditional foods were customarily served at Christmas Eve dinner. The meal began with unleavened wafers dipped in honey. The custom varied, but either the mother or father would use the honey-dipped wafers to make the sign of the cross on each family member's forehead. The main dishes consisted of a special mushroom soup and bite-size rolls in either sauerkraut and butter or poppy seed sauce. Desserts were nuts, fruits, and sweet yeast baked goods, typically filled with ground nuts or poppy seeds. Opening presents and sometimes caroling followed the dinner.

Superstitions influenced some Christmas traditions. With the new year approaching, Slovaks carried out rituals that they believed could foretell their future. On 30 November, people poured lead into boiling water and relied on the shape of the cooled droplets to make predictions about the coming year. On Christmas Eve, young women took part in rituals that they believed could reveal who their husbands would be. Also, it was customary not to remove food from the table. It was left for visitors and deceased family members who, tradition held, would eat the food while the family attended midnight religious services.

Over time, some Easter and Christmas traditions in Slovakia have been modified or abandoned; others have been faithfully upheld. In any case, like other folk traditions, the religious and folk customs associated with an old-fashioned Christmas or Easter are an important part of Slovakia's cultural history.

who drew on Slovak folk traditions. Slovak painters also historically looked to the Slovak countryside and rural life for inspiration. Ladislav Medňanský (1852–1919) was recognized for his beautiful landscapes, and *Trh v Banskej Bystrici* (The Market in Banská Bystrica, 1889) was the most famous oil painting by artist Dominik Skutecký (1849–1921). Martin Benka (1888–1971) and L'udovít Fulla (1902–1980) are twentieth-century painters known for their landscapes, folk themes, and realistic portrayals of rural life.

Folk traditions have not only influenced literature and the fine arts, they have shaped Slovak culture and contributed to its distinctiveness. Indeed, its rich folk heritage is one of the distinguishing characteristics of Slovak culture. Handicrafts, striking folk costumes called *kroje,* music, dancing, and folklore are among the many ways this heritage is evident. Folk dress and arts vary and reflect the regional differences that characterize Slovak society. In some regions, villagers, primarily women, still wear traditional costumes for special occasions and even to Sunday religious services. These colorful *kroje,* which contain several different articles of clothing, are impressive displays of intricate, skilled needlework. Folk art is expressed in several other forms as well. Among the most typical handicrafts are elaborately decorated Easter eggs, wood carvings, figurines constructed of natural materials such as corn husks, embroidered linens, and vividly painted pottery. Annual folk festivals featuring music, dancing, costumes, and handicrafts are regularly held in Slovakia.

As modern-day Slovakia asserts its national identity, it has highlighted this unique feature of its culture. Indeed, the country has been willing to incorporate its folk heritage into the image it projects to the rest of the world. For example, in the same way that it spotlights nationalists, literary masters, and other Slovak figures, independent Slovakia uses

Slovak folk dancers performing. (Lindsay Hebberd/Corbis)

its postage stamps and cards to accentuate its folk heritage. A postage series dedicated to folk customs features dancing and seasonal traditions. Stamps and postcards also commemorate folk festivals.

Finally, religion has significantly influenced the development of Slovak culture. Magnificent art adorns massive cathedrals and small churches alike. Religious paintings, artifacts, and sculptures date as far back as the fifteenth century; a few can be traced to the twelfth century. The Christian motif is particularly strong in numerous public symbols that postindependent Slovakia has chosen to employ. Portraying the apostles Cyril and Methodius on the fifty-crown bank note accents Slovakia's Christian heritage as well as its ancient roots. Casting the ninth-century Prince Pribina on the twenty-crown bill also emphasizes the twin themes of religion and Slovakia's pre-Hungarian history. He is credited with constructing the first Christian church on Slavic territory. Another paper bill depicts the painted wooden Madonna of St. Jacob's Church in Levoča, which boasts the largest wooden altar in Europe. A large number of churches, sacred paintings, and religious artifacts are depicted in public art, stamps, and postcards. Such public expressions attest to the influence that Christianity, especially Catholicism, historically has had—and continues to have—on Slovak culture.

Religion, folk traditions, and a quest to establish a separate national identity have all combined to fashion a distinct Slovak culture. Individuals have, indeed, played an important role in Slovak history and cultural development. The Slovak awakening of the nineteenth century, which was vital to promoting a Slovak national identity, grew from the efforts of committed persons. At the same time, the cultural highlights of Slovak society rest on more than nationalist literature and fine arts promoted by an elite. The distinct features that highlight Slovak culture also rest on folk traditions rooted in a peasant past.

Folk Beliefs and Superstitions

Slovakia has a rich folk culture. Unique aspects of this culture are linked to the nation's agrarian past. Traditionally Slovaks were fervently religious people who believed in divine intervention in their lives. As a consequence, particularly in rural areas, the celebration of the liturgical calendar became closely interwoven with the agricultural seasons of the normal calendar year. In the past, ancient superstitions also shaped popular beliefs. This blending of religion, superstitions, and coping with everyday realities gave rise to an array of rituals and beliefs.

For most of its history, Slovakia was primarily a self-subsistent agrarian society where daily life could be a hard struggle. Slovaks living in rural villages had to grow their own food and raise animals. Peasants and farmers knew that fruitful harvests depended on forces mightier than themselves. Over time, Slovaks living in rural villages tried to influence their situation by appealing to divine forces. For example, the Easter period, which marked the celebration of Christ's death and resurrection, also signaled the arrival of spring and the symbolic awakening of the earth for the planting season. During this time Slovaks prayed for a fruitful harvest. Palm Sunday celebrations, which commemorated Christ's triumphant entry into Jerusalem, welcomed the spring. On some saints' feast days, villagers came together as a community to ask for a favor legendarily associated with a saint's life or unique powers. For example, on the feast of St. Mark (25 April) they appealed for rain and good weather during the growing season. Rituals and pleas were not limited to the spring. Slovak prayer books contained numerous prayers that, throughout the year, entreated the Lord or the saints for something particular that would improve the year's harvest, help the animals, or otherwise benefit the community. On Christmas Eve, the head of the household gave food from the dinner table to the animals in the hope of ensuring the livestock's health.

An array of superstitions permeated rural culture. Communal and individual customs typically blended religion and ancient beliefs. People might ask a clergyman to bless items believed to bring good fortune or good health. Villagers engaged in activities that supposedly chased away demons and witches. They also used charms that they believed would protect their villages from such evil forces.

While superstitions and rituals characterized village life, some practices were common to Slovak culture in general. Death in particular could be accompanied by a host of superstitions. For instance, immediately following a person's demise, Slovaks covered all the mirrors in the deceased's home. They also closed all windows and, if the house had one, locked the gate. They believed that these measures would prevent the deceased from returning and perhaps doing harm.

Twenty-first-century Slovakia is no longer an agrarian society, but rural folk customs, ancient superstitions, and religious beliefs are some of the vibrant traditions that helped shape Slovak popular culture.

ECONOMIC DEVELOPMENT

During most of its history, Slovakia's economy was closely interwoven into the socioeconomic structure of a larger empire or country. Under Hungarian rule, a combination of policies and attitudes blended together to keep Slovakia an agricultural society. The region was essentially assigned a role as the supplier of raw materials for industry elsewhere in the kingdom. As Slovakia moved into the nineteenth and twentieth centuries, its agrarian character was an impediment to its economic development. Like Hungary of earlier years, Czechoslovakia adopted policies that hampered economic change in Slovakia until, during the communist era, Slovakia was industrialized. After the 1989 Velvet Revolution, however, Slovakia had to confront the legacy of an economic strategy that had been too narrowly dependent on heavy industry. Slovakia's history as part of other multinational states thus significantly shaped its economic development.

Slovakia's agrarian roots reach back to when Slavic tribes first migrated into the Danube Basin and established permanent settlements. These were stable communities where inhabitants survived by tilling the fields, raising animals, and hunting local game. The Magyar invasion in the early tenth century did not disturb the self-sustaining agrarian culture that already existed. Instead, feudalism, which started evolving in the mid-thirteenth century, reinforced Slovakia's agricultural economy and helped perpetuate it well into the future. Under the feudal system, peasants were turned into serfs. They had to pay for the right to farm the land as well as pay taxes on their crops and animals. More important, however, serfs were obligated to an overlord and bound to fulfill prescribed obligations, including working for the manor owner. When the system first began, the majority of Slovak serfs were peasant farmers who, after they had met all obligations to their overlord, could freely move somewhere else. Over time this freedom of movement became more and more limited.

The region's mineral wealth also had some impact on Slovakia's early economic development. At approximately the same time that Slovak peasants were being reduced to

Religious sculptures stand on the side altar of the Church of Saint Egidius in Bardejov, Slovakia. (Scheufler Collection/Corbis)

serfdom, mining was getting under way in Slovakia's central region. By the middle of the thirteenth century, iron ore was being dug out of the Slovenské Rudohorie (Slovak Ore Mountains). The discovery of gold and silver caused excavation in Slovakia to diversify and expand. At the end of the fourteenth century, silver, gold, copper, and iron ore were being mined in this northern region of Hungary. Mining gave rise to towns that flourished from the extraction of precious metals and minerals. By the late 1300s, Kremnica probably had forty mills and foundries. While mining spawned additional enterprises in a few towns like Kremnica, generally Slovakia's mineral resources did not foster many allied industries. Instead, raw materials were exported and processed elsewhere, beyond Slovakia. Thus early in its history, outside markets played an important role in Slovakia's economic development.

Despite the growth of mining "industries," the feudal system, which continued to evolve, fated Slovakia to remain a predominantly agricultural area. By the fifteenth century, serfs made up perhaps four-fifths of the Slovak population.

Slovak peasants gather grass to make haystacks. (Scheufler Collection/Corbis)

Some were farmworkers with houses; others worked on property owned by lords; and others were villagers who performed services such as milling grain or working as blacksmiths for the landowner. As time passed, nobles gained more legal control over their serfs and, as a result, their freedom to move away was severely reduced. This erosion of rights continued until, in the early 1600s, geographic mobility by serfs was essentially stopped altogether. They were bound to the land and the landowner. Taxes, crop assessments, and various obligations also meant that serfs were engaged in a constant struggle to eke out an existence.

Hungary's lengthy war to expel the Ottoman Turks helped worsen the economic situation for the serfs. The need to supply Hungary's military posts and soldiers during campaigns against the Turks after the mid-1500s increased the demand for foodstuffs. Since it was financially profitable to grow agricultural products, landlords increased the number of acres they cultivated. Serfs provided the cheap labor that allowed for this expansion. Slovakia thus became an area with huge manors where tremendous amounts of fertile land were concentrated in the hands of a relatively small number of landlords, primarily the nobility.

Through a series of legal measures serfdom was abolished in 1848–1853. The ill effects of this socioeconomic system, which had dominated the economic life of Slovakia for five centuries, were not easily remedied. When the system was ended, many former serfs were left with debt, in poverty, and on plots too small to provide much beyond a subsistence living. The long-term impact of feudalism went even deeper. By keeping a significant segment of Slovaks in an impoverished state and obligated to serve overlords, the feudal system thwarted economic progress. A large segment of Slovakia's population was unable to advance socially or contribute to the region's economic development. Instead of modernizing, agricultural methods remained antiquated. Consequently, into the twentieth century, Slovakia stayed a primarily agrarian, economically undeveloped area with a relatively poor population.

During the centuries dominated by the feudal system, mining was the only major exception to the overwhelmingly agricultural nature of Slovakia's economy. The mining "industry," however, seesawed back and forth between flourishing and bad times. Extracting copper boomed in the sixteenth century but died down by the end of the next century when underground waters flooded many mines and operators lacked the necessary equipment efficiently to pump them dry. Gold and silver mines encountered similar problems. Despite technical difficulties, mining remained the most important part of Slovakia's nonagricultural economy. After technology became available to siphon out water, the industry prospered again, and in the 1700s the amount of silver and gold taken from Slovakia's mines reached all-time highs. At about the same time, copper started to be mined in eastern Slovakia, and the discovery of iron ore deposits stimulated mining in the east as well. Because most of Slovakia's ores and precious metals were exported to lower Hungary or to countries outside the kingdom, its mining industry remained dependent on "outside markets."

During the eighteenth century and into the nineteenth, Slovakia did experience some industrial growth. The economy even became slightly more diversified. The raw materials available in Slovakia determined what types of industrial establishments were created. For example, a textile plant was founded in the early 1700s. In the nineteenth century the number and kinds of factories increased. Paper, textile, leather, iron, and metal as well as food processing plants existed in the region. On the eve of World War I, Slovakia claimed more than half of Hungary's paper mills and a third of its textile plants. There were also sawmills in the heavily forested areas.

By the beginning of the twentieth century, however, the number of factories in Slovakia remained relatively low, and they were small in size. Despite its forests, the region claimed only about one-fifth of Hungary's timber industries and the same proportion of iron and metal processing plants. In 1910 Slovakia had only slightly over 600 industrial plants that employed twenty or more employees; roughly 86,000 persons worked at these concerns. Moreover, because industrial works were located in specific areas, they touched only a small portion of the land and the people. As a result of this concentration of factories, Slovakia claimed just small pockets of industry while most of its territory stayed agricultural. Moreover, agriculture was not commercialized. On the eve of World War I, most Slovak farmers owned only small plots consisting of a few acres. Instead of cultivating produce for sale, they engaged in subsistence farming where persons raised food and livestock for their own consumption. As a result, large pockets of rural poverty existed in Slovakia.

The dissolution of the Austro-Hungarian Empire after World War I ultimately detached Slovakia from its thousand-year bond to the Kingdom of Hungary and made it part of yet another multinational state, Czechoslovakia. Joining in a new nation could not undo the reality that, for a millennium, Slovakia had been part of Hungary and its larger, more complex economy. Under the Hungarians the center of financial activity had been in Budapest and economic decisions affecting the entire kingdom were made there. Slovakia's markets were also primarily in the south; railroad tracks and roads went southward toward Hungary proper.

Liberation from Hungary had serious ramifications for Slovakia because the region now had to integrate into a new economy. Breaking with the Austro-Hungarian Empire meant that Slovakia lost long established markets for its natural resources. Transportation networks that had led south into Hungary needed reorienting in an east-west direction to the Czech Lands. In the new state, Prague replaced Budapest as the financial center.

When Slovakia joined the Czech Lands to form Czechoslovakia in 1918, Slovakia's agrarian base reinforced an economic policy similar to what Hungary had pursued while the region was part of its kingdom. This policy can be described as colonialist, meaning a system whereby one geographic area functions as the source of raw goods for another region. Slovakia was viewed as the supplier of raw materials for Czech factories. Different degrees of economic development in Slovakia and the Czech Lands encouraged this to happen. When Czechoslovakia was created, the Czech Lands were far more industrialized than Slovakia. While more than three-fifths of Slovakia's population was engaged in farming or forestry activities, less than one-third of the Czech populace was involved in some kind of agriculture.

Financial leaders, banks, and the central government in Prague tended to favor Czech enterprises. During the 1920s, using the rationale of modernizing industry, some Slovak factories were eliminated and some new establishments were built. However, all told, the new plants actually employed fewer workers than the number who had lost jobs when the older factories were closed. Slovakia, therefore, endured a higher rate of unemployment than elsewhere in Czechoslovakia, and in industrial development it continued to lag behind the Czech Lands. Although Slovakia remained a basically agrarian region, this did not lead to expansion of commercial farming. Even in agricultural production, Slovakia could not compete because the Czech Lands had developed modern, mechanized farming techniques. At the same time, the majority of farms in Slovakia were small, and farmers consumed most of what they produced. Large estates with sufficient acreage for commercial production remained in the hands of a minority of the population.

The Great Depression of the 1930s inflicted economic hardships on all of Czechoslovakia. To sell its finished goods,

Czechoslovakia depended on outside markets. As a supplier of raw materials, Slovakia therefore could not avoid the ripple effect that the decline in exports had on Czechoslovakia's economy. Not only did the demand for natural resources plummet, factories in Slovakia were shut down and the majority of sawmills closed as well. Still, by 1934, the depression began easing in Slovakia. Adolf Hitler's rise to power in nearby Germany stirred fears about Czechoslovakia's security. In this climate of growing anxiety, Slovakia, which was located farther from Germany, became strategically more important to Czechoslovakia. This situation altered traditional attitudes that had worked against promoting industrialization in Slovakia; consequently, during the 1930s, armament factories were built there.

During World War II, Slovakia experienced an economic boom. This beneficial turn of events, however, was due in large measure to the Slovak Republic's ties to the Third Reich. German investment helped modernize and expand Slovak industries, which manufactured materiel for the German war machine. Overall, by 1943 Slovak industrial production had increased approximately 30 percent over prewar levels.

After the communist takeover of Czechoslovakia in 1948, Slovakia's economic development was controlled by an anticapitalist ideology. It was a doctrine aimed at destroying both private ownership of property and free competition in an independent marketplace. Czechoslovakia adopted centralized planning, which meant that the government took over and managed the economy. The period witnessed the complete nationalization of companies, industries, and consumer-oriented shops. Owners of small businesses were forced to turn them over to the state. The government used various forms of intimidation to force farmers, who still made up nearly half of Slovakia's population, to merge their property into huge cooperatives. This collectivization of farms, which continued in the 1950s, eliminated private ownership of agricultural lands. Individuals were no longer free to cultivate their land or sell their agricultural products. By the early 1960s more than two-thirds of Slovakia's agricultural land was state owned or part of cooperatives. To supplement their incomes, most farmers took second jobs.

Communist rule led to a revamping of traditional views about Slovakia's industrial development. The intensely hostile atmosphere of the Cold War era caused Czechoslovakia's central planners to place strong emphasis on defense-related industries. Five-Year Plans, modeled after the Soviet Union's system to expand industrial output, encouraged construction projects and spurred the expansion of heavy industry. In Slovakia, factories were built to manufacture weapons and armored vehicles such as tanks. In addition, chemical plants and metal industries—including copper, iron, steel, and aluminum—sprang up.

This strong emphasis on heavy industry furthered industrialization in Slovakia, but the standard of living there still lagged behind the Czech Lands. Moreover, in the early 1960s, quality consumer goods were in short supply everywhere in Czechoslovakia, and the country's economy was stagnating. Trying to stimulate the economy and correct inequalities between the regions helped spark the short-lived 1968 reform movement commonly called the "Prague Spring." During "normalization," the period of repression that took place in the aftermath of the failed reform attempt, an ever greater stress was placed on promoting industrialization in Slovakia. The objective was also to improve the standard of living for Slovaks by bringing Slovakia economically on par with the country's western Czech region. The construction of chemical plants and emphasis on heavy industry, especially armaments, thus continued. For Slovaks, building industrial plants had the additional positive effect of creating construction jobs. This opened employment opportunities for more Slovaks and also let farmers, whose property had been merged into huge collectives, supplement their incomes. In the 1980s Slovakia enjoyed 100 percent employment, and the standard of living did reach parity with the Czechs. Rural poverty, in particular, was reduced and life in Slovakia's villages improved.

Under the heavy hand of a centrally controlled regime, then, Slovakia went from a backward agricultural region to an industrialized society. Although a brutally repressive period, the fact is that Slovakia's industrialization occurred primarily during Czechoslovakia's communist era. Centrally managed economic programs led to the modernization of farming methods, but it was in industry where the greatest transformation took place. Policies that fostered full unemployment and raised the standard of living in Slovakia, however, also encouraged inefficiency. Old factories and equipment were often not modernized; the overproduction of goods led to warehouses overstocked with surplus inventory. The strategy of emphasizing heavy industry, especially defense-related products, made Slovakia economically dependent on the Soviet Union and Eastern Bloc countries. Thus following a pattern that had historically characterized Slovakia's economic development, in the late 1980s its prosperity relied on markets outside the region. Moreover, Slovakia's economic progress was overly dependent on a limited range of manufactured goods.

When the communist regime was toppled in 1989, Czechoslovakia set out to reestablish a market economy based on competition and private ownership. In the push to transform the economy, Czechoslovakia's postcommunist government made privatization an important objective. This meant turning former state-owned companies into private properties. The country's privatization program would, ultimately, lead to the elimination of inefficient enterprises that could not compete in the market place.

The economic restructuring following the 1989 revolution hurt Slovakia far more than the Czech Republic. Ironically, the eased international tensions that accompanied the end of the Cold War greatly reduced the demand for defense weapons. The overthrow of communist regimes in Eastern Europe, therefore, resulted in the loss of markets for the types of goods manufactured in Slovakia. The ill effects of an economy too narrowly dependent on armaments and heavy industry quickly became apparent. Slovaks, who had lived under a system of guaranteed employment, were now losing their jobs. By the fall of 1991, unemployment in Slovakia had reached 12 percent; in the Czech Republic it was only 4 percent. Slovak laborers still employed lived in fear that their factories would be shut down. In Slovakia, therefore, popular sentiment favored a more gradual privatization program. Many persons wanted the government to protect their jobs by continuing to subsidize factories, including the inefficient weapons industries. Sharply conflicting views about how quickly the country should privatize industry and reinstitute a free enterprise system contributed to the breakup of the Czech and Slovak Federative Republic in 1993.

Following the Velvet Divorce, Slovakia, for the first time in its history, boasted an independent economy. Its subsequent economic development, however, followed a bumpy course. Slovakia now faced the task of creating a stable economic system that would keep unemployment low, check inflation, and let Slovak businesses participate in a competitive international market. Those advocating independence had promised to slow down the rate of economic change. It was believed that this course of action would spare Slovakia's inhabitants undue hardships and leave them economically better off. The problems that plagued Slovakia before the separation, however, persisted afterward. Slovakia still had a large number of inefficient, state-owned enterprises producing goods for a dwindling market. Workers, used to looking to the government to safeguard their jobs, wanted it to continue subsidizing these factories. Government officials also became embroiled in major controversies over whether banks and energy-producing companies should be privatized.

Although Vladimír Mečiar supported gradual privatization, during the first year of independence he pushed policies that nearly halted the process of turning state owned assets over to private ownership. In 1993–1994 privatization moved slowly. Following the September 1994 elections the process was accelerated but still did not proceed at a rapid pace. On the eve of independence, in 1992, about 30 percent of state-owned businesses suited for privatization had been placed in private hands; by 1995, privately owned enterprises had only grown to slightly over 41 percent. Privatization did subsequently pick up speed. Based on government statistics, by the end of 1997 nearly 97 percent of the country's eligible businesses had been privatized; just over 1,600 were still publicly owned.

As it turned out, however, most state properties privatized under Mečiar's stepped-up program were sold directly to individuals and without public scrutiny. The procedure was fraught with abuses and resulted in cronyism, especially as persons with political connections were allowed to purchase prime real estate and the most lucrative enterprises. Many transactions involved selling properties at costs far below their real value and meant huge financial losses for the national treasury.

Still, during the first three years after independence, Slovakia enjoyed economic growth. During this period, government policies—and its continued intervention in the economy—helped reduce inflation and keep unemployment from worsening. Inflation fell from 23 percent in 1993 to 13 percent in 1994. With a few fluctuations, the unemployment rate dropped slightly; it went from 14 percent in 1993 to 12.5 percent in 1997.

By 1997, however, the economy had moved into a downward spiral. Even before independence, Slovakia had had a difficult time enticing foreign investment. Fears that the Mečiar government lacked a commitment to advancing democratization made foreign financiers even more leery of investing money in the Slovak Republic. Thus, during the entire period from 1989 through 1996, Slovakia reportedly attracted less than $625 million from outside investors. In addition, by 1997 Slovakia had amassed a trade deficit that, together with a rising foreign debt, turned it into a debtor nation. Its financial situation hurt plans to become part of the global economy. In 1995 the Slovak Republic had applied for membership in the European Union. At its December 1997 meeting, for both economic and political reasons, the European Union refused to accept Slovakia into membership at that time. The country was placed on a list for later consideration.

The Dzurinda government, which came into power in 1998, resolved to deal with the republic's economic problems. The new leadership was determined to put the country's financial affairs in order so that Slovakia would qualify for membership in the European Union. The government therefore adopted harsh measures to reduce the debt and increase revenues. This caused unemployment to increase from nearly 14 percent to 17.7 percent in 1999. Inflation also went up nearly eight points to 14 percent. At the same time, in that year Slovakia was able to wipe out its trade deficit. By 2002, the Slovak Republic definitely had not solved its financial problems, and its economic development remained on a bumpy course. Nevertheless, in December, the European Union extended Slovakia an invitation to become a member state as of May 2004. On 16 April 2003, Prime Minister Dzurinda, together with representatives from nine other new-member nations, signed the treaty allowing their respective countries to join. In a national referendum held in May 2003, a majority of the Slovaks who voted indicated that they agreed with the decision to make Slovakia a member state of the European Union. There is still hope that Slovakia's economic development will continue along a path that will allow the republic to participate in the global economy and maintain a decent standard of living for its citizens. Since Slovakia became independent, economic issues have often dominated domestic politics. And Slovakia's ongoing economic development no doubt will be significantly influenced by the course that the government elected in the 2002 national elections chose to follow.

CONTEMPORARY CHALLENGES

Following the Velvet Divorce in 1993, Slovakia became a sovereign nation, but with independence came immediate problems and long-term challenges. The Slovak government now became responsible for safeguarding the welfare of individuals living within its boundaries. Independence meant that, in addition to creating a stable governmental structure, the Slovak Republic had to grapple with forwarding the democratization process and establishing a market economy. These changes, together with the resurgence of ethnic divisions, fragmented Slovak society.

Coping with divisions is among Slovakia's most pressing problems. The economic transformation that took place in the 1990s created a more socially diverse population than had previously existed. In addition, varying perceptions of how well Slovakia has fared since the collapse of communism divides its citizens. A freer, more democratic climate has also allowed a large number of political parties to develop. Slovakia is divided in yet another crucial way. Although Slovaks make up slightly over 85 percent of the population, Slovakia is a multiethnic country. After independence, protecting the rights of ethnic minorities against Slovak nationalism and a potentially tyrannical majority became both a problem and a challenge. In the twenty-first century, Slovakia thus faces the challenge of trying to ensure that all its inhabitants enjoy the benefits of having brought down the communist regime as well as having achieved independence.

One of the principal problems Slovakia has had to confront in the early years of the twenty-first century is to refurbish an international image severely tarnished during the mid to late 1990s. The country still needs to overcome the fact that it was the only Central European country initially denied membership in the European Union on the grounds that it failed to meet the political criteria. Prime Minister Vladimír Mečiar's high-handed tactics and penchant for authoritarianism, together with the perceived mistreatment of ethnic minorities, led to the accusation that Slovakia had a weak commitment to democracy and human rights. Although the Slovak Republic is now a member of the European Union, the earlier rebuff, which included very public criticism of the newly independent country, damaged its standing in the world community. The Mikuláš Dzurinda government, which was inaugurated in the fall of 1998 and reelected in 2002, made strides toward fixing Slovakia's marred image.

Gaining a reputation as a solid democracy is important to Slovakia. Securing international esteem will not only make the Slovak Republic a respected voice in global affairs, it will help attract foreign investment and advance trade with outside countries. But, even though Slovakia's inhabitants might want their country to enjoy international respect, economic and social issues generally take precedence over global prestige. Like the residents of most countries, Slovak citizens typically view politics through the lens of their own self-interest. Such a perspective commonly produces cleavages within a society. In Slovakia, the move to a market economy created more hardships for some segments of the population than for others. These varied impacts have split Slovaks in several different ways.

The most obvious divisions in Slovakia are between those who believe they have benefited in the post-1989 era and those who feel they have not. The more satisfied group tends to encompass the young, the better educated, and individuals who reside in cities. Rural residents, inhabitants of single-industry towns, and the elderly, especially retired persons, belong to the less satisfied category. The ranks of the dissatisfied also can include workers of all ages who lost their jobs when unprofitable factories were closed. They face the same loss of security and reduced standard of living as do older persons whose pensions no longer provide a comfortable existence.

Socioeconomic divisions in Slovakia mirror the situation in other capitalist countries, including the United States. However, in Slovakia societal cleavages are intensified by attitudes and expectations nurtured during the communist era. For all their oppression, communist regimes did provide ordinary persons with basic economic security and social benefits. Thus Slovakia, like other former communist countries, must deal with the legacy of what is often referred to as the "cradle-to-grave" security that citizens believed they had under the old system. Elderly citizens and workers who experienced the benefits of 100 percent employment, a guaranteed pension, and free universal health care feel less secure in the new, post-1989 order. Many Slovaks want the practice of the government taking responsibility for the general welfare to continue.

In the communist era and even during the Czech and Slovak Federative Republic's short existence, assessments of living standards typically compared the Czech Lands and Slovakia. Now, comparisons of living standards are among social classes within Slovakia. These comparisons underscore differences created by the move to a market economy. Postindependence governments, therefore, have been forced to confront class-based tensions that did not previously divide the population. The fact that Slovakia is now an open society means that persons can freely express their grievances. And politicians cannot simply ignore them.

The significance of socioeconomic differences is apparent each time Slovakia holds national elections. Citizen concerns force political parties to address economic issues, which now form an important part of national campaigns. For example, in summer 2002, as Slovakia was gearing up for the fall elections, the media carried reports on nagging economic questions and problems with the country's health care system. Seeking comments from political parties, reporters highlighted the large gap between the minimum wage and the average monthly income. Commenting on economic matters, spokespersons offered their party's solutions for how the situation might be improved.

Economic concerns have contributed to the formation of numerous political parties, but this proliferation also reflects an array of divisions within Slovak society. Indeed, Slovakia's multiparty system is another indicator of just how fragmented the country is. In July 2002, for example, officials announced that twenty-six parties had registered and planned to field candidates in the upcoming fall elections. Given the large number of parties, identifying blocs of supporters is difficult; however, observers tend to agree on some basic points. Persons residing in rural areas and the elderly form pockets of conservative voters who believe that Slovakia was better off before the 1989 Velvet Revolution. Families and individuals whose living standards have been reduced or whose future security seems threatened by unemployment are also drawn to the former Communist and more nationalistic parties. In addition, there is a small hardcore segment still ideologically committed to communism and yearning for a return to the old political and economic order.

Dealing with ethnic divisions within its boundaries is another reality in Slovakia and one of the most formidable challenges confronting the young republic. Slovaks have had to contend with the fact that, although they make up the dominant group, Slovakia is clearly a multiethnic state. Except for the short interim during World War II, the period since 1989 is the first time in nearly eleven hundred years that Slovaks have enjoyed majority status. Gaining independence, which was viewed as finally fulfilling Slovak national aspirations, has intensified nationalist sentiments among the populace. Modern-day politics in Slovakia, therefore, are influenced by a strong Slovak nationalism in the face of minority groups determined to preserve their cultural identity.

Slovakia's constitution addressed the status of subject nationalities by including clauses affirming minority rights. Indeed, beginning with the Preamble, it acknowledges the multinational nature of Slovak society. For the Slovak government, therefore, the challenge is to ensure the fair treatment promised to ethnic minorities; for the Slovak people, the challenge is to avoid becoming a tyrannical majority indifferent or even hostile to the other nationalities in their midst.

Questions involving language rights present a particularly nettlesome problem for the Slovak Republic. The government and Slovaks in general see their language as an expression of national sovereignty. An official state language contributes, theoretically, to national unity. Not surprisingly, Slovaks generally accept the idea that Slovak should be the country's only official language. At the same time, for subject minorities—especially Hungarians—preserving their own language is part of their historical experience and protecting it is a steadfast objective. And they have successfully maintained their cultural identity since the end of World War I, when they involuntarily became part of Czechoslovakia.

Looking back on the decade since independence, Hungarians see a chipping away at minority rights. Even before the breakup of Czechoslovakia, debates over language rights sharply divided the populace and stirred apprehensions among Hungarians that a sovereign Slovak state would try to stamp out their language. From the Hungarian standpoint, when the Slovak National Council passed the State Language Law in 1995, which proclaimed Slovak the only official language, their fears were being confirmed. Hungarians interpreted the law as an outright violation of minority rights guaranteed by the Slovak Constitution. From their perspective, the language legislation reflected more than popular prejudice, which minorities in many countries encounter. It represented official discrimination by the government. The 1995 law thus heightened the difficulties in already strained ethnic relations.

Hungarians are probably aware that not all Slovaks support repressive measures to force the Slovak language on ethnic groups. Indeed, in some regions Slovaks reportedly reacted to language laws by continuing to use Hungarian in their dealings with Hungarians. In the 1990s some Slovaks even responded negatively to Prime Minister Mečiar's attempt to play on nationalist sentiments to shore up support for himself. For their part, Hungarians still remain uneasy about their cultural survival and fear that their legal rights will not be upheld in the Slovak Republic. As a result, in modern Slovakia Hungarians have become a visible, highly vocal minority.

A determination to promote Hungarian interests has caused several political parties to develop. In 2002 there were six such parties in Slovakia. Because Hungarians are overwhelmingly attracted to them, these parties further splinter Slovakia's population as well as the country's political process.

In the main, Hungarian political parties have platforms demanding that minority rights be protected. They seek to ensure Hungarian representation in the government and National Council. Like Slovak nationalists of the nineteenth and twentieth centuries, activists desire more cultural autonomy for Hungarians. They want more authority over local education, a power that would let Hungarians continue to foster Hungarian culture. Coexistence, a more militant political party, has called for granting territorial autonomy to Hungarian areas in southern Slovakia. Hungarian parties, though, have not directly advocated secession.

While Hungarians have been working to preserve their cultural identity, Slovakia's Roma, known as Gypsies in English-language countries, have been dealing with pervasive discrimination. In the modern Slovak Republic, unemployment, poverty, illiteracy, crime, and even disease rates are much higher among the Roma than for other citizens, including other ethnic minorities. The Roma are suffering from the effects of a history of poverty, poor education, and a lifestyle most Slovaks disdain. The period since independence has been a particularly bad time for Slovakia's Roma population. The reduction of social benefits formerly provided by the communist regime has made their already poor existence even worse.

Anti Roma prejudices take several forms. At the national level, there has been government neglect as well as a tolerance of mistreatment and discrimination. In the 1990s Slovakia's political leaders seemed callously disinterested in safeguarding the civil rights of the country's Romany citizens. In addition to Prime Minister Vladimír Mečiar, other national officials openly expressed contempt for the Roma. Instead of helping to moderate popular bigotry, national figures thus helped intensify existing popular prejudices.

In the local arena, bigotry toward the Roma is evident in discriminatory ordinances. By employing former communist-style residency permits, some localities have limited where the Roma can live. Finally, the Roma are the victims of popular stereotypes accepted by most Slovaks. An impoverished, uneducated minority generally living in squalid conditions, they are considered responsible for their dire situation. Their plight is typically blamed on their "way of life." On a more personal level, the Roma have encountered brutal hostility in the form of sporadic attacks, especially by Slovak skinheads. In 2000 the brutal murder of a Romany woman in Žilina who was trying to protect her daughters from men who had broken into their home generated outrage not only in Europe but within Slovakia as well. Whether the publicity about such a horrific incident was a fleeting emotional response or has caused a genuine

Slovak Roma are known in English as Gypsies. All over Europe, Gypsies suffer discrimination. (Shepard Sherbell/Corbis)

reassessment of the ill effects of bigotry toward the Roma is a yet unanswered question, embodying a challenge that Slovak society faces.

Diversity in Slovakia was further enhanced by a surge in ethnic nationalism among Ruthenians (Ruthenian-Ukrainians) after 1989. A small Slavic minority in the country's eastern region, Ruthenians belong to the Greek Catholic (Byzantine) Rite. Although they use the Cyrillic alphabet, their language is similar to the dialect spoken by Slovaks who live in eastern Slovakia. While legislation designating Slovak as the official language does not affect them in the same adverse way as Hungarians, Ruthenians, nevertheless, are increasingly dedicated to preserving their ethnic identity and fighting assimilation into Slovak culture. Language training has been incorporated into school curriculums, where Slovak too is taught. This ethnic revival has also helped boost the number of political parties in Slovakia. By 2002, there were two parties dedicated to promoting Ruthenian interests.

The presence of a tiny Jewish minority presents a special challenge to the rest of the country's populace. Slovaks, in particular, are being called on to guard against a resurgence of anti-Semitism, especially as a reenergized nationalism has prompted some to take a more positive view of the World War II Slovak state and its clerical leader, Josef Tiso.

Slovakia must contend with the fact that questions surrounding minority rights have had an impact that reaches beyond its borders. Specifically, there have been foreign policy ramifications. The treatment of ethnic groups helped bring disrepute to the country in the mid-1990s and contributed to what amounted to a scolding by the European Union (EU) and NATO. Minority issues have prompted outside interference in Slovak affairs. For example, allegations of abuse brought Slovakia under the watchful eye of international groups that monitor human rights. In addition, the language laws that antagonized Hungarians in Slovakia upset the Hungarian government as well. Whether justified or not, Hungary has maintained a keen interest in Hungarian minorities residing in its neighboring countries. In the mid-1990s the Slovak Republic and Hungary negotiated a treaty that, in addition to settling boundary issues, made the Slovak government promise to guarantee human and minority rights. Meddling by Hungary has had the unfortunate effect of nurturing underlying fears that a zealous Hungarian minority could one day turn into a separatist movement. Because persistent, widespread discrimination has led many Roma to seek asylum in other countries, their situation has created an additional international embarrassment. Other countries have generally rejected asylum appeals on the basis that the Roma are economic refugees, not political refugees eligible for protection. Still, their attempt to leave Slovakia spotlights the discrimination against and overall plight of the country's Roma population.

At the beginning of the twenty-first century, Slovakia faces many of the same kinds of problems and challenges as other nations confront. It must contend with economic upswings as well as downturns, unemployment, and inflation. Slovakia cannot escape social problems stemming from an unequal distribution of wealth. Consumer-related concerns have evolved into political issues. It has to cope with environmental problems, especially restoring areas ravaged by industrial expansion during the communist era, when there was little concern about pollution or other adverse environmental impacts.

Like other former communist countries, Slovakia also has to grapple with the peculiar legacy of those years. In particular, these countries cannot escape the lingering impact of a system that, even if it denied political freedoms, provided basic economic security to ordinary citizens of all ages. The transformation to a market economy has created more social classes, and some groups have clearly fared much better than others since 1989. For Slovakia, therefore, a vital challenge is to prevent significant segments of the society from becoming disillusioned with the reformed economic structure.

Slovakia must deal with the reality that it is a divided, often polarized, society. The fact that it is a freer, more democratic country has let suppressed differences surface. The collapse of communism and subsequent Slovak independence also gave rise to a more assertive Slovak nationalism. This heightened Slovak nationalism has accentuated ethnic differences and generated a strong reaction among the country's minority groups. The fight to protect minority languages symbolizes larger, thornier issues. From a practical standpoint, it is reasonable that the Slovak government and Slovaks, who are in the majority, favor a single official language. From the perspective of national minorities, this aim represents an attempt to eradicate ethnic cultures. And from their vantage, Slovaks pose the threat of becoming a tyrannical majority. Slovakia thus faces the ongoing challenge of ensuring that ethnic groups are afforded an opportunity to have their interests heard.

The treatment of minorities has raised doubts about how strong the commitment to democratic principles is among Slovaks in general. Slovakia, though, is not the only country that has had to deal with ethnic tensions. Indeed, some countries have not treated their minorities nearly as well as Slovakia has. For example, at the time of independence, Slovakia conferred citizenship on all residents, including ethnic minorities. Former communist-dominated countries did not universally follow this course. Nevertheless, the practice of discriminatory policies by other nations does not absolve Slovakia or make minority issues any less real or problematic.

For the foreseeable future, ethnic differences will remain a reality of life in the Slovak Republic. There is little doubt that political, social, and demographic differences that fragment Slovak society will persist as well. The economic and political transformations that have taken place since the end of communism seem to ensure that they will. For modern-day Slovakia, the fundamental challenge is to address issues in a way that makes the various social, demographic, ethnic, and political groups believe that, in the long run, they are better off under the reformed economic and political system that has taken hold in this now sovereign nation.

SELECTIVE BIBLIOGRAPHY

Bartl, Július, et al. *Slovak History: Chronology and Lexicon.* Translated by David P. Daniel. Wauconda, IL: Bolchazy-Carducci, 2002.

Berglund, Sten, Tomas Hellén, and Frank H. Aarebrot. *Handbook of Political Change in Eastern Europe.* Cheltenham, UK: Edward Elgar, 1998.

Bradley, J. F. N. *Czechoslovakia's Velvet Revolution: A Political Analysis.* Boulder: East European Monographs, 1992.

———. *Politics in Czechoslovakia, 1945–1990.* Boulder: East European Monographs, 1991.

Brock, Peter. *The Slovak National Awakening: An Essay in the Intellectual History of East Central Europe.* Toronto: University of Toronto Press, 1976.

Bugajski, Janusz. *Political Parties of Eastern Europe: A Guide to Politics in the Post-Communist Era.* Armonk, NY: Sharpe, 2002.

Eberhardt, Piotr. *Ethnic Groups and Population Changes in Twentieth-Century Central-Eastern Europe: History, Data, Analysis.* Armonk, NY: Sharpe, 2002.

El Mallakh, Dorothea H. *The Slovak Autonomy Movement, 1935–1939: A Study in Unrelenting Nationalism.* Boulder: East European Quarterly, 1979.

Felak, James Ramon. *"At the Price of the Republic": Hlinka's Slovak People's Party, 1929–1938.* Pittsburgh: University of Pittsburgh Press, 1994.

Goldman, Minton F. *Slovakia since Independence: A Struggle for Democracy.* Westport, CT: Praeger, 1999.

Henderson, Karen. "Minorities and Politics in the Slovak Republic." In *Minorities in Europe: Croatia, Estonia, and Slovakia.* Edited by Snezana Trifunovska, 175–188. The Hague: Asser, 1999.

———. "Slovakia and the Democratic Criteria for EU Accession." In *Back to Europe: Central and Eastern Europe and the European Union.* Edited by Karen Henderson, 241–258. London: UCL Press, 1999.

———. *Slovakia: The Escape from Invisibility.* London: Routledge, 2002.

Jelinek, Yeshayahu A. *The Parish Republic: Hlinka's Slovak People's Party, 1939–1945.* Boulder: East European Monographs, 1976.

Johnson, Owen V. *Slovakia, 1918–1938: Education and the Making of a Nation.* Boulder: East European Monographs, 1985.

Kirschbaum, Stanislav J. *A History of Slovakia: The Struggle for Survival.* New York: St. Martin's, 1995.

Leff, Carol Skalnik. *The Czech and Slovak Republics: Nation versus State.* Boulder: Westview, 1996.

———. *National Conflict in Czechoslovakia: The Making and Remaking of a State, 1918–1987.* Princeton: Princeton University Press, 1988.

Macartney, C. A. *The Habsburg Empire, 1790–1918.* London: Weidenfeld and Nicolson, 1968.

Mamatey, Victor S., and Radomír Luža, ed. *A History of the Czechoslovak Republic, 1918–1948.* Princeton: Princeton University Press, 1973.

Mannová, Elena, ed. *A Concise History of Slovakia.* Translated by Martin C. Styan and David P. Daniel. Bratislava, Slovakia: Slovak Academy of Sciences, 2000.

Mat'ovčík, Augustín, et al. *Slovak Biographical Dictionary.* Translated by Jana Káčerová et al. Wauconda, IL: Bolchazy-Carducci, 2002.

Paul, David Warren. "Slovak Nationalism and the Hungarian State." In *Ethnic Groups and the State.* Edited by Paul Brass, 115–159. Totowa, NJ: Barnes and Noble, 1985.

Petro, Peter. *A History of Slovak Literature.* Montreal: McGill-Queens University Press, 1995.

Seton-Watson, Hugh. *Eastern Europe between the Wars, 1918–1941.* Boulder: Westview, 1986.

Seton-Watson, R. W., ed. *Slovakia Then and Now: A Political Survey.* London: George Allen and Unwin, 1931.

Svec, Milan. "Czechoslovakia's Velvet Divorce." *Current History* 91 (November 1992): 376–380.

Thomas, Desmond. "Slovakia: Language and National Unity." In *Democracy and Cultural Diversity.* Edited by Michael O'Neill and Dennis Austin, 135–141. Oxford: Oxford University Press, 2000.

Toma, Peter A. "The Czechoslovak Question under Communism." *East European Quarterly,* 3 March 1969, 15–29.

Vietor, Martin. "The Significance and Place of the Slovak Republic in the History of Czechoslovakia." In

Revolutions and Interventions in Hungary and Its Neighbor States, 1918–1919. Edited by Peter Pastor, 431–464. Boulder: East European Monographs, 1988.

Wightman, Gordon. "Slovakia Ten Years after the Collapse of Communist Rule." In *Party Development and Democratic Change in Post-Communist Europe: The First Decade.* Edited by Paul G. Lewis, 126–140. London: Frank Cass, 2001.

Wolchik, Sharon L. "The Czech Republic and Slovakia." In *The Legacies of Communism in Eastern Europe.* Edited by Zoltan Barany and Ivan Volgyes, 152–176. Baltimore: Johns Hopkins University Press, 1995.

———. *Czechoslovakia in Transition: Politics, Economics, and Society.* London: Pinter, 1991.

———. "Czechoslovakia's 'Velvet Revolution.'" *Current History* 89 (December 1990): 413–416, 435–437.

———. "Democratization and Political Participation in Slovakia." In *The Consolidation of Democracy in East-Central Europe.* Edited by Karen Dawisha and Bruce Parrott, 197–244. Cambridge: Cambridge University Press.

CHRONOLOGY

ca. 450–500	Slavs first recorded as residing in modern-day Slovakia.
568	Avars invade the Danube region inhabited by Slavs.
623–658	Period of the Kingdom of Samo.
791–796	Charlemagne's forces expel Avars from the Danube region.
828	Prince Pribina builds a castle and church in Nitra.
833	Mojmír annexes Pribina's land and creates the Great Moravian Empire.
863	The missionaries Cyril and Methodius arrive in the Great Moravian Empire.
870–894	Reign of Svätopluk and height of the Great Moravian Empire.
906–907	Magyars invade the Danube region.
	Great Moravian Empire disintegrates; for the next 1,000 years Slovakia is ruled by the Magyars.
907	First recorded mention of a castle on the site of modern-day Bratislava.
ca. 1200	Germans begin settling in northern Slovakia.
1428	Czech Hussites begin moving into Slovak territory.
ca. 1520	Protestant Reformation gets under way in Slovakia.
1526	Ottoman Turks defeat Magyar forces at Mohács.
1536–1783	Bratislava (Pressburg) is the capital of Royal Hungary.
ca. 1616	Counter-Reformation gets under way in Slovakia.
1619–1711	Religious and civil wars in the Hungarian kingdom.
1635	University is established at Trnava.
1657	University is established at Košice.
1711–1713	Jánošík leads a band of outlaws in northern Slovakia and surrounding areas.
1790	Anton Bernolák publishes a Slovak grammar.
1792	Slovak Learned Society founded in Trnava.
1825	Ján Kollár publishes *Čitanka* (A Reader) in "Czechoslovak."
1843	L'udovít Štúr and followers agree to establish a Slovak literary language.
1848	Demands of the Slovak Nation manifesto are proclaimed in Liptovský Sväty Mikuláš.
	Slovak National Council is created.
	Failed attempt, led by Štúr, to foment a Slovak popular uprising against Magyars.
1849	Slovak delegation presents petition for Slovak autonomy to Emperor Franz Joseph.
1851	Supporters of Štúr and Bernolák agree on a Slovak literary language.
1852	Martin Hattala publishes *Krátka mluvnica slovenská* (A Concise Slovak Grammar).
1861	Memorandum of the Slovak Nation is drafted in Turciansky Svätý Martin.
1863	Matica slovenská is founded.
1867	Dual Monarchy is created; Slovakia falls under direct Hungarian control.
1868	Nationality Law makes Magyar the official language but promises to protect minority language rights.
1870s	Hungarian government renews Magyarization policy.
1871	Slovak National Party is organized.
1874	The government closes Slovakia's three gymnasia.
1875	The government abolishes the Matica slovenská and confiscates its property.
1896	Slovak students form the Czechoslovak Union to foster Czech and Slovak unity.
1907	Černova Massacre.
1913	Slovak People's Party is formally established.
1915	Cleveland Agreement is drafted.
1916	Czechoslovak National Council is formed in Paris.
1918	Pittsburgh Agreement is signed by Tomáš Masaryk.
	New Czech-Slovak state declares independence.
	Declaration of the Slovak Nation is announced in Turciansky Svätý Martin.
	Vavro Šrobár is charged with administering Slovakia; Bratislava is designated Slovakia's administrative capital.
	Slovak People's Party is revived under Father Andrej Hlinka's leadership.
1919	Matica slovenská is reopened.

	Comenius University is founded.
1920	Czechoslovakia's constitution is adopted; it renames the country "Czechoslovakia" and creates a centralized state.
	Treaty of Trianon establishes borders between Czechoslovakia and Hungary.
1925	The Slovak People's Party is renamed Hlinka's Slovak People's Party.
1938	Andrej Hlinka dies in August.
	Monsignor Josef Tiso assumes leadership of the Hlinka's Slovak People's Party.
	Munich Agreement: France and England allow Germany to annex the Sudetenland. In October the Žilina program calling for an autonomous Slovak state is drafted.
	On 22 November, the Prague government implements the Žilina program, and the federated state is renamed "Czecho-Slovakia."
	Josef Tiso becomes prime minister of Slovakia.
1939–1945	The Slovak Republic.
1939	On 13 March, Tiso meets with Hitler, who demands that Slovakia declare independence.
	On 14 March, the Slovak parliament proclaims independence.
	On 15 March, Germany invades Czecho-Slovakia, and the united nation ceases to exist.
	Hungary occupies Slovak territory along the Slovak-Hungarian border.
	On 23 March, Slovak government signs a treaty of "protection" with Germany.
1941	Jewish code establishes restrictive regulations for Jews in Slovakia.
1942	From March to October, Jews are deported to concentration camps.
1944	Slovak national uprising.
	Deportation of Jews resumes in the fall.
1945	Restoration of Czechoslovakia.
	Košice Program is implemented.
	Slovakia temporarily has autonomy.
1946	A centralized government is reestablished.
	Josef Tiso is charged with treason and put on trial.
1947	Josef Tiso is executed.
1948	A bloodless coup establishes a communist government in Czechoslovakia.
1950s	Private property is nationalized.
	Collectivization of agricultural lands destroys private farming.
	Political trials and purges take place.
	Supporting Slovak autonomy—bourgeois nationalism—is a crime against the state.
1960	A new constitution is proclaimed.
	The country is renamed the Czechoslovak Socialist Republic.
	Self-government in Slovakia is crippled.
1963	Slovaks imprisoned for "bourgeois nationalism" are released.
1968	Alexander Dubček is elected first secretary of the Communist Party.
	Prague Spring, a short-lived reform era, gets under way.
	Prague Spring comes to an abrupt halt when Warsaw Pact countries invade.
	Law passed turning Czechoslovakia into a federation of two republics.
1969	Law establishing the Slovak Socialist Republic goes into effect.
	Dubček is replaced by Gustáv Husák as first secretary of the Communist Party.
	"Normalization," a reassertion of Communist Party control, begins.
	Massive purges to eject persons from the Communist Party get under way.
1980s	Political opposition and dissent begin resurfacing.
1988	Police ruthlessly disperse thousands of Slovaks who gathered in Bratislava to pray for religious freedom.
1989	Public against Violence is organized in Slovakia.
	Czechoslovakia's communist government is overthrown in the Velvet Revolution.
1990	Czechoslovakia is renamed Czech and Slovak Federative Republic.
	First elections are held in June.
	Alexander Dubček becomes president of the Federal Assembly.
	Vladimír Mečiar becomes prime minister of Slovakia.
	Privatization plans get under way.
1991	Vladimír Mečiar is forced to resign as prime minister of Slovakia.
	Ján Čarnogurský becomes prime minister of Slovakia.
	Vladimír Mečiar forms a new party: the Movement for a Democratic Slovakia.
1992	In June elections Vladimír Mečiar becomes prime minister of Slovakia.
	In July the Slovak National Council issues a declaration of sovereignty for Slovakia.
	In September the Slovak National Council adopts a constitution for an independent Slovakia.
	In November the Federal Assembly votes to dissolve the federated state.
1993	On 1 January, Slovakia becomes an independent nation.
	Vladimír Mečiar remains Slovakia's prime minister.
	Michal Kováč is elected president.

1994	In March Vladimír Mečiar is ousted as prime minister but is reelected in October.
1995	National Council passes language law making Slovak the official language.
1997	NATO denies Slovakia's application for membership.
	The European Union denies Slovakia's application for membership.
1998	After fall elections, Mikuláš Dzurinda becomes prime minister.
2002	After fall elections, Mikuláš Dzurinda remains prime minister.
	In December the European Union invites Slovakia to join.
2003	In April, Mikuláš Dzurinda signs treaty allowing Slovakia to join the European Union; in May Slovaks vote to approve the decision to join the European Union.
2004	Slovakia becomes a member of NATO.
	Slovakia becomes a member of the European Union.

HUNGARY

ANDRÁS BOROS-KAZAI

LAND AND PEOPLE

Hungary lies at the heart of East Central Europe. Landlocked, it comprises a total of 93,020 square kilometers. Hungary is bordered by Austria (366 kilometers), Croatia (329 kilometers), Romania (443 kilometers), Serbia and Montenegro (151 kilometers), Slovakia (677 kilometers), Slovenia (102 kilometers), and Ukraine (103 kilometers).

Hungary's topography is seldom higher than 200 meters. Mountains reaching heights of 300 meters or more cover less than 2 percent of the country. The highest point in Hungary is Mount Kékes (1,008 meters) in the Mátra Mountains northeast of Budapest. The lowest spot is 77.6 meters above sea level, located in the Great Plain. Hungary has three main geographic regions: the Great Plain (Nagy Alföld), lying east of the Danube River; Transdanubia (Dunántúl), a hilly region lying west of the Danube and extending to the foothills of the Austrian Alps; and the Northern Hills (Északi Középhegység), a mountainous country beyond the northern boundary of the Great Plain.

The Great Plain contains the basin of the Tisza River and its branches. It encompasses more than half of the country's territory. Bordered by mountains on all sides, it has a variety of terrains, including regions of fertile soil, sandy areas, wastelands, and swampy areas. Here is found the *puszta,* an uncultivated expanse with which much Hungarian folklore is associated. With the danger of recurrent flooding largely eliminated in the nineteenth century, the land was placed under cultivation, and animal herding ceased to be major occupations.

The Transdanubia region lies in the western part of the country, bounded by the Danube River, the Dráva River, and the country's border with the former Yugoslavia. The region features rolling foothills of the Austrian Alps. However, large sections of Transdanubia are flat, most notably the Little Plain (Kis Alföld) along the lower course of the Rába River. Transdanubia is primarily an agricultural area, with flourishing crops, livestock, and viticulture. Mineral deposits and oil are found in Zala County close to the southern border.

The Northern Hills lie north-northeast of Budapest and run in a northeasterly direction south of the border with Slovakia. The higher ridges, which are mostly forested, have rich coal and iron deposits. Minerals are a major resource of the area and have long been the basis of the industrial economies of cities in the region. Viticulture is also important, producing the famous wines of the Tokaj region.

The major rivers in the country are the Danube (Duna) and the Tisza. The Danube is navigable within Hungary for 418 kilometers. The Tisza River is navigable for 444 kilometers in the country. Less important rivers include the Dráva (along the Croatian border), the Rába, the Szamos, the Sió, and the Ipoly (along the Slovak border). Hungary has three major lakes. The Balaton (the "Hungarian Sea") is 78 kilometers long

Elizabeth Bridge and cityscape, Budapest. (PhotoDisc, Inc.)

and from 3 to 14 kilometers wide, with an area of 592 square kilometers. It is Central Europe's largest freshwater lake and an important recreation area. Its shallow waters offer good summer swimming, and in winter its frozen surface provides excellent opportunities for winter sports. Smaller bodies of water are Lake Velence (26 square kilometers) in Fehér County and Lake Fertő (Neusiedlersee), with 82 square kilometers within Hungary.

The country's best natural resource is fertile land, although soil quality varies greatly. About 70 percent of the country's total territory is suitable for agriculture, with 72 percent of that being arable land.

Average temperatures in Hungary range from zero degrees Celsius in January to twenty degrees Celsius in July. Average yearly rainfall is 64 centimeters, unpredictably distributed. The western part of the country usually receives more rain than the eastern part, where severe droughts may occur. Weather conditions in the Great Plain can be harsh, with hot summers, cold winters, and scant rainfall.

Hungary's countryside is beginning to show the effects of pollution, from pesticides used in agriculture and rampant industrial pollutants. Most noticeable is the gradual contamination of the country's rivers and lakes, endangering fish and wildlife. Concern has mounted over these threats to the environment, and initial steps have been taken to counter them.

POPULATION

In its recent history, Hungary has exhibited several population trends that parallel those in other industrializing societies. In 1920 Hungary had 8 million inhabitants and by 1941 had grown to approximately 9.2 million. The country lost 5 percent of its people in World War II, and consequently in 1949 the population was only 8.8 million. Since that time, the population growth rate has fluctuated substantially. Until the mid-1950s, high fertility and declining mortality caused rapid population growth. In 1954 the highest postwar live-birthrate was reached, at 23 births per 1,000 population. Then until the mid-1960s the birthrate declined, but the mortality rate was also low. In the late 1960s and early 1970s the birthrate again rose, partly because of stimulating demographic measures introduced by the government. The mortality rate also increased during this period, but it was counterbalanced by the higher rate of live births.

Population grew slowly in the late 1970s and began to decline in 1981. By the mid-1980s, Hungary's demographic growth rate had become one of the lowest in the world. Deaths began to outnumber births. Over the 1980s, population decreased absolutely, after peaking at a post–World War II high of 10.7 million in 1980.

One reason for the overall decline of the birthrate is said to be the increasing number of educated and economically active women who, as in other countries, tend to have fewer children. In the 1980s the typical family had only two children (reflecting a dramatic decrease from the final decades of the nineteenth century, when the average family had five children).

As in many other European countries, the population is aging. A growing proportion of the population is fifty-five or older, and the proportion of the population under fifteen has decreased by 4 percent since 1949. Marriage rates fell steadily from the mid-1970s to the mid-1980s. In 1975 the marriage rate was 9.9 per 1,000. By 1986 that number had declined to 6.8 per 1,000. Moreover, in 1980, for the first time, the number of marriages that ended because of death or divorce outnumbered the number of marriages that took place. In 1980 the number of "marriages ceased" because of death and divorce was 9.2 per 1,000 in the population. That number rose to 9.3 by 1983, then fell slightly back to 9.2 by 1986.

Death rates are relatively high and rising. In 1986 the death rate was 13.8 per 1,000, as compared with 12.4 per 1,000 in 1975. In 1986 life expectancy averaged sixty-eight years, up from sixty-six years in 1975. For women in 1986, the average life span was almost seventy-two years; for men, it was just under sixty-five years.

In 1945 only 35 percent of the population lived in urban areas. After 1945, much of the population moved from the country's less developed counties to Budapest and then to its suburbs and to the industrial counties Hajdú-Bihar and Borsod-Abaúj-Zemplén. The number of urban dwellers grew by more than 50 percent from 1949 to 1984. More people (70 percent) are now living in urban centers than in rural areas. Population density climbed from 100 persons per square kilometer in 1949 to 120 persons per square kilometer in the 1990s. The smallest villages, those with fewer than 5,000 inhabitants, are losing their residents, as the number of people leaving the villages far exceeds the number of incoming residents.

A substantial number of persons of Hungarian origin live outside Hungary, many in neighboring countries. Others live in more distant lands. In the early twentieth century over 2 million ethnic Hungarian peasants fled to the United States to escape rural poverty. After the revolution of 1956, 200,000 people left the country, traveling first to Austria and Yugoslavia and eventually emigrating to Australia, Britain, Canada, France, Switzerland, the United States, and West Germany. As a result, about one-third of all persons of Hungarian descent are living outside Hungary.

Hungary is one of the most ethnically homogeneous countries in Europe. Of its population of 10,045,407 (July 2003 est.), Hungarians (or Magyars) compose 89.9 percent of the population. Over 98 percent of the population speak Hungarian.

The country's ethnic minorities include roughly 230,000 Germans; slightly more than 100,000 Slovaks; 100,000 Serbs, Croats, and Slovenes (often grouped together as South Slavs); and 30,000 Romanians. In the late 1980s the Romanian population increased significantly, as thousands of Romanians sought refuge in Hungary. In addition, 500,000 Gypsies, 150,000 Jews, and 4,000 Greeks live in Hungary. The Jewish community is a mere remnant of the Jewish population that lived in the country before World War II. During the 1940s, as many as 500,000 Jews and 60,000 Gypsies were deported to Nazi concentration camps.

Ethnic discrimination—except toward the Gypsies—is not generally practiced in Hungary. The government makes great efforts to ensure fair and equal treatment for minority nationalities. Foreign policy considerations partially explain this liberal policy: the Romanian and (to a lesser extent) the Slovak governments have subjected ethnic Hungarians in their countries to various kinds of discrimination. As an incentive to relax such pressure, Budapest pursues liberal policies toward its own national minorities and seeks to make its minority policies a model for other countries in Eastern Europe.

The constitution, as well as a sizable body of law, guarantees the cultural rights of recognized national minorities. Minorities are able to promote their national cultures through freedom of association in federations, ethnic clubs, and artistic endeavors. They can use their own language in official procedures, publish newspapers and periodicals, and broadcast radio and television programs in their own tongue.

Hungary's Jews and Gypsies are defined as a "religious community" and an "ethnic community," respectively. The country's 150,000 Jews form the third largest Jewish community on the European continent. They maintain schools, libraries, museums, shops, orphanages, a rabbinical seminary, and dozens of synagogues. Several publications, including newspapers, serve the Jewish population.

Much less favorable is the situation of the half million Gypsies (Roma), traditionally an impoverished, marginal segment of society that is subject to active as well as passive discrimination. About 60 percent of Gypsies live at or below the poverty level, even though half of them live in settled conditions, holding down jobs. Most speak Hungarian. Gypsies have a birthrate more than twice that of the rest of the population. This circumstance, and the widely held view that the Gypsy crime rate is disproportionately high, contributes to a deep-seated hostility toward Gypsies. There are growing efforts to foster a Gypsy ethnic and cultural identity and a sense of community and tradition to enhance the self-esteem of the Gypsy population. In 1986 the Cultural Association of Gypsies in Hungary was founded to help this trend. Still, Gypsies remain particularly vulnerable when the economic climate deteriorates. With minimal skills, education, and training, they are among the first to lose their jobs as unemployment increases. Their health and living standard remain well below the national average.

In traditional Hungary, the family—the basic social unit—had multiple functions, providing security and identity to individuals and reinforcing social values. In rural areas, it was also the basic economic unit; all members worked together for the material well-being of the whole family. Even before World War II, however, family cohesion began to weaken as people became increasingly mobile. But change quickened after the communist takeover. Intensive industrialization and forced collectivization prompted many

The Hungarian Language

Hungarian (Magyar) is a language spoken by nearly 16 million people worldwide. Although most speakers of the language (10.5 million) live in Hungary, another 3.5 million live in Romania (Transylvania), Slovakia, Serbia (Vojvodina), Austria (Burgenland), and Ukraine, with the remainder scattered all over the globe. Hungarian ranks fiftieth in size among the more than 3,000 languages used around the world and twelfth among the sixty-seven languages spoken in Europe.

The word "Hungarian" may have originated from the Old Turkic expression *onogur,* which means *on* (ten) *ogur* (arrows), an ancient tribal designation. Onogurs are first mentioned in the fifth century, a time when the ancestors of Hungarians dwelled between the Dnieper and Volga Rivers alongside Turkic tribes, who were therefore also called Onogurs.

The self-appellation Magyar is a composite, the first part of which may have been based on *mogy,* an ethnic designation, with the addition of *eu,* meaning "man, male." This designation first appeared in a document from around 810.

Unlike most European languages, which belong to the Indo-European family, Hungarian is a Finno-Ugric language related to Finnish, Estonian, and some other languages spoken by peoples in northwestern Siberia. Therefore, both the vocabulary and grammatical structure of Hungarian are different from the majority of European languages. Nevertheless, due to contacts with its mostly Slavic and German neighbors over time, the Hungarian language also reflects their influence.

Hungarian, like other Finno-Ugric languages, is agglutinative. Suffixes are added to the ends of words; these suffixes would be separate words in Indo-European languages. For example, the word *házamban* is translated as "in my house." The word *ház* (house) is followed by the suffixes *am* (my) and *ban* (in).

Hungarian does use the Latin alphabet and includes thirty-nine voiced letters, including sounds that are written with consonant combinations *(cs, dz, dzs, gy, ly, ny, sz, ty, zs),* each representing a single sound. The letters *q, w, x,* and *y* have no role in Hungarian, except when writing foreign terms or names. The vowels *a, e, i, o,* and *u* take diacritical marks, which change the length (and sometimes the quality) of the vowel: *a, á, e, é, i, í, o, ó, ö, ő, u, ú, ü, ű.* Written Hungarian reflects pronunciation more closely than either French or English, and in this it resembles German.

Hungarian has the same principal parts of speech as the Indo-European languages: verbs, nouns, adjectives, pronouns, adverbs, articles, and so on. In the Hungarian sentence the dominant word is the verb.

What is it that the Hungarian language does not have? Here are a few examples: There are no prepositions. Postpositions are used: for example, *a ház mögött* means "behind the house," literally "house behind." There are no genders, which complicate the grammar of many other languages. There are no pronouns indicating gender. In the third person *(ő),* there is only one gender, which in English would be "he," "she," or "it."

The Hungarian vocabulary reflects centuries of cultural exchange within the Carpathian Basin, between north and south and between east and west. Words from Pecheneg, Cuman, and Jazygian were absorbed during the early Middle Ages. Later, Hungarian was influenced primarily by Slavic, German, and Latin. There are Byzantine, Greek, Italian, French, Romanian, and Ottoman Turk influences as well. Hungarian has adopted or borrowed hundreds of foreign words but has always adjusted them to its own linguistic system and was thus able to preserve its own individuality.

peasants to leave agriculture for industrial work in the cities, some commuting long distances between home and work. Patterns of family life changed. A growing number of women worked outside the home, and children spent much of their time in school or in youth organization activities. Families came together only for important ceremonies, such as weddings or funerals.

Family members had greater independence. The role of women changed. By 1987, 75 percent of working-age women were gainfully employed. Even peasant women became wage earners on the collective farms. However, most observers agree that the male is still viewed as the head of the household, if only because of his generally higher income. Women still provide much of child rearing and housework, so they usually work longer hours than men.

Social analysts consider the Hungarian family to be an institution under considerable stress. Statistics support this contention. The divorce rate is on the increase, with every third marriage ending in separation. Almost 15 percent of all Hungarian families are headed by a single parent.

One major source of stress within families, according to many observers, is the scarcity of adequate housing, especially for young families. In many families, members face the pressures and exhaustion of trying to hold down multiple jobs. Another source of tension within families is the prevalence of commuting. A large number of villagers commute to the cities to work.

Still, the cohesive force of the family remains relatively strong. The family continues to be a source of personal comfort and reassurance in the face of worsening economic conditions. The traditional sense of family loyalty and responsibility also seems to survive.

Churches faced extensive harassment and persecution by the antireligious regime of the communist era. The clergy were suspicious of the new, stridently anti-religious system, and the secular authorities denounced such attitudes as traitorous, persecuting the churches as a source of opposition.

The Roman Catholic Church lost much of its wealth in the first postwar land reform, which occurred before the communist takeover. Fifty-nine of the sixty-three religious orders were dissolved in 1948, when religious schools were also taken over by the state. Most Catholic associations and clubs, which numbered 4,000, were forced to disband. A number of members of the clergy, most notably József Cardinal Mindszenty, were imprisoned or deported. Relations between church and state remained strained throughout the following decades.

Churches earned popularity as dissenters under an increasingly unpopular regime. But in recent times, clergymen are aging and decreasing in number, and are able to attract few followers among the young. Nominally, close to 70 percent of Hungarians are Roman Catholic, 20 percent Reformed (Calvinist), 5 percent unaffiliated, and 5 percent Lutheran. Smaller denominations are dubbed Free Churches. Hungary also has 65,000 to 100,000 practicing Jews. The remainder of the population does not subscribe to any religious creed or organization. Nor is any single church or religion associated with national identity in the popular mind, as is the Catholic Church in Poland. Religion does not provide a viable alternative value system that could compete with the predominant secularism and materialism of an increasingly modern society. Thus churches are unlikely to become a vehicle for dissent.

Hungary has faced a severe housing shortage since the late 1940s. However, unlike most other countries in Eastern Europe, since the mid-1970s the government has encouraged citizens to build their own housing. This policy has eased the shortage somewhat, but the lack of adequate housing remains a serious problem.

Although 99 percent of the population participate in the social insurance system and could receive free medical services, there has been much public discussion about serious shortcomings in health care. One topic of discussion is the country's high suicide rate: 44 per 100,000 inhabitants. This has many historical aspects, but the rate has risen noticeably since the 1960s and shows no sign of improvement.

Another source of anxiety for both health authorities and the general public is the downward trend projected for the country's population, which is declining by a rate of –0.29 percent. The postcommunist governments are struggling to devise a comprehensive population policy.

HISTORY

In 1996 Hungarians (Magyars) commemorated 1,100 years of their living in the Carpathian Basin. The land was inhabited as early as 350,000 years ago by a variety of now extinct peoples. In the first century B.C.E. Roman legions brought imperial rule to the western half of the region. With the decline of Rome, the region became a transit zone for new migrations. In the fourth century C.E. the Huns of Attila made the Carpathian Basin their wintering ground. When Attila died (453), this nomadic empire disappeared, opening the region to fresh invaders, among them the Avars. Whether the Avars were eliminated or they formed an early wave of the Magyar arrival, dated around 896, is debated.

Linguistic historians estimate that proto-Hungarians did not emerge as a distinctive entity until the first millennium B.C.E., by which time they were living in the mid- or southern Ural region, probably on the eastern, Asian side of that worn-down mountain chain.

The early Christian era found ancient Hungarians nearer to the Volga River. Threatened from the east, they dropped south toward the Azov Sea and then moved on toward the Black Sea. Peoples inhabiting the grassy, semiarid lands of Inner Eurasia adapted successfully to their harsh environment by assuming the lifestyle of horse-mounted nomadic herdsmen, resorting to farming only intermittently.

Were these proto-Hungarians Asian or European? Their "original homeland" was most likely near the Ural Mountains, which are far from impassable, so it would have been easy for them to move from east to west, from Asia to Europe, and back again.

Magyars reappeared in the eighth and ninth centuries, along the Volga, coexisting with Turkic Bulgars. In the ninth century they were part of the Khazar Empire of the Caspian region reaching into the Don, Dniepr, and Crimean steppes. During this Khazar period, the Hungarian tribes repeatedly journeyed through the steppes from east to west. One region in which they wintered was called Etelköz, meaning "between the rivers." However, since both the Volga and the Don were known at the time as Etel (Etil), it is not easy to be sure about the location of this settlement.

A late-ninth-century Arab traveler visited them somewhere "between the rivers" and described a seminomadic and opulent lifestyle. By this time no longer affiliated with the Khazar Empire, the Magyar warriors constituted a fearsome, mobile army and in their raids had ventured to the borders of the eastern Frankish kingdom.

There is also a mythical account of the journey to the new homeland, preserved in the collective memory and recorded by medieval chroniclers. According to these, Hunor and Magor (sons of Gog and Magog, kings of the Scythians), out hunting one day, saw a miraculous stag and chased it far into unknown regions. Bewitched by the beauty of the landscape, the abundance of herbs, wood, fish, and game, they decided to stay. They found their future wives, daughters of a local prince, and from these unions came the famous and all-powerful King Attila and, much later, Prince Álmos, from whom descended the kings and princes of Hungary. Legends like this fed the Hungarian imagination, merging the plausible memory of an abode near the Azov Sea and an improbable belief in a blood connection with Attila's Huns.

The final push that sent early Magyars into their present homeland was a surprise raid by the Pechenegs (Cumans). The attack must have been catastrophic, since Magyar warriors were busy fighting elsewhere. It was thus as much a flight as a conquest when the tribes crossed the Carpathian passes. Two chieftains, Árpád and Kurszán, led the seven Magyar tribes and their Turkic-Kabar allies. Historians generally give 896 as the date of these events, and by 900 the invaders had reached all parts of the Carpathian Basin.

The land of future Hungary offered numerous advantages to the steppe peoples, and its environment—continental, but relatively moderate—turned them from nomads into settlers. The plains, almost entirely covered with loess, were fertile, intermittently flooded, and richly endowed with fish-filled rivers and lakes.

Árpád and his clan took the center of the Carpathian Basin, with their primary residence probably near what is now Budapest. Other chieftains—the seven Magyars, as they are commonly called—may have maintained sway over their respective lands until central control was enforced. In addition to the chieftains and their close associates, there were the common warriors *(jobbágy),* and the poorest, downtrodden laborers, little better than slaves, who had either arrived with the conquerors or joined, perhaps captured, from the local population during raids.

Until the tenth century, the newly acquired land of the Magyars often appears in Western sources as the Avar Empire, while Byzantine sources write about the "country of the Turks." Soon, however, mentions of the Magyars become more frequent. Practically unknown before, these horsemen of the steppes found fame through their devastating raids into Moravia and Bavaria. The raiders benefitted from disarray in a Europe under attack from several sides (Arabs in the south, Vikings in the north) and torn by rival factions. The often uttered plea, asking divine protection "*de sagitis Hungarorum*" (from the Hungarian arrows), echoed Europe's fear during what some historians call the period of adventures.

Magyar raiders were able to carry on in this manner for fifty years with relative impunity. And yet, their overall strength seems insignificant; in a Europe of some 40 million, Hungary was inhabited by less than 100,000 and could raise an army of no more than 20,000 horsemen. Their military success is all the more astonishing because these armed bands were supported by a society that had yet to be fully organized.

Raids, from wars of plunder to expeditions undertaken in the service of neighboring rulers or the Byzantine emperors, continued unabated until the Battle of Augsburg in 955. A catastrophic Hungarian defeat at the hand of the armies of the Great Moravian Empire ensued, which left no choice but to make peace with Europe. Conversion to Christianity had already begun, and it was in the interests of the Hungarians to establish good relations with both Byzantium and Rome. Prince Géza's reign (972–997) undoubtedly paved the way, even though the honor of being the founder of Hungary is generally accorded his son István, the future St. Stephen. Géza's foreign policy managed to establish stability in a region coveted by two empires. At home he was successful in centralizing power, subtly redirecting Christian conversion away from the Greek Church toward Rome and the Holy Roman Empire.

Géza's methods were more violent than pious. He forced large numbers of lords and warriors to convert whether they liked it or not and persecuted recalcitrant pagans. He was faced with numerous revolts, stemming either from attachments to old beliefs or from resistance against his authority as prince.

Géza's greatest achievement may have been the way he solved the question of succession. His son István (Stephen), born around 970 and originally named Vajk, was baptized and raised as Christian. In 996, in the first of many dynastic unions, he was married to the Bavarian princess Gizella.

Despite his father's legacy of centralization, István I did not begin his reign as the absolute master of his lands. Both before and after his coronation (1000 or 1001), he had to overcome rebels who opposed conversion to Christianity and the ruler's growing authority. Following his father's teachings, István avoided becoming vassal to either the

Painting of St. István, first king of Hungary. (Corel Corporation)

neighboring powerful rulers or the pope. The new kingdom was firmly bound to Western Christianity, but its independence was preserved.

Architectural remains from this period are modest in size. Outstanding among them is the Benedictine abbey of Pannonhalma. However, the spiritual and cultural influence of the Catholic Church was crucial in what must be called a great modernization process. A handful of the first written documents, mostly donation letters, appear in Latin.

The establishment of the Catholic Church, the consolidation of royal power, and the establishment of legal order in keeping with the spirit of the times, attracted many foreigners to the land. Newly introduced laws (which were severe, but no more cruel than others of the time) protected property and provided a degree of security. Social organization was no longer based on the blood ties of the tribal system. Population distribution and settlement were now conducted along county lines (*comitatus* in Latin). The king set about creating about forty counties attached to forts belonging to him. At the head of each of these, he placed a governor, a trusted figure given charge of both the territory and its warriors. Much land was still in the hands of lords, and vast domains belonged to the Catholic Church. Bishoprics were also organized by the king, who divided the country into ten (later twelve) dioceses under the authority of the archbishop of Esztergom.

István's changes ushered in the notion of private property and social stratification according to power, status, wealth, and distribution of labor. Beneath the ruling class, a mixture of established lords, traditional chieftains, and the recently promoted, stood the free warriors, and on the lowest rung, the common people, soon reduced to servitude. The king claimed no less than two-thirds of the county's revenues, leaving one-third at the disposal of his lieutenants. This enabled the king to fulfill his three main domestic objectives: the creation of a state government, the establishment of the Catholic Church, and, finally, regulation of the rights and duties of property owners. At the head of the state, the king reigned supreme, but his power was not absolute. He was surrounded by a council that helped secure integrity and relative peace for the kingdom.

István's death in 1038 was followed by the reign of twenty-two kings from the Árpád dynasty, until the direct line died out in 1301. For nearly three centuries, Hungary held an important position on the European scene, becoming Western Christianity's easternmost bastion on the frontiers of the Orthodox and pagan worlds. At the same time, many of Hungary's problems arose from its location. In addition to being under constant pressure from two empires, the country's geographic situation rendered it isolated in a mostly Slavic environment of Czechs, Moravians, Poles, Russians, Bulgarians, Croatians, Slovenians, Serbians, and others. To establish its authority in the region, the Hungarian kingdom made expansionist moves in Dalmatia and the Balkans, but at the same time also sought alliances through marriages. Six queens came from Slav princely families, others from German, French, and Byzantine dynasties.

Under Kálmán, remarkable progress was made in both legal and literary culture. The use of writing spread. Jesters and jugglers were replaced by chroniclers, authors of *gestae,* who recounted the ancient history of Hungary and the tales of its kings through words and pictures. As well as the doings and exploits of its kings (especially the canonized monarchs István and László), charters of ennoblement and gifts formed central themes within these chronicles. The tradition continued throughout the reigns of Kálmán's successors, and chivalric culture and the poetry of the troubadours also flourished. One of the first poems in the Hungarian language, the very beautiful *Lament of Mary,* was preserved in a thirteenth-century codex.

Hungary became one of Europe's largest and most powerful kingdoms. László, the king-knight, successfully defended his country against invasion by Cumans, the Turkic-Kipchak people who had congregated on the eastern frontiers. But the most important expeditions to be undertaken by László and Kálmán were toward the Balkans. Following in the footsteps of his uncle László, a great warrior, Kálmán gained dominance over Croatia, Slavonia, and Dalmatia. The entire coast, with its splendid merchant towns, recognized his sovereignty with some relief. While siding with the pope in his quarrel with Byzantium, Hungary maintained its autonomy vis-à-vis the Holy See. Historians speak, if not of absolute royal power, of an almost unshakeable hegemony. The extent of royal wealth was a major factor, as was the well-earned prestige of the rulers. In the late twelfth century, the king to stand out was Béla III, not only by virtue of his height (1.9 meters) but also by his qualities as leader and organizer. The son of Géza II and a Russian princess, Béla was raised at the Byzantine court, where he was betrothed to the emperor's daughter and saw himself as destined for the empire's throne. He lost his chance as heir when a son was born to the emperor, but he was still given a royal title and enjoyed great prestige.

Contemporary Western travelers described Hungary as an opulent but none too civilized country. Towns were no more developed than villages, and stone houses were rare. But Hungarians seem to have had enough to eat and enjoyed common freedoms. Hungary's society was also quite diverse, as it welcomed settlers from the west, most of all from German lands, who were attracted by a land that was fertile and less densely populated. Pechenegs, Cumans, and other refugees from various steppe invasions also added to Hungary's population. The mostly rural population lived from cattle herding, agriculture, fishing, viticulture, and crafts. Social strata were numerous, depending on whether one was noble, free, semifree, native, or host.

The king was immensely wealthy due to his inherited properties, which amounted to almost two-thirds of the kingdom, with the rest belonging to the Catholic Church, to descendants of chieftains, to foreign knights, and to the free warrior-peasants. Donations by the king to various beneficiaries, monasteries, bishoprics, or individuals had always existed in some form but increased sharply under András II (1202–1235), described by many as an overly generous monarch. His reign initiated the disintegration of St. Stephen's old patrimonial order and the beginning of the manorial system.

Hungarian Cuisine

In the earliest times, Hungarians' cooking was influenced by their nomadic lifestyle: food had to be easily portable and simple to prepare. Many Hungarian stews and soups to this day reflect the tradition of the *bogrács,* the iron pot permanently simmering over an open fire. The pantry of the early Hungarians was stocked from the flocks of animals they herded, supplemented with plants found along the way, as well as other lightweight, perhaps dried ingredients. Hunting and fishing were also important activities, and archaeological evidence shows that, even though nomadic, Hungarians had some familiarity with planting and growing food. Still, meat and meat products are central in the traditional cuisine. Since most Hungarians were not wealthy enough to consume large amounts of meat exclusively, they had to be creative to feed their families, using relatively small amounts of expensive ingredients. This need explains the large presence of side dishes, stews, and soups in the daily diet of the average Hungarian. (Festive occasions and restaurant meals are quite another matter, since they are often opportunities to celebrate and demonstrate social status.)

The use of onions and other spices, especially paprika, is even more characteristic of Hungarian cooking than garlic, which is most frequently mentioned when talking about Central European food. Meats—most often pork or poultry, less often mutton, the more expensive beef, or fish—are frequently braised with onion or other spices, giving considerable taste intensity to the meal's main ingredient. This is *pörkölt* (braised meat). To counter the richness of the juicy meat, the meal is then stretched, either by turning it into soup or stew, adding large amounts of non-meat ingredients, or creating vegetable-based side dishes called *főzelék,* which can be made out of anything from carrots to zucchini.

Goulash *(gulyás),* a Hungarian dish well known abroad, is actually a soup, not a thick stew. It is prepared with a small amount of diced and braised beef, with its volume expanded by the addition of diced potatoes or pasta and vegetables, and consumed with lots of brown bread.

Paprika, which has come to characterize Hungarian cuisine, was not known until the seventeenth century. It became a defining element of the Hungarian kitchen in the first half of the nineteenth century. Hungarian cooking includes paprika both as a spice and as a vegetable. Both can be mild or spicy and are main ingredients in many Hungarian dishes. A popular, simple dish is *paprikás krumpli,* which is a potato stew with a small amount of sausage, for taste, heavily spiced with paprika. Pepper stew *(lecsó)* is a favorite summer dish when fresh tomatoes and green-yellow peppers are plentiful. Chicken paprikash *(paprikás csirke),* a savory braised dish served with dumplings *(nokedli)* and sour cream, is a mainstay of special-occasion Hungarian meals.

A meatless meal of vegetable soup with a sweet noodle dish, covered with ground walnuts *(diós tészta)* or poppy seed *(mákos tészta),* or with thin pancakes, rolled with filling *(palacsinta),* is still Friday fare in many Hungarian homes.

In a marked departure from Western European practice, the distribution of royal property in Hungary was permanent and hereditary, not given in fief and therefore not tied to the vassal system. These donations created a new class of great barons, without reciprocal obligations to either the royal donor or to the people who became their dependents. Numerous castles and their surrounding villages, even entire counties, were bestowed on the most deserving or clever royal servants. András II also faced criticism for entrusting fiscal affairs to foreigners. Malcontents formed a league and succeeded in extracting from the court a charter of noble freedoms. The Golden Bull of 1222 (somewhat like the English Magna Carta) enshrined the right of nobles to resist royal power. András's successor, Béla IV, initially tried to backtrack in order to undertake more fundamental and considered reforms than his father. The event that changed his mind was the Mongol invasion.

After Chinghis Khan's death in 1227, his successor, Ogoday, sent Batu of the Golden Horde to conquer Russia. The immense project achieved, Batu's army invaded Poland and Hungary. In 1241 the Mongols easily defeated the Hungarians at Muhi. The following winter they crossed the Danube and pursued the king all the way to the Dalmatian islands. The next spring the Mongols suddenly withdrew (whether in response to the death of their great khan or for some unknown motive), leaving behind a destroyed Hungary. The king's reconstruction efforts opened the way to a new era. Béla IV had to start from scratch, so he first reorganized his military forces and the state administration. He proceeded to create a feudal Christian state, giving great power to loyal barons. All high governmental, legal, commanding, and administrative offices in large territorial units were entrusted to barons and bishops. The result proved positive, as Béla's reconstruction soon put the country back on its feet. In subsequent centuries, descendants of these barons would contribute to the weakening of the state, but during this crucial period of renewal, Béla's trust proved well placed. He fortified towns and built new ones, combining military defense with urbanization and the promotion of civic privileges. He laid the foundations of Buda, the castle and the town, making it into an important trade center.

The towns, with their stone churches and houses, markets, municipalities and their inhabitants—many of them foreigners in various trades—generated new wealth for the artisans and tradesmen, and became civilizing centers. Reliable currency (coins with a high silver content) stimulated economic and commercial activities and fiscal income via domestic taxes and duties. Hungary exported beef, wine, and salt and imported cloth, silk, and spices from Venice, Germany, and Moravia. Taxes were fixed according to market conditions. Royalties from the mines (silver, gold, salt) were divided between the treasury and the new entrepreneurs. The new economic activities generated more revenue than the old taxes. Some regions still paid in kind, and the country's Jews paid collectively, in silver. Few were exempt.

With 2 million inhabitants, Hungary was more populous than England, but it still had room for many more people. Béla invited a variety of new settlers. Religious institutions were strengthened. Bishops also provided civil governance over their estates and population, which included the clerical nobility, their servants, and soldiers settled on their land by the bishop. High clergy also had judiciary powers and sat on the Royal Council. The king respected tradition while maintaining control over nominations, retaining investiture for his faithful prelates. Béla's efforts however were almost entirely negated by his son, István II. A bold military leader, he turned against his father, defeated him, and proclaimed himself "king-junior" over the eastern half of the country. The reign of István's son, László IV (1272–1290), ten years old when he succeeded his father, was punctuated by intrigue and chronic instability. The lords of the realm pursued their private wars according to the rules of feudal anarchy. Twenty or so among them seized vast tracts of land, spoils, and positions. With the death of András III in 1301, the lights of the House of Árpád went out.

When Charles-Robert (1310–1342) was crowned, following brief reigns by the Bohemian Vencel (Wenceslas) and Otto Wittelsbach of Bavaria, he had already considered himself king for a number of years. His grandmother, an Árpád princess, had married Charles II of Anjou, king of Naples, and Charles-Robert was brought up at the court, destined for the throne of Hungary since birth. Crowned for the first time when he was only thirteen, he was not to enjoy undisputed kingship until after his third coronation in 1310.

While the young Angevin found his new kingdom in a state of turmoil, the international situation favored his ambitions. The Byzantine and Holy Roman Empires were preoccupied elsewhere. Hungary's immediate neighbor, Austria, had passed into the hands of the Habsburgs in 1278 and did not yet represent a threat. Western Europe was fully occupied with France's wars with the papacy and England. The Black Death (1346–1353) was soon to wipe out a third of the population in the West, and in addition, the continent was suffering a period of severe cold and rain, which brought periods of famine. Hungary was less affected by these calamities. Its population reached 3 million while the whole of Europe, excluding Russia, probably had some 50 million inhabitants before the plague epidemics, and far less than that after midcentury. Under these generally favorable conditions, the Angevins were able to consolidate their internal power and to conduct an active foreign policy.

Charles-Robert's first priority was to put his Hungarian house in order. A handful of powerful magnates ruled over much of the land. Only a smallish region in the center of the country remained under the direct authority of the king. He found that only a few of the barons sided with him. Nevertheless, Charles-Robert had the sense to attack the barons separately. Fortunately for him, neighboring countries preferred not to interfere in Hungary's affairs. Charles-Robert even succeeded in setting up a triple alliance between the Polish, Czech, and Hungarian kings—a Piast, a Luxemburg, and an Angevin—meeting at Visegrád in the 1330s.

Charles-Robert's reign of more than three decades was not particularly violent. He was not as greedy as his predecessors or other European monarchs. Still, he confiscated the possessions of deposed oligarchs, several of whom had taken refuge abroad earlier. His son Lajos pursued the same course, thus recovering much of the estates lost to disloyal magnates. In addition, the Angevins, who already had a huge personal fortune, had discovered a new source of income to be derived from the country's mineral resources. By the end of the century, Hungarian gold accounted for almost three-quarters of the output from all of Europe's mines. Gold coins minted at Körmöc circulated throughout the continent, at a time when high demand boosted the value of a solid currency. During the Angevin period, there were 59 free royal towns, 638 market towns and smaller towns that enjoyed chartered privileges, and around 21,000 villages. Most peasants were still free and enjoyed relatively comfortable living standards, with the more able and fortunate gaining access to economic and social mobility.

Among the larger and medium-size estates, freeholds were far more widespread than in the West, and these farms employed a primitive subsistence farming system. Both large estates and tenanted holdings were starting to produce marketable surpluses within a rapidly developing economic framework. The increasing exploitation of the mines was matched in the villages, as agriculture, livestock farming, forestry, and trade underwent significant growth. There was no shortage of exploitable land in the time of the Angevins. On the contrary, with 3 million inhabitants distributed over a territory of around 300,000 square kilometers (the size of Italy), population density was far lower than in Europe's more developed countries. The kingdom was therefore able to absorb large numbers of immigrants. Its borderlands (such as Transylvania) attracted Romanians, Moravians, Poles, and Ruthenians, joining the Saxons who had established themselves as early as the twelfth century.

Although urban development was under way, the towns and their level of social organization remained inferior to that of Western Europe, with urban settlers accounting for only 3 percent of the population. Medieval Hungarian towns, with the exception of the future capital, offered little more than military security. As the royal seat, Buda attracted increasing numbers of artisans and German merchants who proceeded to rise in municipal circles. Still, urban Hungary was unable to play a role comparable to that of the great Italian, French, or Dutch urban centers.

Nonetheless, it would be fair to see the Angevins' overall contribution to the development of towns, urban civilization, and commerce as substantial. Charles-Robert inherited a land in the grip of anarchy and left behind an ordered, flourishing, and well-governed state. Most people benefited from the consolidation of royal power and social order. Merchants and businessmen, as well as the simple taxpayer, profited from financial stability, safe travel by road, and a coherent household tax, which replaced an inconsistent system. Administrative reforms went hand in hand with a stable royal government, and with social change. Local *comitats* (counties) increasingly turned into autonomous administrative units, even if managed by the nobility. Accordingly, halfway between the traditional patrimonial system based on blood ties and a partially adopted Western feudal model, a "states and orders" system developed, based on a particular concept of civil rights. According to these principles, the kingdom was the property of the Crown, an abstract moral entity, while real political power was regulated by contract between the king and the noble estates.

Charles-Robert had few expansionist tendencies. Through his fourth wife, Elisabeth Lokietek, he maintained good relations with Poland. Bohemia too was part of the triple alliance of Visegrád (1335), and Charles-Robert formed ties with Austria. In the south, he maintained Hungarian dominance over the Slav *banates* and the Adriatic coast, in spite of Venetian ambitions.

The one long-cherished dream of the Hungarian Angevins was to regain a foothold in Naples. Following the death of his father in 1342, it fell to the future Louis the Great to lead the Hungarian side toward Naples. This Angevin's greatness was due to the unprecedented expansion of his kingdoms, which, by the end of his reign, encompassed a vast territory stretching from Poland to the Adriatic. Some of his subjects recognized his greatness: those citizens admitted to the judicial process, the prosperous bourgeois, members of the middle nobility, all felt their views were now being taken into account, as did those barons who shared his external ambitions.

Art and culture flourished at the court, which resided in three sumptuous palaces; and yet even the royal towns of Buda and Visegrád did not measure up to Charles IV's Prague. Louis founded the first Hungarian university in Pécs, as well as several churches and monasteries, but no cathedrals or grand stately castles were built during his reign. There remained a wide cultural divide between the kingdom of Hungary and the realms of Italy, France, and Flanders.

Closer to Hungarian borders, Venetian designs on Dalmatia had resulted in three long wars against Hungary. Stefan Dušan's "great Serbia" was also briefly involved, but it soon fragmented into several petty despotates and then fell to Ottoman rule after the Battle of Kosovo (1389).

The Bulgarian second empire disintegrated too. Between 1353 and 1391, a brief regional Bosnian hegemony emerged under Stephen Tvartko I. Relations between Hungary and Bosnia, several times severed and reestablished, also aimed at preserving influence from the Balkans to the Adriatic coast. Holding on to Croatia and Dalmatia in the face of both Serbian and Venetian opposition was crucial. Louis managed to profit from the situation, failing to foresee the scale of the Ottoman threat. This was in sharp contrast with his piety and proselytizing activities among the non-Catholics in his own country. Hungarian domination in Dalmatia, as well as Serbia, Bulgaria, Bosnia, Wallachia, and even for a brief moment, Moldavia, was unsustainable. In the end, it was the Ottoman Turks, in full expansion, who benefited from the Balkan conflicts.

As one of his best-known achievements, in 1370 Louis seized the Crown of Poland, succeeding his uncle Kasimir III the Great, whom he had assisted on a number of occasions against powerful and expansionist pagan Lithuania. The Hungarian-Polish interlude lasted a mere twelve years and was a personal rather than a state union.

When Louis died in 1382 without a viable heir, his daughter, Maria, was crowned in 1386 at age eleven, enabling her fiancé Sigismund (Zsigmond) of the Luxemburg house to claim, and eventually occupy, the Hungarian throne. Sigismund was a skillful ruler, an accomplished reformer, and a person of considerable talent. Yet, even though he ruled several kingdoms and the Holy Roman Empire, he was in constant financial difficulties and was detested by most of his subjects. Removed from various thrones, he was refused access to the Bohemian one, was held captive by Hungarian barons, and was so deeply in debt that he wagered everything from entire counties and towns down to the silverware from his table.

Sigismund inherited a situation dominated by the oligarchy, which had assumed all powers, including predominance in the diet and tutelage over the sovereign. When, in 1401, he refused the nobles' demand to dismiss his foreign advisers, he was thrown into prison, in the name of a symbol, the Holy Crown, a public legal entity. Nevertheless, through patience and opportunism, not to mention family connections, Sigismund became a prestigious emperor and a Hungarian king of caliber.

Faced with the Ottoman threat, Zsigmond enjoyed a reprieve thanks to Tamerlane (1370–1405), the Central Asian emir who beat the Ottomans and captured Sultan Bayezid. The pace of Turkish advance slowed down as a result, leaving Sigismund to pursue his grand German and imperial policy.

Some of his military endeavors were unprofitable; the number of battles lost far outweighed the victories. Yet he was neither incompetent nor cowardly. His defeats came in the face of formidable enemies, especially the Ottomans.

The Ottomans continued to advance in the Balkans, and Sigismund, determined to stop them, retaliated. In 1396 at Nicopolis (Bulgaria), Sigismund confronted the Turks. A catastrophe ensued, and it was not the last. The military organization of the Ottoman Empire was far more efficient than that of European armies. The king did win a few battles: Nándorfehérvár (Belgrade) was saved provisionally, as was Jajce in Bosnia, though not for long. Then, in 1428, Sigismund was again defeated, this time seriously, at Galambоc (Golubac, Serbia), thus putting a definitive end to Hungarian hegemony in the Balkans.

HUNGARY, THE OTTOMANS, AND THE HABSBURGS

The nobility's right to freely elect a "competent" sovereign (i.e., a king to their liking) was connected to an evolving concept of public life, known as the doctrine of the Holy Crown. It posited the country as belonging to the nation, embodied by the nobility, and represented by the Crown as symbol rather than physical object. The king exercised his powers purely through the latter. Both mystical and legal, the doctrine stipulated the representational nature of royal power and placed the source of sovereignty within the body of the nation's nobility.

Most nobles understood that the fight against the Ottoman threat was a priority and were looking for a sovereign who could rise to the challenge. The young king Ulászló did not disappoint them. Accompanied by János Hunyadi, his most famous general, he went on to conduct numerous campaigns.

János Hunyadi, who was one of a number of leaders in the middle of the fifteenth century who were of humble birth, was probably of Romanian or South Slav descent and settled in Transylvania. Hunyadi served his king well. He accompanied Sigismund to Italy and then Bohemia, participated in the Czech wars and led the campaign against the Turks. By the time of Sigismund's death in 1437, he had great fame but not yet fortune. Soon, however, he became one of the richest men in Hungary.

Hunyadi and Zrinyi

Reflecting the primary challenge of their times, both János Hunyadi (d. 1456) and Miklós Zrinyi (1623–1664) were military leaders who led successful campaigns against the powerful Ottoman forces invading the region. They both also demonstrate the assimilative power of the medieval Hungarian kingdom: Hunyadi (also referred to as Iancu Hunedoara) was a Transylvanian son of a Hungarian-Wallachian marriage; Zrinyi (also written as Zrinski) was a member of the Croatian aristocracy, which made him a subject of the Hungarian Crown, after the merger of the two countries in the twelfth century. They both died at the height of their power, to the great loss of Hungary's national defense.

Hunyadi was a young man of limited means and education, who made his initial fame and fortune rapidly as a small-unit commander in the service of others. His talents were recognized and rewarded, making him one of the country's richest landholders. Count Zrinyi, on the other hand, was born into wealth, acquired considerable erudition from private tutors, became an accomplished poet and writer, and was appointed *ban* (governor) of Croatia.

Hunyadi and Zrinyi embodied unselfish, heroic service to the defense of Hungary and European Christendom at a time when such dedication was becoming increasingly rare. The power struggles of the post-Anjou period led to a breakdown of royal authority and the rise of aristocratic anarchy. The mixed-house rulers of the fourteenth and fifteenth centuries, even the talented Zsigmond, were unable to unify the country's lords in the cause of presenting a strong force in the face of approaching Ottoman threat. In marked contrast with his selfish and reluctant fellow lords, Hunyadi used his leadership ability and his wealth to create and lead armies to major victories. The most important among these was the successful defense of Nándorfehérvár (today's Belgrade) against an Ottoman siege in 1456, which delayed the invasion of Hungary by almost a century. It is in honor of this victory that bells throughout the Christian world ring at noon.

Leading successful raids deep into hostile territory, Zrinyi was a bold military leader at a time when the reputation of Ottoman armies intimidated most Christian generals into avoiding battles and signing accommodating peace treaties. He recognized that Ottoman power was already declining, and called for an all-out military effort to oust the occupiers. Witnessing the reluctance of Habsburg generals, he began to question their commitment to liberating Hungary. During winter breaks from campaigning, he wrote, and he wrote in Hungarian, a pioneering practice. His most memorable work is the epic poem *The Siege of Sziget,* in which he paid homage to his grandfather of the same name, who perished heroically defending a small fortress against Suleiman's grand army. Zrinyi also wrote pamphlets on military strategy and contemporary political affairs, some of them sharply critical of Habsburg designs concerning Hungary. It is not surprising, therefore, that when he was killed in a hunting accident, there was much talk that the wild boar that killed him was in the hire of Vienna.

Hunyadi was appointed *voivode* of Transylvania in 1441 and governor of Hungary between 1446 and 1452, while László V was still under age. Hunyadi's courage as a soldier was legendary, and he was undoubtedly guided as much by his vision of himself as servant of the state as he was by personal interest. His leadership qualities took on historic dimensions in the wars against the Ottoman Empire, on behalf of Hungary and, indeed, Europe. In his "long campaign" of 1442–1444, Hunyadi won several battles, enough to reignite the hope of driving out the Ottoman invaders.

Because of troubles along his Asian borders, Sultan Murad was forced to make peace with Hungary. The young Jagiellon king Ulászló signed the agreement, but in 1444 he went back on his word and set out for war, only to be defeated at Varna on 10 November.

Hunyadi bore no blame for the defeat, but he had trouble dealing with the political infighting at the court. Even though elected as governor, his powers were restricted. Still, he was able to prepare for a new defensive war on the Turkish front. He found an ally in the Albanian hero Skanderbeg and, with encouragement from the Holy See and European promises, chances for another campaign against the Ottoman Empire seemed promising. In 1448 Hunyadi decided to go to war with Murad II, who forced him into a battle at Kosovo. The Field of Blackbirds was once more fatal to Christian armies. Skanderbeg was unable to reach his ally. Hunyadi was beaten.

The fall of Constantinople on 29 May 1453 prompted Christians to mobilize for a common defense. As a frontline nation, Hungary had to be both the initiator of and the decisive factor in the campaign. The 1454 Diet reorganized the army, and Hunyadi worked hard to create a united and efficient military structure, introducing such innovations as the use of mercenaries. To finance an army of 100,000 men, the diet voted for extremely heavy war taxes. Hunyadi's army constituted a formidable force. Allied troops made it to the rendezvous, and for once, despite everything, Europe was ready to fight. In the summer of 1456 Sultan Mohamed II besieged Nándorfehérvár (today's Belgrade) with an army estimated at 150,000 men, 300 cannons, and 200 ships on the Danube. The fortress was defended by Mihály Szilágyi (Hunyadi's brother-in-law) commanding 7,000 soldiers. The great captain himself arrived to rescue the besieged town with 40,000–45,000 men. To everyone's surprise, the

Battle of Mohács, 29 August 1526, where the Hungarian army of King Lajos II met the Turkish army under Suleiman the Magnificent and was decisively defeated. (Getty Images)

Ottoman force lost the battle. Hunyadi was keen to pursue the campaign as far as Constantinople, but he died soon after, probably taken by an epidemic.

The defeat may have shocked the Ottoman Empire but its expansion continued regardless. The invasion of Hungary was, however, postponed.

In 1458 Mátyás became the first national king of Hungary since the extinction of the House of Árpád in 1301, a Hungarian king elected according to the wishes of the nobility. Around 40,000 nobles gathered in Buda to elect Mátyás, and while they were deliberating, he was already being proclaimed king by the crowds. Intelligent, energetic, and willing, Mátyás was certainly well equipped to achieve his goals: to impose his royal authority at home and realize his vision for regional conquest. Bohemia, Austria, and even the crown of the Holy Roman Empire were in his sights. Mátyás's first concern however was to be independent, so he dismissed many of his advisers, even discharging his own uncle Szilágyi. After that, he was free to govern as he wished, because as a descendant of common nobles he enjoyed broad popularity. From the early years of his reign, he was able to assert himself within the country and carry on an imaginative foreign policy. He made peace with Austria as well as the rebellious Bohemian lands.

In the 1460s Mátyás seized Bosnia and pushed back the Turks. However, seeing the grand Christian alliance fall apart on the death of Pope Pius II, Hungary would not fight the Turks again during Mátyás's lifetime. Mátyás turned toward Bohemia, possibly in order to enlarge Hungary's resources. In the midst of succession struggles, the issue of Hussite heretics provided an opportunity for Mátyás to intervene. He eventually conquered Moravia, Silesia, and Lusatia and was crowned king of Bohemia. Czech and Austrian wars were to occupy Mátyás for two decades. During the 1470s, he faced a coalition put together by Frederick and supported by the Jagiellons, which was defeated by Mátyás's Black Army of well-paid, well-trained soldiers. The subsequent Treaty of Olomuc enabled Mátyás to intensify his struggle for the possession of Austria. In 1485 Mátyás occupied Vienna and died there in 1490.

In weighing Mátyás's reign, one can see him as a great Renaissance man, with the goal of fulfilling his desire for glory, as was the case with so many other princes of his time. In this light, Hungary's failure to become a major power is attributable to Mátyás's reluctance to pursue more active anti-Ottoman policies. Mátyás's real innovation was the professionalization of government service. Chancellery secretaries and competent graduates took over affairs of state from the barons and prelates. Tamás Bakócz, of peasant origin, is an example of these new careerists. He was personal secretary to the king and later rose to be archbishop and cardinal; he was even a serious rival of Leo II de Medici for the pontifical crown.

During the reign of Mátyás, the country enjoyed a security it has never known since. His reforms put an end to the arbitrariness and insecurity that had dominated until then. Under Mátyás, an improved legal system was put in place through the establishment of tribunals of the states general at the local level. At a higher level, an appeal court, the Royal Table, was created. Finally, individual towns gained legal autonomy.

The state was far from being a constitutional monarchy, but at least its institutions were more organized. Since he always needed more to finance his wars and sustain his sumptuous court, Mátyás imposed "exceptional subsidiary" taxes, thus adding to the burden shouldered by the Hungarian population. As for the peasantry, the majority still enjoyed the liberties they had either inherited from their status as free men or had acquired in the previous century. They were serfs *(jobbágy),* in the ancient meaning of the term. The proportion of bonded serfs was smaller than before, in some places barely 10 percent of laborers. The standard of living was reputedly decent or sufficient, according to written sources; evidence of a political commitment to protecting peasants from abuse is clear: numerous judgments were passed in favor of "fugitives," or peasants forcibly bonded to the land.

Renaissance humanism had already entered Hungary before Mátyás. The existing tradition was then given new life by his wife, Beatrice of Aragon. The royal courts, both at Buda and Visegrád, attracted scholars, historians, and celebrated artists. The king was probably quite fond of provocative minds and was receptive to the irreverence of the sophisticated scholars at his court. Combining the splendor of Italian style with contemporary wit, Mátyás's court must have been among the most brilliant in Europe. His private library, the Bibliotheca Corviniana, was certainly Renaissance Hungary's prize jewel. It contained over 2,500 illuminated manuscript volumes, and almost no incunabula, even though András Hess's printing shop produced the first printed Hungarian chronicle, *Chronica Hungarorum,* in 1473.

After the death of Mátyás, the fight for the Crown broke out once more. Mátyás did his best to pass it to János Corvin, his out-of-wedlock son, but the designated heir was not recognized. Other pretenders entered the fray, among them Maximilian of Habsburg and two Polish Jagiellons. In the end it was one of them, Vladislas (Ulászló) II, who won.

In Vladislas, the oligarchs had found the weak king they wanted. Described as a handsome young womanizer of mild temperament, the new monarch was totally indifferent to state affairs in his Czech and Hungarian kingdoms. The nickname "Dobze" (Yes, All Right) was bestowed on him, as he approved of anything suggested by the barons who had hoisted him onto the throne. Vladislas II Dobze seems to have spent twenty-six years, saying, "yes, yes" to unbelievable waste and to the impoverishment of the state, as well as to decay in his own court. Hungary was once more under the rule of "little kings," lay and ecclesiastical lords. Peasants who had enjoyed liberties in the past found themselves driven back into serfdom, into the new, or "second," servitude. Social classes that had begun to rise found themselves sinking back, and the whole country sank with them. One explanation for this state of affairs is that since power had been shared by king and nobles until then, the arrival of the weak and ineffectual Vladislas II was bound to create an imbalance. But there is also another way to see the rapid industrial and commercial development in Western Europe in the 1500s and the lack of growth in agricultural producers like Poland and Hungary: the voyages of discovery introduced new currents in world commerce, but left suppliers of basic commodities by and large unchanged. Since cattle herding was a lucrative trade for Hungary's landowners, the spirit of innovation scarcely appeared on the Magyar horizon. During the centuries that followed, this developmental gap continued to widen.

In 1514 Hungary witnessed a peasant revolt unprecedented in size. Vladislas II was still on the throne, but decisions were now more than ever being made by the barons of the Royal Council. The ordinary nobles, meanwhile, were trying, without much success, to organize themselves into a kind of national party under the very popular leader, János Szápolyai, destined to become "national king." The immediate cause for the revolt, however, was elsewhere. Pope Leo X issued an edict calling for a crusade, and Archbishop Tamás Bakócz was entrusted with organizing it. In April 1514, 40,000 peasants assembled outside Pest to take up arms against Ottoman invaders, and more were to join them in Transylvania. The complaints voiced at the camp prompted the mob to start a peasant war. A leader emerged, György Dózsa. The peasant army had some initial victories, but retaliation was not long in coming. Led by János Szápolyai, an army of 20,000 noblemen defeated Dózsa's army at Temesvár. The revenge that ensued was merciless, though the number of rebels killed did not exceed "reasonable" limits, for the simple reason that the landowners needed their labor.

The diet implemented retaliatory legal measures. The principal architect of their decisions was the lawyer István Werbőczi. He compiled a body of laws intended to encompass all political and social spheres, a code called *Tripartitum*. Though it was never fully promulgated, the impact of Tripartitum was considerable. It sealed the unity of the national community by elaborating the doctrine of the Holy Crown, merging the Crown, the sovereign's person, and the nobility into one indivisible whole. However, while it held the political nation together, it tore the population in two, erected an "iron curtain" between Hungarians and Hungarians, until 1848. Serfs were now subject to a ruthless yoke, a state of total lack of liberty.

After Vladislas II died, his son, the ten-year-old Lajos II, succeeded to the Czech and Hungarian thrones. Surrounded by two crowned tutors, the Habsburg Maximilian and King Sigismund of Poland, and the Magyar barons, the king did not have a voice in the assembly. Ottoman forces took Sabac and Belgrade. The country was open to invaders by both land and river. There were serious attempts to organize a national defense in 1526. Pál Tomori, archbishop of Kalocsa and grand commander of Lower Hungary, took charge, aided by János Szápolyai, *voivode* of Transylvania. By August, an army of 25,000 was assembled. A smaller army, led by Szápolyai, was late joining the royal army. Nevertheless, there was optimism in the Hungarian camp, even though the army of Sultan Suleiman was double that of Lajos's forces.

After a number of preliminary skirmishes, the decisive battle took place on the field of Mohács, near the Danube and close to what today is Hungary's southern border. Despite the initial successes of Hungarian charges, within two hours their army had been dislodged and then annihilated. Among the dead were scores of lords and prelates, as well as King Lajos.

The causes of defeat have been the subject of animated debate and historical controversy. Some analysts favored the social explanation, pointing at the ruthless suppression of the Dózsa revolt in 1514, along with the blind and self-serving behavior of the ruling class. There were other factors as well. The seriousness of the Ottoman threat had been realized for some time. It had given rise to the desire to place the country's destiny in the hands of a national king capable of staving off the impending attack. The Hunyadis had met this need and in effect had stabilized the southern frontier. But this had been a temporary solution. Hungary, which in the past had dominated the region, was already on the defensive against this stronger adversary that was pushing forward inexorably, having seized the Balkan buffer states. The Hungarian state, still strong after King Mátyás, had neither the size, the resources, the national leader, nor even the European aid needed to tackle the situation. Weak kings and a new unscrupulous oligarchy had only made the situation worse. By the time Mohács occurred, a conjunction of unfavorable factors had left the country more vulnerable than ever. Hungary lost more than a battle; the state lost its capacity for action.

Suleiman was in no hurry to exploit his victory at Mohács. His plans of conquest certainly included Hungary (and much more of Europe), but he was patient and flexible. Perhaps not realizing that the country was leaderless and disorganized, his armies left Hungary. In November 1526 János I Szápolyai was elected king by his loyal followers. In December, however, a handful of barons met at the Pozsony Diet and, in accordance with the dynastic agreement that the Habsburgs considered the basis of their legitimacy in Hungary, elected Ferdinand I as king of Bohemia and Hungary. With Szápolyai as a national king, and Ferdinand a "German king," there was also the Ottoman sultan; the first had wealth and popularity in his favor, the second was backed by his brother, the Holy Roman Emperor, but it was Suleiman who in fact had much of the country at his feet. In these circumstances, Turkish support given to King János and, later, to his successors in Transylvania, trumped any advantages the Habsburgs might have had.

Hungarian hopes for reunification, illusory as they might have been, were in fact kept alive by the rivalry of the two kings. Treating Szápolyai with "patience," Suleiman was able to use Hungary to threaten Vienna. His clear patronage enabled Szápolyai to take Buda in 1529. Militarily and politically, the Ottoman Empire was to remain present in Hungary for nearly two hundred years. For the moment, instead of occupying the entire country, the Ottomans protected eastern Hungary—soon to become the principality of Transylvania—against Habsburg encroachment.

In the spring of 1541 Ferdinand tried to take Buda, but Ottoman armies foiled the attempt. On 29 August, fifteen years to the day after the Battle of Mohács (the sultan liked symbolism), he occupied Buda without bloodshed. Once

Painting of the capture of Ferenc II Rakoczi, leader of the Hungarian revolt against the Habsburgs. (Archivo Iconografico, S.A./Corbis)

the former royal seat became the first Turkish *vilayet* in Hungary, an Ottoman pasha proceeded to lay down its laws. Partition was complete: Habsburgs were to reign in the west, Ottomans in the center, and the Szápolyai child, with his mother, in the future principality of Transylvania. Between two enemies, Hungary's choices were limited. It had to adopt a survival strategy, fighting incessantly on its borders, adjusting its economy to the circumstances, and being receptive to new influences. In this situation, the developmental gap between Renaissance Europe and an increasingly marginalized Central (or Eastern) Europe grew larger. While the West was shaping modernity, in Hungary and its neighbors living conditions, trade, and urbanization were deteriorating.

The sixteenth century had a severe impact on a people laboring under constant harassment and deprivation, so that Hungary emerged from a long period of adversity with a diminished population. Most historians talk of a net loss of 1 million inhabitants, though others bring evidence that loss of human life was compensated by immigration. Even if immigration compensated for some loss, it also profoundly changed the ethnic composition of the country. Ottoman brutality prompted many Serbs to move northward, and colonization encouraged by Vienna brought large numbers of Slavs, Romanians, and others into Transylvania and Transdanubia. In some regions ethnic Magyars were becoming a minority.

The most widespread social trend during these centuries was the increasing enslavement of the peasantry. The gulf between the "nation of nobles" and the *jobbágy* was ever widening. The phenomenon later became known as the second serfdom, and the term *jobbágy* became synonymous with serf. The supremacy of the nobility manifested itself in politics and in the turbulent relationship between the estates and the king. East of the river Elbe, the society that was emerging was increasingly different from that of Western countries: from the sixteenth century onward, a kind of late feudalism was being created, a type of intermediate society, somewhere between the Western and Eastern models. A large noble class had already arisen in Hungary as early as the thirteenth century. Since then, royal authority had been in decline, and the oligarchy had acquired substantial and often dominating political, economic, and military power. The power of the great lords was further bolstered by the support of the noble's "retainers." Ties between the Hungarian baron and his retainers—based on private agreements and not the vassal ties of Western feudalism—always left the noble a free man, while increasing his economic dependency on the lords. Large estates grew, swallowing up more and more noble property. Economic decay among the lesser nobility was also caused by the accession rights of *aviticitas,* which kept ancestral land within the clan, while ensuring that the inheritance was divided among all legitimate descendants. The resulting impoverishment forced many lesser nobles to became artisans, tutors, or, increasingly, civil servants.

These "gentlemen in sandals," however, had not lost their patent of nobility or their political importance. The traditional legal principle of "one indivisible nobility" endured; though poor, the nobles proliferated. While in Western Europe the nobility was crumbling and shrinking, in Central Europe the proportion of nobles was on the increase, reaching 4–6 percent of the population in Hungary and 8 percent in Transylvania.

Titles of nobility were given by the king and the Roman Catholic Church, ennobling soldiers and peasants as a reward for services. The vast majority of this class were barely better off than the peasants, but their social status remained untouchable. A permanent state of war is one explanation for the survival of this class, as was the shared interest of all nobles opposing central (royal) power. While elsewhere in Europe royal absolutism was on the rise, in Hungary the complicated relationship between a nation of nobles and the sovereign seated in Vienna was to last for centuries. This was probably one of the key factors—if not the factor—which led to a weak middle class. So while Western societies were heading toward a nascent capitalism with a powerful middle class, Hungary was stuck in a system of estates that perpetuated the dominance of the nobility and led to late feudalism, or second serfdom. Static conditions were exacerbated by the fact that much of the very small middle class was foreign, mainly German. A class of half a million privileged dominated millions condemned to eternal servitude, according to the famous legal work, the Tripartitum of 1514.

This socially and economically backward system still proved to be a political force vis-à-vis Habsburg absolutism. The eternal disagreement between the king and the noblemen's Diet was seen as resistance against foreign domination and the defense of public rights of the Hungarian state, its uniqueness, and personality. Thus the role of Hungary's nobility could be seen more positively: by defending its own privileges, the nobility also sustained Hungarian national identity.

During the period of fragmented national existence, 1.5 million people lived in the Habsburg-ruled Kingdom of Hungary, just under a million in Transylvania, and the same number under Turkish occupation, with over 500,000 displaced people who had left their homes or found themselves under one administration and then under another.

Early Ottoman administrations were fairly well ordered, so that in the sixteenth century damage to society was still limited. The "century of Magyar decay" began in the later seventeenth century. Ottoman occupation and resistance to it meant a nearly constant state of war, accompanied by pillage, hunger, pestilence, and a deterioration of communities. Well-cultivated plots were abandoned, and families were decimated by the Ottoman practice of enslaving children from occupied lands. The depopulation of entire regions came about not only because of war but also through a number of economic adjustments. Pastureland was extended in order to accommodate cattle herding, a mobile and thus relatively safe and profitable way of life. It was not in Ottoman interests to pursue a policy based solely on plunder. Hungary, in the sultan's overall plan, was a base from which to invade Europe, fitting into a vision of a great Muslim Euro-Afro-Asiatic empire. It was a dream hindered and eventually shattered by the resistance of Central Europe's peoples, Hungarians and Transylvanians prominent among them.

The Ottomans valued the territories they conquered and set out to profit from them as much as possible. This is one explanation for their relative tolerance of religious diversity. Their administrative methods also had to be flexible to ensure cooperation from the population, yet efficient enough to exploit its economic capacity to the limit. This implied the use of taxes, tributes, and ransoms, making civilian administrators important. They governed the conquered lands, but did not overturn native habits and customs.

For the taxpayer—peasant, craftsman, tradesman, and landlord—life had to go on. Indeed, towns and market towns maintained municipal autonomy. Justice was administered by Hungarian judges in conjunction with Turkish *kadi,* and clergymen carried out their ministry with little discrimination. Indeed, the Reformation spread more easily under Turkish rule, which was indifferent to Christian denominational factions, than in the Habsburg Catholic kingdom.

For Istanbul, Hungary was simply a field of military operations and a country to fleece. The destructive effect of the Ottoman period was enormous, while Turkish contribution to Hungarian life consisted mainly of foodstuffs such as rice, maize, tobacco, perhaps paprika, and coffee. The overall balance is indisputably disastrous.

In northwestern Hungary, the most densely populated and richest part of the former kingdom, Ferdinand respected the rights of the Hungarian orders and avoided confrontation. Six rulers from his family succeeded him during the Ottoman occupation, with most of them adopting an increasingly absolutist and intolerant attitude toward Protestants. In the decades immediately after Mohács, a spirit of relative societal peace prevailed. Habsburgs ruled as kings elected according to Hungarian public law and by virtue of their succession rights—in the Habsburg interpretation—but not in any sense by absolute divine right. Hungary did not belong to them but to the Holy Crown. At the same time, Vienna bore the bulk of military expenses, maintaining 20,000 or so soldiers along the military frontiers. It was therefore in the interests of the nobility, jealous guardians of their privileges, particularly fiscal ones, to maintain the political status quo.

THE REFORMATION

As a consequence of the Protestant Reformation, Hungary witnessed a rebirth of humanism, was exposed to the teachings of the great German and Helvetic (Swiss) reformers, participated in the great debates of ideas, and, last but not least, experienced the blossoming of literature. Protestant ideas had found an audience as early as 1525, mainly among the (largely German-speaking) urban population. Among Hungarians, these ideas were often divisive. From the 1540s, Magyars from all walks of life began to follow Helvetic Protestantism, soon referred to as Calvinism. It was propagated by preachers of varying temperaments, but all of them developed their calling in the heat of religious disputes. The education of each of these men was determined by the university they attended, in Wittenberg, Geneva, or elsewhere, but with each adding his own personal touch.

The purification of the Catholic Church, corrupted by its prelates, its wealth, the sale of letters of indulgence, made a strong impression. Additional attraction was provided by the purification of places of worship, the abolition of priestly celibacy, a simpler hierarchical system, and the disappearance of submission to Rome.

The adoption of the mother tongue for prayer, the translations of the Bible and the Psalms, the theological debates and publications in Hungarian were also hugely significant. It was not only churchmen who participated enthusiastically in these debates but the lay public too. Protestants primarily targeted the sins of the "papists" but also extolled hopes for deliverance from the Turkish yoke through a purified "true Christian faith." The Protestant God had to deliver his Hungarian people, just as he had done for the Jews held captive in Babylon and Egypt.

The all-powerful, wealthy Catholic Church of the Middle Ages was becoming a thing of the past. Several rulers had divested it of properties and traditional sources of revenue, distributing them among their servants or simply expropriating the lot. The Mohács debacle and Turkish occupation had left many bishoprics empty. Ferdinand, together with a number of magnates, was quick to take advantage of the situation and appropriated them. Reformed Churches proliferated throughout towns and market centers, among diligent and industrious people. The magnates and nobles who had converted to the new denominations dragged with them their entire entourage: relatives, town dwellers, and peasants. Vast numbers thus switched religious allegiance.

Disputes and conflicts did engender violence and sometimes bloodshed. This did not bring irreparable damage, however, and the spirit of tolerance survived. People learned to live together; the absolute domination of a single state church was no longer possible. Hungary's religious freedom was indeed remarkable when compared to the zealous excesses occurring elsewhere in Europe. The Reformation eventually won over most Hungarians and forced Catholicism onto the defensive. Many schools, as well as the print works and publications of the period, were either Lutheran or Calvinist until the end of the sixteenth century. After that, the Catholic Church threw its energies into the Counter-Reformation, especially with the rise to prominence of Péter Pázmány, cardinal and archbishop of Esztergom, a master of religious polemic.

The legacy of diversity led to an extraordinary event for the period. In 1568 the Transylvanian Diet of Torda decreed religious freedom, although limited to the four recognized rites, Catholic, Evangelical Lutheran, Reformed Calvinist, and Unitarian, and excluding the large numbers of Orthodox Romanians, as well as the handful of Jews and Muslims.

The number of schools and publishing opportunities increased. Protestant colleges were set up in Transylvania, in both Saxon and Hungarian areas, as well as at Debrecen, Sárospatak, and a dozen other towns. There were two hundred elementary schools by the late sixteenth century, and dozens of outlets published Hungarian translations of the Bible (the first by the Protestant Gáspár Károlyi in 1590), prayers, psalms, and a lively literature of polemics. More promising was the fact that books were now appearing in Hungarian, either to propagate religious renewal or to instruct and entertain, representing the first buds of a truly national literature.

TRANSYLVANIA

Wars, famine, and natural calamities at the turn of the sixteenth century had caused demographic and economic disaster in the kingdom, and the situation in Transylvania was not much better. Half of the population is said to have disappeared, and 90 percent of property is thought to have been damaged. These figures may seem exaggerated, but they indicate the extreme gravity of the situation. Transylvania soon recovered, however. Indeed, the seventeenth century came to be seen as its golden age. By 1660 the population had grown to 955,000, made up of six main nationalities (and several smaller ones). Magyars and Szeklers constituted the majority (500,000), followed by Romanians or Wallachians (280,000), Saxons (90,000), Serbians, Ukrainians, and others (85,000). Five languages were spoken and six religions practiced, excluding the Jewish faith and smaller sects.

Magyar settlement in the region has its roots in the migrations, when the variously identified indigenous populations were submerged. Most of the new conquerors left Transylvania in search of pasture on the plain, but the region remained under their military control and soon was resettled by Magyars and Szeklers.

The Szeklers (Székely in Hungarian) arrived with the conquerors in 895, probably as army auxiliaries; they spoke Hungarian and are thought to have been of Magyar or Turkish origin. Deployed to guard the eastern frontiers, by the thirteenth century the Szeklers constituted a homogeneous and tightly knit community that preserved its own social and cultural characteristics. Traditionally all were free and equal; there were neither bondservants nor nobles among them, and their leaders were seen as chieftains. By the sixteenth century, the old military and social structures were eroding, but it was still a closed society, fiercely protective of its freedoms, as proved by numerous uprisings. The Szeklers allied themselves with the two other Transylvanian nations, the Magyars and the Saxons. Together, the three made up the diet of Transylvanian States, which seized its independence from the Hungarian Diet of the royal territory.

The origins of the Saxons in Transylvania date back to the early Árpád period. First invited to settle by Géza III in the twelfth century, they came from Flanders, the Rhine region, and Wallonia, rather than Saxony. They were given considerable privileges to maintain their independent administrative and judiciary system, as they introduced advanced agricultural techniques and artisanship and founded thriving urban centers. Primarily Lutheran and Melanchtonian evangelicals, their churches and Gothic buildings are among the country's most beautiful monuments. Hardworking and commercially prosperous, the Saxons provided the economic base for the golden age of the seventeenth-century princes.

The Romanians, although quite numerous, did not enjoy the same rights as the "three nations." The Orthodox religion was tolerated but not recognized to the same extent as Catholicism and Protestantism. Most Romanians, except for the village chiefs and boiars, who were assimilated into the Hungarian nobility, were serfs. Romanian communities certainly existed in Transylvania around the same time as the Szeklers and Saxons, but the issue of the origins of Romanians in the region divides Hungarian and Romanian historians, reflecting national ideological differences, and seems likely to remain disputed for some time to come.

In the middle of the sixteenth century Transylvania became a distinct and recognized state. The rise and survival of specific administrative and cultural structures culminated in a key historical turning point, a series of anti-Habsburg wars. The first of these was led by Count István Bocskai, who formed an army of free soldiers, called *hajdú,* and was then joined by Transylvania's "three nations." A great fighter of Ottomans in the Fifteen Years War, Bocskai turned against the Habsburgs in 1604 and conducted a successful campaign, reaching the gates of Vienna. Eventually he was forced to sign the Treaty of Vienna (1606), which guaranteed Transylvania's independence and religious freedom, and was followed by a twenty-year tripartite peace treaty with the sultan.

Bocskai's brief era was a historical turning point. It ushered in a century of anti-Habsburg struggles, mainly led by Transylvanian princes. Their objective was always the same: to unify the country under Hungarian sovereignty. The dilemma too was the same: how to drive both Turks and Habsburgs out of Hungary. Though weakened as a result of the Treaty of Westphalia at the end of the Thirty Years' War (1648), the Habsburgs still had an empire behind them. As for the Ottoman Empire, it numbered 30 million subjects and possessed an army that was reputedly invincible. Faced with these two giants, Transylvania, with its 1 million inhabitants and limited resources, was not up to the confrontation, even though it did succeed more than once in rallying the Habsburgs' Hungarian subjects.

Still, Transylvania had its golden age. The country found its brightest star in Gábor Bethlen (1613–1629). He had played an important role under Bocskai and in the struggles over succession. When elected prince, he had to make humiliating concessions to the Ottoman Empire, and he also made a number of internal mistakes, only later realizing that the prosperity of his subjects was better for the treasury than despoilment or irregular and unpredictable fiscal policies. His subsequent economic policy proved fruitful; regulated foreign trade brought in revenues, and everyone profited. Urban centers developed, Renaissance buildings sprang up, and public education reached unprecedented levels. This most eastern Protestant country—back to back with the Habsburgs—was soon drawn into the Thirty Years' War, beginning with a conflict between the Czechs and Ferdinand II, an implacable foe of the Reformation. Bethlen joined the Czechs and campaigned as far as the gates of Vienna. In 1620 the diet offered him the Hungarian Crown, but the Czech defeat at the Battle of the White Mountain cut him short. Nonetheless, the emperor was in a perilous position, and Bethlen was quick to take advantage of this, negotiating a very favorable compromise. Under the Treaty of Nikolsburg (1621), he renounced the royal crown but maintained control of seven counties in Upper Hungary. His sovereignty over Transylvania was never questioned.

Bethlen made several attempts to realize his anti-Habsburg plans, but never achieved national unification. The equation remained the same: the Habsburgs could only be kept out with the support of the Ottoman Empire, but in order to get rid of the latter, Bethlen would have to call on the Habsburgs. In the end, enthusiasm waned. Transylvanian lords were unwilling to mobilize in support of a policy perceived as Bethlen's personal ambition, while the kingdom's nobility wanted to curb powers conferred on him by his elevation to royal status, which Bethlen had in any case turned down.

At a time when absolutism was on the rise throughout Europe, the authority of the Transylvanian princes was of a more personal nature. They were local nobility, preceded by princes from the Báthorys, and succeeded by those of the Rákóczi family, members of which were skilled at amassing wealth. When György Rákóczi died in 1648, he left behind a country that was well governed, prosperous, and with an acquired habit of religious tolerance. His son György Rákóczi II nurtured larger ambitions, though he turned out to be far less successful, mounting a foolhardy incursion into Poland. He never recovered from the defeat, and Transylvania's star fell with him. Successors of little significance followed and Transylvania's golden age came to an end. It was invaded by the Turks and later occupied by the imperial army of Leopold I.

THE HABSBURGS

As Ottoman power weakened during the seventeenth century, Hungary's political center of gravity moved to the Habsburg-ruled kingdom. Despite its misfortunes, the country remained a bastion against the Ottoman invasion. Amid the wars and ravages, new spiritual and cultural waves swept across the entire country, and even its economy managed to survive. Vital links within this fragmented country remained intact, and a tacit contract united Magyars, born of a desire to liberate the entire country, though there was no consensus on how to go about achieving this.

Unlike the absolutist Bourbons, the Habsburgs had to adopt a measured approach toward the various states that made up their rather heterogeneous family empire. Czech resistance was easier to overcome, but the Magyar insistence on sovereignty, defended by a large and powerful nobility, was a greater challenge. Indeed, the Hungarian noble lawmakers did not yield to absolutism until the second half of the long reign of Leopold I (1657–1705), and even then only temporarily. Until that point, Vienna's interventions had been limited.

For centuries, an aristocracy of rich and powerful barons had risen from within a socially differentiated nobility. Over time, through titles and influence, they had become a superior class. The kings ruling from Vienna wanted these magnates as allies and had therefore made several of them counts, even hereditary princes, among them the Pálffy, Nádasdy, Eszterházy, Wesselényi, Forgách, and Csáky families. This new upper class later formed the upper chamber of the diet.

The Counter-Reformation changed the cultural and political landscape. Most squires returned, under duress or for convenience, to Catholicism, and the resulting alliances and quarrels with either the Turks or the Habsburgs, as well as differences in religious loyalties, had serious political repercussions and were not easily overcome. Religious tolerance remained far greater in Transylvania than in the kingdom, and the success of the Counter-Reformation was not unequivocal; Hungary was once again predominantly Catholic, but it remained a multifaith country. Cultural pluralism survived despite the Counter-Reformation's excesses. The Catholic Church regained its former preeminence in public life, with considerable influence in literature, education, and the arts.

The Habsburgs' goal was to keep the peace both at home and abroad, so they left Hungary's noblemen pretty much alone and did not interfere with their treatment of the peasantry, who were now reduced to serfdom, a fate escaped only by the most enterprising. Vienna intervened more readily in commerce than in political matters. It created trade monopolies, entrusting them to foreigners, among whom were the Oppenheimer and Wertheimer families, prosperous Viennese bankers who dealt in army supplies. Monopolies in the trade of cattle, ore, glass, and other products seriously reduced the scope for a free market and the income of the proprietors. Only a handful of rich and enterprising magnates threw themselves into "undignified" commercial activities.

Still, the Magyar lords had not forgotten that their primary duty was to prepare for the decisive war against Turkish occupation, despite the reticence of the Habsburgs. To achieve this, they were ready to cooperate with Vienna. The Treaty of Westphalia (1648) had raised hopes that Europe's Christian forces could at last unite to drive out the Ottomans. But Ferdinand III was more interested in negotiating peace with the Ottomans than in risking confrontation. Such evasion was not well received in Hungary. Particularly impatient, and effective, among Hungary's lords was the warrior-poet Count Miklós Zrinyi (1620–1664), *ban* (governor) of Croatia, whose literary work and military-political role earned him an extraordinary reputation. Zrinyi disseminated the idea of a national kingdom, asserting that under the leadership of a strong—even absolutist—national king, the Turks could be driven out and the country reunited. In contrast with the prevailing wisdom of the times, according to which waging war was essentially a matter of money, money, and more money, Zrinyi called for "weapons and the determination of valiant men" (cited in Makkai 1996, 89–90).

The war of liberation for which Zrinyi had longed finally arrived in the 1660s. After a series of setbacks, Christian forces crushed the Turks at St. Gotthard in 1664. The victory was rendered meaningless, however, by the ensuing peace treaty signed at Vasvár. Although Turkish power was by now on the decline, the short but efficient "Küprülü Renaissance" brought major reforms to the Ottoman Empire, and its rule in Hungary was still strong.

While common sense called for moderation, royal absolutism was on the rise, and Leopold I even suspended Hungary's constitution. The closing decades of the seventeenth century thus ushered in the anti-Habsburg *kuruc* movement (the name derives from the Hungarian word for "crusader"), made up of fugitives from imperial justice, and dismissed soldiers. A young baron named Imre Thököly became the first leader of the kuruc. He won battles and conquered much of Upper Hungary, so the Ottomans supported him and even referred to him as Hungary's king. But Thököly is perhaps best remembered for marrying Ilona Zrinyi, widow of a Transylvanian prince who held the fort of Munkács for three years against imperial forces and for being the stepfather to the child Ferenc Rákóczi II.

Thököly—courageous, colorful, and energetic—embodied the ambiguities and contradictions of his time. He had tried to unite the "two Hungarys" with the help, or consent, of the Ottoman occupiers. A wave of paradoxical "Turkophilia" arose throughout the kingdom.

The final attempt by the Turks to take Vienna came in 1683. Saving Vienna was a great Christian victory and was followed by the retaking of numerous Hungarian fortresses. Ottoman-occupied Buda held for another three years. Pope Innocent XI succeeded in forming a new Holy League, supported by huge monetary contributions, and in 1686 an allied army set off toward Buda, under the command of the duke of Lorraine, this time with a large Hungarian contingent.

The siege began in June and lasted seventy-eight days, with a dramatic end: eight hundred tons of gunpowder exploded under the ramparts, hastening victory for the Christians. Ottoman soldiers resisted to the last man, but on 2 September, Buda was liberated. Christian Europe celebrated, but the war of liberation dragged on for two decades. Finally, in 1699, a peace treaty at Karlóca (Karlowitz) put an end to 173 years of Ottoman presence on Hungary's soil.

THE RÁKÓCZI REBELLION

Ferenc Rákóczi II (1676–1735) grew up in Vienna and overcame his Habsburg education only on witnessing conditions in his native land. He then associated himself with the kuruc rebels. After his first attempt to establish a French alliance failed (resulting in his brief imprisonment and exile to Poland), he returned to Upper Hungary in 1703 to lead the already brewing insurrection. The cornerstone of his policies, an alliance with France, made good sense. Louis XIV welcomed the idea of an insurrection in the rear of his Austrian rival, so he granted Rákóczi a sizable annual subsidy out of the French military budget. But the French alliance always remained somewhat tentative, even after Rákóczi's loyalists forced the Ónod Diet (1707) to proclaim the House of Austria dethroned.

The kuruc cause was very popular, but Rákóczi's peasant armies were outsoldiered by the regular imperial troops. Nevertheless, Rákóczi, somewhat naively, continued to wage war until 1711. As the main cause of dissatisfaction—Leopold's harsh treatment of Magyars—was replaced by the more conciliatory approach of Joseph I, and as Louis XIV seemed ready to make peace with the Habsburgs, Rákóczi's hopes evaporated. In 1711 his commanding general signed a peace treaty at Szatmár. The terms offered by the imperial generals were quite fair. The king granted the rebels total amnesty, the restitution of their confiscated property, religious peace, respect for the constitution, and the safeguard of tax exemptions.

Rákóczi's insurrection may fairly be seen as a lost cause. The loyalty of Magyar nobility was divided, the peasantry was exhausted, and the prince's foreign allies had abandoned him. The long-suffering towns had now been subjected to war for two centuries, and Hungarian currency was worthless. It has also been asserted that Rákóczi was primarily obsessed with his Transylvanian principality, which by this time was firmly under Viennese administration.

Maria Theresa, Empress of Austria by Martin Mytens the Younger, 1744. (Archivo Iconografico, S.A./Corbis)

COMING TO TERMS WITH VIENNA

The Szatmár peace treaty—sketched out between two opposing generals with both *kuruc* and *labanc* being Hungarian lords—was based on a tacit agreement: the Magyar nation, represented by its nobility, would cease rebelling, and the imperial winner would negotiate an honorable compromise. The king pledged his goodwill to the diet and promised to govern in keeping with its traditional laws, which ensured noble prerogatives. The legislative body was essentially dominated by nobles. Prelates and barons had sat at the table of the diet with the magnates and two noble deputies from each of the fifty-two counties, while members of the clergy and of the towns sat at the lower table. The estates formed a counterbalance to royal power, except during periods of absolutism.

Habsburg rulers of the eighteenth century were more interested in pacifying the dominant classes than in breaking them. The latter, rather than continue to chase the mirage of total national independence, were by and large ready to profit from the compromise. One example of this was the diet's acceptance of the Pragmatic Sanction, recognizing royal succession by the Habsburg female branch.

Maria Theresa was twenty-three years old when she became archduchess of Austria in 1740; she became queen of Hungary and Bohemia a year later. With her husband the prince consort, she established the Habsburg-Lorraine dynastic line. Her long reign began with serious problems: Prussia started the War of the Austrian Succession (1740–1748) and invaded Silesia, to be joined by Bavaria and France. Thus the young ruler found herself in desperate need of Hungarian military support. At the diet of 1741, Hungary's nobles offered her their "lives and their blood" (Sugar 1984, 147). This meant that more than 100,000 Hungarian soldiers fought in the wars of the coming century and became instrumental in saving the dynasty's rule.

Maria Theresa's absolutism was moderate. She made concessions that favored the Hungarian estates, but the modus vivendi was fragile, and the compromise required constant renegotiation. For example, the territorial integrity of historical Hungary was not entirely restored. In Transylvania, Romanian and Székely territories were separated and organized into military frontier defense regions under the command of the Military Council in Vienna.

Military reforms were necessary both to ensure the kingdom's security and to support the wars with Prussia. The old system of raising armies, called "noble insurrection," was no longer effective. A permanent army of around 300,000 to 400,000 men, one-third Hungarian, was placed under the Viennese Military Council; its general officers and language of command were German. In the spirit of enlightened absolutism, such measures existed side by side with Maria

Theresa's considerable gratitude and benevolence toward the Hungarians.

Maria Theresa was devout, maternal, and marked by the contrasting traits of her age (the baroque), a mixture of mysticism, pathos, and glitter. She was both a modernizer strongly attached to traditional values, and a devout Catholic quite tolerant toward Protestants. An important element of Maria Theresa's reign was her striving to end confrontation and her search for equilibrium. Thanks to her reforms, the life of her subjects improved. It is fair to say that Maria Theresa and her son, coruler then king Joseph II, transformed the political and social landscape before a new era of national and literary revival began in Hungary.

Catholic teaching orders (Jesuits, Piarists) became active in education. After the demise of the Jesuits in 1773, Maria Theresa's reforms gave public education new impetus. The tradition of attending Protestant universities abroad in Wittenberg, Jena, and Halle continued. Alongside Latin, Hungarian literature was also coming into its own. Its flourishing began in the 1780s, due in part to the spread of rationalist ideas and also to an original initiative of Maria Theresa: she founded a Hungarian Guard unit, attracting to it Magyar cadets who served and studied in Vienna for five years before returning home and contributing to public life.

According to the first reliable census, taken in 1784–1787, the Habsburgs ruled over 23 million people, half of whom lived under the Hungarian Crown, in historical Hungary, Transylvania, and Croatia. Hungary was important for the Viennese monarchs; it was the size of their empire's population that made the Habsburgs a great power. This meant that after the breakup of Poland (1772–1795), Russia, France, and Austria (with Hungary) loomed large on the continent, in terms of both territorial mass and their respective populations, while Prussia dominated militarily and England ruled the seas. The sixth power, the Ottoman Empire, was still significant, but would soon become the "sick man" of European politics.

Hungary held an important position in the new European configuration, despite its limited sovereignty and its state of convalescence. Under the Habsburgs, abandoned or sparsely populated territories were systematically colonized by both old and new immigrants, including a million Germans who settled in various regions. These newcomers were settled by special state committees. Priority was given to skilled farmers and artisans, who received material and financial assistance. As well as Serbs, numerous Slovaks and other Slavs joined older settlers, together totaling some 3 million. Adding 1.5 million Romanians, almost half of Hungary's inhabitants were non-Magyars.

The nation's ethnic composition had been reversed. Even though this was to bring on a number of conflicts later, it was not an issue at the time; statistics did not even take ethnicity into account. The new migration wave also changed the religious makeup of the country. Along with Catholics and Protestants, there were now large numbers of Eastern Orthodox and Greek Catholics (Uniates). There were also Armenian Christians and Jews, estimated to number 10,000 at the beginning and over 50,000 by the end of the century. As for the Protestants, despite churches and schools being restored to them, the Catholic Counter-Reformation was pursued with great success. Joseph II's Edict of Tolerance in 1781 ensured religious freedom for all.

For the first time in centuries, Hungary entered a long period of relative peace and prosperity. Society was able to pick itself up, despite its cumbersome and archaic social structure, which consisted of a huge majority of landless peasants on the one hand and a dominant nobility on the other, representing almost 10 percent of the inhabitants. In between the two was a weak stratum of bourgeoisie, soldiers, and civil servants, largely of foreign birth. The magnates and prelates were at the top of the pyramid. The 200 richest families included foreigners who were integrated with the Hungarian aristocracy. They lived a cosmopolitan lifestyle and were familiar with world culture. The 400,000 nobles, on the other hand, were literally and figuratively stuck in the past. Inequality between magnates and common nobles was enormous. Inequalities among peasants were less differentiated. The luckier or more enterprising among them inhabited a tenure of around twenty hectares or more, while the poorest lived in a shack with a backyard. Some of them sold their products on the market, settled in the market towns, and escaped rural servitude. Then there were those who swelled the ranks of agricultural laborers, much in demand by landowners seeking profits from growing markets.

Grievances over this "second servitude" exploitation reached the royal court and did not pass unnoticed. But vis-à-vis the nobility, its hands were tied. In exchange for possessing the Czech and Hungarian crowns (which made Maria a powerful European monarch), she guaranteed the lords' special feudal rights, and she needed their support. The Court promulgated reforms in Austria and Bohemia, but encountered resistance from the Hungarian orders and counties, where the nobility enjoyed a system of self-rule and used it to preserve its privileges. Maria nevertheless succeeded in implementing the Urbarium, a 1767 royal decree regulating peasant-lord relations.

In all respects, a new civilization was being born. There was no lack of books: the first literary dictionary (1766) contained biographies of more than five hundred Hungarian writers. These were astounding statistics for an economically underdeveloped country. Publications in Hungarian increased in number, as did secular, literary, historical, and scientific works.

Hungary's economy remained markedly rural. Factories were rare; in 1790–1800 there were around 125 factories and small manufacturers. Thus Hungary was more closely linked to the spiritual life of Europe than to its industrial revolution. Its wealth came primarily from agriculture. Habsburg court policies discouraged industrialization: Hungary was to remain the empire's supplier of meat, cereals, potash, and wine.

Though still far from giving rise to a genuine urban class, made up of bourgeois, free laborers, and intellectuals, the education system was nonetheless transformed. The first *Ratio educationis* in 1777 subjected schools to state directives and created a uniform system. Training for public health professions was instituted. A welfare system of sorts was created, concerned with orphans, widows, and the education of the children of Gypsies. Justice was dispensed according to set laws and separate from the administration. Maria Theresa put an end to witch trials and torture.

The traditionalist Maria Theresa changed a great many things, not because she was fond of reforms but because she saw them as necessary for the dynasty's survival. All this changed with the arrival on the throne of Joseph II, a zealous and impatient reformer. He contributed toward progress in many ways, but his ten-year reign was too short and resistance too strong for any real change to take place. Maria Theresa was certainly an authoritarian and a reformer, but not to the point of imposing her will without consideration for the interested parties (and certainly not to the extent of alienating magnates and nobles). Joseph, on the other hand, seemed driven by an ardent desire for change for its own sake. The spirit in which he imposed his designs was more modern and enlightened than his mother's; he was undoubtedly more in tune with the times but certainly not with his subjects. Joseph wanted to transform society immediately, while strengthening Austria against other powers.

Upon coming to power, Joseph II immediately set about integrating Hungary into his conception of a unitary state. In so doing, he attacked the privileges of the nobility, the rights of the state, and Hungarian cultural identity. He refused coronation in order to avoid direct confrontation with that jealous guardian of Magyar particularity, the diet. Nevertheless, a number of his decrees were enacted without much resistance. A relaxation of censorship was a notable case in point, as was the Edict of Religious Toleration in 1781. The edict abolished most discrimination against Protestants, Jews, and Orthodox Christians. Joseph II also eliminated Catholic orders with the exception of teaching and care-providing ones, turning hundreds of convents into schools. Civil marriage was introduced and church offices were reorganized. Joseph II wanted to be the architect of a modern state, for the good of both his empire and his people.

In 1784 Joseph II decreed that the official language in all the states was to be German. He did this in order to govern better: German, once extended to education, could train the elite capable of managing a modern state. The decree set three years to execute the project, but nothing, or very little, was to come of it, since in addition to provoking national resistance, the decree was impossible to implement. Even the more enlightened elements in society saw Joseph's measures as unrealistic. Realizing that his reforms were detested by all, Joseph II withdrew all his decrees on his deathbed in January 1790, except for the Edict of Toleration.

His successor, Leopold II, an enlightened and efficient ruler, was able to appease his subjects, before turning back to authoritarianism. His foreign policy proved successful, but in the subsequent decades all the problems of the old regime resurfaced.

NATIONAL AWAKENING

In Francis I a reactionary brute came to the Habsburg throne, a man in sharp conflict with the spirit of Enlightenment and the French Revolution, the influence of which was felt even among tradition-bound Magyar nobles who continued to believe that sovereignty belonged to the "privileged people."

The nation's intellectual elite were even more drawn to the ideas of the Enlightenment, finding them useful to voice their own aspirations. In view of the heavy-handed absolutism of Vienna, they felt that the only path to revival was within the cultural framework. To the reformers, knowledge was the key to development, and language the key to knowledge. The leading organizer and indisputable leader of Hungary's language reform was Ferenc Kazinczy, who spent 2,387 days in a Habsburg prison for having been implicated in a Jacobin conspiracy. He withdrew to his estate and dedicated his life to writing and to guiding a revival of the Magyar language and its literature. In this effort, he became a "dictator" of cultural life, a ruthless critic, imposing an elevated classicist style, stripped of frills, on his fellow writers.

The Magyar language had to adapt to modern life and become useful for conveying new notions. Kazinczy's "neologists" set out to reform grammar and lighten and enrich the vocabulary so as to keep abreast of cultural and technical developments in Europe. They created new words based on Hungarian roots, by borrowing foreign words and then Magyarizing them, or by image association. Reaction among their opponents, called "orthologues," was fierce, but the nation at the time had genuine and complex needs, which the reform movement could meet. To complicate matters and press the urgency of language reform, there were three languages in use throughout the land: Latin was the language of the Catholic Church, the law, and politics; German was used by the Viennese administration; and Hungarian was the language of the people and the new national elite. The promotion of Hungarian, the language of the dominant Magyars, was a major objective, as well as a cultural and political necessity.

At the same time, a growing number of grievances further poisoned the relationship between the court and Hungary. The devaluation of paper money, together with mandatory payment of taxes in silver coin, arbitrary levying of recruits, and lastly, the prolonged absence of the diet, forced the Austrian court to appease the Magyars. The diet was therefore finally summoned in 1825, but the all-powerful chancellor, Metternich, remained hostile toward national grievances as well as toward social radicalism. (The Metternich era was characterized by great power in the hands of a small circle at the court, the *camarilla,* a network of informers, and heavy-handed police intervention.)

The laws voted in by the diet in 1825–1827 and sanctioned by the king restored constitutional rights, abolished arbitrary levying of taxes and recruits, and promoted the use of Hungarian as the official language, but they did not widen the debate of ideas and reforms. This task was taken on by the county diets, and by the young radical reformers whose writings appeared in newspapers and books. Reform did not mean a complete break with the past; small, gradual steps prevailed. Social transformation from one session to another was consequently slow and difficult. Any denunciation of the old regime was punished, and during the 1830s a number of young liberals received prison sentences.

Lajos Kossuth (1802–1894) and István Széchenyi (1791–1860) came to represent the two radically different approaches to reforming Hungary's public life. Széchenyi came from a family of aristocrats who had long patronized the arts and intellectual progress. He founded the Hungarian Acad-

Lajos Kossuth, nineteenth-century Hungarian nationalist and revolutionary. (Library of Congress)

emy of Sciences as well as social clubs for aristocrats, and published his ideas about banking, credit, and industry, aspects of modernization he had come to know during his travels. His projects included river regulation to facilitate navigation, the creation of a steamboat company, and the building of a permanent suspension bridge between Pest and Buda. For this English-style reformer, this kind of project was the way to progress, rather than social subversion or nationalist demagoguery. And yet Vienna considered him dangerous, seeing a threat coming from conservative magnates and nobles as well as those more radical, especially Kossuth.

There was a fierce argument between the two over the nationality issue. Széchenyi believed that assimilation would come about through the beneficial effects of general progress; Kossuth hoped that Magyarization would occur as a result of Hungarian democracy, culture, education, and administration. Public opinion sided with the latter view, inflamed by its own national demands against Austria, combined with a desire for preponderance over Slav and Romanian minorities in this multinational kingdom. Széchenyi's fear that an alliance between clamorous Magyar nationalism and the narrow-minded reactionary nobility, his worst nightmare, would become a reality, may have been exaggerated, but it was not unfounded. Still, the count, once praised for awakening the nation, lost popularity, whereas Kossuth, the first to have succeeded in conducting a policy that moved the masses, carried the day and assumed the role of the nation's leader.

Kossuth's dazzling career was due to his personal qualities; the task that was incumbent on him, through a combination of personal qualities, background, and circumstance, was no less than that of knitting together a land whose development had been curbed by external misfortune. Both progress and national freedom had to be fought for simultaneously. He became a highly respected figure in European public opinion and, after his defeat, received a hero's welcome from London to Washington.

Having recently completed a three-year prison sentence because of his seditious journalism, in early 1841 Kossuth launched a journal that was to be the focus of the entire opposition, *Pesti Hirlap* (Pest News), which became especially famous for its dazzling editorials. It was then that Kossuth's political genius really took off. He realized that the platform of the assembly could not on its own generate a sufficiently broad change in public opinion. He needed the press. He knew that the social foundation of his bold reform program was the "middle ground," the ordinary nobility, the intelligentsia, and the bourgeoisie—a middle class in the making. Among them, the subgroup requiring the most delicate handling in order to be won over to his cause consisted of the local squires. With infinite patience, Kossuth cajoled them into gradually giving up some of their privileges and very tentatively introduced the idea of a modest property tax. Even this proposal failed in the 1843–1844 county diets and the national diet, during which there were violent outbursts against the reformers.

This setback did not stop Kossuth, however, who had emerged triumphant from his arguments with Széchenyi. The aristocrat had been eclipsed by the lesser noble who was not, as he himself liked to point out, "born with a silver spoon in his mouth." Kossuth remained leader of the nationalist liberal trend throughout these prerevolutionary years.

REVOLUTION AND WAR OF INDEPENDENCE

In 1848 Hungary and Transylvania had over 14 million inhabitants, 600,000 of whom were nobles, and only 120,000 wealthy lords. But the new middle class, composed of nobles as well as the free professions and the bourgeoisie, constituted a considerable political and economic force. It was a force that operated like a kind of third estate, with the difference that the assorted city dwellers, who were neither noble nor bourgeois, and the large peasantry were mere spectators, waiting for the outcome of the reforms, especially the abolition of serfdom.

Agriculture, unmodernized save for a few experimental farms, was the dominant economic activity. Landowners and tenured peasants continued to use old-fashioned farming methods and had no money for improvements. Industry was no longer in its infancy, there were a thousand factories (and yet this was only a tenth of the number of Austrian and Czech industries).

Urban development continued, and the dusty towns grew and changed. By 1848 Pest-Buda-Óbuda had a population of 120,000, a beautiful suspension bridge designed by two English engineers, a permanent theater, new hospitals, schools, and administrative buildings.

Széchenyi and Kossuth

István Széchenyi (1791–1860) and Lajos Kossuth (1802–1894) represent the great dichotomy in nineteenth-century Hungarian public life. Each sought to move Hungarians to take—at times sharply divergent—action to reach a goal they shared: independent national progress. Much of their initiatives met with tragic failure, but their memory remains honored in Hungary, as Washington's and Lincoln's are in the United States; their images appear on currency, streets, parks, and prizes, and associations are named after them.

Their background had little in common. Count Széchenyi was the scion of a wealthy aristocratic family, was raised speaking German, and fought for Habsburg interests as a cavalry officer. Kossuth was born into a Hungarian-Slovak family of modest means, studied law, and took up journalism. During the reform period of the 1820s and 1830s, Széchenyi took his inherited seat in the Upper House of the Hungarian Diet, while Kossuth became a deputy in the Lower Chamber. Both became activists: Kossuth was inspired by reading the radical ideas of European revolutionaries, and Széchenyi by traveling abroad and witnessing the economic and social progress made in industrializing Western Europe, especially in England.

Seeing the miserable living conditions most Hungarians had to endure, they came to different conclusions. Kossuth blamed the country's dependent status and the Habsburg court's policies for Hungary's backwardness and called for radical reforms in political life, starting with far greater freedom from Vienna's increasingly authoritarian policies. Széchenyi saw Hungary's outmoded social institutions and practices as the prime causes of the country's condition, and set out to change them. Indeed, his initiatives laid the bases for modernizing the country. Among the ideas he promoted, and enthusiastically supported, were the construction of steamships and the regulation of rivers, building railroads and a permanent bridge connecting Buda and Pest, social clubs to promote the exchange of ideas, the establishment of a National Academy of Sciences, and organized horse racing in order to improve the native breeds. He was tireless in raising and providing funds for these projects, even though one of his most significant proposals—calling for doing away with the nobles' inalienable right to their lands, and thus making way for the introduction of credit so desperately needed for economic improvements—made him quite unpopular among his peers. Széchenyi took advantage of his position in public life and his family's great wealth to bolster his arguments (and even learned to make speeches in Hungarian), while Kossuth used his considerable journalistic and oratorial skills, which made him popular among young radicals, as well as earning him a term of imprisonment on sedition charges.

In public they showed great respect for each other, but the two unavoidably became political rivals. Although it was Kossuth who took the lead in turning the 1848 revolution into a yearlong war of independence (which almost brought about the fall of the Habsburg Empire), Széchenyi's ideas and actions could be seen as more radical, as they held the promise of more thorough and significant changes. While Kossuth called on Hungarians to take up arms and continue fighting even when there was no hope for military victory, Széchenyi worked to remake Hungarian society. He called on his fellow noblemen to give up many of their privileges, abandon their lives of rural indolence, and take practical steps to make Hungary economically powerful, a course that in his view would give the country a stronger bargaining position vis-à-vis Vienna, inevitably leading to independence without bloodshed and upheaval.

The choice of action offered by these two patriots set a pattern for the rest of Hungary's recent history, including the recent decades: the debate between those who, following Széchenyi's example, work for gradual, "careful" progress, and those who call for radical changes, continues.

Debate among liberal Hungarians focused on the modalities and the pace of change and not on the suitability of another policy. The issue of national minorities was now high on the political agenda; and it was not limited to languages. There were legal, economic, educational, and cultural aspects too.

About half of the population belonged to non-Magyar ethnic groups. In contrast to the past, their assimilation was seldom spontaneous. Though no one yet spoke of national identity as such, a vague national awareness, diffused and mixed in with the social and religious, had been awakened.

The nation was both multiethnic and multidenominational, strongly influenced by cultural and political nationalist awakenings. The Croats, subjects of the Crown but with their own diet and enjoying considerable state autonomy, constituted a particularly complex problem. In the 1840s the Croat nobility had severed its traditional alliance with the Hungarian lawmakers. The Croat National Party and the Illyrian movement, an outcome of Napoleon's Illyrian Provinces created between 1809 and 1813, squared off against pro-Hungarian Croats.

Equally strong cultural nationalist currents existed among the Slovaks in Upper Hungary, the Serbs in the south, and the Romanians in Transylvania. The intellectuals and patriots of these nationalities were unhappy with the introduction of Hungarian as the official language, the concept of one state, one nation, and the assimilationist policy of the Hungarian political class. As for the Viennese court, in accordance with its age-old tactic of divide and rule, it encouraged the minorities to pursue their demands.

In three-nation Transylvania (Magyar, Szekler, and Saxon), the fourth nation, the Romanian, had raised its head, influenced by its intellectuals. The vision of a Greater Serbia as an ideology was also promoted by the Serbian minister of the interior, Ilija Garasanin. As for Serbians living within the kingdom of Hungary, their most important journal, *Serbske narodne novine* (Serb National News), published in Pest, leaned more toward Hungarian reformism. In Upper Hungary, a "war of languages" raged between Magyars and Slovaks. Two intellectuals led the Slovak movement, Jan Kollár and Ľudovít Štúr, both opponents of Magyarization. Kollár's profile illustrates well the complexity of the situation; he was a Lutheran pastor living in Pest, wrote in Czech and adopted a pro-Austrian and Austro-Slav policy. Austro-Slavism, as opposed to Russian Pan-Slavism, envisaged the union of the Slavs of the Habsburg Empire, a vision dear to the great figure of Czech nationalism, František Palacký. Nevertheless, from the Hungarian perspective, Austro-Slavism and the pro-Russian Pan-Slavism were indistinguishable in that both of them threatened the integrity of the kingdom's territory.

The Jewish minority constituted a special case; in the mid-nineteenth century there were some 250,000 Jews in Hungary. Due to a massive influx of Jews from Bohemia and Moravia, followed by another from Galicia, no other ethnic group or religion underwent such a dramatic increase in numbers over a century. These immigrants were on the whole well received. Documents attest to a Jewish presence in Hungary since the ninth century. As with other Jews in Europe, they were dependent on powerful lords, the king first and foremost, from whom they received protection in exchange for services or straightforward ransoms. They were subjected to the customary discriminations: the wearing of distinctive insignia and clothes was compulsory; there were restrictions concerning property and profession; cohabitation with Christians was forbidden, although this last rule was not very strictly enforced. And yet Hungary's few thousand Jews fared far better than those living in other lands. They were spared the massacres perpetrated during the Crusades and, aside from a few isolated cases, were not subjected to violence or mass expulsions. After the reign of Mátyás, things changed. The mainly German urban bourgeoisie let loose its fury on these rival foreigners who practiced "strange rites." Thus alongside religious anti-Judaism, a modern day anti-Semitism emerged. Nonetheless, Hungary had far less persecution and offered a higher guarantee of security to Jews than other countries. In tolerant Transylvania, cases of anti-Judaism were rare except in Saxon towns.

The Habsburg era was particularly difficult for the Jews; the diet practically outlawed them, and a number of towns once again expelled them. In 1783 Joseph II promulgated the "systematic regulation" of the Jews' status, which accorded them a number of civic rights, including access to towns, participation in industry, and admission to Christian schools without having to wear any distinctive identification.

With medieval anti-Judaism fading, competitive anti-Semitism persisted. While the urban bourgeoisie remained on the whole hostile, enlightened intellectuals and nobles favored Jewish emancipation and further immigration. Legal and social integration went ahead, because, unlike most minorities, Jews were willing to modify their ways. They adopted the Magyars' language, customs, and even patriotism. Their contribution was invaluable at a time when pressure from other national minorities began to weigh on the Magyars.

In 1848 revolution broke out in Paris. As the news from Paris reached Hungary, Kossuth went on the political offensive at the Pozsony Diet with his liberal-radical program, which was soon relayed to Pest. The Opposition Circle drafted the "demands of the Hungarian nation," the famous Twelve Points constituting the essence of Kossuth's program and reflecting the ideas of the Pest radicals. The twenty-five-year-old poet Sándor Petőfi, drafted the fiery "National Song," and the next day the young revolutionaries had the poem and the Twelve Points printed without the censor's approval.

The Twelve Points expressed what the nation demanded: freedom of the press, abolition of censorship, a cabinet of responsible ministers and a National Assembly in Buda-Pest, equality of civic and religious rights, equal and universal contribution to public expenses, abolition of tax privileges, a national bank and national armed forces, freeing of political prisoners, legal reforms, and union with Transylvania. The revolution wanted to abolish restrictive and discriminatory laws, indeed, the entire political and economic system. At the Pozsony Diet, conservatives in both chambers were swept aside by Kossuth's party, a victory due partially at least to the rumor that a peasant army led by Petőfi was set to march on the city.

At the imperial capital, the March revolution succeeded because the government was weak and psychologically destabilized. After Metternich's dismissal, the feeble King Ferdinand and his court ratified the key laws of the Hungarian Diet, the "April laws." The promulgation of these laws meant that the revolutionary achievements became legalized. A government accountable to the assembly was to be installed, serfdom abolished, and the road to universal suffrage opened. The main national demands had been granted. The new Hungarian council of ministers, presided over by Count Lajos Batthyány, included Kossuth as minister of finance and Széchenyi as minister of public works and transport.

On 11 April, the ancient diet was dissolved and replaced by the National Assembly, elected by direct suffrage constituted by the nobles, the bourgeoisie, and wealthy peasants. Hungary was now a constitutional parliamentary monarchy, governed by an accountable ministry. The Habsburg emperor, however, remained king of Hungary; Hungarian sovereignty was not internationally recognized, and there was no foreign office in Pest. A national currency, the forint, was soon in circulation, and a Hungarian National Guard and army were established. Finally, following a general election, the first National Assembly of 415 deputies, mainly from the provincial nobility, opened on 5 July, with few radicals elected.

Transylvania proclaimed reunification with Hungary, and the issue of military frontiers under Austrian rule was also resolved. The demands of ethnic minorities were listened to, placated, but basically refused. Hungarian liberals of 1848 were not ready to renounce the concept of a unitary state and to concede autonomous territories to the different nationalities. They felt that liberating the serfs and ensuring equal civic rights to all citizens, regardless of ethnicity or creed, would solve the minority problem.

Croatia constituted a special case. It was part of the Hungarian Crownlands, but enjoyed considerable autonomy and its own diet, while also dependent on the authority of the civil governor designated by the king of Hungary. Neither the *ban,* General Josip Jelačić, a strong national figure, nor the more powerful section of the Croatian political class wanted to march alongside the Magyars. Vienna initially approved Hungary's position with regard to the national minorities and went as far as recalling Jelačić, but quickly restored him. The intention was to put an end to the Hungarian revolution. Victories against the rebels in Italy and in Bohemia, and news that the Paris barricades had fallen, had restored Austria's confidence.

The Habsburg government tried to reverse the political concessions it had made in its moment of weakness and set about encouraging ethnic separatism within Hungary. In the face of danger, the Buda-Pest government hastened its own preparations for war. A national army—called Honvédség, "defender of the Homeland"—was set up, armament and equipment factories bought, political and social rights broadened, and patriotic propaganda increased. "The fatherland is in danger," a slogan launched by Kossuth, reverberated throughout the land. His speech to the assembly led the deputies to vote for recruiting 200,000 men and extending a sizable military credit.

On 11 September, 1848, Jelačić's army entered Hungary. Austria was still negotiating, but clearly Jelačić's war was Vienna's. After Batthyány's resignation, Hungary came to be governed by a Defense Committee, which the assembly vested with all powers. It was Kossuth's moment—his speeches fanned the fires of patriotism and mobilized the population.

On 29 September, the Honvéd army stopped Jelačić at Pákozd. After this, the monarchy dissolved parliament and replaced Batthyány; the Hungarian Assembly declared these decisions null and void. On 6 October, the people of Vienna rebelled, forcing the court to escape to Olmütz (Olomouc) in Moravia. Two days later, the assembly in Pest nominated Kossuth to be president of the Defense Committee, with almost dictatorial powers.

By December, Austria had a new emperor, Franz Joseph. The eighteen-year-old emperor-king soon demonstrated his ambition to reestablish absolute authority at all costs and without compromise. Meanwhile, the legendary Polish general, Józef Bem, had offered his services to Hungary and taken command of the Transylvanian army. Having won several battles, the Austrian commander, General Windischgrätz, told the emperor that Hungarian resistance was over. Vienna, encouraged by the news, issued a manifesto that nullified the 1848 laws and subjected Hungary to the government in Vienna. This caused serious dissent within Kossuth's army and unrest in the Hungarian Peace Party, which was opposed to the pursuit of war. Kossuth's eloquence and his policies won over the peasantry, inspired the army, and rallied the moderates and the undecided—but not the entire political class.

Vienna's absolutist circles wanted to drown Hungarian ambitions once and for all. There was little room for negotiations. Kossuth saw only two courses of action: either to fight until victory had been achieved, which he still thought possible, or to capitulate unconditionally. He chose the former. On 13 April 1849, despite opposition from members of the legislature, Kossuth proposed a Declaration of Independence of the Hungarian state and the dethroning of the House of Habsburg-Lorraine before the National Assembly. The bill was unanimously approved the following day at a public meeting of an enlarged Assembly. Kossuth now had behind him not only the majority of parliament, but also, he claimed, the loyalty of the army and popular support. The break with Vienna and the king was now complete.

Hungary was not proclaimed a republic. The constitutional shape the Hungarian state was to take would be decided later. For the moment, Kossuth was elected president-governor, but, contrary to the wishes of a small radical left, the assembly did not confer full powers on him. Kossuth was more representative of the dominant middle nobility in the assembly than of the Left or, indeed, the opposition, which favored accommodation with Vienna. His principal objective had been achieved. Hungary had become independent.

Despite initial optimism and success, Hungary's days of independence were numbered. Responding to his imperial cousin's call, Russia's Tsar Nicholas decided to deploy his army against the Hungarians. In June the Russians invaded Hungary, and the Hungarians found themselves caught in a stranglehold. Austrian and Russian superiority of forces was overwhelming.

Kossuth's government concentrated on its military effort, while pursuing its liberal democratic policymaking. On 28 July, it emancipated the country's Jews, and an enlightened nationalities law was promulgated on the same day. This legislation gave minorities the freedom to use their mother tongue at the local administrative level, at tribunals, in primary schools, in community life, and even within the national guard of non-Magyar councils. It was the first law in Europe to recognize minority rights. These actions, however, were too late to influence events in the two weeks leading up to military defeat.

After the Russian invasion, hopes of saving the country were slim. On 9 August, General Haynau beat and dispersed the main Hungarian army. Kossuth abdicated, transferred all powers to General Artur Görgey, and sought refuge in Turkey. Three days later, the War Council decided to surrender to the Russians at Világos, near the city of Arad.

The war ended and repression began. The tsar sent his son to Vienna to persuade Franz Joseph to act with clemency, but the Austrians executed thirteen top generals along with the former president of the Council of Ministers, Count Lajos Batthyány, and several other military and civil individuals. Nicholas was able to save only the life of Görgey. Many were condemned to death by war tribunals, others were simply massacred, and thousands received long prison sentences.

The poet Petőfi died two weeks before the end, fighting with Bem's army. He was twenty-six years old. Count Széchenyi fell into a depression in September 1848. His tortured soul found a degree of tranquillity in a psychiatric establishment near Vienna, where he continued to write and to receive friends; he took his own life in 1860.

TOWARD THE COMPROMISE OF 1867

An uneasy calm was reestablished in the Habsburg kingdoms and provinces. The emperor assumed total control, to the point of presiding over the Government Council in person. Proconstitutional ministers resigned one after another. Alexander von Bach, the minister of interior, became the architect of the neoabsolutist turn that began in 1850. He replaced Hungary's counties with five districts, administered Transylvania and Croatia separately from the kingdom, applied harsh censorship, suppressed civil associations, and introduced foreign penal and civil codes.

At the same time, some important 1848 reforms came into effect under the Bach regime: the repurchase of peasant servitude, for example, accompanied by (unsuccessful) antifeudal propaganda aimed at dividing nobility and peasantry. Indeed, the population's state of mind remained surprisingly united around the memory of the lost war of independence; everyone awaited Kossuth's return.

The most original feature of this decade of oppression was passive resistance, which became a way of life and an ethical code. Thinly concealed vitriolic anti-Habsburg references appeared in the press and in literature, and when the government introduced a tobacco monopoly, many quit smoking in protest. Following a decade characterized by hatred and despair, the sense of distress and trauma was to be the basis for the conciliation constructed by the architects of the future 1867 compromise.

Several thousand chose exile, a significant number at the time. Many of these political refugees soon returned, but a thousand or so dispersed in Europe and in the Americas tried to influence public opinion abroad. Kossuth was warmly received in England and in the United States but could not translate public sympathy into action on behalf of the Hungarians. He became the heroic representative of an honorable but hopeless cause.

The notion of returning to the ancien régime was unpopular in Hungary and impossible given the European situation at the time. Austria was unlikely to concede independence around the negotiating table with the rebels. The best minds in Hungary therefore set about formulating a compromise. The compromise was nurtured by liberal moderates, among whom the jurist Ferenc Deák played the key role. The spirit of reconciliation matured in the imperial capital as well. Responding to defeat against Italy and internal rumblings of discontent, Franz Joseph reorganized the government and his states, though without giving in to true constitutionalism and even less to liberalism. The 1860 October Diploma and the 1861 February Patent were the first steps toward a constitutional regime of sorts. But, as distrustful of magnates as he was of liberals, the ruler imposed a centralizing bill which took into consideration the "individuality" of the kingdoms that constituted the monarchy without really giving them satisfaction.

The Hungarian Assembly, convened at last in 1860, responded to the royal move in a moderate petition rather than a resolution proposed by the more intransigent. The emperor rejected the petition and dissolved parliament, handing moderates a defeat. After a few years of maturing, however, political life reemerged, primarily as a result of the celebrated 1865 "Easter article," in which Deák proposed a compromise with a joint Austro-Hungarian administration for shared external and military affairs. The decisive turning point came in July 1866 when Prussia decimated Francis Joseph's imperial army. The Koniggrätz (Sadowa) defeat forced Vienna to reach an agreement with the Hungarians.

Another year passed before the *Ausgleich* (Compromise) of 1867 was put into effect, formalizing relations between Vienna and the lands of the Hungarian Crown. The compromise created a new state system composed of two constitutionally distinct entities united under a single sovereign and sharing governmental institutions—a characteristic that made it more than a personal union. Dualism was, for the moment, the optimal solution for safeguarding both the Magyar sense of identity and dynastic rule.

Aside from sporadic hostile reactions, Hungarian public opinion appeared more satisfied than frustrated, and not without reason. Compared with the 1723 Pragmatic Sanction, the 1867 law was more acceptable to the Magyars. Hungary was under the king's rule but was not directly subject to the Austrian imperial government. The Hungarian half of the empire was far better defined than its other components, and the Magyar sense of identity was respected. Still, the ingenious legal edifice of the compromise did not reflect the actual economic relationship between a rich and powerful Austria and a Hungary handicapped in several ways. In addition, Hungary was not free in foreign and military affairs. In diplomacy, war, and international law, Hungarian national sovereignty was incorporated into Austria-Hungary.

When it came to "common affairs," two equally representative delegations had to be elected by the two parliaments, to deliberate on the financing of foreign and military affairs, each managed by a common ministry. The delegations had no legislative power, and their deliberations took place separately, communication between the two conducted strictly by written notes.

In the fifty years of its existence, this system was the object of incessant controversy, particularly from the Hungarian nationalist left. Political life was dominated by the rivalry between the party of 1848 and Deák's Liberal Party. Until 1905, the latter retained a three-quarters parliamentary majority. The Dual Monarchy survived; its accomplishments pacified the people and turned a reviled emperor into an accepted and even finally well-liked sovereign.

The real losers in this solution were neither the Hungarians nor the Austrians, but Hungary's other nationalities. During the neoabsolutist 1850s, they shared the fate of the Hungarians. Under the new system, the non-Magyar nationalities, who constituted almost half the kingdom's population, were returned to the fold of the Hungarian Crown.

The dualist system and parliamentarianism worked without major hitches, and its liberalism promoted economic growth. Count Gyula Andrássy, head of the Hungarian government, then minister of Austro-Hungarian foreign affairs from 1871 to 1879, worked with Bismarck toward strengthening the Austro-German alliance, keeping Russia at arm's length and defending Austrian interests in the Balkans.

Kálmán Tisza's government ruled between 1875 and 1890. The Tisza era marked both the zenith of liberalism and the beginning of its decline. Internal stability was assured, thanks to the abilities of this prime minister and the preponderance of the Liberal Party, a combination that managed to mix a small dose of "1848" with a strong dose of "1867." It went on to win elections for thirty years, taking between two-thirds and three-quarters of parliamentary mandates.

Apart from a small conservative party and rather weak representation of non-Magyar nationalities, the opposition consisted of independents who relied for support on a nostalgic provincial nobility and on the Magyar peasantry of the Great Plain, who gained little from the development of capitalism. Nor did the new tax-based voting system work in their favor: only 24 percent of the male adults had the right to vote, and voting rights based on noble titles remained in place. National policy was now conducted in the parliament, not at the county level. Alongside magnates and nobles, the benches of parliament, of political clubs and casinos, the editorial boards of newspapers, and the management boards of banks and factories were filling with the bourgeoisie and representatives of the liberal professions, mainly lawyers. Political decisions were often made in the corridors of the National Casino, the exclusive preserve of the aristocracy, or in less exclusive clubs frequented by the nobility and bourgeoisie.

The two liberal-conservative decades corresponded to a period of unprecedented progress in terms of the economy, urbanization, and education. Even though acute problems of social injustice darkened the horizon, the state did not interfere in the citizens' private affairs, and ethnic groups were free to pursue economic activities, to practice their respective religions, and to develop their identities. The country's political class lacked the will and talent to address the new conflicts or to resolve old ones. As the end of the century loomed, Tisza's successors seemed even more inclined to consolidate the gains of the wealthy to the detriment of the less fortunate. They failed to halt either the decline of liberalism or the erosion of dualism.

INTO THE TWENTIETH CENTURY

The thousand-year anniversary of Hungary's settlement by the Magyars was celebrated during the 1896 millennial festivities. The stability of the country seemed secure, justifying the optimism and enthusiasm of the crowds, and its economic health was also promising for the time being. In 1910, when the last general census was undertaken, Hungary (without autonomous Croatia) had 18.3 million inhabitants. Ethnic Magyars, at 10 million, made up 54.5 percent of the inhabitants, compared with 51.4 percent in 1900. Other ethnic groups decreased in number slightly, although Germans still constituted 10.4 percent, Slovaks 10.5 percent, Romanians 16.1 percent, and Ruthenians, Serbs, and others combined, more than 8 percent. Nearly half the population was Roman Catholic, 22 percent Protestant. There were almost a million Jews.

The impact of voluntary assimilation, notably of large numbers of Germans, along with a policy of Magyarization, was significant, as was the assimilation process of the Jews, who practiced their faith but readily adopted Hungarian as their mother tongue. For Slav and Romanian nationals, on the other hand, the situation became more precarious, since Magyar nationalism was beginning to overshadow liberalism. With the upsurge of nationalism, the roots of cultural-political conflicts no doubt lay in the idea itself of the one and indivisible Hungarian state. The 1868 nationalities law was certainly a very liberal law that opened the way to assimilation. What the law did not recognize was the collective, corporate right of nationalities to cultural and administrative autonomy. Hungary constituted a single political nation in which all citizens were equal without distinction, but within the framework of a unitary state with Hungarian as the official language. There was, however, a lack of long-term perspective on the part of Magyar liberals. It was unrealistic to count on the assimilation of minorities living in a country in which they constituted almost half the population. Furthermore, the tactics used by over-zealous authorities in their attempt to Magyarize the minorities were counterproductive, as they created antagonism (save in the case of Jews, who assimilated and identified themselves with the Magyars).

Hungary's best thinkers had worked for a modern, industrial, and urbanized Hungarian society and for the creation of a multitude of educated individuals ever since the time of István Széchenyi. Their most vehement opponents often came from Hungary's new civil servants. This rather large body attracted the landed and landless gentry, and came to constitute a political class whose members would later call themselves the "gentlemanly Christian middle class," a specifically Hungarian self-identification. Its members had a strong tendency toward social posturing, reflecting the attitudes and lifestyles of the nobility, whether authentic or borrowed.

In 1910 agriculture employed more than 60 percent of the population; industry, 18 percent; and services, 22 percent. Social divisions were marked, especially in agriculture. Five thousand of the wealthiest families owned 27 percent of the cultivated land, 3.5 million peasants worked tiny plots, and 5 million were practically landless. Still, more of the wealth came from industry, industrialized arts and crafts, transport, and other services than had been the case. The number of factories increased, and the industrial workforce doubled in size. The state promoted and aided industrial growth, railroad building, and the regulation of rivers, as a result of which arable land increased by 4 million hectares. Infrastructure and road building had been taking place throughout the century, but railroad building was even more rapid, especially after 1890, when Hungary's rail network grew to be second only to that of France.

All of these changes had a beneficial impact on developments in education and urbanization, as well as lifestyle and material and cultural civilization. Compulsory state education caused illiteracy rates to fall dramatically. Within thirty years, two-thirds of the male population had an elementary education. A second university was established at Kolozsvár in 1872, and others were set up in Debrecen and Pozsony. In 1895 the Eötvös College was founded, modeled on the École Normale Supérieure in Paris. Education was open to all, and several thousand elementary and secondary schools used languages other than Magyar in teaching.

The economic transformation brought about by industrial and commercial activities, and the increasing contribution of factories to the national revenue, along with other indicators of development, were evidence that bourgeois society was on the rise. The value of industrial production rose from 175 million crowns in 1860 to 1,400 million in 1900, and to 2,539 million in 1913. The industrial growth index soared to 1,450, while the national revenue index climbed from 100 to 453.

These signs of a developing capitalism concealed a society split in two; modern and dynamic on the one hand, and moving at a snail's pace on the other. This contrast explains the sharply divergent views that have been formed about Hungary. Some underline its outmoded, even feudal, structures; others highlight its scientific and technical achievements, the expansion of urban centers, of civil society, the arts, and literature. Life in the villages had changed little, whereas the large towns, especially Budapest, had risen close to the same level as in other European cities.

The capital was created in 1873 out of the unification of three separate towns: Óbuda, an ancient settlement, Buda, the royal seat, and Pest, a small town of peasants, craftsmen, and merchants. Unified Budapest had 887,600 inhabitants, nearly three-quarters of them living in Pest. With all the growth, historic Buda did not lose its "old town" look. On the left bank, Pest revealed a disconcerting blend of styles: neo-Gothic, neobaroque, neoclassical, *Jugendstil* (secessionist), or simply of no particular style. The boulevards and the town center, with the Opera, the neo-Gothic Parliament, the museums, schools and theaters, the palatial banks, the stock exchange, and well-to-do middle-class apartment houses, were reminiscent of imperial Vienna, though less opulent. The capital became Hungarian at the same speed with which it became a modern urban center. In 1850 only 36 percent of its residents were Magyar, with Germans, Slovaks, and others making up the majority. Fifty years later, 85 percent were Hungarian, resulting from immigration and spontaneous assimilation.

Social divisions remained, but class barriers were crumbling in favor of the middle classes. The distinction between persons "of good birth" and commoners did not disappear, but education did have a certain equalizing effect. The growth of bourgeois society was also evidenced by the growing number and diversity of people participating in social, professional, and cultural organizations. These ranged from small clubs to large trade associations, and more and more labor unions.

In particular, the lifestyle of new urban (mostly Jewish) writers, poets, and journalists influenced Budapest entertainment and mass communication, and its practitioners became household names. The capital had half a dozen theaters, large publishing houses, and twenty newspapers representing diverse points of view. Fine arts flourished, and a certain un-definable Hungarian School, presented at the 1900 Paris World's Fair, was admired for its bold and brilliant virtuosity, having no particular characteristic but a certain exoticism. Officially, Budapest of the early 1900s cultivated a conservative national art rather than the fin de siècle art of Vienna, Berlin, Paris, or London. The educated majority, fearing the dilution of national cultural identity, remained suspicious of anything labeled "modern." Béla Bartók and Zoltán Kodály were undertaking their research into and rediscovery of Magyar folk music, which was later blended into their modernist music.

Hungary thus entered the twentieth century under the fascination of its thousand-year past and pleased with its successes. Most of its citizens were confident, had a clear conscience, and failed to notice the clouds gathering on the horizon. The nation's leaders were able to discard any proposal to move from a Dual Monarchy to a more inclusive federation, or any other notion that called into question Magyar political supremacy within the kingdom.

The first troubling incidents arose from the difficulty of managing the monarchy's "joint affairs," that is, those dealing with finances and the army. Since the joint affairs were the cornerstones of the empire, and since the army was the tool of social and supranational integration of the monarchy's peoples, where individuals could advance regardless of class or nationality, Franz Joseph took a firm stand against critics of the military. He even threatened Hungary's lawmakers with the introduction of universal suffrage, which might have led to the defeat of the Independence Party. The ploy worked. Opposition deputies accepted the emperor's conditions concerning the army and formed a coalition government including politicians of diverse hues.

In 1910 the former liberals, now the National Workers Party, led by István Tisza, came to power. Tisza's personal qualities—intelligence, steadiness, and courage—were undisputed, but he also had a strong authoritarian attitude. He put an end to the nationalist opposition that threatened the monarchy, but was also a supporter of a pro-Magyar policy at the expense of the minorities.

Non-Magyar politicians found in Archduke Franz Ferdinand, the emperor's nephew and heir to the throne, a powerful potential ally. He was above all a defender of Habsburg interests and its power, but he was also decidedly anti-Hungarian. He developed a strong aversion to the Magyars, whom he saw as obstacles to his plans to reorganize the monarchy along federal lines.

Meanwhile, the monarchy had to face even more acute crises abroad. In October 1908 Bosnia-Hercegovina, occupied since the Congress of Berlin (1878), was formally annexed by Vienna. Hungarians did not particularly want an increase in their Slav population, so Bosnia-Hercegovina was shared by the two states of the monarchy, without being made part of Hungary. After some conflicts with the local Muslims, Bosnians by and large came to accept Austro-Hungarian administration. The Bosnian Serbs, however, did not. They looked to Serbia, where the accession of the Karadjordjević dynasty gave rise to the idea of "Greater Serbia." South Slav unrest was a growing cause of concern for the Hungarian kingdom. Even among Croats the idea of separation from the Hungarian Crown was gaining popularity.

Seeing the political crises of the new century, especially in the Balkans, some of Hungary's progressive minds began to advocate a radical transformation of society and cultivated a democratic "counterculture," open to modern ideas. Their guiding light was the poet Endre Ady; the breeding ground for their ideas were journals like *Huszadik század* (Twentieth Century) and *Nyugat* (West), and associations like the Social Sciences Society. One leading mind of this movement was the sociologist Oszkár Jászi. He raised and tackled a variety of issues, including socialism, agrarian reform, and the struggle for political democracy. It was he who developed the modern democratic concept of solving the nationality problems based on cultural freedom for all minorities, but not necessarily calling for autonomy. He retained the concept of the integral and unitary Magyar state, which he hoped would evolve toward a citizens' democracy.

WORLD WAR I

No one foresaw what was to follow the events of 28 June 1914, when Gavrilo Princip, a member of the secret Serbian Black Hand Society, assassinated Franz Ferdinand, heir to the Habsburg throne, and his wife in Sarajevo. The belief that Belgrade was behind the assassination led to an Austro-Hungarian ultimatum and subsequent declaration of war. A short punitive expedition was envisioned, and even Russia's likely involvement did not unduly worry the monarchy's leaders. Only the Hungarian prime minister, István Tisza, opposed the war, fearing irreparable consequences if Serb complicity could not be proven and if military and diplomatic conditions were not optimal. When Tisza was finally pressured into agreeing with Vienna's decision, he became one of the strongest supporters of a decisive military solution.

As in all of the belligerent countries, the war was popular. Even the Social Democratic Party gave up its opposition to the war, and Hungary contributed half of the 8 million soldiers eventually fighting on the monarchy's fronts. For a while, even the ethnic minorities exhibited considerable loyalty to the emperor.

Hungarian armies first fought on the southern front against Serbia, then on the Russian front, and finally in the Alps against Italy. Despite the valiant efforts of both soldiers and officers, Hungarian units suffered more than their share of defeats. High command was partially responsible, as were organizational weaknesses and lack of equipment and provisions. The human cost was high. A total of 661,000 Hungarian soldiers lost their lives, more than 700,000 were wounded, and a similar number became prisoners of war.

The final debacle began in 1918 on the Italian front. Along the Piave River, the Austro-Hungarian army was almost annihilated. After the Germans sustained a fatal defeat near the Somme and the Bulgarians withdrew from the war, October brought the second defeat on the Piave, and the monarchy sued for peace on 3 November. Meanwhile, Franz Joseph died after a sixty-eight-year reign and was succeeded by Charles (Karl) IV. The decline of the empire had already begun with the military defeats and economic deterioration in its rural hinterland. Yet, despite military setbacks, desertions, mutinies, strikes, and agitation by the minorities, the destruction of Austria-Hungary was not a foregone conclusion. Woodrow Wilson's Fourteen Points, proclaimed in January 1918, did not envisage it, nor was it part of the Entente's war aims. Due in large part to the activities of émigré politicians representing the monarchy's nationalities, the Allied attitude changed, and by the end of May 1918, even the United States agreed to the dismantling of Austria-Hungary. The creation of Poland, Czechoslovakia, and a South Slav state became part of the war aims. Historical Hungary was finally eliminated when Transylvania was awarded to the Romanian kingdom. The Paris peace treaties, specifically the Treaty of Trianon, which was signed by Hungary on 5 June 1920, satisfied a number of peoples, while brutally carving up the historic homeland of others.

The Hungarian national leaders stuck firmly to their intransigent position, unwilling to give away an inch of their ancient prerogatives. They rejected any trialism or federal project that would have placed the monarchy's ethnic minorities on an equal footing with the Magyars. This position made Hungary the stumbling block to any reorganization of the monarchy. Without Hungary's agreement, the project could not be carried out. Austria was cobbled together through the centuries, piece by piece, into a heterogeneous empire. It was a mosaic of states and provinces with a supranational character, headed by the shared sovereign in the Hofburg. But the Hungarian "mosaic" was drawn on the canvas of a thousand-year historical Hungary. Renouncing this unity could have been seen as generous. According to Magyar public opinion, however, it would have also been something no other nation was asked to undertake—a suicide act.

Hungary now entered a Europe forged by the victors, a small, defeated country of less than 8 million inhabitants. As soon as the monarchy collapsed, successor states occupied the most coveted parts of the kingdom: to the north, Upper Hungary was claimed by the Slovaks and Czechs; to the south, Serbs joined with Croats and Slovenians and created a common kingdom; to the east, Transylvanian Romanians opted to join Romania. After Charles IV abdicated, and his former realm became the Republic of Austria, Hungary was alone to face its vengeful neighbors as well as the Entente army that had already defeated Bulgaria and was advancing to its southern borders.

Attacked on all sides, the country underwent a year of torment. On 25 October 1918, three opposition parties—the Radicals, the Social Democrats, and Count Mihály Károlyi's Independence Party—created a National Council. Károlyi proclaimed Hungary to be a republic before an enthusiastic crowd.

The new premier was a complex individual: son of a historic aristocratic family who became a leftist; a large landowner who distributed one of his domains among the peasants; a pacifist who had served as a cavalry officer. He was a pro-Entente politician, a rival of Tisza, a Wilsonian, and a patriot. Some called Károlyi a "republican royalist"; indeed, he was the last Hungarian statesman to swear allegiance to the king. His government however was too radical for the right and not radical enough for the communist left. Consequently, the "Red count" is remembered as a slightly eccentric man of the Left who represented no one.

In November 1918 the government asked for an armistice on the Balkan front. At a meeting with the Allied commander Franchet d'Esperey in Belgrade, Károlyi insisted on the territorial integrity of Hungary and wanted its frontiers guaranteed until the peace treaty.

The Hungarian leader evidently nurtured certain illusions, whereas the Allies wanted to satisfy the Czechs, Slovaks, Serbs, and Romanians (to whom the Bucharest Treaty of 1916 promised Transylvania and vast adjoining territories). The West also had military plans against Soviet Russia, which left the Hungarians with no room for maneuver. As the country's borders were pushed back, Károlyi was unable to maintain his legitimacy. His government resigned. The Social Democrats and the Communist Party—they had merged the day before—proclaimed the Hungarian Soviet Republic on 21 March 1919.

The two workers parties were very different. The Social Democratic Party, founded in 1878, had as its basis skilled workers and, unlike the Communists, had earned respectability. The Communist Party, founded in 1918, followed Russian Bolshevik orders and was composed of left-wing dissident Social Democrats, anarchist theoreticians, and communists trained in Moscow. A militant journalist, Béla Kun, gained leadership of the Party and of the Soviet Republic.

The success of the Communists' power grab can be attributed to the malaise among the unemployed, the wandering demobilized soldiers and wounded veterans, and the demoralization of millions of landless poor. Hungary's masses were in disarray and ready for a revolutionary adventure. In addition, the Communists' condemnation of the punitive Treaty of Trianon and their plans to seek an alliance with the new Soviet Russian government raised hope among many Hungarians.

The first regime formed on Russia's Bolshevik model, Hungary's Republic of Councils, lasted 133 days. It nationalized enterprises, banks, insurance companies, wholesale trade, and apartment blocks. The press, cultural activities, and the professions were subjected to government control. Hardship, rationing, and inflation soon followed. Lands confiscated from large landowners were turned over to cooperatives rather than to the landless peasants and agricultural workers.

Within weeks, the novelty and promise of the communist regime were replaced with disillusionment and resentment. In April Hungary was attacked by a Czecho-Slovak army, leading to war on the northern front, where a Hungarian counteroffensive achieved considerable success. Some among the Allies were willing to negotiate with the Hungarian Soviet regime, while others, especially the French, wanted to send in troops against "Lenin's allies." The issue soon became irrelevant, as the Hungarian Red Army suffered a decisive defeat on the Romanian front, bringing down the regime on 1 August.

INTERWAR HUNGARY

The Romanian army advanced into Budapest, pillaging and requisitioning along the way. The makeshift governments that succeeded the Communists were powerless. The Entente finally ordered the Romanians to go home in mid-November. Meanwhile, several political parties were formed, as was a national army under the command of Miklós Horthy, which entered the capital the day after the Romanians left, on 16 November 1919. Horthy's army was a nationalist force of law and order, targeting communists and their real or supposed accomplices. The victims of its paramilitary detachments included many Jews, socialists, and even democrats. An unprecedented wave of anti-Semitism swept the country, tolerated by Horthy. This "White Terror" can be seen as a reaction to the "Red Terror" of preceding months, but it had other, more disturbing aspects, paralleling developments in other parts of Europe. The brief but bloody rule of the Communist Party undeniably contributed to the upsurge of anti-Semitism and virulent anticommunism. As for the number of victims, estimates vary (as they do for the Red Terror) between a few hundred and several thousand. The Horthy regime was installed in 1920. On 1 March, a national assembly elected Horthy regent of the kingdom. The new government that took office soon after had the task of signing the Treaty of Trianon on 5 June.

Miklos Horthy, Hungary's Regent from 1921 to 1944, and somewhat reluctant ally of Germany during World War II. (Corbis)

There were no negotiations leading to the Trianon treaty. The outcome was a "diktat." The terms imposed on Hungary by the victors were more draconian than those imposed on Germany. Even Austria, also labeled as contributing to the war's start, received a part of the Hungarian kingdom. Hungary's 283,000 square kilometers were reduced to 93,000 square kilometers; its population dropped from 15.2 million to 7.6 million (growing to approximately 8 million by year's end, when Magyars from annexed territories were repatriated). In all, 3,425,000 Magyars, including sizable homogeneous communities, found themselves separated from their motherland in territories given to the monarchy's successor states. Romania received a territory that was larger than that of truncated Hungary. Newly created Czechoslovakia was given territory inhabited by more than 1 million Magyars. Another half a million Magyars found themselves in the Serb-Croat-Slovene kingdom, 60,000 in Austria, and 6,000 in Italy.

Trianon was seen as a national disaster. Though its measures may have been foreseeable since 1919, their flagrant injustice traumatized the Magyars within and beyond the new frontiers. Apart from the economic consequences, the post-Trianon shock drove many Hungarians to nationalism and isolated the country from its neighbors, the future Little Entente, who watched every move Budapest made.

Hungary between the wars has been labeled variously as semifascist, authoritarian, nationalistic, anti-Semitic, semifeudal, and archaic. Reality was more complex, but certain traits of the regime do support these summary judgments. Horthy's rise to power was accompanied by violence and an outburst of anti-Semitism, which was noted at the peace conference. After introducing a *numerus clausus* law to limit Jewish enrollment in universities, Hungary came to be seen as a champion of anti-Semitism. Later, the government of István Bethlen curbed the excesses, and Regent Horthy also distanced himself from the extremists to obliterate memory of his reliance on paramilitary detachments and of his march on Budapest, "the guilty city."

Under Bethlen, Hungary's parliamentary system and the lawful nature of the state were firmly established. However, the regime remained undemocratic, and its tradition-bound ideology was evident throughout its twenty-five-year existence. The countryside was tightly policed by the gendarmes, its rural social structures remained unchanged, and the electoral system was rigged to forestall real radical, or even democratic, changes. Still, Hungary had little in common with Mussolini's populist and corporate Italian fascism. What the two regimes shared was a sense of revisionism, which brought Budapest closer to Rome in the second half of the 1920s.

The perceived injustice of Trianon rallied the middle classes, if not under a common political banner then at least under the banner of erstwhile greatness and of lost ideals. This nostalgia for the past was not shared with equal fervor by the Hungarian masses. Nonetheless, the policies of nearly every interwar government were steered by it.

Bethlen was the most broad-minded Hungarian statesman of the interwar period. His domestic policy was a strange mixture of conservatism and liberalism. The Communist Party was banned—not surprisingly—as was freemasonry. The law came down heavily on clandestine communists as well as extreme right-wing activists. Much to the latter's displeasure, the *numerus clausus* was moderated and lost some of its anti-Semitic dimension. Newspapers of all persuasions proliferated. Censorship was abolished, and the media were able to maintain their autonomy.

The economic domination of large landowners remained intact, but without hindering the development of state-supported financial and industrial capitalism. In politics, the government tried to limit party fragmentation while exploiting splits and mergers in order to gather the center right in its Unity Party. The party was able to hold an overall majority in parliament until Bethlen's resignation in 1931. In the 1926 elections, the party secured 170 mandates (70 percent) out of 245, the National Christian Party 35, the Social Democrats 14, and the smaller groups shared the rest.

Bethlen's diplomatic efforts were entirely concentrated on seeking rectification of the Treaty of Trianon and on obtaining concessions for Magyars separated from their motherland. Thanks to persistence at the League of Nations, Magyars who opted for Hungarian citizenship received partial compensation.

The pro-British Bethlen made overtures to the Entente but in the end had to make do with Italian support, granted to him from 1927. The English expressed a degree of goodwill, but it never went further. France pursued its pro–Little Entente line, and Germany had little interest in its former Danubian ally.

With regard to economics, the Bethlen decade was modestly healthy. The introduction of the new currency, the pengő, in 1927 concluded a consolidation program. The ailing Hungarian economy was badly hit by the Depression of the early thirties, which forced Bethlen's departure. After Gyula Károlyi's brief spell as head of government, Gyula Gömbös led the country until his death in 1936, followed by two short-lived cabinets and then, in 1939, by Pál Teleki.

By 1930, the population of the dismembered Hungarian state had reached 8,688,000, of which 92 percent were ethnic Magyars. Denominational homogeneity had also increased. Catholics now constituted around 66 percent, Protestants 27 percent, Uniates and Orthodox 2.8 percent, and Jews 5.7 percent. Altogether, some 3.2 million Magyars lived in neighboring countries.

Economic adaptation to the country's reduced geography was hard. The Great Plain and Transdanubia provided the bulk of national products. Aside from a little coal, there was no source for energy or industrial raw materials. Waterways had been cut at the new frontiers, and roads and railway lines came to dead ends. There was no outlet to the Adriatic; the forests were in the now foreign Carpathians. The economic consequences of peace were as disastrous as those of war.

Admittedly, there were also some advantages, such as a more educated workforce, low rates of illiteracy, higher industrial concentration, and a slight decrease of the agrarian sector, which, in 1930, nonetheless still employed half of the workforce. The proportion of industrial workers increased to 26.7 percent. Budapest had over 1 million inhabitants, followed far behind by Szeged and Debrecen. There were more railways, more primary schools (7,000 with 30,000 teachers), high-quality secondary schools, and prestigious universities. Also growing were the numbers of newspapers, books, theaters, and physicians: of the last, 96 per 10,000 people in 1930 and 106 in 1940, one of the highest rates in the world. All in all, the composition of society became a little more bourgeois than before, and the level of modernization rose, though still below that of the developed countries.

Growth in industry and mining, however, was considerable. Coal extraction increased by 30 percent, the discovery of rich bauxite deposits gave birth to metallurgy, and electricity production quadrupled. Mechanical industry thrived in some sectors, producing notably locomotives, motorcycles, radios, and other popular consumer products. The electro-technical industry, lightbulb production, and a few chemical and optical products also flourished, even though many new trends, such as personal car manufacture, were neglected. The textile industry developed rapidly, overtaking traditional food industries. On the whole, compared with the prewar period, industrial output increased by 18 percent by 1938, the number of workers by 16 percent, and industry's share of the national revenue reached 36 percent. Still, these factors of modernization could not make up for the slump in agriculture, transport, trade, and crafts, which resulted from Hungary's diminished size, combined with the world crisis. Hungary remained an underdeveloped (though not poor) European country.

The middle classes now occupied a higher rung on the social ladder. Even faced with slow modernization, the period's richest legacy was university, intellectual, literary, and artistic life in all its diversity and richness. A growth in post-secondary education, producing 30,000 graduates annually, was a measure of this progress.

Upward mobility took place among some social strata. A section of the peasantry rose to middle-class level; civil servants were reasonably well off and enjoyed considerable prestige; the urban proletariat who could at least defend their social position acquired through work and union struggles (even though facing poverty and bad housing conditions). Still, there were almost 3 million people at the bottom of the ladder, who were, if not beggars, then at best, rural paupers, half of them living in subproletarian conditions. There were, thus, two Hungarys: one on the road to modernization and becoming a middle-class, liberal society; the other stuck in the past.

In the mid-1930s a hundred or so families and the Catholic Church still owned almost one-third of cultivated land. Beneath them, some 11,000 middle landowners worked 1.7 million hectares. Together, the two groups owned 48 percent of the cultivated land. Halfway up the ladder, some 233,000 landowners and their families shared one-third of the property, farms ranging in size between 8 and 50 hectares. This reveals an inequality of land ownership even among those who were above the poverty line. Far more serious was the condition of the 1.3 million peasants subsisting on plots of one to three hectares. Finally, at the bottom were the "penniless": 1.5 million agricultural laborers and servants, along with the equally destitute domestic servants. These added up to the 3 million beggars, one-third of the population.

The Széchenyi reformers, who wanted to modernize Hungary without resorting to radicalism, had been forgotten. In the view of reformist conservatives, apart from Trianon, a moral degeneration and social disintegration were largely responsible for this state of affairs: the selfishness of the upper classes, their contempt for the underdog, combined with the latter's deference toward those higher up, a system based on connections and nepotism, and foreign, principally Jewish, infiltration. The narrow-mindedness that prevailed in Hungary's interwar "neobaroque" society hindered the adoption of civic values and the rise of a confident middle class that would be industrious and devoted to the public good.

There were signs of change. Notions of public honesty, a work ethic, the value of education, and urbanity in relationships were evolving. Imitating the gentry was becoming a matter of cheap comedy. Despite obstacles, a civil European society was slowly taking shape, sometimes treading on conservative and nationalist sensibilities.

The capital city was the target of both conservatives and populists, for some of whom anticapitalism went hand in hand with anti-Semitism, though they failed to win over the general public. Budapest tended to favor integration rather than segregation for its 250,000 Jews—a quarter of its population. The city's Jewish writers, journalists, thespians, and liberal professionals cultivated a mocking, caustic humor, without provoking rejection by the majority of the population. Urban morality had changed, much to the regret of conservatives, the Catholic Church, and the antiliberal press.

A mindset that emerged after the war, commonly called populism, gained considerable following among young intellectuals of the period by advocating a "third way" between communism and capitalism. Engendered by writers and sociographers, it focused on Hungarian society's most pressing problem, the condition of the peasantry. Known also as village explorers, populists criticized the latifundium system and were strongly anti-German, so it is difficult to call them fascists, even though their writings contained anti-Semitic passages and a few of them associated with extreme right-wing movements.

The vast and rich domain of "pure" literature was dominated by Mihály Babits, a gifted poet and a literary authority. A host of composers, conductors, and performers became internationally renowned under the giant shadows of Béla Bartók and Zoltán Kodály. Bartók's music was not well understood in his native country, probably because its universal and cosmic dimension was disturbing, even though it was rooted in popular traditions. Despite the political turn to the right after the mid-1930s, art and literature remained animated until the eve of World War II.

In 1931 Bethlen withdrew from the political scene, replaced by individuals of far more limited vision and far less tolerance. Gyula Gömbös, who came from a family of civil servants, was a career officer and founding member of the Race Protection Party. He shared a Greater Magyar nationalism with his aristocratic predecessors, but Gömbös favored the middle class and sought dialogue with the populists and even with labor. In foreign policy, continuity meant pursuing friendship with Italy and Austria and, after Hitler's accession to power, closer ties with Germany. Internally, Gömbös had only to hold to his predecessors' anticommunist line. Gömbös proclaimed a corporatism designed to forge a national unity between work, capital, and intellectual talent. He presented a national work plan aimed at national union, revealing a determination to create a government that would play a more active role in getting out of the crisis and curbing the decline in living standards, mass bankruptcy among small farmers, and social conflict. In the same spirit, he rose up against ultraconservatives in his own party and distanced himself from the extreme right. This combination inevitably seduced intellectual reformers to some extent as well as wider public opinion; his Party for National Unity won by a landslide in 1935. (Shortly before the Berlin–Rome axis was formed, Gömbös died, and his successors continued the political slide toward Germany.)

After incorporating Austria in March 1938, Germany shared a border with Hungary and was able to exert greater influence in the latter's affairs. Despite protests not only from the Left but from several conservatives, Hungary's course—strengthening links with Germany in the hopes that, with its support, the Treaty of Trianon would be revised—was set. This called for the adoption of state anti-Semitism. The first anti-Jewish law was ratified in May 1938. Berlin made it clear that without Hungary's alignment with the German course in the treatment of Jews, there would be no question of territorial revision. In May 1939 the second anti-Jewish law, this time racially based, came into effect, and a third was introduced in 1941.

From this time on, protofascist movements organized into several parties began to grow. In 1939 they won forty or so parliamentary mandates and became a formidable extremist political force, under the leadership of the future Hungarian Führer, Ferenc Szálasi. Parliamentary plurality survived, but the number of Social Democratic deputies dropped to five, and the bourgeois parties along with the Smallholders Party—the remaining antifascist opposition—were growing weak. The press was still fairly active, although several newspapers were outlawed, censorship was introduced, and Jewish journalists had their work proscribed by the race laws.

Not satisfied with the anti-Jewish measures in effect, Hungary's protofascists increased their pressure on the government. British concessions made to Hitler in the Munich agreements of September 1938 were widely interpreted to mean that the West had abandoned the countries of Central Europe. Horthy still wanted to maintain a degree of independence: he refused to participate in the attack on Czechoslovakia.

To be sure, Hungarians saw some good news in the aftermath of Munich. The Vienna Award returned nearly 12,000 square kilometers of Czechoslovakia—with 870,000 inhabitants, 86.5 percent of whom were Magyars—to Hungary. The following year, a second arbitration took place in Vienna, this time at Romania's expense; Hungary gained northern Transylvania and other regions, in which 1.1 million Magyars made up 51.4 percent of the population. Further annexations in Yugoslavia—home to nearly 275,000 Magyars—ensued the following year. Approximately 2,300,000 Magyars from the separated territories now found themselves back on Hungarian soil. At the same time, Hungary was beginning to pay a price for these developments, first by allowing the Germans to move into Romania across its soil. And, in November 1940 Hungary added its support to the Italian-German-Japanese tripartite agreement.

In 1941 Hitler decided to invade Yugoslavia and invited Horthy to join the attack. Having to choose between a possible British alliance and a pro-German policy—both with punishing consequences—Hungarian Prime Minister Pál Teleki committed suicide. His act of despair changed nothing. In April 1941 Hungarian units entered Yugoslavia in support of a German invasion. Two months later, on 24 June 1941, two days after the German invasion of Russia, Hungary broke off diplomatic ties with Moscow, despite Molotov's assurances that the USSR's intentions toward it were not hostile.

WORLD WAR II

Budapest was waiting for Berlin to ask Hungary to enter the war, whereas the Reich was trying to get the Hungarians to volunteer. A casus belli was provided when, on 26 June, planes identified as Soviet but more likely flown by Slovak pilots, bombed the Hungarian town of Kassa (now Košice). Hungary joined the German attack on the Soviet Union.

With no other goal than further territorial gains in Yugoslavia, Romania, and a dismembered Czechoslovakia, Hungarians were reticent when Germany demanded troops and supplies. There were even tentative moves to reach a separate peace with the Allies, especially after the Allied landing in Africa (November 1942), which aroused speculation that a similar action in the Balkans might follow. For a while, Budapest even resisted German demands for "solving the Jewish problem"—mass deportation to death camps. After the loss of the entire Second Army at Voronezh on the Don and the Battle of Stalingrad, getting out of the war became more attractive. The key idea was to get Hungary into a "neutral" position, fighting Bolshevik Russia but not the English and Americans. This tactic aroused a degree of interest, as did any move likely to weaken Germany, but no more. German intelligence suspected that Hungary was trying to defect and kept a close watch on Horthy's "secret" diplomatic activities.

As far as the Germans were concerned, Hungary's bad faith was no longer in doubt, and the decision to invade the country was soon made. In March 1944 eight German divisions moved into Hungary. The handful of Hungarians who tried to organize resistance were quickly eliminated. Measures were introduced to place Hungary's economy at the service of the German war machine. In Russia, the First Hungarian Army took the place of the Second, which had been crushed at Voronezh. To hasten the Final Solution of the Jewish problem, Adolf Eichmann's team of "experts" arrived. With the collaboration of Hungarian gendarmes, Jews in the countryside were rounded up and sent to the extermination camps.

By August-September 1944, the country was on the brink of becoming a theater for Soviet army operations. Horthy, pushed by those close to him, finally decided to take action. On 15 October, he announced on the radio that he had asked for an armistice and ordered Hungarian units to cease fighting. Only a handful of generals obeyed. The others moved toward the Germans who, informed in advance, immediately occupied strategic positions, while a commando unit kidnaped the regent's only son. Cornered and broken, Horthy capitulated and placed Ferenc Szálasi, leader of the Hungary's Nazis, the Arrow Cross Party, in the post of prime minister. The Hungarians, who already had at least 40,000 dead and 70,000 prisoners of war at the front, found themselves dragged into a suicidal battle alongside a routed Wehrmacht. And as the Red Army headed toward Budapest, the Arrow Cross unleashed terror.

The war's closing months were tragic for Hungary's Jews, once numbering close to half a million and representing the single largest Jewish community in Europe. Nearly all of them were gathered into ghettos and then deported between May and July 1944. A few thousand escaped persecution, and 100,000 survived the camps. The fate of Budapest's Jews took a somewhat different course. On 8 July, Horthy halted deportations from the capital, in response to protests from abroad, but also because he was more concerned about the fate of assimilated Budapest Jews than about the rural Jews. The latter, victims of ceaseless discrimination, had a brief reprieve until the Nazi advance on 15 October. After previous losses, there were still 230,000 Jews in the capital. Thanks in part to Horthy's decision, more than half of these, 119,000, were saved.

Atrocities resumed when Szálasi and the Arrow Cross came to power and continued for the next four months. Switzerland, Sweden, and the International Red Cross were most active in saving the persecuted. Much of the credit for saving lives goes to the Swedish diplomat Raoul Wallenberg, who later disappeared (and perished) in a Soviet prison, but there were also unnamed Hungarians—peasants, workers, priests, resistance workers, or simply neighbors—who came to the rescue of the persecuted.

German resistance to the advancing Soviet armies reduced Budapest to rubble and condemned its freezing inhabitants to famine. More than 25,000 civilians perished, and a quarter of the city's dwellings were destroyed.

By 4 April 1945, resistance on Hungarian soil ceased. Meanwhile, in Debrecen, closely watched by the Soviets, a provisional national government was formed. Hungary now fell under Stalin's authority. This was decided by the Allies at the Yalta Conference in February 1945, but was also the result of earlier bargaining between Churchill and Stalin over zones of influence, FDR's informal consent, and, perhaps most importantly, the position of various armies. "Whosoever occupies a territory, imposes its system," went the cynical explanation.

In Hungary, the Allied Control Commission was controlled by Soviet Marshal Voroshilov. A national government existed under Allied control, until a peace treaty would restore full sovereignty. In reality, Hungary was a supervised democracy under Soviet occupation.

A provisional National Assembly had appointed a provisional government, dominated by the Communist, Social Democratic, Peasant, and Independent Smallholders parties. It was a delicate composition: the Smallholders, existing under the prewar regime, represented continuity, whereas the former opposition parties and the Communists stood for more or less radical change. Communists were still a distinct minority, holding only two cabinet posts out of eleven, although they could count on several fellow travelers.

This provisional government remained in office for nearly a year. It signed the armistice, declared war on Germany, set up a public administrative machinery, brought war criminals to justice, outlawed fascist organizations, and revoked anti-Jewish laws. Life began again: supplies improved, people returned to work, trains started to run again, and children went back to school.

A long-awaited agrarian reform completely abolished the old system of land ownership. Large properties were confiscated and distributed to agricultural laborers and the poorest peasants.

Hungary faced great economic problems. The Germans had blown up all the Danube bridges and seized public and private property, locomotives, wagons, carriages, and horses. War damages were the equivalent of five years of national product. The country had also had to provide for the Soviet army of occupation and was subjected to looting and rape by Red Army soldiers. To cap it all, Hungary was required to pay heavy reparations—$300 million—to the Soviet Union, Czechoslovakia, and Yugoslavia.

In November 1945 Hungarians elected a new National Assembly. These were the first and last free elections during forty-five years of Soviet domination, and the results disappointed Moscow. Although the Communists took 17 percent of the votes (as did the Social Democrats), the clear winner was the Smallholders Party, with 47 percent of the votes. Its leader, Zoltán Tildy, formed a coalition government out of the four National Independent Front parties. The Smallholders ended up with only half of the ministries, due to an arrangement imposed by Marshal Voroshilov.

THE COMMUNIST PARTY'S RISE TO POWER

After their brief period of power in 1919, members of the Hungarian Communist Party faced severe repression and twenty-five years of clandestine existence. By the time the future leader Mátyás Rákosi and his jailed comrades were handed over to the Soviets in 1940 (in exchange for Kossuth's flags carried off by Russian armies in 1849), the Hungarian Communist Party was completely marginalized and had no popular base. The Party had shrunk to a literal handful of members. But there were many Hungarian communists in Moscow.

Upon returning to Hungary, therefore, the Communist Party had to start from scratch. In no time, it was back on its feet, and with Soviet support it enjoyed a disproportionately high political profile. On Stalin's orders, it played a "moderate" game and refrained from talking about dictatorship of the proletariat on the 1919 model. Instead, it called for a "people's democracy."

The Kremlin, confident of winning in the end, decided not to rush things. Moreover, Hungary was not on the cutting edge of geopolitical struggle. All the same, the country's shaky democracy was under close watch by the Red Army and Soviet secret policemen, who stayed around long after the signing of the 1947 peace treaty.

In order to break the Smallholders Party, Rákosi and his comrades used not only intimidation, but also demonstrations, sabotage, and strikes. Initially, the Party left the Catholic Church alone. By 1948, however, church schools were brought under state control, and convents were shut down. Hundreds of priests and monks were arrested and sentenced. Two years later, the churches, worried about being able to remain alive, signed a concordat and various agreements with the state.

Capitalism on a small and medium scale was left to function alongside the nationalization of banks, mines, and the giants of heavy industry. Staggering inflation meant that Hungarians literally worked for nothing in the eighteen months preceding the introduction of a new currency, the forint, in August 1946. For the state, the moment was ripe, and a three-year reconstruction plan was launched. Meanwhile, the Soviet Union seized properties and created "joint companies," requisitioning plants, equipment, and buildings.

These actions not only resulted in a handsome profit but also constituted a leverage of power for Moscow.

Soon, "domestic enemies" and "suspects" were exposed to persecution by the state security apparatus (ÁVO, ÁVH). Fully operational from 1948, within a few years the ÁVH was able to implicate Ferenc Nagy, president of the Council of Ministers, and Béla Kovács, two leaders of the Smallholders Party, in drummed-up conspiracy plots. After Kovács was arrested and taken to the Soviet Union, Nagy resigned. Other noncommunist party leaders fled the country, resigned one after another, or found themselves imprisoned. The parliamentary facade was maintained, but from 1948 the semidemocratic pretense ceased. The 1949 elections could be seen as the beginning of complete takeover: 96.27 percent of the ballots went to an artificial Popular Front, dominated entirely by the Communist Party.

At the same time, Hungarians went to work and the reconstruction plan launched by the Communists and supported by the other parties was an undisputed success. Factories were running again; artisans and small traders ran their workshops and businesses; intellectuals participated in a lively cultural life. As has already been stated, the distribution of large estates among 642,000 agricultural laborers and destitute farm workers amounted to a revolution and entirely changed the country's profile. The optimists expected the Red Army to withdraw after the signing of the peace treaty in 1947. This did not happen, and the transition to a single-party system put an end to a relatively free and promising period.

Instead of a "people's democracy," Hungary became a single-party dictatorship on the Soviet model: state control of the economy, enforced industrialization plans, collectivization of agriculture. Churches came under attack; there were mass purges and arrests; the intellectuals were brought into line, and a campaign was launched to unmask "traitors who have infiltrated the party" (Lendvai 1988, 438).

The transition to brutality affected everyone. There were mass dismissals in the ministries, municipalities, army, and publishing houses. Imprisonment, without real trials, of Social Democratic leaders, added to the already numerous politicians and officers in prison. The old party of the workers, the Social Democratic Party, had been swallowed up by the Communist Party in 1948. Two years later, the collaborating architects of this forced merger were themselves imprisoned, to join others whom they betrayed a few years ago.

The 1949 trial and execution of the minister of interior, László Rajk, along with several other veteran Communists, ushered in a new fear of a different kind. Between 1948 and 1953, nearly 1.3 million people came before the "people's tribunals," which issued 655,623 condemnations ranging from a fine to capital punishment (all in a country of 9.5 million inhabitants). The exact number of political executions and political prisoners incarcerated, beaten, and tortured is not known.

The primary victims were the working-class people of Hungary. They were deprived of their Social Democratic Party, genuine trade unions, and decent working and living conditions. They were as badly paid and housed as under the regime of the lords, but now they were subjected to the pressures of "production norms" and daily propaganda harassment, when it was not imprisonment for "sabotage" or for stealing a piece of wire. Everyone was a potential "class enemy."

Shortage was one thing of which there was plenty. Millions queued up, physically and metaphorically. Food shortages were of course linked to collectivization. Both old and newly established peasants were forced to abandon their "capitalist" farms and to join the cooperatives. And yet the results of the collectivization campaign of 1949–1950 were poor; without producing more food, it created disruption in society.

In June 1953 Mátyás Rákosi was replaced by Imre Nagy, a little-known member of the Politburo, according to instructions from Moscow. Nagy, though a communist since his youth and an erstwhile Red Army soldier, did not belong to the core leadership of the Hungarian Party in Moscow. He had also run afoul of the Party line because of his opposition to forced collectivization. Perhaps it was precisely this that motivated his promotion, at a point when agrarian policy was failing and an economic crisis was shaking the stability of Communist power. Furthermore, unlike the other four top leaders, Nagy was not Jewish.

Nagy broadcast his program on radio, causing relief after so many years of terror and deprivation. His program included the slowing down of frenetic industrialization, the lifting of constraining measures against peasants, permission to dissolve the kolkhozes, and release of detainees from internment camps. Nagy's patriotic warmth and his speech—part professorial, part rural—made him the first popular Communist politician. Since promises were kept, he earned the trust of his compatriots and the hatred of the Party apparatus, Rákosi in particular.

The June program resulted in relentless infighting between Rákosi and Nagy. Confident of his position, Nagy relied on the power of the word and on public opinion. Until October 1954, he was able to count on Khrushchev's support, but then things changed. The Federal Republic of Germany was allowed to join NATO, and the communist bloc set up the Warsaw Pact.

REVOLUTION OF 1956

Nagy was ousted in April 1955. His refusal to subject himself to the ritual of self-criticism cost him his Party membership card. Rákosi once again held exclusive power. However, at the Twentieth Congress of the Soviet Party, 14–25 February 1956, Khrushchev delivered his celebrated speech condemning Stalin's crimes and the damaging effects of the "personality cult." Rákosi and the Party apparatchiks were now on the defensive. Hungarian intellectuals organized debate after debate on the most sensitive issues, such as the economy, historiography, Marxist philosophy, and the role of the press. The debate on the latter took place in June 1956, with people listening to speeches broadcast to the street over loudspeakers. After this, events gathered momentum.

In mid-July Rákosi was dismissed at the insistence of the Soviets and went into exile in the USSR. A reshuffle brought to power Ernő Gerő, who tried to implement a halfhearted policy change. A few ÁVH torturers went to prison; a few hundred of their victims were rehabilitated.

This halfhearted thaw did not appease the public mood. The opposition now called for a state funeral and rehabili-

Hungarian Premier Imre Nagy dances with a peasant girl at a reception of the Patriotic People's Front Congress in 1955. A year later student uprisings would call for Nagy's reappointment as premier; after the Soviet suppression of Hungary's move towards independence, Nagy was executed. (Bettmann/Corbis)

tation for Rajk and the other trial victims who had been secretly buried following their execution. For the first time under a communist regime, a crowd of 100,000 demonstrated. At the funeral, the public interrupted the speeches regularly, as Party functionaries rubbed shoulders with surviving victims.

The collective mood was clearly saying, "Enough is enough." Gerő, an unshakeable Stalinist, believed he could carry on, but the majority of Hungary's 860,000 Communists wanted change. There were reformists hoping for "communism with a human face." There were the radicals, who no longer believed in a renewal of society without a decisive break with communism. This was also the general feeling among the Hungarian people, who wanted above all to shake off Soviet domination and to achieve a better life and freedom.

On 23 October, students demonstrated in support of the striking Poles. Young people led the march, writers made speeches, and an actor recited the poem that had signaled the start of the 1848 revolution. The points formulated by students included demands for national independence, Russian withdrawal, free elections, and support for Nagy. The massive procession swelled to 300,000. The atmosphere was celebratory; popular songs were intoned, including the "Marseillaise," and sometimes the "Internationale." Significantly, the communist red star was cut out of the tricolor national flag.

Concessions would have sufficed to appease the public mood, as happened in Poland, but no such response occurred. One section of the crowd laid siege to the radio station, another, to the Party newspaper, a third set about dismantling the symbol of tyranny, the immense statue of Stalin. The night had barely begun, and the regime, armed to the teeth, collapsed like a house of cards.

Communist leaders turned to the only force that could save them, and soon two Soviet divisions stationed close by arrived in the capital. The people of Budapest resisted and retaliated; Russian tanks were blown up with Molotov cocktails. Soldiers and sometimes entire units joined the insurrection. It was the beginning of a national revolution, an uprising supported by a civil population. For five days, the skirmishes raged in Budapest and provincial towns.

The once strong Party was reduced to a handful of leaders in a state of panic. They had no choice but to call on Nagy to speak out against the insurrection. He promised

Revolutionaries and demonstrators wave a flag as they drive through the streets of Budapest on top of a tank at the height of the anticommunist demonstrations. (Hulton-Deutsch Collection/Corbis)

amnesty, not realizing that this was no longer a fight for a softer communism, but a fight for freedom. For the first time in a communist system, a revolution was taking place, an antitotalitarian revolution.

Nagy finally understood—too late for public opinion and the insurgents, far too soon in the eyes of the Stalinists. Until then, Nagy was a prisoner of his militant past and his belief in the possibility of reforming communism without abandoning it. On 28 October, however, the Hungarian side of his personality took over. He declared a unilateral cease-fire and announced the immediate abolition of the security police, the commencement of negotiations for the withdrawal of Soviet troops, and other radical measures, to bring an end to the fighting. The Communist Party disbanded; its most hated leaders fled to Moscow, and a directorium of six took over, aided by a reduced cabinet formed on 30 October. Within forty-eight hours, Nagy made two more crucial moves: he denounced the Warsaw Pact and proclaimed Hungary's neutrality. From here on, changes could not have been more radical: the multiparty system was reborn. The fighting stopped, but insurgents demanded guarantees from the government that promises would be kept.

On 30 October, the Soviet leaders publicly acknowledged their "errors" in dealing with Hungary and the other people's democracies. The text, published in *Pravda,* announced that the Soviet government was ready to negotiate "concerning the presence of Soviet troops on Hungarian soil" (Hoensch 1988, 218). It was a huge step, but significantly it did not include acceptance of Hungary's withdrawal from the Warsaw Pact, which Nagy raised as a point of negotiations the next day.

One sign of change was the spontaneous creation of self-governing bodies. Calling themselves national committees, revolutionary or workers councils, they took on administrative tasks or the management of institutions or factories. This momentum was leading toward a pluralist civil society. Of course, no one had even heard of a civil society, and yet, from the villages to the large factories, everyone seized a share of the power that belonged to them as citizens.

József Mindszenty, archbishop of Esztergom, was freed and took up a position criticizing the government, referring to its members as "heirs of a deposed regime" and articulating a conservative vision of society and of "cultural nationalism" (Molnar 2001, 317). His speech was broadcast on 3 November. At dawn the next day, Soviet tanks invaded the country.

The fate of Hungary was settled when the Soviets and visiting Chinese leaders opted for military intervention. Hungary declared its neutrality, indicating that it had no intention of moving over to NATO. Moscow gave assurances that it would not threaten Hungary. The Soviets pretended they had every intention of keeping their word. They invited Imre Nagy to negotiate the withdrawal of their troops. Soviet generals arranged to meet their Hungarian counterparts, including General Maléter, at their headquarters near Budapest, to continue negotiations. It was an ambush: the Hungarians were arrested by the KGB in the middle of talks. Meanwhile, plans were made for a dawn attack.

The events in Hungary made front-page news worldwide, but the United Nations discussed the "Hungarian affair" only after the November invasion, and a resolution was passed demanding the withdrawal of Soviet troops. It was in vain, of course. Having crushed the revolution, the Red Army stayed in Hungary for thirty-five years.

To escape arrest, Nagy went to the Yugoslav embassy. The last minister remaining in the parliament building, István Bibó, wrote a brief memo of the situation. A handful of broadcasters transmitted the final messages, while armed resistance continued in various places for weeks. The first antitotalitarian revolution had ended in a bloodbath. War with the Soviet Union was unthinkable, and no sensible Hungarian would have wanted a third world war. Still, the uprising was an affirmation of selfhood and provided Hungarians with moral capital, though with paltry dividends. National identity had been rescued. Beyond the frontiers, the 1956 revolution demonstrated for the first time that totalitarianism was not to last for a thousand years.

Hungarian politician János Kádár (1912–1989), one of the leading figures of the Communist regime. (Hulton-Deutsch Collection/Corbis)

1956–1989

On 1 November 1956, János Kádár announced in a broadcast speech that "the uprising of the Hungarian people has achieved freedom and independence" and promptly left Budapest (Kontler 1999, 430). He went to the Soviet ambassador, Yuri Andropov, and from there, fled to Russia, returning on 7 November in a Red Army truck as the head of a Soviet-appointed government.

The new masters at first presented themselves as successors of the revolution, set only to redress its mistakes. There was no talk of a counterrevolution or of punishing the guilty. The uprising was declared just and the old regime—Rákosi and his allies—were largely blamed for having provoked it. Kádár even talked of Nagy returning to political life. This overture was nothing more than a sham. The leaders of the new Party (rebaptized the Hungarian Socialist Workers Party, MszMP) had their course firmly set. The issue of Imre Nagy was solved by the Kremlin in a customary fashion. On 22 November, as Nagy and his friends, trusting their safe conduct, left the Yugoslav embassy to board a bus for home, they were kidnapped at gunpoint by the KGB and taken to Romania. They ended up in a Hungarian prison, where the principal leaders were tried behind closed doors and executed in 1958.

Armed resistance continued for several weeks. The Workers Councils called a strike, and economic life was paralyzed. In December the government dissolved the Workers Councils and National Committees and arrested their leaders, thus cutting the last fictive tie with the revolutionary events. Dozens of Hungarian intellectuals had been executed, committed suicide, disappeared, or were imprisoned.

The Kádár regime now undertook the change in direction that made the Western media describe it later as the champion of communist freedom. The general amnesty in 1963 closed the period of repression and marked a phase of consolidation. Kádár had a sharp political mind, the skill to manipulate others, and the capacity to thwart political intrigue on all fronts. With the opposition broken or at least muzzled, he found himself fighting the exiled Rákosi, as well as plots hatched within his own party's Central Committee. Supported by Khrushchev, he was able to overcome every obstacle. The removal of Khrushchev in 1964 undoubtedly shook him, but his position remained solid. His Socialist Workers Party had half a million members by 1966, and, having eliminated his rivals and opponents, Kádár held all the reins of power. The Soviet leaders no doubt appreciated his success in pacifying Hungary, even if it meant discarding several elements of the Soviet model.

In the early 1960s the regime again adopted old Stalinist methods, forcing peasants into collectives. They were more successful this time than in the Rákosi era, and only a few private farms remained. After a collectivization drive, however, cooperatives were given considerable managerial, productive, and commercial autonomy. This turned into the exception in the socialist universe—something that actually worked. Food shortages disappeared.

Rákosi and Kádár

The two men whose names are associated with lengthy periods of post–World War II Hungary's history, Mátyás Rákosi and János Kádár, did not share much beyond a lengthy membership in the Communist Party. Rákosi was born into a family of small town merchants and was educated to be a banker. Kádár was the son of urban factory workers, whose only experience with higher education was limited to ideological seminars. Rákosi became a communist in a Russian POW camp, and was groomed by Moscow to become a leader of Hungary's small communist movement. He spent many years in the Soviet Union, married there, and spoke fluent Russian. By contrast, interwar Hungary left him with nothing but failure. His role in the short-lived communist dictatorship of 1919 endeared him to few people, and later he was imprisoned for illegal political activities. Possibly the only thing Hungarian he liked was a set of flags, taken by the Russian invaders in 1849, which Stalin's government returned in exchange for his freedom. (Rákosi's Jewish background is hardly worth mentioning: he was not persecuted for it, he rejected all religious belief, and he mistreated people regardless of their religious denomination.) Kádár, by contrast, lived in Budapst as a factory worker and was active in Hungary's tiny communist underground.

After World War II, Rákosi became the uncontested leader of the Party and, after 1948, the dictator of Hungary. Even though he never won an election, he gained a certain popularity because of the Communists' role in land distribution and the rebuilding of the economy. By the 1950s, however, his one-man rule and the brutal repression of any dissent (he even had Kádár jailed and tortured), made him the most hated man in the country. It was in large part Rákosi's slavish imitation of Stalinist practices that brought about the 1956 revolution, and he was one of the first persons to disappear from Hungary's political scene, to live out his years in Krasnodar, Russia, as a total failure.

Kádár was a member of Imre Nagy's government during the few days when the 1956 revolution appeared to have succeeded. Just days later, however, he rode the tanks of the invading Red Army to power. He was genuinely hated by most Hungarians for this betrayal and for the harsh measures he introduced to eradicate dissent in Hungary. The initial years of his long rule were marked by brutality (thousands arrested and scores executed in open disregard for legality) and a dull, rigid paranoia. Kádár had to demonstrate his mastery of the country to his ideological masters in Moscow. By the mid-1960s, however, it was obvious that he had a better insight into the thinking of Hungarians than Rákosi ever had. He saw the need to make material concessions, realizing that most Hungarians, weary of resistance in the face of overwhelming force, were ready to settle for a semblance of "good living" and make peace with his regime. Hungarian policies, guided by the principle of "he who is not against us is with us" (originally uttered by Imre Nagy) must have made the Soviet leaders uneasy. The Party line they tried to enforce was more and more often ignored in Hungary, especially in such areas as private economic initiatives, a relative freedom of conscience and expression, and a commitment to raise the standards of living. From the 1970s on, Kádár's Hungary became "the happiest barracks in the Socialist camp," and the once despised Party leader was seen by most Hungarians as "Old Uncle János." By the time he faded from the scene in 1988, his countrymen thought of him as a modest, plain-living caretaker who "did the best he could for us."

The post-1989 changes in Hungary's economic, political, and social life have created problems as well as blessings. To many, the past does not look so bad. While there are few apologists for the Rákosi era, Kádár's thirty-two-year rule, somewhat like the sixty-eight years Hungarians lived under Franz Joseph's reign, is beginning to take on the appearance of the good old days.

The regime inherited a planned economy, modeled on Soviet lines. Its predecessors had built up heavy industry without the technical means, the know-how and the raw materials, and managed it by a central planning office that was in turn subject to ideology-driven directives. The brief reformist interlude under Imre Nagy was unable to eliminate altogether the negative consequences and the poverty of the population. Behind the spectacular, and often fake, statistics, real growth was minimal and purchasing power lower than before.

Food shortages dropped, thanks to agricultural productivity, but a remedy for inefficiency and reform of an almost nonexistent service sector remained. Reopening the ludicrously overnationalized small businesses soon bore fruit. Restructuring large enterprises, however, was never fully achieved in two decades of the Kádár era. Still, its beginnings were promising and showed some successes.

Economic reforms had their roots in Nagy's attempt to have experts guide some projects. Ten years went by before the experiment was renewed, inspired by the Czechoslovak example, but also due to the political will of the Hungarian leadership and the competence of several brilliant economists. It resulted in an ambitious restructuring plan, introduced in 1968, cautiously named the New Economic Mechanism (NEM). Moscow considered the Hungarian regime's survival more important than ideological conformity. The reforms were launched and pursued, though not without hitches, for four years.

NEM's aim was the creation of a profitable and competitive economy. In order to achieve this in an interventionist system, planning had to be dismantled, structures decentralized, prices freed, and enterprises enabled to manage production, administration, salaries, and marketing as close as possible to market principles. NEM continued until 1972, when the "left-wing" opposition within the Party slowed things down. This marked the end of reformist experiments, until their partial revival in 1980.

Hungary's economy continued to develop appreciably better than those of its socialist neighbors. Progress was especially notable in the private and semiprivate sector (where small contracted groups were self-employed within a state company), a unique feature of the "Hungarian model." The semiprivate sectors, a modest capitalist presence representing 7 percent of the active population, was putting out as much as 30 percent of Hungary's domestic production, contributing significantly to the country's growth. Hungary's socialist market economy was in fact neither socialist nor market, but it did produce results. National revenue doubled in twenty years, the agrarian workforce became much smaller, and real per capita income rose for years.

The economy, however, came up against insurmountable political limitations, first and foremost the single-party system, which had no intention of reforming, much less abandoning its position. The other worrying factor was the issue of debts. By the mid-1980s, the nation's debt had tripled. Hungary's political leaders chose indebtedness to compensate for the slowing down of the economy. The index of real income began a breathtaking fall in the 1980s.

THE COLLAPSE OF COMMUNISM

In Kádár's Hungary, there were no free elections or reliable opinion polls, and the press was as servile as in other communist countries. And yet, the regime, initially held in contempt, produced a relative contentment, and a leader as detested as Kádár became almost popular. His years in power can only be understood if approached through the ambiguities and contradictions involved.

It was said that Hungary was the "happiest barrack in the socialist camp." Living in the Hungarian "barrack" was not overly harsh; it provided satisfactions, material pleasures, and even the prospect of social promotion. In the 1970s Hungarian living standards seem to have been at around the 80–90 percent level of the European average. This represented considerable progress. The average Hungarian had an income that allowed the satisfaction of dreams like buying an East German Trabant car, building a cabin in the mountains or along a lake, or traveling abroad (although seldom all three). Political constraints on individuals, and their private and social lives, had relaxed, and Hungarians were fairly satisfied with their living conditions. It was not freedom, but it was far better than the social and moral bondage of the pre-1956 years.

At the same time, it has been said that Kádár's regime infantilized Hungarians, reducing them to consumers of material goods. Indeed, a consumer society (though a third-rate one) had developed under Kádárism, but who could blame the citizen for being happy to consume? Hungary was slowly becoming a middle-class society, with all of the implications of that label. Creature comforts were no substitute for freedom; they only made nonfreedom more tolerable, and the soft stupidity that had replaced harsh dictatorship was simply less suffocating.

The weakness of this fake liberalism soon became apparent. Since stability and consensus relied entirely on increasing purchasing power and the relaxation of constraints, the first signs of a downward turn evoked rumbles of discontent. Events showed that Hungarians had not completely lost their cultural identity, their desire for freedom, or their civic aspirations.

The year 1989 is remembered as the year when the entire communist system collapsed like a house of cards. The conditions for its collapse had been in place since at least 1985. Among the most immediate factors, stark economic deterioration undoubtedly played a role, if only as a spark. This explanation, however, is far from sufficient. What led to the final crisis—slowly and by process of accumulation—was a transformation in the thinking of both the leaders and the people, the authorities and society. The two parted ways to an extent that no ideology could reconcile. The Hungarian model of communism was never ideologically pure. It allowed a civil society to awaken, which changed the rules of the game. The autonomy acquired by so many individuals in various spheres of public life—in politics, the economy, the media, and in the Party itself—rendered governance within the framework of existing institutions impossible. As for Marxist ideology, it had been reduced to shreds long ago.

Miklós Németh, the last president of the defunct regime's Council of Ministers, admitted that there was nothing that could be done to "normalize" the situation. Power ended up in possession of a civil, diverse society, inarticulate but united in the desire for change.

The "second society" was no longer an underground one. Once the absence of control became evident, no one cared about the remaining taboos—Soviet occupation, Party rule, the authority of a charismatic leader, and finally even 1956, the official memory of which had crippled Hungarian thinking for decades. The failure of "scientific socialism" was no longer even a topic of debate, nor was the conclusive success of private enterprise. The arts, literature, and historiography, which all had been hijacked by a boring ideology, now calmly took up their real tasks as conscientiously as their individual practitioners found it within their powers.

In 1988, after it was already consigned to the scrap heap of history, the Communist Party tried to rescue the situation by hardening its tone and discipline. But it was too late. There was infighting even among Communist leaders, and opposition to the regime was in the open. For over a decade a group of antiestablishment intellectuals had been fighting for their ideas, publishing samizdats (underground publications) and rallying sympathizers, while braving police intimidation.

In May 1989 the government of Hungary made the historic step to dismantle the Iron Curtain, by opening the route to hundreds of East Germans on their way to West Germany via Austria. On 13 June, negotiations began between the party in power and representatives of opposition groups. The outcome of these roundtable discussions was the dissolution of the Communist Party, the introduction of a multiparty system, and the transition to democracy.

Another event signaling the beginning of a new era was the public rehabilitation of Imre Nagy and a solemn funeral honoring the victims of repression. The Committee for Historic Justice, which had been in full operation for over a year, its efforts focused on exposing the truth and extracting a recognition of guilt from the authorities, organized the funeral. It did so without letting Communists exploit the memory of the revolution to their own ends—a measure of its moral authority. The Party was not even represented at the funeral.

Moscow's hope that remnants of its empire could be salvaged by introducing "reform communism" proved to be unrealistic. There is no evidence, on the other hand, of any will to use force in order to preserve the status quo. In the case of Hungary and Poland, the Velvet Revolution was also a negotiated revolution.

Árpád Göncz, president of Hungary (1990–2000). (Embassy of Hungary)

SINCE 1989

The Hungarian Republic was solemnly proclaimed on 23 October 1989, the anniversary of the 1956 revolution. Miklós Németh's ministers kept showing up at their offices until spring 1990, when Hungarians decided their future at the ballot box. The election was essentially a loud and clear denunciation of communism. The two successors to Kádár's ideas, the Communist and Socialist parties, received 4 percent and 11 percent of the votes, respectively. The Socialist Party's position on the new landscape was consequently modest, with 33 deputies in the National Assembly. The Christian Democrats obtained 21 mandates, and the Smallholders Party 44 parliamentary seats.

They joined the overall winner, the Democratic Forum, with 165 mandates out of a total 386. Four years later, this balance of power was changed, but the parties who got through in 1990 still occupied the key positions, thus ensuring stability despite alternations. For the first time in a century, Hungarian liberals became significant players in politics. Thirty percent of the electorate voted liberal. Despite being unknown to most until the late 1980s, the Hungarian Democratic Forum, with its eclectic program and composition, presented a reassuring image as being national, Christian, liberal, and, above all, anticommunist. It was invited to lead the ruling coalition for four years. The government was headed by a historian, József Antall, and portfolios were distributed between the coalition parties.

The National Assembly elected as president of the Republic Árpád Göncz, a lawyer, writer, and translator who had spent five years in Kádár's prisons. He became a popular statesman and was reelected for a second term. The republic's foundations were now solid, based on the principle of a division of powers, since a very important institution was created, the Constitutional Court. Its role was to scrupulously monitor respect for the letter and the spirit of the fundamental laws. Local self-government completed the new state structure. The traditional county councils now played a less significant role compared to the past. The 3,000 or so rural councils, towns, and villages, on the other hand, were given substantial autonomy.

Hungarian democracy matured under Antall's government, among the first in the region to move peacefully from communism to democracy and capitalism. It delivered results as far as the consolidation of the institutional system and respect for public and individual freedoms were concerned. Its foreign policy was resolutely European in outlook. Its conduct was low profile, even if its rhetoric was at times criticized for traces of nationalism.

Antall, catapulted into his post by the leaders of the national-popular wing of the Democratic Forum, had to perform a balancing act between the different tendencies within his party and at the same time with the other components of the government majority. Thus pressed by the Smallholders, Antall worked to transform agricultural property structure in favor of a social class that had still to be invented: independent farmers. This called for two measures: issuing compensation coupons to enable former owners to buy back their land and dismantling agrarian cooperatives. Both ended in controversy. Compensation, extended, and rightly so, to other injured parties, disrupted the economy without really repairing the damage and created chaos in the villages. Coupons were often bought up by intermediaries, and few peasants were able to use them well. Moreover, cooperatives remained alive: only 200 disappeared out of 11,000. As for the net agricultural production index, it fell significantly. This can be attributed to the end of exports to the Soviet bloc, compounded by the financial burden of surplus manpower. Government action contributed to internal dissension in the Democratic Forum. Confident of its clear popular mandate, it set about aligning society to its own ideas—which included a renewed relationship with the country's religious majority, at the expense of militant secularism.

Though Antall had surrounded himself with trusted ministers, his charismatic authority did not prevail throughout his heterogeneous party. The nationalist right was far from being under his authority, and it continued to make statements that were easy to present as controversial by the media. The Forum thus came to have an embarrassing internal opposition in its own right wing, especially its guiding force, the popular-populist writer István Csurka. He professed nationalist and antiliberal ideas, deviating from the party's national liberal image and the more moderate views of its majority. The prime minister was slow to distance himself from the right, due to political necessity and probably also to personal loyalties.

Despite his weaknesses, Antall was a sincere democrat and would never have allowed his regime to be controlled by extremists. It was due to his moral steadfastness that, in the end, it was Csurka who, unable to get a hearing in the Forum, broke away in order to form his own openly nationalist movement.

The issue of punishment of those responsible for crimes committed under communism also occupied political center stage and remained unresolved, perhaps unresolvable. The process hit legalistic obstacles: the statute of limitations had expired in most cases; difficulties arose with defining crimes against humanity; or the guilty had simply died. Indeed, the incriminating facts dated back decades, and the men serving the communist regime, however responsible and morally guilty, were "just obeying legal orders." As in all postcommunist countries, justice went as far as accusing the handful of officers who gave orders to open fire on border crossers. The real criminals, if they were not dead, lived out their retirement peacefully—earthly justice would not touch them. As for the agents provocateurs and other informants of the political police, their names never became public. This aroused widespread indignation, but the desire for revenge abated with the passage of time.

The newly freed mass media criticized authorities and continued to support the opposition rather than government action. This in turn provoked lively responses from the people and parties affected, leading at times to less than civil debates. This was perhaps to be expected, but the sharp, personal, and intolerant tone damaged the political class as a whole.

Indignation over the decline in public civility failed to overshadow the more positive development, a successful shift to a legal and democratic state in four years. Even the noisy claims made by a small group of right-wing intellectuals were seen as signs of maturing diversity in the reemerging political arena.

The issue of ethnic Magyars living beyond the frontiers, apart from its diplomatic aspects, had preoccupied generations of Hungarians since the Treaty of Trianon. The concern, both legitimate and enduring, had also probably been altered by experience. When it became apparent that the old frontiers would not be restored, the rational and desirable solution seemed to be for all the region's countries to work for permeable boundaries, with cultural and, if possible, territorial autonomy for minority communities.

When the communist era came to an end, Hungary was considered the best prepared among the bloc countries for a transition toward a market economy. In reality, the glass was half full, half empty. Among other problems, there were no plans for paying back the mountainous debt (US$11 billion at the end of the communist era). The fiction of full employment was maintained; a dilapidated industry was kept afloat by subsidies, as was a productive but expensive agriculture. The situation was nonetheless manageable, with sufficient reserves of hard currency and, thanks to Hungary's reputation, an intact credit rating.

From 1990 through an economic policy resolutely geared toward the market, Hungary could have maintained its lead and come out of the transition difficulties at least as rapidly and as well as Poland. At the outset, Antall's government took the right direction, stabilizing public finances, launching privatization, and other reforms. At the same time, due to timidity and half-measures, the "classic" problems of transition arose. Antall's government added US$8 billion to the debt and operated with a huge budgetary deficit. Direct foreign investments, the highest among former communist countries, helped, but state or local council ownership remained dominant. The state spent four out of every ten forints; GNP decreased significantly; unemployment was at 12 percent; and inflation fluctuated at around 30 percent.

Living conditions were deteriorating. Enormous sacrifices were demanded of the population, with no evidence that the high price of transformation would lead to financial recovery, to structural reform, and finally to growth. The government tried to navigate between the necessary restrictions and a threatening social crisis. If it did not take draconian measures, it would soon be accused of being lax and populist. If it did, it would be seen as a lackey of the International Monetary Fund. The road from communism to capitalism had never been explored before. It would have been difficult to do better than the Antall government did.

The verdict of the 1994 election discredited the Democratic Forum and its coalition partners. The semimajority system enabled the winners, the new socialists, to gain a majority in parliament. The extreme right and left parties were literally swept aside. As in 1990, the Social Democratic Party was practically absent.

The fact that the same six parties shared most seats in the assembly demonstrated a degree of stability, and the Hungarian Socialist Party (MSzP), with its absolute majority, could have governed alone. Gyula Horn, its leader and future prime minister, decided otherwise. The Free Democrats (SzDsZ) were invited into the government, if only in order to share responsibilities. This unnatural coalition of two former opponents was created in June 1994. There was nothing innovative in the Horn government's political program, but its audacity in economic matters was, for a socialist party, astonishing. Its stabilization program was rather more liberal in tone than socialist, despite being the brainchild of the socialist finance minister László Békési. However, the Békési program remained on paper, and no serious measures were introduced. Then, the unenviable post of chancellor of the exchequer was filled by a neoliberal economist, Lajos Bokros. It was a dramatic turn of events.

In March 1995 the new finance minister presented a program of restrictions called the Bokros package. It was the first time that the question of budgetary balance had been seriously addressed. Among its many measures was the reduction in social loans from a providential state, soon provoking a general outcry, making Bokros the most hated man in Hungary. His package had nonetheless been approved by parliament, with predictable reticence on the part of several socialist deputies and the unions.

The Bokros package was duly carried out, going beyond even the monetary measures prescribed by the IMF: a rehaul of the tax and customs-duty systems, a devaluation of the forint, deregulation, reform of the health service and pensions, plans for the reform of state finances. Considerable savings were made, but the package weighed heavily on citizens; real income fell by 11 percent, along with social benefits and provisions. Dissatisfaction grew, as did nostalgia for the good old days of relative (and artificially maintained) prosperity. However, by 1997, pensioners and other underprivileged sections of society began to feel the benefits of economic growth, a growth largely due to the dynamic privatized industries, to the hundreds of billions gained from privatization, and to the influx of foreign capital. The state was able to spend the equivalent of DM8 billion on reorganizing the economy and repaying foreign debts. The foundations of growth were in place, but this did not alleviate poverty in a growing segment of the population, especially among the Gypsies. The none too rich but satisfied lower middle classes of the era were disappearing.

Adding to the problem of economic reforms, social and national problems came to the surface: anti-Semitism, corruption, public disorder. Budapest, and other Hungarian cities as well, became targets of a new criminal underworld. In four years, 140 bomb explosions (allegedly perpetrated by the "foreign Mafia") remained unsolved. Public opinion accused the police of complicity. Once known as a "safe" city, the Hungarian capital appeared on the verge of being taken over by organized crime imported from Russia, Ukraine, and the Balkans.

The socialists' four years in office were studded with corruption and scandals: obscure bank dealings, assignments of public funds, underworld connections. Leading the opposition was the League of Young Democrats (FIDESZ), who went on to win the 1998 elections. The image of FIDESZ was national and bourgeois. The league was also accused of mild anti-Semitism, but the main representatives of these tendencies was Csurka's extreme right-wing Party of Hungarian Justice and Life (MIÉP). The young, Western-educated operatives of the FIDESZ easily exploited the weaknesses of Horn's dull and old-fashioned socialist government, even turning the socialists' few merits—its ideological neutrality and economic pragmatism—to their own advantage. The already waning popularity of Hungary's postcommunist left was also severely tarnished by its involvement in major scandals.

Count István Szechényi, Kossuth's major rival in the reform movement of the 1820s and 1830s. (Archivo Iconografico, S.A./Corbis)

The Horn government fell in the 1998 elections, losing much of its base of popularity among the rising managerial class. The extremely complex, part proportional, part majority electoral system went in favor of FIDESZ. Of 388 mandates, FIDESZ gained 148, its ally, the Smallholders Party 48. The rest of the parties preferred to support FIDESZ in parliament, including 14 members of parliament from the right-wing MIÉP, led by Csurka.

POLITICAL DEVELOPMENTS

Magyars brought with them to the Carpathian Basin a political system that was shaped by the necessities of nomadic pastoralist lifestyle. Family units resided miles apart from each other, and this implied nearly unlimited freedom in the daily affairs of the individual. Whenever the entire clan, tribe, or tribal federation took to the field, however, this freedom disappeared. Since even the smallest action could mean disaster for all, discipline during these community undertakings was strict, whether they were a joint search for new pasturage, a massive hunting expedition or, especially, a military campaign. Loyalty was to the clan or the tribe and their leaders, offices to which one could rise through succession, which was often influenced by other considerations. Popularity was one such factor, based on perceived leadership qualities and achievements. Most leaders thus chosen were proven military leaders, but the pastoralists also valued other qualities, and often elected a co-ruler recognized for his wise and judicious practices during peacetime. Thus, even though ruling dynasties existed, there was no great social distance between members of these and common pastoralists, and there was a chance for nearly every male to rise to a leadership position.

This "steppe democracy" came to an end when Hungarians converted to Christianity, adopting at the same time the prevailing European social practice of centralized royal authority, along with those of county administration and an increasing stratification that was part and parcel of feudalism. Gone was the free, individualistic roaming of nomadism. Instead, people were increasingly forced to live in villages, which came more and more under the authority of the large landholding lords. As more and more commoners became impoverished, they were forced to become servants, and later serfs, in the service of barons. While the number of serfs increased, so too did the number of those who retained their titles of nobility, but lost all or almost all of their property. The nobility, composed of wealthy landholders and a growing number of common noblemen, together came to consider themselves the "one and indivisible noble Hungarian nation." They attended the diets (periodically assembled legislative meetings), and they made and enforced the laws, most of the time with royal cooperation, but at times in conflict with it. In exchange for performing these duties, and in recognition of their service as the armed defenders of the nation, they were exempt from paying taxes of any kind, a privilege they guarded jealously well into the nineteenth century.

Social injustice aside, this stratification of Hungarian society poisoned public life for much of the modern period. Unfortunately, not all noblemen were endowed with fairness in the way they treated their serfs, the wisdom to manage the nation's affairs, or a sense of patriotic unselfishness. On the contrary, more and more of them took on attitudes that proved destructive for the nation's interest. Some of the wealthiest barons did their utmost to weaken royal authority, attracting many of the lesser nobles to their causes. To be sure, they distinguished themselves in the long anti-Ottoman wars of defense. Their ranks were thinned in battles and replenished by newly created aristocrats, often imported from other lands. Not surprisingly, few of Hungary's aristocrats opposed the Habsburg-supported Catholic Counter-Reformation, and even fewer were enthusiastic supporters of Prince Rákóczi's *kuruc* war of independence.

The common nobility took a more independent position both regarding Protestantism and the anti-Habsburg struggle. They were, by and large, enthusiastic supporters of both causes, even while stubbornly safeguarding their increasingly meaningless privileges. After the defeat of the kuruc armies, this class, which represented a very large proportion of Hungarian society, became disillusioned and fatalistic. Most of its members assumed the parochial stance of passive resistance, withdrawing from national affairs into the ancient, familiar institutions of the counties. Dealing only with local affairs (and only in Latin), refusing to travel, consider, or even read about the new ideas streaming in from the west of Europe, this loudly "patriotic" nobility thus evaded its responsibility to lead Hungary out of its state of severe underdevelopment.

In general, European nobility exhibited contradictory attitudes toward the ideas of the Enlightenment, and especially toward the notions of revolutionary romanticism. In Hungary and Central Europe, however, the situation was made worse by the nearly total absence of a middle class, the stratum of society that was instrumental in bringing about much of Western Europe's modernization in the eighteenth and nineteenth centuries. In part because of the centuries-long wars in the region, and in part because of the shortsighted insistence of the nobility to preserve their countries' social institutions, the societies of Central and Eastern Europe did not encourage the rise of commercial-entrepreneurial-professional classes. This was not a matter of education alone. Noblemen were literate (though not widely read), and an increasing number of commoners attended secondary schools. But working in typically middle-class professions (e.g., merchant, manufacturer, or writer) was not seen as befitting a "real Hungarian," and especially not a Magyar nobleman. The one exception was the legal profession. A mushrooming of complicated and time-consuming lawsuits, and the intricate machinery of country administrations, provided a "gentlemanly" opportunity for lawyers. Hungary's business life and fledgling manufacturing activities, on the other hand, were largely nurtured and controlled by Germans, Serbs, Greeks, and Armenians, among others. The presence of the growing Jewish population in these activities was also noticeable. Pest and Buda, along with the few small cities of the late eighteenth century, had an increasingly large proportion of foreign-born inhabitants, and this marked the beginning of the great urban–rural alienation so characteristic of the region.

The weakness and marginalization of Hungary's middle class, combined with the common nobility's retreat from national affairs and the aristocrats' loyalty to Habsburg interests, meant that there was scarcely anyone promoting genuinely pro-Hungarian social-political reforms. There were isolated cases of a few radicals conspiring to break away from Vienna's control, but they were easily uncovered and eliminated by the increasingly efficient police organizations.

In the end, the leaders of the early-nineteenth-century reform movements still came from the two classes that showed few signs of being interested in public affairs. Without forming political parties or creating grassroots movements, a few inspired aristocrats—Count István Széchenyi and Baron Miklós Wesselényi prominent among them—began to sound the voices of reform, in politics as well as in social practice. Wesselényi called for greater independence from Vienna, while Széchenyi was needling his fellow aristocrats to make serious sacrifices in the cause of national progress. The enlightened aristocrats found allies in the ranks of the common nobility. They were first brought together by their shared interest in such nonpolitical issues as reforming the Hungarian language, promoting literature and theater in the vernacular, or founding economic and trade organizations. And, of course, there was a great deal of diversity in their methods and goals, ranging from radical republicans on the left to cautious reformers on the more conservative side. Their increasingly lively debates during the 1830s and 1840s, and the reporting of these exchanges in a burgeoning press, led to the birth of modern political life in Hungary.

The common nobleman turned journalist-activist Lajos Kossuth and the wealthy man of the world István Széchenyi, for example, remained worlds apart politically, even while paying homage to each other's greatness. Kossuth agitated for an immediate and even violent break with Vienna, while Széchenyi promoted such seemingly nonpolitical issues as river regulation, steamship transport, railroad- and bridge building, and the establishment of academies, social clubs and credit institutions, asserting that if Hungary were to become an economic power, independence would follow.

Followers of these two great personalities in fact created Hungary's first political parties, even if they formally established such organizations only after the defeat of the war of independence. The "'48ers" remained stubbornly loyal to the exiled Kossuth's ideas, while their opponents leaned toward a compromise with the Habsburg authorities. Owing to skillful and moderate negotiating by Ferenc Deák, a provincial jurist who came to be called "the sage of the nation," a compromise *(Ausgleich)* was reached in 1867, creating the Austro-Hungarian (Dual) Monarchy.

The era of dualism had several stages of development in Hungary's political life. Even though it was somewhat of an anomaly—two realms ruled by one person who was king of Hungary and emperor of the Austrian lands at the same time, governed by two independent governments, except for the common affairs of defense and foreign affairs—the system worked reasonably well for decades. The aristocracy in both halves of the monarchy retained its leadership role, the nobility preserved some of its privileges, and the numerous ethnic minorities were pacified with token concessions but denied real political power. Elections were regularly held, but the franchise was severely limited, and the formation of political parties, while permitted, was closely scrutinized. A narrow coalition of conservatives remained in power for decades, winning elections by any means and governing with a firm but legalistic and reasonably humane approach.

The unsatisfied land hunger of rural masses, combined with the growth of urban proletariat, contributed to the formation of radical parties and the mobilization of organized labor. However, their growth was hindered by the traditionalist mindset of Hungarians and their mistrust of foreign-inspired radical ideas. The left remained fragmented and weak, its ideas entertained mostly by urbanite intellectuals, until World War I brought a number of additional miseries, and ended up destroying the monarchy and breaking up "historical Hungary."

Defeat and subsequent revolutions had overthrown the bloc of Liberal magnates and bourgeoisie, and created an internal political vacuum. It was filled at first by the agrarian group of conservative landowners and gentry organizations that had formerly played secondary political roles. The leaders of the gentry organizations came from conservative landowners, civil servants, officers, and right-wing intellectuals. Their number and weight were significantly increased by the masses of unemployed former officers, unable to find lucrative employment, and refugee government officials from the detached territories.

This new right wing wanted not merely restoration, but redistribution, that is, a share in political power and positions in the top ranks of the Hungarian army. Its members also wanted leading positions in the civil service and yearned to dominate the professions. They clamored for the imposition of high taxes on the "plutocrats" of finance and industry and the supervision of laissez-faire policies by the state. They intended to implement statist, authoritarian rule in order to sustain the dominance of a gentrified elite. The extreme right wing of this new movement consisted of former leaders of officers' detachments and members of secret racist associations, including paramilitary pressure groups. They were vaguely supported by an antiliberal, anti-Semitic middle class and petit bourgeoisie.

The postwar sense of malaise and hopelessness called for astute national leadership, of which there was little. After a brief period as a bourgeois republic under the government of the naive liberal Count Mihály Károlyi, Hungary became the second country to become a communist-ruled dictatorship. Governed by a body of commissars, led by Béla Kun, who became a communist while in a Russian POW camp, Hungary's Republic of Councils lasted 133 days. It enjoyed a certain popularity at first, because it dismantled the army, nationalized the nation's industries and cultural institutions and promised a land reform. It might have lasted longer if its leaders had moderated their terror and pacified the fears of the victorious Allies. Since they failed to do either, and they managed to alienate most Hungarians, the Communists were forced out by the Allied-supported Royal Romanian Army, which invaded the country in the summer of 1919.

The interwar period was marked by the name of Miklós Horthy, formerly an admiral in the Habsburg navy and a member of Hungary's Protestant gentry. In a country that formally remained a kingdom, even though it was forbidden to have a king, Horthy was elected regent for life, and he asked a number of conservative politicians to form governments. The regularly held elections (with a still severely limited franchise) were lively and provided some room for political opposition. The communists, however, were only able to operate underground, as their party was not allowed to exist. Even if it were, it would not have attracted many supporters. The brief Red Terror of 1919 turned most Hungarians into anticommunists. At the same time, Horthy's government was not widely popular, either. It was blamed for a brief but brutal period of White Terror (in the aftermath of Béla Kun's rule), and even for signing the 1920 Trianon peace treaty, which deprived Hungary of two-thirds of its territory and over half of its population. In addition, the Horthy governments failed to address the issue of agrarian poverty through a comprehensive land reform, preserved the country's anachronistic class system, and in foreign affairs proved to be unable to remedy Hungary's diplomatic isolation.

Hungary's best political minds were, thus, in a difficult position. Feeling betrayed and rebuffed by the liberal democracies of the West, disillusioned by the unfulfilled promises of the radical Left (as it showed its true nature in

Stalin's Soviet Union as well as in Hungary's 1919 Republic of Councils), they were driven to experiment with various "native" ideologies. Most of these were based on an idea that could be called "Hungarian exceptionalism." According to this, the Magyars—having no ethnic relatives nearby and having shown a strong nation-building and maintaining ability in the face of serious threats—ought to rely on their own well-developed political instincts to guide them along a third road, an alternative to both the bourgeois liberal capitalism of the West and the Marxist-Stalinist absolutism of the East.

During the Bethlen consolidation, nationalist extremists were ousted from political positions, but their influence was by no means eliminated; they retained their press organs and a leading role in the army. The executive branch and the armed forces gained the upper hand over liberal parliamentarianism and the democratic strivings of a civil society. Thus the conservative gentry continued to thrive throughout the period of consolidation, only to add to their strength and power during the 1930s.

The economic and political power of the bourgeoisie still, however, continued to grow, and the main tendency of restoration was moving toward liberalization. Bethlen was determined to revive the prewar alliance between magnates and the bourgeoisie in government as well as in local administration. Organizations safeguarding the interests of capitalists were filled with fresh vigor and their influence over the economic ministry increased. Banks and entrepreneurs played a leading role by investing the huge loans acquired by the state. Thus the trust of Hungarian and international monied circles, and economic prosperity in general, were among the firm bases of consolidation.

Portrait of Bela Kun, early-twentieth-century Hungarian communist revolutionary. (Hulton Archive/Getty)

The ideology and propaganda of the new regime were also modified. Efforts to end the prevailing chaos had begun under the banner of militant antiliberalism and anti-Semitism. The adjective "Christian" was not used in a religious sense, as a slogan for moral revival, but with a distinctively anti-Semitic, discriminatory edge. Furthermore, the emphasis on "national character" unambiguously implied territorial revision to prewar boundaries

The institutions, open activities, and propaganda of the White Terror were suppressed. Militant anti-Semitism was on the decline: the government moderated the *numerus clausus* quota law and even encouraged the Jewish middle class to participate in public life. Racism was also eliminated from the interpretation of national character, and the sense of the nation as a political unit was brought back into use. From the mid-1920s on, this concept came to mean the partial or total revision of the Trianon peace treaty. On this point a full national consensus was achieved. Growing professionalism in the techniques of government, authoritarian paternalism, revival of religiosity, patronage of the arts and sciences, and parliamentarianism after the European model were the features with which the system was endowed. Horthy's was a peculiar, neobaroque style of government. The adjectives fascist or semifascist, which the communists used to describe the era, are simply not applicable.

The Depression sharpened social conflicts. Strikes by industrial workers were matched by mass demonstrations in Budapest on 1 September 1930. The Communists made their first reappearance since 1919 in these struggles. The Social Democratic Party also gained strength, and the opposition to the government became more outspoken. The Smallholders, who had been integrated into the government party, began to organize separately once again, as the Independent Smallholders Party. As the left was reinvigorated, right-wing elements also began to mass their forces. Repressed after the White Terror, the extreme right was now reactivated. Frustrated by the misery and the crisis in which they found themselves, many of the lower middle class and unemployed joined these extremists.

The new extreme right could look to Italy and Hitler's emerging movement in Germany for support, especially after Gyula Gömbös, the chairman of the right-wing Hungarian National Military Association, was named prime minister by the regent in 1932. He announced a ninety-five-point "national unity program." Its points included gaining material well-being and security for the population, restricting the "harmful growth of capitalism," establishing safety in the workplace, and restructuring land ownership in a more equitable way. Gömbös's scheme envisioned a unity of labor, capital, and intellectual talent. One important organizational element in his scheme was the corporation à la Mussolini, in which workers and employers would reconcile their interests in disputed matters, with the state serving as mediator. The plan failed because of the strong resistance by capitalists and labor unions alike.

In the 1930s a new force appeared among middle-class intellectuals. The new group called itself *népiek* (the most common translation is "populist"). This group was made up of intellectuals of peasant background who sympathized with the plight of the rural poor. They were also concerned with the difficulties facing members of the middle class of peasant origin. Sociographers such as Zoltán Szabó, Géza Féja, and Ferenc Erdei, the poet Gyula Illyés, the teacher and essayist László Németh, as well as Imre Kovács and József Darvas, were the leading personalities of this progressive, literary, and sociopolitical movement. They referred to themselves as the populist writers. The Hungarian populists differed from the Russian and other Eastern European *narodniks,* as somewhat similar populists were called, in that they did not have a messianic, social-revolutionary creed; they were also different from the romantic populists of Germany, many of whom identified with fascism. The Hungarian populists were, first and foremost, antifeudal and anticapitalist in their ideology. Their primary goal was to elevate the peasantry to a higher status, because they considered it to be the backbone of the Hungarian nation. They wished to rejuvenate the national ideal advanced by the gentry, blending it with the fresh vigor of the peasantry. Their ideology was based on the notion of the "third road," a peculiar Hungarian version of socialism that was national but not fascist, socialist but not Soviet Communist, and one that would bring about "cooperative socialism."

The populists were open to the ideas coming from the democratic left. However, they were also willing to listen to the anticapitalist tendencies and anti-Semitism of the right. When Gömbös flirted with the idea of the New Intellectual Front, these tendencies were quite visible. The populist writers were quick to realize what Gömbös was up to and broke off their relations with the governing party. In the following year, part of the populists began to lean toward the left, while another segment moved over to the right.

The Hungarian fascist movement began to take shape during the first half of the 1930s. By 1935, the various racist and chauvinistic groups were drawn together by Ferenc Szálasi, a former staff officer of the army. In that year, Szálasi founded the Party of Hungarian Will, which, two years later, took the name Hungarian National Socialist Party. Its symbol became two arrows forming a cross, giving it the popular title of Arrow Cross Party. Its leading elite was composed of petit bourgeois individuals, although there were a handful of eccentric aristocrats and chauvinist gentry scions among the members. For some time, the gentry elite of Hungary did not take the Arrow Cross Party seriously. Its members were not admitted to the casinos frequented by the upper class. The elite was contemptuous of the masses even more than of the socialist workers.

Though Hungary was nominally an ally of Germany, by the end of the war Hungary and its political life ended up under German control. Germans were assisted by a newly appointed government headed by Döme Sztójay, a notoriously pro-German former diplomat. Mass arrests and internment of anti-German politicians, leaders of the opposition, and the left were immediately undertaken. In May the deportation of the over 500,000 Jews in the country began and was accomplished within three months. Only the Jews of Budapest were saved from deportation, though profascist thugs took victims there by the thousands as well. (The losses suffered by Hungarian Jewry came to 564,307 people killed, 75 percent of the Jewish citizenry of Hungary. Only 120,000 returned from the Nazi camps, and about the same number survived in Budapest.)

Was Hungarian society responsible for this genocide? Research shows that, were it not for the effective assistance of Hungarian authorities, the German machinery would have been unable to arrange for the mass deportations. As for society at large, a great range in attitudes toward the deportations existed. Apart from a racist minority, the vast majority remained passive, indifferent, or fearful, and several thousand people sympathized with the Jews and took risks to save some of them.

After the failed attempt on 15 October 1944 to disengage Hungary from the war, Horthy ceded power to the Arrow Cross Party and Ferenc Szálasi; this was followed by a five-month reign of random terror. In April 1945 the Red Army removed the last German units and their allies from Hungary. It was, indeed, considered a liberation by most Hungarians. However, liberty did not arrive immediately.

In December 1944 a provisional government was formed in Debrecen by a coalition comprised of the Hungarian Communist Party, the Independent Smallholders and Agricultural Workers Party, the Social Democrats, the National Peasant Party, and the Civic Democrats. The Communists gathered earlier and declared their readiness to cooperate with "democratic forces." Their leaders were mostly "Muscovites" following in the wake of the Red Army: Mátyás Rákosi, Ernő Gerő, József Révai, Mihály Farkas, Zoltán Vas, and Imre Nagy. The Smallholders were led by Béla Vargha, Ferenc Nagy, Zoltán Tildy, and Béla Kovács. The principal Social Democrats were Károly Peyer and Anna Kéthly. Árpád Szakasits, editor in chief of the party daily, *Népszava* (People's Voice), also belonged to the party elite. The National Peasant Party was established by left-wing populist intellectuals in 1939, with few members. The Civic Democrats drew members from the relatively ideology-free urban middle classes, who wanted simply to restore order and rebuild Hungary and, consequently, had never played a significant role in politics.

The Red Army remained master of life and death in Hungary. Stalin hesitated to include Hungary in the Soviet empire, but he had the means to do so. There were hundreds of thousands of Hungarian POWs in the Soviet Union, and their return depended on the behavior of the Hungarians at home. The amount of war reparations was not determined immediately, so Stalin could increase his demands as he pleased. For the time being, however, he settled for favorable trade deals and the establishment of joint Soviet-Hungarian companies (in air transport, shipping, and bauxite and oil production, among others). In this manner, long before Soviet political control over Hungary was established, Moscow had already achieved a stranglehold on the economy of the country.

Noncommunist politicians expected that the Red Army would leave Hungary soon, so that they could create a democratic country in the shadow of Stalin's Soviet Russia. But their plans were endangered as soon as the political police, controlled by Rákosi, was organized in 1945. It proved to be a useful instrument, as it was staffed by thugs, former members of the Arrow Cross, and vengeful radicals, who cared little about laws, human rights, or even elementary rules of decency.

Genuinely free elections took place in late 1945, with the Communists receiving 17 percent, and the Smallholders 57 percent of the vote after a clean but heated campaign. Social Democrats outpolled the Communists by 0.5 percent. A coalition government was created, in which the ministerial posts were to be distributed according to the strength of each participating party. This served Communists well, for they were able to obtain important cabinet posts. Inexperienced and naive Smallholder leaders were unable to stand up to the pressure of the Communists and their allies, which included the Red Army. In response to physical violence, expulsion of deputies, Communist-organized mass demonstrations, and strikes, the Smallholders, winners of the elections, caved in. The political police now had a free hand to arrest "enemies of the state." Social Democrats, who showed greater resistance to Rákosi, became his next target.

Lászlo Rájk was an interesting figure in the struggle for power. Not a Muscovite, he fought in the Spanish Civil War and ended up in a French detention camp. While working with the antifascist underground in Hungary, he was arrested, and his life was saved by his brother, who was a member of the Arrow Cross "cabinet" after 15 October 1944. Rájk was a convinced Marxist and an anti-Semite, for which he earned the special respect of Communists who had formerly been Arrow Cross members. By 1946, the police apparatus was under Rájk's control, who reported directly to Rákosi, not to the prime minister. The police openly participated in terror campaigns against the opponents of the leftist bloc.

By 1947, Stalin had decided that all Eastern European states would be included in the Soviet empire. By then the struggle for power was over, and Rákosi and his Muscovite collaborators were rulers of Hungary in all but name. The prime minister, Ferenc Nagy, was attacked for "harboring criminal elements." In May 1947, while vacationing in Switzerland, he was told that he was under investigation for alleged activities against the republic. Nagy agreed to resign on condition that his four-year-old son be permitted to join him in exile.

New elections were held in August 1947. This time, Communists were not leaving anything to chance: their voters received absentee ballots (the so-called blue slips) and thousands of them roamed the country—in Red Army trucks—voting at every conceivable election booth. Even after this, the Communists received only 22 percent of the total vote. But this made them the largest single party, since the rest of the votes were fragmented. Rákosi could now "legally" take power. Soviet troops were to stay "temporarily" in Hungary, ostensibly to secure communications with forces stationed in Austria. In reality they were to secure Communist control of Hungary. Opposition parties were now banned. In 1948 Rákosi forced a fusion between the Social Democrats and Communists. The takeover was completed, and the Stalinist phase of Hungarian history began.

The politics of terror did not end. The Hungarian branch of the Soviet NKVD (the AVO-AVH) became a huge and busy apparatus, the real executive organ in Hungary. In 1948 the target was the Roman Catholic Church, closely followed by Rajk himself. A show trial was ordered by Stalin, and Rákosi delivered. Rajk and several other top Communist officials were tried in September 1949, after lengthy torture. They confessed to every false charge leveled against them, to no avail. Six of them, including Rajk, were hanged on 15 October. Other show trials followed.

A new Stalinist constitution went into effect on 20 August 1949 (also, ironically, St. István's Day, honoring the nation's founder). The document named the Communist Party as the leading force in the process of building socialism in Hungary. New laws were enacted, giving the ÁVO a free hand against political opposition.

The system imposed on Hungary was a dictatorship that recognized no legality except its own. This was real Soviet-style socialism. Rákosi developed his own personality cult. He was, indeed, the "best pupil of comrade Stalin," as he liked to be called. No other Eastern European communist leader was trusted more by the Soviet dictator, and no other leader was so willing to execute and overfulfill Stalin's orders.

Rákosi and the members of his ruling circle—Ernő Gerő, József Révai, Mihály Farkas—were devoted citizens of the Soviet Union, and their rule in Hungary was based on brute force alone. Between 1949 and 1953, well over 750,000 people out of a population of 10 million were investigated, and 150,000 ended up in prison or in labor camps. Two thousand were executed on trumped-up charges, and thousands were maimed by sadistic investigators. Even high Party officials were not safe: Sándor Zöld, Rajk's successor in the interior ministry, was berated by Rákosi for having the wrong type of friends. Fearing arrest, Zöld killed his wife and children and committed suicide. János Kádár, György Marosán, and countless others were also thrown into jail.

The Hungarian educational system was ordered to create a "new socialist man." From kindergarten to the universities, Marxism became the guiding light. Compulsory Russian language study, together with the study of the falsified history of the Soviet Communist Party, was introduced. With all this, mind-killing boredom and confusion became a matter of everyday life. At the same time, education was made widely available, and illiteracy all but disappeared. Engineering and technological subjects received high priority, along with Marxist studies, while learning about Hungarian history was deemphasized. Children with the "wrong" background were excluded from the universities, while offspring of Party officials received preference in admissions, regardless of their talents. This was affirmative action, Stalinist style.

No questioning was tolerated. Listening to the broadcasts of Radio Free Europe or the BBC could land one in jail or in a labor camp. Hungarian literature consisted mainly of anti-Western propaganda. Many Soviet books were translated into Hungarian, mostly of the "socialist realist" variety. The Russian classics were neglected, but thousands of copies of Lenin's and Stalin's works were distributed to libraries and Party offices.

Communists may have won the power struggle and accomplished a cultural coup, but the ruthlessness of leaders and their openly Russifying policies left the people cynical and demoralized. During the 1940s, the peasants were forced into Soviet-style collectives. A series of Five-Year Plans intended to create a "country of steel and iron" out of Hungary, calling for the constant raising of work norms and a hidden but obvious lowering of wages. Emphasis was placed on heavy industry, with consumer needs neglected.

Only by maintaining a constant level of terror could such a system survive. But the Party, quite capable of creating fear, was unable to earn respect for itself. Similarly, there was no respect for law. Morality changed; stealing, cheating, and petty pilfering were no longer considered wrong. "The factory is yours," the simple worker said; "take home as much of it as you can." The situation was no different in the rural areas. There was a huge and widening discrepancy between ideology and reality. Living standards plummeted at a time when the Party preached prosperity.

By 1953, it became obvious that the Party and its ideology served nothing but the goals of Soviet imperialism. The pitiless servility and self-criticism it demanded were rooted in human weakness and fear. When Stalin died, he was replaced by a collective leadership dominated by Malenkov and Khrushchev. The new leaders soon expressed dissatisfaction with the Hungarian situation. In a stormy meeting in Moscow they collectively berated Rákosi and ordered the reorganization of the leadership of the Hungarian Workers Party. Subsequently, Imre Nagy became prime minister, but Rákosi retained the position of first secretary of the Hungarian Workers Party. Révai and Farkas were removed from the political committee. It seemed to all but Rákosi that his policies were repudiated. But the "best pupil of Stalin" did not give up easily. He was convinced that, given time, the new Soviet leaders would recognize his indispensability.

The new prime minister, Imre Nagy, was also a faithful Muscovite. He was not interested in airing the guilty secrets of Rákosi's rule. The major difference between him and his predecessor was that Nagy did not want power for its own sake. He wanted to use his new authority to improve the lives of Hungarians. He naively believed that good relations with Moscow could be maintained without the exploitation of Hungary.

Nagy proclaimed that the forced industrialization of Hungary could no longer be maintained. He hoped that the regime of socialism could gain public support if living standards were improved quickly. He knew he could count on at least some of the Soviet leaders for support.

But the Soviet leadership was divided. Some members supported Nagy, others still favored Rákosi. The Hungarian Party apparat, fearful for its privileges, stood solidly behind Rákosi. Nagy failed to obtain majority support in the Central Committee of his party. The government, tied to the Party apparat by thousands of threads, followed the new prime minister only reluctantly.

In June 1953 the new course proposed by Imre Nagy was reluctantly accepted by parliament. Nagy wanted to reduce support for heavy industry and ordered increased support for the consumer goods industry instead. He permitted the dissolution of collectives if their membership so desired. He closed the concentration camps and ordered the rehabilitation of the unjustly accused. But Nagy was stymied everywhere. The subcommittee of the political committee charged with supervising economic development was headed by Ernő Gerő. Rákosi was the chairman of another subcommittee charged with the rehabilitation of the unjustly accused. They did everything to sabotage Nagy's instructions.

In the meantime, the country breathed a sigh of relief. Collective farms dissolved themselves, their members taking with them their tools and animals. Soon the peasants produced more foodstuffs than before. The end of the persecution of better-off peasants, the so-called kulaks, created a more relaxed atmosphere in the villages. The service industry began to recover from the paralysis of state-imposed restrictions. But the ministry of heavy industry stymied Nagy's plans for reduced investments.

In May 1954 the third congress of the Hungarian Communist Party was held. Rákosi was the keynote speaker and he delivered a vicious attack against Imre Nagy's policies. Nagy, in order to counter the apparat, began to organize a Patriotic People's Front. He thought that this mass multiparty organization would unite the people. He proclaimed that the Party alone could not build socialism. He formulated the thesis later expropriated by his executioner, János Kádár, that "those who are not against us are with us."

In January 1955 the long simmering feud within the Soviet Politburo over policy in Hungary came to the fore. At this time a Hungarian government delegation was visiting Moscow and had to listen to criticism by every member of that august body. In February Imre Nagy suffered a mild heart attack. While he was recuperating, Rákosi made his move. On 14 April 1955, the political committee of the Hungarian Workers Party relieved Imre Nagy of all his Party functions and expelled him from the Central Committee. Rákosi had won a meaningless victory. Although Soviet leaders would not permit him to reinstitute terror, he partially revived previous economic policies and threatened the peasants with recollectivization.

Former Party members who had been jailed began to reappear. János Kádár, Géza Losonczy, Sándor Haraszti, to mention only a few, were walking the streets of Budapest once again and spoke to their friends about the horrors to which they had been subjected. The people, especially Hungary's young, committed writers, listened to their stories with feelings of betrayal. Then the question was raised: "What happened to those who disappeared forever? Why did they have to die?" By the summer of 1956, everyone in Hungary knew that the victims of the show trials were innocent of the crimes of which they were accused. Everyone recalled the announcements of Rákosi as he "discovered" ever newer "conspiracies" against socialism, and personally "unmasked Rajk and his gang." Party propagandists desperately tried to place the blame on Gábor Péter, former head of the ÁVO-ÁVH, now himself in jail. Rákosi continued to boast, but to no avail. There was a general feeling of revulsion toward the dictator.

In 1955 the Austrian State Treaty was signed, and Soviet troops were withdrawn from that fortunate country. Soon

House of Parliament, Budapest. (PhotoDisc, Inc.)

the great powers agreed in Geneva to tone down Cold War rhetoric. Soviet leaders then decided to patch up their feud with Yugoslavia, and Tito's price was to end Rákosi's rule in Hungary.

The Hungarian Workers Party was now in shambles. Party members no longer believed their leaders. On the other hand, the Muscovites and their protégés still tried to hold onto power. Khrushchev and Bulganin visited Tito in Belgrade, but Rákosi refused to make peace with the Yugoslavs.

On 11 May 1955, leaders of Moscow's European satellites signed the Warsaw Pact treaty. This encouraged Rákosi, since the agreement's purpose was the legalization of Soviet occupation in each Eastern European state. In June 1956 the Soviet leaders finally gave in to Tito and removed Rákosi from the Hungarian Party and government. He retired to the Soviet Union, where he lived for the rest of his life. However, he was replaced by Ernő Gerő, who was closely identified with Rákosi's repudiated policies. This should not have surprised anyone: Soviet leaders counted on Gerő to keep Hungary toeing the line.

Then, in October, workers in Poland began striking for better living conditions. This left a lasting impression on the Hungarians, who had always considered the Poles as their friends. On 6 October the Hungarian Workers Party reburied a posthumously rehabilitated Lászlo Rájk. Two hundred thousand people silently marched by his coffin. On 23 October, university students and workers demonstrated on the streets of Budapest, demanding reform. They toppled Stalin's giant statue and demanded that their reform proposal be aired by Budapest radio. The ÁVO-ÁVH opened fire on the demonstrators. The revolution was on.

The Hungarian Revolution—ten days that shook the Kremlin—was one of the most written-about events of the Cold War. Shooting was initiated by the security organs, and Soviet forces, "temporarily stationed in Hungary," were already moving on Budapest. But their intervention was halfhearted and proved to be a mistake. Soviet tanks and armored vehicles were fired on by the revolutionaries, causing severe casualties. The rebels got arms from the Hungarian army whose soldiers were supposed to disperse them. Workers in the armament factories around Budapest also delivered arms. The fighting continued sporadically until 25 October. On that day, a huge crowd gathered in front of parliament, asking for Imre Nagy to address them. They were fired on by hidden ÁVH troops from across the square. Hundreds were killed, and hundreds more wounded. The next day revolutionaries, seeking revenge, besieged the headquarters of the Hungarian Workers Party and killed several of the defending ÁVH troops. Given the butchery committed by the secret police, there were remarkably few incidents of this sort during the revolution.

By 28 October, the Hungarian revolutionaries were victorious. The Soviet government withdrew its troops from

Mátyás Rákosi on trial in 1925. After becoming a communist in a World War I prisoner-of-war camp, he was sent back to Hungary to play a leading role in the short-lived Hungarian Soviet Republic of 1919. He was arrested for organizing the underground party and spent sixteen years in prison. He led the 1948 communist takeover of Hungary and ruled as a dictator. The Post-Stalin Thaw and the 1956 revolution removed him from power, and he died in the Soviet Union. (Bettmann/Corbis)

Budapest and began negotiations for the complete withdrawal of the Red Army. A government headed by Imre Nagy was formed; he was trusted by most of the population to lead the country toward democracy. His government included János Kádár and Colonel Pál Maléter, one of the rebel leaders.

On 1 November, however, some prominent Communists, including János Kádár and Ferenc Münnich, disappeared. They left Budapest in Soviet vehicles. By then, fresh Soviet divisions, 200,000 Soviet soldiers and 2,000 heavy tanks and fighting vehicles, were in Hungary. On 4 November, a Sunday, while a Hungarian delegation was negotiating with Soviet representatives about the troop withdrawal, they were treacherously arrested by NKVD operatives led by General Serov. A concerted attack was made on Budapest and other centers of revolutionary activity. In desperation, the Nagy government declared Hungary's withdrawal from the Warsaw Pact and asked for help from the United Nations.

The Soviet attack was swift and overwhelming. It was aided indirectly by the preoccupation of Western powers with the Suez crisis and by the impending U.S. election. The Nagy government eventually took asylum in the Yugoslav embassy, trusting in Tito's sympathy for Hungary's independent course. But the Yugoslav leader betrayed the Hungarians.

Nagy and his entourage were forced to leave the Yugoslav embassy and were promptly arrested by NKVD troops. They were deported to Romania. For more than a year Hungary's legal prime minister was held prisoner in a foreign country. On 16 June 1958, after a short, closed trial, he and several members of his government were executed and secretly buried in unmarked graves.

Before the end of 1956, 200,000 Hungarians had fled to the West. János Kádár's betrayal of Imre Nagy and the brutal revenge that his police force exacted from the population in his name made him the most hated person in Hungary. His counterrevolutionary terror lasted well into the early 1960s. The atrocities and judicial murders were no less brutal and vicious than those in Rákosi's time.

By the mid-1960s, however, it was obvious that the reorganized Communist Party, now renamed the Hungarian Socialist Workers Party (MszMP), attracted only the most cynical opportunists. Marxist-Leninist ideology was but a dogma in which few believed. By 1968 the regime had grown desperate for legitimacy. It introduced a set of reforms (NEM) intended to stimulate the economy. These reforms were based on modified plans originally introduced by Imre

Nagy in his first premiership in 1954. They established the rights of individual peasant proprietors to cultivate private plots of land as part of their share in their collectives. They were permitted to sell their products on the open market at uncontrolled prices. This way the peasantry's unmitigated hatred for the collectives (reestablished in 1959–1961) was somewhat eased. The prices of essential consumer goods (such as bread, sugar, flour, and meat) were still subsidized and regulated. The state retained its monopoly on foreign trade, but controls over internal trade were relaxed.

The reforms brought about unprecedented economic activity. They also brought a certain measure of prosperity for Hungary. The stores soon filled up with long-missed consumer goods, and the population began to recover from the misery to which it had been subjected since 1947. Commerce with the Soviet Union and the people's democracies, which brought in automobiles and other industrial products such as freezers and television sets, began to expand. Hungarians were increasingly permitted to visit relatives and friends abroad, and a trickle of former refugees, now citizens of their adopted countries, began visiting Hungary. The press was permitted to criticize lower Party officials for misusing their power. But there were also taboos that could not be touched: no one was permitted to question Soviet-Hungarian relations, and the revolution of 1956 could be discussed only in derogatory terms.

In August 1968 Hungary participated in the suppression of the Prague Spring, which seemed to confirm the Kádár line, namely, that no independent course was possible for the Eastern European Soviet satellites. In time, however, Kádár took a further step; he coopted many Hungarian intellectuals if they were willing to abide by his rules. These rules were determined by subjects that were supported, others that were tolerated, and again others that were forbidden. Those who refused to cooperate had to keep silent. But the Kádár regime needed experts in technical fields and had to support talented individuals in these areas regardless of their political opinions. Thus Kádár adopted the slogan, originally coined by Imre Nagy, that "those who are not against us are with us." Nevertheless, this was not a regime moving toward democracy. Kádár remained an old-fashioned dictator whose word was final.

All in all, however, Hungarians began slowly to prosper. The country was becoming, as the popular saying went, "the happiest barrack in the socialist camp." Kádár was gradually accepted as the architect of a better life. This was the basis of his own *Ausgleich* (compromise); as long as life continued to improve and forbidden subjects were left alone, his system was accepted. The populations of other Eastern European socialist countries watched Hungary with envy. Soon Western reporters were claiming that Kádár could win even in a free election, but of course their assertion was never tested.

In 1972 there was a slowdown in the reform process. Further reforms were stopped or were even reversed. It seems that Kádár went too far. There were complaints by hardliners that the peasants were too greedy and that they earned more than industrial workers in whose name socialism was being built. Instead of paying more to workers, Kádár decided to tighten the screws on the peasants. The new policy, however, backfired. Food production slowed down, and there were empty shelves in the stores, forcing Kádár to hastily reverse course. Then the oil crisis of 1973 hit Hungary hard. Although the Soviet Union continued to supply Hungary with oil and natural gas at somewhat below world market prices, the subsequent reordering of the world market created great difficulties. The opening to the West that Kádár attempted faced grave difficulties. Hungary's industry was not modern enough to compete. The volume of exports declined while production costs continued to increase. Yet Hungary was able to obtain loans from Western banks, and these loans eventually reached US$20 billion. Kádár's greatest mistake was that he did not insist on using the loans for the modernization of Hungary's industry. Instead, the loans were used for subsidizing products that otherwise could not be sold, especially for products delivered to the Soviet Union. Therefore Hungary's loans were actually helping the Brezhnev leadership postpone *their* economic reform program. The repayment and interest charges on the Western loans soon became a real burden for Hungary. Kádár tried to hide the fact from the population, but by the mid-1980s, his compromise had begun to unravel.

The ascendance of Mikhail Gorbachev to power signaled a real turning point. Eastern European communist leaders learned soon enough that they could no longer count on Soviet tanks, nor could they call in the KGB to help out in case of difficulties. At the same time, intellectuals were emboldened to demand greater freedom of expression, and dissent increased. Suddenly history became a very important subject. Its practitioners, both amateurs and professionals, increasingly resorted to underground publications to inform their readers about an alternative to "official" Marxist-Leninist history. This was particularly damaging in Kádár's Hungary, where the true history of the 1956 revolution remained a sore point in the nation's memory. The Marxist-Leninist interpretation of history, long questioned, lost its last vestiges of credibility.

Kádár was becoming old and feeble, yet he clung to power. Perhaps he believed that he alone knew how to deal with the "Soviet comrades." But younger members of his party's central committee were becoming restless. In March 1988, at a meeting of the political committee of the HSWP, János Kádár was relieved of his post as first secretary. The Kádár era was over. Károly Grósz, a gray apparatchik, became his successor, and Rezső Nyers, Imre Pozsgay, and others took the reins of the Party into their hands.

The Communist Party created by Kádár could not survive his demise. Dissenting voices could be heard even at the highest levels of the Party. Imre Pozsgay broke with his colleagues first. On the basis of a study concluded by members of the Hungarian Academy of Sciences, he proclaimed that the 1956 "events" were a popular uprising against abuses by the Party. Suddenly he was not alone, and the hardliners were in a minority. In May 1989 Kádár was retired. In June, Kádár's victims were reburied in the presence of hundreds of thousands of mourners. On the day Imre Nagy was rehabilitated, Kádár died, a lonely man, not hated but considered irrelevant.

Miklós Németh, a young member of the Party's political committee, formed a new government with dynamic young supporters. Németh soon declared the complete separation of the government from the Party. The new minister of education, Ferenc Glatz, a historian, abolished the compulsory teaching of the Russian language and Marxism in the schools. Gyula Horn, the minister of foreign affairs, began to forge an independent foreign policy for the Hungarian state. In the summer of 1989 President George Bush visited Hungary and delivered a rousing speech at the Economics University (formerly named for Karl Marx).

In October the last congress of the Hungarian Socialist Workers Party was held. It was dominated by the reformers, who beat back several attempts by hardliners demanding "administrative measures" to restore the Party to power. In the end, the Party declared itself dissolved. Two successors emerged, one led by the reformers who took the name Hungarian Socialist Party, and the other the old MszMP. Both parties proved irrelevant in the new order. By then a multiparty system was rising in Hungary.

In the first free elections held since 1945, in June 1990, a new party called the Hungarian Democratic Forum emerged as the strongest, with 24 percent of the total votes. Its closest rival, the left-of-center Association of Free Democrats (SzDSz) gained 21 percent. The revived Smallholders Party and a new Christian Democratic Party gained 11 percent and 7 percent respectively. The Socialist Party received 11 percent, and the most dynamic party, the Alliance of Young Democrats, received 10 percent of the votes.

The Németh government had already committed itself to the democratic reorganization of Hungarian society. It opened the border with Austria to a flood of East German refugees. This indirectly contributed to the collapse of the Honecker regime in East Germany. Soon Czechoslovakia followed with its "Velvet Revolution," and the Eastern European segment of the Soviet empire dissolved.

In July 1990 the freely elected Hungarian parliament approved the formation of a coalition government headed by József Antall from the Hungarian Democratic Forum. Negotiations with the Soviet government were already under way for the complete removal of Soviet troops from Hungary. An agreement signed in March 1990 stipulated that all Soviet personnel and military equipment had to leave by July 1991.

The Warsaw Pact dissolved in March 1991. The Antall government rapidly moved toward the establishment of an economic system based on the private ownership of property. The last vestiges of communist rule were being removed; the media were now completely free and often criticized the government with great enthusiasm.

During the 1990s, genuinely autonomous associations of a newly forming civil society once again began to emerge. By 1993, more than 10,000 new voluntary associations had been registered, ranging from the Chamber of Society and the Alliance of Social Associations to such special-interest bodies as the Chamber of Retired Persons, the Associations of the Virgin Mary, the Association of Friends of the Arts, or the Association of Danubian Fishermen.

Neither democracy nor civil society can exist without each other, and this is why the strengthening of civil society is such an important phenomenon in the current history of the Hungarian nation. This development promises to bring about the renewal of Hungarian culture as well as the democratization of society. The flowering of civil society is one of the best guards to block the rise of authoritarian trends. This is true even when the number of such associations appears to be excessive, or when their aims and interests are too varied or deviate too far from society's general mores. The teaching of tolerance and ethical behavior will have to be included in the curricula of all schools. Only such a nationwide effort can lead to success and provide for a favorable environment for the full development of democratic institutions.

Hungarian democracy could be an achieved fact within a very short time. If the problems of the economy created by nearly four decades of mismanagement can be solved, Hungary should enter a new era of prosperity the likes of which it has not recently experienced. This may all end in a debacle, however; as early as 1991, old "values" emerged in Hungary, among them nationalism, anti-Semitism, and impatience with dissenting opinions. Unless strong efforts are made to avoid the pitfalls represented by such trends, Hungary may find itself in a precarious position once again.

CULTURAL DEVELOPMENT

Perhaps nothing has had as great an influence on the development of Hungarian culture as its transitory, borderline nature, rooted in Hungary's location and reinforced by recurring clashes between civilizations. When Magyars first settled in the Carpathian Basin some 1,100 years ago, they brought with them a strong sense of ethnic identity and a set of cultural values. In time, their national identity and their culture were forced to evolve to accommodate (more or less successfully) the diverse coinhabiting ethnic groups. One might ask, in light of the above, how were Hungarians able to preserve their culture, unique language, and ethnic characteristics? Other peoples in the region—Huns, Avars, Yazygs, Cumans, or for that matter Romans—simply disappeared, and their cultures also disappeared or were swallowed up by latecomers.

Around the year 1000, the newly created kingdom of Hungary was accepted into the Christian community of European nation-states; thus it became a border outpost of Christianity. The freshly (and not all that easily) converted Hungarians became soldiers in the service of a militant faith. Along with peoples of the Balkan peninsula, the Bohemian Czechs, the Poles, and the Lithuanians (Christianized a few centuries later), they became guardians protecting the eastern edge of feudal Europe against the continuous incursion of aggressive newcomers from the East.

There was much to learn. Beyond the strict, often harsh discipline of Christianity, which prescribed building churches, supporting a clerical hierarchy through taxes, and abandoning old ways, the move away from nomadic pastoralism called for permanent settlements, adopting agriculture as a primary support of life, and accepting centralized authority, giving up the rough individual "freedom and equality" of their former tribal existence. Slavery, for example, was not unknown in nomadic societies, but it was by and large limited to captive outsiders or individuals punished for transgressions. The overwhelming majority of Magyars at the time of the settling were free and equal individuals, obeying their tribal chiefs out of personal loyalty, which was earned through a combination of individual virtue, leadership abilities, and success. The new ways called for the establishment of dynasties (houses), whose members succeeded to the throne in accordance with rigid rules and whose all-encompassing authority was supported not only by secular force but also by the spiritual authority of the Catholic Church. Refusing to obey a royal command was not only a severely punishable crime, it also became a sin, a transgression against the divinely sanctioned order of the world, condemning the offender to eternal damnation.

The "new ways" were introduced into newly Christianized Hungary by representatives sent from neighboring countries. These were realms in which both Christianity and the prevailing social order of Europe, feudalism, were firmly established. Clergymen, courtiers, and knights arrived from mostly German-speaking lands immediately west of Hungary.

Hungary's rulers were relentless in enforcing the new order, and they succeeded in creating a new European nation out of their reluctant subjects. Peace, stability, and order resulted from the adoption of the new ways. At the same time, there arose a sense of losing individual freedoms and ethnic identity, and this vague but persistent dissatisfaction continued to run as a thread through Hungarian history.

Two elements of this attitude are especially worth mentioning. The old ways were held to be worth preserving and in order to support this position, were presented in an unrealistic, romanticized manner. It was asserted that the pre-Christian, pre-European ways of life—pseudonomadic pastoralism, combined with a raid-and-trade attitude toward their neighbors—suited the Hungarians naturally, served them well and brought them victories, security, and success. Supporters of this view, of course, ignored the disastrous defeats suffered by Hungarian raiders in the mid-tenth century and the tightening ring of hostile alliances surrounding the Carpathian Basin. Sooner or later, these factors would have forced Hungarians to choose between retreating to the steppe lands or being militarily eliminated.

The new ways were also opposed because they were introduced and often enforced by foreigners, whom Hungarians, having extensive experience with duplicity and betrayal during their long migration through Central Eurasia, never came fully to trust. This attitude may have originated from the archetypal suspicion that the proselytizer-civilizer (or liberator) has ulterior motives, wishing to tame or even subjugate the unsuspecting object of his attention. In fact, there were to be numerous episodes throughout history when such antiforeign suspicion appeared to be justified. The territory of Hungary came to be a desirable piece of real estate and figured prominently in the expansionist designs of neighbors.

This is not to suggest that Hungary ever became inhospitable. Nor could Magyars afford to become hostile to non-Magyars. From its beginnings, the country's population was marked by ethnic and linguistic (and later denominational) diversity, which was welcomed by rulers and subjects alike. The first king, István, married a Bavarian princess, Gizella, who brought with her a retinue of "Germans." The practice was followed throughout the rule of the Árpád dynasty, and the influx of foreigners swelled when rulers invited settlers, especially Saxons from German lands, to repopulate regions devastated by the 1241 Mongol devastation. Throughout these centuries, the number of original Slavic and Romanian coinhabitants grew and was augmented by new immigrants, attracted by the wealth and hospitality of the Hungarian land.

The nation's culture was beginning to show signs of division along a different line. While the rural majority lived their lives in the traditional way, altered only superficially by the regulations imposed by the Catholic Church and their lords, the ruling elite pursued a lifestyle and accepted standards of behavior that were Western European and communicated in Latin. Until the sixteenth century, we know of only a few fragments of texts that were written in the Hungarian language. Perhaps the best known among them is a bilingual Latin-Hungarian funeral oration from the early thirteenth century.

Education was under the control of the Catholic Church and was limited to learning rudimentary Latin and a modicum of theological, rhetorical, and musical skills needed to perform Christian services. Before the eighteenth century, attempts to establish full-fledged universities on Hungarian soil proved to be short-lived. Learning beyond the middle grades had to be sought abroad, at Italian, French, or German universities, where secular, humanist approaches were beginning to make inroads. Graduates of these universities were the pioneers of literary and scientific activities in Hungarian. They were also the first secular men (less frequently women) of letters. Going beyond the limits of their religious education, many of them became wandering intellectuals in the service of lords or rulers, since there was no literate public to support their literary activities. Among these freelancers, Sebestyén Tinódi, the lutanist chronicler of the sixteenth-century anti-Ottoman struggle, stands out. The outstanding men of letters in late Renaissance Hungary, however, were of more privileged status: Janus Pannonius, the learned humanist cleric and one of King Mátyás's closest advisers, who recorded his impressions in witty Latin poetry; Bálint Balassi, the dispossessed aristocrat who used Hungarian to craft lyrical poems about his amorous attachments and his soldiering, which took him to a battlefield death; and Miklós Zrinyi, the *ban* of Croatia and daring military commander of the southern borderlands, who penned epics dedicated to the nation's defense and sharply worded prose on public affairs.

The teachings of the Protestant reformers, especially Calvin, reached Hungary in the middle of the sixteenth century and spread rapidly. There was no need to be a Roman Catholic to be distinguished from the invading Muslim Turks (who were generally tolerant of nonbelievers; nonbelievers, after all, were the *reaya* [flock] whose taxes maintained the sultan's magnificence and power). During the sixteenth and seventeenth centuries, Calvinism came to be seen as the true Hungarian religion, while Roman

Catholicism increasingly was identified with the Habsburg Empire. The majority of Hungarians became Calvinists, which meant being both a non-Muslim and an opponent of the Austrian-German Habsburgs at the same time. Protestant organizations also took over some of the culture-preserving functions of the Roman Catholic Church. Not surprisingly, successive Habsburg governments considered Calvinist Hungarians especially rebellious and independent minded.

The Protestant Reformation also energized Hungarian writing. Beginning with the translation of the Bible (first accomplished by the Calvinist Gáspár Heltai in 1551, and soon to be followed by Catholic translations) and religious texts, professional writers of hymns, homilies, and religious propaganda appeared among Catholics as well as among followers of the new denominations. The spreading practice of book printing (the first application of which was a short-lived shop set up in Buda in 1472) brought literacy to more and more commoners, though schooling was still far from universal.

The virtual state of war, imposed by the Turkish military presence as much as by the struggle between the various domestic factions, slowed Hungary's cultural progress. It was only after the Ottoman occupation ended in 1699, and decades later, when the anti-Habsburg *kuruc* struggles came to an end, that Hungarians could consider rebuilding and reorganizing their country. The independence campaigns led by Thököly and Rákóczi produced a large amount of rebellious songs, a few issues of a periodical publication, and touching philosophical memoirs by the exiled leaders.

There was, however, a new threat represented by the Habsburg court's announced aim to remake Hungarians into German-speaking, Catholic, and obedient subjects. The Catholic Counter-Reformation succeeded to a great extent, and the resources of the devastated country just as quickly came under the control of Habsburg or pro-Habsburg aristocrats. Indeed, much of seventeenth- and eighteenth-century Hungary's culture—from postsecondary education to scientific work and theater—was shaped on the baroque Austrian-German model. During the heated seventeenth-century struggle between Protestants and Catholics, many writers devoted their talent to producing religious texts, supporting their denomination and attacking the opposition. Among the best known of these writers was Péter Pázmány, who was archbishop of Esztergom, a patron of Hungarian education, and a particularly effective polemicist.

Transylvania, Hungary's easternmost province, escaped direct Ottoman occupation by virtue of its location and skillful diplomats. As a consequence, it did not suffer huge population losses, and it remained a relatively wealthy, orderly, and even powerful political entity. It preserved some "ancient freedoms" for many of its citizens, wise and enlightened government practices, a relatively peaceful coexistence among its ethnic groups, and a considerable degree of religious tolerance in an increasingly intolerant region. As a result, Transylvania became a bridge between the various neighboring cultures, a haven for refugees, and a place where such cultural activities as book printing, the funding of schools, scientific research, and even artistic, literary, and musical undertakings were favored and patronized. This golden age of Transylvania nurtured multiethnic urban centers, accomplished scientists, and a number of internationally recognized printers.

After surviving between "two pagans" (as a contemporary Hungarian writer described the Ottoman and Habsburg threats to his nation's independence), Hungarians stubbornly resisted all Habsburg attempts to turn them into German speakers. At times, during the kuruc campaigns of Thököly and Rákóczi, they even accepted Turkish alliance to frustrate Vienna's imperial plans. There was a rationale behind such an "anti-European" behavior. While the Ottoman occupation was exploitative and often brutal, turning all non-Muslims into second-class citizens, it interfered little with the Hungarians' way of community life, their religious practices, or their cultural activities. Conversion to Islam was rarely attempted by force, nor were Hungarians required to learn to speak Turkish. As for the Habsburgs, their claim to the Hungarian throne was legally sound, and the role of Habsburg-led Christian armies in the country's liberation was undeniable. It was also recognized by many Hungarians that Habsburg efforts to modernize and "civilize" Hungary had the potential to improve the everyday life of its population. In spite of this, the growing Austrian influence on Hungarian life, bolstered by the growing Habsburg military-administrative control, soon came to be considered as far more dangerous to national identity than the Ottoman threat ever was.

Recurring struggles against armed Hungarian insurgents and the stubborn legalistic obstructions raised by the Hungarian county administrations prompted the Viennese court to moderate its goal of Germanizing the country, choosing instead to enlist the aristocracy in its empire building. With the court's promise to respect the nation's "time-honored" institutions, the lords of Hungary were allowed to maintain their feudal practices (including serfdom, which kept the rural poor tied to the land and subject to harsh exploitation) in exchange for which they were expected to become loyal to the ruling house. Since many of the aristocrats, not all of whom were ethnic Magyars, benefited from the redistribution of properties after the Turks were expelled, the bargain was not difficult to make. There were even certain elements of this cooperation that ended up benefiting the Hungarian language and literature. Empress Maria Theresa gathered a number of young nobles from Hungary into a guard unit. The intent was to civilize and tame these young men by exposing them to the cosmopolitan life of the court, but a number of these former guards decided to transplant what they had learned in Vienna to their native soil. Their writings may have been imitative of baroque sentimentality, but they wrote the first novels, dramas, and scientific books in Hungarian.

The bargain prevailed until the 1780s, when the Habsburg court, motivated by a combination of rationalist governing principles and absolutist tenets of royal authority, mounted an attack against the Hungarian language and culture. This was the wrong time to irritate the already suspicious Magyars and widen the rift between them and Vienna. Nurtured by the ideas of the Enlightenment and

Mathematics and Sciences

Scholarly research and discovery have a long tradition in Hungary that began at the end of the fifteenth century and gained worldwide recognition starting in the eighteenth century. The Bolyais, Farkas Bolyai (1775–1856) and later his son, János Bolyai (1802–1860), pioneers of non-Euclidean geometry, achieved international recognition for their work. Hungarians assumed an increasingly active role in scientific and intellectual life.

Loránd Eötvös (1848–1919), after whom the University of Budapest is named, was the greatest Hungarian scientist of theoretical and experimental physics. Eötvös's research resulted in the so-called Eötvös Law (1866), which Albert Einstein considered a pillar of his theory of relativity. For many years Eötvös studied the problem of gravity and designed the world-renowned Eötvös torsion balance (pendulum), which is still used all over the world for gravity measurements and for geophysical explorations.

In the late nineteenth century two Hungarian schools of mathematics gained prominence: one group worked at the Technical University of Budapest, another at the University of Kolozsvár-Cluj (which later moved to Szeged). Perhaps the best-known representative of this generation was János (von) Neumann (1903–1957), a 1927 Budapest Ph.D. who later joined Princeton's Institute for Advanced Studies. He developed the binary code, the basic element of modern computer operations, pioneered research in quantum mechanics, and participated in work leading to the development of the atomic bomb. Others in the same field included John G. Kemény (1926–1994), a mathematician on the Manhattan Project, one of Einstein's assistants, and codeveloper of BASIC computer language, and Pál Erdős (1913–1997), whose interest was focused on the theory of numbers and the calculus of probabilities.

Three Hungarian born physicists, Edward Teller, Leó Szilárd, and Eugene P. Wigner, worked closely with Enrico Fermi. The four of them persuaded Albert Einstein to write his historic letter in 1939 to President Franklin Roosevelt that led to the start of the Manhattan Project, making them the primary architects of the atomic age. Teller was later instrumental in the development of the hydrogen bomb, submarine-launched rockets, and the conceptualization of the Star Wars missile defense system, while Szilárd became an advocate for the peaceful use of atomic energy and the international control of nuclear weapons, efforts for which he received the Atoms for Peace Award in 1959.

romanticism, a new political attitude—modern political nationalism—appeared on the scene. The 1784 language ordinance of Emperor Joseph II ordered that all official business in the Habsburg Empire be conducted in the German language. There were good reasons for issuing this edict: the unification and modernization of the multilingual empire and the need to rationalize the state and municipal administrations justified such a step from the point of view of enlightened absolutism. Nevertheless, the imperial edict awakened the national pride of the nation's intellectual elite.

A broader awakening of national identity was also taking place. It was prepared by the continent-wide thirst for knowledge and self-knowledge known as the Enlightenment, combined with ideas engendered by the French Revolution and the attitude of romanticism, with its emphasis on "the spirit of peoples." The first two were applicable in the sciences and in politics, while romanticism championed the cause of cultural diversity, as expressed by the multitude of languages. It became fashionable to use Hungarian, not just at home but in writing for the public.

It was found, however, that the long underutilized and marginalized Hungarian language was not fully capable of conveying the notions of the times. A few committed intellectuals set out to remedy this by initiating an energetic language reform movement, the major cultural initiative of the 1820s, unconnected to any religion. Led by the most enlightened minds of the times, first among them Ferenc Kazinczy, the movement promoted the rediscovery of ancient Magyar words and the creation of new ones in accordance with the sense and music of the language, and the use of this renovated language in all spheres of life. The efforts of the language innovators were opposed, and their excesses often ridiculed, but their ranks were swelled by the best writers and publicists of the times, and they proved to be victorious in a few decades. One gem of the reform movement is Hungary's national anthem, written by Ferenc Kölcsey, a moving masterpiece that stood the test of time very well.

The reformed and invigorated Hungarian language was put enthusiastically to use by the great generation of poets and writers during the century's middle decades. Central among them was Sándor Petőfi, whose name still evokes the native genius of Hungarian poetry. A descendant of a lower middle-class rural family, thoroughly assimilated into Hungarian life although of Slavic descent, Petőfi was the quintessential poet of his age. Somewhat of a social misfit, he dedicated his entire short life to poetry. Folk elements provided much of his early inspiration, combined with sentimental, but always fresh, themes of love. When he joined a circle of like-minded dissidents in Pest, who came to be known as the Young Hungary movement, his lyricism took on an increasingly radical republican edge,

Sándor Petőfi *[the poet],* in His Study, *by György Vastagh. (Archivo Iconografico, S.A./Corbis)*

which fit the spirit of the 1840s. His poem "National Song" is thought to be one of the sparks that set off the bloodless revolution of 15 March 1848, and Petőfi's name is as closely connected with the subsequent war of independence as those of Kossuth or the generals. Fittingly, the "comet of the revolution" was killed on a battlefield, probably by a Russian lancer, during the final days of Hungary's anti-Habsburg struggle. His poetry, easy to recite and difficult to translate, remains central to appreciating Hungarian literature.

Hungary's men of letters supported the revolutionary cause almost without exception, even if some of them lost hope, or accepted defeat, sooner than others. Brooding over the lost cause of national independence remained the central theme of cultural life for decades. Perhaps to explore the wealth of the Magyar language, or perhaps to get away from dismal reality and boast instead with past glories, a full-blown nationalist-romantic attitude made its appearance in literature, as well as in the music and arts of Hungary. Wealthy patrons and an enthusiastic public supported the creation of oversized paintings of historical events that still decorate public buildings, and the numerous Hungarocentric musical compositions of the period. In literature, the most popular and prolific representative of this escapist trend was Mór Jókai, who produced more than one hundred volumes of fiction in his long life. His novels and stories have been widely translated and remain on every Hungarian's reading list.

To complicate matters, the Kingdom's non-Magyar coinhabitants discovered their own ethnic identities at just about the same time as the ruling Magyars did. Their demands, in such areas as language rights or local school issues, were often diametrically opposed to perceived Hungarian national interests. At times, in fact, they appeared to threaten the continued existence of historical Hungary. The stage was thus set for bitter interethnic struggle in various areas of public life. Yet, until the mid-nineteenth century, the Hungarian public remained quite tolerant toward national minorities and their cultural aspirations. After 1849, however, things changed. The nationalities, especially the Romanians and the Croats, played an active military role in defeating the Hungarian revolutionary cause, and this was long remembered. Magyar nationalists now called for an assertive program of assimilating ethnic groups into Hungarian culture. Some of the best minds called for moderation and tolerance in this regard, but their views were seldom heeded, with disastrous consequences for interethnic relations in the coming decades.

The late-nineteenth-century modernization of Hungary (now as the larger half of the Dual Monarchy created by the 1867 compromise) brought both positive and negative results. Railroads and factories were built and an excellent industrial system for cloth and food production was created. The cities, especially Budapest, developed rapidly in the demographic, economic, and cultural sense alike. At the same time, the nation's social problems remained unsolved: the rural population lived in neglect and misery, and the common nobility—traditionally considered to be the nation's patriotic backbone—became the impoverished, déclassé gentry. Some of their members were absorbed by the civil service bureaucracy as low-level officials, while others became employees in business or manufacturing firms or managers of estates owned by aristocrats and foreign, largely Jewish absentee landlords. Hungary's gentry thus came to form a perpetually discontented segment of society. Its members considered themselves the traditional nation-making elements of the population. In their frequently and loudly expressed opinion, the "alien" industrialists and financiers (many of them foreign born or Jewish) marginalized and oppressed "true Magyars," and hastened the destruction of Hungarian culture. As they saw it, that culture could be found only in the villages, whose dwellers were "bravely struggling" for survival against the "alien" cities.

Budapest was the proud capital of dualist Hungary, with its smokestacks, cafés, ever taller apartment buildings, electric streetcars, and a population that in 1910 was more than one-quarter Jewish, German, and otherwise non-Magyar. Moreover, the city's cultural and intellectual life was decisively altered. Budapest was now a metropolis, where a well-educated citizenry sought out its own kind of news and entertainment. The scores of daily newspapers and theaters, along with the clubs, cafés, and other signs of modern urban life turned the nation's capital into a separate, at times indeed contrasting, entity in the heart of the country.

Budapest's artists and intellectuals held the key to modernizing the taste and outlook of Hungarian readers, acquainting them with new styles and radically different attitudes concerning various aspects of their society. They gravitated toward newly established journals of arts and opinion, of which *Nyugat* (West) had the greatest impact. Started in 1906, it immediately attracted a talented corps of contributors, among them Endre Ady, Hungary's preeminent modern poet, who broke with all traditions in form and content alike. He and his followers broadened the scope of Hungarian literature, leaving behind the adoration of rural (populist) traditions, and often braving the extreme limits of the public's tolerance on such matters as religion or patriotism. While most of them were ethnic Magyars, of gentry background, their writings appeared in publications often financed or edited by non-Magyars. The new bourgeoisie of the capital was generous in supporting culture, but it wanted its own culture. This enabled the traditionalists to set up the dichotomy between Budapest and "real Hungary" (a depiction that is sometimes detectable even in today's attitudes).

By the twentieth century, the conservative national movement, by now fossilized into formalism, was still in official command of cultural life. The man who for decades was recognized as the leading writer of semifeudal Hungary was Ferenc Herczeg, a "gentleman writer" who began by describing the life and pastimes of the urban gentry—a devil-may-care life lived with elegant nonchalance—and he described it with the facility of a confirmed insider. He was genuinely favored by this class, which went so far as to identify itself with the nation. It is their position and problems that we see reflected and solved in Herczeg's (once widely read) historical novels and plays. Bitterly opposed to any new literary trend, Herczeg was lauded as "author laureate" of interwar Hungary. His most durable works are a number of short stories, written with a technique similar to Maupassant's, in which he gives a realistic portrayal of his environment. By this time, however, a new Hungarian culture—still fraught with contradictions—was already in the making.

The urbanizing wave of 1890 produced only initial and ambiguous results—a ferment was aroused, a restless searching for new ways; the rising Hungarian urban bourgeoisie found its voice. At the outset, the new trends found a literary organ in the review *A Hét* (The Week), started in 1890 under the editorship of József Kiss, a successful Jewish poet. Although uneven in content, it managed to rally more than one writer seeking a way out of the suffocating atmosphere of formalism that overhung the literary scene at the end of the century. Intellectually alert and lively in tone, marked by an urbanism that mocked at rigid authority, *A Hét* strove, in essence, to create a modern, big-city literature as opposed to the manorial provincialism of the traditionalist school.

Throughout Europe, a dominant trend and school of thought of the period was naturalism, calling for a more profound, unvarnished, raw representation of life, a greater emphasis on psychological analysis, a physiological and biological outlook, free thought, antireligious views, and materialism. The new poetry was characterized largely by a loosening of old forms and manners, and a freshness, lightness, and urbanism of content. Among the forerunners of modern Hungarian culture we find writers, each speaking in his own individual voice, who were representatives of critical realism, cultivating chiefly the psychological short story. The careers of nearly all of them, after promising starts in the last decade of the nineteenth or the early years of the twentieth century, were soon to be broken off as some died young, others lost interest, or their ambition spent itself.

The modern era of Hungarian literature, which began to take shape around the turn of the century, is usually regarded as dating from 1905 when Endre Ady first appeared on the scene with his entirely new intonation in poetry. A fermentation began in cultural life, inseparable from the social turmoil. The Dual Monarchy was caught in constant crisis; the heterogeneous economic and social structure raised burning questions for which there was no solution; the poor peasantry began to stir; the organized working class gathered strength and a radical group formed within the middle class, small in number but aggressive and consistently fighting for bourgeois transformation.

The pioneers of this cultural revival sprang from different strata of the bourgeoisie and middle class. They followed diverse aims but were unanimous in their opposition to the derivative flatness and chauvinism, the sentimentality and the lack of higher aspirations that characterized the dominant national literature; they were out for more advanced trends instead. They had a healthy interest in foreign works of philosophy, literature, music, and the arts. Owing to Hungary's peculiar historical and social background, many of the successive trends in the arts and literature of developed bourgeois countries made their impact felt simultaneously; Nietzsche and Bergson, Spencer and the positivists, Baudelaire and the French symbolist poets, the naturalists and their opponents, the soft-toned fin de siècle lyrics of Vienna and the slum poetry of German naturalism, all arrived and found followers at about the same time. A strong influence on the prose genres was exercised by the great critical realists—Tolstoy, Ibsen, and France; no less was the effect of Dostoevsky and Zola. Yet all this was not mere imitation; the writers of the period were consciously adhering to, and wished to carry on, the traditions of Hungarian literature. Interest revived for everything that was truly national and genuinely vernacular. From the mannerism of the end-of-century sham populism, creative intellectuals turned toward the original treasures of Hungarian peasant culture and of Hungary's past, to find those models of harmony and perfection that had ceased to exist in their own epoch.

The world outlook and political consciousness of the new literary movement was very diverse. Some of the writers were motivated by no more than a search for new tones, new flavors, new sensations, new styles. There were those who realized that the revolution in letters heralded a social transformation, and that the literary tumult was necessarily linked with ideas and was part of the fight for a new Hungary.

Some only fought for the consistent application of liberal views, for full freedom of writing; others strove for a ruthless exposure of reality. Often these conflicting aspirations would be apparent not only in the same review or within the same literary coterie, but also in the various stages of the careers of individual artists, writers, and critics. Two tendencies were distinguishable, both in the review *Nyugat* and in the new literary movement: one of a more bellicose spirit, bent on politics, readily responding to changes, influenced by bourgeois radicalism, interested in socialism and emotionally siding with plebeian trends; the other leaning rather to liberal conservatism, with a nimble sense for everything new and artistic. The first can be characterized by the names of Endre Ady and Zsigmond Móricz, the second by those of Mihály Babits and Dezső Kosztolányi.

In its critical approach, however, the movement was lacking a defined and consistent program; its partisans and critics (Ernő Osvát, Aladár Schöpflin, Lajos Hatvany) saw the essence of their mission as waging war against conservative nationalism and made a point of linking the fresh values of the movement to the mainstream of national literature, and were otherwise advocating liberal views, the free evolution and self-assertion of the individual. The main combatants of *Nyugat,* their personalities and works, with Ady as their leader, became the subject of heated and loud polemics. Some of the conservatives borrowed weapons from the political armory (with charges like "high treason" and "alien mentality") and, to a lesser degree, fought with arguments of literary aestheticism.

The central figure and star of Hungarian literature, in fact of the entire cultural scene, was Ady, the greatest creative genius of Hungarian poetry after Sándor Petőfi. He was born into a family of lesser nobility, and received a Protestant education imbued with a passion for national independence in the *kuruc* tradition. He went to Debrecen to study law, but soon took up journalism. He was introduced to the world of theatre, literature, and journalism. A turning point in his life came at the end of 1899 when he went to Nagyvárad (today Oradea, Romania). In this bustling and spirited city, whose intellectual, political, and social life went far beyond that of the provinces, the backwardness of Hungary came home to Ady as a startling realization. He became first a convinced liberal, then an increasingly militant radical. Here also he emerged as a brilliant journalist with a sharp eye and farsighted knowledge. He came to represent Hungarian political journalism waging a spirited battle against chauvinism, obscurantism, and ignorance.

At first, Ady wrote the light, cynical parlor poetry of the fin de siècle, but his second volume showed his future greatness. In the summer of 1903, after many passing affairs, he fell in love with the attractive wife of a local businessman, Léda. Theirs was a great, sensuous, tormenting love and it gave birth to hundreds of outstanding poems. It was with Léda's support that Ady went to Paris in 1904 and in 1906–1907. The trips were liberating and stimulating; he saw the justification of what he had been trying to formulate at home. Those were the years when the French radicals began their secularizing campaign and seeing this affected Ady's ongoing dispute with clericalism. He also came to see the contradictions of bourgeois democracy and the controlling role of wealth. At times this realization would make him embrace Nietzsche and plunge him into disillusion and despair; at other moments it would make him feel that social conditions (in France and Hungary alike) called for radical political changes.

After his Paris visits, Ady's verse was entirely different from anything that Hungarian poetry had produced up to that time in both tone and message. His first volume of this type of verse, *Új versek* (New Poems; 1906), was followed by a rapid succession of other innovative volumes, along with a torrent of short stories and newspaper articles. What was the striking novelty of his writing? Ady's was a great self-contained world, his language was powerful and individual; the wide range of his themes included the heroes, ideas, and movements of Hungarian national history, including the disappointing contemporary vision of the "Hungarian wasteland"; the agony of the poet in a materialist world, fighting a "Great Lord with the Boar's Head." Another group of themes included the thousand and one aspects of love, the unashamed presentation of his love for Léda, songs of all the warped complexities of love, and evocations of passing, sensual love affairs. Another strand was that of poems evoking death, fleeting time, downfall, fear, and solitude, verses that conveyed the restlessness, strain, and worries of the modern big city dweller, seeking refuge in God or quarreling with God. Two new themes of crucial importance were the proclamation of his historical mission and a repeated evocation of his own personality. Ady's poetry was at the same time modern and ancient; it was also in the mainstream of the latest European intellectual trends and rooted in the time-honored core of Magyar tradition. The richness of his verbal flow, and the multitude of his own coinages or revivals from the archaic vocabulary of the language combined into a fascinating idiom, unlike that of anybody else.

The other outstanding figure of twentieth-century Hungarian literature, also a member of the *Nyugat* circle, was Zsigmond Móricz, a master of Hungarian prose. After attending a distinguished Calvinist school, he became a divinity student and studied law, only to end up as a low-paid, conservative-minded country journalist in metropolitan surroundings. He was thirty when the *Nyugat* published his first short story "Hét krajcár" (Seven Pennies), making Móricz a celebrated writer. Ady's poetry and later friendship gave him stimulus and guidance, while his own stodgy, considerate temperament hailed the ardent self-consuming genius of the poet. From the writing of "Seven Pennies" until his death, Móricz's output was unbroken; he published one of the most voluminous and most impressive oeuvres in Hungarian literature. He attracted notice primarily as a new portrayer of peasant life, evoking the Hungarian village writhing in the stranglehold of the estate system, a world overshadowed by the figures of his peasant heroes. Yet some of Moricz's best novels and short stories portrayed the life of the Hungarian gentry at the turn of the century—a picture of decay going on behind a glittering facade. The effect thus produced was one of extraordinary authenticity.

Others from the *Nyugat* circle included Margit Kaffka, Hungary's first woman writer of note, a friend of Ady, who made her debut as a poet in the fin de siècle style. Subsequently, she took to writing short stories, intrigued by the problems that faced the modern woman—moral, social, human, and vocational problems. Endowed with great sensitivity and a gift for portraying the emotional life of her characters, she evolved an individual impressionistic staccato style and a way of creating atmosphere, introducing subjectivity into her description of objective processes, such as the decline of rural gentlefolk and the succession of generations. Hers was an impressionistic idiom, peculiarly emotional and charged with tension, attentive of details, and evocative. In November 1918 she died in the influenza pandemic that swept across Europe.

Among the poets of the period, Árpád Tóth stands out as a masterful lyricist and one of the most likable and original figures of the *Nyugat* generation. His writing speaks in the voice of a quiet, melancholy man, longing to find refuge in other, imaginary, worlds. Ady's tone found a continuation of great fidelity in the poetry of Gyula Juhász, a poet of landscapes, portraits, descriptions, and moods condensed into sonnets with strong pictorial quality, a keen sense of color and many ties with the traditions of Hungarian history and literature. His poetry of hopeless desire—the devoted pieces of the Anna Cycle addressed to the distant woman—are among the most often quoted masterpieces of Hungarian lyric poetry.

Not all *Nyugat* poets resembled Ady in tone or in lifestyle. In fact, two of his greatest contemporaries represented different trends. Mihály Babits was a great poet, novelist, essayist, and translator, the prime authority in Hungarian letters during the 1930s and an outstanding humanist. Fitting in well with the mildly conservative Hungarian intelligentsia at the turn of the century, marked by respect for classical culture and holding liberal views that had taken on a conservative complexion, the young provincial teacher believed in art for art's sake. He was a virtuoso in playing with styles, a master of verse forms displaying high artistry in his use of language, a thinking poet with a philosophical turn of mind, a master in bold and unusual verse constructions, and in the use of words. He avoided Ady's radical fervor and desire for action. In politics too, he leaned toward the conservative side; the mob scared and repulsed him. After the tragedies of World War I and the resulting Trianon treaty, he withdrew to the liberal-conservative stand of politically disinterested observer who entrenched himself behind aesthetic arguments. Babits came to the defense of all that was positive in culture and literature against challenges from the political side.

Dezső Kosztolányi's oeuvre is the most extensive and, in its influence, the strongest after that of Babits, so distant from Ady. He was born into provincial intelligentsia, the son of a teacher proud of his noble ancestry. He also took up journalism and settled in Budapest as a fashionable publicist. His poems—colorful, musical, and embodying a facility and high artistry of form—display all the requisites of the art nouveau. Kosztolányi was a sovereign artist and knew the secrets of the Hungarian language, which he loved passionately. In his novels and especially in his short stories, the best Hungarian linguistic heritage is allied with the polish and clarity of French; the pointed sentence construction of the early twentieth century is combined with sensuously colorful images. He was one of the most zealous adherents and propagators in Hungarian letters of the Freudian achievement.

Frigyes Karinthy achieved wide popularity as a humorous writer, even while he was one of the most versatile, many-sided talents of *Nyugat*. Born into a family of Budapest intellectuals and growing up as the prototype of a city dweller, the principal scenes of his life were the café, the editorial office, and the street. The meaning and essence of his work was to criticize and reassess the philosophy, social conditions, manners, and morality of his times, with an outlook that was a blend of French rationalism, Freudian interpretation, and respect for sciences. Philosophical thinking marks his short stories, reflections, and novels.

Gyula Krúdy was a truly singular figure. Born into the gentry, the impoverished provincial nobility, his life was that of the struggling Budapest journalist and author. He created a prose style of his own in which "atmosphere" overshadows plot and character development, and construction is dissolved in a web of reflections and rambling digressions, giving readers a peculiar dream world where present and past are blurred and blended together, and the characters lose their contours to dissolve into local color.

Running parallel to the *Nyugat* movement there existed, on the one hand, a more pungent, sardonic, militantly outspoken style giving utterance to the lower-middle-class outlook, as well as a neo-Catholic literary movement, and a type of Hungarian drama that attracted great popularity abroad. Ferenc Molnár was the most gifted among these playwrights. He started as a journalist, but soon became one of the best-known and most sought-after writers for the stage; his plays scored one success after another both abroad and at home. After World War I, he spent more and more time abroad, and he lived in New York until his death. Molnár was a many-sided author; his short stories and light sketches are the works of a sharp-eyed, perceptive man capable of caustic satire. His writing is stamped with some cynicism and, at the same time, a measure of often spurious sentimentalism. His most popular prose work is the much translated *A Pál-utcai fiúk* (The Paul Street Boys), a novel for adolescents that, by its unstudied and objective treatment of its subject, poignantly captures all the beauty and torment of childhood. Molnár's rise as a successful dramatist began with *Liliom* in 1909, a piece that is half drama, half mystery play, with the local color typical of Budapest in those days. (Based on this play, the musical *Carousel* was a great success on Broadway.)

Although many of Hungary's leading men of letters voiced criticism of the country's social order, few became committed leftists. This was especially true after the 133-day Republic of Councils in 1919, during which Hungarians gained their first and lasting impression of communism. One early figure of the organized socialist movement was Lajos Kassák, who roamed all over Europe, working in factories. He developed an individual style, reminiscent of those of Italian futurists and German expressionists. He became a revolutionary anarchist, a maverick both in literature and in politics, fiercely opposing both the Social Democrats and the meandering policies of the Communists.

Sports and Games

Centuries of living on the steppes of central Eurasia kept alive in Hungarians the urge to compete in physical activities, as these skills often ensured survival. This innate predisposition was encouraged throughout the centuries. During the Middle Ages, horseback riding and the use of various weapons was widely practiced. Physical education was among the earliest subjects introduced at the country's schools, and the most popular leaders of the nineteenth-century reform era, István Széchenyi, Lajos Kossuth, and Miklós Wesselényi, were themselves practicing athletes. The Physical Training Institute (later to become the College for Physical Education) was established in the nineteenth century to train coaches and athletes alike. Not surprisingly, when the Olympic games were revived in 1896, seven Hungarians competed against athletes of thirteen other nations and won two Gold, one Silver, and two Bronze Medals.

The tradition continued, even during periods of economic hardship and political oppression. In addition to seeking personal distinction (a kind of "nobility"), being a winner in sports also became a means through which young Hungarians could escape the limitations and restrictions in their lives. During the decades of Communist rule, for example, athletic skill qualified one to become a member of teams traveling to Western countries, a rare and coveted privilege.

Hungarians have been enthusiastic supporters of the modern Olympic Games, one of the few global venues in which the size or wealth of a nation does not necessarily determine the outcome of competition. During the first hundred years of the Games, Hungary won a total of 141 Gold, 123 Silver, and 151 Bronze Medals. The country's athletes have been particularly successful in water polo, soccer (although not recently), women's and men's swimming, boxing (with László Papp winning Gold Medals at three consecutive games), Greco-Roman wrestling, men's gymnastics, men's and women's fencing, the pentathlon, kayak and canoe racing, and table tennis.

The game of chess was brought to Hungary by Beatrix, queen of King Mátyás (1458–1490), who was an outstanding player of her time. In modern times, players such as József Szén and Géza Maróczy led the Hungarian team to several world championships. In recent decades, the Polgár sisters have achieved great success in world tournaments.

Several athletes of Hungarian birth or descent have become well-known in the United States, including the golfer Julius Boros, the Super Bowl champion New York Jets quarterback, "Broadway Joe" Namath, Larry Csonka of the Miami Dolphins, the place-kicking Gogolák brothers, the tennis star Monica Seles (Szeles), and the championmaking gymnastics coach Béla Károlyi.

Breeding and training dogs can be seen as a sport, even though Hungary's canines have more often been considered useful work mates than pets. The best-known Hungarian breed in the United States is the puli, a medium-sized dynamo with long black hair matted into dreadlocks, and a perpetual urge to herd something. A larger look-alike of the puli is the white komondor, also used for tending flocks as well as a formidable watchdog. The kuvasz, with retriever-like white hair of medium length, is a popular rural household dog. The vizsla, with smooth, reddish-gold hair and thoughtful eyes, is an excellent hunting companion, as is the agár, Hungary's variant of the speedy whippet, and the Transylvanian kopó, a black-and-white medium-size pointer.

Some Hungarian writers hailed the Bourgeois Revolution of 1918 and the Council Republic of 1919, looking to them for the solution to national and social problems. However, most of them became disillusioned even before those 133 days came to pass. In a way, the response to the Hungarian Council Republic became a cultural touchstone; every trend and every group took a stand for or against it.

A lost war, distorted revolutions, a harsh period of counterrevolutionary terror, and the overriding tragedy of the country's dismemberment by the Trianon peace treaty was a burdensome legacy that marked the interwar cultural life of Hungary. In 1920 a kingless kingdom of Hungary was established and consolidated, giving a strongly feudal character to the state, even though some capitalist development did take place. The establishment was conservative and proreligion; old prejudices and privileges were now mingling with chauvinism and a rising anti-Semitism.

In cultural life, as in other areas, the best minds of Hungary were seeking answers to some of the great problems of the age. Their struggle assumed various forms. Some saw the solution in improving Hungary's economic and social structure and a continuation of the bourgeois revolution; others in a land reform; yet others called for the demolition of the obsolete framework of the Hungarian state body. These trends dominated the culture of the period; they left their mark on almost all writing, whether political essay, descriptive poem, reportage, or pieces of sociography or journalism.

A host of writers, bringing a new mentality and coming from new social strata, appeared on the scene. A few self-educated writers from the poor peasantry and the working class had already entered the nation's cultural scene earlier. But it was during the interwar period when Hungary saw the rise of popular talent. A few of them came from the industrial working class, but far more from the ranks of land workers, poor peasants, and small farmers; they brought with them the gift of expressing deeply rooted emotions and representing formerly unknown domains of reality. Their emergence from the social depths did not necessarily coincide with a progressive world outlook, and certainly not with any radical ideology. But they combined their experience of life with awareness, and sometimes with progressive ideas, and gave birth to grand compositions in verse and prose.

This was also a time of striving after new forms appropriate to the demands of the times; it involved a more profound and differentiated rendering of the human frame of mind and behavior, a reshaping of literature to match the conditions of a changed world. All this led to thriving new forms in various genres such as the novel, the short story, the analytical poem, and so on.

Upon closer inspection, three main trends were distinguishable. The first was a trend toward the unsophisticated, the genuine, and the straightforward. A sincere desire was at work here to renew the means of expression in the arts and literature, to make them more creative by the addition of something that is at once new and old, simple and peculiarly intricate. This trend, which had its European counterparts, was associated in Hungary with two political drives (sometimes allied, more often divergent): a plebeian democratic movement and a right-leaning nationalist one.

The second trend ran parallel to European avant-garde movements. Its aim was to extend the expressive power of language; introducing new domains into the scope of literary representation; giving poetry a multiplicity of facets, rendered with greater passion and ardor; adding a measure of lyricism to the novel and a grain of epic to verse; setting off and giving greater prominence to the poet's ego or merging it in the community. Although the influence of the avant-garde movement on Hungarian literature was less decisive in determining its physiognomy than it was on the French or even the Czech, the results and achievements, viewed collectively from a higher angle, have left their traces with almost every writer of the age.

The third main trend was that of the analyzing intellect. It manifested itself in lyrics as a leaning toward philosophy, a strong bent for contemplation, a subtle analysis of the poet's personality, and a ready response to the slightest impulse, emotional or intellectual; partly in prose as the psychoanalytical approach and a more differentiated portrayal of milieu in the analytical novel. Scholarship was characteristic of these late *Nyugat* followers, sometimes called "a generation of essayists."

However, the greatest men of the epoch, who expressed the essential message of their times more convincingly than other contemporaries, were also receptive to many diverse trends and responsive to most new ideas. In Attila József and Béla Bartók, we find a popular simplicity of approach combined with avant-garde revolts and an analyzing intellect, all summed up and resolved in a classical harmony. Still, the official culture of Horthy's Hungary harkened back to the nationalist school of the late nineteenth century, in order to avoid the most radical aspects of the Nyugat followers. This traditional trend of Hungarian prose writing found a continuation in Ferenc Móra. He strived for a deeper and more diversified knowledge of Hungarian country life, of which he was a masterful interpreter endowed with the gifts of a fully individual style, mild irony, profound erudition, and a rare sense of humor.

The "third generation" of the *Nyugat* made its appearance in the 1930s under difficult conditions: the growing pressure of fascism and an increasingly dehumanized world bore down on its members. They arrived equipped with considerable learning in world literature and a high degree of responsiveness to foreign cultures, which suggested translation as an almost natural form of expression. By means of translations and essays, they tried to introduce into Hungarian culture and learning the assets of bourgeois literature as a quasi-defense against the cruelty of their age. Their ways branched off in many directions: some withdrew into splendid isolation, others sought refuge in irrationalism. Several eminent members of this generation were murdered by Nazism. The most gifted survivors, after periods of varying length, came perhaps grudgingly to approve of socialism.

A poet who is characteristic of this generation is Sándor Weöres. He was a boy when he first published his poems, and soon came to impress everyone by his superb mastery of form in almost every style and tone. A man of universal erudition, he translated everything from ancient Indian texts to T. S. Eliot. The basic themes of his poetry are the total senselessness of life and society, tinged with nihilism, trying to find consolation in irrationalist philosophies and pseudo-Oriental myths. World War II, and the years that have elapsed since, have confirmed his aloofness. He was a brilliant versifier and a great master of form; he has created an almost entirely new rhythmic pattern and held up bright and undreamed of possibilities inherent in Hungarian verse. Unique are his torrents of color and scene, his gift for creating myth and atmosphere, his evocative power.

A unique figure in Hungary's interwar cultural life was Dezső Szabó. Except for Marxist socialism, he advocated every major intellectual trend of his age and, as an impelling character with a keen interest in politics, he exerted considerable influence, especially on youth. Originally he prepared for a linguistic career and was an admirer of French literature. After spending a year in Paris, he became an assistant schoolmaster in the provinces, a young man bursting with energy, self-esteem, and a sense of mission. From a clerical anti-Semite, he changed into an extremist radical; after philology and politics, his interest turned to literature, and he joined the editorial staff of *Nyugat* in 1911. In his political writings, he put his finger on the crucial issues of his time. The philosophical foundation of Szabó's writings was a combination of Nietzscheanism and positivism, marked by extreme antirationalism, antidemocratic views, and a yearning for a "new unity." He was against capitalism but his response to it was a desire to turn back the clock. Eventually racialism came to dominate his thoughts, the idolization of the "Hungarian race," the cult of the Hungarian peasant as the vehicle of the vital national force. Szabó's most impressive novel after a series of remarkable, striking short stories and novelettes was *Az elsodort falu* (The Village That Was Swept Away), a three-volume saga written in an expressionist free-flowing, torrential style; in it, through the mythically magnified figures of a few heroes, he depicts the diminution of the Hungarian race, extols the primitive soundness of the Hungarian village, and shows the depraving, enervating influence of the town against a full panorama of Hungarian life before the war. This is a distorted view of Hungarian life. Everything is presented as a part of the struggle between Hungarians and Jews, and every problem is simplified into a contest between the peasantry and foreign capital. Szabó's critique is mordant, ruthless, and exterminating when his intent is to demolish, while his concepts are hazy, mystical, and undefined when he means to construct.

The impact of *The Village That Was Swept Away* was tremendous. Its pathos and expressionist-romantic style, its readily acceptable anti-Semitism and racialism, its peasant cult and its social criticism fitted the hazy discontent and increasingly reactionary temper of post-1919 youth and petit bourgeoisie. Thus it happened that the former contributor to *Nyugat,* the learned teacher who had been groomed on French culture, came to be seen as one of the ideological forerunners of Hungarian fascism. Yet, within a few years, Szabó saw German domination as threatening as he had seen the Jewish "danger" earlier. He now turned the blade of his racial theory against the "Swabians," pouring his venom on the influence of German culture that hamstrung the Hungarian intelligentsia. This new element was expressed in his articles and new novels with their verbal torrents, dimly drawn characters and hardly a trace of plot. He became more and more isolated; his quaint, unsociable nature, his self-worship and merciless criticism, which was right and wrong at the same time, alienated the literary world from him. From 1934 almost until his death, he published his own articles and booklets. With the advance of German Nazism his life took a strangely tragic turn: his assault on Nazi racial theory from a racial standpoint was doomed to failure from the start. Szabó died, most likely of starvation, during the 1945 siege in battered-down Budapest.

The group whom it is customary to call populist intellectuals (often but not always of peasant origin themselves), was a complex political and cultural entity. Basically, it was an intellectual "third force" movement, which looked to the peasantry as its mainstay. The failure of the 1919 dictatorship gave rise to the notion that only through an alliance between the peasantry and the bourgeois-nationalist intelligentsia would it be possible to settle the great social problems of rural Hungary. Beginning in the 1930s, an outlook began to manifest itself, widely called "third road" or "third force," popularized and kept alive by a political movement with an impressive cultural record. Its chief characteristic was a conception of a "special Hungarian road," the insistence on a "third course," somewhere between the extremes of capitalism and socialism. It rendered a great service by calling public attention to the social problems of rural Hungary, doing so in political writings and sociological studies as well as fiction, and in propagating its democratic concepts with much vigor. Its aspirations, however, were often thwarted by nationalist trends clinging to it.

The heyday of the populists came after 1935. This was when members of the group wrote their most significant works, and their magazine *Válasz* (Answer) came to be one of Hungary's fearlessly militant periodicals. However, external pressure from the fascist state power, as well as internal strife, soon disrupted the group. After 1938, the greater part of the movement's members withdrew into passivity; a good many drifted to the political right, while a minority joined the antifascist resistance.

Characteristic of populist artists is a focus on the life of poor peasants, portrayed with a fidelity to the facts and with the authenticity of self-confession. They demonstrated a more realistic way of seeing things, occasionally with a scrupulous care for detail and naturalistic undertones. Populists drew a vivid picture of rural Hungary, the relationship of the various strata of the peasantry to one another and to other social classes and the diversity of these relations. Those joining the movement included poets like Gyula Illyés, novelists and short story writers like Péter Veres, József Darvas, and Iván Boldizsár, historians of literature like Géza Féja, sociologists like Zoltán Szabó, political writers like Imre Kovács, as well as economists, ethnographers, demographers, and art historians. The greater part of intellectual Hungary, especially the younger generation, turned with great interest toward the populists.

Gyula Illyés, the leading figure of modern Hungarian literature, was born in a Transdanubian manor, a descendant of shepherds. His parents had made great sacrifices to give their son an education. After university studies, he lived for years in Paris, where he formed friendships with French writers, including Tzara, Aragon, Eluard, Breton, and others. His literary career too dates back to the Paris years of free verse and surrealist and expressionist experiments.

After his return home in 1926, Illyés became one of the most valued young contributors to *Nyugat*. In his first two volumes, he laments for the plight of poor villagers in sweeping, rhythmical free verse. The young poet's rebellion strikes a note of vigorous defiance, blending *Nyugat* traditions and those of the contemporary French school with an innate respect for reality, a vivid imagination, and sudden outbursts of stifled anger. With each passing year, his tone became more strident, developing into a kind of community art, expressing the destitute, oppressed peasants' troubles and sorrows with conscious self-discipline in a highly polished form. Illyés created realist lyrics marked by transparent construction of Gallic lucidity, an almost inevitably epic flavor, a thorough knowledge and skillful evocation of everyday life, a free manner and the cadence of informal speech, and a blending of rustic impulses with European civilization.

By the mid-1930s, Illyés stood at the centre of the populists, in a political as well as ideological sense, while acting as a liaison with the *Nyugat* circle. This was when he wrote his major works, among them two remarkable prose works, *Puszták népe* (People of the Puszta) and *Petőfi* (both in 1936). *People of the Puszta* is a sociological study, but its literary craftsmanship, latent irony, and the broad perspective of vision have made it into a major artistic work. *Petőfi,* at once an essay and a biography, is one of the finest books ever written on the great Hungarian poet. It is an analysis and a personal confession, an assessment of the stature of the poet-revolutionary and an appraisal of his significance.

Illyés hailed the liberation of Hungary in 1945 and the ensuing land reform; he saluted the national reconstruction efforts and the Hungarian peasant entering on a new life. During the years of Stalinist terror, his writings evinced weariness and dejection, a voice of reservation and concern about Hungary's lot. This was when he wrote *One Sentence on Tyranny,* a long, bitter outcry against communist dictatorship, published only after 1956.

A contemporary of Illyés, Béla Balázs became a disciple of communism after he had made a name as a bourgeois writer. He was one of the eminent members of the first *Nyugat* generation, a teacher and aesthete. He was most consistent in carrying out the great command of twentieth-century lyric poetry; brushing aside the outside world, he turned inward in order to probe the world of the spirit in a number of singular poetical short stories and dramas. Bartók's *Prince Bluebeard's Castle* was composed to a Balázs libretto. There formed around Balázs in the 1910s a small coterie of admirers, one of whom was György Lukács, then a fledgling writer. The Great War dislodged this sensitive, introvert author from his groove: he volunteered for the army. When the true aspect of war was brought home to him, he became a socialist, among the first to join the newly founded Communist Party of Hungary, and commissar of theatres for the Hungarian Council Republic.

Political exile took Balázs to Vienna, Berlin, and, finally, Moscow. Filmmaking attracted him, and his *Der sichtbare Mensch* (The Visible Man) and *Der Geist des Films* (The Spirit of the Screen) became fundamental works of cinema aesthetics.

The 1930s saw the rise and maturing of Attila József, the greatest and most tragic poetic genius of interwar Hungary. His father, a worker in a Budapest soap factory, emigrated when his son was three years old, leaving his mother to fend for her little family by taking in washing. During World War I, József's family sank into dire poverty. After his mother died, the talented young József obtained a scholarship to attend Szeged University. He was only seventeen when his first volume of verse, *A szépség koldusa* (Beggar of Beauty) was published to acclaim. There followed one year in Vienna, and one in Paris, a period when the young man gained his introduction into literature and politics. In 1927 he returned to Budapest and for the rest of his life tried to eke out a living by writing poetry. In the 1930s he joined the underground Communist Party but soon broke with it. The final years of his life saw his mental health worsen, even while he continued writing. On 3 December 1937, József took his life by jumping in front of a speeding train.

The most salient characteristics of József's lyrics are a profound knowledge of conditions and a fundamental realism. He speaks in the voice of a poet who had the capacity of discerning the contradictions as well as the distress and predicaments, and the greatness of mind never to varnish human conditions.

József's influence can be felt on nearly all of his contemporaries. The most prominent member of this group was the lyricist Miklós Radnóti. Although Radnóti was an erudite, highly gifted poet and translator with a teacher's diploma, he was refused employment everywhere on account of his Jewish extraction and was compelled to do odd jobs and translations for a living. Beginning in 1941 he was called up several times to do service spells in forced labor camps, and finally, in 1944, was sent to one of the most brutal German extermination camps in Bor, Yugoslavia. A few days before the end of the war, when the captives were force-marched toward Germany, the exhausted poet was shot dead by an SS guard.

Radnóti's voice soared highest in the last few years of his life, in the years of humiliation and persecution, of horror and extreme peril. In eight eclogues (the last of which was written behind the barbed-wire fences of Lager [Camp] Heidemann in Bor), he expresses in dialogue through the rigorous discipline of the classical verse form and by using delicate shades of meaning, his perturbation at the ever more savage horror of the era, and despite all that, his confidence in an idyllic peace that would come, perhaps when he was dead. Radnóti kept writing poems until the last moment; he evoked the world of concentration camps with a rare degree of perceptivity, describing each stage of his calvary with more and more perfect versification, in an exceptionally condensed and mature poetry.

Hungarian culture began to live again in the early months of 1945. The way was now clear for all trends and ambitions; only openly fascist writers were denied any opportunity of expression. The cultural scene was marked by a coexistence of diverse trends: progressive and conservative, socialist and antisocialist trends; all were thriving side by side.

The year 1948, when the Communist Party came to rule Hungary, saw the dissolution of various cultural groups and publications that represented diverse trends of political opinion. Between 1949 and 1953, the reading public expanded, and a substantial number of writers came to accept the goals of the new regime.

From 1949 onward, especially after 1950, the brutality that characterized the Stalinist period became increasingly apparent. The goal of building socialism was replaced by the efforts of a dogmatic leadership to maintain itself in power. The standard of living had ceased to rise; the pace of industrialization was forced; and unlawful and brutal acts were committed in cities as well as villages. Patient persuasion and constructive debate were supplanted by authoritarianism. The meaning of socialist realism was interpreted in a doctrinaire, narrow-minded, and inflexible manner. Artists assumed and perfected a tendency to varnish the unpalatable truth. Dissenters were silenced, imprisoned, even eliminated. These tormenting problems and the artists' crisis of conscience were reflected in a number of outspoken literary works created during the 1953–1956 period of cultural thaw. In the autumn of 1956 the Union of Hungarian Writers, along with other cultural associations, sided enthusiastically with the workers and students demanding their rights. The few days during which Hungary's press was free saw the publication of Illyés's "One Sentence on Tyranny," along with a torrent of similar expressions of pent-up anger, aroused by communist tyranny.

The Kádár regime at first repressed all signs of intellectual dissent, whether it came from writers, students, or from the general public. Thousands of artists, students, and intellectuals were imprisoned, and scores were killed. Kádár heeded Khrushchev's advice to crack down on writers who were potential dissidents. The best literary periodicals ceased publication, and the Writers Union remained disbanded until 1959.

In 1960 there was an amnesty, and most writers were released. A second amnesty in 1964 released all political prisoners. Hungary's cultural life gradually became cautiously tolerant to a relatively wide variety of trends. The Moscow-dictated dogma of socialist realism was scarcely paid even lip service. As a consequence, many artists, long silenced, returned to the cultural scene. The spirit of Helsinki, providing for the free flow of information across borders, had come to prevail. Even a variety of Western art, cinema, and foreign literature became available. The tolerant policy governing culture was derived from the political slogan "Those who are not against us are with us," voiced by the once hated Party first secretary, János Kádár. His regime gained a degree of legitimacy because of giving a "longer leash" to Hungary's citizens. The 1960s and 1970s were often referred to as the "Age of the Three T's" (the letters standing for the Hungarian words for "support, tolerate, and prohibit": *támogat, tűr,* and *tilt*). An increasing number of artists were supported or tolerated, and fewer remained in the last category.

The "year of miracles," 1989, opened the floodgates of free expression throughout East Central Europe. Hungari-

Hungarian or Hungarian-Born Winners of the Nobel Prize

The physicist Fülöp Lénárd was the recipient of the Nobel Prize in 1905 for his work on cathode rays.

Róbert Bárány received the 1914 Nobel Prize in Physiology and Medicine for his studies concerning the physiology and pathology of the human ear's vertibular apparatus and its balancing function. (He accepted the award two years later when released from a Russian prisoner of war camp.)

In 1925 the chemist Richard Zsigmondy received the Nobel Prize for elucidating the heterogeneous nature of colloidal solutions.

Albert Szent-Györgyi (1893–1986) was awarded the 1937 Nobel Prize in Physiology and Medicine for his discoveries in connection with biological combustion processes, with special reference to vitamin C.

George Charles Hevesy developed isotopes as tracers in chemical research, which earned him the 1943 Nobel Prize for Chemistry. He also discovered the new element Hafnium, and ended up receiving the Faraday, Copley, and Bohr Medals, the Enrico Fermi Prize, and the Atoms for Peace Award.

George Békésy was awarded the 1961 Nobel Prize in Physiology and Medicine for his research on the mechanism of stimulation of the human inner ear.

Eugene P. Wigner received the 1961 Nobel Prize in Physics. He clarified the mechanics and interaction of protons and neutrons in the atomic nucleus, and was instrumental in building the first atom bomb.

Dénes Gábor won the 1971 Nobel Prize in Physics for his pioneering work in the development of holography.

The writer and human rights activist Elie Wiesel, who was born in Hungary, was recognized for his fight against violence, oppression, and racism with the 1986 Nobel Peace Prize.

In the same year, John C. Polányi was awarded the Nobel Prize in Chemistry for his work in chemical reaction dynamics.

In 1994 the chemist George Oláh received the Nobel Prize for developing new ways to use hydrocarbons.

Also in 1994 John Harsányi received the Nobel Prize in Economics for his proof of equilibrium in the theory of noncooperative games.

In 1998 the Organization Against Land Mines received the Nobel Peace Prize. One of the five organizers and leaders of this organization was Judith Majláth, a 1956 refugee from Hungary.

Due perhaps to the scarcity of writings translated from their language into any of the "major" languages, Hungarian writers or poets have had few chances to compete for the Nobel Prize in Literature. Finally, in 2003, the novelist and short story writer Imre Kertész was awarded that prize in recognition of his lifetime activity recording the struggle between inhumanity and hope.

ans had been watching the deadly boredom of communist culture making a series of retreats ever since 1956, and acknowledged its final capitulation with quiet satisfaction. In tandem with political liberalization, cultural life has also rid itself of all arbitrary restrictions. Long-forgotten works of art are presented, staged, and performed. State controls have been removed, which (perhaps unfortunately) also means that cultural commodities (books, periodicals, theater tickets) have become less affordable to a public that is struggling with the negative consequences of privatization, cutbacks, and rampant competitive marketization. All in all, however, few Hungarians wish to return to the era of cheap paperback volumes of Soviet pseudo-literature and low-priced tickets to watch films glorifying fake Soviet achievements. In a free and democratic society, Hungarians once again have the opportunity to create their own truly Hungarian and at the same time open and diverse national culture.

ECONOMIC DEVELOPMENT

The past century of rapid worldwide economic development did not leave Hungary untouched, notwithstanding the country's numerous misfortunes in other regards. Hungary's economy has advanced from a nearly feudal condition to a midlevel stage of industrial development. Perhaps the most spectacular growth took place around the turn of the century, with great advances made in food processing, foundry, and transportation. Much of this progress was cut short by the Trianon peace treaty of 1920, which deprived the nation's industry of nearly all of its natural resources and much of its markets, as well as disrupting the well-developed rail network. The rampage of political extremism following World War I did not help, nor did the worldwide depression of the 1920s, during much of which Hungary remained isolated in the economic as well as political sense. By the late 1930s, however, there was a certain amount of consolidation taking place. The price for this recovery proved to be steep, though, since much of it was accomplished by developing closer ties with Nazi Germany and fascist Italy, and led to Hungary's involvement in World War II as an ally of the Axis powers. In addition to the huge human losses at the front, this also meant that some of the most desperate closing skirmishes of the Second World War were fought on Hungarian soil. As a result, in 1945 the country's capital city lay in ruins, with all of its bridges and about half of the residential dwellings destroyed, and its factories incapacitated. The decimated and undernourished population, however, accomplished the challenges of reconstruction energetically and heroically. By the 1950s, Hungary may have appeared drab and poor, but its economy was able to provide basic necessities for the population.

After 1948–1949, when the Communists established themselves as the ruling and sole political party, the government controlled by Mátyás Rákosi began to slavishly imitate the Soviet course of economic development. It used the most brutal coercion to force peasants, who had just received land for the first time in history, to join collectives, and proceeded to squeeze profits from them to finance rapid expansion of heavy industry. At first, Hungary concentrated on manufacturing the same assortment of goods it had successfully produced before the war, such as locomotives and railroad cars. Soon, however, heavy industry came to receive more than 90 percent of investment, disregarding the country's poor resource base and its favorable opportunities in other areas of production.

The Soviet Union became Hungary's principal trading partner, supplying crude oil, iron ore, and much of the capital for Hungary's iron and steel industry. Heavy Soviet demand also led Hungary to develop shipbuilding and textile industries. Soviet pressure, Western trade restrictions, and the new Hungarian practice of favoring domestic and regional autarky combined to reduce the flow of goods between Hungary and the West to a trickle.

The government's wage controls and a two-tier price system made up of producer and consumer prices (controlled separately) were used to limit domestic demand and cut relative labor costs by raising consumer prices and holding back wages. Popular dissatisfaction increased in the wake of material shortages and export difficulties. Agrarian growth also stagnated, and the area of cultivated land actually decreased.

With the onset of a relative thaw after the Soviet dictator Joseph Stalin died in 1953, Imre Nagy became Hungary's prime minister and, following the Soviet example, implemented major reforms. He halted the collectivization drive, allowed farmers to leave collective farms, eased production quotas, raised procurement prices for farm products, and increased investment in agriculture. He also shifted investment from heavy industry to consumer goods production. But the changes were too timid, and productivity actually worsened after 1953. In 1955 hard-liners regained control, and the reforms were halted.

The brutal defeat of the popular revolution of 1956 was followed by a standstill for Hungary's economy. The new Party leadership under János Kádár realized that notions of Marxism-Leninism, as dictated from Moscow, had little to do with reality, and began to consider economic policies that would actually improve the people's living conditions. This course had some immediate results: by the early 1960s, the real income of Hungarians nearly doubled, household consumption grew accordingly, and the wave of popular resentment that faced Kadar had diminished considerably. A second effort to collectivize agriculture began in 1959. Instead of coercion, however, the government this time offered incentives to those who would join cooperative or collective farms. By 1962, more than 95 percent of agricultural land had come under the state sector's control. Major investments were made in agriculture, mechanization rose by 50 percent, and farm prices were raised to make the sector viable.

Heavy controls were relaxed in other areas as well. Engineering and chemical branches received greater support, resulting in the production of buses, machine tools, precision instruments, and telecommunications equipment, as well as artificial fertilizer, plastic, and synthetic fiber. These resulted in increased imports of energy, raw materials, and semifinished goods. Hungary's economy was growing during the 1960s, and the population's living standard was improving, but continuing growth was not foreseen. In addition to the limited

Three steel workers convene on the train tracks in front of the mill's smokestacks in Dunaújváros, Hungary. Dunaújváros was an important center for iron and steel industry in Hungary, ca. 1950–1980. (Paul Almasy/Corbis)

supply of natural resources, Hungary had also exhausted its labor force reserves. By the mid-1960s, it was clear that the policies followed since 1949 were no longer viable.

Hungary's industries lagged far behind those in the West; its communication and transportation infrastructures were so weak that they stood in the way of further growth. The USSR and other socialist countries were in no position to help, so Hungary's leaders realized that they would have to seek these critical inputs from the West. The government introduced the NEM (New Economic Mechanism) in 1968. In order to improve enterprise efficiency and make its goods more competitive, the government abolished universal compulsory planning, granted enterprises greater autonomy, and unleashed some market forces. (The program stalled, or was made to stall, within four years, but a burgeoning balance of trade deficit, slumping performance, deteriorating terms of trade, and other problems prompted the leadership to start the reform process anew in the late 1970s.)

The NEM and a favorable economic environment contributed to good economic performance for a few years. The economy grew steadily; neither unemployment nor inflation was apparent, and the country's balance of payments improved as exports grew. Cooperative farms and factories provided much needed goods and services. By about 1970, Hungary had reached the status of a medium-developed country. Its industry was producing 40–50 percent of the gross domestic product, while agriculture was contributing less than 20 percent.

The energy price increases of the 1970s had a disastrous effect on Hungary's trade. In response, the country's leadership made a number of major policy errors, the worst among them being the assumption that Hungary's economy could be shielded from the world's energy crisis. Many NEM reform measures were negated or crippled, and by the late 1970s Hungary was forced to turn to the convertible currency market for loans. A partial reinstatement of the command economy and a hasty recentralization combined to exacerbate Hungary's economic woes.

The NEM was brought back into force in 1978, but it was too late to undo the damages. To avoid bankruptcy, Hungary obtained loans from the IMF (International Monetary Fund) and the World Bank, introduced a stricter stabilization program and obtained bridge financing from the Bank for International Settlements. The leadership also renewed its support for economic reforms, which creditors viewed as a positive step toward more efficient use of resources and improvement of the country's balance of payments.

Under the new stabilization program, Hungary had slashed its investment spending to about a quarter of the earlier level, and increased prices steeply, calling for greater austerity, efficiency, and profitability. It has also streamlined its ministries, dismantled some huge enterprises and trusts, stimulated the growth of small and private firms, implemented a competitive pricing system, decentralized foreign trade, created small stock and bond markets, enacted a bankruptcy law, carried out banking reform, and levied value added and personal income taxes.

In spite of all these measures, growth remained far below the expected level during the seventh, and last, Five-Year Plan (1986–1990). The country enjoyed favorable treatment from international capital markets, mainly because its reporting system was considered the most reliable in the region, it had good debt-servicing records, and there was no lack of economic and entrepreneurial talent on the scene. In the latter half of the 1980s Japanese banks even increased their loan portfolio and sought to make low-risk loans to East European countries, particularly Hungary, which took the loans to restructure its industry, renovate power stations, implement its energy rationalization program, upgrade its telecommunications system, and finance foreign trade. As a result of a deteriorating convertible currency account, Hungary's debt has continued to grow.

In addition to the standard characteristics of East Central European socialist states (central planning, budgetary policies driven by ideology, state ownership of means of production, and chronic shortages), Hungary also inherited high external indebtedness from its forty-year experiment with socialism. At the same time, some early, clumsy attempts at reprivatization were also detectable. In 1980 the public sector's share in the "official" GDP (which ignored the burgeoning "unofficial economy") was 90 percent, with 10 percent domestic, and 0 percent foreign private owned. During the final decade or so of the socialist era, the shares of these sectors in the GDP changed dramatically. In 1990 the respective percentages were 76, 23, and 1; in 1991 they were 70, 27, and 3; in 1992 they were 56, 36, and 8; and in 1993 they were 42, 45, and 13. If one was to include the unofficial "gray" sector of the economy, the actual public-private-foreign ratios were 83, 17, and 0 in 1980; and 37, 50, and 13 in 1993. These are perhaps the most telling numbers about the changes in the Hungarian economy. The corollaries of this restructuring were not entirely positive: output declined by 20 percent of the GDP between 1989 and 1994, and incomes dropped by 8–10 percent in real terms between 1990 and 1994. There was also a shift in the occupational structure: far more persons came to be employed in the service sector of the economy.

Suddenly there were three working environments available to Hungarian workers. State employment provided greater job security, better fringe benefits, and lower pay. The "competitive" private sectors, domestic or foreign, offered less job security, fewer fringe benefits, longer hours, and 24–30 percent higher pay. The third alternative was the unofficial economy in which people from both sectors traded marketable skills for unreported, untaxed incomes.

The growing number of unemployed and unemployable was the inevitable result of a budget and market driven rush of downsizing because of obsolescent skills and/or of poor physical health. Combined with demography and the high ratio of pensioners, this placed crushing burdens on the active wage earners. The ratio of economically inactive dependents to 100 active wage earners was 117 to 100 in 1987 and 167 to 100 in 1993.

Hungary is referred to as an upper-middle income country in the World Bank's world development reports, and its comparative economic performance among twenty-eight postcommunist states is generally praised. However, neither assessment takes account of the social impact of rapid economic change.

The Kádár era generated new patterns of social mobility and stratification. With the exhaustion of the economy's growth potential and the onset of political entropy, both processes came to a standstill in 1983. Upon the change of the political regime and the revival of the private economy, new patterns of social mobility and stratification surfaced after 1992.

According to one estimate, 1 million people, or 20 percent of the active labor force, were "winners," and the rest were victims of stagnant or rapidly declining incomes and deteriorated living standards. The principal winners were those with higher education (8.1 and 14.5 percent of the labor force in 1980 and 1993, respectively), those with market-convertible skills, and specific elite groups with discretionary access to incomes generated by the market and "unofficial economy" and the recipients of preferential resource allocations by government agencies.

Income inequality did not begin with the onset of economic transformation in Hungary, but it did gain momentum. Trends indicate a gradually widening gap between the lowest and the highest 20 percent of recipients. It is the lifestyle and conspicuous consumption of the upper 1 percent that is seen as unjustifiable by market criteria, as well as morally reprehensible by the public's quasi-egalitarian standards. Groups and individuals who have become vulnerable on this score are the new—partly managerial, partly "Wild East" entrepreneurial—business elites and the new kleptocracy of politically well-connected executives of industry, banking, and commerce. The wealth and power, converted into ever higher positions, splendid homes, and luxury cars tend to catalyze public skepticism about social justice in a parliamentary democracy.

Hungary's postcommunist governments have gone to great lengths to cushion the impact of economic transformation. Still, even the disbursement of 26–28 percent of the budget (arguably the highest percentage in Europe) for social welfare purposes has failed to slow down the growth in the number of those living at or below the poverty level. Their numbers were 1 million in the 1980s, 1.5 million in 1991, 2 million in 1992, and 3.0–3.5 million in 1994. (To be sure, using the yardstick of the old bankrupt welfare state is an unrealistic device with which to measure poverty. Thus World Bank and IMF numbers of around 10 percent ought to be closer to the mark. This is not to deny the severity of hardships faced by social victims of economic transformation.)

Equally essential, however, is to see the "winners" of postcommunism and efforts by the well-off intelligentsia to keep politicians on the defensive. They use the poverty issue to forestall, as long as possible, the full implementation of economic restructuring and, with it, the inevitable decline of public welfare, often in the form of state patronage of cultural activities, disbursed to intellectuals.

Challenges to the economy are more than merely structural. Rapid industrialization and the priority of plan fulfillment over environmental concerns have resulted in serious air and water pollution problems in Hungary. One-third of the country's population lives in regions where air pollution exceeds international standards. Electric plants burning high-sulfur coal and automobiles emit most of the pollutants that foul Hungary's air. (Sulfur dioxide emission is particularly great.) Prevailing winds from the west and southwest carry much of Hungary's sulfur dioxide emissions into neighboring countries, and acid rain has damaged 20–30 percent of the country's forests.

Pollutants also foul the rivers and ground water. The Tisza, Duna, Szamos, Sajó, and Zagyva are Hungary's most polluted rivers, and the water supply of many towns and villages is only marginally fit for human consumption. Hungary emits almost 2 million cubic meters of polluted water per day. Industrial waste from chemical, rubber, iron, paper, and food processing industries accounts for 70 percent of the polluting effluent, less than half of which is treated. Even an adequate residential sewage system is available only to 65 percent of the population.

Hungary produces more than 5 million tons of hazardous waste annually, and it reportedly accepts huge amounts of similar waste from Austria, Switzerland, and Germany in return for hard currency. After years of public protest, in the late 1980s Hungary constructed an incinerator in Dorog capable of burning 25,000 tons of hazardous waste per year. Hungary operated a nuclear waste dump between the villages of Kisnémedi and Püspökszilágy, but precise information on the disposal of radioactive waste from the country's nuclear power plant is unavailable. Hungary has antipollution agreements with Czechoslovakia and Austria, but has no such agreement with Romania and complains about Romania's chronic discharge of phenol, oil, and even arsenic and other hazardous pollutants into the Tisza and smaller rivers.

The future of the economy is tied in many respects to its resources. Hungary's geology is dominated by young sedimentary rock that has few minerals and raw materials except bauxite, soft coal, and small deposits of uranium, natural gas, oil, iron ore, manganese, and copper. On the other hand, Hungary has large tracts of fertile land and a favorable climate. The country's shortage of raw materials has necessitated vigorous foreign trade, especially after 1920, when Hungary lost much of its pre–World War I territory. Raw materials, semifinished products, spare parts, fuels, and electricity accounted for the bulk of imports, and their cost equals one-quarter of Hungary's gross domestic product.

Hungary's coal deposits total 4.5 billion tons and include hard coal (15 percent of the total), brown coal (30 percent), and lignite (55 percent). Hungarian coal generally has a low energy content and lies at great depths in thin seams, making mining difficult and costly. Deep mines in the Mecsek Mountains near Pécs and Komló yield some coal suitable for coking. Thick layers of higher-quality brown coal lie 200–300 meters beneath Tatabánya and Dorog, while lower-quality brown coal lies under the Carpathian foothills near Miskolc and in the central Danube Plain. The Várpalota Basin in Veszprém County and the southern slopes of the Mátra Mountains yield lignite. Hungarian experts predict that the country's coal reserves will last 400 years at the present production levels.

Hungary's natural gas and oil deposits are far smaller than its coal reserves. The country's largest natural gas deposits are located near Szeged, Hajdúszoboszló, and Miskolc. Geologists predict that natural gas reserves would be used up by the middle of the twenty-first century. Small crude oil deposits lie beneath Szeged, Zala County, and other areas. The Zala crude is highly viscous and difficult to transport. Wells at Lispeszentadorján, Lovászi, and other sites yield high-quality oil, but they are almost exhausted. In the late 1970s drillers struck oil in the mid-Danube-Tisza region (the central part of the country) and near Sárkeresztúr, Endrőd, and Ullés. However, geologists anticipate no new major oil discoveries and expect the wells to run dry soon.

Hungary began mining uranium near Pécs in the 1950s with Soviet assistance. Estimates of the actual size of the country's uranium deposits are vague, but official sources indicated that Hungary had uranium reserves sufficient to supply its domestic needs until the year 2020.

Chronic coal mining problems and shrinking domestic hydrocarbon reserves have plagued the economy since the

Paks nuclear power plant. (Serge Attal/Corbis Sygma)

mid-1970s. The reliance on imported energy increased steadily from 37.2 percent in 1970 to 51.3 percent in 1986. The Soviet Union furnished most of Hungary's energy imports, but Soviet production setbacks and demands for better trade terms complicated Hungary's energy supply problems after the mid-1980s.

Hungary slashed investment in coal mining in the late 1960s and 1970s, when Soviet oil and natural gas were less expensive alternate fuels. Consequently, coal's share of domestic energy production dropped from 62.7 percent in 1970 to 36.6 percent in 1986. Coal accounted for 26 percent of Hungary's energy consumption. In the early 1980s rising oil and natural gas prices prompted Hungary to reopen the flow of investment into coal mining but the country still suffered from a severe shortage of miners, and its mines were unable to keep pace with rising demand. The government approved substantial pay increases for miners in order to attract new workers. In 1986 Hungary's mines employed 79,566 workers who labored between sixty and seventy hours per week and produced coal worth $779 million. Total annual coal output has hovered around 24 million tons since 1975, but hard coal production actually fell by 23 percent between 1975 and 1986, and the calorific value of coal output declined by 18 percent in the same period. Coal, coke, and briquette imports totaled US$268 million in 1986.

Hydrocarbons, including oil, propane, natural gas, and gasoline, accounted for 61 percent of total energy consumption in 1986. Natural gas production has increased considerably since the mid-1960s, exceeding 7 billion cubic meters in 1986 and 1987. Domestic consumption, however, has far outstripped production since 1970, nearly doubling from 5.9 billion cubic meters in 1975 to 11.5 billion in 1986. Hungary's wells supplied 94.8 percent of its natural gas consumption in 1970 but only 66.1 percent in 1986. Natural gas imports totaled 4.8 billion cubic meters in 1986 and cost US$366 million. The Soviet Union supplied Hungary with 90 percent of its natural gas imports.

Hungarian wells have pumped 2 million tons of crude oil yearly since 1975, mostly from the Szeged region, but observers expected production to decline after 1990. Oil imports totaled US$1.1 billion in 1986, while exports added up to US$332 million. Hungary exported oil by reselling Iranian and other Middle Eastern oil acquired in various compensation schemes.

Hungary launched an energy rationalization program in the early 1980s aimed at maintaining levels of domestic oil and gas production attained in the mid-1980s, increasing exploration, and substituting natural gas and other fuels for oil. The conservation program, backed by stiff price hikes, netted positive results. Oil consumption dipped from 12.5 million tons in 1979 to 9.1 million tons in 1985, and Hungary's imports of petroleum and petroleum products dropped from US$1.3 billion in 1985 to US$1.1 billion in 1986.

Hungary's power plants had a 6.8 billion kilowatt capacity in 1986 and generated 28 billion kilowatt-hours of electricity, almost double the amount generated in 1970. The increase failed, however, to keep pace with demand as consumption rose from 17.9 billion kilowatt-hours in 1970 to 38.6 billion in 1986. Hungary overcame the 1986 shortfall by importing 11.9 billion kilowatt-hours of electricity. Transmission lines from the Soviet Union carried one-third of Hungary's imported electricity.

In the late 1980s thermal power stations generated 70 percent of Hungary's electricity and burned 65 percent of Hungary's brown coal production and nearly all of its lignite output. Hungary has constructed large thermal power stations in the last fifteen years, including a 1.9 million kilowatt heat and power plant at Százhalombatta in Pest County that generated almost 40 percent of the country's electricity.

Southern Hungary's uranium reserves supplied the 880 million kilowatt Paks nuclear power plant in Tolna County, the country's only nuclear power facility. The plant's first reactor went on line in 1983, and its second followed a year later. In 1986 the plant generated 7.4 billion kilowatt-hours, or 26.5 percent of the nation's electricity output and 19.2 percent of its consumption. Hungary and the Soviet Union agreed in 1986 to build four additional 440-megawatt reactors at Paks in the next decade. Officials hoped that the plant would supply 40 percent of Hungary's electricity by the early 2000s.

In the late 1980s Hungary's hydroelectric power stations generated less than 1 percent of the country's electricity, but Hungary has joined with Czechoslovakia to build two hydroelectric power stations on the Danube at Gabcikovo in Czechoslovakia and at Nagymaros in Hungary. The project, which was scheduled for completion by 1993, received Austrian financial assistance. However, in May 1989 the Hungarian government suspended work on the power station because of public concern over the damage it threatened to cause to the environment. The power stations' total projected capacity was 3.6 billion kilowatt-hours per year, and their estimated cost was US$1.4 billion.

The Bakony and Vértes Mountains contain 10–12 percent of the world's known bauxite reserves and deposits of manganese ore, the only alloy necessary for steel production found in Hungary. The only iron ore mine, located at Rudabánya, produces ankerite and siderite that contain only 24–27 percent iron and require lime before smelting. In the late 1980s the country's limestone and dolomite reserves satisfied the needs of its iron industry. Copper mines at Recsk remain undeveloped because of lack of financing and because of copper's low price on world commodity markets.

The aluminum industry developed rapidly after World War II and in the late 1980s employed more than 40,000 workers. The production of bauxite (used in making aluminum) more than doubled since the war, reaching more than 3 million tons in 1986, while alumina (aluminum oxide) output totaled 856,000 tons in the same year. Increased bauxite production was depleting deposits near the surface, however, and costly deep mining had become necessary. Conversion of alumina into aluminum is highly energy intensive, and a lack of inexpensive electricity prevented Hungary from converting more than 25 percent of its alumina output.

Soviet technology and raw material inputs were key factors in the development of Hungary's iron and steel industry. The large steel mills at Dunaújváros in Fehér County, Ózd, Miskolc, and Budapest have used local low-grade iron ore, but more than 80 percent of their raw material input originated in the Soviet Union. In the late 1980s the industry suffered from several major problems. First, Hungary's iron and steel mills were less cost effective than West European mills because, among other factors, Hungary had to pay to transport and process Soviet ore that had only a relatively low (45–50 percent) iron content. Second, the prices Hungary received for its iron and steel exports to convertible currency markets had fallen. These exports generated losses for the industry, but Hungary continued the trade for several reasons: the domestic market could not absorb enough output to maintain satisfactory use of the country's mill capacity, the state subsidized losses on metallurgical exports, and export income provided the industry with the grounds to increase wages. The industry underwent a sweeping reorganization as part of a 1987 restructuring program that included the elimination of 2,400 jobs. Hungary produced no iron ore in 1986, and analysts expected the country to reduce iron and steel output by up to 10 percent in 1988.

Arable land, pastures, meadows, vineyards, and gardens occupy 70 percent of the total land area. Hungary has large tracts of fertile black soil, especially in the Great Plain region. Even though the climate can be harsh, it is generally favorable for agriculture. Concentrated in mountainous areas, the forests occupy 1.5 million hectares and contain mostly deciduous trees of little value except for holding moisture. The government launched an extensive reforestation effort after World War II, but domestic timber still supplies only a small percentage of the country's needs.

The future of the Hungarian economy also depends on its workforce. Until the 1980s, many Hungarians supplemented their income by working outside jobs, tilling household plots, or operating private businesses. Most enterprises used labor inefficiently, creating underemployment and relatively low productivity. The postcommunist measures are forcing enterprises to operate more efficiently and thus threaten the loss of many jobs. Compared with Western countries, however, Hungary's unemployment problem was relatively small: a 4 percent unemployment rate is generally considered full employment in a free market economy; in Hungary this percentage would amount to 240,000 people.

Women joined the workforce in great numbers after World War II and contributed significantly to reconstruction and the government's industrialization drive. Families supported the entry of women into the workforce because they could not survive on a single income or they desired a higher living standard. In 1949 29.2 percent of active earners were women; by 1987 they accounted for 46 percent. Likewise, whereas 34.5 percent of working-age women were active earners in 1949, 75 percent were active earners by 1987. Fifty-nine percent of Hungary's working women were manual workers; the remainder worked in white-collar jobs. (About 70 percent of men were manual workers, and 30 percent had white-collar jobs.) Women dominated low-paying jobs in the textile industry, the service sector, canneries, and commerce; in the white-collar area, women dominated in education, health, and clerical office jobs.

PROSPECTS

According to most experts, the economies of East Central Europe will take a long time to catch up with those of their Western neighbors. It is estimated that if the fifteen countries of the current EU enjoy economic growth of 2 percent a year, and the countries joining in the next few years grow by 4 percent a year, then it will take the new members, on average, more than fifty years to draw level with the old ones. Of course, other factors may be at work, and growth and convergence rates will probably vary widely from country to country, but in this scheme of things, it will take thirty-four years for Hungary to "catch up" with the West.

What is clearer to most observers is that Hungary's economy can grow only if its factories and farms become more efficient and competitive. There are three complicating factors. First, except for excess workers in existing enterprises, Hungary no longer has an untapped labor pool, such as the one that existed after World War II in the female and peasant populations. Second, the country has few natural resources, and raw materials have become more costly on both Western and regional markets. Third, Hungary can pay for imports of raw materials and efficiency-improving Western technology only by exporting goods whose quality and price compete in the world market.

Joining the EU may not in itself bring an economic boom. In the event Hungary's growth rate does not meet expectations, the advantages of EU membership could be balanced by serious burdens. The country will be saddled with the rules and expenses of a club meant for the rich, while its income remains far below the average and may even decline in relative terms. Problems may also arise from adjusting to the EU's common visa and border regime. Border controls, already gone from most of the EU, will disappear from the new members in three or four years. By that time the new members are expected to have perfected tough border controls of their own against non-EU countries, including friends and trading partners. This prospect worries Poland, which would prefer a more open border with Ukraine, and Hungary, which would like to keep ties with ethnic Hungarian minorities in the neighboring countries.

There is also the possibility of tensions between the EU's older members and those newer ones that, like Hungary, have regained their freedom and, in some cases, their independence, relatively recently, after decades spent taking orders from Moscow. The forces of nationalism that helped oust the communist order in East Central Europe in 1989–1991 are still strong here, and not always far from the political mainstream. Like all Central Europeans, Hungarians would prefer to join an EU in which their country is respected, not one in which they are bossed around casually by France or Germany. Hungary's interests might be best served by opposing policies that impose new costs on industry and new regulatory burdens on government, and by insisting on the freedom to keep taxes low, public spending down, and labor cheap.

CONTEMPORARY CHALLENGES

More than a few of the 15 million Hungarians alive today worldwide may find the pace of change staggering. Many were born in a kingdom governed by a regent and saw their native land change, in rapid succession, first into a pseudo-fascist dictatorship fighting a losing war; then a devastated and occupied republic led by a weak coalition; then a satrapy of Stalin's empire; then a short-lived republic frantically led by idealistic amateurs; then a cowed and vengeful police state; then a fake socialist resort; and then, quite suddenly, a fully constitutional parliamentary democracy at the mercy of global forces.

Since 1989, when Hungary regained its national sovereignty and found itself in a position to make genuine progress toward democracy and the rule of laws, the nation was faced with a number of challenges. Some of these derived from Hungary's location, its societal makeup or from its history, while others—just as problematic—arose from the new European realities. The lessons of the past and the actualities of a new Europe made it clear for all Hungarians that their country could scarcely go its own way.

The changes of 1989, while truly revolutionary in their depth and breadth, came about as a result of relatively civil negotiations, conducted at a roundtable. Efforts were made to include or represent as many elements of society as possible, and there was a surprising degree of patience exhibited by the parties. The Communists showed unusual humility, and speakers for the incoming power did not press their obvious advantage. (Of course, the kid gloves came off during the elections of subsequent years.)

Hungary's institutional transition was essentially completed by 1994, but the country's socioeconomic transformation is still in progress. After decades of living in the stifling comfort of central planning, this is a difficult process. It is made even more complicated by two major challenges to the country's leaders: On the one hand, they are called on to democratize public life, marketize the economy, and establish a rule of law. At the same time, Hungary's citizens keep loudly reminding their government not to forget *their* priorities, which add up to a set of nearly unrealizable expectations when it comes to providing goods and services. Underlying it all is the issue of cultural and spiritual survival, as well as political and economic survival. After surviving for 1,100 years in the face of numerous invasions, occupations, and periods of oppression, many in public life sound cautious, even alarmed, seeing the multitude of new forces on the Hungarian scene.

THE PRESENCE OF THE PAST

Four decades of communist rule ended in 1989, but the communist legacy is likely to be felt for some time. The forced adaptation of the Soviet model changed practically all of Hungary's political, social, and economic institutions. This is true for the other formerly socialist countries of the region. Hungary's communist period, however, has a number of characteristics that, considered together, may distinguish it somewhat from the experience of its neighbors. As pointed out by leading observers of the Hungarian scene, these elements include (1) the exceptional harshness of the Stalinist years between 1948–1953, (2) the spontaneous popular revolution of 1956, (3) János Kádár's coercive, terroristic policies, which later turned into a sustained commitment to legitimacy building through economic reforms and seeking a national consensus, (4) an increasingly civil and self-moderating interaction between the regime and its internal opposition, and (5) the surprisingly pragmatic cooperation between the outgoing and incoming political elites during the year of change, 1989.

After the Yalta regime gave free rein to Soviet expansion into East Central Europe, the Hungarian people and their neighbors had only two available options: accommodation and survival, or resistance and inevitable repression. The second option, that is, an armed uprising against the regime and its Soviet masters in October 1956, was not a premeditated choice but a collective act of public outrage. It was rooted in two widely shared aspirations: the nation's attempt to regain its freedom, and the people's seeking to reclaim their sense of personal dignity and civic identity. With this in mind, it can thus be argued that there was an intrinsic causality between intolerable oppression and the revolution of 1956, on the one hand, and between that singular and regionally unique event and the rest of the hypothesized attributes that characterized people–regime interactions in Hungary in the next three decades, on the other.

The precedent of the 1956 revolution is not meant to be an all-purpose explanation for what came to pass in Hungary during the next thirty-three years. Other factors, such as the country's relatively minor strategic importance for the USSR, the peculiar chemistry of Kádár's personal relations with his Kremlin superiors, and many other external factors were also responsible for the relatively sheltered environment in which the people and the regime came to craft a common survival pact after the defeated revolution.

Freedom, or at least a longer leash in a cage, can be earned in many ways. Hungary's choices in October 1956 were either to fight or to submit to the tyrant. In any case, the record is clear that the Hungarian people paid dearly with blood on the streets of Budapest, with the execution of hundreds, the incarceration of thousands, the forced exodus of many tens of thousands to the West, and the relative personal autonomy that the denizens of the Soviet bloc's "jolliest barrack" came to enjoy in the 1970s and in the 1980s.

The attainment of normalcy, or at least the absence of debilitating political and economic crises, has been the East European societies' age-old aspiration. This is to be expected in the part of Europe that served as a battleground in two world wars, was the scene of the Holocaust and other acts of genocide, and was the bloody political testing ground for transplanting the Soviet model to alien soil. In any case, Kádár's Hungary in the 1970s came close to "normalcy" and managed to instill a consequent sense of public well-being that most people still consider as the benchmark against which to measure living conditions and the performance of the political incumbents in the mid-1990s.

Hungary's "homo Kadaricus" (Kadarian man) was unambiguously materialist, but with a twist. Whereas the predominantly materialistic Western European public could afford the luxury of preoccupation with consumption and the even greater luxury of pursuit of both materialist and idealistic postmaterialist goals under the solid shelter of liberal democratic political institutions, the average Hungarian was bereft of choices of this kind. The regime's repressive tolerance helped foster a new context of social interaction. It gave relatively free rein, in the Hungarian sociologists' terminology, to the realization of personal interests in the nonpolitical realm. As a result, a "survival of the fittest" (or best connected) bargain culture was born in Hungary. The upshot was the rise of an adulterated sense of civic identity and political infantilism. Corruption and misuse of power above and widespread disregard of laws and administrative rules below were two facets of a symbiotic whole of moral decay and diminished civic competence. These behaviors have remained largely unaffected by legal and institutional changes in the postcommunist period.

The task at hand is the redefinition of the ruling party's style of governance from the "vanguard" to the "system management" mode and the consequent empowerment of the state for the implementation of the party's political will.

NATIONAL SECURITY

At the end of the communist era, the Hungarian People's Army numbered around 160,000 in personnel, and military expenditure exceeded 3.5 percent of the nation's gross domestic product. In 2000 the Hungarian Defense Forces included 53,000 persons, and defense expenditure was 1.61 percent of GDP. As for alliances, in the summer of 1990 Hungary and several other member states suggested a review of the Moscow-dominated Warsaw Treaty Organization, and soon after moved for its dissolution, which took place in 1991. Simultaneously, the Budapest government succeeded in getting the Red Army to withdraw from Hungary (after forty-six years), and in the summer of 1991, the Moscow-controlled economic and trade block Comecon was disbanded as well.

The newly acquired independence raised the issue of how to guarantee national security. Hungary's foreign policy priorities proclaimed by the first freely elected government, led by the historian József Antall and his Hungarian Democratic Forum, cut across political parties and included (1) striving for Euro-Atlantic integration, (2) maintaining good neighborliness to ensure regional stability, and (3) actively supporting Hungarian minorities living abroad primarily in neighboring countries (altogether a community of 3 million ethnic Hungarians). All Hungarian governments in office since that time have considered and continue to consider these goals to be of primary importance.

EU ENTRY

In May 2004 Hungary, along with the Baltic states, Poland, the Czech Republic, Slovakia, Slovenia, Cyprus, and Malta, joined the European Union (EU). The preparations for entry gave these countries the motivation and the models they needed to entrench or restore democratic institutions and market economies, replacing the communist and socialist ones previously imposed there. Even the skeptics in the new member countries should be pleased with this. A country well equipped to join the EU is a country well equipped to make its way in the world otherwise, if it chooses to do so.

As it happens, voters in all the East Central European countries eligible to join the EU have supported entry, often by large majorities. Now they are preparing for the shocks and strains, as well as the opportunities and rewards, that lie ahead. Of course, EU entry does not in itself bring wealth. The countries of East Central Europe will take decades to catch up with their Western neighbors. Any East Central European country where the growth rate sags will suffer for it. It will be saddled with the rules and expenses of a club meant for rich people, while its income per person remains far below the average and may even decline in relative terms.

East Central Europeans also face challenges in adjusting to the EU's common visa and border regime. Border controls have already disappeared across most of the EU. They should disappear among the new members too, but only after three or four years. By that time, the new members are expected to have perfected tough border controls of their own against non-EU countries, including friends and trading partners. This prospect presents a certain concern for many Hungarians, who desire to remain in close contact with the Hungarian minorities in Romania, Serbia, and Ukraine.

The EU may yet emerge the stronger for all this, if the assertiveness of the Central Europeans emboldens them to push harder for policies that make the Union work better. As poor countries with threadbare institutions, their interests should lie in opposing policies that impose new costs on industry and new regulatory burdens on government. They should insist on the freedom to keep taxes low, public spending down, and labor cheap. Those are also good policies, as it happens, for stagnant rich countries, of which the EU has more than its share.

There is the possibility of tensions arising between the EU's older members and those newer ones that have re-

Hungarian men and women on stilts dancing with EU and Hungarian flags at the monument of the statues of Hungarian kings at the Heroes Square of Budapest on Saturday 1 May 2004. Hungary celebrated the EU enlargement as nine other European countries, Cyprus, the Czech Republic, Estonia, Latvia, Lithuania, Malta, Poland, Slovakia, and Slovenia joined the European Union. (AFP/Getty Images)

gained their freedom and, in some cases, their independence, relatively recently, after decades spent taking orders from Moscow (or Belgrade, in the case of Slovenia). The currents of nationalism that helped overturn the communist order in East Central Europe in 1989 still run strong there, and not always far from the political mainstream. Central Europeans want an EU in which they and their countries are respected, not one in which they are bossed around casually by countries such as France or Germany. President Jacques Chirac's outburst that the Central Europeans should have remained silent instead of supporting U.S. policy on Iraq, betrayed the patronizing and bullying attitude that future EU members least want to encounter in Brussels. Forewarned by Chirac, they will enter the Union in a more combative mood, complicating their future relations with France and its increasingly like-minded ally, Germany.

TOLERANCE IN POLITICAL DEBATE

Hungary's sharp political debates serve a purpose, in that they decide who wins and loses elections. However, in the bitter and desperate manner in which they are more and more frequently conducted, they are also breeding attitudes that negate the very purpose of the debate. One of the approaches that tend to embitter these debates (in Hungary and elsewhere) is the attempt to forge a number of small facts, which may be statistically correct, into one all-encompassing construct of "truths," and then declare this newly forged model to be "the Truth." The manufacturing of such political truth calls for a considerable amount of commitment, even fanaticism. In the past, such fanaticism was often fueled by religious faith, and in the modern world by equally strong adherence to secular, man-made ideologies. Believers in a truth are totally dedicated to it, and are convinced that there is only one road to travel to serve the interest of their community or nation. (This practice of worshiping a single saving truth is, of course, not limited to Hungary or even East Central Europe. After all, National Socialism and fascism originated in Western Europe, and Marxism was the manufactured dream of the German Karl Marx and his mentor and ally, the German industrialist Friedrich Engels, only to be taken to its extreme conclusion by the Russo-Tatar Lenin and the Georgian Stalin.)

Political discussion in Hungary was long distorted by the fact that the various partners each believed in a single truth. Whether this meant a strict loyalty to the Holy Crown, an abiding faith in the basic goodness of the Magyar peasant, or a worshipful imitation of models concocted in the British Library, beliefs of such intensity called for intolerance of "others" who could not or would not see "the Truth." It became an accepted tenet that doubters and questioners were either stupid, in which case they could be ignored, or liars and scoundrels, in which case they were labeled not just political opponents and debating partners but enemies to be destroyed or made impotent by any and all means. On a personal level, this attitude has led to brawls, even murders, in pubs or in legislative chambers. In a more damning manner, it provided the justification for the wide variants of hatreds that dominated Hungary and the region in the past century.

Believers in a single truth simply are incapable of making compromises in politics. Therefore, politics, which in democratic societies is the art of compromise, in East Central Europe led to vendettas and prompted political figures to work for the physical destruction of their "enemies." This attitude continues to be the major reason for the slow development of genuine participatory democracy throughout East Central Europe.

Hungarian society is ready for a transformation. The country is no longer surrounded by implacable enemies, and the West is paying a lot more attention to developments in the region. This means that there is no excuse for reviving the spirit of extremist nationalism that caused so much human and civilizational harm during the past century, and which, by the way, proved to be counterproductive as regards to alleviating the nation's ills. After 1989, there were some voices calling for just such a return to the 1930s. Hungarians heard the extemists' simplistic slogans, read their overheated arguments, and saw mass demonstrations.

Nevertheless, such exclusive nationalism no longer represents a significant force in the thinking of Hungarians. Although the scarcity of true democratic traditions continues to cause problems in Hungary's efforts to become a stable democratic society, the elections since the collapse of the communist regime have shown that Hungarians have finally accepted the rules of Western-type participatory democracy. The greatest progress has been made in the explosive growth of civil society.

Society as a whole, however, is still threatened by the dominance of the idea of the single truth. This idea has penetrated Hungarian mentality to such an extent that it will be very difficult to eliminate. To discover and then to defend the one Truth "to the death" has become a matter of honor for most citizens in every sphere of life, including the family. Few political parties or educational institutions have realized that this way of thinking simply must be changed.

The attitude demanding devotion to the idea of a single truth is so pervasive that its elimination will require the cooperation of all segments of society. It will be necessary to start teaching children about its dangers at an early age, and to inculcate them with tolerance and respect for the laws, as well as for those who do not conform to social norms laid out by the single truth. The teaching of tolerance and ethical behavior will have to be included in the curricula of all schools. Only such a nationwide effort can lead to success and provide for a favorable environment for the full development of democratic institutions. As long as the political parties and all social strata do not see this need clearly, history will remain an "enemy" of Hungarian democracy, even if economic conditions of the country take a turn for the better.

It is, of course, quite possible that the question of the continuing survival of the Hungarian nation, its language, and its culture eventually will become moot, in light of globalization and the information revolution. This may be the fate of all the nations of Europe. In such a future (which, of course, is by no means inevitable), all European nations will be amalgamated into a European Union dominated by a universal culture that will not be English, German, French, or Italian but European. The Union also will bring about the Europe-wide spread of uniformly democratic institutions.

The glass appears to be more than half full: institutional changes have become irreversible; free enterprise has taken deep roots and will soon dominate the economy; and the people, however dissatisfied with inept politicians and clumsy policies, do believe in democracy and do vote for the party and the candidate of their choice. Hungary is no longer a barracks, but the half-built home of 10 million free, albeit somewhat discontented citizens. Democracy works, and it is here to stay.

SELECTIVE BIBLIOGRAPHY

Aczél, Tamás, and Tibor Méray. *The Revolt of the Mind.* New York: Praeger, 1960.

Ash, Timothy Garton. *The Uses of Adversity: Essays on the Fate of Central Europe.* New York: Random House, 1989.

Bak, János M., and Béla K. Király, eds. *From Hunyadi to Rákóczi: War and Society in Medieval and Early Modern Hungary.* New York: Social Science Monographs, 1982.

Balogh, Sándor. *Autonomy and New World Order: A Solution to the National Minority Problem.* Toronto: Matthias Corvinus, 1999.

Barany, George. *Stephen Széchenyi and the Awakening of Hungarian Nationalism.* Princeton: Princeton University Press, 1968.

Bartha, Antal. *Hungarian Society in the 9th and 10th Centuries.* Budapest: Akadémiai Kiadó, 1975.

Batkay, William A. *Authoritarian Politics in a Transitional State; István Bethlen and the Unified Party in Hungary, 1919–1926.* Boulder: East European Monographs, 1982.

Bayerle, Gustav. *Ottoman Diplomacy in Hungary.* Bloomington: Indiana University Press, 1972.

Békés, Csaba, Malcolm Byrne, and János Ranier, eds. *The 1956 Hungarian Revolution: A History in Documents.* Budapest: Central European University Press, 2002.

Berend, T. Iván, and György Ránki. *The Hungarian Manufacturing Industry: Its Place in Europe, 1900–1938.* Budapest: 1960.

———. *Hungary: A Century of Economic Development.* New York: Barnes & Noble, 1974.

Bernard, Paul B. *Jesuits and Jacobins: Enlightenment and Enlightened Despotism in Austria.* Chicago: University of Chicago Press, 1971.

Bibó, István. *Democracy, Revolution, Self-Determination.* Edited by Károly Nagy. New York: Social Science Monographs and Atlantic Research and Publications, 1991.

Birnbaum, Marianna. *Janus Pannonius.* Zagreb: Jugoslavensko akademija znanasti I umjetnasti, 1981.

Blanning, T. C. W. *Joseph II and Enlightened Despotism.* London: Longman, 1970.

Bödy, Paul. "Joseph Eötvös and the Modernization of Hungary, 1840–1870: A Study of Ideas of Individuality and Social Pluralism in Modern Politics." *Transactions of the American Philosophical Society* 62, no. 2 (1972).

Borsody, Stephen, ed. *The Hungarians: A Divided Nation.* New Haven: Slavica, 1988.

Brada, Josef C., and István Dobozi, eds. *The Hungarian Economy in the 1980s.* Greenwich, Conn.: JAI Press, 1988.

Braham, Randolph L. *The Destruction of Hungarian Jews.* New York: World Federation of Hungarian Jews, 1963.

Bridge, F. R. *Great Britain and Austria-Hungary, 1906–1914.* London: London School of Economics and Political Science, 1972.

Cadzow, John F., Andrew Ludányi, and Louis J. Éltető, eds. *Transylvania: The Roots of Ethnic Conflict.* Kent, Ohio: Kent State University Press, 1983.

Chászár, Edward. *The International Problem of National Minorities.* Toronto: Matthias Corvinus, 1999.

Collinder, Björn. *An Introduction to the Uralic Languages.* Berkeley: University of California Press, 1965.

Csapodi, Csaba. *The Corvinian Library.* Budapest: Akadémiai Kiadó, 1973.

Cushing, George Frederick. *Hungarian Prose and Verse.* London: Athlone, 1956.

Czigány, Lóránt. *The Oxford History of Hungarian Literature.* Oxford: Clarendon, 1984.

Deák, Francis. *Hungary at the Paris Peace Conference.* New York: 1942.

Deák, István. *A Lawful Revolution: Louis Kossuth and the Hungarians, 1848–1849.* New York: Columbia University Press, 1979.

Deme, László. *The Radical Left and the Hungarian Revolution of 1848.* Boulder: East European Monographs, 1976.

Dienes, István. *The Hungarians Cross the Carpathians.* Budapest: Corvina, 1972.

Engel, Pál. *The Realm of St. Stephen: A History of Medieval Hungary, 895–1526.* London: L. B. Tauris, 2001.

Enyedi, György. *Hungary: An Economic Geography.* Boulder: Westview, 1976.

Fejto, Francois. *A History of the People's Democracies: Eastern Europe since Stalin.* Harmondsworth, U.K.: Penguin, 1974.

Fél, Edit, and Tamás Hófer. *Proper Peasants: Traditional Life in a Hungarian Village.* Chicago: Aldine, 1969.

Felkay, Andrew. *Hungary and the USSR, 1956–1988.* New York: Greenwood, 1988.

Fenyo, Mario. *Horthy and Hungary: German-Hungarian Relations, 1941–1944.* New Haven: Yale University Press, 1972.

Ferge, Zsuzsa. *A Society in the Making: Hungarian Social and Societal Policy, 1945–75.* White Plains, N.Y.: Sharpe, 1979.

Fodor, István. *In Search of a New Homeland: The Prehistory of the Hungarian People and the Conquest.* Budapest: Corvina, 1982.

Fügedi, Erik. *Castle and Society in Medieval Hungary, 1000–1437.* Budapest: Akadémiai Kiadó, 1986.

Gabriel, Astrik. *The Medieval Universities of Pécs and Pozsony.* Notre Dame, Ind.: University of Notre Dame Press, 1969.

Gáti, Charles. *The Bloc That Failed: Soviet–East European Relations in Transition.* Bloomington: Indiana University Press, 1990.

Gerevich, László. *The Art of Buda and Pest in the Middle Ages.* Budapest: Akadémiai Kiadó, 1971.

Glatz, Ferenc, ed. *Hungarians and Their Neighbors in Modern Times, 1867–1950.* New York: Social Science Monographs, 1995.
Hajdú, Tibor. *The Hungarian Soviet Republic.* Budapest: Akadémiai Kiadó, 1979.
Hanák, Péter, ed. *One Thousand Years: A Concise History of Hungary.* Budapest: Corvina, 1988.
Haraszti, Miklós. *The Velvet Prison: Artists Under State Socialism.* New York: Basic, 1987.
Held, Joseph. *Hunyadi: Legend and Reality.* Boulder: East European Monographs, 1985.
Held, Joseph, ed. *The Columbia History of Eastern Europe in the 20th Century.* New York: Columbia University press, n.d.
Hoensch, Jörg K. *A History of Modern Hungary, 1867–1986.* New York: Longman, 1988.
Hóman, Bálint. *King Stephen the Saint.* Budapest: Sárkány, 1938.
Horthy, Admiral Nicholas. *Memoirs.* New York: Robert Speller, 1957. New edition annotated by Andrew Simon. Safety Harbor, Fla.: Simon, 2000.
Ignotus, Paul. *Hungary.* New York: Praeger, 1972.
Illyés, Elemér. *Ethnic Continuity in the Carpatho-Danubian Area.* Boulder: East European Monographs, 1988.
———. *National Minorities in Romania: Change in Transylvania.* Boulder: East European Monographs, 1982.
János, Andrew C. *The Politics of Backwardness in Hungary, 1825–1945.* Princeton: Princeton University Press, 1982.
Jászi, Oscar. *The Dissolution of the Habsburg Monarchy.* Chicago: University of Chicago Press, 1929.
Jones, D. Mervyn. *Five Hungarian Writers.* Oxford: Oxford University Press, 1966.
Joó, Rudolf, and Andrew Ludányi, eds. *The Hungarian Minority's Situation in Ceausescu's Romania.* New York: Social Science Monographs, 1994.
Juhász, Gyula. *Hungarian Foreign Policy, 1919–1945.* Budapest: 1979.
Kállay, Miklós. *Hungarian Premier.* New York: Columbia University Press, 1958.
Kann, Robert A. *A History of the Habsburg Empire, 1526–1918.* Berkeley: University of California Press, 1974.
———. *The Multinational Empire: Nationalism and National Reform in the Habsburg Monarchy, 1848–1918.* New York: Columbia University Press, 1950.
Kann, Robert A., Béla K. Király, and P. S. Fichtner, eds. *The Habsburg Empire in World War I.* Boulder: East European Quarterly, 1977.
Kecskeméti, Paul. *The Unexpected Revolution.* Stanford: Stanford University Press, 1961.
Kertész, Stephen. *Between Russia and the West: Hungary and the Illusions of Peacemaking, 1945–1947.* Notre Dame, Ind.: University of Notre Dame Press, 1984.
Király, Béla. *Hungary in the Late Eighteenth Century: The Decline of Enlightened Despotism.* New York: Columbia University Press, 1969.
Király, Béla K., ed. *Lawful Revolution in Hungary, 1989–94.* Boulder: East European Monographs, 1995.
Király, Béla, and Paul Jonas. *The Hungarian Revolution of 1956 in Retrospect.* East European Monographs, no. 40. New York: Columbia University Press, 1978.
Király, Béla K., Peter Pastor, and Ivan Sanders, eds. *Essays on World War I: Total War and Peacemaking: A Case Study of Trianon.* New York: Social Science Monographs, 1982.
Kohn, Hans. *The Habsburg Empire.* Princeton: Van Nostrand, 1961.
Kontler, László. *Millennium in Central Europe: A History of Hungary.* Budapest: Atlantisz, 1999.
Kopácsi, Sándor. *In the Name of the Working Class.* New York: Grove, 1986.
Köpeczi, Béla, Gábor Barta, István Barna, László Makkai, and Zoltán Szász, eds. *The History of Transylvania.* Budapest: Akadémiai Kiadó, 1994.
Kosáry, Domokos. *Culture and Society in Eighteenth-Century Hungary.* Budapest: Corvina, 1987.
Kovács, Éva, and Zsuzsa Lovag. *The Hungarian Crown and Other Regalia.* Budapest: Corvina, 1980.
Kovrig, Bennett. *Communism in Hungary from Kun to Kádár.* Stanford: Hoover Institution Press, 1979.
Lendvai, Paul. *Hungary: The Art of Survival.* London: I. B. Tauris, 1988.
Macartney, Carlile A. *The Habsburg Empire, 1790–1918.* London: Weidenfeld & Nicolson, 1968; New York: Macmillan, 1969.
———. *A History of Hungary.* New York: Praeger, 1956.
———. *Hungary.* London: E. Benn, 1934.
———. *Hungary: A Short History.* Chicago: Aldine, 1962.
———. *Hungary and Her Successors, 1919–1937.* London: 1937.
———. *The Magyars in the IXth Century.* Cambridge: Cambridge University Press, 1930.
———. *October Fifteenth: A History of Modern Hungary, 1929–1945.* 2d ed. Edinburgh: University Press, 1962.
Makkai, Adam, ed. *In Quest of the "Miracle Stag": The Poetry of Hungary.* Chicago: Atlantis-Centaur, 1996.
May, Arthur J. *The Passing of the Hapsburg Monarchy, 1914–1918.* Philadelphia: University of Pennsylvania Press, 1966.
McCagg, William O., Jr. *Jewish Nobles and Geniuses in Modern Hungary.* Boulder: East European Quarterly, 1972.
McGowan, Bruce. *Economic Life in Ottoman Europe: Taxation, Trade, and the Struggle for Land, 1600–1800.* Cambridge: Cambridge University Press, 1981.
Molnár, Miklós. *A Concise History of Hungary.* Cambridge: Cambridge University Press, 2001.
Nagy, Imre. *On Communism.* New York: Greenwood, 1957.
Nagy-Talavera, Nicholas M. *The Green Shirts and the Others.* Stanford: Hoover Institution Press, 1970.
Nelson, Joan M., ed. *Fragile Coalitions: The Politics of Economic Adjustment.* New Brunswick, N.J.: Transaction, 1989.
Pamlényi, Ervin, ed. *A History of Hungary.* London: Collet's, 1975.
Ránki, György, ed. *Hungarian History-World History.* Budapest: Akadémia kiadó,1984.
Robertson, Priscilla. *Revolutions of 1848: A Social History.* Princeton: Princeton University Press, 1968.

Roider, Karl A., Jr. *Maria Theresa.* Englewood, N.J.: Prentice-Hall, 1973.

Rothenberg, Gunther E. *The Army of Francis Joseph.* West Lafayette, Ind.: Purdue University Press, 1976.

Rothschild, Joseph. *East Central Europe between the Two World Wars.* Seattle: University of Washington Press, 1974.

———. *Return to Diversity: A Political History of East Central Europe since World War II.* New York: Oxford University Press, 1989.

Rounds, Carol. *Hungarian: An Essential Grammar.* London: Routledge, 2001.

Rounds, Carol, and Erika Sólyom. *Colloquial Hungarian: The Complete Course for Beginners.* London: Routledge, 2002.

Schöpflin, George. *Hungary between Prosperity and Crisis.* London: London Institute for the Study of Conflict, 1981.

Seton-Watson, Robert W. *Racial Problems in Hungary.* London: Constable, 1908.

Simon, Andrew L. *Made in Hungary: Hungarian Contributions to Universal Culture.* Safety Harbor, Fla.: Simon, 1998.

Sisa, Stephen. *The Spirit of Hungary: A Panorama of Hungarian History and Culture.* 2d ed. Morristown, N.J.: Vista, 1990.

Somogyi, Ferenc, and Lél F. Somogyi. *Faith and Fate: A Short Cultural History of the Hungarian People through the Millennium.* Cleveland: Kárpát, 1976.

Spira, György. *A Hungarian Count in the Revolution of 1848.* Translated by Richard E. Allen. Budapest: Akadémiai Kiadó, 1974.

Sugar, Peter F. *Southeastern Europe under Ottoman Rule, 1354–1804.* Seattle: University of Washington Press, 1977.

Sugar, Peter, et al. *A History of Hungary.* Bloomington: Indiana University Press, 1984.

Szabad, György. *Hungarian Political Trends between the Revolution and the Compromise, 1849–1867.* Studia Historica, no. 128. Budapest, 1977.

Szász, Béla. *Volunteers for the Gallows: Anatomy of a Show Trial.* London: Norton, 1971.

Szelényi, Iván. *Socialist Entrepreneurs: Embourgeoisement in Rural Hungary.* Madison: University of Wisconsin Press, 1988.

Taylor, A. J. P. *The Habsburg Monarchy, 1815–1918.* London: H. Hamilton, 1949.

Tezla, Albert. *Hungarian Authors: A Bibliographical Handbook.* Cambridge: Cambridge University Press, 1970.

Tilkovszky, Lóránt. *Pál Teleki, 1879–1941.* Budapest: Akadémiai Kiadó, 1974.

Tőkés, Rudolf. *Béla Kun and the Hungarian Soviet Republic.* New York: Praeger, 1967.

Toma, Peter A. *Socialist Authority: The Hungarian Experience.* New York: Praeger, 1988.

UN General Assembly. *Report of the Special Committee on the Problems of Hungary.* New York, 1957.

Váli, Ferenc A. *Rift and Revolt in Hungary: Nationalism versus Communism.* Cambridge: Harvard University Press, 1961.

Várdy, Steven Béla. *Historical Dictionary of Hungary.* Lanham, Md.: Scarecrow, 1997.

———. *Modern Hungarian Historiography.* Boulder: East European Monographs, 1976.

Várdy, Steven Béla, and Ágnes Huszár Várdy, eds. *Triumph in Adversity: Studies in Hungarian Civilization.* Boulder: East European Monographs, 1988.

Várdy, Steven Béla, Géza Grosschmid, and Leslie S. Domonkos. *Louis the Great.* Boulder: East European Monographs, 1986.

Varga, Domokos. *Hungary in Greatness and Decline: The Fourteenth and Fifteenth Centuries.* Atlanta: Hungarian Cultural Foundation, 1983.

Verdery, Katherine. *Transylvanian Villagers.* Berkeley: University of California Press, 1983.

Vermes, Gábor. *Count István Tisza.* Boulder: East European Mongraphs, 1985.

Wagner, Francis S. *Hungarian Contributions to World Civilization.* Center Square, Pa.: Alpha, 1977.

Winter, Stanley B., and Joseph Held, eds. *Intellectual and Social Developments in the Habsburg Empire from Maria Theresa to World War I.* Boulder: East European Quarterly, 1975.

CHRONOLOGY

1st millennium B.C.E.	Finno-Ugric period of the Hungarian people. Separation of the Finno-Ugric languages in western Siberia. Separation of the Ugrians, Magyar people group in the southern Ural region (Bashkiria).
5th–8th c.	Hun then Avar rule in the Carpathian Basin.
8th–9th c.	Migration of the Hungarian tribes from the Urals to the Black Sea region.
896–900	Hungarian settlement of the Carpathian Basin.
	Árpád is chosen chieftain; his male descendants become hereditary rulers.
899–970	Hungarian raids into Western Europe and the Balkans.
955	Hungarian raiders defeated at Lechfeld (Augsburg) by German-Moravian forces.
	Prince Géza is baptized into the Roman Catholic Church.
1001	Coronation of Géza's son, István I (later St. Stephen).
1046	Vata's pagan rising.
1077–1116	László I (St. Ladislas) (1077–1095) and Kálmán I (1095–1116) expand into Croatia and Dalmatia.
1142–1162	Saxon settlements in Transylvania; struggle against Byzantine expansion.
c. 1192–1195	The Pray Codex, containing the oldest Hungarian text.
1222	The Golden Bull, first charter of rights for the nobility.
1241–1242	Mongol invasion devastates the country, followed by reconstruction.
1301–1308	Struggle for the Hungarian throne between Wenceslas Przemysl, Otto von Wittelsbach, and Charles of Anjou; won by latter.

1308–1342	Dynastic marriages link Hungary to Naples and Poland.
1343–1382	Lajos I (Louis the Great) reconfirms the Golden Bull.
1349	The Black Death in Hungary.
1370–1382	Lajos becomes king of Poland.
1416–1456	Wars against Ottoman threat.
1442–1443	János Hunyadi defeats Ottomans in Transylvania and Serbia.
1444	Hunyadi is defeated at Varna (Bulgaria). Ulászló I dies in battle.
1446–1452	János Hunyadi rules Hungary as regent for infant king.
1448	Hunyadi's defeat at Kosovo Polje.
1456	Hunyadi stops Ottoman expansion at Nándorfehérvár (Belgrade).
1458–1490	Mátyás I Corvinus, Hunyadi's son, reconstructs the kingdom and introduces Renaissance culture.
1472–1477	First Hungarian printing press in Buda.
1505	Decision of Diet at Rákos to elect a king, excluding a foreign ruler.
1514	Peasant uprising led by György Dózsa. István Werbőczi's Tripartitum reduces peasants to serfdom.
29 August 1526	At Mohács, army of Suleiman I defeats the Hungarian army. Two rival kings, János Zápolyai (1526–1540) and Ferdinand I (1526–1564), divide the country between them.
1540–1570	Rule of János Zsigmond (Zápolyai) in eastern Hungary.
1541	Ottomans occupy Buda and central Hungary. Division of Hungary into three parts. The Reformation reaches Hungary.
1566	Suleiman's last campaign in Hungary; the fall of Szigetvár (September).
1568	Transylvanian Diet at Torda proclaims religious freedom.
1570	Treaty of Speyer: Eastern Hungary becomes Principality of Transylvania.
1571–1586	István Báthory, future king of Poland (1576–1586), Prince of Transylvania.
1581–1602	Zsigmond Báthory rules as Prince of Transylvania.
1591	Habsburgs invade Transylvania.
1598	Zsigmond Báthory hands over Transylvania to the Habsburg king.
1604–1606	Campaigns against the Habsburgs led by István Bocskai.
1606	Peace of Zsitvatorok with Ottomans.
1606–1608	Zsigmond Rákóczi rules as Prince of Transylvania.
1608–1613	Gábor Báthory rules as Prince of Transylvania.
1613–1629	Transylvania's golden age under Gábor Bethlen.
1630–1648	György Rákóczi rules as Prince of Transylvania.
1644–1645	Campaign of György Rákóczi I, in alliance with the Swedes. Peace of Linz: religious freedom for the serfs.
1657–1705	Leopold I introduces Habsburg absolutism in Hungary.
1664	Miklós Zrinyi's winter campaign; Battle of St. Gotthard. Peace of Vasvár leaves Turkish conquest intact.
1672	The beginning of the *kuruc* liberation struggle.
1683	Ottoman siege of Vienna; defeat of Ottoman forces.
1686	Recapture of Buda from Ottomans.
1687	Transylvania falls under Habsburg rule. Diet at Pozsony recognizes Habsburg right of succession in Hungary.
1691	*Diploma Leopoldinum:* Transylvania becomes independent principality.
1697	*Kuruc* rebellion in the Tokaj region. Eugene of Savoy wins a decisive victory over Ottomans at Zenta.
1699	Peace treaty of Karlowitz ends Ottoman rule in Hungary.
1687–1918	Hungary under the Habsburgs.
1703–1711	War of liberation led by Ferenc Rákóczi II.
1711	Treaty of Szatmár ends rebellion and results in compromise between Habsburg monarchy and Hungarian rebels.
1722–1723	Hungarian Diet accepts Pragmatic Sanction. Habsburgs agree to rule Hungary subject to constitution and laws.
1767	Urbarial Patent regulates size of serfs' land holdings and labor services.
1781	Edict of Tolerance: religious freedom to non-Catholics.
1785	Decree of Joseph II reorganizing public administration in Hungary; abolition of perpetual serfdom.
1786	Romanian peasant insurrection in Transylvania.
1790–1792	Leopold II softens Habsburg policy.
1800–1848	Movement to reform the Hungarian language.
1802	Founding of the Hungarian National Museum.
1805	Laws printed in Hungarian and Latin, first achievement in the struggle for the recognition of the Hungarian language.
1830	Publication of *Hitel* (Credit) by Count István Széchenyi.
1832–1848	Period of reforms in the Diet. Lajos Kossuth leads the liberal-radical

	opposition. Diet makes Hungarian the country's official language. Opening of the National Theater at Pest. First railway line.
1848–1849	Hungary's War of Independence against Austria. A revolution against the absolute monarchy breaks out in Pest (15 March). Abdication of Emperor Ferdinand. Franz Joseph is enthroned. After the victorious spring campaign the Hungarian army retreats. The National Assembly, transferred to Debrecen, proclaims Hungary's independence and the dethronement of the Habsburgs (14 April 1849). Armies of Tsar Nicholas I invade Hungary to rescue Habsburg rule. Hungarian army lays down its arms to the Russians at Világos (15 August). Franz Joseph revokes Hungarian constitution and assumes absolute power.
1849–1850	General Haynau's martial rule in Hungary.
1851	Proclamation of the Principles of Government and open absolutism.
1860	István Széchenyi commits suicide. October Diploma issued.
1861	February Patent issued. First, brief parliament of the neoabsolutist period.
1866	The Austrian army is defeated by the Prussians at Sadowa (Königgrätz).
1867–1918	Dual Monarchy.
1867	Austro-Hungarian Compromise *(Ausgleich)* based on mutual concessions.
1867–1871	Count Gyula Andrássy's government.
1868	Hungarian parliament adopts liberal laws regarding education and the rights of the national minorities in the kingdom. In Hungarian-Croatian compromise, Croatia gains autonomy and control over its domestic affairs.
1871–1879	Gyula Andrássy serves as minister of foreign affairs of Dual Monarchy.
1873	Pest, Buda, and Óbuda are united, Budapest is born.
1879	Austro-Hungarian Monarchy and Germany form the Dual Alliance.
1882	Germany, the Austro-Hungarian Monarchy, and Italy form Triple Alliance.
1894	Funeral of Lajos Kossuth. Libel trial of Romanian politicians (Memorandum trial). Sanctioning of laws on church–state relations.
1908	Annexation of Bosnia-Hercegovina by Austria-Hungary. Launching of the progressive literary periodical *Nyugat* (The West).
1910	Mass emigration to America (more than 1.5 million).
28 June 1914	Assassination of Archduke Franz Ferdinand, at Sarajevo; outbreak of World War I.
1915	Count Mihály Károlyi forms Independence Party.
1916	Franz Joseph dies.
1918	General political strike. Defeat and disintegration of Austro-Hungarian monarchy (October). Democratic revolution. Abdication of King Charles IV. Formation of Hungarian National Council presided over by Mihály Károlyi.
11 January 1919	Károlyi becomes president of the republic.
1919	Law on land reform published.
21 March 1919	Hungarian Soviet Republic proclaimed under Communist leader Béla Kun.
1919	Anti-Bolshevik committee formed in Vienna under Count István Bethlen. Romanian forces occupy Budapest.
16 November 1919	Admiral Miklós Horthy's paramilitary forces enter the capital.
1920–1945	Trianon Hungary.
1 March 1920	Horthy elected regent of the kingdom.
4 June 1920	Under the Treaty of Trianon, Hungary loses two-thirds of its territory, 60 percent of its population, and most of its natural resources.
6 November 1921	Dethronement of the House of Habsburg.
1922	Hungary joins the League of Nations.
1927	Italian-Hungarian friendship treaty. Monetary stabilization.
1932–1936	Under Prime Minister Gyula Gömbös, a turn to the right, toward Germany and Italy, takes place.
1934	Rome Protocol on Hungarian, Italian, and Austrian cooperation.
1938	First anti-Jewish laws. First Vienna Award restores southern Slovakia to Hungary.
1939	Hungary regains Magyar-inhabited region of Carpatho-Ukraine. Second anti-Jewish laws. Rise of the Hungarian Nazis, the Arrow Cross Party, at the elections.
1940	Second Vienna Award restores northern Transylvania to Hungary. Adherence to the tripartite pact of Berlin-Rome-Tokyo.
1941	Hungary joins German attack on Yugoslavia. Hungary enters the war against Soviet Union (June) and declares war against Allies (December).

1942–1943	Prime Minister Miklós Kállay attempts peace overtures toward the Allies.
1943	The Hungarian Second Army is annihilated at Voronezh on the Don.
	Secret negotiations with Britain.
1944	Germany occupies Hungary (19 March).
	Deportation of almost half a million Jews from the provinces.
	Red Army crosses Hungarian border.
1944	Horthy proclaims armistice on the radio (October 15).
	Germans occupy strategic points.
	Horthy appoints Arrow Cross leader Ferenc Szálasi as head of the Council of Ministers.
	Assassination or deportation of 105,000 Jews.
	Anti-German provisional government formed in Debrecen.
1945–1989	Postwar and Communist Hungary.
1945	Soviet troops drive all German troops out of Hungary (April 4).
	Legislative elections (November 4): Smallholders Party 57 percent, Communist Party 17 percent. Coalition government includes four Communists.
1946	Proclamation of the Republic; Zoltán Tildy becomes first president.
	Nationalization of banks and the iron and steel industry.
1947	Three-year plan of reconstruction.
	Peace treaty signed in Paris (February 10).
	Arrests and sham trials of non-Communist politicians.
	Forced resignation of Premier Ferenc Nagy.
1948	Forced fusion of the Social Democratic Party with the Communist Party; further nationalization.
	Closing of church-operated schools.
1949	Hungarian People's Republic proclaimed with Soviet-style constitution (August 20); Cardinal József Mindszenty and other Church dignitaries arrested and tried.
	Trial and execution of Communist Minister of Internal Affairs László Rajk.
1949–1953	Stalinist political, economic, and social systems are imposed.
1953	Stalin dies.
1955	Reformer Imre Nagy becomes prime minister, implements New Course.
1956	Twentieth Congress of the Soviet Communist Party (February).
	Opposition group of Hungarian intellectuals (Petőfi Circle) grows.
	Solemn funeral of Rajk and other victims of Stalinist terror (October) culminates in mass demonstrations in Budapest.
	The Hungarian Revolution erupts (23 October).
	Soviet army invades Hungary (4 November) and installs János Kádár.
	Hungarian Workers Party renamed Hungarian Socialist Workers Party.
	Exodus of 200,000 Hungarians.
1957–1963	Period of repression.
	Imre Nagy and associates tried and executed (June 1958).
	Trial of writers and freedom fighters; over 300 executions.
1961	Recollectivization of agriculture.
1963	General amnesty; relaxation of repression.
1968	Launching of economic reforms: "New Economic Mechanism."
1984	Hungary begins to establish semi-independent foreign policy.
1987	Democratic opposition spreads.
1988	Károly Grósz replaces Kádár as Communist Party leader.
	Creation of democratic political parties.
1989–	Post-Communist era.
1989	The year of changes.
26 January	Exhumation and reburial of Nagy and his associates is authorized.
	Workers are granted the right to strike.
10–11 February	Central Committee formally endorses the idea of multiparty system.
20–21 February	Central Committee approves draft of new constitution, omitting leading role of the Communist Party.
11 March	Hungarian Democratic Forum (MDF) holds its first congress.
23 March	Revived Smallholders Party holds its first congress.
6 April	Withdrawal of 10,000 (of the 62,000) Red Army troops from Hungary announced.
8–9 May	Central Committee relieves János Kádár of his party posts.
14 June	Tripartite roundtable talks begin for a democratic transition.
16 June	Reburial of Imre Nagy and associates; hundreds of thousands attend.
6 July	János Kádár dies; Imre Nagy rehabilitated by Supreme Court.
11–12 July	U.S. President George Bush visits Budapest.
September	Foreign Minister Gyula Horn announces "temporary suspension" of agreement with East Germany; East German citizens are allowed to cross into Austria.
10 October	Central Committee changes party's name to Socialist, led by Rezső Nyers.
23 October	Republic of Hungary proclaimed.

March 1990	Legislative elections: Democratic Forum forms center-right coalition government, headed by historian József Antall. Árpád Göncz, president of the republic.
1994	Legislative elections. Socialist (ex-Communist) Party gets an absolute majority. Gyula Horn forms a coalition government with Liberal Democrats.
1996	Commemoration of the eleventh centenary of the arrival of the Hungarians in the Carpathian Basin.
1997	Protocols signed for Hungary to join NATO.
2004	Hungary joins the European Union (EU).

CROATIA

MARK BIONDICH

LAND AND PEOPLE

GEOGRAPHY

The Republic of Croatia (in Croatian, Republika Hrvatska) is situated in Southeastern Europe. It is located in the northwestern part of the Balkan Peninsula, bounded by Slovenia in the northwest, Hungary in the northeast, Serbia-Montenegro in the east, Bosnia-Hercegovina in the south and east, and the Adriatic Sea in the west. Croatia is a comparatively small country with a total area of 56,538 square kilometers, with a coastline that extends 5,790 kilometers (mainland 1,778 kilometers, and the islands 4,012 kilometers).

Croatia is composed of four historic provinces: Croatia proper (with Zagreb), Slavonia, Dalmatia, and Istria. Croatia proper, which is composed of the areas known as Medjimurje, Hrvatsko Zagorje, Moslavina, Banija, Kordun, Lika, and Gorski Kotar, is the most heavily populated area and also the industrial and agricultural center of Croatia. According to the census of 31 March 2001, Croatia proper had a population of 2,571,764, or 57.9 percent of Croatia's total population. The principal towns are Karlovac, Petrinja, Sisak, and Čakovec. Slavonia is a fertile agricultural and forested lowland bounded in part by the Drava River in the north and the Sava River in the south. Wheat and corn are the primary crops; the leading industry is food processing. It also has oil and natural gas deposits. According to the 2001 census, this province had 797,870 inhabitants, or 18 percent of the total population of Croatia. The principal towns of Slavonia are Osijek, Slavonski Brod, and Vukovar. Dalmatia extends along the Adriatic Sea. In 2001 it had 861,482 inhabitants, or 19.4 percent of the total population of Croatia. Its principal towns are Split, Zadar, Šibenik, and Dubrovnik. The local economy is oriented toward the sea; the scenic location and historic monuments make Dalmatia an important tourist destination. Split is the largest town and a leading commercial center. Shipbuilding and the production of plastics, chemicals, and cement are the major industries. The town of Zadar is also a leading tourist center, in addition to having industries that produce liqueur, processed fish, textiles, and cigarettes. The city also has several Roman monuments and medieval churches and palaces. Šibenik is a seaport and naval base, with shipbuilding, metalworking, and aluminum industries. Dubrovnik is also an important tourist and cultural center. Istria is a mountainous peninsula approximately 3,900 square kilometers in size. Although the vast majority of the peninsula is part of Croatia, a smaller part of the northwestern portion belongs to Slovenia and Italy, including the city of Trieste. The area is thickly forested and predominantly agricultural. In 2001 Istria had a population of 206,344, representing about 4.7 percent of Croatia's total population. Pula is the principal town and a shipbuilding center. It is a major seaport and industrial center, with shipyards, docks, and varied manufactures.

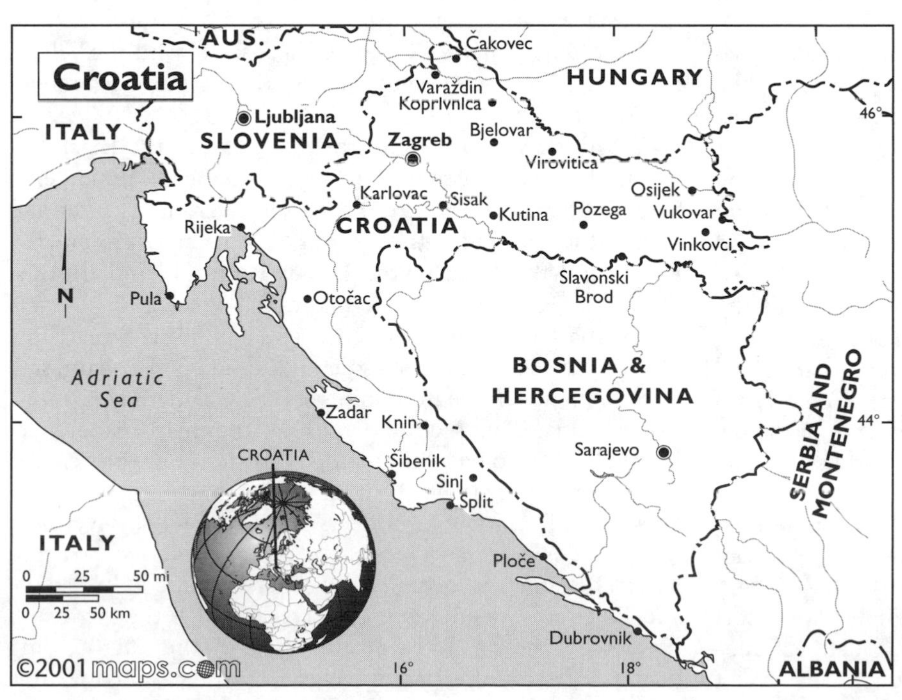

Clock tower in Zagreb. (Tim Thompson/Corbis)

Croatia is a geographically diverse land composed of three distinct zones: the Adriatic (or Littoral), the Mountainous (or Dinaric), and the Continental (or Lowland). The Adriatic zone consists of the relatively narrow strip of territory running along the Adriatic coastline, consisting of the peninsula of Istria, the Croatian Littoral, Dalmatia, and the islands. The coastline extends 5,790 kilometers. The climate in this zone is characterized by hot and dry summers and mild and rainy winters. The Adriatic zone may be divided further into a northern part, consisting of Istria and the Kvarner, and a southern part, which includes Dalmatia.

The Croatian Adriatic has a total of 1,185 islands and islets with a total coastline of 4,012 kilometers. Of the 1,185 islands and islets, 718 are islands in the conventional sense, of which only 66 are inhabited. There are an additional 389 "rocks" and 78 reefs. There are fourteen islands with a total size of more than 50 square kilometers. Eight of these islands are larger than 100 square kilometers: Krk (409 square kilometers), Cres (405.8 square kilometers), Brač (394.6 square kilometers), Pag (299.7 square kilometers), Korčula (284.6 square kilometers), and Hvar (276 square kilometers), Dugi Otok (114.4 square kilometers), and Mljet (100.4 square kilometers). The inhabited islands are sparsely populated. According to the 1991 census, only four islands had more than 10,000 inhabitants: Korčula (17,038), Krk (16,402), Brač (13,824), and Hvar (11,459).

The Continental (or Lowland) zone is composed of Croatia proper with Slavonia. The western part of this zone lies in the Dinaric Alps; the eastern part, drained by the Sava and Drava rivers, is mostly low lying and agricultural. Slavonia is a fertile agricultural region and hence the country's chief farming region and a center of livestock breeding. The northwestern part of this zone, and especially the capital Zagreb with its environs, is industrially the most developed part of the whole country. The climate in this entire zone may be termed continental. Winters are normally cold and snowy while summers are short and humid. More than one-third of Croatia is forested and consequently lumber is a major export. There are also some natural resources like oil, bauxite, copper, and iron ore.

The Continental and Adriatic zones are separated by the Mountainous (or Dinaric) zone, which consists of low mountains and highlands. This transitional zone is a barren, rocky region lying in the Dinaric Alps and consisting of the Lika region and the Velebit range. This hilly and mountainous area is economically the least developed part of Croatia. A considerable part of Croatia lies at an altitude of over 500 meters, but there are no mountains higher than 2,000 meters. The highest mountains are found in the Mountainous zone (e.g., Risnjak at 1,528 meters, Velika Kapela at 1,533 meters, and Plješivica at 1,657 meters) or close to the sea (e.g., Velebit at 1,758 meters). The highest mountains in Dalmatia are Biokovo (1,762 meters) near the sea and Dinara (1,831 meters) in the hinterland.

Croatia has no mountains exceeding 2,000 meters, although it has twenty-one mountains with peaks exceeding 1,000 meters above sea level. The five tallest peaks (and the mountain ranges where they are located) are Dinara (in the Dinara Mountains) at 1,830 meters, Kamešnica (in the Kamešnica range) at 1,810 meters, Sveti Jure (in the Biokovo range) at 1,762 meters, Vaganski vrh (in the Velebit range) at 1,757 meters, and Ozeblin (in the Plješivica range) at 1,657 meters.

Croatia's rivers belong to the Adriatic and the Black Sea basin. The rivers in the interior are large and calmer (e.g., Sava, Drava, and Danube). The coastal rivers are shorter and have a higher gradient. The longest coastal rivers are the Mirna and the Rasa in the Istrian Peninsula and the Zrmanja, the Krka, and the Cetina in Dalmatia.

Croatia has approximately thirty small lakes. Only three of these are larger than 10 square kilometers. The largest is Lake Vrana (30.7 square kilometers) near Biograd-na-moru in Dalmatia. The second largest is the man-made Lake Peruča (13.0 square kilometers) located on the Cetina River near Sinj, also in Dalmatia. The third largest is Lake Prokljan (11.1 square kilometers) along the Krka River near Šibenik. There are also a number of artificially constructed lakes. The largest is Lake Peruča; others include Lakes Lokve and Bajer in Gorski Kotar and Trakošćan in the region of Hrvatsko Zagorje. Lake Kopačevo and the surrounding swamp forests in the Baranja region of eastern Croatia are a

Plitvice Lakes, a World Heritage site. (Corel Corporation)

major bird habitat. The most famous lakes in Croatia, and also an important tourist destination, are the Plitvice Lakes. This chain of sixteen lakes is designated as a national park with a total area of 19,479 hectares.

Croatia has eight national parks: Kornati (30,200 hectares in size), Plitvice Lakes (19,479 hectares), Krka (14,200 hectares), Paklenica (3,617 hectares), Mljet (3,100 hectares), Risnjak (3,014 hectares), Brijuni (2,700 hectares), and Northern Velebit (10,900 hectares). Additionally, there are six "nature parks" totaling 317,502 hectares in area, two "strict" reserves totaling 2,395 hectares, and sixty-nine "special" reserves totaling 30,372 hectares. There are also twenty-eight protected nature areas totaling 17,544 hectares. These state-protected nature zones amount to roughly 7.5 percent of Croatian state territory.

Croatia has a total of 3.15 million hectares of agricultural land of which roughly 2 million is cultivated. The rest consists of pastures, moors, and fishponds. The majority of cultivated land (81.5 percent) is privately owned. There is 59,000 hectares of land allotted to vineyards. In 2001 there were 1,142 companies employing 22,300 employees in the agricultural sector. Of the three geographic zones in Croatia, only the Lowland zone (i.e., Slavonia), with its fertile soil and continental climate, is favorably suited for agriculture.

POPULATION

According to the last Croatian census, conducted on 31 March 2001, the total population of Croatia was 4,437,460. Croats compose the vast majority of the population, numbering 3,977,171 persons, or 89.63 percent of the total population. Of the country's minorities, the most numerous are the Serbs, who number 201,631 or 4.54 percent of the population. Nearly a dozen other nationalities compose the remaining 258,658 inhabitants (5.83 percent). The 2001 census indicates that important changes have taken place in Croatia's population since the last census, which was conducted in March 1991. These changes can be attributed almost entirely to the breakup of Yugoslavia and the war in Croatia (1991–1995).

According to the 1991 census, which was conducted on the eve of the war in Croatia, the Republic of Croatia had 4,760,344 inhabitants, that is, 322,884 more people than it had in March 2001. In 1991 Croats composed 77.9 percent of the population while in 2001 that percentage had increased to 89.6 percent. Conversely, the Serb component of the population has declined over the same period from 12.2 to 4.5 percent. Historically, Serbs have been the largest non-Croat nationality in Croatia and were settled primarily in those regions that had formed from the sixteenth to the nineteenth centuries parts of the Habsburg "military

The Croatian Language

Croatian is the official language of the Republic of Croatia. It is the mother tongue of over 5 million persons in Croatia and other parts of former Yugoslavia. The Croatian language belongs to the South Slavic group of the Slavic branch of Indo-European languages. It is virtually identical to Serbian and closely related to Slovenian, Macedonian, and Bulgarian.

The Croatian language may be divided into three dialects, each named according to the word used for "what": Kajkavian *(kaj),* Čakavian *(ča),* and Štokavian *(što).* The Čakavian and Kajkavian dialects have a relatively limited territorial base within Croatia: the latter is spoken in Zagreb, its wider environs, and the region of Hrvatsko Zagorje, and the former in Istria, part of the Croatian Littoral, and some of the northern Adriatic islands. Štokavian is the most widely spoken dialect in Croatia. The Štokavian dialect may be further grouped into three subdialects, according to the treatment of vowels in certain words. On this basis, Štokavian may be grouped into ekavian, ikavian, and ijekavian variants. The modern Croatian literary language is based on the ijekavian variant, while the ekavian variant, which is spoken in Serbia proper, forms the basis of modern literary Serbian.

The Croatian language has a rich and long literary history. The earliest written records in Croatian date from the ninth to the eleventh centuries and are in Old Church Slavonic, a liturgical language developed by the Greek missionaries Cyril and Methodius. Old Church Slavonic was based on the Macedonian Slav vernacular of Salonika's hinterland, which Cyril and Methodius adapted to written form. The script employed to write this language was known as Glagolitic; in Christian Orthodox societies it was eventually replaced by the Cyrillic script, while in Catholic Slavic countries it was replaced by the Latin script, in the Croatian case by the fourteenth century. Thus the Croatian variant of Old Church Slavonic in the Glagolitic script represents the earliest form of literary Croatian.

The first major text written in Croatian Old Church Slavonic was the Baška Tablet (ca. 1100) recording the donation by the Croatian King Zvonimir of a property to the Benedictine convent of the island Krk. Written in the Glagolitic script, the tablet is so named because it was found in St. Lucy's church near Baška on the island of Krk. It stands as a cornerstone of Croatian literary development, although fragments of earlier inscriptions written in Glagolitic and dating from the eleventh century have been found on the islands of Krk and Cres (the Valun Tablet) and in Istria.

The Croatian language flourished during the Renaissance, particularly in Dalmatia and Dubrovnik. The most famous literary figure of the time, the humanist writer Marko Marulić (1450–1524) of Split, wrote his famous epic poem *Judita* (Judith; 1501) in Croatian and had it published in Venice in 1521. A younger contemporary, the playwright Marin Držić (1508–1567) of Dubrovnik, also distinguished himself. The first Croatian grammar, the *Institutionum linguae Illyricae* (Rome, 1604), was published by Bartol Kašić (1575–1650) in this same era. Although Kašić's native dialect was Čakavian, he urged the use of the ikavian variant of Štokavian as the basis of Croatian. It was one of the earliest attempts at standardizing the Croatian literary language. Kašić also began translating the Bible into Croatian; Matija Petar Katančić completed his project in the early nineteenth century. The city-state of Ragusa (Dubrovnik) produced a number of outstanding humanist and Renaissance writers. In addition to Marin Držić, it produced great writers like Ivan Gundulić (1589–1638) and Julije Palmotić (1605–1657). Ivan Belostenec published the first Latin-Croatian dictionary in 1740.

(continues)

frontier," that is, Kordun, Banija, Lika, and western Slavonia, although a sizable minority settled also in northern Dalmatia. In 1991 Serbs composed an absolute majority in eleven Croatian municipalities. During the war in Croatia these municipalities and some adjoining territories seized by the Yugoslav People's Army formed part of the so-called Republic of Serb Krajina. In August 1995, during the Croatian Army's Operation Storm, the Serb population of this region either fled or was expelled. The other national minorities have not witnessed major changes, although the category of "Yugoslav" has disappeared entirely; in 1991 Yugoslavs composed 2.2 percent of the population.

According to the 1991 census, Croatia had a total of 6,694 settlements: 205 urban settlements (i.e., towns, cities) and 6,489 rural settlements (villages, hamlets). In all, 57.1 percent of the Croatian population lived in urban settlements. By far the largest city is Zagreb. In 2001 it had a population of 779,145. The three largest cities after Zagreb are Split, Rijeka, and Osijek.

(continued)

Although the center of gravity of Croatian culture and literature lay in Dalmatia until the seventeenth century, after that point the center shifted north to Croatia proper. In the nineteenth century the Croat national awakeners, known as the Illyrian movement, had a critical role in the further evolution of Croatian literature and language. In the 1830s Zagreb became both the political and cultural center of the Croat lands. However, the Illyrianist awakeners first had to contend with the name of the spoken language. They initially referred to it as "Illyrian" and later as "Croatian or Serbian." For the remainder of the nineteenth century, the language was referred to as "Croatian" or "Croatian and Serbian." After the creation of the Kingdom of Serbs, Croats, and Slovenes in December 1918, the term "Serbo-Croatian" became official. The proponents of Yugoslavist unitarism believed that just as the Croat, Serb, and Slovene "tribes" would be melded into a hybrid Yugoslav nationality, so too would the "Croatian or Serbian" tongue merge into a single literary language. However, this proved problematical on many levels. As Yugoslavia's political experience soured and resistance to state centralism stiffened among the non-Serbs, resistance to linguistic unity grew also.

This raises one of the controversial aspects of the Croatian language question, namely, its relationship to the Serbian language and whether the two are really the same language. In 1850 a group of Croat, Serb, and Slovene intellectuals signed the so-called Vienna Literary Convention, calling for the creation of a common language of Croats and Serbs. Many Croat intellectuals rejected it; nevertheless it raised the whole issue of linguistic unitarism. For nineteenth century Croat intellectuals of a Yugoslavist cultural orientation, it was hoped that linguistic unity would nurture cultural and perhaps, at some distant future point, even political unification of the South Slavs.

Thus what initially began as "Croatian or Serbian" subsequently became "Croato-Serbian" or "Serbo-Croatian," first in royalist and then communist Yugoslavia. The communist authorities at first referred to Croatian and Serbian languages, but in 1954 twenty-five Serb, Croat, and Montenegrin writers and linguists met at Novi Sad to pass a new law designating "Serbo Croatian" as the official language and passed a resolution calling for the publication of a common Serbo-Croatian/Croato-Serbian orthography and dictionary. In Croatia this decision was resisted, implicitly or explicitly, on both political and cultural grounds. Politically it was seen as a manifestation of Belgrade centralism and culturally as a degradation of Croatian to the status of a regional dialect. In March 1967 eighteen Croatian scholarly institutions published the "Declaration Concerning the Name and Position of the Croatian Literary Language," which emphasized that although Croatian and Serbian possess the same linguistic basis, they are nonetheless two separate languages. The declaration was an early indicator of the level of dissatisfaction of many Croat intellectuals with the treatment of Croatian culture, and indeed the Croat nation generally, in communist Yugoslavia. This growing dissatisfaction culminated in the Croatian reform movement known as the so-called Croatian Spring, which was crushed in 1971 but not before it renounced the Novi Sad Agreement. Following the demise of communism in Yugoslavia and the move toward Croatian independence, Croatian was proclaimed in December 1990 as the official language of the Republic of Croatia.

In 1991 Croatia had a population density of 84.2 inhabitants per square kilometer. The most densely populated areas of Croatia are the cities of Zagreb, Split, Rijeka, and Osijek, in addition to the Medjimurje region. The cities of Split and Zagreb have population densities (persons per square kilometer) of 1,386.7 and 544.5, respectively, while Osijek and Čakovec municipality (in Medjimurje region) have population densities of 249.7 and 164.1, respectively. The population density (per square kilometer) of other selected towns and municipalities is: Donja Stubica municipality (123.4), Ivanec municipality (120.3), the city of Karlovac (126.9), Rijeka (393.6), and Varaždin (250.7).

Among the twenty counties (and the city of Zagreb), the population is distributed as follows:

County	*Number*	*Percentage of Total*
Bjelovar-Bilogora	133,084	3.0
Dubrovnik-Neretva	122,870	2.8
Istria	206,344	4.7
Karlovac	141,787	3.2
Koprivnica-Križevci	124,467	2.8
Krapina-Zagorje	142,432	3.2
Lika-Senj	53,677	1.2
Medjimurje	118,426	2.7
Osijek-Baranja	330,506	7.4
Požega-Slavonia	85,831	1.9
Primorje-Gorski kotar	305,505	6.9

(continues)

(continued)

County	*Number*	*Percentage of Total*
Šibenik-Knin	112,891	2.5
Sisak-Moslavina	185,387	4.2
Slavonski Brod-Posavina	176,765	4.0
Split-Dalmatia	463,676	10.4
Varaždin	184,769	4.2
Virovitica-Podravina	93,389	2.1
Vukovar-Srijem	204,768	4.6
Zadar	162,045	3.7
Zagreb (county)	309,696	6.9
Zagreb (city)	779,145	17.6
Total	4,437,460	100.0

Among the four provinces the majority of the population is found in Croatia proper:

Province	*Population*	*Percentage of Total*
Croatia proper (with Zagreb)	2,571,764	57.9
Dalmatia	861,482	19.4
Istria	206,344	4.7
Slavonia	797,870	18.0
Total	4,437,460	100.0

From the census of 1890 until 2001, the population of Croatia has grown by close to 1.6 million people:

Evolution of the Population of Croatia, 1890–2001

	1890	*1921*	*1948*	*1991*	*2001*
Total	2,854,558	3,443,375	3,779,858	4,784,265	4,437,460

In 2001 the estimated population growth was 1.48 percent, reflecting a birthrate of 12.82 per 1,000 inhabitants (the death rate is 11.41 deaths per 1,000). The infant mortality rate is 7.21 deaths per 1,000 live births. Life expectancy is approximately 73.9 years (70.28 years for men and 77.73 years for women).

Croatia is a highly homogeneous society, with most of the population (96.12 percent) identifying Croatian as their native language. (Another 1.01 percent identify Serbian as their "mother tongue," 0.16 percent Serbo-Croatian, and 2.71 percent as "other" or "unknown.") The literacy rate for persons over ten years of age is 98.23 percent (99.33 percent for men and 97.23 percent for women).

Of the total population of 4,437,460 in the 2001 census, the single largest religious denomination is the Roman Catholic, with 3,897,332 adherents, representing 87.83 percent of the population. There are 6,219 followers of the Greek Catholic and 303 followers of the Old Catholic rites, representing 0.14 percent and 0.01 percent of the population, respectively. The largest non-Catholic denomination is the Orthodox Christian with 195,969 followers representing 4.42 percent of the population. The religious composition of the remainder of the country is as follows: Muslim 56,777 (1.28 percent); Jewish 495 (0.01 percent); Adventist 3,001 (0.07 percent); Baptist 1,981 (0.04 percent); Evangelical 3,339 (0.08 percent); Jehovah's Witness 6,094 (0.14 percent); Calvinist 4,053 (0.09 percent); Methodist 15 (0.00 percent); Pentecostal 336 (0.01 percent); other 4,764 (0.11 percent); agnostic 132,532 (2.99 percent); atheist 98,376 (2.22 percent); unknown 25,874 (0.58 percent). The statistics on religious affiliation generally reflect the country's nationality composition. For example, the Orthodox Christian population (4.42 percent) is predominantly of the Serb nationality (4.54 percent) and most Croats (89.63 percent) are Roman Catholic (87.83 percent).

The 1990 Constitution of the Republic of Croatia provides for freedom of conscience and religion and free public profession of religious conviction. Croatian governments since 1990 have in practice generally respected these rights. Although Croatia has no official state religion, the Roman Catholic Church has since the end of World War II been a powerful national symbol. Since 1990, it has enjoyed a special relationship with the state not shared by other denominations; the line separating the Roman Catholic Church and the state has occasionally appeared blurred since the first democratic elections. The then ruling Croatian Democratic Union (HDZ) periodically attempted to identify itself more closely with the Catholic Church. Under Franjo Cardinal Kuharić, the former archbishop of Zagreb, the Catholic Church identified itself with the Croat national cause. More often than not, however, the Catholic Church retained an independent role in society and was occasionally critical of the political situation in Croatia and some of the semiauthoritarian measures of the government. Since 1997, under the new head of the Catholic Church, Archbishop Josip Božanić, the Catholic Church has publicly promoted reconciliation, dialogue, and the return of refugees.

The Croatian government requires that religious training be provided in schools, although attendance is optional. Schools filling the necessary quota of seven minority students per class offer separate religion classes for these students. In classes not meeting this quota, minority students may fulfill the religion requirement by bringing a certificate that they had received classes from their religious community. Since 1990 the Croatian government has not imposed any formal restrictions on religious groups or their ability freely to conduct public services. The Roman Catholic Church receives direct subsidies, as well as state financing for some salaries and pensions for priests and nuns through the government-managed pension and health funds. Other religious communities still do not have such an agreement with the state, nor is there yet a law that regulates these issues. Catholic marriages are recognized by the state, eliminating the need to register them in the civil registry office. The Muslim and Jewish communities have sought a similar status, but the issue has yet to be resolved to their satisfaction.

The official coat of arms of the Republic of Croatia is a historical Croatian coat of arms in the shape of a shield. The checkered pattern has twenty-five alternating red and white fields, so that the upper left corner of the shield is red. Above the shield is a crown with five peaks, which touches the left and right upper ends of the shield, bending in a slight arch.

The crown is divided into five small shields with historical Croatian coats of arms, in the following order, from left to right: the oldest known Croatian coat of arms, then coats of arms of the Dubrovnik Republic, Dalmatia, Istria, and Slavonia. The height of the smaller fields in the crown is 2.5 times the size of the fields in the main shield, while the width of both sets of fields is the same. The oldest known Croatian coat of arms has a yellow (golden) six-pointed star and a white (argent) new moon on a blue shield. A golden rim borders the entire coat of arms. The coat of arms of the Dubrovnik Republic has two red beams on a navy blue shield. The Dalmatian coat of arms has three yellow (golden) crowned leopard heads on a blue shield. The Istrian coat of arms has a yellow (golden) goat with red hoofs and horns facing left, on a navy blue shield. The Slavonian coat of arms has two horizontal white (argent) beams on a blue shield. Between the beams there is a red field with a marten in motion facing left. There is a yellow (golden) six-pointed star in the chief blue field. A red line trims the entire coat of arms.

The flag of the Republic of Croatia consists of three bands of color—red, white, and blue—with the Croatian coat of arms in the center. The length is twice the width. Its colors, in the order red, white, and blue, are laid horizontally, each one-third the width of the flag. The Croatian coat of arms is placed in the center of the flag so that the upper part of the coat of arms (the crown) overlaps the red field of the flag, and the bottom part of the coat of arms overlaps the flag's blue field. The center of the coat of arms is placed at the point where the diagonals of the flag meet. The Croatian tricolor was first used during the Revolutions of 1848–1849.

The national anthem of the Republic of Croatia is "Lijepa naša domovino" (Our Beautiful Homeland). Composed by Antun Mihanović (1796–1861), it was first published as a poem under the title "Croatian Homeland" in the 14 March 1835 issue of the journal *Danica* (The Dawn). The original poem was much longer than the official national anthem; only the first and last eight verses were adopted for the official version. In 1846 the Croatian Serb Josip (Josif) Runjanin composed the musical score. The anthem was first played as such in 1891. The text of the anthem of the Republic of Croatia is:

Lijepa naša domovino,	Our Beautiful Homeland
Oj junačka zemljo mila,	O so fearless, o so gracious.
Stare slave djedovino,	Our fathers' ancient glory,
da bi vazda sretna bila!	May God bless you, live forever!
Mila, kano si nam slavna,	You are our only glory,
Mila si nam ti jedina.	You are our only treasure,
Mila kuda si nam ravna,	Yes, we love your plains and valleys,
Mila, kuda si planina!	Yes, we love your hills and mountains.
Teci Dravo, Savo teci,	Sava, Drava, keep on flowing,
Nit' ti Dunav silu gubi,	Danube, do not lose your vigor,
Sinje more svijetu reci,	Deep blue sea, go tell the whole world,
Da svoj narod Hrvat ljubi.	That a Croat loves his homeland.
Dok mu njive sunce grije,	When his fields are kissed by sunshine,
Dok mu hrašće bura vije,	When his oaks are whipped by wild winds,
Dok mu mrtve grobak krije,	When his dear ones go to heaven,
Dok mu živo srce bije!"	Still his heart beats for Croatia!

HISTORY

SETTLEMENT AND NATIVE RULE TO 1102

Relatively little is known of the early medieval history of the lands that today compose Croatia or of the people who bear the Croat name. The name Croat (in Croatian, *Hrvat*) is of unknown origin but was apparently first mentioned in the third century C.E. in an inscription discovered near the Sea of Azov. Many scholars now believe that the original Croats were not Slavs but nomadic Sarmatians who roamed Central Asia and permanently entered Europe around the third or fourth century C.E. This theory proposes that these Croats settled in a land called White Croatia, in what is now southern Poland near Cracow, where they established a short-lived and rudimentary state. These Croats, some scholars have claimed, ruled over and were eventually assimilated by the far more numerous indigenous Slavic-speaking tribes of that region; eventually they bequeathed to these Slavs their name.

According to a tenth century Byzantine source, in the seventh century C.E. the Byzantine Emperor Heraclius enlisted the Croat tribes of White Croatia against the Avars, a people who were threatening Byzantine control of the western Balkans. At that point, around 630, the Croat tribes migrated southward and eventually settled in their present-day homeland, thereby establishing the Croat presence in the western Balkans. In their new homeland the Croats gradually displaced or assimilated the indigenous population, which consisted of Illyrian tribes, Vlachs, and a Romanized element in the towns of Dalmatia.

At the time of the Croat settlement of the Balkans, the Roman presence and culture had already permeated the region for half a millennium. In 35 B.C.E. the Roman emperor Octavian had conquered the eastern Adriatic coastal region and by 14 C.E., Rome had subjugated the indigenous Celtic and Illyrian tribes of the western and central Balkans. The Romans brought with them law and order and bequeathed many lasting monuments. In order to govern more effectively their Balkan possessions, the Romans

Diocletian's Palace

The Roman emperor Diocletian (r. 284–305 C.E.) was born in Salona, the capital of the Roman province of Dalmatia, in 245. At the end of the third century, Diocletian built a palace in what is today the city of Split, just a few kilometers from Salona. Following his abdication in 305 (the motives for which still remain unclear), he retired to the palace.

Today the palace lies in the heart of Split. The importance of Diocletian's Palace far transcends local significance because of its level of preservation and the buildings of succeeding historical periods, stretching from the Roman period onward, that form the very fabric of old Split. The palace is one of the most famous architectural and cultural constructs on the Adriatic coast and holds an outstanding place in the Mediterranean, European, and world heritage. In November 1979 UNESCO added the historic Split inner city, built around Diocletian's Palace, to its register of World Cultural Heritage sites.

Despite its obvious importance, Diocletian's Palace is hardly an archeological site. That is to say, its shape and style need to be extrapolated from its remains, which have been altered because of construction over the centuries. The ground plan of the palace is an irregular rectangle with towers projecting from the western, northern, and eastern facades. It combines the qualities of a luxurious villa with those of a military camp. Only the southern facade, which rose directly from the sea, was unfortified. The elaborate architectural composition of the arcaded gallery on its upper floor differs from the more severe treatment of the three shore facades. A monumental gate in the middle of each of these walls led to an enclosed courtyard. The southern Sea Gate has a simpler design, perhaps because it was originally intended as the emperor's private access to the sea or as a service entrance for supplies.

The dual nature of the architectural scheme is also evident in the arrangement of the interior. The transverse road linking the eastern and western gates divided the complex in two. The more luxurious structures (such as the emperor's apartment) were located in the southern half. Although for many centuries almost completely filled with refuse, most of the substructure is well preserved. A monumental court formed the northern access to the imperial apartments. It also gave access to Diocletian's Mausoleum on the east, and to three temples on the west. The northern half of the palace, which was divided in two parts by the main longitudinal street leading from the North Gate, is less well preserved. It is believed that each of these parts formed a large residential complex, housing soldiers, servants, and other facilities. The palace is built of white limestone, tufa (or porous stones) taken from the nearby river beds, and brick. One can still find along the road from Split to Salona the impressive remains of the original aqueduct, which was restored in the nineteenth century. Diocletian's Palace is one of Croatia's historical and archeological treasures.

divided their territories into separate provinces linked by roads, towns, and fortresses. Three Roman provinces encompassed what later became the Croat lands: Dalmatia (i.e., Dalmatia, most of Bosnia-Hercegovina), Pannonia (i.e., eastern Slavonia, northeastern Bosnia), and Savia (i.e., western Slavonia, Croatia proper). But perhaps the greatest legacy of Rome was the separation of the empire, in 395 C.E., into western (Roman) and eastern (Byzantine) halves. This division eventually became a cultural chasm, following the church schism of 1054, and a permanent feature of the European cultural landscape. It likewise separated the South Slavs. The Croats settled on the territorial cusp of this chasm.

By the late eighth century, two powerful empires were contesting the Croat lands: the Germanic Frankish Empire to the northwest and the Byzantine Empire to the southeast. Most of the Croat tribes lived under loose Byzantine rule, but in reality the Croats alternated between Frankish and Byzantine control in this period; the Franks dominated in the north (the Roman provinces of Savia and Pannonia) and Byzantium in the south (Dalmatia). However, the Byzantine Empire continued to exert a far greater political and cultural influence at the time.

It was in this context that an obscure figure named Ljudevit, apparently the ruler of a rudimentary principality in Pannonia, led a revolt in 818 against the Franks. The revolt was suppressed by 823, but the first steps in Croatian political development had been taken. With Ljudevit's revolt suppressed, the focus of Croatian politics moved to Dalmatia, where Croats had already established their first port towns (e.g., Šibenik, Biograd, Nin), a small navy, and a seat of government (Knin). The most notable of these early Croat rulers in Dalmatia was a tribal chief named Trpimir (r. 845–864), who gave his name to the dynasty (Trpimirovićes, r. 845–1089) that governed first the Croatian principality and then the independent kingdom. Trpimir led successful military campaigns against the Bulgarians and the Byzantine Empire in Dalmatia and issued the first charter in which he is mentioned as the prince of Croatia.

Under Branimir (r. 879–892), the Croatian principality in Dalmatia established close links with the papacy; in 879, the year of his accession, he obtained the pope's recognition of Croatia as an independent principality. The Christianization of the Croats, undoubtedly a lengthy process, began in this period. Missionaries came to Croatia in greater number during his reign. Most of them were disciples of Sts. Cyril and Methodius; they brought with them liturgical texts in the Old Slavonic language and in the Glagolitic script, which the two saints had developed. From that point, liturgical services were held in this language and church books were written in this script. This was the beginning of the written word among the Croats.

Under Tomislav (r. 910–928), Croatia became an independent kingdom and a powerful state in the western Balkans. He organized a strong military and defeated the Magyars who had recently arrived from the Russian steppe and forced them permanently across the Drava River, which today forms the border between Croatia and Hungary. As a result, he brought Slavonia under his rule, thereby unifying the two Croatian principalities. As an ally of Byzantium, Tomislav helped defeat the Bulgarians and was granted in return the right to administer the coastal towns (e.g., Zadar, Split, and Trogir), thus rounding off his state from the Adriatic Sea to the Drava River. In 925 Tomislav was crowned king, apparently by or in the presence of a papal legate.

Several able rulers succeeded Tomislav, foremost of whom were Držislav (r. 969–997) and Petar Krešimir IV (r. 1058–1074), during whose reign Croatia achieved its greatest territorial extent. Both rulers bore the title of "King of Dalmatia and Croatia," administered the relatively prosperous Dalmatian towns, and successfully resisted encroachments by Venice in the west and Byzantium in the southeast. During the reign of Dmitar Zvonimir (r. 1075–1089), a Charter containing his name and title was engraved in stone. Known as the Baška Tablet, it is the oldest artifact written in the Croatian language, in the Glagolitic script. However, the death of Dmitar Zvonimir marked the end of the native dynasty and independent statehood.

At that point a struggle ensued for the Croatian throne. A faction of nobles or tribal chiefs contested the succession and offered the Croatian throne to the King of Hungary, László I (Ladislas, r. 1077–1095), who was the late Zvonimir's brother-in-law. In 1091 László accepted, and in 1094 he founded the Zagreb bishopric, which later became the ecclesiastical center of Croatia. Another Hungarian king, Kálmán I ("the Book Lover," r. 1095–1116), crushed the opposition after the death of László and won the crown of Dalmatia and Croatia in 1102. Kálmán forged a lasting link between the Croatian and Hungarian crowns. The nature of that link has long been contested, however. Croats have maintained that the 1102 union was based on an agreement *(pacta conventa)* of equals (i.e., the Croatian nobility and the Hungarian king), whereby the two kingdoms were joined in a personal union under the Árpád dynasty. According to the terms of this union, Croatia managed for centuries to remain a sovereign state. However, Hungarians have long asserted that Hungary annexed Croatia outright in 1102. Although Hungarian influence in Croatia remained significant after 1102, the fact remains that Croatia retained its own prorex, or viceroy *(ban),* privileged landowning nobility, and an assembly of nobles, the diet *(Sabor)*. This union remained in place until 1918.

CROAT LANDS (1102–1526)

One of the main trends in the political history of Croatia in this period was the political fragmentation of the Croat lands (i.e., Croatia proper, Slavonia, Dalmatia, and Istria). This trend was not immediately apparent, since the Hungarian-Croatian state was initially a significant political and military force in the area between the German (i.e., Holy Roman) and Byzantine Empires and a rival to the Venetian state in the Adriatic. Despite the devastations wrought by the Tatar invasion of 1242, the Croats and Hungarians managed to resist their more powerful neighbors. Only the internal weaknesses of the kingdom, which were caused by the strengthening of noble prerogatives at the expense of the monarchy, enabled the fragmentation of the Croat lands.

Although much of Bosnia (though not Hercegovina) had originally formed part of the Croatian principality and kingdom, from the twelfth century, Bosnia began increasingly to disassociate itself from the Hungarian-Croatian kingdom. Bosnia first became a separate principality under ban Kulin (r. 1180–1204), who managed to solidify Bosnian autonomy at the expense of its more powerful neighbors. This autonomy proved ephemeral, however. Only in the fourteenth century did Bosnia become a formidable state. The first Bosnian monarch was ban Stefan Tvrtko I (r. 1353–1391), who in 1377 became "King of Bosnia and Raška (Serbia)" and later conquered parts of Croatia and Dalmatia. However, the Ottoman Turks conquered most of Bosnia in 1463, followed by Hercegovina in 1483.

Much of Dalmatia was lost in this same period. Between 1115 and 1420, the Hungarian-Croatian kingdom and Venice waged twenty-one wars for control of the province. The Dalmatian cities repeatedly changed hands. Both Serbia and Bosnia also competed for Dalmatia; the coastal area around the Gulf of Kotor became part of the Serbian state around 1196, and the Bosnian kingdom dominated parts of Dalmatia in the fourteenth century. The only part of Dalmatia to avoid direct foreign rule was the Republic of Dubrovnik, known by its Italian name Ragusa, which became an important mercantile center, in addition to being a focal point of medieval Croat and South Slavic culture and literature. It had been founded in the seventh century by Romans fleeing Slavic incursions, but was gradually "croatized." Ragusa became a powerful merchant republic by skillfully cultivating relations with its far more powerful neighbors. It was a protectorate of the Byzantine Empire until 1205, of Venice until 1358, of Hungary-Croatia until 1440, and finally of the Ottoman Empire until 1806. It was the first Christian state to establish treaty relations with the Ottoman Turks. It remained independent throughout these centuries until it was abolished in 1806 by Napoleon and incorporated into his Illyrian Provinces.

Following the extinction in 1301 of the native Hungarian Árpád dynasty, Charles Robert of the Italian branch of the French Anjou dynasty ascended the throne. King

Charles I (Károly, r. 1308–1342) and his son Louis/Lajos ("the Great," r. 1342–1382) temporarily restored royal power, which had been undermined by the Croatian and Hungarian magnates. Louis defeated Venice, and at the Peace of Zadar (1358), he restored virtually the entire Croatian coastline to his rule and placed Dubrovnik under his protection. Following his death, however, a period of internal anarchy commenced and the enormous territorial expanse of Hungary-Croatia was reduced. In 1409 a large part of Dalmatia was lost to Venice, when Ladislas of Naples, a claimant to the Hungarian-Croatian throne, sold Venice his rights to Dalmatia. Between 1420 and 1428 all of Dalmatia was lost to Venice, with the exception of Dubrovnik. The internal weakness of the Hungarian-Croatian state prevented the kingdom from slowing or stopping the Ottoman Turks, whose advance into Europe posed the greatest danger to the Hungarian-Croatian state. In the mid-fifteenth century the Ottomans moved into the Balkan Peninsula. In 1417 the Romanian principality of Wallachia submitted to Ottoman rule, and after 1440 Dubrovnik accepted Ottoman protection against Venice. The Ottomans then conquered Constantinople (1453), Serbia (1456), Bosnia (1463), and Hercegovina (1483). Ottoman armies inflicted decisive defeats against a Croatian army at Krbava (1493) and far more importantly, a Hungarian army at Móhacs (1526). The latter defeat destroyed the independent Hungarian-Croatian state and brought the Habsburg dynasty of Austria possession of the throne.

CROAT LANDS (1526–1790)

Following the battle of Mohács, most of Croatia came under Ottoman rule. On 1 January 1527, the Croatian Landed Estates, meeting at Cetingrad, elected Ferdinand I of the House of Habsburg as King of Croatia in return for his pledge of support in defending the kingdom against further Ottoman incursions. He also pledged to respect their political rights and social privileges. During the following century, Croatia served as a Habsburg outpost in the defense of central Europe against the Ottomans. Between 1527 and 1699, much of Croatia remained under Ottoman occupation. A smaller portion, known as Royal Croatia, was under Habsburg rule while Dalmatia and much of Istria remained in Venetian hands.

By the middle of the sixteenth century, the Croat lands had, as a result ofVenetian and Ottoman encroachments, become politically fragmented. For centuries to come they would remain divided into Croatia proper (Royal Croatia, centered at Zagreb), Slavonia, Dalmatia, and Istria. The region of Slavonia was after 1526 incorporated directly into the Ottoman Empire. It was recovered from the Ottomans only in 1699 by the terms of the Treaty of Karlowitz (Srijemski Karlovci). However, after 1699 Slavonia was administered as a province distinct from Croatia proper. The two provinces, Slavonia and Croatia proper, were permanently reunited only in two stages, in 1868 and 1881. Dalmatia had been contested by Venice and Hungary-Croatia ever since the twelfth century. By the 1420s, the coastal islands and most of Dalmatia, with the exception of Dubrovnik, had become Venetian possessions. Istria (in Croatian, Istra) had by the fifteenth century been absorbed by the Habsburg dynasty of Austria and Venice, which controlled its northeastern and southwestern parts, respectively.

In the Habsburg monarchy, Croatia managed to preserve its internal administration, that is, the diet (Sabor) and viceroy (ban). But the rights of the native nobility were progressively diminished to the benefit of the Habsburg dynasty. In order to enhance the prestige of his dynasty and to avoid future succession conflicts, Ferdinand I arranged for his heirs to be recognized as future kings of Bohemia (after 1549) and Hungary-Croatia (after 1563), which in practice (though not in theory) meant that these kingdoms became hereditary Habsburg possessions. Habsburg rule in Croatia never seemed secure, however, largely because of the Ottoman threat. The Habsburg rulers formed a defensive cordon, lined with fortifications, known as the military frontier (in Croatian, *Vojna krajina*). The first section of this frontier was formed in 1538, under the control of the Croatian diet and ban. However, by 1630 the military frontier had been removed from the administration of the Croatian diet and was governed directly by agents of the Habsburg dynasty. Since the ongoing warfare against the Ottoman Turks had taken such a devastating demographic toll on the native population, the Habsburg authorities settled thousands of agricultural colonists in the military frontier, who, in return for land, served in military units. These frontiersmen (in Croatian, *graničari;* in German, *Grenzer*) were composed mainly of Croats, Serbs, Germans, and others. In this way, the nationality composition of Croatia was changed and the country became an ethnically far more heterogeneous society.

Disenchantment with and resistance to the Habsburgs grew over time. The most noted incident in Croatian history, which is known to Croatian historiography as the Zrinski-Frankopan conspiracy, was in fact part of a larger anti-Habsburg conspiracy centered in Hungary, where it is remembered as the Wesselenyi conspiracy. Following the Peace of Westphalia (1648), which brought an end to the Thirty Years' War, the Habsburgs again asserted their dynastic prerogatives in Hungary-Croatia. Habsburg absolutism and the existence of the military frontier to the detriment of Croatian political autonomy fueled hostility to the dynasty. In 1663 hostilities were initiated between the Ottoman Turks and the Habsburg monarchy. In the initial stages of this war, Habsburg armies managed major gains. Many Croatian and Hungarian nobles hoped that the Habsburg monarch, Leopold I, would retake all the territory that had been lost to the Turks in the sixteenth century. However, on 10 August 1664 the Habsburgs hastily concluded peace with the Ottomans at Vasvár. That led a number of prominent Hungarian and Croatian nobles to rebellion, in the hope of restoring the independence of Hungary-Croatia. Among the conspirators were the Hungarian Palatine Ferenc Wesselenyi, the bishop of Esztergom, Gyorgy Lippay, the Croatian ban Nikola Zrinski, his brother Peter Zrinski, and their brother-in-law, Krsto Frankopan. Eventually, the Hungarian conspirators, Peter Zrinski, and Frankopan were arrested. They were condemned for high treason and executed at Wiener Neustadt on 30 April 1671. The conspiracy put an end to Croatia's two leading magnate families.

In 1699, by the terms of the Treaty of Karlowitz (Srijemski Karlovci), the Ottoman Turks were forced to cede to the Habsburgs all of their Hungarian and Croatian territories. By 1718, the Ottomans no longer posed a danger to Dalmatia. Thus, at the dawn of the eighteenth century, the Croat lands achieved "liberation" from the Turks. Liberation came at a price, however. Slavonia and other Croatian regions (e.g., Lika, Krbava) were henceforth administered separately from Royal Croatia (Croatia proper), which was also referred to as Civil Croatia. Although the Ottoman threat progressively receded in the eighteenth century, the military frontier remained a separate administrative region beyond the control of the Croatian diet; it was abolished and incorporated into Croatia only in 1881. Nevertheless, the diet continued to assert Croatian political sovereignty. In 1712 it accepted, independently of the Hungarian diet, the so-called Pragmatic Sanction, which stipulated that a female could assume the Habsburg throne; the Pragmatic Sanction enabled Maria Theresa to become empress. However, because of Maria Theresa and (her son) Joseph II's policies of absolutism, centralization, and administrative Germanization, the rights of the Croatian kingdom were gradually reduced even further. In fear of these centralizing tendencies, the Croatian nobility firmly allied itself with their far more powerful Hungarian counterparts, who were able to offer firmer opposition to the Habsburgs. Joseph II's reforms exposed latent ethnic and linguistic rivalries within the monarchy. By attempting to bring the empire under strict central control and decreeing that German replace Latin as the official language of the empire, Joseph II brought Hungary to the verge of rebellion, a fact that would have important consequences for Croatia.

THE NATIONAL AWAKENING (1790–1848)

The French Revolution (1789) and the Napoleonic era (1795–1814) introduced to Croatia and all of Eastern Europe the ideologies of nationalism and liberalism. The Napoleonic era also brought about extensive territorial changes in Europe, and the Croat lands were no exception. More importantly, this era saw the first stirrings of national awakening in the Croat lands. From the 1790s onward, the Croatian nobility was confronted by both Habsburg absolutism and growing Hungarian national assertiveness, which challenged the traditional nature of the Croato-Hungarian relationship. In addition to the traditional threat posed by Habsburg absolutism and administrative Germanization, the Hungarian nobility now posed, in the era of nationalism, a threat in the form of Magyarization (the imposition of Hungarian culture and institutions).

During this same period, French revolutionary ideas and armies established themselves in the region. As a consequence of Napoleon's military campaigns in northern Italy in 1796–1797, the Republic of Venice disappeared. According to the Treaty of Campo Formio (April 1797), signed by France and Austria, the Habsburgs acquired Venice, Istria, and Dalmatia. In this manner, Croatia-Slavonia was again united with Dalmatia under the same dynasty, although they were administered as separate provinces. However, according to the Treaty of Schönbrunn (October 1809) between Napoleon and Austria, the Habsburgs were forced to cede part of Carinthia and Croatia south of the Sava River, which together with Istria and Dalmatia formed the so-called Illyrian Provinces (1809–1813), which were attached directly to France. Napoleon's army had entered Dubrovnik in 1806 and the French proclaimed the dissolution of the Dubrovnik Republic. After the defeat of Napoleon, all of these regions were ceded to the Austrian empire. Although the Illyrian Provinces had only a brief existence and were directly under French rule, they subsequently provided Croat Romantic nationalists of the 1830s and 1840s, who adopted the Illyrian name, with political inspiration.

Under the influence of the French Revolution, and because of resistance to Germanization and Magyarization and the internal development of rich cultural and state traditions, a national revival occurred in Croatia after 1836. The Croat national awakening became known as the Illyrian movement (1836–1848) and was led by Ljudevit Gaj (1809–1872). The Illyrian movement laid the basis of a standardized Croatian literary language and alphabet; it formed the first national newspapers and national institutions. The Illyrian movement also prompted the use of Croatian in the diet, in place of Latin; from 1847 the diet began using Croatian in its deliberations. The appeal of the Illyrian movement was limited, however, almost entirely to the Croat intelligentsia of Croatia-Slavonia and much later, of Bosnia-Hercegovina, Istria, and Dalmatia. Slovene and Serb support was weak from the outset.

The most significant factor shaping modern Croat national identity and nationalism has been the concept of historical rights, that is, the belief that the medieval Croatian kingdom had never completely lost its independence, despite the union first with Hungary (1102) and then the Habsburgs (1527). Like their counterparts in Hungary, the Croatian nobility ("political nation") had defended their social privileges, identity, and political rights by associating them with the institutions of the Kingdom of Croatia-Slavonia. All Croat nationalists, even those of a South Slavic orientation, operated within a framework of historic state right. The second factor shaping Croat nationalism was the identification with other Southern Slavs, which was a reflection of Croat numerical inferiority in relation to the Habsburg monarchy's Magyars and Germans. It also stemmed from the fact that there was a numerically significant Serb minority in Croatia.

Both factors, the state-oriented, historically rooted perception of nationalism and emphasis on Slavic solidarity, were evident in the Illyrian movement. Like national awakeners everywhere in Eastern Europe at the time, Gaj and his associates had to ask themselves a basic question: what is the Croat nationality? They opted for a linguistic definition, but by doing so they ran into a peculiar problem. Of the three dialects spoken in Croatia, two (Kajkavian, Čakavian) were purely Croatian, but the third (Štokavian) was spoken not just by the majority of Croats, but all Bosnian Muslims and Serbs. They opted for the Štokavian dialect, calling it "Illyrian" in order to appeal to Croat and Serb intellectuals alike, but a dilemma persisted. If Croats were to be identified as speakers of Croatian ("Illyrian") residing in historic Great Croatia, then how were those people who regarded themselves as Serbs, spoke virtually the same language, and composed roughly 25 percent of the population of Croatia, to be identified? The problem of identity thus proved particularly problematical in the Croat case.

Equestrian statue of Josip Jelačić by Anton Dominik Fernkorn. (Charles Philip/Corbis)

THE NATIONAL PROGRAM (1848–1918)

During the revolutions of 1848–1849, the two most important Croat political leaders were Gaj and ban Josip Jelačić (1801–1859), who headed the Croatian royal administration. Their political program, and that of the Illyrian movement, was the unification of all the South Slavs of the Habsburg monarchy around an autonomous Croatian kingdom, within a federalized Habsburg monarchy. The Croatian diet adopted a "national" program that abolished serfdom, expressed loyalty to the dynasty, and firmly established the idea of the unification of all Croat lands (the so-called Triune Kingdom of Croatia-Slavonia-Dalmatia) within a reformed monarchy. Because of the dangers posed by Magyar nationalists, who were led in the Hungarian revolution (War for Independence) of 1848–1849 by Lajos Kossuth, the Croat national program was based on resistance to the Hungarians, who did not recognize Croatian autonomy, and support for the Habsburg dynasty, which was viewed as an ally against Magyar nationalism. In 1848 representatives of the Illyrian movement attended the Slavic Congress in Prague and supported František Palácky's plan for a federalized Habsburg monarchy. The Illyrianists did not, it is worth pointing out, advocate the creation of a Yugoslav state encompassing Serbia and Bosnia-Hercegovina. Gaj and the Illyrianists did win some support from Serb intellectuals of the Habsburg monarchy, that is, the Serb leaders of Croatia and southern Hungary. This political cooperation reflected the greater danger posed at the time to Croat and Serb alike by the Magyars, who were intent on creating a Magyar nation-state and Magyarizing all non-Magyars.

Following the suppression of the 1848–1849 revolutions, the Habsburgs introduced a period of absolutism. Only in 1860 did the Habsburg authorities restore constitutional life and initiate a series of political experiments concerning how the monarchy should be governed. When this period of political experimentation ended in 1867, Croat national leaders would be greatly disappointed. The year 1867 represented an important turning point in the history of the monarchy. After being defeated by Sardinia-Piedmont (1859) and Prussia (1866), the Habsburg authorities realized the need to restructure the monarchy and to come to terms with the Magyars. The *Ausgleich* (Compromise) of 1867, which was negotiated by Emperor Franz Joseph and the Magyar ruling oligarchy, transformed Austria into the Dual Monarchy, or Austria-Hungary (also known as the Austro-Hungarian Empire). According to the terms of the *Ausgleich,* Hungary and the "Austrian" lands became two states joined in personal union through a common monarch (the Habsburg emperor of "Austria" and king of Hungary); the two states shared joint ministries of war, finance, and foreign affairs. Otherwise, they were independent states.

The Ausgleich perpetuated the division of the Croat lands. Croatia-Slavonia and the military frontier were regarded by the monarchy as historically belonging to Hungary. Istria and Dalmatia, however, belonged to the non-Hungarian half of the empire, which was officially referred to as "the kingdoms and crown lands represented in the Imperial Parliament." Dalmatia was designated as one of three Austrian kingdoms, while Istria had the status of a margraviate. In 1868 the Croato-Hungarian *Nagodba* (Agreement) was signed, whereby the Kingdom of Croatia-Slavonia was recognized by the Magyar ruling oligarchy as a "political nation," with autonomy within the Kingdom of Hungary. A Croatian diet dominated by pro-Hungarian deputies adopted the Nagodba. Croatia-Slavonia obtained autonomy in internal matters, retained its own Sabor (diet), administration, and education system, all of which employed the Croatian language. In 1881 the Croatian military frontier was incorporated into Croatia-Slavonia. However, Hungarians continued to wield significant influence over internal Croatian affairs. For example, the king appointed the Croatian ban on the recommendation of the Hungarian minister-president; since the ban could influence the autonomous Croatian administration, the Hungarian government was able readily to manipulate internal Croatian politics and administration. Indeed, under Károly Count Khuen-Hédervåry (who was ban from 1883 to 1903), this proved to be the case, as Croatian autonomy was reduced to a bare minimum. Throughout the era of dualism (1867–1918), Hungarian leaders continued to believe that the Nagodba provided ample (indeed, too much) autonomy to Croatia, but Croat patriots always remained strongly opposed to its terms.

After 1868, there were two opposing Croat political movements in Croatia-Slavonia. One emphasized a purely Croat identity, while the other continued in the Illyrian tradition, albeit in a different form. The first movement was Ante Starčević's Party of (Croatian State) Right, formed in 1861, which adopted a program based on historical state right. Frustrated by the Croat failure to gain autonomy in 1848, and by the lack of Serb support for Illyrianism, in which he had participated as a student, Starčević advocated a purely Croat identity. Starčević claimed that the Croatian kingdom's state right had never been abolished and that it was thus de jure an independent entity. Starčević adopted a political concept of nationality, inherited from the old notion of a noble "political nation," and defined Croats simply as all people residing in Great Croatia, be they Catholic, Muslim, or Orthodox Christian. Great Croatia encompassed present-day Croatia, Bosnia-Hercegovina, and Slovenia. Although he recognized the existence of Serbs in Serbia proper, he refused to recognize the existence of "political Serbs" (or any other nationality) in those lands regarded as historically Croatian, for there could only be one nation on the territory of the Croatian state. Thus the Serbs of the Habsburg lands remained, in the minds of the Party of Right, Orthodox "Croats," just as the Bosnian Muslims were viewed as Muslim "Croats." Starčević's nationalism revealed the powerful hold of historical state right on the thinking of all of Croatia's nineteenth-century intellectuals.

The other Croat political movement was the National Party of Josip Juraj Strossmayer. Strossmayer was a leading Croatian Catholic bishop and proponent of cultural Yugoslavism. Strossmayer and his supporters continued in the Illyrian tradition; they promoted the cultural unity of all South Slavs in the Habsburg lands. They believed that cultural interaction and cooperation would eventually lead to greater political cooperation between the Croats, Serbs, and Slovenes of the monarchy. Like the Illyrianists before them, the proponents of cultural Yugoslavism in the 1870s and 1880s hoped at the very least to achieve Croatian autonomy within a federalized Habsburg monarchy. However, Strossmayer's influence, and the appeal of Yugoslavism, was limited only to the small liberal intelligentsia in Croatia, and almost entirely to Croat intellectuals. It was essentially a Croat program and reflected a continued sense of Croat weakness; as an ideology it was designed to strengthen the Croat position, together with Serbs and Slovenes, within the monarchy. Strossmayer's Yugoslavism failed to attract many Serb intellectuals, who continued on the whole to look to Serbia for leadership and saw Yugoslavist ideology as a Croat attempt to assimilate Croatian Serbs to a Yugoslav or Croat identity. It is worth remembering that Strossmayer's National Party, although recognizing the "genetic" distinctiveness of Serbs in Croatia, refused to recognize Serbs as a "political nation" in Croatia. To do so would have meant opening the door to separate Serb rights in or even demands for territorial autonomy within Croatia. The thinking of the Croat political elites thus fit the Central European pattern of "historic" and "nonhistoric" nations, with the Croats (like the Magyars, Germans, Poles, and Czechs) falling into the former and all other nationalities into the latter. Strossmayer's achievements were primarily in the cultural sphere. He founded the Yugoslav Academy of Arts and Sciences (1866) and was instrumental in the creation of the University of Zagreb (1874). Ultimately, both the Party of Right and National Party were neutralized by Khuen-Hédervåry, who ignored the Nagodba and exploited Croat-Serb rivalries to promote Magyar rule in Croatia.

Croatia's Serbs established their own political party in 1881, known as the Serb Independent Party, following the incorporation of the military frontier into Croatia-Slavonia. Adopting a linguistic definition of nationality, the Serb intelligentsia initially argued that all speakers of the Štokavian dialect were Serbs. The disparities in Croat and Serb nationalist ideologies made cooperation between the two nationalities increasingly difficult in late-ninteenth-century Croatia. This was a pressing matter, given the fact that in 1881 Serbs constituted one-quarter of Croatia-Slavonia's population. The Serbs were concentrated in those parts of Croatia that had formerly been part of the military frontier (e.g., Lika, Kordun, Banija, parts of Slavonia, Srijem). Initially the Croatian Serbs hoped to defend their traditional religious autonomy, but as the Orthodox population began acquiring a Serb identity, religious demands gave way to demands for national rights, such as the use of Cyrillic script and cultural and political autonomy. Most Croatian Serbs wanted the former military frontier removed from Croatian administration; many hoped for eventual unification with Serbia. At the dawn of the twentieth century, there was little common ground between Croat and Serb in the Habsburg lands.

In the first years of the twentieth century a younger generation of Croat and Serb politicians, dissatisfied with the Croat and Serb predicament in the Austro-Hungarian Empire, forged a new cooperation. In 1905 an important alliance of the leading Croat and Serb parties in Croatia was formed, known as the Croato-Serb Coalition, consisting of Croat and Serb politicians who believed their fortunes would be best served by cooperating in Croatia against the Habsburg authorities. The greatest contribution of this coalition was to put an end (albeit temporarily) to Croat and Serb political rivalries in Croatia. By 1908, the "Croato-Serb Coalition" won a majority in the diet. The Habsburg authorities hoped to break the coalition; they brought charges of treason against Croatian Serb leaders, but the subsequent trials scandalized European opinion and strengthened the Croato-Serb Coalition. This coalition dominated Croatian politics to 1914, and during World War I some of its most prominent leaders chose political exile to advocate among the Western Allies the creation of a Yugoslav state.

Two characteristics distinguished this generation of supporters of "Yugoslavism" from Strossmayer's generation. First, they increasingly thought in terms of creating a Yugoslav state, which would encompass all the South Slavic regions of Austria-Hungary (i.e., Croatia, Dalmatia, Slovenia, southern Hungary, Bosnia-Hercegovina) and Serbia and Montenegro. This tendency reflected the intense and growing dissatisfaction with Austro-Hungarian rule. Second, they adopted an innovative but in retrospect flawed belief that the South Slavic peoples (Croats, Serbs, Bosnian Muslims, Slovenes) constituted one (a Yugoslav) nationality, and that Yugoslav identity would gradually supplant Croat, Slovene, and Serb identities. This variant of Yugoslavism is referred to as "integral" Yugoslavism or Yugoslavist "unitarism": it was the notion that Croats, Serbs, and Slovenes were simply "tribes" of a single Yugoslav nationality, just as Prussians, Bavarians, and Saxons were "tribes" of a single German nationality. Some of the more radical followers of this "integral" Yugoslavism began forming revolutionary societies in the decade before World War I and employing violence against Austrian and Hungarian officials in Bosnia-Hercegovina and Croatia. Gavrilo Princip, the Serb student who assassinated Archduke Franz Ferdinand in 1914, came from one such revolutionary organization. Thus, in the period from 1905 to 1914, the "South Slav Question" emerged as an important issue in Austro-Hungarian domestic politics, and an issue of European significance.

WORLD WAR I AND THE FORMATION OF THE YUGOSLAV STATE

What made the South Slav Question an issue of European significance was the emergence of Serbia as a regional Balkan power during the Balkan Wars of 1912–1913. During those wars, a pro-Russian Serbia had doubled in size and thus was perceived by the Austro-Hungarian government as a serious threat, especially given the growth of revolutionary societies in Croatia and Bosnia-Hercegovina. It was Vienna's perception of a Serbian threat, combined with growing radicalism in Croatia and Bosnia-Hercegovina, which prompted the Habsburg authorities to go to war against Serbia in 1914, which, in turn, sparked World War I.

Following the outbreak of the war, many Croat politicians and intellectuals left the monarchy to work for the cause of Yugoslav statehood. In April 1915 a number of these exiled politicians, led by the Croats Ante Trumbić and Frano Supilo, formed the Yugoslav Committee in London. Fearing Italian pretensions toward Dalmatia and Istria, Trumbić and the Yugoslav Committee promoted the cause of a South Slavic state, encompassing the South Slavic lands of the Habsburg monarchy and Serbia-Montenegro. Dalmatia in particular was contested by a number of powers. According to the terms of the secret Treaty of London (1915), the Allies promised Dalmatia to Italy in return for Italian support in the war against the Central Powers.

In July 1917 the Serbian premier Nikola Pašić and Trumbić signed the Corfu Declaration, which called for a common state of Serbs, Croats, and Slovenes with a single democratic, constitutional, parliamentary system, under the Karadjordjević dynasty of Serbia. The Declaration promised equality for the three national names and flags, the three predominant religions, and both scripts (Cyrillic and Latin). However, it did not indicate whether the new state would be highly centralized or a federation of historic provinces. Pašić advocated the former, Trumbić and the Yugoslav Committee the latter.

The Dual Monarchy's authority over its South Slav lands ended abruptly in October 1918. At that time, a "National Council" of Slovenes, Croats, and Serbs was formed in Zagreb and became the de facto government of the monarchy's South Slavic regions; the Slovene politician Anton Korošec headed the National Council, and its vice presidents were Svetozar Pribičević and Ante Pavelić (who was no relation to the leader of the Croatian fascist movement from 1929–1945). On 29 October, the Croatian Sabor annulled the eight-century-old union between Croatia and Hungary and authorized the "National Council" to act as the supreme political authority in a new state, called the "State of the Slovenes, Croats, and Serbs," which encompassed all of the South Slavic lands of the former Habsburg monarchy. In November 1918 Pašić, Trumbić, and Korošec met in Geneva and signed an agreement providing for a joint provisional government but recognizing the jurisdiction of Serbia and the National Council in the areas under their respective control, until a constituent assembly could convene. However, the rapid conclusion of the war, and the fact that Italy began seizing parts of Dalmatia and Istria, prompted the National Council to rush headlong into union with Serbia. It did so in spite of the objections of the Croat Peasant Party leader Stjepan Radić, who would soon become the dominant politician in Croatia, and without obtaining guarantees of autonomy. Leaders in Bosnia-Hercegovina and Vojvodina favored union; on 24 November, the Montenegrins deposed the Petrović dynasty and declared unification with Serbia. On 1 December 1918, Prince Regent Alexander Karadjordjević and delegates from the National Council, Vojvodina, and Montenegro announced the founding of the Kingdom of Serbs, Croats, and Slovenes. The Paris Peace Conference recognized the new kingdom in May 1919.

KINGDOM OF SERBS, CROATS, AND SLOVENES (YUGOSLAVIA) (1918–1941)

Formed on 1 December 1918 and proclaimed in Belgrade, the Kingdom of Serbs, Croats, and Slovenes (which was renamed the Kingdom of Yugoslavia in 1929) was from its inception plagued by numerous political, nationality, social, and other problems. The question of centralism versus federalism bitterly divided Serb and Croat; a lasting democratic solution eluded the country's leaders and led to the imposition in January 1929 of royal dictatorship. Only in 1939, on the eve of World War II, did Croat and Serb leaders manage to reach a political settlement. However, that agreement came far too late and failed to satisfy nationalists on either side.

The creation of Yugoslavia fulfilled the dreams of many Croat intellectuals of Yugoslavist persuasion but ignored some fundamental differences in national ideologies, histories, and cultures among the different nationalities. Serbs, Croats, and Slovenes had conflicting political and cultural traditions, and the Yugoslav state possessed significant non-Slav minorities (including, among others, Germans, Albanians, Magyars, Romanians, and Turks). Confessional differences were a divisive rather than integrative factor; the Orthodox, Roman Catholic, Islamic, Jewish, and Protestant faiths were well established and normally cut across territorial and nationality lines.

After 1918, many Croats would repeatedly point to the fact that the decision to join Serbia in a new kingdom was never authorized by the Croatian diet, which had broken all ties with the Habsburg monarchy on 29 October 1918. Although it had then ceded to the short-lived State of Slovenes, Croats, and Serbs, and its executive, the National Council, some of its sovereignty, it never authorized the subsequent act of unification. Had it been given the chance to do that, in all likelihood it would have authorized unification. That is because the Croat lands (like the Slovene territories) were threatened in the fall of 1918 by Italy, which as one of the victors of the war began occupying territory on the Adriatic coast. Furthermore, in the fall of 1918 massive rural disturbances swept through the Croatian countryside; the middle-class Croat politicians in Zagreb feared the social revolutionary implications of these disturbances, which prompted them, together with the Italian threat, to move even more quickly toward unification with Serbia.

However, once the rural disturbances had been quelled and the Italian threat had receded, the new state's political and other problems quickly surfaced. To Serb politicians, the new kingdom was first and foremost a state of all Serbs; it represented the unification of all Serbs within a unitary state under the scepter of the Serbian Karadjordjević dynasty. The Serbian establishment (i.e., the middle class, bureaucracy, and army) believed that the best way to safeguard the recently obtained unity of Serbs was to have a highly centralized state that ignored local historical individualities. Croats and other non-Serb nationalities were as a consequence deprived of their national rights and increasingly experienced the Yugoslav kingdom as a Great Serbian state; Serbs dominated the government, police, and military. The two leading Serb parties were the Democratic Party, which attracted the support of some non-Serb unitarists, and the National Radical Party, which was a Great Serbian Party. The national question in Yugoslavia was essentially a Croat-Serb rivalry over state organization; it was a clash between uncompromising visions of centralist rule versus historical identities and rights. The main political conflicts of the interwar era stemmed from this Croat-Serb dispute.

In the 1920s the dominant Croat party was the Croat Peasant Party (HSS, Hrvatska seljačka stranka), which had been founded in 1904 by Stjepan Radić (1871–1928) and his brother Antun (1868–1919). (The party's nomenclature changed many times. From 1904 to 1920 it was known as the Croat People's Peasant Party [or HPSS], from 1920 to 1925 as the Croat Republican Peasant Party [HRSS], and after 1925 as the Croat Peasant Party [HSS]). Its strength was rooted in Croatia's socially dominant countryside; it demanded Croatian political sovereignty and peasant social right. The HSS had been opposed to the nature of Yugoslavia's unification in 1918. In November 1920, in the elections to the Constituent Assembly, the HSS reaped the benefits of this opposition. Radić's HSS emerged as the only serious political party in Croatia. Its hold over the Croatian countryside was reaffirmed in the March 1923 elections, when it expanded for the first time to Dalmatia and Bosnia-Hercegovina. From 1920 to 1924, the HSS adopted a policy of abstention; it refused to participate in the Constituent Assembly (1920–1921) or Parliament thereafter (1921–1924). When other anticentralist groups left the assembly in 1921, the National Radicals and Democrats won by default an opportunity to adopt a centralist constitution. The 1921 constitution (the Vidovdan Constitution, so named after the date of its promulgation, 28 June, or St. Vitus Day) provided standard civil and political liberties but, far more importantly from the perspective of the new multiethnic state, allowed no room for local historical individualities and gave non-Serbs inadequate representation.

Having adopted abstention from Belgrade as a policy in itself, Radić took his Croat campaign for autonomy to the outside world. He had hoped in 1919 to send a representative to the Paris Peace Conference but was thwarted by the Yugoslav authorities. In 1922 his party issued a memorandum to the Genoa conference, but the Great Powers ignored it. In 1923 he secretly left the country for London and then, in 1924, the Soviet Union. In the meantime, the Democratic Party, the Slovene People's Party, and the Yugoslav Muslim Organization formed a political coalition that toppled the National Radical Party. In March 1924 Radić, who at the time was in Vienna, ordered the HSS to end its boycott and go to Belgrade. In July 1924 King Alexander gave Ljubomir "Ljuba" Davidović, the leader of the Democratic Party, a mandate to form a new government. Davidović hoped to bring the HSS into his government and thus ease political tensions in the country. Radić returned to Yugoslavia in August 1924, but not before visiting the Soviet Union where he enrolled the HSS in the Soviet-sponsored Peasant International. In October 1924 Alexander forced the resignation of the Davidović government for its flirtation with the now allegedly communist HSS. The National Radicals were returned to power and at the end of December 1924 banned the HSS and ordered the arrest of Radić and the entire party leadership.

Radić would remain in prison from January to July 1925. Political realities and the possible dissolution of his party forced him to make a deal with Alexander. In July 1925 he recognized the monarchy and the HSS joined a government coalition with the National Radical Party, still led by Pašić. This seemingly unnatural union lasted until January 1927, even managing to survive a major corruption scandal that forced Pašić to resign in April 1926. After leaving government early in 1927, the HSS campaigned for decentralization, tax equality for the non-Serbian regions, and political reform. In the fall of 1927 Radić formed a political alliance with his former nemesis, the Croatian Serb politician Svetozar Pribičević, leader of the Independent Democratic Party (SDS, Samostalna demokratska stranka). Their alliance, known as the Peasant-Democratic Coalition, represented a united Croatian front for political reform and decentralization, against Belgrade. On the other hand the two major Serbian political parties, the National Radicals and Democrats, were increasingly torn by factionalism. Their internal party divisions facilitated the growing political importance of King Alexander. Political tensions grew in 1928. In June 1928 a Montenegrin Serb deputy, a member of the National Radical Party, shot Radić and three other HSS deputies during a session of parliament. Two deputies died instantly and Radić died two months later. The HSS and its Croatian Serb ally, the SDS, withdrew from Belgrade and demanded sweeping political reform. On 6 January 1929, King Alexander Karadjordjević abrogated the constitution, dissolved the parliament, banned political parties, and declared a royal dictatorship.

The 6 January dictatorship, as it was known, proved more destructive than Alexander and his advisers originally believed. Civil liberties were suspended, existing institutions of local self-government were abolished, and strict laws against sedition, terrorism, and propagation of communism were imposed. The dictatorship only heightened existing differences, as non-Serbs viewed the dictatorship as an instrument of Serbian hegemony. The king named a Serb army officer, General Petar Živković, as premier and officially changed the name of the country to the Kingdom of Yugoslavia. As part of his campaign to erase "tribal" differences and identities, the king replaced traditional provinces with new territorial units, called *banovine* (sing., *banovina*), named mainly after the country's major rivers. In this way, Croatia was divided between Sava and Primorje provinces; the former was named after a river and encompassed Croatia proper and much of Slavonia, while the latter, meaning "Littoral," encompassed Dalmatia and some parts of Bosnia-Hercegovina.

In the end, Alexander's policies backfired. Not only did they further antagonize the non-Serbs, many of whom saw the dictatorship merely as a vehicle of Great Serbian interests, but Serbs too. For democratically inclined Serb politicians, the price paid for state unity was far too high; the dictatorship further diminished the already fragile unity within the Serbian political establishment. The dictatorship failed to produce an understanding of common national interests and ultimately strengthened the country's centrifugal forces. In Croatia, the royal dictatorship unified Croat opinion in its opposition to the perceived threat of Serbian hegemony. The government's policy in 1932–1933 of prosecuting Vladko Maček, successor to Radić, for terrorist activity proved disastrous; it further alienated the Croat population. The extreme nationalists of the Croat political right fled abroad in 1929; Italy granted asylum to Ante Pavelić, the leader of the Ustaša (insurgent) movement. The movement's singular objective was the liberation of Croatia and creation of an independent Great Croatian state, one that could be formed only with the destruction of Yugoslavia.

Champion of the Croat peasant cause Vladko Maček. (Time Life Pictures/Getty Images)

In 1931 Alexander formally ended his personal rule by promulgating a constitution that provided for the restoration of limited democracy. Political parties were legalized, but "tribal" groups (religious, ethnic, and regional) and all organizations that threatened the integrity and order of the state were banned. The Croat and Serb opposition leaders could not agree on a common platform. The HSS hoped for the restoration of democratic governance, but its primary goal was achieving Croatian sovereignty within Yugoslavia. The Serb opposition was interested in a return to parliamentary life but deeply divided on the question of Croatian autonomy, which most Serb politicians were unwilling to concede. Political developments and tensions in the early 1930s were exacerbated by the worsening economic crisis, which hit Yugoslavia particularly hard. Foreign trade slumped, unemployment rose, and the large agrarian sector stagnated. The economic crisis brought renewed accusations from Croats (and Slovenes) that Belgrade was exploiting Croatia (and Slovenia).

In October 1934 a Macedonian terrorist working with the Ustaša movement assassinated Alexander at Marseilles while he was on an official state visit to France. Prince Paul, cousin of Alexander, nominated a three-person regency that ruled for Alexander's son, Peter II, who was still a minor. Paul hoped to liberalize the regime and reconcile

Serb and Croat without amending the 1931 constitution. To that end, the Belgrade government freed Maček and in 1935 held elections that revealed significant dissatisfaction with the existing political system. Paul then called upon the Serb politician, Milan Stojadinović, to form a cabinet. His new government granted amnesty to political prisoners and permitted political parties additional leeway, but it refused to restore democracy and failed to solve the "Croat Question."

Maček realized that growing domestic and international tensions worked in favor of a positive resolution of the Croat Question and potentially even a federalist solution; he refused to compromise with the Stojadinović government. On the other hand Stojadinović alienated many Serb nationalists by signing a concordat with the Vatican; the National Assembly canceled the concordat, after the Serbian Orthodox Church denounced it. Stojadinović also initiated a rapprochement with Rome, designed in part to neutralize the Ustaša extremists who were protected by fascist Italy. Paul forced Stojadinović's resignation in February 1939 and named Dragiša Cvetković the new premier.

By this point, domestic political strife and portents of war induced Prince Paul to instruct Cvetković to reach an agreement with the HSS. For its part, the HSS managed to maintain its political stronghold in Croatia and the predominantly Croat-populated areas of Bosnia-Hercegovina. On 26 August 1939, after months of negotiation, Cvetković and Maček reached an agreement *(Sporazum)* that created an autonomous Croatia. Under the *Sporazum,* Belgrade controlled defense, internal security, foreign affairs, trade, and transport; but an elected Sabor and a Crown-appointed ban (viceroy) would decide internal matters in Croatia. Paul then appointed a new government with Cvetković as premier and Maček as vice-premier. The *Sporazum* failed to satisfy nationalists on either side. Maček was denounced by the Croat political right for renouncing Croatian independence and some supposedly historic Croatian territories (i.e., Bosnia-Hercegovina), while Serb nationalists attacked Cvetković for conceding far too much territory, abandoning Croatia's Serbs to Zagreb, and for not restoring parliamentary rule in the country. This arrangement returned autonomy and some attributes of statehood that Croats had lost after unification in 1918. This might have been a step toward the federalization of the state and a solution to the Croat Question, but World War II rendered all of this temporary.

WORLD WAR II (1941–1945)

Despite the outbreak of World War II in September 1939, Yugoslavia managed to remain neutral until 1941. When Greece repelled an Italian invasion in October 1940, Germany was forced to come to Italy's assistance. In late fall of 1940 and winter of 1940–1941, Germany pressured the Balkan states to join the Tripartite Pact; Romania and Bulgaria signed in November 1940 and March 1941, respectively. Virtually surrounded by hostile states, neutral Yugoslavia desperately sought allies. It recognized the Soviet Union in 1940 and signed a nonaggression agreement with Moscow in 1941. When Berlin pressed Yugoslavia to join the Axis, Paul and his cabinet concluded that their military situation was hopeless. On 25 March 1941, Yugoslavia joined the Tripartite Pact. In exchange, Germany promised not to violate Yugoslavia's sovereignty.

However, on 27 March, military officers overthrew the Cvetković-Maček cabinet, declared the sixteen-year-old Peter II king, and formed a new cabinet under General Dušan Simović. The new government affirmed Yugoslav loyalty to the Tripartite Pact because of the country's perilous position. Nevertheless, the putsch provided Germany with a pretext to invade. In a twelve-day lightning offensive beginning on 6 April 1941, in which Italy, Hungary, and Bulgaria also participated, the Yugoslav army was crushed. The king and government fled, and on 17 April remaining resistance forces surrendered unconditionally.

Germany and its Axis allies partitioned the country. The largest single entity emerging from this partition was the Independent State of Croatia (NDH, Nezavisna država Hrvatska), which consisted of present-day Croatia (minus Istria and much of Dalmatia), Bosnia-Hercegovina, and Srijem (part of Vojvodina). However, Italy controlled Istria (as it had since 1919), and in 1941 Rome annexed most of Dalmatia as well. The NDH was in actual fact an Italo-German condominium. Both Nazi Germany and fascist Italy had spheres of influence in the NDH and stationed their own troops there. The Croatian fascist movement, the Ustaše (sing., Ustaša), headed by Ante Pavelić, was a relatively small group that had lived in political exile since 1929. The agenda they espoused was basically a Croat nationalist program that was influenced only to a small degree by fascist and Nazi ideologies. During the war, the movement unleashed a brutal and murderous policy against those minorities deemed to be "alien" to Croatia and her national interests. As a consequence, Ustaša authorities slaughtered tens of thousands of Serbs. The Croatian authorities also collaborated with the Nazi authorities in implementing the Final Solution. As a result, approximately 32,000 Croatian and Bosnian Jews perished in the Holocaust. Most were killed at Croatian camps, like Jasenovac, although approximately 7,000 were deported to Auschwitz.

The dominant political party in Croatia, the HSS, disintegrated during the war. Although Maček refused collaboration with the Axis, he never contemplated active resistance. As a result, the HSS inner leadership withdrew into the political shadows. To ensure his quiescence, the Ustaša regime had Maček imprisoned; he spent nearly a year in the Jasenovac camp and then the remainder of the war under house arrest. One segment of the HSS right wing sided, actively or passively, with the Ustaša regime or was coopted by it, believing that statehood had at long last been achieved; the left wing gradually opted for the Popular Front led by the Communists.

Armed resistance to the Axis in wartime Croatia (and generally throughout partitioned Yugoslavia) took one of two forms. On the one hand remnants of the Serb-dominated Yugoslav army formed small guerrilla units known collectively as Četniks. They were led by Colonel Dragoljub "Draža" Mihailović, a Serb nationalist and monarchist, who hoped for a return to the status quo ante. However, following the Nazi invasion of the Soviet Union, the Communist Party of Yugoslavia (KPJ, Komunistička partija Jugoslavije) launched its own resistance to the Axis while simultaneously articulating a program opposed to that of the Četniks and government in exile. The Communist-led Partisan movement eventually became the most effective resistance movement in Croatia and Yugoslavia. Although the KPJ had been banned in 1921 and then decimated by police repression, internal Party factionalism, and, not least of all, the Stalinist purges of the 1930s, it was the only entity in 1941 to possess a "Yugoslav" political program. The KPJ/Partisan leader, Josip Broz "Tito" (1892–1980), a native of Kumrovec, Croatia, had become a communist as a POW in Russia after 1917. In 1937 he became general secretary of the KPJ, and in the years immediately preceding World War II, Tito reorganized the Party and attempted to give it a stronger organizational base. In 1937 he oversaw the creation of a Communist Party of Croatia (KPH, Komunistička partija Hrvatske), essentially an extension of the KPJ.

In wartime Croatia both the Četniks and Partisans recruited heavily from the Serb population, which was exposed to the murderous policy of the Ustaša regime. For much of 1941, the line separating Četnik and Partisan units in the field was imprecise. Both had the same pool of recruits, and in the early days of the war they were willing to collaborate for the sake of survival. However, in the winter of 1941–1942 Četnik-Partisan conflicts erupted into open warfare. Henceforth, the Četnik movement turned increasingly to collaboration with the Axis, first with the Italians in Croatia and Montenegro, and eventually with the Germans and even the Ustaša authorities. The Partisan movement in Croatia, headed by Andrija Hebrang, established itself within the framework of the broader, Yugoslav communist movement; part of their appeal in Croatia, among Croats, was that they advocated a federal system in which Croatia would become one of the constituent republics of a new Yugoslavia. As support for the Ustaša government waned in 1941–1942, because of its arbitrary policies and persecution of Serbs, Jews, and Croat opponents, the Partisans benefited. In some parts of Croatia (e.g., Dalmatia, which was annexed by Italy), the local population sided with the Communist resistance in the first days of the occupation. However, the Croat element in the resistance began substantially to grow only in the winter of 1942–1943.

In November 1942, at Bihać in northwestern Bosnia (then part of the NDH), Partisan leaders convened a meeting of the Antifascist Council for the National Liberation of Yugoslavia (AVNOJ, Antifašističko vijeće narodnog oslobodjenja Jugoslavije), a committee of Communist and noncommunist Partisan representatives from all of Yugoslavia. AVNOJ became the political umbrella organization for the people's liberation committees that the Partisans had established to administer territories under their control. AVNOJ proclaimed support for democracy and the rights of all nationalities. A second session of AVNOJ was convened in November 1943. It included representatives of various ethnic and political groups and built the basis for Yugoslavia's postwar regime. AVNOJ formed a National Committee to act as the temporary government, named Tito a marshal and prime minister of Yugoslavia, and issued a declaration forbidding King Peter from returning to the country until a popular referendum had been held on the status of the monarchy. At the Teheran Conference in December 1943, the Allied leaders (Franklin D. Roosevelt, Winston Churchill, and Joseph Stalin) decided to support the Partisans. In June 1944 the exiled King Peter appointed the Croat politician, Ivan Šubašić, who had been prewar ban of Croatia, as prime minister of the government in exile. Šubašić accepted the resolutions of the second AVNOJ conference, and Peter agreed to remain outside Yugoslavia. In September 1944 the king succumbed to Allied pressure and summoned Yugoslavs of all nationalities to back the Partisans. The following month, the Soviet Red Army helped the Partisans liberate Belgrade; from that point, the German retreat from the NDH and all of partitioned Yugoslavia intensified. The last German and Ustaša forces left Croatia in early May 1945.

World War II was devastating for Croatia and its people. It also provided a vivid new set of memories to kindle future hostility between Croat and Serb. In four years of war, approximately 1.1 million persons were killed in the different parts of partitioned Yugoslavia. Although the figures are still contested, it is now believed that roughly 60 percent of all deaths were on those territories that were part of the Independent State of Croatia. The Serbs, of whom approximately 350,000 died on the territory of the NDH, suffered the largest number of casualties. It is believed that roughly 200,000 Croats and 86,000 Bosnian Muslims died between 1941 and 1945. Many of Croatia's towns, production centers, and communications systems were either ruined or heavily damaged; malnutrition and disease were common. The formal cessation of hostilities in Europe, which occurred on 8 May 1945, did not bring immediate peace. Collaborators were hunted down and usually executed without trial. The Ustaša militia and regular Croatian army retreated to Austria in early May 1945, accompanied by thousands of civilians fearing communist rule. After surrendering to British forces, they were repatriated to the Partisans near the town of Bleiburg. Many of these soldiers and civilians were summarily executed; others were marched back to Yugoslavia where they ended up in camps or prisons.

COMMUNIST YUGOSLAVIA (1945–1990)

After 1945, the most salient feature of Croatian life was a communist dictatorship. Yugoslavia's new communist authorities suppressed all manifestations of Croat (and other) nationalism, labeling advocates of Croat national interests Ustaše, even if they had no ties to the wartime fascist regime. The political oppression and administrative centralization experienced under the KPJ (later renamed to League of Communists of Yugoslavia or SKJ, Savez komunista Jugoslavije) harkened back to the days of interwar Yugoslavia, especially the period of King Alexander's royal dictatorship (1929–1934), when Croat national rights were suppressed. Croat nationalists had long objected to Croatia's perceived exploitation, and by the 1960s even some of Croatia's Communists eventually began to feel that Croatia was again being exploited by Belgrade. This oppression was not limited to political or economic life but allegedly extended to the cultural realm. National aspirations would peak again in the late 1960s and early 1970s during the Croatian Spring. Only with the collapse of communism in 1989 was Croatia gradually able to move toward independence and democratic governance.

One of the many political changes introduced by the Communists in 1945 was a federal system; it was their attempt to resolve the national question that had plagued Yugoslavia since its creation in 1918. Croatia now became one of six federal republics. In a sense, 1945 represented the unification of the Croat lands. The new Croatian republic acquired those parts of Dalmatia that had been occupied by Italy between 1918 and 1920 and held throughout the interwar era. The Italo-Yugoslav peace treaty of 1947 gave Yugoslavia (i.e., Croatia) the islands that had been ceded to Italy in 1920. Most of the Istrian Peninsula, together with the town of Rijeka, which had in 1919 passed to Italy, was ceded in 1947 to Yugoslavia.

Despite this "national unification," democratic institutions and political parties were suppressed. The exiled King Peter had surrendered his powers to a three-person regency in late 1944. On 7 March 1945, a provisional government took office with Tito as prime minister and war minister and Šubašić in charge of foreign affairs; all the remaining cabinet posts went to Tito's followers. In November 1945 the Communist authorities organized elections for a Constituent Assembly. Alleged wartime collaborators were barred from voting. Moreover, all candidates were supposed to be nominated by the Communist-controlled People's Front, the successor to the wartime People's Liberation Front that encompassed all noncollaborationist political parties and organizations. Noncommunist politicians were harassed. Šubašić and other noncommunist ministers resigned in protest, while the HSS (whose leader Maček fled the country in May 1945), Serb Radicals, and other parties boycotted the election.

The Communist-dominated Constituent Assembly then proceeded to abolish the monarchy and on 29 November 1945 established a Federal People's Republic of Yugoslavia. In January 1946 the Constituent Assembly adopted a constitution based on the Soviet model; Yugoslavia became a federation of six people's republics held together by a strong central government. The constitution included direct KPJ control over all aspects of state activity. Tito was head of the KPJ, government, and armed forces. Only after the break with the Soviets in 1948 did Tito and the KPJ gradually move away from this rigid Stalinist model.

Between 1945 and 1948, the government ruthlessly punished wartime collaborators. Many members of the Croatian army as well as smaller numbers of Slovene and Serb collaborators (along with civilian refugees) repatriated in May 1945 to the Partisans were summarily executed. In Croatia, the Communist authorities also used allegations of collaboration to stifle legitimate political and religious opposition. The HSS leadership either fled or was suppressed. The Roman Catholic Church, which strongly opposed the new communist system although a segment of it had collaborated with the wartime Croatian fascist regime, was exposed to persecution. The archbishop of Zagreb, Alojzije Stepinac, protested government "excesses." In September 1946 he was sentenced to life imprisonment for war crimes and his alleged collaboration with the wartime Croatian fascist authorities. He served five years before the regime released him; he lived the rest of his life in his native village, under virtual house arrest. Communist oppression took a heavy toll against real and alleged collaborators. According to some estimates, after the war the Communist authorities executed over two hundred priests and nuns who allegedly collaborated with the Ustaša regime in some capacity. Consequently, Yugoslav-Vatican relations deteriorated. The Yugoslav government severed relations in 1952 when Pope Pius XII named Stepinac a Cardinal. The authorities permitted the funeral and burial of Stepinac in Zagreb in 1960, after which Yugoslav-Vatican relations gradually improved. Diplomatic relations were reestablished only in 1970.

The break with the Soviet Union in 1948 prompted a number of domestic political changes. Among them was Tito's belated decision to permit greater political rights to the six constituent republics. A greater degree of regional autonomy was now deemed necessary in order to maintain his own internal political support. A few prominent Yugoslav Communists had defected to the Soviet side in 1948, and for years thereafter the Yugoslav authorities imprisoned thousands of suspected pro-Soviet Communists. One of the more prominent victims of this anti-Stalinist purge was the Croat Communist leader Andrija Hebrang, who had led the wartime Croat Partisan movement and risen to high rank after 1945. However, in 1948 he was purged and probably murdered in prison for his alleged anti-Tito behavior. In actual fact, he was probably removed because he had established a significant power base in Croatia, which posed a potential threat to Tito.

Despite the 1948 break with Stalin, the Yugoslav Communists attempted to prove their allegiance to Marxist-Leninist theory by implementing Stalinist social and economic policies. The Stalinist course was reversed at the Sixth KPJ Congress in 1952, which proved to be a watershed in Yugoslav political change. Henceforth the KPJ (now renamed SKJ, for League of Communists of Yugoslavia, or Savez komunista Jugoslavije) attempted to articulate a path to socialism distinct from the Stalinist model. The constitution that was adopted partially separated Party and state functions and restored some political rights to Croatia and the other constituent republics. Constitutional foundations were also laid for worker control over enterprises and expanded local government power. The 1953 constitution established the Federal People's Assembly, which was composed of two houses: a Federal Chamber, representing the regions; and a Chamber of Producers, representing economic enterprises and workers groups. The executive branch, called the Federal Executive Council, included only the ministries dealing with national affairs and foreign policy.

Economic decentralization was also instituted, representing a step away from the harsh Stalinist practices of collectivization of agriculture and suppression of market. This

During the funeral for Cardinal Alojzije Stepinac. (Time Life Pictures/Getty Images)

decentralization also led to friction among the republics, which now sought preferences in the national allocation of resources. By the 1960s, this friction generated new intrarepublican tensions. In fact, the 1963 constitution decentralized the political system even further, to the benefit of the six republics. The Federal Assembly was divided into one general chamber, the Federal Chamber, and four chambers given specific bureaucratic responsibilities. In an effort to end regional conflict and promote national representation of the peoples of Yugoslavia, the constitution directed that individual republics be represented in the Chamber of Nationalities, which was a part of the Federal Chamber.

Although the 1963 constitution reflected the "liberal" and reformist leanings of the Yugoslav leadership in those years, substantial power existed outside the institutional structures. Aleksandar Ranković, the state secretary of the federal security police, led an obstructionist bloc that opposed economic reform and advocated a return to the pre-1953 strong Party role. In the many deadlocks between the reformist and conservative groups, Tito remained the ultimate arbiter. In general, he supported economic reform while resisting those tendencies that sought the decentralization of state and Party power. Tito's decision to remove Ranković in 1966 was a victory for the SKJ reformist wing, represented by the likes of Edvard Kardelj, the chief theoretician of Yugoslav socialism, and the Croat Communist Vladimir Bakarić. His ouster removed one of the most important Party conservative elements from power. After 1966, the media were permitted to discuss more freely Party policies. Central control over some economic enterprises was loosened. The SKJ also decentralized its structure, allowing for more power at the level of the republican parties. Increasingly all major decisions required compromise. That in turn led occasionally to stalemate on some issues, in particular pertaining to economic development. In Croatia and Slovenia, the two wealthiest republics, resentment mounted in the late 1960s at what they perceived as economic exploitation by Belgrade to the benefit of Serbia and the poorer regions (Macedonia, Kosovo, and Montenegro).

The decentralization of the 1960s engendered regional reformist tendencies for political liberalization. In Croatia this movement became known as the Croatian Spring (1966–1971), which was as much a call for political liberalization as it was for greater Croat national rights within Yugoslavia. Demands were openly voiced in Croatia and even within the reform-minded wing of the League of Communists of Croatia, headed by Miko Tripalo and Savka Dabčević-Kučar, for decentralization, greater rights for Croatia and the other republics, economic reform, and political pluralism. Croat nationalists, based in powerful cultural institutions like Matica Hrvatska (Croat Literary-Cultural Foundation), urged the reformist wing of the Croatian League of Communists to adopt even tougher attitudes vis-à-vis Belgrade. Eventually they went beyond Party policy and even voiced separatist demands. In 1967 a group of Croat intellectuals, including Miroslav Krleža, the most respected literary figure in twentieth-century Croatia, signed a statement denying the validity of "Serbo-Croatian" as a historical language and promoting Croatian as a distinct language. Croat historians recalled exploitation of Croatia by the Serb-dominated interwar government, and Croat economists complained of disproportionate levies on Croatia for the federal budget and development fund. Party leaders in Zagreb won popularity by defending the economic interests of Croatia. Finally, in November 1971, university students went on strike and demonstrators marched through the streets of Zagreb demanding political reform and greater national freedoms. At that point, Tito urged the Croatian Party leadership to suppress the nationalist movement in Croatia.

When the Croatian Party failed to comply, Tito intervened personally in the winter of 1971–1972 to suppress the Croatian Spring, which by that point had taken on overtly separatist dimensions. The intervention involved an extensive purge of the reformist wing of the Croatian Party. The Croatian purge and the imposition within the Party of a more conservative wing created a more pliant Party leadership in Croatia that supported Tito's Party centralization. The new Croatian Party leaders were politically far more reliable. Eventually the purge extended well beyond Party ranks. Thousands of persons were arrested, some were killed, while many others chose political exile. The University of Zagreb's ranks were purged and the authorities temporarily disbanded Matica Hrvatska. Nationalists and liberals were purged from other Croatian institutions. The rise of nationalism halted the liberalizing tendency in the federal Party. In 1972 Tito also conducted a purge of the Serbian Party; the reformist wing (e.g., Latinka Perović, Marko Nikezić) was ousted in favor of a more conservative faction of Party veterans. After 1971–1972, Tito called for stricter adherence to democratic centralism. In 1974, at the SKJ's Tenth Congress, Tito was elected president of the Party for life. The press was muzzled, dissidents were harassed and arrested, universities were forced to remove professors deemed politically unreliable, and a renewed effort was placed on promoting Tito's cult of personality.

Despite crushing reformist tendencies in Croatia and elsewhere in 1971–1972, Tito addressed some of the concerns raised by republican leaders. Among these were the question of decentralization and the nature of the Yugoslav federation. A new constitution, promulgated in 1974, stipulated that each of the six federal republics was a state with its own borders. In doing so, the new constitution decentralized the Yugoslav political system even further; Tito believed the reform would satisfy Croat (and other non-Serb) demands for increased republican autonomy and thus dampen secessionist sentiment. In effect, the 1974 constitution enshrined many of the decentralizing tendencies of the late 1960s. It also created new representative federal institutions and a complex system of political checks and balances, designed to enhance the power of the SKJ. The most important legacy of the 1974 constitution was that it transferred numerous powers from the center to the republics. Although the Croatian Spring had been suppressed, and a new leadership imposed that stifled political creativity for the next seventeen years, some of the concerns raised by Croat reformers had been adopted.

After 1971, Tito gradually withdrew from decisionmaking. Although he continued to address Party cadres and appoint Party officials to the Presidium, by the late 1970s, he no longer presided over meetings of the SKJ Presidium or new State Presidency. The latter institution consisted of nine members, that is, Tito and one representative from each republic and autonomous province, with equal representation for each republic and province. In his last years he began paving the way for a power sharing government-by-consensus, which he believed to be the best hope of binding the federation after his death. The 1974 constitution had given substantial new powers to the republics, which obtained veto power over some federal legislation, and now both government and Party became increasingly stratified between federal and regional organizations. In 1979 the Presidium, which was chief executive body of the SKJ, began annual rotation of its chairmanship. After Tito died in May 1980, his power to name Presidium members devolved to a special commission including regional Party leaders. This was yet another step toward Party decentralization. Rotation of the Presidium chairmanship continued through the 1980s on a regular schedule, following a formula that divided the position equally among the eight federal jurisdictions. Although Tito had devised the rotational system to prevent Party domination by one individual, he had placed great importance on a strong central Party surviving him. By 1980, however, the centrifugal political forces gradually building in the previous decades had already significantly eroded the single-party structure.

FROM TITO TO DISINTEGRATION (1980–1991)

Although the causes of Yugoslavia's breakup predate Tito's death on 4 May 1980, that event serves as a symbolic turning point in the political history of the country. Henceforth, Yugoslavia was governed by a rotating Federal Presidency, consisting of one representative from each of the six republics and two autonomous provinces. Consensus politics were the order of the day. However, by 1980 the SKJ was no longer a monolithic entity. It was merely the sum of its constituent parts and represented the interests of its republican constituencies. Given the country's complex nationality composition, consensus rule proved increasingly difficult over the long run.

Thus Tito's death inaugurated a period of political uncertainty. Yugoslavia's collective presidency assumed full control in a fairly smooth transition, but the country's strongest personality and unifying force had disappeared. Yugoslavia had clearly entered a new era. The divisive issues that Tito had held in check became more pronounced; the political system that he bequeathed to the country was a structure torn by regional and nationality divisions. Tito's death undeniably weakened Yugoslavia and served to strengthen centrifugal forces. The internal breakup of Yugoslavia commenced, albeit slowly. The 1980s were a time of gradual political and economic deterioration and a period that saw intrarepublican and nationality hostilities boiling just below the surface of the Yugoslav political culture. It was also a decade singularly lacking in strong political leadership.

For example, in 1981 riots occurred in the Autonomous Province of Kosovo, where Albanians called for republican status for their autonomous province, which was part of Serbia. It was the first post-Tito crisis and revealed differences within the Yugoslav polity. The political crisis prompted radically different responses from different quarters of the SFRY. The Serbian leadership and Yugoslav People's Army (JNA, Jugoslavenska narodna armija) urged a hard line; the leadership of Slovenia urged reform. In Serbia, which had historically been the dominant political entity within Yugoslavia, the response to two decades of decentralization and fragmentation was recentralization. In 1984 the Serbian Party officially demanded repeal of the autonomy granted in 1974 to Kosovo and Vojvodina. In 1986, the Serbian Academy of Arts and Sciences composed a "Memorandum," subsequently stolen from the Academy's offices and leaked to the press, which spoke of alleged discrimination against Serbs in communist Yugoslavia. The memorandum attacked the 1974 constitution for limiting Serbia's control of its two autonomous provinces and also for further weakening Serb unity within the SFRY. The memorandum alleged that, since Serbs lived scattered across a number of republics outside Serbia (i.e., Croatia, Montenegro, and Bosnia-Hercegovina), decentralization only exposed them to cultural assimilation and political and social marginalization in these republics, to the benefit of dominant groups (Croats in Croatia, Montenegrins in Montenegro, and Bosnian Muslims in Bosnia-Hercegovina). The memorandum was not so much a blueprint for future action as it was a list of popular grievances long felt in Serbian educated society. When Slobodan Milošević became secretary of the League of Communists of Serbia in 1987, his political program spoke to the grievances articulated in the memorandum.

The Kosovo crisis of 1981 prompted the passage of a number of constitutional amendments that consolidated the principles of rotational government. However, neither the Twelfth nor the Thirteenth SKJ Congresses (1982, 1986) gave the Party a new political direction. Regional divisions were now more pronounced and resulted in stalemate between the forces of centralism and federalism (or decentralization). Serbia, historically the most outspoken exponent of strong central power, was increasingly at odds with Slovenia and Croatia, which historically had supported regional autonomy and resented the central government's policy of redistributing their relatively greater wealth to impoverished regions of the south. By the late 1980s, the resentment of exploitation turned into resistance, which was both economic (withholding revenue from the federal treasury) and political (threatening secession unless granted substantial economic and political autonomy within the federation). Intrarepublican disputes prevented the emergence of a political consensus on the Yugoslav level.

The 1989 collapse of communism in Eastern Europe undoubtedly quickened the pace of Yugoslavia's dissolution. The governing SKJ held its last Party congress, the Fourteenth Extraordinary Congress, in Belgrade in January 1990. In the course of this congress, the League of Communists split along republican lines. It could not agree on how to reform Yugoslavia politically, now that communism had disappeared in Eastern Europe, or in which general direction to proceed. There was only a vague consensus that reform was needed and that democratic elections were inevitable. But how Yugoslavia would look after these reforms were implemented or whether it would survive them at all was open to heated debate. On 22 January 1990, the delegates of the League of Communists of Slovenia, which had agreed in the fall of 1989 to permit democratic elections in Slovenia in the New Year, urged the federal Party to legalize a pluralist system. Delegates of the League of Communists of Croatia, which had in December 1990 also agreed to hold multiparty elections in Croatia, supported them. However, on 23 January 1990, the League of Communists of Yugoslavia rejected the Slovenian reform proposals. At that point, the Slovenian and Croatian delegations left the Congress and the federal Party disintegrated.

Following their withdrawal from the Belgrade Congress, the Croatian Communists moved ahead with plans for multiparty elections. These elections were conducted in two stages, on 22 April and 6 May 1990. The Croat Democratic Union (HDZ, Hrvatska demokratska zajednica) of Franjo Tudjman won a plurality of votes (41.5 percent) and secured a majority of seats (197, or 60 percent) in the Croatian parliament, known as the Sabor. The new Sabor then elected the HDZ candidate Tudjman president of Croatia; he was inaugurated on 30 May. The HDZ hold over Croatian politics remained intact until Tudjman's death in December 1999. The HDZ saw itself as the defender of Croat national rights, Croatia's territorial integrity and sovereignty, which it held to have been long suppressed within Yugoslavia. It was a Croat nationalist party and quickly moved forward with its goal of greater political rights for Croatia within a restructured, decentralized, and noncommunist Yugoslavia. On 25 July 1990, the new Croatian parliament ratified amendments to the Croatian constitution. The "socialist" adjective was dropped from Croatia's official nomenclature, and the Communist flag was replaced by traditional nationalist symbols. In December 1990 a new constitution was promulgated.

Portrait of Franjo Tudjman, president of Croatia (1990–1999). (Embassy of the Republic of Croatia)

The leading Croatian Serb party, which was formed on 17 February 1990, was the Serb Democratic Party (SDS, Srpska demokratska stranka). It was the handiwork of three Croatian Serb intellectuals, Jovan Rašković, Dušan Zelenbaba, and Jovan Opačić, who served as the party's first president and vice presidents, respectively. Founded at the town of Knin, Croatia, the SDS quickly established itself as the undisputed leader of Croatia's Serbs. On 20 May 1990, the SDS withdrew its deputies from the newly elected Croatian Parliament and declared a boycott. At the same time, one of its deputies, Milan Babić, announced the establishment of an Association of Serb Municipalities in Croatia. This association was supposed to link all the predominantly Serb populated municipalities of Croatia, where the SDS has scored its major electoral gains. On 26 July, one day after the Croatian Parliament ratified a number of amendments to the Croatian Constitution, the SDS declared that the Serbs had a right to hold a referendum on autonomy within Croatia. The SDS created a Serb National Council, which ostensibly was supposed to serve as the supreme political authority of the Croatian Serbs. The Croatian government immediately rejected the idea of a Serb referendum, and in August 1990 it began trying to disarm Croatian Serb police and replacing Serbs in the police and reserve forces. At the same time, an oath of loyalty was required of all Serbs in the public sector.

The SDS had a Serb nationalist agenda, but originally it advocated only territorial and cultural autonomy for Serbs within Croatia. Only later did it move toward outright secession of the predominantly Serb-populated areas from Croatia. According to Babić, under the influence of propaganda from Belgrade, which claimed that the new Croatian authorities were preparing to commit genocide against the Croatian Serbs, the SDS shifted from a relatively moderate, autonomist position to a more radical and uncompromising position. Rašković had favored negotiations with the Croatian government, but this course was rejected by almost all other leading figures within the SDS. As a result, Rašković was gradually marginalized within the SDS, which accepted Milošević's concept of Serb unification. If the Croats had a right to break away from Yugoslavia, then the Croatian Serbs had the right to remain in what was left of Yugoslavia.

To that end the SDS organized, on 9 August and 2 September 1990, a referendum on Serb "sovereignty and autonomy" within Croatia. The vote took place in Croatian municipalities where the Serbs formed either an absolute or relative majority of the population and was limited only to Serb voters. The result was overwhelmingly in support of Serb autonomy. The Croatian government declared the Serb referendum illegal and redoubled its attempts to disarm the Serb police. On 30 September the Serb National Council, presided over by Milan Babić, declared the autonomy of the Serb people in those municipalities of Croatia where they possessed either an absolute or a relative majority. The Croatian Serb leadership would accept autonomy within Croatia as long as it remained part of Yugoslavia; if Croatia opted for independence, the Croatian Serbs indicated their readiness to secede from Croatia. Days later, on 4 October, the JNA seized possession of all territorial defense weapons stockpiles in Croatia, which would later be given to the SDS. On 21 December, the SDS announced the creation of three Serb Autonomous Districts (SAO, Srpske autonomne oblasti): SAO Krajina (encompassing the following regions of Croatia: northern Dalmatia, Lika, Kordun, Banija); SAO Western Slavonia (the municipalities of Grubišno Polje, Pakrac, Daruvar, and parts of Novska and Nova Gradiška); and SAO Slavonia, Baranja, and Western Srijem (eastern Croatia). When the SDS attempted to establish its control of local government and police in these three areas, it clashed with the Croatian authorities. Overt conflict between Serbs and Croatian police forces erupted in the spring of 1991.

In October 1990 Slovenia and Croatia had proposed to the other republics that Yugoslavia be restructured as a loose confederation of sovereign states, each with its own army and foreign policy. Based on the model of the European Community (EC), the formula included monetary union and a common economic market. In February 1991 Croatia and Slovenia passed resolutions to dissolve the Yugoslav federation into separate states as the next step after their 1990 declarations of the right to secede. The respective assemblies also passed constitutional amendments declaring republic law supreme over federal law and essentially overriding the authority of the 1974 federal constitution. The Serbian leadership dismissed these plans; the large Serb minorities of Bosnia-Hercegovina (31 percent in 1991) and Croatia (12 percent) would become citizens of foreign countries.

The Serbian leadership, which was still run in 1990 by a conventional communist regime headed by Milošević, attempted to halt Yugoslavia's fragmentation by reviving its historical tradition of geopolitical dominance in Yugoslavia. Milošević's call for the union of all Serbs in one state coincided with those outside Serbia agitating for the creation of a Great Serbian state on the ruins of Yugoslavia. The Milošević regime forged a close alliance with the new Croatian Serb leadership and intervened in the nascent conflict between the Croatian authorities and Croatian Serbs, supposedly to protect the latter from alleged oppression at the hands of the former. As a result, tensions mounted between Serbia and Croatia. The purpose of this alliance between Belgrade and Knin was to carve out a purely Serb area in Croatia that would remain part of a rump Yugoslavia (or Great Serbian state) in the event of Croatian secession. The plan forged at the time in Milošević's inner circle called also for the forcible removal of the majority of the Croat and other non-Serb population from the approximately one-third of Croatia that was supposed to become part of a new Serb-dominated state. These areas included those regions designed by the Croatian Serbs as SAO Krajina, SAO Western Slavonia, and SAO Slavonia, Baranja and Western Srijem. Following the Croatian Serb declaration of independence from Croatia on 19 December 1991, the Serb authorities collectively referred to these three SAOs as the Republic of Serb Krajina (RSK, Republika Srpska krajina).

The Croatian Serbs began receiving increasing support from the Serbian government. Before Croatia's secession from Yugoslavia in June 1991, this support was largely logistical and financial. Following secession and the outbreak of open warfare, this support included arms and personnel. Serb volunteer and police forces in Croatia were being supplied and led by officials of the Serbian Interior Ministry. Ultimately, they were able also to rely on the support of the JNA. The project to create a Great Serbian state had Milošević in a central command responsibility, in his capacity as the president of Serbia. But he worked closely with or exercised substantial influence over numerous key persons who influenced the actions of the Federal Presidency, the Serbian Interior Ministry, the JNA with affiliated Serb-run militia (known as the Territorial Defense) and Serb volunteer groups, and the Croatian Serb leadership. The objective of this combined project was the creation of a Great Serbian state on the ruins of Yugoslavia.

In 1990–1991 Milošević exercised control over four of the eight members of the Federal Presidency of Yugoslavia, thereby managing to set its agenda or neutralize its effectiveness as the need arose. The four members of the Federal Presidency who in 1991 formed the so-called Serb Bloc were Borisav Jović (Serbia), Branko Kostić (Montenegro), Jugoslav Kostić (Autonomous Province of Vojvodina), and Sejdo Bajramović (Autonomous Province of Kosovo). From May 1989 to April 1992, Jović was the representative of the Republic of Serbia and held different positions within the Federal Presidency, including vice president and president. Milošević used Jović and the others as his agents in the Federal Presidency and through them he directed the actions of the Serb Bloc. After 1 October 1991, from which point there were no longer any representatives in the Federal Presidency from Croatia, Slovenia, Macedonia, and Bosnia-Hercegovina, the four members of the Serb Bloc exercised fully the powers of the Federal Presidency, including that of collective commander in chief of the JNA.

The collaboration of the JNA, which was led in 1990–1991 by Generals Veljko Kadijević (federal secretary of national defense, 1988–1992) and Blagoje Adžić (JNA chief of staff, 1989–1992), was essential for both Milošević and the Croatian Serb leadership. During the war in Croatia, the JNA participated in the ethnic cleansing of the Croat and other non-Serb population from the Serb Krajina. It carried out the policies of the Serbian government in Croatia by directing the actions of local Croatian Serb police and security forces. They also introduced Serb volunteer groups into Croatia and supported their activities. The JNA leadership was in constant communication and consultation with Milošević, his inner circle, and the Croatian Serb leadership. The Serbian Interior Ministry was also instrumental to the Serbian war effort in Croatia. It provided arms, funds, training, and other assistance to Croatian Serb regular police units and to paramilitary organizations in Croatia.

The leading Croatian Serb figures in 1990–1991 were Jovan Rašković, Dušan Zelenbaba, Jovan Opačić, Milan Martić, Milan Babić, and Goran Hadžić. In late 1990 Rašković was marginalized within the SDS because of his decision to hold talks with the Croatian government. Al-

Two Croatian soldiers hold a Yugoslavian flag bearing a hole in the center, after fights against the Yugoslavian army and the Serbian militias, during the siege of Vukovar. (Antoine Gyori/Corbis Sygma)

though his two vice presidents, Zelenbaba and Opačić, had opposed these negotiations, they were seen in Belgrade as too close to Rašković and were ultimately themselves marginalized. The new SDS triumvirate in 1991 consisted of Martić, Babić, and Hadžić. Martić served as head of internal affairs (January–May 1991) and defense minister (May–June 1991) of the SAO Krajina, and then as minister of internal affairs for the SAO Krajina (later the RSK, June 1991–January 1994). In this position he commanded the Croatian Serb police force (referred to as Martić's Police, or Martićevci). Babić served as president of the Executive Council of the SAO Krajina (January–May 1991), then as president of the SAO Krajina (May–December 1991), and finally as president of the RSK (December 1991–February 1992). In these political posts, he helped organize and administer the actions of the Croatian Serb forces. Finally, Hadžić held a number of important administrative posts in the Croatian Serb leadership from March 1991 to February 1992. From February 1992 to January 1994 he served as president of the RSK. In these posts, he helped establish, command, and direct police and militia operations. Through Serbian government and JNA channels, the Croatian Serb leadership was given logistical assistance and directions for the take-over of those areas deemed to be Serb and the subsequent forcible removal of the Croat and other non-Serb population.

In 1990–1991 the latent tensions in Croatia between the Croatian authorities and SDS prompted the Serbian government formally to demand intervention on the part of the JNA. Led by an officer corps that was predominantly of Serb and Montenegrin nationality, the JNA took a dim view of political pluralism that threatened the power of central institutions. Especially troubling were Slovene and Croat assertions of republic sovereignty, which threatened the very existence of the Yugoslav state. On 9 January 1991, the Yugoslav President Borisav Jović sought the Federal Presidency's approval for authorization of JNA force against Croatia and Slovenia; the JNA would be permitted to disarm the militias of those two republics. The Macedonian and Bosnian representatives, Vasil Tupurkovski and Bogić Bogićević, respectively, voted against the proposal, ensuring its defeat. However, the secondary proposal, ordering all paramilitary groups in Croatia and Slovenia to disarm within ten days, was passed. The following day, the JNA issued a ten-day ultimatum for the dissolution of the Slovenian and Croatian militias and all paramilitary formations in those republics. The Croatian and Slovenian governments ignored the order and on 17 January agreed to coordinate mutual defense policy. Eight days later, the JNA ordered the arrest of the Croatian defense minister, Martin Špegelj, who was forced to go into hiding. In the spring of 1991 the JNA would intervene in dozens of battles between separatist Serbs and Croatian police in Croatia, ostensibly as a peacekeeping force preventing a wider conflict. In actual fact, the JNA eventually openly supported the Croatians Serbs and actively participated in the occupation of Croatian territory.

On 21 February 1991, the Croatian Parliament declared that all federal laws not in compliance with the amended republican constitution of December 1990 were null and void. The Croatian declaration restricted any use of federal emergency measures and stated that Croatia would secede from Yugoslavia by June 30. A similar timetable was adopted by Slovenia. The Serb National Council at Knin declared that the Croatian Serbs would remain part of Yugoslavia if Croatia seceded. In March 1991 the conflict between the Croatian authorities and Croatian Serbs intensified when Croatian Serb police forces attempted to consolidate power in those areas with significant Serb populations. The Serb police, headed by Martić, took control of the police station in the town of Pakrac, and battles erupted when Croatian Special Forces attempted to retake the station and establish Croatian authority in the town and municipality. On 31 March 1991, a second and more serious armed confrontation occurred between regular police forces of the Croatian Interior Ministry and Croatian Serb paramilitaries at Plitvice National Park. One Serb and one Croat were killed. The Federal Presidency ordered the withdrawal of the Croatian police from Plitvice. The JNA then moved into Plitvice, ostensibly interposing itself between the combatants. On 1 May, another armed confrontation occurred between Croatian regular police from Osijek and Serb villagers at Borovo Selo, a suburb of Vukovar in eastern Croatia. Two Croatian policemen were wounded and two taken prisoner. When a larger detachment of Croatian police were sent to rescue the prisoners at Borovo Selo, twelve of the Croatian policemen were killed and over twenty were wounded. On 3 May, the JNA occupied Borovo Selo. The Croatian Serbs declared that they would not obey Croatian laws that were not in accordance with federal laws; on 12 May, the Croatian Serbs held a referendum to stay in Yugoslavia. A week later, Croatia held a sovereignty referendum in which 93 percent of those voting opted for Croatian independence. The Croatian Serbs boycotted the referendum. Five weeks later, on 25 June, Croatia and Slovenia declared their independence from Yugoslavia.

The Yugoslav Federal Parliament declined to recognize Slovenian and Croatian secession on the following day and authorized the JNA to occupy strategic points in Slovenia on the pretext of defending Yugoslav territorial integrity against an illegal secession. The JNA operations in Slovenia proved disastrous, however. The Slovenian militia had managed to capture roughly 2,000 JNA soldiers within days. On 18 July, the Federal Presidency authorized the withdrawal of JNA units from Slovenia, thereby acceding to its secession and the dissolution of Yugoslavia.

The cease-fire in and JNA withdrawal from Slovenia moved the conflict decisively to Croatia, where there was a noticeable intensification of the fighting. The war that was waged in Croatia from July to December 1991 between Croatian militia and police, on the one hand, and Croatian Serb forces and the JNA on the other, proved particularly brutal. Many large towns were devastated (such as Vukovar) while others suffered tremendous damage (including Dubrovnik and Karlovac). JNA and Croatian Serb forces seized roughly one-third of Croatian territory, which was organized, after 19 December 1991, into the self-styled Croatian Serb state called the Republic of Serb Krajina (RSK, Republika srpska krajina). From these territories they systematically expelled Croats and other non-Serbs. For example, on 18 August 1991 the Croatian Serb police chief, Milan Martić, issued an ultimatum to Croats to leave the village of Kijevo in the Serb-held Krajina. One week later, on 26 August, a combined JNA–Croatian Serb police attack was launched on the village and the Croat population was expelled.

On 22 August 1991 the Croatian president, Franjo Tudjman, issued an ultimatum to the JNA ordering it to withdraw from Croatia immediately or be treated as an occupying force. The ultimatum was ignored, and on 25 August the JNA began an assault on the town of Vukovar in eastern Croatia, thereby initiating the three-month long Battle of Vukovar. The JNA undertook operations against other towns in eastern Slavonia, resulting in their occupation by JNA and Serb police forces. In response, after 14 September 1991, Croatian forces began their blockade of all remaining JNA garrisons in Croatia, somewhat improving their decidedly inferior military position. On 1 October, the JNA began shelling the city of Dubrovnik.

One of the central objectives of Serbian government and Croatian Serb policy during the fighting in Croatia between July and December 1991 was ethnic cleansing, that is, the deportation or forcible transfer of the non-Serb civilian population from Serb-held territory. During that period, the JNA enabled the Croatian Serbs to carve out their own statelet (i.e., the Krajina or RSK) in Croatia. Serb forces (JNA units, militia, police contingents, paramilitary units) attacked towns and villages. (The two most prominent paramilitary leaders during the Croatian war were Željko Ražnatović, "Arkan," and Vojislav Šešelj.) In 1990 Arkan created the Serb Volunteer Guard, commonly known as the Arkanovci, "Arkan's Tigers." They were under the command of the Serb militia (Territorial Defense) in eastern Croatia. Arkan's Tigers maintained a significant military base in Erdut, near the town of Vukovar, which served as the training center of other militia units and also as a detention facility. Arkan himself functioned as the commander of the base in Erdut. Šešelj, who was president of the Serb Radical Party (SRS) and a supporter of the Great Serbian cause, recruited and provided substantial support to Serb volunteers, commonly known as Četniks (*četnici*), who perpetrated crimes in Croatia. In order to achieve a nationally homogeneous Krajina, Serb forces surrounded non-Serb settlements and demanded that their inhabitants surrender all weapons. Then the settlements were attacked.

After the takeover, these forces in cooperation with the local Serb authorities established a regime of persecutions (torture, murder, other acts of violence) intended to compel the non-Serb population to leave. Sometimes they rounded up the remaining Croat and other non-Serb civilian population and forcibly transported them to locations in Croatia controlled by the Croatian government or deported them to locations outside Croatia, in particular Serbia and Montenegro. On other occasions, the Serb forces in cooperation with the local Serb authorities imposed restrictive and discriminatory measures on the non-Serb population and engaged in a campaign of terror designed to drive them out of the territory. Almost all of the non-Serb population was eventually killed or forced from these occupied zones. According to the March 1991 census, the non-Serb population of the areas that became part of the RSK was approximately as follows: Croat, 168,026, and other non-Serb, 55,895. Virtually the whole of this non-Serb population of over 220,000 was ethnically cleansed (i.e., forcibly removed, deported, or killed) from the RSK in 1991–1992.

The most devastating example of wanton destruction and ethnic cleansing in the Croatian war took place in the town of Vukovar. The siege of Vukovar lasted from late August until 18 November 1991, when the town finally fell to combined JNA and Serb paramilitary forces. During the course of the siege, the town was largely destroyed by JNA shelling, and hundreds of persons were killed. When the JNA/Serb forces occupied the city, hundreds more Croats were killed by Serb troops; the non-Serb population of the town was expelled. Between 18 and 20 November, after the termination of the military operations in and around the town of Vukovar, the JNA deported thousands of Croat and other non-Serb inhabitants to the territory of the Republic of Serbia. In one well documented incident that occurred on 20 November, military forces under the general command of the JNA removed approximately 255 Croats and other non-Serbs from Vukovar Hospital. The victims were transported to the JNA barracks and then to the nearby Ovčara farm, where they were beaten and then executed. Their bodies were buried in a mass grave. According to the prosecutor of the International Criminal Tribunal for the former Yugoslavia (ICTY), at least 20,000 Croat and other non-Serb inhabitants were deported from Vukovar, at least 5,000 from Ilok, and at least 2,500 from Erdut near Vukovar. Homes, property, cultural institutions, and historic monuments were deliberately destroyed.

On 23 November 1991, former U.S. diplomat Cyrus Vance, who in October had been appointed U.N. special envoy to Yugoslavia, negotiated an agreement in Geneva between Milošević, General Kadijević, and Tudjman. It called for lifting the Croatian militia's blockade of JNA barracks and withdrawing JNA forces from Croatia, which began on 28 November. Both sides committed themselves to an immediate cease-fire. On 4 December 1991, the Croatian delegate on the Federal Presidency, Stjepan Mesić, resigned his post of president of Yugoslavia. On 2 January 1992, Tudjman and Milošević signed at Sarajevo a final cease-fire agreement that paved the way for the implementation of the so-called Vance Plan. On 14 January, the first U.N. cease-fire monitors arrived in Croatia. On 12 February, Vance recommended to the secretary-general of the United Nations the deployment of U.N. peacekeeping forces in Croatia. Nine days later, under Security Council Resolution 743, the United Nations established a U.N. Protection Force (UNPROFOR) in Croatia that was to be stationed in four U.N.-protected areas (UNPAs), which had been taken by Serb forces during the fighting. The JNA was to complete its withdrawal from Croatia, and displaced persons from the UNPA zones were supposed to be permitted to return to their homes. The UNPROFOR peacekeeping force numbered 14,000. Meanwhile, on 15 January 1992, most European and some non-European states recognized Croatia as an independent state, and in May 1992 Croatia became a member of the United Nations.

The six-month Croatian war wrought mass destruction, claimed over 10,000 lives, and produced nearly 500,000 refugees and displaced persons. By early 1992, overt hostilities between Croatia and rump Yugoslavia had ceased. The JNA completed its withdrawal from Croatia by spring 1992, but large portions of its weaponry and personnel were turned over to the police and militia of the so-called RSK. Displaced persons were not allowed to return to their homes, as envisaged by the Vance Plan. The UNPROFOR mission in Croatia merely froze the territorial status quo that had been established in January 1992; Croatia's Serbs, who hoped to remain part of a Yugoslav or Great Serbian state, held nearly one-third of Croatia. Their RSK remained a dependency of Milošević's Serbian regime. In 1993 the RSK authorities staged a referendum resoundingly in favor of integration with the Serbs of Bosnia-Hercegovina and Serbia. However, in 1995 the Croatian Army retook the RSK in two separate operations, code-named Flash (May 1995) and Storm (August 1995), which led to the forced exodus of much of the remaining Serb population. The only area to remain under Serb control at that time was eastern Slavonia, and on 12 November 1995, during the Dayton peace negotiations that brought an end to the war in Bosnia-Hercegovina, the Croatian and Serbian government negotiators agreed to the peaceful reintegration of eastern Slavonia into Croatia.

The "Basic Agreement" allowed for a transitional period of demilitarization and government by an international administration backed by an implementation force. In January 1996 Security Council Resolution 1037 established the UNTAES (UN Transitional Administration for Eastern Slavonia). Control of the region was handed back to Zagreb on 15 January 1998, and with the government's agreement, an OSCE mission took over some of the UNTAES tasks, including police monitoring. As of 2002, only a small U.N. contingent of fewer than thirty observers remained in Croatia's Prevlaka Peninsula, which had been occupied by the JNA in 1991.

POLITICAL DEVELOPMENTS

After 1945, the most salient feature of Croatian political life was communist dictatorship. Only with the collapse of communism in 1989 has Croatia gradually moved toward democratic governance. At the end of World War II, Croatia again became part of a reconstituted Yugoslavia after its brief wartime "independence." One of the many changes introduced by the Communists in 1945 was a federal system in an attempt to resolve the national question, which had plagued Yugoslavia since its creation in 1918. Croatia now became one of six federal republics. However, democratic institutions and political parties were suppressed in Croatia as elsewhere. The Catholic Church was persecuted and the archbishop of Zagreb (later a cardinal), Alojzije Stepinac, was sentenced to life imprisonment for his alleged collaboration with the wartime Croatian fascist authorities. Communist oppression took a heavy toll on real and alleged collaborators.

Croat nationalism was suppressed but nevertheless persisted in Communist Yugoslavia. The political oppression and administrative centralization experienced under the League of Communists of Yugoslavia harkened back to the days of interwar Yugoslavia, especially the period of King Alexander's royal dictatorship (1929–1934), when Croat national rights were suppressed. Croat nationalists had long objected to Croatia's perceived exploitation, and after 1945 even Croatia's Communists began to feel that Croatia was again being exploited by Belgrade. This oppression was not just limited to political or economic life, but allegedly extended to the cultural realm; for example, the use of the Croatian language was prohibited in favor of "Serbo-Croatian." The so-called Croatian Spring of 1966–1971 was as much a call for political liberalization as it was for greater Croat national rights within Yugoslavia. Demands were openly voiced in Croatia and even within the reform-minded wing of the League of Communists of Croatia, headed by Miko Tripalo and Savka Dabčević-Kučar, for decentralization, greater rights for the Croatian and other republics, economic reform, and political pluralism.

The Croatian Spring was forcefully crushed in late 1971, as were reform movements in other parts of Yugoslavia. In Croatia thousands of Croats were imprisoned, some were killed, and many emigrated. Despite crushing political reform tendencies in Croatia and elsewhere in 1971, the Yugoslav leader, Marshal Josip Broz Tito, decided to address some of the concerns raised by republican leaders. One of those issues was decentralization and federalism. The new constitution, promulgated in 1974, stipulated that each of the six republics was a state with its own borders. Thus the 1974 constitution decentralized the Yugoslav political system tremendously; Tito believed the reform would satisfy Croat (and other non-Serb) demands for increased republican autonomy and thus dampen secessionist sentiment.

The death of Tito in May 1980, however, weakened Yugoslavia and increased demands for secession. The internal breakup of Yugoslavia began. The country was henceforth governed by a rotating presidency, consisting of one representative from each of the six republics and two autonomous provinces. Consensus rule proved increasingly difficult. The federal Party, the League of Communists of Yugoslavia, was by this time merely the sum of its parts and not an independent force. In 1981 riots occurred in Kosovo, where Albanians called for republican status for their autonomous province, which was part of Serbia. It was the first post-Tito crisis and revealed differences within the Yugoslav polity; the Serbian leadership and Yugoslav People's Army (JNA) urged a hard line while the leadership of Slovenia urged reform. In the end, martial law was imposed. In 1986 the Serbian Academy of Arts and Sciences composed a memorandum, subsequently leaked to the press, which spoke of alleged discrimination against Serbs in Communist Yugoslavia and the need to address various contemporary threats to the Serb nation. According to many observers, the memorandum articulated a Great Serbian program that was subsequently adopted by Slobodan Milošević. When Milošević became the secretary of the League of Communists of Serbia in 1987, the implementation of this program began in earnest.

The unified League of Communists of Yugoslavia held its last Party congress in Belgrade in January 1990. Divided over the question of how to reform the country politically, now that communism had collapsed in Eastern Europe, the League of Communists disintegrated. Democratic elections now became possible. In the spring of 1990 both Slovenia and Croatia held democratic elections that brought noncommunists to power. The Croat Democratic Union (HDZ) of Franjo Tudjman, which was a Croat nationalist party demanding greater political and national rights for Croats within Yugoslavia, won the Croatian elections of April and May 1990. A referendum in May 1991 resulted in over 90 percent of the population voting for Croatian independence. The Croatian Serbs boycotted. A month later, on 25 June 1991, Croatia and Slovenia seceded from the Socialist Federal Republic of Yugoslavia.

The Sabor is the home of the Croatian parliament in Zagreb. (Richard Klune/Corbis)

GOVERNMENT AND STATE AUTHORITY

Croatia is a parliamentary democracy with a republican form of government. State authority is divided into legislative, executive, and judicial branches. The legislative branch is represented by a unicameral parliament known as the Sabor. The judiciary is independent and includes district, constitutional, and supreme courts. The executive branch is composed of a president and a prime minister with his cabinet. The prime minister, whose cabinet implements those policies designated by the Croatian Parliament, heads the government of the Republic of Croatia. The government organizes and directs legislative issues, initiates general domestic and foreign policy, and directs the work of state administrative bodies. The cabinet, known officially as the Council of Ministers, has its members appointed by the prime minister and then approved by the parliament.

Although Croatia possessed a constitution in the communist era while it was still part of the Socialist Federal Republic of Yugoslavia, the communist authorities had drafted it without any serious input from the population. Following the collapse of communism in 1989 and the democratic elections of the following year, a new Croatian constitution was adopted on 22 December 1990. It asserted the sovereignty of the Croatian republic within Yugoslavia and affirmed that Croatia was the national state of the Croat nation. The constitution also guarantees basic civil, human, and political rights to all citizens. These include the right of free political association, equality before the law, and the same rights and freedoms for all, regardless of race, gender, language, religion, political or other belief, national or social origin, property, birth, education, social status, or other characteristics. Members of all national minorities in theory have equal rights, including the freedom to express their nationality, to use their language and script, and cultural autonomy. Freedom of conscience and religion are also guaranteed. All religious communities have equal rights before the law and are separated from the state. Religious communities are free publicly to perform religious services and to open schools and social and charitable institutions and to manage them.

All citizens are guaranteed the right of public assembly and peaceful protest and the right to freedom of association for the purposes of protection of their interests or the promotion of their social, economic, political, national, cultural, and other convictions and objectives. For this purpose, everyone may freely form trade unions and other associations. All citizens who have reached the age of eighteen years have universal and equal suffrage exercised through direct elections by secret ballot. Military service is the duty of every capable citizen, although conscientious objection is permitted for religious or moral reasons. Such persons are obliged to perform other duties specified by law. Primary education is compulsory and free. Secondary and higher education are equally accessible to everyone according to abilities.

A unicameral Croatian parliament, the Sabor, represents the legislative branch of government. Constitutionally it must have no fewer than 100 and no more than 160 members, elected on the basis of direct universal and equal suffrage by secret ballot. Members are elected for a term of four years. The Croatian parliament normally meets in two regular annual sessions: 15 January–15 July and 15 September–15 December.

The specific duties of the parliament are defined in Article 80 of the constitution. These include but are not limited to: enacting and amending the constitution; passing laws; adopting an annual state budget; adopting a strategy of national security; maintaining civil control over the armed forces and security services; calling referenda; carrying out elections and making administrative appointments; supervising the work of the government; granting amnesty for criminal offenses; and conducting other affairs as specified by the constitution.

The parliament may call a referendum on a proposal for an amendment of the constitution, on a bill, or for any other issue within its competence. The Sabor is obliged to call a referendum on a specific range of issues if at least 10 percent of all registered voters in the Republic of Croatia sign a petition to that effect. At such a referendum, the majority of the voters make a decision, provided that the majority of the total number of electors has taken part in the referendum. Decisions made at referenda are binding. Constitutional amendments may be proposed by at least one-fifth of the members of the Sabor, the president, or the government. The parliament decides by a majority vote of all representatives whether to start proceedings for the amendment of the constitution. The decision to amend must be made by a two-thirds majority vote of all the members of the Sabor.

The president of the Republic of Croatia represents the republic at home and abroad. According to Article 93 of the constitution, the president "shall take care of regular and harmonized functioning and stability of the state government" and is "responsible for the defense, independence and territorial integrity of the Republic of Croatia." The president is elected in direct, secret balloting, on the basis of universal and equal suffrage, for a term of five years. The president is elected by a majority vote. If none of the candidates obtains an absolute majority, new elections are held after fourteen days. The two candidates who obtained the largest number of votes in the first round have the right to run in the second and final round. No one may be elected to the post of president for more than two consecutive terms. Since declaring independence in June 1991, Croatia has had two presidents: Franjo Tudjman (1991–1999) and Stjepan Mesić (since 2000).

The duties of the president, as defined by Article 97, include but are not limited to the following: calling elections for the parliament and convening its first session; calling referenda; confiding the mandate to form a government to the person winning parliamentary elections; granting pardons; and conferring decorations and other awards specified by law. The constitution mandates that the president and the prime minister (i.e., the government) cooperate in the formulation and implementation of foreign policy. The president may, with the prior countersignature of the prime minister, establish embassies and consular offices and appoint diplomatic representatives. The president is also the commander in chief of the Armed Forces of the Republic of Croatia. He may appoint and dismiss military commanders. On the basis of the decision of the Croatian Parliament, the president may declare war and conclude peace. In case of an immediate threat to the independence and existence of the state, the president may, with the countersignature of the prime minister, order the activation of the armed forces even if a state of war has not been declared. During a state of war, the president may issue decrees with the force of law "on the grounds and within the authority obtained from the Croatian Parliament." In case of an immediate threat to the independence, unity, and existence of the state, or if governmental bodies are prevented from performing their constitutional duties, the president may, with the countersignature of the prime minister, issue decrees with the force of law. However, these must be submitted for approval to the Sabor as soon as the parliament is in a position to convene or they cease to be in force.

The president and the government jointly direct the operations of the security services. The appointment of the heads of the security services is first approved by the authorized committee of the Croatian parliament and is then countersigned by the president and the prime minister. According to Article 104, the president is impeachable for any willful violation of the constitution. Parliament may institute proceedings by a two-thirds majority vote of all representatives. The Constitutional Court of the Republic of Croatia then decides on the impeachment of the president by a two-thirds majority vote of all the judges.

The government of the Republic of Croatia, the specific role of which is defined in Articles 107 through 116 of the constitution, exercises executive powers. The government consists of a prime minister, one or more deputy prime ministers and ministers. The prime minister nominates members of his cabinet. When the government is formed, the prime minister presents his government and its program to the parliament and asks for a vote of confidence, following which the government assumes its duties. The Croatian government has a total of nineteen ministries: Defense; Internal Affairs; Foreign Affairs; Finance; Public Works, Reconstruction and Construction; Agriculture and Forestry; Culture; Economy; Education and Sports; Health; Homeland War Veterans; Justice, Administration, and Local Self-Government; Labor and Social Welfare; Maritime Affairs, Transportation, and Communications; Science and Technology; Tourism; Environmental Protection and Physical Planning; European Integration; and Crafts, Small and Medium Enterprises. In addition to these ministries, the government operates a number of offices (e.g., Office for Human Rights, Office for National Minorities, General Administration Office, etc.), Agencies (e.g., Croatian Securities Exchange Commission, etc.), directorates, and commissions.

The government proposes legislation and other acts to the Croatian parliament, drafts an annual state budget, implements laws and other decisions of the parliament, articulates both foreign and internal policies, directs the operation of the state administration, and implements an economic policy. The government is responsible to the Croatian parliament. According to Article 115 of the constitution, at the proposal of at least one-fifth of the members of the Sabor, a vote of confidence in the prime minster, in individual members of the government, or in the government as a whole, may be put in motion. The prime minister may also request a vote of confidence in the government. A no confidence decision must be accepted if the majority of all members of the Croatian parliament have voted for it. If a no-confidence vote is passed, the prime minister and government must submit their resignation.

Judicial power is exercised by courts and is autonomous and independent. The Supreme Court of the Republic of Croatia, as the highest court, ensures the uniform application of laws and equal justice to all. The president of the Supreme Court is appointed by the Croatian Parliament on the proposal of the president, following a prior opinion of the general session of the Supreme Court and of the authorized committee of the Sabor. The president of the Supreme Court is appointed for a four-year term of office. Court hearings are open to the public and judgments are pronounced publicly in the name of the Republic of Croatia.

Judges enjoy immunity and cannot be called to account for an opinion or a vote given in the process of judicial decisionmaking. A judge may not be detained in criminal proceedings initiated for a criminal offence committed in performance of his or her judicial duty without prior consent of the National Judicial Council, which decides on all matters concerning discipline. Judges are normally appointed for a five-year term. After the renewal of the appointment, the judge assumes his or her duty as permanent. Whether appointing or dismissing a judge, the National Judicial Council, which consists of eleven judges chosen by the parliament, must obtain the opinion of the relevant committee of the Sabor. Members of the National Judicial Council are elected for a four-year term and no one may be a member for more than two consecutive terms. The president of the National Judicial Council is elected by secret ballot by a majority of the members of the National Judicial Council for a two-year term of office.

The Office of Public Prosecutions is an autonomous and independent judicial body empowered to prosecute those individuals and institutions that commit criminal offenses. The Croatian parliament, on the recommendation of the government, appoints for a four-year term a chief public prosecutor. Deputy public prosecutors are appointed for five-year terms. After the renewal of the appointment they may assume their duty as permanent. Deputy public prosecutors are appointed by the National Council of Public Prosecutions, which is elected by the Sabor. The majority of members of the National Council of Public Prosecutions are drawn from the ranks of deputy public prosecutors.

The Constitutional Court of the Republic of Croatia consists of thirteen judges elected by the Croatian parliament for a term of eight years. The Constitutional Court elects its own president for a term of four years. Judges of the Constitutional Court enjoy the same immunity as members of the Croatian parliament. The Constitutional Court issues decisions on the conformity of laws and other regulations with the constitution, and on constitutional complaints against individual decisions of governmental bodies, when these decisions violate human rights and fundamental freedoms as guaranteed by the constitution. It also decides on jurisdictional disputes between the legislative, executive, and judicial branches, on the impeachment of the president, on the constitutionality of the programs and activities of political parties, and on the constitutionality and legality of elections and national referenda.

The constitution defines local and regional self-government as rights of all citizens. This right is realized through local and regional representative bodies, composed of members elected on the basis of free elections by secret ballot on the grounds of direct and equal suffrage. The two basic units of local self-government are municipalities *(općine),* of which there are over four hundred, and towns *(gradovi).* The basic unit of regional self-government is the county *(županija),* of which there are twenty-one in addition to the capital city of Zagreb. Municipalities and cities are permitted to carry out the affairs of local jurisdiction, in particular those related to housing, urban planning, public utilities, child care, social welfare, primary health services, education and elementary schools, culture, physical education and sports, customer protection, protection and improvement of the environment, fire protection, and civil defense. Counties are mandated to perform all affairs of regional significance, and in particular the affairs related to education, health service, economic development, traffic infrastructure, and the development of networks of educational, health, social, and cultural institutions. Units of local and regional self-government have a constitutional right to their own revenues.

POLITICAL LANDSCAPE (1989–2002)

The collapse of communism in 1989 brought a proliferation in the number of political parties in Croatia. The following is a brief description of the major political parties that have been active in Croatia since 1989.

The Social Democratic Party of Croatia (SDP, Socijaldemokratska partija Hrvatske) is the successor to Croatia's former Communist Party, known until 1989 as the League of Communists of Croatia. The SDP leader is Ivica Račan. Support for the SDP has grown steadily throughout the 1990s; in 1995 it became the strongest opposition party in Croatia. Since January 2000, the SDP has been the largest government party and Račan has served as prime minister. As a left-of-center party, the SDP advocates the development of a modern social welfare state based on a democratic political system with rights and freedoms for all. The SDP advocates a policy of reconciliation with Croatia's neighbors and noninterference in the internal affairs of Bosnia-Hercegovina. The SDP strives for integration in the European Union and NATO membership.

The Croat Democratic Union (HDZ, Hrvatska demokratska zajednica), as of late 2002, was the largest party in the Croatian Parliament. It was founded in 1989 by Franjo Tudjman as a Croat national party seeking to assert Croatian sovereignty within Yugoslavia. In April-May 1990 Tudjman led the HDZ to electoral victory; from that point to 1999, he and the HDZ governed Croatia. The HDZ won the 1992 general elections and was able to consolidate its dominant position in parliament again in 1995 and 1997. The HDZ was composed of diverse elements, including but not limited to former Communist officials, nationalist dissi-

President of the Croatian Democratic Union (HDZ) and new Prime Minister Ivo Sanader speaks to the press under the historic Croatian coat of arms, after receiving a mandate for the new government from Croatian President Stjepan Mesić, 9 December 2003, in Zagreb. Sanader, a Croatian nationalist leader, was formally named prime minister following his party's victory in November's legislative elections. (AFP/Getty Images)

dents, and at least initially, some liberals. When Tudjman died on 10 December 1999, the latent fissures within the HDZ surfaced, and the party was left in a shambles. Power struggles erupted between moderate reformers and nationalists. Ivo Sanader currently leads the HDZ.

The Croat Social Liberal Party (HSLS, Hrvatska socijalno liberalna stranka) is a moderate center-right party, advocating social and liberal economic policies, individual rights, and a limited state role in society. The HSLS was founded in 1989 and is headed by Dražen Budiša. From the start, the HSLS mixed liberal, democratic, and nationalistic elements in its program. Between 1992 and 1995, the HSLS was the strongest opposition party in Croatia but lost this position to the SDP in 1995. Like most other Croatian political parties, the HSLS has suffered several internal party disputes. As a result, the HSLS received only 12 percent of the vote in 1995, and in 1997 the Liberal Party (LS, Liberalna stranka) of Vlado Gotovac split from the HSLS. Internal consolidation on the one hand and cooperation with the SDP on the other hand led to a renewed popularity from 1998 onward. From January 2000 to the summer of 2002, it was a member of the coalition presently governing Croatia.

The Croat Peasant Party (HSS, Hrvatska seljačka stranka) is the successor to Croatia's largest interwar political party. It is a moderate conservative party that advocates farmers' social rights and economic protection, in addition to traditional family and nationalist values. It is currently led by Zlatko Tomčić.

The Croat Party of Right (HSP, Hrvatska stranka prava), founded in 1990, is a nationalist party with a history of internal dissension. Its paramilitary wing, the Croat Defense Forces (HOS), was founded in the early days of the war in Croatia but was eventually suppressed by the Croatian authorities. Its first party leader was Dobroslav Paraga. The current party leader is Ante Djapić.

The Croat Party of Right 1861 (HSP-1861, Hrvatska stranka prava 1861) as of 2002 had no seats in the Croatian Parliament. The party was founded in 1995 as a splinter group of the larger HSP. Much like the original HSP, it is a nationalist party and regards itself as politically conservative. It is headed by Dobroslav Paraga.

The Istrian Democratic Assembly (IDS, Istarski demokratski sabor) is a regionally organized party and defender of Istrian interests. Istria has always been one of the richer regions of Croatia. The IDS advocates a decentralization of power and is in some respects a reaction to the decade of Tudjman rule, when administrative centralization was the norm. It is a liberal and centrist party with a majority of seats in Istria's regional parliament. The IDS is led by Ivan Jakovčić.

The Liberal Party (LS, Liberalna stranka) split from the larger HSLS in 1997. It plays a marginal role in Croatian politics. Originally led by Vlado Gotovac, who died in 2000, the party is currently headed by Ivo Banac.

The Croat People's Party (HNS, Hrvatska narodna stranka) is a centrist party, similar in some respects to the HSLS. It is generally of marginal political significance and repeatedly operated in election coalitions, being too small to gain any seats on its own. The prominence of the HNS grew in 2000, however, when its candidate, Stjepan Mesić, was elected president of Croatia. The HNS leader is Vesna Pusić.

The Serb People's Party (SNS, Srpska narodna stranka), founded in May 1991, is the party of the majority of Serbs who remained in Croatia during its war of independence (1991–1995). The SNS is committed to securing cultural and political rights for the Serb minority. It is led by Milan Djukić.

The Croat Christian Democratic Union (HKDU, Hrvatska kršćansko-demokratska unija) is a conservative, Christian Democratic party with only a marginal presence in Croatian politics. Its leader, Marko Veselica, was a dissident in the communist period. It is primarily due to his charisma and history as a dissident that the party is able to maintain any presence in the Croatian political arena.

Independent Croat Democrats (HND, Hrvatski nezavisni demokrati) is a centrist party founded in April 1994 when, following a split in the ruling HDZ, Josip Manolić and Stipe Mesić left the HDZ largely because of their opposition to Croatian policy toward Bosnia-Hercegovina. The HND is an insignificant factor in Croatian politics. It is led by Manolić.

Social Democratic Action (ASH, Akcija socijaldemokrata Hrvatske) was founded in October 1994 and is led by Silvije Degen. It is a left-of-center party and only a marginal factor in Croatian politics. The party consists of former members, mainly intellectuals, of the Socialist Party of Croatia, the Social Democratic Party, and the Social Democratic Union.

From April to May 1990, when the first democratic elections since World War II were held in Croatia, to the January 2000 elections, the dominant political party in Croatia was the Croat Democratic Union (or HDZ) of Franjo Tudjman. The HDZ, which was formed by Tudjman in the spring of 1989, saw itself as the defender of Croat national rights and of Croatia's territorial integrity and sovereignty, which they held to have been long suppressed within Yugoslavia. In the 1990 elections the HDZ won 42 percent of the vote and 60 percent of the seats in the Croatian Parliament. Its hold over Croatian politics was broken only with Tudjman's death in December 1999.

Tudjman was a Croat nationalist. As a former high-ranking Communist official and retired general of the JNA, Tudjman possessed an authoritarian demeanor. Hence the transition from Communist to HDZ rule in 1989–1990 did not dramatically or immediately improve democratic institutions in Croatia. The manipulation of laws and legal harassment of the independent media were means to control political life and public political discourse. Moreover, the constitution provided Tudjman with great powers; he attempted to govern Croatia as a presidential state. The electronic media was almost completely muzzled. Press freedom was restricted. The government used the courts and the administrative bodies to restrain newspapers, radio, and independent television that were critical of the government or not under government control. Journalism fell victim to censorship and government intimidation resulted in self-censorship by journalists. Tudjman was assisted in this respect by the opposition, which was unable, at least until 1999, to overcome its own divisions and make common cause against the HDZ. Freedom of assembly was restricted under Tudjman. Freedom of association was circumscribed by a law that prohibited groups from forming or meeting unless expressly authorized to do so by means of a lengthy registration process.

Parliament was from 1991 to 2000 a bicameral institution consisting of a lower house known as the House of Representatives (Zastupnički dom) and an upper house known as the House of Counties (Županijski dom). The HDZ never managed to achieve a two-thirds majority in the Croatian parliament, which would have enabled it to ride roughshod over the opposition. Nonetheless, it was able to influence the upper house more readily than the lower house. The House of Counties had 68 deputies, 63 of whom were elected locally on the basis of proportional representation for a four-year term; each county (including the city of Zagreb) sent three deputies to the House of Counties. Tudjman appointed an additional five deputies, thus enabling him to exert influence over the upper house. The number of deputies in the House of Representatives may vary from term to term, from 100 to 160. At least 80 deputies were supposed to be elected under a system of proportional representation and 28 in one-member constituencies according to a simple majority system. Twelve parliamentary seats were originally reserved for representatives of the Croatian Diaspora, which largely voted throughout the 1990s for Tudjman's HDZ, and 8 for the national minorities.

The first parliamentary elections to be held in independent Croatia occurred in August 1992. They were for the House of Representatives. The HDZ won 44 percent of the vote and gained 85 of 138 seats. Presidential elections were held simultaneously, which were won by Tudjman. The first elections to the House of Counties were held in February 1993, and the last in April 1997. In the 1993 elections the HDZ gained 45.5 percent of the vote and 37 of 68 seats. In the next parliamentary elections, held in October 1995, the HDZ consolidated its position; it won 75 of 127 seats in the House of Representatives. The regional and municipal elections of April 1997 were also won by the HDZ, which gained a majority in 40 percent of the counties. That same year, in June 1997, Tudjman was reelected in presidential elections with 61.4 percent of the popular vote. The Social Democratic Party (SDP) candidate, Zdravko Tomac, gained 21 percent of the vote, while the Croat Social Liberal Party (HSLS) candidate, Vlado Gotovac, gained 17.6 percent. However, the Organization for Security and Cooperation in Europe (OSCE) declared the elections undemocratic, since it believed that the opposition parties had lacked access to the media.

Since Tudjman's death, the Croatian political landscape has changed dramatically. Encouraged by the divisive leadership struggle within the HDZ that accompanied Tudjman's last days, the opposition forged a coalition consisting of Ivica Račan's SDP and Dražen Budiša's HSLS. It was supported by a smaller four-party coalition consisting of the Croat People's Party (HNS), Croat Peasant Party (HSS), the Istrian Democratic Assembly (IDS), and the Liberal Party (LS); this coalition won 47 percent of the vote in the January 2000 elections to the House of Representatives. Although the HDZ remained the single largest party in the Croatian Parliament, with 46 deputies, the six-party coalition had over 90 deputies and thus formed the new government. In the concurrent two-stage presidential campaign, held January–February 2000, Stjepan Mesić of the Croat People's Party (HNS) emerged victorious; in the first round, Mesić and HSLS-SDP candidate Dražen Budiša defeated Mate Granić, Tudjman's former foreign minister who had left the HDZ in early 1999, and in the second round, held on 7 February 2000, Mesić defeated Budiša with 56 percent of the vote. Mesić was inaugurated as president on 18 February 2000.

Since then, Prime Minister Račan and President Mesić have pursued economic and political reform programs, including a restructuring of the Croatian military and state bureaucracy, and they have worked toward the creation of an independent public broadcasting service and liberalization of the media. They have also worked to develop a new approach to Croatia's ethnic minorities, particularly the Serbs. And in order to avoid a repeat of the abuses of the Tudjman era, the new SDP-HSLS government has limited the powers of the presidency. Although the president is hardly a ceremonial figure, which is what the SDP-HSLS government hoped to make him, the scope and range of his powers have definitely decreased; the president remains the head of the armed forces and the intelligence agency. Moreover, a constitutional amendment of 28 March 2001 transformed the parliament into a unicameral body, and the House of Counties was dissolved.

POLITICAL DEVELOPMENTS AND THE HOMELAND WAR

Almost all major political developments in Croatia since the collapse of communism have been affected in one way or another by the country's war of independence (1991–1995), known in Croatia as the Homeland War *(Domovinski rat)*. Following the April-May 1990 multiparty elections in Croatia, then still part of the Socialist Federal Republic of Yugoslavia, the League of Communists of Croatia relinquished power to the HDZ. The HDZ quickly moved forward with its goal of greater political rights for Croatia within a reformed Yugoslavia. In 1990 the term "socialist" was dropped from Croatia's official nomenclature, a new constitution was promulgated, and a revival of nationalist sentiment was experienced. Following the failure of a series of talks with the leaders of the five other Yugoslav republics, which had been designed to reformulate the Yugoslav federation, on 25 June 1991 Croatia, together with Slovenia, declared its independence.

Even before the Croatian declaration of independence was made, fighting had erupted between the Croatian authorities and Croatian Serbs who, having rebelled against Zagreb, were aided by the Serbian regime of Slobodan Milošević and armed by the Serb-dominated Yugoslav People's Army (JNA). In 1990, as Croatia moved ever closer to independence, the Croatian Serb intellectual Jovan Rašković formed the Serb Democratic Party (SDS). In August 1990 the SDS organized a referendum on Serb autonomy within Croatia. Shortly thereafter armed Serb-Croat confrontation flared up. The referendum resulted in the Knin-based SDS declaring autonomy in October 1990 for the so-called Serb Autonomous Region of Krajina. In May 1991 this autonomous Krajina region announced its independence from Croatia. Violent clashes between Zagreb and the Croatian Serbs continued throughout this period.

When Croatia declared its independence, the fighting only intensified and became more brutal. The Serbian authorities and the JNA responded by helping the Croatian Serb leadership carve out a Serb territory in Croatia. Following intense fighting between June and December 1991, during which time the Croatian town of Vukovar was destroyed and Dubrovnik was shelled indiscriminately by the JNA, in December 1991 Croatia's Serb autonomous regions united to form the so-called Republic of Serb Krajina (RSK). On 2 January 1992, the American mediator Cyrus Vance brokered a cease-fire whereby a United Nations mandated force, called U.N. Protection Force (UNPROFOR), was to be sent to Croatia. In February 1992 the U.N. Security Council approved a 14,000-member peacekeeping force to monitor the cease-fire. Meanwhile, on 15 January 1992, most European and some non-European states recognized Croatia as an independent state, and in May 1992 Croatia became a member of the United Nations. The six-month Croatian war had claimed over 10,000 lives and wrought mass destruction. By early 1992, overt hostilities between Croatia and Yugoslavia ceased.

However, the problem of the Croatian Serb entity, the RSK, which Croatia considered an illegal Serb occupation of its sovereign territory, remained unresolved. The RSK was from its inception a satellite and dependency of Slobodan Milošević's Serbian regime. A protégé of Milošević, Milan Martić, was elected its president in 1993. The UNPROFOR mission in Croatia merely froze the territorial status quo that had been established in January 1992; Croatia's Serbs, who hoped to remain part of a Yugoslav or Great Serbian state, held nearly one-third of Croatia. In 1993 the Serb authorities in the RSK staged a referendum resoundingly in favor of integration with the Serbs of Bosnia and Serbia.

However, in two separate lightning offensives in 1995 the Croatian army recaptured all the territory controlled by the RSK. In the first in May 1995 (called "Flash") and in the second in August 1995 (called "Storm"), all of the RSK was retaken except for eastern Slavonia. On 12 November 1995, during the Dayton peace negotiations that brought an end to the war in Bosnia-Hercegovina, the Croatian government and Serbian negotiators agreed to the peaceful reintegration of eastern Slavonia into Croatia. The basic agreement allowed for a transitional period of demilitarization and government by an international administration backed by an implementation force. In January 1996 Security Council Resolution 1037 established the UNTAES (U.N. Transitional Administration for Eastern Slavonia). Control of the region was handed back to Zagreb on 15 January 1998, and with the government's agreement, an OSCE mission took over some of the UNTAES tasks, including police monitoring. As of 2002, only a small U.N. contingent of fewer than thirty observers remained in Croatia's Prevlaka Peninsula, which had been occupied by the JNA in 1991.

From its outbreak in 1992, Croatia was involved in the war in Bosnia-Hercegovina. At that time, Croats composed approximately 17 percent of the population of Bosnia-Hercegovina. When the war began, the Bosnian Croats were united with the Bosnian Muslims (44 percent of the population) in their determination for independence, while the Bosnian Serbs (31 percent), who were backed by the Serbian leadership in Belgrade, opposed independence. Although allied to the Bosnian Muslim government, the HDZ headed the Croat political leadership in Bosnia-Hercegovina. The first HDZ leader in Bosnia-Hercegovina, Mate Boban, proclaimed a Croat Community of Herceg-Bosna, which was supposed to serve as a Croat parastate in parts of Bosnia that were predominantly inhabited by Croats. It had its own military, known as the Croat Council of Defense (HVO). However, in 1993 conflict erupted between the Bosnian Croats and Bosnian Muslims for control of central Bosnia. Croatia became indirectly involved in this conflict as a financier and supplier of the HVO and Bosnian Croat leadership. Only after the American administration applied strong pressure on Zagreb did the Croatian government agree to the territorial integrity of Bosnia-Hercegovina and the formation of a loose confederation with its Bosnian neighbor. In April 1994 the Bosnian president, Alija Izetbegović, and Tudjman agreed to the so-called Washington Agreement, forming a Bosniak-Croat Federation within Bosnia-Hercegovina and a loose economic confederation between Zagreb and Sarajevo.

The presidents of Croatia, Bosnia, and Serbia signed the Dayton Accords, which ended the war in Bosnia-Hercegovina, in December 1995. In practice, however, throughout the Tudjman era, the Croat-populated parts of Bosnia were treated as an extension of Croatian territory, just as Serb-populated areas were treated as an extension of Serbia. For that reason, the international community expressed concern over Croatia's slow implementation of the Bosnian peace treaty and continued support of the nationalist Bosnian Croat leadership. Moreover, opposition to the return of Serb refugees to Croatia, alleged human rights abuses, and Tudjman's autocratic rule led eventually, by the late 1990s, to Croatia's international political isolation.

Only after the January 2000 elections did a major change occur in Croatia's relations with the international community and its neighbors, particularly Bosnia-Hercegovina. The new Croatian foreign minister, Tonino Picula, immediately pledged that the new government would respect its obligations toward Bosnia-Hercegovina under the Dayton Accords and that it considered Bosnia-Hercegovina's borders inviolable. The new government also ended Zagreb's extensive financial subsidies to the Croats of Bosnia-Hercegovina, where the dominant Croat party was still the HDZ. Cooperation has also been established with the International Criminal Tribunal for the former Yugoslavia (ICTY) at The Hague. In February 2000 Croatia was invited to join the NATO-sponsored Partnership for Peace program. Croatia has also been admitted to the World Trade Organization (WTO) and the Council of Europe. Today, more than at any other point in the past half-century, the prospects for liberal democracy in Croatia appear genuinely strong.

CULTURAL DEVELOPMENT

Although Croatia has a rich cultural history and an equally rich contemporary cultural scene, any discussion of culture must begin with the importance of language and the evolution of a literary language. In short, the literary and spoken language is perhaps the most important element of culture and the cultural heritage of a people. Language is particularly important in the context of Central and Southeastern Europe, as it has served in the era of nationalism as the main criterion in defining nationality.

The Croatian language is a Slavic language that is almost identical to Serbian and Bosnian and closely related to Slovenian, Macedonian, and Bulgarian. It may be divided into three dialects, each named for the word it uses for "what": Kajkavian *(kaj),* Čakavian *(ča),* and Štokavian *(što).* Čakavian and Kajkavian now have a relatively limited territorial base in Croatia. The Kajkavian dialect is spoken in Zagreb, its wider environs, and the region of Hrvatsko Zagorje to the north of Zagreb. Čakavian is spoken in Istria, part of the Croatian Littoral, and some of the northern Adriatic islands. Štokavian is the most widely spoken dialect in Croatia. The Štokavian dialect may be further grouped into three subdialects, according to the treatment of vowels in certain words. On this basis, Štokavian may be classified into ekavian, ikavian, and ijekavian variants. The modern Croatian literary language is based on the ijekavian variant, while the ekavian variant, which is spoken in Serbia proper, forms the basis of modern literary Serbian.

The Croatian language and literature have a rich history dating back to the medieval period. The earliest written records in Croatian date from the ninth to the eleventh centuries and are in Old Church Slavonic, a liturgical language developed by the Greek missionaries Cyril and Methodius. Croatian medieval texts were written largely in the Glagolitic script and Old Slavonic language. Almost all the texts from this period are either legal or religious documents, such as the Baška Tablet (ca. 1100) and Vinodol Law (1288). Perhaps the most important medieval text is the *Chronicle of the Priest of Dioclea* (Ljetopis popa Dukljanina), dating from the late twelfth century.

The term "Croatian Latinists" refers to writers whose works were written in Latin and who belong to the humanist and early Renaissance traditions. Most of these writers were from Dalmatia, the heart of the Renaissance in Croatia; the cities of Dubrovnik, Split, and Hvar were important cultural centers. Unlike Croatia proper, which was being laid waste from the late fifteenth century onward by Ottoman incursions, Dalmatia experienced relative peace and prosperity. Among the leading figures of the period was Marko Marulić (1450–1524), probably the greatest humanist figure in Croatia. The development of a specifically Croatian literature in Dalmatia is attributed to him; his major work was the epic poem *Judita* (Judith), written in 1501 and published in Venice in 1521. Although Marulić was the most significant Renaissance figure in Croatian literature, Marin Držić (ca. 1508–1567) of Dubrovnik and the poet Petar Hektorović (1487–1572) of Hvar were also important. Držić was a priest, literary figure, and playwright. His studies in Sienna exposed him to a rich cultural life, especially in the realm of theater and contemporary drama. He achieved his fame based on a number of farces or short comedies, the best known of which is *Novela od stanca* (A Novella in Stanzas), which was first shown in 1550. With these works he became a central figure in Dubrovnik's theater life. The philosopher and theologian Matija Vlačić Ilirik (Matthias Flacius Illyricus) (1520–1575) was another prominent Latinist. A follower of Martin Luther and the Reformation, his most significant work was *Catalogus testium veritatis* (A Catalog of Witnesses of the Truth). Ivan

The Internet and Eastern Europe

Just as Central and Southeastern Europe entered a new world with the collapse of communism in the late 1980s and early 1990s, so too has the region become more accessible for those seeking to learn more about the region, thanks to the Web. Croatia provides a model example of what will be increasingly available to those seeking to learn more about the region in the twenty-first century.

The most useful gateway to Internet resources about Croatia is the Croatian homepage, located at www.hr. In addition to a section containing basic facts about Croatia, it categorizes Web pages into more than a dozen different categories, from "Arts and Culture" to "Tourism."

Croatia

Croatia in English (http://www.croatia-in-english.com) This site is for English-speaking people who have an interest in Croatia and especially for persons of Croat descent who were born outside Croatia and Bosnia-Hercegovina and other places where the Croat population is indigeneous. The focus is primarily genealogical, with some information on customs and travel.

Inside Croatia (http://www.insidecroatia.com). This site contains a good deal of basic information about the Republic of Croatia.

Handbook for Foreign Visitors to Croatia (http://centar-cons.tripod.com). The handbook offers an overview of the Republic of Croatia. It is useful for both tourists and those merely looking for information. It offers a broad range of historical, economic, political, and tourist data.

HIDRA: Croatian Information Documentation Referral Agency (http://www.hidra.hr). HIDRA is the official service of the government of Croatia for the dissemination of information, documentation, and referral.

Additional information may be found at the Web sites of various academic institutes and centers specializing in the region (e.g., the Balkans, Eastern Europe). Among the more useful sites are the following: (1) the Russian and East European Network Information Center (or REENIC) of the University of Texas at Austin, http://reenic.utexas.edu/reenic/index.html; (2) the Center for Russian, East European, and Eurasian Studies at the University of Texas, http://reenic.utexas.edu/creees/index.html; (3) the Balkan Studies Center and Program at Columbia University in New York, http://www.columbia.edu/cu/sipa/REGIONAL/HI/balk.html; (4) the Russian and East European Studies Virtual Library of the University of Pittsburgh, http://www.ucis.pitt.edu/reesweb; (5) the Center for Russian, East European, and Eurasian Studies at Stanford University, http://www.stanford.edu/dept/CREES; (6) the Center for Russian and East European Studies at the University of Michigan, http://www.umich.edu/~iinet/crees. All of these Web sites have useful links.

Arts and Culture

An Overview of Croatian History, Culture, and Science (http://www.hr/hrvatska/Croatia-HCS.html). This text was written by Darko Žubrinić and provides an overview of Croatian culture and history.

Croatian Portal for Art, Architecture, and Design (http://www.punkt.hr). This site was conceived as a starting page for all information relating to Croatian culture, the visual arts, architecture, and design. Daily news, list of exhibitions, galleries and contests, as well as personal homepages of artists, architects, and designers can be found here.

Croatian Cultural Association (http://www.hrsk.hr). This is the official Web site of the Croatian Cultural Association, with a good deal of information about orchestras, folk and dance ensembles, and writers.

Business and Economy

Useful Internet sites dealing with the Croatian economy are (1) the Ministry of the Economy (http://www.mingo.hr); (2) the Croatian Chamber of Economy (http://www.hgk.hr), a great source for basic indicators on the Croatian economy; (3) Croatian Bureau of Statistics (http://www.dzs.hr); (4) the Croatian National Bank (http://www.hnb.hr); (5) the Ministry of Finance (http://www.mfin.hr); (6) the Business Forum (www.poslovniforum.hr), for information technology and business services; and (7) the Croatian Business Information Centre (http://www.cbic.efzg.hr), which provides the most important resources of business studies in Croatia.

(continues)

Education

Ministry of Education and Sport (http://www.mips.hr). The Ministry of Education and Sports in the Republic of Croatia is responsible for preschool, primary, and secondary education. Its duties encompass teacher training, development, textbooks, verifications of school certificates and international cooperation, inspection, and financing of schools. It carries out projects related to civic education; human rights, rights of the child, and minority rights; heritage education; and special education needs children.

For other Web sites devoted to education in general and specifically to academic institutions in Croatia, follow the links under "Education" at http://www.hr/index.en.shtml, and visit the Web sites of the Universities of Zagreb (http://www.unizg.hr), Split (www.unist.hr), Rijeka (http://www.uniri.hr), and Osijek (http://www.unios.hr). See also the Ministry of Science and Technology (www.mzt.hr).

History

On Croatian history, see the relevant links at http://www.hr/index.en.shtml. A great deal of information (e.g., book reviews, discussion logs, etc.) can be found through the Habsburg Discussion Network, http://www.h-net.msu.edu/~habsweb, and at the links found on that page. Also useful are the Web sites of the various university institutes in the United States listed under "About Croatia."

Current Events and Media (Journalism, Press, and Television)

Croatian Radio and Television (http://www.hrt.hr). The Web site of Croatian Radio and Television, known by its Croatian acronym HRT (with three stations), also contains useful links to Croatian regional radio.

Croatian Information and News Agency (http://www.hina.hr/nws-bin/ehot.cgi). Known by its Croatian acronym HINA, Croatia's official news service is a good starting point for Croatian news.

Croatian Information Center (http://www.hic.hr). A useful link providing the latest news from the Croatian press. It also contains links to audio news from HRT.

Croatian Journalists' Association (http://www.hnd.hr). Contains information about the activities of the Croatian Journalists' Association and links to various newspapers. Most of Croatia's print press, like *Vjesnik, Večernji list, Obzor, Globus, Nacional, Slobodna Dalmacija,* and *Hrvatsko slovo,* have their own Web sites, but these are still usually only in Croatian.

For Western-based and English-language sources dealing with current events, consult the Web sites of the following organizations: (1) Radio Free Europe/Radio Liberty (http://www.rferl.org), for news and an overview of political developments; (2) Institute for War and Peace Reporting (http://www.iwpr.net), which produces "Balkan Crisis Reports," as well as "Tribunal Updates," summarizing the week's developments at the International Criminal Tribunal for the former Yugoslavia (ICTY); (3) the U.S. Department of State (http://www.state.gov/p/eur/ci/); and (4) the CIA's *World Factbook* (http://www.cia.gov/cia/publications/factbook/index.html).

Museums

Those interested in Croatian museums may consult the relevant Web sites listed below, all of which have English-language pages with detailed descriptions of the histories and holdings of the museums. Among the more important museums are (1) Trakošćan Castle (http://www.mdc.hr/trakoscan), (2) the Archeological Museum of Istria (http://www.mdc.hr/pula), (3) the Archeological Museum of Split (http://www.mdc.hr/split-arheoloski), (4) the Dubrovnik Museums (http://www.mdc.hr/dubrovnik), (5) The Museum of Croatian Archeological Monuments (http://www.mhas-split.hr), (6) The Museum of Modern Art Rijeka (http://www.mgr.hr), (7) the Ethnographic Museum of Istria (http://www.emi.hr), (8) the Peasants Revolt Museum (http://www.mdc.hr/msb), (9) the Gallery of Fine Arts (Osijek) (http://www.mdc.hr/glu_osijek/), (10) Klovićevi dvori Gallery (http://www.galerijaklovic.hr), (11) the Zagreb Municipal Museum (http://www.mdc.hr/mgz), (12) the Croatian Museum of Naive Art (http://www.hmnu.org), (13) the Archeological Museum (Zagreb) (http://www.amz.hr), (14) the Ethnographic Museum (Zagreb) (http://www.mdc.hr/etno), (15) the Museum of Contemporary Art (Zagreb) (http://www.mdc.hr/msu), (16) the Museum of Arts and Crafts (Zagreb) (http://www.muo.hr), and (17) the Croatian Natural History Museum (http://www.hpm.hr).

(continues)

Politics, Law, and Administration

The official Web site of the government of Croatia (http://www.vlada.hr) offers a detailed description of Croatian political institutions and civil service, accompanied by biographical profiles of each member of government. A range of general information documents can also be accessed from the site, in particular the text of the Croatian Constitution and the government's political program. The site also features a database containing press releases, accounts of cabinet meetings, and a weekly news bulletin. A monthly newsletter is also published on the site.

The different ministries have their own Web sites, all of which have English pages. Each site offers a detailed description of the role of the ministry and features short biographical accounts of the Minister and other members of the ministry. An organizational chart detailing the structure of the Ministry is usually also contained on the site. The following is a list of Croatian government ministry Web sites: Ministry of Foreign Affairs (http://www.mvp.hr), Ministry of Finance (http://www.mfin.hr), Ministry of Defense (http://www.morh.hr), Ministry of Internal Affairs (http://www.mup.hr), Ministry of the Economy (http://www.mingo.hr), Ministry of Family, Veterans and Intergenerational Solidarity (http://www.mhbdr.hr), Ministry of Culture (http://www.min-kulture.hr), Ministry of Agriculture and Forestry (http://www.mps.hr), Ministry of the Sea, Tourism, Communications, and Development (http://www.mmtpr.hr), Ministry of Justice, Administration, and Local Autonomy (http://www.pravosudje.hr), Ministry for the Protection of the Environment (http://www.mzopu.hr), Ministry of Education and Sport (http://www.mips.hr), Ministry of Labor and Social Assistance (http://www.mrss.hr), Ministry of Tourism (http://www.mint.hr), Ministry of Health (http://www.miz.hr), Ministry of Science and Technology (http://www.mzt.hr), Ministry for European Integration (http://www.mei.hr), and the Ministry of Manual Trade, Small, and Medium Enterprise (http://www.momsp.hr).

The Croatian president maintains his own site at http://www.predsjednik.hr. The Supreme Court has a site at http://www.vsrh.hr. The Croatian parliament (the Sabor) also has its own Web site (http://www.sabor.hr). Most Croatian political parties maintain their own Web sites. The Social Democratic Party's (SDP) site is at http://www.sdp.hr, the Croatian Social Liberal Party's (HSLS) site is at http://www.hsls.hr, the Croat Democratic Union (HDZ) site is at http://www.hdz.hr, the Croat Peasant Party (HSS) site is at http://www.hss.hr, the Croat Party of Right is at http://www.hsp.hr, the Croat People's Party site is at http://www.hns.hr, and the Liberal Party is at http://www.liberali.hr.

On Croatia's twenty-one counties, see the respective county Web sites: Istria (http://www.istra-istria.hr), Littoral-Gorski kotar (Rijeka) (http://www.pgz.hr), Karlovac (http://www.karlovacka-zupanija.hr), Lika-Senj (http://www.lickosenjska.com), Zadar (not available), Šibenik-Knin (http://www.sibenik-knin.com), Split-Dalmatia (not available), Dubrovnik-Neretva (not available), Zagreb (http://www.members.tripod.com/~zagzup), city of Zagreb (not available), Sisak-Moslavina (not available), Krapina-Zagorje (http://www.kr-zag-zupanija.hr), Varaždin (http://www.varazdinska-zupanija.hr), Medjimurje (http://www.zupanija-medjimurska.hr), Koprivnica-Križevci (http://www.tz-koprivnicko-krizevacka.hr), Virovitica-Podravina (http://www.viroviticko-podravska-zupanija.hr), Bjelovar-Bilogora (not available), Požega-Slavonia (not available), Slavonski Brod-Posavina (http://www.tel.hr/zupbrps), Vukovar-Srijem (not available), Osijek-Baranja (http://www.osjecko-baranjska-zupanija.hr).

Religion

Freedom of Religion in Croatia (www.vjerska-sloboda.com). This is the Web site of the Association for Religion Freedom in the Republic of Croatia, a nongovernmental and nonprofit organization that brings together believers from twenty-four churches and religious communities in Croatia.

Bahá'í Religious Community of Croatia (Bahai) (http://www.bahai.hr). Website of the Bahá'í community of Croatia, with an introduction to the Bahá'í faith, Bahá'í writings, activities of the Bahá'í community in Croatia, and links to the worldwide Bahá'í Web pages.

Jehovah's Witnesses (http://www.watchtower.org/languages/c/library/rq/index.htm). The Jehovah's Witnesses are a Christian religious organization that actively witnesses about Jehovah God and his purpose for mankind.

Evangelical Methodist Church (http://www.metodisti.hr). Site of Evangelical Methodist Church in Split, Croatia.

Serbian Orthodox Church Borovo Naselje (http://www.spco-borovonaselje.org). This site is dedicated to the work and life of the Serbian Orthodox Church in Borovo Naselje, Vukovar.

(continues)

Croatian Catholic Press Agency (http://www.ika.hr). This is the official Croatian Catholic Press Agency, based at Zagreb, which provides daily news about the Catholic Church in Croatia.

Catholic Bishops Conference (http://www.hbk.hr). This is the official site of Croatia's Catholic bishops, and hence of the Catholic Church in Croatia.

Sport

For information on Croatian soccer, see the links at http://www.hr/index.en.shtml and the Croatian Football Association at http://www.hns-cff.hr. Most Croatian soccer clubs have their own Web sites. Tennis fans can visit the Web site of the Croatian Open, which is held every year in Umag (Istria), at http://www2.croatiaopen.hr, and the Web site of the Zagreb Open at www.zagrebopen.hr.

Tourism

A legion of Web sites is devoted to the Croatian tourist industry and its various branches. A useful starting point is the Croatian homepage under "Tourism and Traveling" at the Croatian Homepage (http://www.hr/index.en.shtml). For detailed information on Croatia's eight national (nature) parks and protected nature areas, see Kornati (http://www.archaeology.net/kornati), Plitvice Lakes (http://www.archaeology.net/plitvice), Krka (http://www.npkrka.hr), Paklenica (http://www.tel.hr/paklenica), Mljet (http://www.mljet.hr), Risnjak (http://www.archaeology.net/risnjak), Brijuni (http://www.np-brijuni.hr), and Velebit (http://http://www.pp-velebit.hr). For travel, see the Web site of Zagreb Airport at http://www.tel.hr/zagreb-airport and that of Split Airport at http://www.split-airport.tel.hr/split-airport. The Web site of Croatia Airlines is http://www.croatiaairlines.hr. The Web sites of Croatian Railways (http://www.hznet.hr), Croatia Line (http://www.croatialine.com), and Jadrolinija (http://www.jadrolinija.tel.hr/jadrolinija) are all useful for travel purposes.

War Crimes

International Criminal Tribunal for the former Yugoslavia (ICTY) (http://www.un.org/icty). This is the official Web site of the UN tribunal based in The Hague. The site contains a number of public documents, official transcipts, and indictments.

Institute for War and Peace Reporting (http://www.iwpr.net). This IWPR produces a weekly report called *Tribunal Update,* summarizing developments at the ICTY.

Women's Issues

Ona (http://www.ona-hr.com). An up-to-date Web site dealing with a range of issues for women.

The International Women's Club Zagreb (http://www.iwcz.org). Founded in 1994 to bring together women of all nationalities living in Zagreb, the International Women's Club (IWC) offers friendship and support to members, with monthly get-togethers and a varied program of visits, activities, and fundraising events.

B.a.B.e.—Be active, Be emancipated (http://www.babe.hr/eng). B.a.B.e. is a strategic lobbying and advocacy group located in Zagreb, Croatia, working for the affirmation and implementation of women's human rights. The organization lobbies for the recognition and improved status of women's human rights, such as the right to be free of violence, both at home and in the public sphere; the right to reproductive choice and reproductive health, including the right to decide when to create and how to raise children; and the right to equal and full participation in all aspects of society, especially in leadership roles and important decisionmaking. It also supports the civil scene in Croatia and cooperates with peace, human rights, and ecological groups in Croatia.

Women's Infoteka (http://www.zinfo.hr). The Web site of a women's information and documentation center founded in Zagreb in December 1992 as the first of the sort in Croatia and Eastern Europe. The basic activities are collecting and disseminating data and information, a lending service library, publishing (books and the magazine *Kruh i ruže* [Bread and Roses]), organizing training seminars and international conferences, conducting research projects, and providing help in research projects.

Center for Women's Studies, Zagreb (http://www.zenstud.hr). The Center for Women's Studies in Zagreb, founded in 1995 by feminist scholars, activists, and artists, is the first and only independent educational center in Croatia

(continues)

and acknowledged center for civil education in Southeastern Europe offering a place for academic discussion on women's and feminist issues. The main activities of the center are women's studies, public education (for women leaders, politicians, and activists), research, cultural activities, and publishing. The center provides its students with basic insights, theoretical knowledge, and critical reflection into a wide range of women's studies topics, including feminist epistemology, women in cultural theories, theories of identity, and women's awareness of the self, by providing new models of education that fulfill and complement the formal education obtained within the university sphere.

Center for Education and Counseling of Women (http://www.zamir.net/~cesi). CESI is a women's nonprofit, nongovernmental organization established on International Women's Day, 8 March 1997, in response to problems of the violation of human rights, in particular women's and minority rights, nationalism, militarization, and the deterioration of economic standards in the postwar period. It was founded by members of several women's and peace initiatives, all of whom have many years of professional experience working with women war survivors. The main goal is to empower women to gain control over their lives, to improve their psychological, economic, and physical well-being, and to promote values of gender equality.

Česmički (Janus Pannonius) (1434–1472) composed satirical epigrams, panegyrics, and elegies.

The leading figure of the baroque in Croatia was Ivan Gundulić (1589–1638), a patrician from Dubrovnik who penned dramas and epic poems. He authored numerous works, the most famous of which is *Osman*. This epic poem, although running 11,000 lines, remained unfinished at the time of his death. It was inspired by a 1621 Polish victory against the Ottoman Turks and glorified the great courage of the Slavs. Pavao Ritter Vitezović (1652–1713) is the best-known Croat writer of the late seventeenth century and in some respects is the father of Croat historicism. He authored numerous historical, literary, and lexicographical works in Latin and Croatian. Also of significance in this period were Andrija Kačić Miošić (1704–1760), Adam Baltazar Krčelić (1715–1778), and the philosopher Rudjer Bošković (1711–1787). Bošković is one of the most important Croat cultural and scientific figures of the eighteenth century. An astronomer, mathematician, and physician, he is best known for his philosophical and poetic works, of which he authored over a dozen in Latin.

Although the center of gravity of Croatian culture and literature lay in Dalmatia up to the seventeenth century, after that point it shifted north to Zagreb. In the nineteenth century national awakeners in Croatia had a critical role in the further evolution of Croatian literature and language. Indeed, modern Croatian literature began with the Illyrianist movement (1836–1848) of Ljudevit Gaj and the literary-cultural circle that the movement spawned. Illyrianism was suffused with romanticism and nationalism; the latter theme expressed itself throughout the nineteenth century partly in terms of antagonism to Habsburg and Hungarian rule. In the 1830s Zagreb became both the political and the cultural center of the Croat lands. However, the Illyrianist awakeners in Croatia first had to contend with the name of the spoken language. They initially referred to it as "Illyrian" and later "Croatian" or "Serbian." After the creation of the Kingdom of Serbs, Croats, and Slovenes in 1918, the term "Serbo-Croatian" became official. At the time it was hoped by Yugoslavist unitarists that just as the Croat, Serb, and Slovene "tribes" would be melded into a hybrid Yugoslav nationality, so too would "Croatian" and "Serbian" merge into a single literary language. This proved highly problematical on many levels, however. As Yugoslavia's political experience soured and resistance to state centralism stiffened among the non-Serbs, resistance to linguistic unity stiffened also.

The Illyrianist movement counted among its followers Ivan Mažuranić (1814–1890), who penned the epic *Smrt Smail-Age Čengića* (The Death of Smail-Aga Čengić; 1846), which tells of Christian-Muslim conflict in Turkish-ruled Hercegovina. Stanko Vraz (1810–1851) and Petar Preradović (1818–1872) were also important in the movement. The main figure in late nineteenth-century Croatian literature was August Šenoa (1838–1881), who dealt mainly with historical themes. His two main works were *Seljačka buna* (Peasant Uprising; 1877) and *Diogeneš* (Diogenes).

The rise of literary realism in the second half of the nineteenth century furthered the development of the novel. Literary realism included among its followers Silvije Strahimir Kranjčević (1865–1908), Eugen Kumičić (1850–1904), Ante Kovačić (1854–1889), Ksaver Šandor Gjalski (1854–1935), and Milan Begović (1876–1948). Particularly important in this respect were Kumičić and Šenoa. Many novelists of the period also wrote poetry and drama. The late nineteenth century also saw a growing interest in the psychology of motives and morals, a trend influenced by the writings of Russian novelists. Historical themes, which had predominated in Šenoa's work, gave way to psychology, which gradually displaced the cult of history. The best known of the psychological novelists in Croatia was Gjalski, who in a series of some twenty novels depicted the whole range of contemporary Croatian life.

During the first quarter of the twentieth century, modernists sought to assimilate literary trends imported from France and Germany. Croatian literary modernism was represented by Milivoj Dežman Ivanov (1873–1940), Milan

Marko Marulić (1450–1524)

Marko Marulić was a Croat poet, writer, and scholar from Split, which after 1420 was part of the Venetian Republic. Marulić wrote the first secular work of Croatian literature, the *Istoria svete udovice Judit* (The History of the Holy Widow Judith). This Croatian epic tells the biblical story of Judith, who killed the Assyrian general Holofernes; it is an allegory of Croatia's struggle against the Ottoman Turks. It was published in five editions in Venice between 1521 and 1627. The poem proved to be very popular with a large section of educated Dalmatian society. In the preface to the book, Marulić wrote: "In reading this history I was minded to translate it into our [Croatian] tongue, so that it might be understood by those who are not learned in Latin or clerical writing" (Croatian Information Centre). The ethical message of Judith appears to be a call to Christian faith, devotion, and unity in the struggle against the Ottoman Turkish infidel. Marulić sounded an urgent call to his people to hold firm to Christianity, which alone would give them the moral force to withstand the Turk.

Marulić also wrote in Latin a series of works of religious morality, some of which were highly regarded by contemporaries: *Evangelistarium* (Book of Gospels; 1487); *De Institutione bene vivendi per exempla Sanctorum* (Instructions for a Good Life Based on the Examples of the Saints; 1498); and *Dialogus de laudibus Herculis* (A Dialogue on the Great Deeds of Hercules; 1524). He authored other noteworthy works in the areas of poetry, history, and archaeology, most of which were published in several editions, as well as being translated into German, Italian, French, Czech, and Portuguese. Related works in Croatian concerned with the Ottoman threat include his *Molitva suprotiva Turkom* (Prayer against the Turk), and *Tuzenie grada Hjerozolima* (The Plaint of the City of Jerusalem). *Prayer against the Turk* denounces the destruction, pillage, and massacres perpetrated by Ottoman Turkish soldiers in the Croatian hinterland. Although a layman, Marulić devoted his life to religious contemplation and to the improvement of his fellow man. His religious writings were known throughout Europe.

Although his classical education and his interest in Roman monuments stamp him as a humanist, Marulić was deeply rooted in medieval Catholic theology. His books were moralistic and didactic and attracted many readers and admirers throughout Europe. His *De Institutione bene vivendi per exempla Sanctorum* was not only reprinted but translated into many languages. The main reason for its popularity was that during the whole of the Counter-Reformation it was considered an effective book for Catholics to use in the defense of their faith. Marulić shared the common belief of the Renaissance era that the Croats had been in Dalmatia from time immemorial. He translated from Croatian into Latin an old chronicle (*Ljetopis popa Dukljanina;* Chronicle of the Priest of Dioclea) under the title *Regum Dalmatiae et Croatiae gesta* (Deeds of the Kings of Dalmatia and Croatia). Concerned with the rapid advance of the Ottoman Turks in the Balkans and the disunity prevailing in Christendom, Marulić wrote the moving *Epistle to Pope Hadrian VI* (Rome, 1522), begging him humbly to intervene in favor of the poor persecuted Christians. Marulić wrote that many of his countrymen had been killed, others enslaved, their properties destroyed, villages burned, and fields either wasted or left without their cultivators. Marulić's impressive opus has earned him the reputation of being the father of Croatian literature.

Marjanović (1879–1955), Vladimir Nazor (1876–1949), and Antun Gustav Matoš (1873–1914), among others. Nazor's prose dealt with the epic world of legend and mythology. His novel *Pastir Loda* (Pastor Loda) is a panoramic description of his native island Brač; his *Zagrebačke novele* (Zagreb Novellas) provides a reconstruction of Zagreb in his last years.

The cause of Croatian literature has been greatly assisted by the Society of Croat Writers (DHK, Društvo hrvatskih književnika), which was formed in 1900. From its inception, the DHK has been a remarkably active cultural institution. It has published several periodicals, such as *Ljetopis* (Annals; 1903) and *Savremenik* (The Contemporary; 1906). In 1909 it also began publishing a major series of literary works under the rubric, Contemporary Croat Writers; between 1909 and 1938, it published sixty-four volumes. The series was resumed in 1957. In 1954 the DHK began publishing its Little Library, intended as a venue for young writers. In 1966 it began publishing *Most/The Bridge,* with translations of Croatian poetry and literary works into foreign languages. It is published to this day by the DHK.

Undoubtedly the greatest Croat writer, poet, essayist, and playwright of the twentieth century was Miroslav Krleža (1893–1981). He left behind a rich opus consisting of novels, dramas, poetry, and political essays. Born in Zagreb, which was then part of the Austro-Hungarian Empire, he received his primary schooling there but in 1908 entered a preparatory military school in Peczuj and then attended the Lucoviceum Military Academy in Budapest. In 1912, during the first Balkan War, he volunteered for service in the

Serbian army. Suspected of being an Austrian spy by the Serbs, he was forced to return to Austria-Hungary, where the authorities arrested him. He was deprived of his officer's rank; during World War I, he served on the Galician front as a common soldier.

In his early literary career, Krleža was an idealist and romanticist. But World War I shattered many of his illusions; his embittered prose reflected his strong antiwar feelings. After 1918, Krleža opposed the Great Serbian monarchist regime of Yugoslavia and in 1919 founded *Plamen* (The Flame), a left-wing review, and then in 1923 *Književna republika* (Literary Republic), among others. Deeply impressed by the Soviet revolution, he became a Marxist and was a member of the Communist Party from 1919 until 1939, when he was expelled.

Krleža's early dramas, *Legenda* (The Legend; 1914), *Kraljevo* (1918), and *Adam i Eva* (Adam and Eve; 1922) reveal his transformation from an idealist into a socially conscious and antiwar writer. Krleža's plays are characterized by straightforward dialogue and merciless revelation of social injustice. *Hrvatski bog Mars* (The Croatian God Mars; 1922) was a short story collection depicting the miserable condition of the Croat soldier in the Austro-Hungarian army and the exploitation of the peasant; it is a powerful antiwar statement. The dramatic trilogy *Gospoda Glembajevi* (The Glembays; 1928), *U agoniji* (Death Throes; 1928), and *Leda* (1932) depicts the disintegration of the Glembay family and the downfall of bourgeois society.

Krleža's significance as the leader of socially oriented writers grew steadily in the interwar era, when he produced most of his best work. Perhaps his best known work outside Croatia is *Povratak Filipa Latinovicza* (The Return of Philip Latinovicz; 1932), which is a dissection of Croatia's aimless bourgeoisie in the aftermath of the Great War. His novel *Na rubu pameti* (On the Edge of Reason; 1938) is set in the same period and portrays bourgeois society as a form of self-deluding madness. Krleža excelled as a political commentator. In the interwar period he was Croatia's (and Yugoslavia's) leading Marxist intellectual. His best-known work of political commentary is *Deset krvavih godina* (Ten Bloody Years), which is a collection of essays from the 1920s. In the poetry collections *Knjiga lirike* (Book of Songs; 1932) and *Pjesme u tmini* (Poems in the Dark; 1937), Krleža predicted the victory of socialism. But in *Dijalektički antibarbarus* (Dialectical Antibarbarus; 1939) he mocked Stalinism, for which he was expelled from the Communist Party of Yugoslavia. The satirical novel *Banket u Blitvi* (Banquet in Blitvia; 1938–1939) dealt with the political situation in Europe in the interwar period in the imaginary country Blitvia. *Balade Petrice Kerempuha* (The Ballads of Petrica Kerempuh; 1936), a collection of poems, was written in Croatia's regional Kajkavian dialect and was a synthesis of the author's entire poetic oeuvre.

After World War II, Krleža was rehabilitated. In 1947 he was chosen vice president of the Yugoslav Academy of Sciences and Arts, and in 1951 he became director of the Croatian Institute of Lexicography, which today bears his name. He was also the editor in chief of the *Encyclopedia Yugoslavia*. From 1958 to 1961 Krleža was president of the Writers' Union. His most ambitious work is the six-volume novel *Zastave* (Banners; 1967), which paints a panoramic overview of European life in the decade after 1912. Throughout his life Krleža stood in the forefront of the struggle against reactionary social and political attitudes. He wrote with enormous creative energy and defended his views fiercely. Although a Marxist to the end, he expressed his disdain for Stalinism and totalitarian systems generally.

Dubravka Ugrešić and Slavenka Drakulić are perhaps the two most outstanding writers of Croatian posmodern literature. Both writers emigrated in the 1990s, largely because of their disillusionment with Croatia's drift to the nationalist political right. Ugrešić has written *Culture of Lies, Have a Nice Day* (the English translation of *Američki fikcionar*) and many other works. Drakulić is a noted feminist writer who began her career as a journalist and political commentator, writing for a number of Zagreb periodicals. Her better-known works include three books of journalism, *How We Survived Communism and Even Laughed, Rain Express,* and *Café Europa,* as well as the four novels *Holograms of Fear, Marble Skin, The Taste of a Man,* and *As If I Am Not Here.* Her books have been translated into more than a dozen languages. She also contributes political columns to a number of European newspapers.

MUSIC AND DANCE

The oldest preserved relics of Croatia's musical culture are of religious provenance and are related to medieval Latin liturgical manuscripts with Gregorian chants. The earliest known Croatian manuscript is the Osor Evangelistary (ca. 1080), a neumatic manuscript from the convent of St. Nikola in Osor on the Island of Cres. It is written in Beneventan, a medieval script employed chiefly in southern Italy, and contains a prayer for the pope, the Byzantine emperor, and the Croatian king Zvonimir; it is held in the Vatican Archives. Also of historic significance is the Dubrovnik Missal (twelfth century), now kept in the Bodleian Library at Oxford University. Written in Latin, in the Beneventan script, it contains prayers and chants. Glagolitic church singing holds a special place in the history of Croatian music. The earliest mention of Glagolitic singing in Croatia dates to 1177, when Pope Alexander III visited the town of Zadar in Dalmatia. In the Missal of Duke Novak (1368), which is kept at the National Library in Vienna, there are symbols above the Glagolitic text that appear to denote singing. The same holds for the Hrvoje Missal (1404) held in the Library of Turkish Sultans at Istanbul.

In Dalmatia the extant sources belong to the Beneventan script, demonstrating the close cultural connection between Dalmatia and Italy. The music of medieval northern Croatia, on the other hand, is intimately associated with the formation of the Zagreb bishopric (1094). Because the Zagreb bishopric was under the jurisdiction of Hungarian ecclesiasts until 1180, its musical codex was based on those in Hungary. The oldest liturgical and musical relic written in Zagreb is the Zagreb Missal (1230), which is kept in the Franciscan monastery at Güssing, Austria.

Croatia can boast a number of important Renaissance and baroque composers. The first is Julije Skjavetić, who from 1557 to 1573 lived in Šibenik, where he conducted the choir of Šibenik Cathedral. The Franciscan monk Ivan Lukačić (1584–1648), a Renaissance composer who was also from Šibenik, was conductor and organist in Split Cathedral. In 1620 he published a collection, *Sacrae cantiones,* containing twenty-seven motets accompanied by organ. The only extant copy is held in the Jagiellonian Library in Cracow, Poland. Another important representative of Croatian church music was Vinko Jelić (1596–1636), an early baroque composer who is noted for introducing new techniques like chromatics and sequences into his music. In 1622 he published a collection consisting of twenty-four motets, *Parnassia militia,* in Strasbourg. Canon Kristofor Ivanović of Budva published his *Memorie teatrali* (Venice, 1681), which was the first history of Venetian opera, covering the period from 1637 to 1681.

The first national operas in Croatia were composed in the middle of the nineteenth century. Vatroslav Lisinski (1819–1854) composed the Croatian opera, *Ljubav i zloba* (Love and Malice; 1846). Ivan Zajc (1832–1914) was perhaps the most productive Croat composer, however. His most important operas are *Mislav, Ban Legat,* and *Nikola Šubić Zrinski,* among others.

Folk musician in traditional clothing, Vrbovec. (Corel Corporation)

In the modern period, Croatian folk music has been the exemplar of popular musical culture. It is diverse and reflects the varied cultural influences of the Mediterranean, Central Europe, and the Balkans on Croatian culture. Traditional folk music still forms an important part of everyday life in many of Croatia's towns and villages, where local folklore societies have tried to preserve knowledge of native song and dance. The folk music of eastern Croatia is characterized by the *tambura* (or *tamburica,* its diminutive form), a lutelike instrument that is plucked to produce a sound that is similar to the mandolin. The instrument was probably brought to the Balkans by the Turks and was gradually adopted by the Slavic-speaking peoples. By the nineteenth century, the tamburica was the most common musical instrument in much of Croatia. During the nineteenth century national revival, the instrument was seen as an authentic symbol of indigenous Croat (and Slavic) popular culture. Tamburica troupes were formed in villages and regions, which played popular folk tunes. In the twentieth century this particular sound, which was especially popular in eastern Croatia (especially Slavonia), came to symbolize Croatia as a whole and has remained popular to this day. That is not to say, however, that other musical variants are not popular. For example, in the Zagorje region north of Zagreb, music and dance center on the polka and waltz, which are common to Central Europe. In southwestern Croatia (e.g., Lika) and in the Croat-populated areas of Hercegovina, *gange* are popular; this is a dissonant form of singing that is commonly heard at village festivities of one kind or another. In Istria and Dalmatia, other forms predominate.

One can hear folk music in Croatia today by attending the performances of one of any number of folklore societies. For example, Lado, the state professional ensemble, performs dances all over Croatia. There are also numerous folklore festivals in Croatia, which provide a window on Croatian popular culture. Croatia's annual International Folklore Festival, held in Zagreb, brings together an array of performers from all over the country and the world. Much of the traditional Croatian folk music has made its way into the Croatian commercial mainstream. Groups like Zlatnik dukati (Golden Ducats) and Gazde (The Bosses) have melded folk music themes with modern pop sound and have gained broad appeal in Croatia.

Like folk music and many other aspects of traditional culture, the traditional folk dance repertory in Croatia is conditioned by the specific cultural heritages of the country's diverse regions. The richness and wide variety of dance styles, including the accompanying songs, music, and instruments, resulted from the convergence of various cultures. Central European cultural influences were of crucial importance for lowland and central Croatia. The mountainous region of Croatia fell under Southeast European influences. On the other hand, Mediterranean qualities are characteristic for the Adriatic islands, its coast and hinterland.

In the 1930s folk dances began to be performed on stage with a view to preserving them as part of the nation's cultural heritage, and also in order to present regional identities at national and international festivals. The work of

Sport

Sport occupies an important position in Croatian society, not least because this country of 5 million has produced and continues to produce a large number of talented and successful athletes and teams. Croatia's success in sport has enhanced national pride, particularly in the difficult period of the War of Independence (1991–1995) and since then.

Soccer is without a doubt Croatia's national sport and by far the most popular national pastime. The Croatian football federation is one of the oldest in the country, having been formed in 1912. Two Croatian clubs have stood out, Hajduk Split and Dinamo Zagreb. They were often the best in Croatia and among the best in former Yugoslavia. In addition to many domestic titles, Dinamo Zagreb won the UEFA Cup (then known as the Fairs Cup) in 1967. At the 1998 World Cup in France, which was Croatia's first appearance at a World Cup, the Croatian National Team finished third behind France and Brazil.

Next to soccer, basketball is the most popular sport in Croatia. Croatian clubs were among the best in former Yugoslavia, in particular Cibona of Zagreb. In 1985 and 1986, Cibona won the European championship. From 1989 to 1991, this title was won by Split. The Croat contribution to the Yugoslav national team was also important and certainly helped the squad win the gold medal at the Moscow Olympic Games (1980) and at the World Championships (1970, 1978, 1990). Yugoslavia also won gold at the European Championships in 1973, 1975, 1977, 1989, and 1991. Among the best-known Croat basketball players are Dražen Petrović, Toni Kukoč, and Dino Radja. The Croatian national team was formed in 1992 and quickly distinguished itself by reaching the finals of the 1992 Olympic Games in Barcelona, where the U.S. "Dream Team" defeated them. The following year the Croatian national team won third place in the European Championship at Munich and repeated that finish at the World Championships of 1994 in Toronto and the European Championships of 1995 in Athens.

Croatia has long produced many talented tennis players. Although the names Željko Franulović and Nikola Pilić are unfamiliar to most Westerners, Goran Ivanišević is certainly not. He is undoubtedly the best Croatian player of all time. He has reached the Wimbledon finals four times, winning at his fourth appearance in 2001. Known for his remarkably powerful serve, he was also very popular with tennis fans because of his aggressive style. On the women's side, Iva Majoli has established herself as a solid performer on the women's circuit and spent some time as a member of the Top 10.

Croat players have excelled at many other sports, among them handball. Croatian clubs were among the leading teams in former Yugoslavia, and Croat players contributed to the successes of the Yugoslav national team—the gold medal at the Munich (1972) and Los Angeles (1984) Olympic Games. In independent Croatia, the national squad has won bronze at the European Championships in 1993, silver at the World Championship in 1995, and gold at the 1996 Atlantic Summer Games. The Zagreb men's club Badel 1862 was European champion for two consecutive years (1992, 1993) and lost on three other occasions in the finals. The women's club Podravka, from Koprivnica, won the 1996 European championship.

Seljačka sloga (Peasant Concord), a cultural and charitable organization founded in 1926 by the Croat Peasant Party, was particularly important in this respect. After World War II, a number of urban amateur cultural troupes and societies continued to promote this form of national culture. The most important of these, Lado, was established in 1948. Lado performs folk dances, and the Institute for Ethnology and Folklore Research in Zagreb deals in the research, documentation, and popularization of folk dancing.

ART

Croatia is especially renowned for its naive artists—generally self-taught artists who lacked or rejected formal training and who used vibrant colors, definite shapes, extreme detail, and nonscientific perspective to characterize their style. Naive art in Croatia was born in the interwar era and owes a great deal to the academically trained painter, Professor Krsto Hegedušić (1901–1975). While studying in France he became an admirer of naive artists like Henri "Le Douanier" Rousseau. When he returned to Croatia, he discovered the work of young Croat naive artists. In September 1931, Hegedušić organized an exhibition of the works of the Zemlja (Earth) group of academic painters, sculptors, and architects, which opened at Zagreb's Art Pavilion. This was the Croatian public's first opportunity to see the works of peasant-painters Ivan Generalić (1914–1992) and Franjo Mraz (1910–1981), both of whom were from the village of Hlebine in Croatia's Podravina region. The basic orientation of the Zemlja group was toward socially committed art; that

Naive Art

Naive artists are self-taught artists or artists who imitate the self-taught. Naive art may thus be defined as the work of artists in advanced or sophisticated societies who lack or reject formal training. Vibrant colors, definite shapes, and nonscientific perspective characterize their style. Naive artists should not, however, be confused with hobbyists; they create with the same passion as trained artists but without formal knowledge of methods. Naive works are often extremely detailed, with a tendency toward the use of brilliant, saturated colors and a characteristic absence of perspective, which creates the illusion of figures floating in space.

Naive art in Croatia was born in September 1931, when the third exhibition of the Zemlja (Earth) group of academic painters, sculptors, and architects opened at the Art Pavilion in central Zagreb. It was organized thanks largely to the academically trained artist, Professor Krsto Hegedušić, who acquired an interest in naive art while studying in France. In the 1930s Croatian naive art was closely associated with the works of peasant-painters Ivan Generalić and Franjo Mraz, both of whom were from the village of Hlebine, in Croatia's Podravina region. The basic orientation of the Zemlja group was toward socially committed art; that is, art that served the needs of the people, was understood by them, and that contributed to the improvement of their cultural standards. The most important artists of the group, in addition to Generalić and Mraz, were the peasant sculptor Petar Smajić and Mirko Virius. Generalić, Mraz, and Virius constituted the so-called Hlebine Group, named after their village. In 1936 the Hlebine Group held its first exhibition in Zagreb's Ulrich Gallery; organized by the painters themselves, it was one of the first exhibits of naive art anywhere. Without any financial backing or official sponsorship, the group fought for the recognition of naive art as a legitimate form of contemporary art. After World War II, naive art gradually established itself as a modern trend and gained international recognition. After 1945 a number of Croat naive artists came to prominence, among them Franjo Filipović, Dragan Gaži, Ivan Večenaj, Mijo Kovačić, and Ivan Lacković Croata. Many of the most important works of Croat naive artists are housed in the Croatian Museum of Naive Art, which has about 1,500 items in its holdings (paintings, sculptures, drawings, and prints). The focus is on artists belonging to the well-known Hlebine School of naive art and several highly regarded independent naive artists. Alongside these artists, the exhibit also includes some works by major international naive artists of other nationalities.

is, art that served the needs of the people, contributed to the betterment of their cultural standards, and was understood by them. Such an orientation supplied the setting for Croatian naive art.

Other important artists of the group were the peasant sculptor Petar Smajić (1910–1985) and Mirko Virius (1889–1943). Generalić is regarded as the first Croat naive painter to develop a personal style and to reach a high level of artistic mastery. Social themes predominated in his earliest works, from the 1930s, which gave way in the postwar period to more complex compositions. Like Generalić, Mraz and Virius presented the life of their village and the beauty of the countryside. In 1936 their so-called Hlebine Group (named after their village) held its first exhibition in Zagreb, one of the first exhibits of naive art anywhere. After World War II, naive art gradually established itself as a modern trend and gained international recognition. After 1945 a number of Croat naive artists came to prominence, among them Dragan Gaži (1930–1983), Ivan Večenaj (b. 1920), Mijo Kovačić (b. 1935), and Ivan Lacković Croata (b. 1931). In 1952 the Croatian Museum of Naive Art was established in Zagreb. It treated naive art as a legitimate orientation in its own right within contemporary art. From the outset, the museum's objective was to promote and foster Croatian naive art domestically and internationally. To that end, an exhibition of Ivan Generalić's works was held in Paris (1953), while the Hlebine School was represented at the Sao Paolo Biennale (1956). Croat naive artists were represented at other international exhibitions of naive art: Basel and Baden-Baden (1961), Rotterdam and Paris (1964), Bratislava (1966, 1969, 1972), Zagreb (1970, 1973), and Munich and Zurich (1974, 1975).

Two of Croatia's internationally renowned sculptors are Ivan Meštrović (1883–1962) and Antun Augustinčić (1900–1979). Meštrović was a famous Croat sculptor who designed several imposing buildings throughout Croatia and the former Yugoslavia, including the Croatian History Museum (Zagreb) and the Njegoš Mausoleum (Mt. Lovćen, Montenegro). From 1900 to 1905, he studied at Vienna's Academy of Art and then moved to Paris where, from 1908 to 1911, he executed more than fifty sculptures. In 1911 he moved briefly to Belgrade and then to Rome. The turning point in his career was the 1911 international exhibit at Rome, where he won first prize for sculpture. Oral epics, folk songs, and historical ballads common among the peasantry of his native Dalmatia powerfully influenced his early works. Epic heroes inspired him to carve in wood and stone. His works glorified in bronze and stone the heroes who had fought the Turks in the famous Battle of Kosovo (1389). He presented them to the European public as symbols of the patriotic aspirations of the South Slavs for political freedom and independence.

Politics and art were intimately interwoven throughout his life. During World War I he became actively involved with a group of Croat and other South Slav émigrés who formed in 1915 the Yugoslav Committee, to work for a postwar Yugoslav state that would include Croatia and his native Dalmatia. These exiles, based in London and Paris, had learned that the Allies were secretly negotiating with Italy to enter the war on their side. As its price, Italy demanded Croatian and Slovenian territory. At that point two Croat politicians, Ante Trumbić and Frano Supilo, formed the Yugoslav Committee. During the war Meštrović became well known to the British public. His works were displayed at the Victoria and Albert Museum in London; his exhibition drew the British public's attention to the cultural achievements of Croats in particular and South Slavs generally and underscored the solidarity of Croats, Slovenes, and Serbs of Austria-Hungary. During the 1919 Peace Conference, he had a series of exhibits at the Petit Palais in Paris.

Returning in 1919 to his homeland, which was now part of the new Yugoslav state, Meštrović turned his attention to numerous projects, including monuments and statues, many of which embellish public squares and museums throughout Croatia. He would become far better known in the interwar era. He received commissions in Europe and the Americas; he executed numerous monuments and held exhibits in Europe and the Americas. His first American exhibition came in 1924, when he exhibited 132 pieces at the Brooklyn Museum in New York. He became a member of the Academy of Arts and Sciences in Belgrade and Zagreb, Grand Officer of the Legion d'Honneur in France, and bearer of the Cross of St. George in England. He also became an honorary member of many art academies and universities in Europe and America.

In 1946 Meštrović was offered a professorship at Syracuse University. He arrived in New York in January 1947. Later that spring he was invited by the Academy of Arts and Letters to mount an exhibit at the Metropolitan Museum, where he displayed marble, bronze, and wood sculptures that he had crafted during the war. His sculptures now expressed the cruelty and tragedy, injustice and endurance of the human condition. His best known pieces from the period include *Job, St. Francis, Pieta,* and *Woman under the Cross,* all of which speak to supreme sacrifice and the promise of salvation. In 1954 he became an American citizen at a special ceremony conducted by President Eisenhower at the White House. Before his death, Meštrović donated fifty-nine sculptures to his homeland, which are now displayed in various museums.

Augustinčić was also an important artist, who in fact studied under Meštrović in the early 1920s. Educated in Zagreb and Paris, he became a renowned sculptor and representative of contemporary Croatian art. He is known to the wider public primarily for his outstanding public monuments, such as *Peace,* which stands in front of the United Nations Building in New York, and the *Monument to the Peasants' Rebellion and Matija Gubec* in Gornja Stubica, Croatia. He began studying sculpture in 1918 at the College

The Necktie

The necktie began as a simple garment; over the centuries it has assumed more importance, finally becoming a distinct symbol of elegance and refinement. The necktie originated as a simple handkerchief (or neckerchief), but it has achieved a remarkable position in men's fashion in light of its humble origins.

The world first discovered the tie in the seventeenth century. At the time, and probably in earlier times also, Croat soldiers and mercenaries wore the tie around their necks, probably for hygienic reasons. According to François Chaille, author of *La Grande Histoire de la Cravate* (The Book of Ties), during the Thirty Years' War (1618–1648), which was fought almost entirely in the German lands, and in which thousands of Croat troops saw action on behalf of the Habsburg dynasty of Austria, the Croat soldiers impressed the French with their costume. The traditional outfit of these Croats aroused interest because of the picturesque scarves distinctively tied about their necks. The scarves were made of various cloths, ranging from coarse material for common soldiers to fine cotton and silk for officers. This elegant Croatian style immediately enchanted the French, who adopted the tie soon thereafter. In fact, the French word for "tie," *cravate,* is derived from the Croatian word *Hrvat,* meaning "Croat." For the French officers, the advantage of the Croatian neckerchief was its enviable practicality. In contrast to the lace collar, which was then the norm and had to be kept white and carefully starched, the neckerchief was simple and loosely tied around the neck. In addition to being less awkward, it was also elegant and easier to wear, and it remained visible beneath the soldiers' long hair.

Shortly thereafter, in 1661, the French King Louis XIV instituted the position of "tie maker" for the monarch, a gentleman who was assigned to help the king arrange and knot his necktie. Nine years later, the duchess of Lavallière, one of the king's favorites, was the first woman to wear a tie. The Croatian scarf was thus accepted in France, above all at the court, where military ornaments were much admired. In the nineteenth century the duchess of Lavallière's name was given to the most graceful of masculine ties. Thus the tie (or at least something resembling the modern tie) first appeared among Croat soldiers and mercenaries in the seventeenth century.

of Arts and Crafts (Zagreb), where he briefly studied under Meštrović (1922–1924). In 1924 he received a scholarship from the French government and studied at Paris's L'Ecole des Arts décoratifs and L'Académie des Beaux-Arts. In 1925 he held an exhibition at the French Artists Showroom. He returned to Zagreb in 1926, where he staged his first exhibition. During the 1930s he focused more on public monuments and soon gained a reputation as a master of monuments, particularly equestrian monuments. In 1940 he became a corresponding member of JAZU (Yugoslav Academy) and in 1946 a professor at the Visual Arts Academy (Zagreb). Augustinčić's bronze sculpture *Peace* was struck between 1952 and 1954, commissioned by the then Yugoslav government as a gift to the United Nations. When it was completed, the 10-meter-high stand and 5.5-meter-high equestrian sculpture were shipped to New York and placed in the vicinity of the United Nations Building. In 1970 he donated all his works to his native Klanjec, where the Antun Augustinčić Gallery opened in 1976.

CULTURAL AND ACADEMIC INSTITUTIONS

There are four universities in Croatia: Osijek, Rijeka, Split, and Zagreb. The University of Zagreb is the oldest and largest. In September 1669 the Habsburg ruler Leopold I granted the Jesuit academy in Zagreb the status of a university. The Jesuit academy never became a university in the proper sense of the word, however. Only in 1861 did the Croatian diet adopt a University bill, which the Habsburg monarch Franz Joseph signed in 1869. The University of Zagreb was officially founded in October 1874. Today it has twenty-eight faculties, three art academies, and two higher institutes. In the 1991–1992 academic year the university had 47,913 undergraduate and 2,407 graduate students. The university also operates a campus at Dubrovnik. The University of Rijeka was founded in May 1973. It has ten faculties in Rijeka, Pula, and Opatija, two institutes, two libraries, and a student center. In the 1991–1992 academic year it had 10,544 students. The University of Split was founded in June 1974. It has nine faculties, two scientific institutes, two libraries, and two student centers. In addition to the main campus in Split, there are campuses in Zadar and Dubrovnik. In 1992–1993 it had 10,000 students. Finally, the Josip Juraj Strossmayer University is located at Osijek in eastern Croatia. It was founded in 1975. It has seventeen faculties, institutes, and libraries. During the 1992–1993 academic year, the university had 6,500 students. In the academic year 1998–1999, the four Croatian universities had approximately 80,000 students.

The National and University Library is the largest and by far the most significant research library in Croatia. It is also an important cultural repository. Its origins date to the seventeenth century when the Jesuits founded their own gymnasium, residence, and library in Zagreb. In 1776 the Jesuit library was transferred to the newly founded Academy of Science. In 1913 the library moved to a new building on Marulić Square in central Zagreb, where it remained until 1994. In 1914 the library's collection was enriched when it received the library of the archbishop of Zagreb. The library has in its possession books, manuscripts, and incunabula; it currently has over 2 million volumes.

The Croatian Academy of Sciences and Arts (HAZU, Hrvatska akademija znanosti i umjestnosti) is one of the leading scientific, cultural, and intellectual institutions in Croatia. Located on Strossmayer's Square in central Zagreb, HAZU was founded in 1866 by Josip Juraj Strossmayer, the bishop of Djakovo, and was originally known as the Yugoslav Academy of Sciences and Arts (JAZU). It is responsible for nurturing artistic, scientific, and humanistic research in Croatia. According to its own statutes, the three main tasks of the Croatian Academy are (1) to promote and organize scientific research and encourage the application of the findings of this research, and to develop artistic and cultural activities, and concern with Croatian cultural heritage and its affirmation throughout the world; (2) to publish the results of scientific research and artistic creation; and (3) to promote arts and sciences in fields that are of special importance to the Republic of Croatia. HAZU has nine departments to carry out its scientific and artistic activities. Additionally, it has numerous scientific councils and committees, as well as scientific and research institutes. HAZU works closely with other academies of sciences and arts, universities, scientific institutions, and cultural and other institutions, as well as with individual scholars and artists from Croatia and abroad.

Among the most important HAZU publications are *Gradja za povijest književnosti hrvatske* (Documents for the History of Croatian Literature, 34 vols.); *Diplomatički zbornik Kraljevine Hrvatske, Dalmacije i Slavonije* (The Diplomatic Codex of the Kingdom of Croatia, Dalmatia, and Slavonia, 19 vols.); *Noviji pisci hrvatski* (Modern Croatian Writers, 12 vols.); *Hrvatski latinisti* (Croatian Latinists, 11 vols.); *Gradja za gospodarsku povijest Hrvatske* (Documents for the Economic History of Croatia, 21 vols.); *Djela* (Works, 80 vols.), a series of monographs on Croatia as a country and its history and language; *Prirodoslovna istraživanja* (Natural History Studies, 107 vols.); *Pomorsko pravo* (Maritime Law, 6 vols.); and *Gradja za pomorsku povijest Dubrovnika* (Documents for the Naval History of Dubrovnik, 6 vols.). HAZU has published the following dictionaries: Ivan Mažuranić's *Prinosi za hrvatski pravno-povijesni rječnik* (Contributions for a Croatian Historical Dictionary, 11 vols.), Julije Benešić's *Rječnik hrvatskog književnog jezika od preporoda do I. G. Kovačića* (Dictionary of the Croatian Literary Language from the National Revival to I. G. Kovačić, 12 vols.); and *Rječnik hrvatskoga kajkavskog književnog jezika* (A Dictionary of Croatian Literary Kajkavian, 8 vols.). Work on the monumental *Rječnik hrvatskog ili srpskog jezika* (Dictionary of the Croatian or Serbian Language, 97 vols.) went on for almost one hundred years.

The Croatian Academy had its origins in the Croat national awakening of the early nineteenth century. At that time, Croat patriots realized that such an institution was needed to help the nation resist the threat posed by cultural Magyarization. The leader of the Illyrianist movement, Ljudevit Gaj, proposed the creation of an academy in 1836 in his weekly newspaper, *Danica* (The Dawn). His proposal was supported that same year by the Croatian diet but was not approved by the Habsburg emperor. Its creation was again raised during the revolutions of 1848–1849, but the failure of the revolutions and the introduction of an absolutist regime delayed its creation yet again.

The bishop of Djakovo, Josip Juraj Strossmayer (1815–1905), took up the cause of the Croatian Academy in 1860. His role in the development of Croatian culture in the nineteenth century was unprecedented. Originating from a Croatized German family of Osijek, he became a major philanthropist and an important political figure. Strossmayer studied theology at the Catholic seminary at Djakovo before moving to the High Seminary in Budapest, where he obtained a doctorate in philosophy. Ordained in 1838, from 1840 to 1842 he studied in Vienna, where he obtained a doctorate in theology and served briefly as a professor of canon law at the University of Vienna. In 1847 he was ordained court chaplain and director of the Augustineum in Vienna. He was named bishop of Djakovo in November 1849.

From 1860 to 1873, Strossmayer acted as the leader of the National Party. The Croatian diet adopted his proposal for an academy in April 1861, but the Habsburg emperor Franz Joseph sanctioned the academy's charter only on 4 March 1866. That date is taken to be the formal creation of the Yugoslav Academy of Sciences and Arts (JAZU), the first of its kind in Southeastern Europe. That same year, the Croatian diet appointed JAZU's first sixteen members. Bishop Strossmayer was named its patron and the historian Canon Franjo Rački its first president. Under the leadership of Strossmayer and Rački, the academy gradually developed into an important scientific institution and one of the leading centers of learning in Southeastern Europe. It had been given the name "Yugoslav" because Strossmayer hoped the academy would help in the scientific and cultural enlightenment of other South Slav peoples and nurture their cultural cooperation. Throughout its existence, however, the academy remained a Croatian institution.

In 1867 the academy began publishing its official organ, *Rad* (Work). In 1887 the first volume of *Ljetopis* (Annals), which became a regular annual publication of the Academy and its administrative herald, was published. Because the study of Croatian history was one of its central tasks, the Academy began in 1868 to publish the *Monumenta spectantia historiam Slavorum meridionalium* (Annals for the Study of the History of the South Slavs), in which were published lengthy archival documents. To date, over 52 volumes have been published. In 1869 the academy began publishing *Starine* (Antiquities), as well as to circulate shorter archival fragments from Croatian history and literature. There followed a series of related tomes, such as *Monumenta Ragusina* (Dubrovnik Annals), *Spomenici Hrvatske krajine* (Annals of the Croatian Frontier), and works of older Croatian historians under the title of *Scriptores* (Historical Writers). In the series entitled *Monumenta historico-iuridica* (Historical-Juridical Annals), the academy began publishing statutes of the Dalmatian towns and medieval laws originally issued in the Croatian language (13 vols.). In 1896 the Academy began publishing the *Zbornik za narodni život i običaje Južnih Slavena* (Anthology of National Life and Customs of the South Slavs); over fifty volumes have been published. In 1877 Bishop Strossmayer initiated the project of building a palace for the academy in central Zagreb, which would house his gallery of art works; it was completed in 1880. In 1884 the Academy received a gift of 256 art pieces from Strossmayer. During World War II, the Academy was known as the HAZU, but from 1947 to 1991 it was again known as JAZU. Following Croatia's secession from Yugoslavia in June 1991, the academy changed its name to HAZU.

Another important cultural institution is Matica Hrvatska (Croat Literary-Cultural Foundation). Founded in February 1842 as Matica Ilirska (Illyrian Literary-Cultural Foundation), during the period of the Croat national awakening, it was renamed Matica Hrvatska in 1874. At the time it served primarily as a publishing house to enable publication of books and related periodicals in Croatian. These works were deemed important for the nation's cultural revival and the promotion of its cultural heritage. Its creation was prompted by the threat posed at the time by cultural Magyarization and was modelled on existing Maticas among the Czechs and Serbs. The first president of Matica Ilirska, Count Janko Drašković, remarked in his inaugural speech that the main task "of our society is to promote science and language of our own national language and to educate our youth on a national basis" (Matica Hrvatska). In 1869 the Matica began publishing the first fiction newspaper of Croatian literature, entitled *Vijenac* (Wreath), which it publishes to this day.

Following the creation of JAZU (i.e., HAZU) in 1866, the Matica worked closely with the Academy to publish literary and scientific books. Matica soon became the largest publishing house in Croatia, with the purpose of promoting books that were deemed to have cultural merit and that promoted scientific advancement. The main literary editions in Croatia were regular editions published by Matica and its magazine *Vijenac*. The Croat writer and essayist Antun Barac, who also served as Matica's president in the late 1920s, once noted that "Matica published almost everything that was of value in Croatia or, that is to say, the history of Matica is in some way the history of Croatian culture" (Matica Hrvatska). In fact, almost every Croat writer and poet of note in the nineteenth century published his works through Matica.

After World War I, in the newly founded Kingdom of Serbs, Croats, and Slovenes (Yugoslavia), Matica's role as cultural institution and publishing house underwent important changes. It became even more politicized. Although the intellectuals who ran the organization originally welcomed the new state, the experience of political centralism bred resistance and opposition in the cultural sphere. Despite its financial problems in the 1920s, after 1928 Matica began publishing a number of new periodicals, the most important of which was *Hrvatska revija* (Croatian Review). After World War II, Matica suffered because of the political restrictions imposed by the new communist authorities. But the greatest single publishing accomplishment of Matica was launched in 1962; it was known as *Five Centuries of Croatian Literature,* and it presented the historical and artistic development of Croatian literature from the Middle Ages to the present.

However, only after the cautious political liberalization of the late 1960s was Matica again able to publish under more favorable circumstances. In fact, during the late 1960s Matica became the focal point for the reformist and nationalist movement in Croatia, which is known as the Croatian Spring (1966–1971). In 1967 Matica presented a declaration on the name and status of the Croatian literary language. The signatories to the declaration argued for the equality of all four literary languages existing in Yugoslavia at the time: Slovenian, Croatian, Serbian, and Macedonian. What they opposed in particular was the designation "Serbo-Croatian," which they claimed enabled the Serbian literary language to be imposed on Croats and Bosnian Muslims. The declaration was an attack against linguistic and literary unitarism. Most of the signatories were purged from Matica following the collapse of the Croatian Spring. In 1972 Matica was temporarily suppressed by the Communist authorities, and many of its most prominent members, like Šime Djodan, Vlado Gotovac, Franjo Tudjman, Marko Veselica, to name only a few, were imprisoned because of their political and nationalist views. Following the democratic transition in Croatia in 1989–1990, the Matica and its branch offices were fully restored. Today, Matica Hrvatska has more than 120 branches in Croatia, Bosnia-Hercegovina, and other countries.

MUSEUMS

The visitor to Croatia has the option of visiting any number of excellent museums. The Trakošćan Castle was built in the thirteenth century in what was then part of Croatia's system of defensive fortifications against the Ottoman Turks. It was a rather small observation fortress for monitoring the road from Ptuj to Bednja Valley.

The Archeological Museum of Istria is located in Pula and was founded in 1902 as the Pula Municipal Museum. The discovery of local stone, ceramic, and metal objects led to its creation. In 1925 the Municipal Museum was merged with two other regional museums to form the current institution. It is a rich repository of classical monuments and other objects. The museum was first opened to visitors in 1930, when Pula (as well as Istria) was part of Italy. The museum reopened in 1949 as the Archaeological Museum of Istria, which was now part of Croatia (Yugoslavia), with some slight changes introduced in some of the collections. Systematic work was done to restore part of the archaeological material that was returned from Italy in 1961. In 1968 a collection of stone monuments was set up in the refurbished rooms and halls on the ground floor of the museum and in 1973 followed the opening of the prehistoric collection exhibition halls on the first floor and the classical Roman and medieval collections on the second floor of the museum. The exhibition halls are constantly enriched with new finds from archaeological sites throughout Istria, including prehistoric caves, hill-forts, and necropolises, Roman commercial complexes, buildings, and cemeteries, and sacral objects dating from the early Christian and Byzantine periods.

The oldest museum in Croatia, the Split Archaeological Museum was founded in 1820 by the municipal authorities of Zadar, then the capital of Dalmatia. The original museum building was erected in 1821 next to the eastern walls of Diocletian's Palace, but soon became too small to house the growing number of monuments. The present-day home of the Archaeological Museum was built in 1914 and opened to the public only in 1922. It holds some 150,000 artifacts dating from prehistoric times to the early medieval period. Of special interest is the collection of over 6,000 stone inscriptions from Salona and the collection of Hellenic ceramic objects, Roman glass, ancient clay lamps (around 1,600), and bone and metal articles, as well as the collection of gems. In addition, the museum houses an extensive collection of ancient and medieval coins (over 70,000) and a rich library with an archive. The new permanent display opened in 1999.

The Dubrovnik Museums were formed in February 1872 with the foundation of the Dubrovnik Regional Museum on the initiative of the chamber of commerce. A valuable natural history collection represented the nucleus of the museum to which a cultural, a historical, and an archaeological collection were added. In 1932 the museum collections were moved to St. John's Castle, and in 1940 the collection of stone monuments and the ethnological collection were relocated to what was formerly Rupe Granary. The cultural history collection was moved to the Rector's Palace in 1948. The Dubrovnik Museums constitute today a regional institution made up of six distinct institutions: the Archaeological Museum, the Ethnographic Museum, the Cultural-Historical Museum, the Maritime Museum, the Modern History Museum, and the Marin Držić Home. All six museums are under the unified management of the Dubrovnik Museums. The rich museum holdings are displayed in four locations: the Rector's Palace, the Rupe Granary, St. John's Castle, and the Marin Držić Home. However, neither the Archaeological nor the Modern History Museum has a permanent location where it can display its holdings.

The Museum of Modern Art was founded in Rijeka in 1948. Although it houses the works of a number of twentieth-century Croatian and foreign artists, most of its collection is composed of the works of artists who lived in Rijeka from the late nineteenth to the middle of the twentieth century. Because of the lack of space there is no permanent exhibition; the museum's five collections are exhibited occasionally.

The Gallery of Fine Arts in Osijek holds some twelve to fourteen exhibitions annually. These exhibitions are diverse and thematically range from the historical to the contemporary. The curators organize some of these exhibitions while others are on loan from Croatian museums. At least once a year the museum organizes an exhibition of a modern artist from Osijek, as well as an exhibition of an artist who worked in Osijek and contributed to the promotion of art in the city.

The Mimara Museum in Zagreb is named after Ante Topić Mimara (1898–1987), who donated his art collection of over 3,700 pieces to the museum. Based in large

Archaeology Museum in Split. (Hans Georg Roth/Corbis)

part on his donation, the museum has become one of the richest and most versatile art collections in Croatia. The museum's collections span three millennia with works of art from virtually every style, epoch, and civilization. The archaeological section consists of nearly two hundred pieces dating from prehistoric times (Egypt, Mesopotamia, Persia, Greece, pre-Columbian America, Rome, and early medieval Europe). The Far East collection consists of over 350 exhibits from China, Japan, Cambodia, Indonesia, and India. Another important collection consists of over 550 glass pieces, representing the development of glass production from ancient Egypt to the late nineteenth century. There is also a textile collection consisting of eighty carpets manufactured between the sixteenth and nineteenth centuries in Persia, Morocco, and Turkey. There is also a collection of household utensils and vessels consisting of more than a thousand pieces and made from various materials and dating from the early medieval period to the nineteenth century. There are more than two hundred sculptures from ancient Rome and Greece, over two dozen Russian, Armenian, and Greek Orthodox religious icons, eighty Italian Renaissance paintings, sixty paintings by the Dutch masters, fifty by the Flemish masters, and more than thirty by the Spanish masters, among others. Also represented are works by Belgian, Swiss, German, Austrian, Czech, Hungarian, and Russian painters.

The Klovićevi Dvori Gallery in Zagreb holds roughly fifty art collections of the broadest cultural and national importance. The gallery is among the most important Croatian institutions of its kind. The gallery is housed in the former Jesuit Collegium, which was transformed in 1982 into a gallery space. Although it holds a large variety of exhibitions, including those of contemporary art, most of its exhibitions deal with Croatian national treasures. Among the more popular exhibitions it has organized are *Treasures of the Zagreb Cathedral* (1983), *The Written Word in Croatia* (1985), *The Golden Age of Dubrovnik* (1987), and *A Thousand Years of Croatian Sculpture* (1991), among others.

The Zagreb Municipal Museum was founded in 1907 by the Družba Braće hrvatskog zmaja (The Brethren of the Croatian Dragon Society). Until World War II, it was located in the Art Pavilion, but in 1945 the museum moved into a larger building in Zagreb's Upper Town. The permanent display presents in chronological order the development of Zagreb to the beginning of the nineteenth century.

The Croatian Museum of Naive Art opened in 1952 but was known at the time as the Peasant Art Gallery. In 1956 it became the Gallery of Primitive Art and in 1994 it adopted its current name. It purports to be the first museum of naive art in the world. Today it has approximately 1,500 items in its holdings (paintings, sculptures, drawings, and prints), mostly by Croat naive artists. The focus is on artists belonging to the Hlebine School of naive art. Some works of major international naive artists are also held by the museum.

The Archaeological Museum in Zagreb has a number of permanent collections and exhibitions, among which are included stone monuments from the Greek and Roman periods. The museum also contains an Egyptian collection and a numismatic collection, one of the largest in Europe.

Zagreb's Ethnographic Museum was established in 1919 and is located in a remarkable Secession building, built around 1903, that once used to seat the Crafts Hall. It was established in 1919 upon the initiative of Salamon Berger, textile merchant and industrialist, originally from the Slovak Republic. He donated to the Museum one that is among the first and largest folk costumes and textile collections. The Berger Collection, the Croatian National Museum Collections, and the Museum of Arts and Crafts ethnographic collections constituted the museum's initial holdings, today including around 80,000 items.

The holdings include predominantly Croatian ethnographic heritage, classified in two principal groups: Croatian Folk Costumes and Selected Items of Popular Art and Handicraft.

The items associated with Croatia have been divided into three cultural zones (Pannonian, Dinaric, and Adriatic). The non-European cultures department includes traditional culture items of the peoples of Africa, Asia, Latin America, Australia, and Oceania. The materials are associated mostly with explorations conducted toward the turn of the century by Dragutin Lerman and Mirko and Stjepan Seljan. It is constantly being enriched through donations by artists, explorers, and missionaries.

Ever since its establishment, the museum employed or was managed by renowned Croatian ethnologists and museologists, such as Vladimir Tkalčić, Milovan Gavazzi, and Jelka Radauš-Ribarić. The museum's collection on permanent display dates back to 1972, including 2,750 exhibits.

The Museum of Contemporary Art in Zagreb was established in 1954 with the aim of promoting and documenting contemporary art events, styles, and phenomena. The largest part of the museum's collection consists of the works of Croat artists after 1950, although there is a smaller part dating back to the first half of the twentieth century.

The origins of the Croatian Natural History Museum in Zagreb date to 1829, when Ljudevit Gaj, the founder of the Illyrianist movement, first raised the idea of such a museum. In 1836 the Croatian diet proposed the formation of a "Friends of the National Illyrian Learned Society" and a museum within its framework. But the museum was not founded until 1846, when the Zagreb municipal authorities purchased a palace in the Upper Town, which became a National Home. It immediately housed museum objects. In 1867 the museum was formally proclaimed a national institution, on the initiative of Bishop Strossmayer of Djakovo, and placed under the care of the Yugoslav Academy. The museum contains a wealth of information on the natural history of Croatia (zoology, botany, geology, paleontology, and mineralogy) and contains many important scientific collections and exhibitions.

ECONOMIC DEVELOPMENT

For the better part of the modern era, Croatia has been an agrarian society in which a majority of the population derived its livelihood from farming and related sectors. At the beginning of the nineteenth century, most Croats were peasants and only a small number lived in towns and could be classified as professionals, artisans, merchants, or nobles. Given the agrarian nature of the Croatian economy, the dominant social institution in Croatia-Slavonia was the *zadruga,* or extended family household. Composed of two or three generations of a single family, the extended household was both a social and economic unit. It provided for joint ownership of land and the tools used to work it and a joint division of goods. This institution predominated in a society where market forces were not yet pronounced and the system of land tenure could be compared to feudalism. Generally speaking, in Croatia-Slavonia peasants were still bound to the soil and met their obligations to their lords through the *zadruga.* Serfdom was abolished only in 1848, although in the military frontier it had not formally existed at all. In Dalmatia the small middle class of the towns was culturally Italian. Since the land in Dalmatia was not as fertile as in Croatia-Slavonia, much of the population was active in fishing and the merchant marine. However, most peasants continued to farm the land under sharecropping arrangements and feudal regulations, cultivating mainly olives and grapevines.

The modernization process, measured in terms of industrialization and urbanization, was initiated in the nineteenth century but would remain sluggish and uneven to World War II. With the abolition of serfdom, the introduction of private property, and a money economy, market forces began to play a leading role in socioeconomic change. The agrarian sector of the economy began to change and a nascent industrial sector was born in the second half of the nineteenth century. The main industries were food and agricultural raw materials processing. Lumber played a particularly prominent role in this regard. However, of all the lands of the Habsburg monarchy, Croatia-Slavonia still had in 1890 the second highest (after Dalmatia) proportion of population (84.6 percent) deriving its livelihood from agriculture. The bourgeoisie and industrial proletariat were numerically and socially weak as well as politically insignificant. Urbanization had hardly advanced since the mid-nineteenth century; in 1910 only 8.5 percent of the population of Croatia-Slavonia lived in urban settlements. At the time, Zagreb was still a small provincial town with a population of roughly 75,000 inhabitants. The slow rate of economic modernization in Croatia-Slavonia in the quarter century before World War I, when combined with rural overpopulation, created a situation where emigration became endemic. In 1850 Croatia-Slavonia had a population of roughly 1.6 million; by 1914, that figure had risen to nearly 2.7 million. In roughly the same period (1840–1910), Dalmatia's population grew from 399,000 to 646,000. Between 1899 and 1913, nearly a quarter of a million persons emigrated from Croatia-Slavonia, accounting for over 6 percent of the total population. According to one estimate, between 1880 and 1914, roughly 400,000 persons emigrated from Croatia-Slavonia, Dalmatia, and Istria.

In 1918 Croatia became part of Yugoslavia. In the interwar era, Yugoslavia was one of Europe's least developed countries. This period brought little improvement in the way of either urbanization or industrialization, although the process of modernization undoubtedly intensified. A large segment of the Croatian population still lived at subsistence levels, dependent on small, inefficient peasant farms. A land reform was introduced in 1919, but it was directed mainly against the German and Hungarian landowners in eastern Croatia, Slovenia, and Vojvodina. Croatia remained a land of peasant smallholders; the country still suffered from rural overpopulation, which the land reform failed to address. Economic growth was modest. Industry advanced only slowly, given the weak internal market, few resources, and unskilled labor force. In 1938 per capita income in Yugoslavia was 30 percent below the world average.

The partition of Yugoslavia during World War II destroyed all semblance of normal economic life. In all Yugoslavia, it is estimated that over 50 percent of livestock and 80 percent of equipment were destroyed or confiscated during the occupation. The communications network was virtually destroyed; over half the railroads and rolling stock was demolished. Inflation was rampant, and barter became the prime means for transacting business. The most devastating blow to Yugoslavia fell on its peoples: approximately 1.1 million people of all nationalities were killed, 10.8 percent of the population; nearly a third of all deaths occurred in Croatia. The occupation and war had devastated both the agricultural and small industrial sectors. By the end of 1946, Yugoslav national income was restored to its 1938 level.

Only after World War II did Croatia experience a rapid industrialization and urbanization. The country's socioeconomic structure changed profoundly as a result. This change mirrored the wider social and economic changes in Yugoslavia and Eastern Europe, brought on as a result of the establishment of Communist rule. The Communist Party of Yugoslavia (KPJ, Komunistička partija Jugoslavije) was strictly Marxist-Leninist in economic outlook, fiercely loyal to Stalin, and painfully aware of its country's relative socioeconomic backwardness. To remedy this situation, that is, in order to expand the small industrial base, which was located mainly in Slovenia and Croatia, and transform the agrarian economy, the KPJ resorted to a command economy on the Soviet model for rapid industrial development. Following the example of the Soviet Constitution of 1936, the Yugoslav Constitution of 1946 initiated the process of bringing all sectors of the economy under state control. At the core of this program, encapsulated in the first Five-Year Plan (1947–1951), were the nationalization of industry, redistribution of private land, and collectivization of agriculture. All mineral wealth, power resources, means of communication, and foreign trade were nationalized. By 1948, all domestic and foreign-owned capital, excluding some retail trade and small craft industries and most of agriculture, had been nationalized and brought into the social sector. The industrialization plan relied on high taxation, fixed prices, reparations, Soviet credits, and export of foodstuffs and raw materials to generate additional capital.

The Communist authorities also instituted a land reform. In August 1945, under the new land reform law, over one million hectares of land were confiscated from private owners and institutions; most of this property formerly belonged to banks, churches, monasteries, absentee landlords, private companies, and the expelled German minority. A state-controlled land fund was established to hold and redistribute the land to peasants and state-operated farms. Local authorities set the exact amount of land peasants could retain, within the state parameters of twenty to thirty-five hectares. Forced collectivization of agriculture was instituted only in January 1949, bringing the last privately owned portion of the economy under state control. At the program's inception, 94 percent of Yugoslav agricultural land was privately owned; by the height of the collectivization drive in 1950, nearly 96 percent was under the control of the social sector. Yugoslav planners expected that rapid collectivization and mechanization of agriculture would increase food production, improve the people's standard of living, and release peasants to work in industry. The result, however, was a poorly conceived program that was abandoned three years later. Between 1949 and 1951, the Yugoslav authorities induced nearly two million peasants to join roughly 6,900 collective or state-run farms. The campaign caused a decrease in agricultural output and the use of coercion eroded peasant support for the authorities. Since Croatia, together with Slovenia and the province of Vojvodina, had the most developed agrarian sector, collectivization proved more painful than elsewhere. Peasant resistance and a 1950 drought stalled and then killed the collectivization drive, the cancellation of which was announced in 1951.

By the time the first Five-Year Plan was officially completed, Yugoslavia was burdened with an oversized balance of payments deficit, significant foreign debt, low labor productivity, and inefficient use of capital. In the short term, however, the centrally directed planning approach managed to mobilize national resources to achieve rapid postwar development. As inefficient as the system may have been, the relatively high rate of investment in the first Five-Year Plan ensured increased output during the second Five-Year Plan (1957–1960). Throughout the 1950s, industrial output rose faster in Yugoslavia, in both per capita and total output, than in almost any other European country. Because of Communist modernization, urbanization and industrialization intensified rapidly. For example, the population of the Croatian capital, Zagreb, grew from roughly 180,000 in 1931 to roughly 280,000 around 1950 to nearly 800,000 in 1991.

A movement toward greater market freedom spurred economic reforms in the 1960s. During that decade, Yugoslav Communist authorities instituted economic policies unknown in the Soviet Bloc, which contributed greatly to the economic development of Croatia and Yugoslavia. Economic reformers were able to make a case for decentralized control over investment policies and a greater role for market forces as the solution to Yugoslavia's long-term economic development problems. The 1963 constitution introduced a system of "market socialism." Decisionmaking was decentralized, the federal government further loosened its control over investment, prices, and incomes, and market forces were allowed greater play. The so-called workers' self-management system thereby received more power and responsibility in the economic development of the country. The authorities now emphasized policies that increased personal consumption, production growth, and labor productivity by loosening government controls on wages and increasing investment in the production of energy, steel, chemicals, and capital equipment. Particular attention went to investment in the less developed republics and to mechanization of agriculture. A more liberal trade policy devalued the currency (the Yugoslav dinar) and reduced tariffs and import restrictions. The authorities permitted workers to emigrate to Western Europe, especially West Germany, as guest laborers; this policy brought substantial hard currency reinvestments to Yugoslavia and relieved labor surpluses at home. By loosening border restrictions, the Yugoslav authorities opened the country's scenic beaches to Western tourists, who increasingly provided a reliable source of hard currency from the 1960s on. It was in this period that Croatia's Dalmatian coast became a popular tourist destination for many Europeans. Hard currency remittances from tourism and guest workers became important sources of relief for Yugoslavia's weak balance of payments, especially when other parts of the economy declined in the 1970s and 1980s.

The new system of market socialism was enshrined in roughly thirty laws issued in July 1965. One of the primary objectives of the new legislation was to allow economic enterprises to keep a greater share of their earned income, much of which had previously gone to the state. To achieve this goal, the government lowered taxes, limited state control of investments, removed price controls on some goods, devalued the dinar, and reduced customs duties and export subsidies. Whatever the failings of the system, growth was experienced. Between 1954 and 1965, gross industrial output increased at an annual rate of 12.2 percent; industrial employment, 6.6 percent; social sector employment, 5.9 percent; exports 11.7 percent; and fixed investments 9.2 percent. After 1965 (and well into the 1970s and 1980s), these rates steadily declined because of growing inflation, balance of payments deficits, and high unemployment.

Nonetheless, on the eve of Yugoslavia's dissolution, Croatia was, next to Slovenia, the most industrialized, urbanized, and prosperous of the Yugoslav republics. Its economy and social structure had undergone a tremendous transformation since 1945. Moreover, given the greater economic liberalism of Yugoslav communism, Croatia (like Yugoslavia) was ahead of the East Bloc countries in terms of wealth and per capita income. However, following the collapse of communism, Croatia's economic development was retarded by two closely related factors: the war in former Yugoslavia of 1991–1995 with its attendant damage to infrastructure (bridges, factories, commercial buildings, and houses), costs related to refugees and displaced persons, and disruption of old economic ties; and the troubled transition from a communist (planned) economy to a market-oriented one, affected by the still evident legacy of communist mismanagement of the economy.

In 1991 over 80 percent of Croatian economic production was in state hands while only 18 percent was generated by the nascent private sector. At that time the most significant sectors of the Croatian economy were industry (composing 32.8 percent of domestic product), trade (22.5 percent), communication (11.4 percent), and agriculture and fishing (11.4 percent). In industry, the most important areas were food processing (17 percent), textiles (8.1 percent), and machine production (8.0 percent). By 2001, Croatia's gross domestic product (GDP) was US$20.7 billion. Its per capita GDP was US$4,726.

CURRENCY AND BANKING

The legal currency of Croatia is the kuna; its domestic symbol is *Kn* but its international abbreviation is *HRK*. The kuna consists of 100 smaller units called lipa *(lp)*. The name kuna, meaning "marten," has its origin in the medieval era, when the marten's fur was used as a unit of trade. The first known use of the kuna dates from 1256. The word "lipa" means linden (tree). The kuna has been the new form of currency since 1994, when it replaced the Croatian dinar. Historical Croatian personalities are featured on one side of the kuna note, with famous Croatian landmarks on the reverse. The 5 kuna note features ban Petar Zrinski and Duke Fran Krsto Frankopan, two seventeenth-century Croat nobles, with the Varaždin Fortress on the reverse. The 10 kuna note features Juraj Dobrila, a noted Croatian bishop who promoted Croatian cultural rights and advanced the Croatian language. On the reverse is found the Roman Amphitheater at Pula. The 20 kuna note features ban Josip Jelačić, the military hero of the 1848 revolution in Croatia, and the Eltz Castle in Vukovar with the Vučedol Dove. The 50 kuna note features Ivan Gundulić, perhaps the greatest Croat poet of the seventeenth century, and the city of Dubrovnik as its landmark. The 100 kuna note features Ivan Mažuranić, the first nonnoble person to hold the title of ban, and the Church of St. Vitus in Rijeka. The 200 kuna note features Stjepan Radić, the founder of the Croat Peasant Party. On the reverse is found the Town Command in Osijek. The 500 kuna note bears the image of Marko Marulić, the greatest Croat poet of the fifteenth and sixteenth centuries, and Diocletian's Palace in Split. Finally, the 1,000 kuna note features Ante Starčević, the leader of the Party of (Croatian State) Right, with a monument to King Tomislav and the Zagreb Cathedral.

As of 2000, Croatia had forty-four banks and a National Bank, which serves as the country's central bank. In 2001 the National Bank's foreign reserve was US$4.61 billion. According to the most recent Law on Banks (1998), there are few restrictions for foreign investors who wish to form a bank or invest in the banking sector. The minimum stock capital needed to establish a bank is between 20 and 60 million HRK, depending on the nature of its operations. Furthermore, newly formed banks have a time limit imposed on them for performing certain business operations. They must operate for at least three years before being allowed to collect deposits and savings from citizens in both domestic and foreign currency. After a bank has been issued a license by the Croatian National Bank and registered with the Commercial Court, it becomes a legal business entity. A single shareholder may control more than 10 percent of the shares with voting rights only with the prior approval of the Croatian National Bank. Foreign banks are permitted to establish subsidiaries in Croatia.

Of the forty-four banks in Croatia in 2000, twenty-one were owned completely or largely by domestic shareholders, while twenty were owned completely or largely by foreign entities. A total of three banks were owned completely or largely by the state. Although most of the banks were Croatian-owned, foreign-owned banks controlled 83.7 percent of all banking assets, while the figures for Croatian and state-owned banks were 10.2 and 6.1 percent, respectively. By far the two largest and most important Croatian banks are the Zagrebačka banka (Zagreb Bank) and Privredna banka (Economic Bank) with total stock capital of 3.46 billion HRK and 2.39 billion HRK, respectively. Their total stock capital exceeds the combined total capital of the next eight largest Croatian banks. In 2000 these two banks had total assets exceeding 10 billion HRK each. The Croatian Bank for Reconstruction and Development (HBOR) is the first investment bank established by the state, which in turn guarantees its obligations. This bank provides credit financing for the reconstruction and development of the Croatian economy; rebuilding of apartments, houses, and infrastructure; exports; and insurance of exports against noncommercial risks.

The use of debit cards and automatic teller machines (ATMs) is now common, as Croatian banks have modernized many of their technologies and operations. Over 2.4 million debit and credit cards were in use in 2001. There were in the same year 848 ATMs operating in the country. The first ATM was installed in January 1996. The Croatian ATM network, linking all Croatian banks using debit and credit cards, is known as MBNET.

There are two securities markets in Croatia: the Zagreb Stock Exchange and the Varaždin Over the Counter Market. More than fifty brokerage houses perform transactions on these two markets, which are supervised and regulated by the Securities Commission of the Republic of Croatia. Total foreign investments in Croatia from 1993 until September 2001 amounted to US$5.92 billion. The three largest sources of direct foreign investment in this period were Austria with US$1.74 billion, Germany with US$1.19 billion, and the United States with US$1.18 billion. The European Bank for Reconstruction and Development (EBRD) has invested only US$101.8 million.

AGRICULTURE, FISHING, FOOD, AND TOBACCO INDUSTRIES

In 2000 Croatia had 842 companies registered in the food, beverage, and tobacoo industry; these sectors employed roughly 45,000 workers, or 17 percent, of the workforce in the manufacturing sector. A few large companies play a dominant role in the Croatian market, such as Podravka in Koprivnica and Franck and Kraš, both located in Zagreb. Despite the importance of this sector to the Croatian economy, in the 1990s production declined in most sectors (especially wheat flour, bread, canned fish, condiments, sugar, and spirits) or remained stagnant (such as pasta, canned vegetables, concentrated soups, and biscuits). Only in a few sectors (fruit juices, cheese, and cigarettes) has there been a substantial increase. Agricultural and food products compose approximately 18 percent of the total export and import market. However, the export value of this industry has declined steadily. In the period between 1997 and 2001, exports of food and tobacco products declined from US$460 million to US$366 million. In the same period, imports declined from US$636 million to US$581 million.

Croatia has a total of 3.15 million hectares of agricultural land, 63.5 percent of which is cultivated and the rest pastoral. The vast majority (81.5 percent) of the cultivated land is privately owned. Cattle raising has always played an important role in Slavonia. Over 80 percent of livestock is privately owned. Agriculture and fishing generate 8.1 percent of Croatian GDP. The production of food, beverages, and tobacco generates 20.6 percent of Croatian GDP (gross domestic product).

The Croatian food industry includes some of the most successful companies in Croatia: twelve out of the fifty Croatian companies with the highest revenues in 2000 were producers of food, beverages, and tobacco. The major export products of these companies are Vegeta (food seasoning), biscuits and wafers, chocolate, canned fish, soups, olive oil, cigarettes, beer, and alcoholic beverages. The wine-making industry is also an important sector. The total area used for vineyards amounts to 59,000 hectares. Thirty larger wine-making companies, thirty-five production cooperatives, and about 250 family businesses represent wine production. Wines made of indigenous grape varieties are becoming increasingly popular on the European and world markets.

Production of Selected Products, 1996–2000

Type	*Amount*	*1996*	*1998*	*2000*
Cereals	'000s tons	2,760	3,207	2,768
Wheat	'000s tons	741	1,020	1,032
Corn	'000s tons	1,886	1,982	1,526
Grapes	'000s tons	373	421	354
Cattle	'000s heads	461	443	427
Pigs	'000s heads	1,197	1,166	1,233
Poultry	'000s heads	10,993	9,959	11,256
Milk	Millions of liters	593	663	607
Eggs	Millions	848	818	774

During the first half of the 1990s, agricultural production witnessed a substantial decline associated with the war in Croatia (1991–1995) and the transition to a market economy. The Croatian government has throughout this period provided subsidies to most sectors of agriculture in an effort to revive production and increase incomes. Although Croatia has now achieved self-sufficiency in the production of wheat, corn, poultry, eggs, and wine, some sectors of agriculture remain well below their prewar levels.

Fishing, fish farming, and processing have traditionally been an important source of income, in particular for the population of Dalmatia and the islands. In 2000 there were fourteen factories for fish processing in Croatia, which produced 15,000 tons of various fish products; three quarters of this total is canned sardines. The 2000 output of freshwater fish amounted to about 4,800 tons, and saltwater fish and other seafood to about 24,000 tons. Large quantities of fish are exported.

Aquaculture (fish and shellfish breeding) is another important sector of the fishing industry. The breeding of freshwater fish is centered in continental Croatia, where roughly 12,000 hectares of carp ponds are allocated for such production. An additional 30,000 square meters is allocated to trout ponds.

Sea-fish, Fresh-fish, and Shellfish Breeding

Type (in tons)	*1997*	*1998*	*1999*	*2000*
Carp	2,607	2,299	1,993	2,013
Trout	453	296	471	680
Sea Bass and Gilthead	1,500	1,747	1,750	2,100
Tuna	507	906	970	1,200
Mussels	790	900	1,100	1,111
Oysters	30	53	52	37

Since the dissolution of Yugoslavia, this sector of the Croatian economy has been reoriented toward the foreign market. Tuna fish alone account for 64 percent of all fishing-related exports. The most important markets are Austria, Bosnia-Hercegovina, Macedonia, and Serbia-Montenegro.

Export of Fish and Fish Products

Type (in tons)	*1996*	*1997*	*1998*	*1999*	*2000*
Live fish	1,137	700	790	623	456
Fresh and refrigerated fish	4,642	8,615	6,134	6,260	6,076
Frozen fish	73	282	57	354	611
Fish fillets	29	37	13	6	6
Dried, salted, smoked fish	19	49	20	385	1,401
Crustaceans, mollusks	1,441	2,126	977	1,208	1,126
Canned fish	9,796	12,952	11,122	8,859	8,565

Import of Fish and Fish Products

Type (in tons)	*1996*	*1997*	*1998*	*1999*	*2000*
Live fish	16	31	151	38	341
Fresh and refrigerated fish	16	474	116	93	35
Frozen fish	3,493	4,162	4,090	5,800	14,879
Fish fillets	2,020	2,958	2,388	1,862	1,504
Dried, salted, smoked fish	312	292	247	236	179
Crustaceans, mollusks	4,507	4,233	3,795	3,727	4,474
Canned fish	2,756	1,301	2,067	2,632	3,936

INDUSTRIAL PRODUCTION

The Croatian industrial sector has been in a state of flux since the dissolution of former Yugoslavia. Although the industrial sector has undergone some privatization and a reorientation of export markets toward the countries of the EU, as a whole it has not advanced rapidly. The industrial sector currently represents about 20 percent of Croatia's GDP. In 1999 the value of industry's production level was estimated to be around 93 billion HRK (or approximately US$13.0 billion) with 293,000 employees, representing 27 percent of Croatia's workforce. Industrial goods account for 97 percent of Croatia's total exports.

TOURISM

Croatia has long been one of the most important tourist destinations on the Mediterranean and boasts a long tradition in tourism. The advantages of Croatian tourism are primarily a well-preserved natural environment (a beautiful coast, more than 1,000 islands, eight national parks, and ten nature parks), cultural and historic heritage (including numerous cultural monuments protected by UNESCO, such as Diocletian's Palace in Split, the towns of Trogir and Dubrovnik, and Euphrasian's Basilica in Poreč), a mild Mediterranean climate, and its vicinity to European markets. A variety of forms of tourism are offered in Croatia, from summer and nautical tourism (44 marinas and roughly 15,000 berths) to health tourism and hunting and fishing. The most important tourist regions are Istria, Dalmatia, and the cities of Dubrovnik and Zagreb. In 2001 Croatia had 160,000 hotel beds and beds in tourist facilities, 306,000 beds in private accommodations, and 180,000 places in campsites. That same year, Croatia had 6,544,217 foreign tourists who made 38.3 million overnight stays. The majority of these tourists were from Germany (1,299,729) and Italy (1,059,810), with Slovenia, the Czech Republic, and Austria occupying the next three spots. The average tourist stay lasted five days; foreign tourists averaged six and domestic tourists four days. The largest number of tourists and overnight stays in 2001 were recorded in Istria (37 percent), Kvarner (23 percent), Dalmatia (27 percent), Dubrovnik (7 percent), and Zagreb (2 percent). The revenue generated by international tourism is of great importance to the Croatian

The Palace of Diocletian faces the harbor in Split. (Jonathan Blair/Corbis)

economy. According to the Croatian National Bank, international tourism revenue amounted to US$3.3 billion in 2001, or 16.3 percent of GDP.

Revenue (USD mil) from International Tourism and Percentage Share of GDP, 1995–2001

	1995	*1997*	*1999*	*2001*
Revenue	1,345.9	2,529.8	2,493.4	3,335.0
Share	7.2	12.6	12.4	16.3

In 2001 there were 559 registered travel agencies and tour operators in Croatia. The travel industry employed approximately 3,300 people that year. In 2001 Zagreb hosted 148 conferences with more than 25,000 participants.

BUILDING AND CONSTRUCTION

The building and construction sector remains a significant industry in Croatia. In 2001 the sector employed 62,773 persons in 11,762 registered companies, up from 819 companies in 1990. The total value of construction contracts carried out abroad amounted to US$142.7 million. In 2000 around 12,000 apartments with a total area of approximately 1 million square meters were built. Despite the overall importance of the construction industry, whether measured as a share in the total value of GDP or the total number of persons employed, it has been steadily declining since 1990. In 1990 a total of 118,700 workers, or 7.6 percent of all employees in Croatia, were employed in construction. By 1999, the number of persons employed in construction had fallen to 71,302, or 6.7 percent of all employees in Croatia. In 1999 the value of completed construction works amounted to 10.557 million HRK. Work on road infrastructure composed 41.2 percent of the total value of the construction industry in 1999, followed by nonresidential buildings at 26.4 percent, residential buildings at 16.3 percent, pipelines and communications at 13 percent, industrial sites at 1.5 percent, and 1.6 percent on other sectors.

SHIPBUILDING

Croatia has a long history of shipbuilding and seafaring. In 2001 Croatia produced fifty-six ships, making it sixth in the world in production. According to the Global Orders Ledger, in that same year Croatia was ranked, in terms of deadweight (in tdw), fifth in the world at 2,784,930 tdw of ships contracted, behind South Korea, Japan, China, and

Poland. In 2000, the last year for which figures are available, Croatia generated 5.899 billion HRK in total income from the shipbuilding sector, which employed 13,952 persons. The shipbuilding industry has about a 10 percent share in export and about a 2 percent share in import in the commodity exchange with foreign countries. The shipbuilding industry composes a number of shipyards of varying size. The primary and largest shipyards are Uljanik (at Pula); 3. Maj, Viktor Lenac, and Kraljevica (all at Rijeka); Brodotrogir at Trogir; and Brodosplit at Split. There are eight secondary or midsized shipyards located at Pula (Tehnomont and Heli), Mali Lošinj (Lošinjska plovidba Brodogradilište), Krk (Punat), Ugljan (Wolf Lamjana), Murter (Brodogradilište Betina), Šibenik (Remontno brodogradilište Šibenik), and Vela Luka (Greben). There are also a number of tertiary shipyards and repair centers.

FOREIGN TRADE

Croatia's foreign trade is geared toward the European Union (EU). In 2001 Croatia's total exports amounted to US$4,659,286,000. Of this total, US$2,547,109,000 (or 54.7 percent) went to the countries of the EU. Another 12.1 percent (or US$565,682,000) of exports went to the seven countries of the Central European Free Trade Agreement (CEFTA), which includes Poland, the Czech Republic, Slovakia, Hungary, Slovenia, Romania, and Bulgaria. The remaining 33.2 percent of exports (US$1,546,494,000) went to other countries.

Croatia's total imports amounted to US$9,043,699,000. In all, 56.0 percent of all imports, with a value of US$5,060,711,000, originated from the EU zone. CEFTA countries accounted for 15.7 percent of all imports or US$1,420,220,000. All other countries accounted for the remaining 28.3 percent of imports (US$2,562,768,000). Croatia's ten most important trading partners in 2001 (in thousands of U.S. dollars), according to the Croatian Chamber of Commerce, were:

Country	*Exports*	*Percentage*	*Imports*	*Percentage*
Italy	1,104,447	23.7	1,524,139	16.9
Germany	688,877	14.8	1,546,726	17.1
Bosnia-Hercegovina	559,575	12.0	-	-
Slovenia	426,135	9.1	711,558	7.9
Austria	267,787	5.7	630,939	7.0
France	163,106	3.5	398,293	4.4
Yugoslavia	146,813	3.2	-	-
Liberia	115,075	2.5	-	-
United States	107,392	2.3	296,925	3.3
Russia	83,360	1.8	653,594	7.2

(continues)

Tugboats and wharves in the harbor city of Rijeka in Croatia. (Nik Wheeler/Corbis)

Country	*Exports*	*Percentage*	*Imports*	*Percentage*
Hungary	-	-	238,039	2.6
UK	-	-	225,115	2.5
Czech Republic	-	-	209,267	2.3
Total of Above	3,662,567	78.6	6,434,595	71.2
Total Exports/Imports	4,659,286	100	9,043,699	100

Exports by Main Branches of Industry (2001)

Branch of Industry (Manufacture/production of)	*Value (USD '000)*	*Percentage*
Transport equipment (shipbuilding)	730,381	15.7
Chemicals and chemical products	452,531	9.7
Wearing apparel	440,092	9.4
Petroleum derivatives	431,517	9.3
Food products and beverages	248,892	5.3
Electrical machinery	207,202	4.4
Nonmetallic products	193,922	5.3
Leather, footwear	172,848	3.7
Communication equipment	150,600	3.2
Fabricated metal goods	116,005	2.5
Total from above	3,143,990	67.5
Total exports	4,659,286	100

Imports by Main Branches of Industry (2001)

Branch of Industry	*Value*	*Percentage*
Petroleum derivatives	991,781	10.9
Transport equipment (shipbuilding)	458,160	5.1
Food products and beverages	413,052	4.6
Chemicals and chemical products	351,663	3.9
Wearing apparel	342,177	3.8
Electrical machinery and apparatus	257,402	2.8
Leather (tanning/dressing), footwear	144,130	1.6
Rubber and plastic products	129,301	1.4
Communication equipment	127,070	1.4
Metals	123,232	1.4
Total from above	3,337,968	36.9
Total imports	9,043,699	100

TRANSPORTATION

The transportation sector encompasses all areas of economic activity involving the transport of people and goods, whether by road, rail, water, air, or pipeline; auxiliary activities relating to this transport; postal services and telecommunications; and renting of vehicles and equipment. The share of the transportation sector in GDP is 8 percent and in overall number of employees, 7 percent. Given Croatia's important geographic position between Central and Southeastern Europe, the transportation sector is an important one to the country's economy. Currently this sector suffers from a number of shortcomings, however. Harbors and railways are in need of modernization. Road and railway infrastructures are not equally well developed in all parts of the country. Existing and new infrastructure are in need of investments.

Croatia has a total of 27,840 kilometers of roads. Road transportation remains the most important branch of the transportation sector since the road network covers all parts of the country, and for many areas this network remains the only available connection to the rest of the country and the outside world. However, the volume of traffic has outpaced the ability of both government and the private sector to expand the capacity of this network. In 1999, the last year for which reliable information is available, 109,387 freight trucks and 9,317 combined vehicles (i.e., for passenger and freight transport) were registered in Croatia. In April 2001 two companies were established to manage, construct, and maintain the road network: Hrvatske autoceste d.o.o. (Croatian Motorways, PLC) and Hrvatske ceste d.o.o. (Croatian Roads, PLC). They are authorized to collect tolls and road taxes and finance the construction of motorways and roads; they will manage the 200 kilometers of new roads that are expected to be built in Croatia by 2011.

Croatia has 2,726 kilometers of railway lines. The railway system connects all major Croatian cities except Dubrovnik. Croatia has direct railway links with its neighbors (Slovenia, Hungary, Bosnia-Hercegovina, and Yugoslavia) and through them indirect links to the European railway network. Railway transport has suffered immensely because of the war in Croatia from 1991 to 1995. Since the Croatian Serb Krajina severed the rail link between Croatia proper and Dalmatia during those years, a number of railway lines had to be terminated; the volume of traffic decreased and the number of employees working for Croatian Railways (HŽ, Hrvatske željeznice) was halved. Half of HŽ's total income continues to come from the government's budget. In 2000, 45 percent of all transport on Croatian railways involved transit of passengers and goods, 24 percent involved internal transport of passengers, 16 percent export goods, and 15 percent import goods.

As in the case of railways, the marine sector has not experienced any major modernization in the 1990s. In the decade since 1991 there has been a reduction in the size of the Croatian merchant marine, in harbor transport, and in the transport of passengers. The main Croatian seaports are Rijeka, Split, Zadar, Šibenik, Pula, and Dubrovnik. None of these harbors has seen an improvement in infrastructure since 1991. The total length of inland waterways for ships under 150 tons is 922 kilometers in the Danube, Sava, Drava, and Kupa Rivers. The river transport sector has not been modernized since 1991. River harbors and piers are in need of reconstruction and the fleet used for river transport is outdated.

On the eve of the war in Croatia and the dissolution of Yugoslavia, Croatia's airports averaged 4–5 million passengers per year. In 1991 the number of passengers was 1.16 million, but in 1992 this number fell to 0.45 million. Passenger volume has been growing steadily since the end of the war in 1995 and is expected to reach 7.5 million passengers by 2010. The two primary Croatian airports are Zagreb and Split. There are five secondary airports (Dubrovnik,

Pula, Zadar, Rijeka [Krk], and Osijek) that can accommodate aircraft of all sizes, with tertiary airports at Brač, Lošinj, Vrsar, and Osijek-Čepin. But apart from the Zagreb airport, there has been relatively little investment in airports. The Croatian national air carrier is Croatian Airlines, which flies between Zagreb and most major European cities and between Zagreb and a few select domestic destinations (such as Dubrovnik and Split). As of 1999, it had four Boeing 737–200s, 3 ATR 42-300s, one Airbus A320, and two Airbus A319s.

Croatia has 601 kilometers of oil pipeline and 1,769 kilometers of gas pipeline. Pipeline transport remains the cheapest way to transport energy products to market. However, like railway transport, the pipeline network was adversely affected by the war in Croatia. It has not been fully restored to prewar levels and is in dire need of modernization.

The transport sector remains in need of rapid modernization and investment. In 1999 road transport accounted for 73.26 percent of total passenger transport, with railways transport accounting for 19.29 percent, marine and coastal transport 7.42 percent, and air transport 1.03 percent. In the case of the transport of goods, marine and coastal transport accounted for 56.9 percent of total transport, railway transport accounted for 19.4 percent, pipeline transport 13.2 percent, road transport 9.0 percent, inland waterway transport 1.4 percent, and air transport 0.1 percent.

CONTEMPORARY CHALLENGES

Contemporary Croatia is confronted by a range of problems and challenges, which may be grouped for simplicity's sake into the following five broad categories: relations with neighbors; relations with the international community; cooperation with the ICTY (the International Criminal Tribunal for the former Yugoslavia) and prosecution of war crimes and crimes against humanity; treatment of minorities; and postcommunist transition, which encompasses a range of issues.

RELATIONS WITH NEIGHBORS

Since Croatia was born in war and in the context of the dissolution of the Yugoslav state, its relations with its immediate neighbors were bound to remain strained. Since 1991, this meant above all the rump Yugoslavia, consisting of Serbia and Montenegro. But with the outbreak of war in Bosnia-Hercegovina, and Zagreb's overt support of the Bosnian Croat leadership, relations with the Bosnian Muslim–led government also deteriorated. Relations with Slovenia remained tense, in large part because of unsettled territorial disputes.

The death of Franjo Tudjman in December 1999 and the defeat of his Croat Democratic Union in the 2000 elections brought about a dramatic improvement in relations between Zagreb and most of Croatia's neighbors. The impact of Premier Ivica Račan's and President Stjepan Mesić's policies has been greatest in Bosnia-Hercegovina. Under President Tudjman, Croatia recognized the Bosnian government in Sarajevo in 1992, but in 1993–1994, it supported the Bosnian Croats in their struggle against that same government. Although Zagreb altered course in 1994, and supported the formation of a Bosnian Muslim–Bosnian Croat alliance under pressure from Washington, the Croatian authorities failed fully to implement the spirit of the Dayton Peace Agreement, which brought an end to the war in Bosnia-Hercegovina in 1995.

After gaining office, Račan and Mesić promised an end to these policies and have moved rapidly to place Croatian support for the Bosnian Croat armed forces on a transparent footing. Indeed, President Mesić's first foreign visit was to Sarajevo, where he managed to mend fences with the Bosnian government and was welcomed as a friend of Bosnia-Hercegovina. Relations also have improved with Serbia-Montenegro, especially following the demise of the Slobodan Milošević government in late 2000. Diplomatic relations have largely been normalized with Belgrade and recipocral diplomatic visits at the highest levels have taken place. Many Croats still vividly recall the activities of the Serbian authorities during the war in Croatia; complete reconciliation may not be possible until all those accused of war crimes have been brought to trial.

Despite the improving climate, there are a number of unresolved territorial disputes between Croatia and its neighbors. Discussions continue with Bosnia-Hercegovina on sections of the Una River and villages at the base of Mount Plješevica. Relations with Slovenia are still strained because of land and maritime boundary disputes in Istria; according to the terms of a recent but unratified agreement between Zagreb and Ljubljana, Croatia would have ceded most of Pirin Bay and maritime access to Slovenia, which in turn would have ceded several villages to Croatia. In late 2002 Croatia and Serbia-Montenegro adopted an interim agreement to settle territorial claims in the disputed Prevlaka Peninsula, allowing the withdrawal of the UN monitoring mission (UNMOP). Discussions continue to be complicated by internal problems in Serbia-Montenegro, however. Croatia and Italy continue to debate bilateral property and ethnic minority rights issues stemming from border changes following World War II. Despite these lingering problems, relations between Croatia and its neighbors have improved steadily since 2000.

RELATIONS WITH THE INTERNATIONAL COMMUNITY

Croatia's primary foreign policy priority since 2000 has been improving its relationship with both the European Union and the United States. That relationship had been tested severely during the Tudjman years, especially his last years. For the most part, the center-left government elected in 2000 has made significant progress on both fronts. Croatia has since joined the Partnership for Peace (May 2000) and the World Trade Organization (June 2000). On 12 May 2001, Croatia signed the Stabilization and Association Agreement, the first step toward a closer relationship with the EU. The United States has stepped up its political, legal, and military assistance to Croatia ever since. But integration with the European Union and improved relations with

Washington continue to be plagued by issues related to the prosecution of war criminals.

ICTY AND WAR CRIMES COOPERATION

Most problematic is Croatia's relationship with the International Criminal Tribunal for the former Yugoslavia (ICTY). Nationalist elements in Croatia continue to denounce the ICTY as a politically motivated and anti-Croat court. The Croat nationalist right views the criminal indictments against Croats, issued by The Hague tribunal, as an attempt by the international community to criminalize Croatia's Homeland War of 1991–1995, which is seen as a just, legitimate, and defensive war. Conservative elements in Croatia's Catholic hierarchy have shown dissatisfaction with the policies of the Račan-led center-left coalition government. In January 2001 conservative Dalmatian Catholic bishops boycotted President Stjepan Mesić's annual reception for religious communities, apparently to register their dissatisfaction with the government's policies. In February 2001 several Dalmatian clergy publicly supported right-wing demonstrations in support of General Mirko Norac, who was indicted for war crimes by the ICTY.

As of 2003, relations with the ICTY were strained for two reasons: General Janko Bobetko and General Ante Gotovina. General Bobetko had been indicted by the ICTY for his role, as commander in chief of the Croatian Armed Forces, in the September 1993 "Medak Pocket" incident, during which the Croatian army allegedly killed dozens of Serb citizens. The Račan government failed to turn him over to the ICTY, because such a bold step would have undoubtedly spelled the demise of the governing coalition. Although Bobetko passed away in the spring of 2003, harm had been done to Zagreb's relations with The Hague. Furthermore, the indicted General Gotovina remains at large. Most observers believe he is hiding in Croatia. Whether or not the authorities know of his whereabouts, they have not moved energetically on this front for the same reason they failed to comply with the ICTY's demands on Bobetko. They continue to pledge their commitment in principle to the ICTY's overall mission, however. The ICTY indictment of Gotovina alleges that as overall operational commander for part of "Operation Storm," the Croatian army's August 1995 campaign to capture the Croatian Serb statelet known as Krajina, he was either implicated in a range of crimes including killing and expelling local Serb civilians, or was aware of the acts committed by his men and did nothing to prevent or punish them. In June 2003 Gotovina gave an interview to the Croatian weekly *Nacional,* in which he again denied the allegation. He agreed to surrender to the ICTY if it agreed to revoke its indictment. A large segment of Croatian public opinion continues to see Gotovina as a hero, just as it saw Bobetko as a hero.

Partly in order to get around this problem, in early May 2003 the Croatian government indicated its willingness to consider the formation of a special domestic court or tribunal to try war crimes and crimes against humanity. In June 2003 Croatia's minister of justice, Ingrid Antičević-Marinović, again indicated that her cabinet was considering its own war crimes legislation. The move, if accomplished, would make Croatia the third former Yugoslav republic, along with Bosnia-Hercegovina and Serbia-Montenegro, to announce plans to establish its own war crimes court. Zagreb's announcement was welcomed by the ICTY. That is apparently because, in an effort to finish its own proceedings by 2008, the ICTY has been trying to focus only on high-level war crimes suspects. It may eventually try to turn over cases of intermediate and lower level perpetrators to national courts in Croatia and the other Yugoslav successor states.

Thus, ICTY officials have indicated that they would consider passing some of the less significant cases to the relevant national authorities. The case most likely to be handed over to Croatia is that of General Rahim Ademi, an ethnic Albanian who served in the Croatian army. Ademi was indicted along with General Bobetko for the murder of Serb civilians in the Medak Pocket in September 1993. However, few domestic war crimes trials have been conducted to date in Croatia (or elsewhere). Those that have gone forward have received generally poor reviews.

The establishment of a war crimes court is not just a reflection of Croatia's new willingness to confront atrocities committed in its name. It is also a politically expedient move by Račan. His Social Democrats have been fiercely criticized by the increasingly popular nationalist political right for being too cooperative with The Hague. Creating a local war crimes court would help his party placate nationalist opinion by obviating the need to extradite suspects to The Hague. Thus far Croatia had conducted only two significant trials arising from the war of Yugoslav dissolution. The first was the trial of the Bosnian Muslim rebel leader and Croatian citizen Fikret Abdić. However, he was prosecuted for war crimes and crimes against humanity perpetrated against other Muslims in Bosnia-Hercegovina from 1993 to 1995; a court in Karlovac sentenced him to twenty years in prison, the highest penalty under Croatian law. And in 2003, a court in Rijeka tried the Croatian General Mirko Norac for war crimes committed against Serb civilians in Gospić in 1991. Although Norac was found guilty and sentenced to twelve years in prison, Račan was able to neutralize nationalist criticism by pointing out that he had ensured that the trial was held in Croatia and not The Hague. Thus when ICTY officials indicated that they might be willing to hand some cases over to local courts, Račan's government announced its intention to form a tribunal of its own.

Since the death of Bobetko, only Ademi and one other war crimes suspect, General Gotovina, remain in Croatia. Račan's government offered a 50,000 euro reward for information leading to his arrest. However, if Račan is unable to find the fugitive general and can ensure that Ademi is tried in Croatia, he will be able to tell his critics that he has not sent anyone to The Hague. The existence of a war crimes court is also expected to aid Croatia in its bid for European Union membership, which it hopes to achieve by 2007. Croatia's ability to try war criminals is of crucial importance for achieving EU integration.

The International Criminal Tribunal for the Former Yugoslavia called on the UN operation in Eastern Slavonia for assistance in exhuming a mass grave at Ovčara. Workers inspect the site where two hundred civilians were massacred in 1994. (United Nations/DPI)

TREATMENT OF MINORITIES

Croatia has long been a multiethnic society. During the recent war of independence, that multiethnic structure was demolished. The last Croatian census was conducted on 31 March 2001. It revealed that Croatia's total population was 4,437,460, with Croats composing the vast majority (3,977,171 persons or 89.63 percent). Of the country's minorities, the most numerous are the Serbs, who number 201,631 or 4.54 percent of the population. Nearly a dozen other nationalities compose the remaining 258,658 inhabitants (5.83 percent). The 2001 census confirmed what observers had suspected for years, namely, that important demographic and ethnic changes had taken place since the last prewar census, which was conducted in March 1991. These changes can be attributed almost entirely to the breakup of Yugoslavia and the war in Croatia (1991–1995). According to the 1991 census, Croatia had 4,760,344 inhabitants, that is, 322,884 more people than in 2001. In 1991 Croats composed 77.9 percent of the population (as compared to 89.6 percent in 2001) while the Serb component of the population has declined over the same period from 12.2 to 4.5 percent. Historically, Serbs have been the largest non-Croat nationality in Croatia and were settled primarily in those regions that had formerly been part of the "military frontier" in the Habsburg era. In 1995, during the Croatian army's Operation Storm, which recaptured the Croatian Serb Krajina, tens of thousands of Serbs either fled or were chased out.

Hence, facilitating the return of refugees, especially those of Serb nationality, is one of the many challenges confronting the Croatian authorities. To be sure, since 2000 they have made important advances in a number of areas relating to returns. But many ethnic Serbs who wish to return to Croatia, including Serbian Orthodox clergy, have continued to encounter difficulties recovering their prewar property and reconstructing damaged or destroyed houses. There were no reports of specific discrimination against Serbian Orthodox clergy beyond that faced by other ethnic Serb citizen refugees. Notions of religion and ethnicity are linked closely in society, but the majority of incidents of discrimination are motivated by ethnicity rather than religion.

There have been no property restitution agreements between the government and other religious groups. The Serbian Orthodox community has filed several requests for the return of seized properties, and some cases have been resolved successfully. However, several buildings in downtown Zagreb have not been returned, nor have properties that belonged to monasteries, such as arable land and forest. This uneven progress may be the result of a slow judicial system rather than a systematic effort to deny restitution of Serbian Orthodox properties. Several Jewish properties, including some Zagreb buildings, have not been returned. No properties have been returned to the Jewish community since March 2000. The Croatian government failed to amend discriminatory clauses of the Law on Compensation for Property Taken during Yugoslav Communist Rule that were struck down by the Constitutional Court in 1999. It failed to meet a court-mandated 31 March 2001 deadline to enact the amendments. The new amendments are expected to extend compensation to Jews whose property was confiscated between 1941 and 1945, as well as to foreigners. The previous HDZ government implemented property restitution in a discriminatory manner. In 1998 the government signed a concordat with the Vatican that provided for the return of all Catholic Church property confiscated by the communist regime after 1945. This agreement stipulated that the government would return seized properties or compensate the Catholic Church where return was deemed impossible. Some progress has been made, but there has been no compensation to date for nonreturnable properties.

POSTCOMMUNIST TRANSITION: CIVIL SOCIETY AND MARKET REFORM

For the better part of the 1990s, Croatia's politics and economy faltered under the weight of war and a failed postcommunist transition. However, the parliamentary elections of 2000, which brought Ivica Račan's reformist center-left government to power, triggered signs of recovery both in the depressed economy and in political life. The Croatian economy may be poised to take off, but it has a long way to go. Since the death of Franjo Tudjman in December 1999 and the 2000 elections, the prevailing international attitude toward Croatia has changed tremendously and for the better. Foreign investors have reentered the Croatian market, although not as quickly as Zagreb would have liked.

According to a September 2003 World Bank study, Croatia's economy has undergone a profound transformation since independence and especially since the last elections. Market laws and institutions have been introduced and the enormous real output decline of the first war-torn years of independence have been virtually recuperated. These achievements have been made despite a highly unstable geopolitical environment. The current government has accelerated this transformation by opening Croatia to global markets by joining the World Trade Organization (WTO) and Central European Free Trade Association (CEFTA), cooperation with neighbors in Southeastern Europe, the signing of the Stabilization and Association Agreement (SAA) with the EU, and accelerating the implementation of key economic reforms.

Foreign investment alone will not solve all of Croatia's economic problems, however. The privatization of state industries is of central importance. As of 2000, roughly 70 percent of Croatia's major companies were still state-owned. That includes water, electricity, oil, transportation, telecommunications, and tourism. Government expenditures account for almost 60 percent of Croatia's gross domestic product (GDP). Other signs of a struggling economy include high unemployment, which is still over 20 percent, and relatively low salaries even by regional standards. Croatia also has a significant foreign debt of approximately US$9.5 billion. Privatization and deep cuts in government spending are central to market reform and economic recovery. Despite the problems, Croatia embarked in 2000 on its real transition to a market economy. To be sure, the transition started earlier but at a very slow pace. The privatization of large government-owned companies was practically halted during the war and in the years immediately following the conclusion of peace.

Another area of concern is the development of a civil society; in the most basic terms, civil society may be taken to mean those individuals and organizations in a society that are independent of the government and which are able to exercise rights of free speech and association. Where there is an active civil society citizens can freely organize and advocate for their beliefs and causes. Yet another area, related to the development of civil society, is the rule of law. The relatively inefficient Croatian justice system is one of the most significant impediments to investment, fundamental protection of human rights, and democratic development. It is under enormous pressure for systemic reform and improved performance. With the advent of the reformist government in 2000, however, a number of foreign sponsors, both American and European, helped launch legal and judicial reforms. They have also assisted the Ministry of Justice in developing an efficient and effective court case management system.

The media have also been an area of concern for reformers. In the 1990s, under the government of Franjo Tudjman's HDZ, the independent commercial media was controlled through legislation that prevented access to a national audience and placed it under central government control. Since 2000, media freedoms have improved measurably. Through foreign assistance, Croatia has developed its first independent television and radio network. As a result, as of 2003 there were 24 media outlets (13 radio, 4 print, and 7 television stations) now generating self-sustaining revenue. Croatia's only independent television network is now financially independent. The Croatian government has also adopted legal reforms that support independent media.

Thus Croatia has managed to make important advances in introducing market mechanisms and institutions, as well as in strengthening civil society. Since 2000, the Croatian government has received the active support and assistance of EU agencies and the U.S. government, a marked difference when compared to the 1990s. Many challenges still need to be overcome, however. There is still a need to deepen and accelerate those reforms that have been launched, in order to enhance Croatia's competitiveness and raise living standards. The country's laws, institutions, and policies still need to be aligned with those of the EU, if the process of integration is to succeed. The challenge for Croatia remains to create conditions that will attract investment, produce growth, enshrine the rule of law, and strengthen civil society.

SELECTIVE BIBLIOGRAPHY

Alexander, Stella. *Church and State in Yugoslavia since 1945.* Cambridge: Cambridge University Press, 1973.

———. *The Triple Myth: A Life of Archbishop Alojzije Stepinac.* Cambridge: Cambridge University Press, 1987.

Almond, Mark. *Europe's Backyard War: The War in the Balkans.* London: Heinemann, 1994.

Banac, Ivo. *The National Question in Yugoslavia: Origins, History, Politics.* Ithaca: Cornell University Press, 1984.

———. *With Stalin against Tito: Cominformist Splits in Yugoslav Communism.* Ithaca: Cornell University Press, 1988.

Banac, Ivo, ed. *Eastern Europe in Revolution.* Ithaca: Cornell University Press, 1992.

Bennett, Christopher. *Yugoslavia's Bloody Collapse: Causes, Course, and Consequences.* New York: New York University Press, 1985.

Biondich, Mark. *Stjepan Radić, the Croat Peasant Party, and the Politics of Mass Mobilization, 1904–1928.* Toronto: University of Toronto Press, 2000.

Boban, Ljubo. *Croatian Borders, 1918–1993.* Zagreb: Školska knjiga, 1993.

Bracewell, Catherine Wendy. *The Uskoks of Senj: Piracy, Banditry, and Holy War in the Sixteenth-Century Adriatic.* Ithaca: Cornell University Press, 1992.

Burg, Steven L. *Conflict and Cohesion in Socialist Yugoslavia.* Princeton: Princeton University Press, 1983.

Carmichael, Cathie. *Croatia.* Santa Barbara, CA: Clio, 1999.

Crnja, Zvane. *Cultural History of Croatia.* Zagreb: Office of Information, 1962.

Croatian Information Centre. "Latin as a Literary Language among the Croats," http://www.hic.hr/books/latinists/01latin.htm (accessed 8 August 2004).

Čuvalo, Ante. *The Croatian National Movement, 1966–1972.* Boulder: East European Monographs, 1990.

———. *Historical Dictionary of Bosnia-Herzegovina.* Lanham, Md.: Scarecrow, 1997.

Cviic, Christopher. *Remaking the Balkans.* London: Royal Institute of International Affairs, 1991.

Djordjevic, Dimitrije, ed. *The Creation of Yugoslavia, 1914–1918.* Santa Barbara, CA: Clio, 1980.

Dvornik, Francis. *The Making of Central and Eastern Europe.* Gulf Breeze, FL: Academic International, 1974.

———. *The Slavs: Their Early History and Civilization.* Boston: American Academy of Arts and Science, 1956.

———. *The Slavs in European History and Civilization.* New Brunswick, NJ: Rutgers University Press, 1962.

Eterovich, Francis, ed. *Croatia: Land People, Culture.* 3 vols. Toronto: University of Toronto Press, 1964.

Fine, John. *The Late Medieval Balkans: A Critical Survey from the Late 12th Century to the Ottoman Conquest.* Ann Arbor: University of Michigan Press, 1987.

Franolić, Branko. *An Historical Survey of Literary Croatian.* Paris: Nouvelles éditions latines, 1984.

———. *Language Policy in Yugoslavia: With Special Reference to Croatian.* Paris: Nouvelles éditions latines, 1988.

Gazi, Stjepan. *A History of Croatia.* New York: Philosophical Library, 1973.

Goldstein, Ivo. *Croatia: A History.* London: Hurstand, 1999.

Guldescu, Stanko. *The Croatian-Slavonian Kingdom, 1526–1792.* The Hague: Mouton, 1970.

———. *History of Medieval Croatia.* The Hague: Mouton, 1964.

Hoptner, J. B. *Yugoslavia in Crisis, 1934–1941.* New York: Columbia University Press, 1962.

Irvine, Jill A. *The Croat Question: Partisan Politics in the Formation of the Yugoslav Socialist State.* Boulder: Westview, 1993.

Kann, Robert A. *A History of the Habsburg Empire.* Berkeley: University of California Press, 1974.

Kann, Robert A., and Z.V. David. *The Peoples of the Eastern Habsburg Lands, 1526–1918.* Seattle: University of Washington Press, 1984.

Magaš, Branka. *The Destruction of Yugoslavia: Tracing the Breakup, 1980–92.* London: Verso, 1993.

Magaš, Branka, and Ivo Žanić, eds. *The War in Croatia and Bosnia-Herzegovina, 1991–1995.* London: Frank Cass, 2001.

Matica Hrvatska. http://www.matica.hr/www/mhwww.nsf/english.htm (accessed 9 August 2004).

Pavlowitch, Stevan K. *The Improbable Survivor: Yugoslavia and Its Problems, 1918–1988.* London: Hurst, 1988.

Ramet, Sabrina P. *Nationalism and Federalism in Yugoslavia, 1962–1991.* 2d ed. Bloomington: Indiana University Press, 1992.

Ramet, Sabrina P., ed. *Yugoslavia in the 1980s.* Boulder: Westview, 1985.

Rothenberg, Gunther. *The Austrian Military Border in Croatia, 1522–1747.* Bloomington: University of Illinois Press, 1960.

———. *The Military Border in Croatia, 1740–1881: A Study of an Imperial Institution.* Chicago: University of Chicago Press, 1966.

Rothschild, Joseph. *East Central Europe between the Two World Wars.* Seattle: University of Washington Press, 1974.

Rusinow, Dennison. *The Yugoslav Experiment, 1948–1974.* Berkeley: University of California Press, 1977.

Sedlar, Jean W. *East Central Europe in the Middle Ages, 1000–1500.* Seattle: University of Washington Press, 1994.

Seton-Watson, Robert William. *The Southern Slav Question and the Habsburg Monarchy.* 1911. Reprint, New York: Fertig, 1969.

Singleton, Fred. *A Short History of the Yugoslav Peoples.* Cambridge: Cambridge University Press, 1985.

———. *Twentieth-Century Yugoslavia.* Cambridge: Cambridge University Press, 1976.

Stallaerts, Robert, and Jeannine Laurens. *Historical Dictionary of the Republic of Croatia.* Lanham, MD: Scarecrow, 1995.

Sugar, Peter F. *Southeastern Europe under Ottoman Rule, 1354–1804.* Seattle: University of Washington Press, 1977.

Tanner, Marcus. *Croatia: A Nation Forged in War.* New Haven: Yale University Press, 1997.

Wolff, Robert Lee. *The Balkans in Our Time.* Cambridge: Harvard University Press, 1956.

CHRONOLOGY

Seventh century	Croat settlement in western Balkans.
818–823	Ljudevit, apparently the ruler of a rudimentary principality in Pannonia, leads a failed revolt against the Franks.
845–864	First notable Croat ruler in Dalmatia, a tribal chief named Trpimir who gave his name to the dynasty (i.e., Trpimirovićes, r. 845–1089) that governed Croatia. Referred to as prince of Croatia *(Dux Croatorum).*
879–892	Branimir establishes links with the papacy; in 879, the year of his accession, he obtains the pope's recognition of Croatia as an independent principality.
Ninth to eleventh centuries	Earliest written records in the Croatian language.
910–928	Croatia becomes a kingdom under her first king, Tomislav.
1058–1074	Greatest territorial extent under Petar Krešimir IV (r. 1058–1074), known as King of Dalmatia and Croatia.
1075–1089	Reign of the last Croatian king, Dmitar Zvonimir.
1094	King of Hungary, László (Ladislas) I, establishes the Zagreb bishopric.
1102	Personal union between Hungary and Croatia based on an agreement *(pacta conventa)* of equals (the Croatian nobility and the Hungarian king).
1242	Tatars invade.
1115–1420	Much of Dalmatia is progressively lost to Venice.
1493	Croatian army is defeated by Ottomans at Krbava.
1521	*Judita,* by Marko Marulić (1450–1524), is published.
1526	After the Battle of Móhacs, much of Croatia is incorporated into the Ottoman Empire.
1527	Croatian Landed Estates elect Ferdinand I of Habsburg, King of Croatia.
1538	Beginnings of the military frontier take shape.
1595	Publication of the first Croatian dictionary by Faust Vrančić (1551–1617).
1699	Treaty of Karlowitz (Srijemski Karlovci) restores Slavonia.
1797	Dalmatia is incorporated into the Austrian Empire.
1836–1849	Illyrianist movement of Ljudevit Gaj.
1836	The first Croatian weekly newspaper, *Danica* (The Dawn), is published.
1842	Matica Ilirska (or Matica Hrvatska) is founded.
1846	Ivan Mažuranić's (1814–1890) epic *Smrt smail-age Čengića* (The death of Smail-Aga Čengić) is published.
1846	First Croatian opera, *Ljubav i zloba* (Love and Malice), is composed by Vatroslav Lisinski (1819–1854).
1866	The Yugoslav Academy of Sciences and Arts (JAZU) (now the Croatian Academy, HAZU) is founded.
1867	The *Ausgleich* (Compromise) is negotiated between Emperor Franz Joseph and the Magyar ruling oligarchy, transforming Austria into the Dual Monarchy, or Austria-Hungary. Croatia-Slavonia and the military frontier remain in the Hungarian half of the empire. However, Istria and Dalmatia remain in the Austrian half.
1868	The Croato-Hungarian *Nagodba* (Agreement) is signed, whereby the Kingdom of Croatia-Slavonia is recognized by the Magyar ruling oligarchy as a "political nation," with a right to autonomy within the Kingdom of Hungary.
1861	Formation of the Party of (Croatian State) Right of Ante Starčević.
1881	The military frontier is incorporated into Croatia-Slavonia.
1905	The Croato-Serb coalition, the dominant political force in Croatia to 1918, is founded.
1914–1918	World War I.
1915	Yugoslav Committee is formed in London to promote the cause of a South Slav state encompassing the South Slav lands of the Habsburg monarchy and Serbia-Montenegro.
1917	Corfu Declaration signed by Yugoslav Committee and Serbian government, calling for a common state of Serbs, Croats, and Slovenes in one state with a single democratic, constitutional, parliamentary system, under the Karadjordjević dynasty, after the war.
29 October 1918	Croatian parliament declares Croatia's independence.
1 December 1918	The Kingdom of Serbs, Croats, and Slovenes is formed.
1920	Elections to the Constituent Assembly, in which the Croat Peasant Party (HSS, Hrvatska seljačka stranka) emerges as the leading Croat party in the country.
28 June 1921	Promulgation of centralist Vidovdan Constitution, imposing a centralist state system in Yugoslavia.
1922–1932	Publication of Miroslav Krleža's *Hrvatski bog Mars* (The Croatian God Mars, 1922) and *Povratak Filipa Latinovicza* (The Return of Philip Latinovicz, 1932).
1925	HSS dissolved by the authorities; its leader, Stjepna Radić, is jailed.

1928	Radić and four other HSS deputies are shot during a session of parliament; Radić dies two months later.
6 January 1929	King Alexander Karadjordjević abrogates the constitution, dissolves the Skupština (parliament), bans political parties, and declares a royal dictatorship.
1934	Alexander is assassinated on a state visit to France by an agent of the Croat fascist Ustaša (Insurgent) movement.
26 August 1939	An agreement (the so-called *Sporazum)* is negotiated between Belgrade and the HSS, creating an autonomous Croatian province *(banovina)* in Yugoslavia.
6 April 1941	Yugoslavia is invaded by the Axis; an "independent" Croatian state is proclaimed on 10 April under Axis auspices.
1941–1945	Partisans and Četniks fight German occupiers and each other.
1945	End of World War II; Yugoslav Communists assume power in Croatia and Yugoslavia; Federal People's Republic of Yugoslavia founded.
August 1945	Communist-dominated Provisional Assembly is convened, which organizes elections for a Constituent Assembly (November).
1945–1948	Show trial of wartime collaborators and "traitors," many real and some imagined.
1946	Trial of Croatia's archbishop of Zagreb, Alojzije Stepinac.
1948	Tito-Stalin split; purge of leading Communists, including the Croat Communist Andrija Hebrang.
1962–1971	Political liberalization in Yugoslavia.
1966–1971	Croatian Spring.
1974	New Yugoslav constitution establishes many of the decentralizing tendencies of the late 1960s.
May 1980	Tito dies.
1986	Memorandum of the Serbian Academy of Arts and Science composed, alleging discrimination against Serbs in Communist Yugoslavia.
1990	League of Communists of Yugoslavia hold their last congress, dividing along republican and nationality lines.
April and May 1990	Elections in Croatia; the Croat Democratic Union (HDZ) of Franjo Tudjman wins handily.
December 1990	Croatia adopts a new constitution.
1991	Ninety percent of the population vote for Croatian independence; Croatian Serbs boycott the election.
25 June 1991	Croatia and Slovenia secede from the Socialist Federal Republic of Yugoslavia. Open war begins between Croatia and the rump Yugoslavia (Serbia and Montenegro).
December 1991	Croatian Serbs declare the existence of their own statelet in Croatia, known as the Republic of Serb Krajina.
15 January 1992	The EU and most other countries recognize Croatia.
May 1992	Croatia joins the UN.
August 1995	Operation Storm, leading to Croatia's recapture of the Krajina; exodus of as many as 200,000 Serbs.
1997	Franjo Tudjman wins presidential elections (61.4 percent).
1999	Tudjman dies.
January 2000	The ruling Croat Democratic Union, which had governed Croatia since 1990, is defeated by a six-party coalition that wins 47 percent of the vote to the House of Representatives.
January–February 2000	Stjepan Mesić of the Croat People's Party (HNS) wins presidential vote with 56 percent of the vote.

SLOVENIA

BRIGIT FARLEY

LAND AND PEOPLE

"Draw a straight line across Europe from Gibraltar to Moscow and another one from Scotland to Crete," Slovene writer Alenka Puhar told a British visitor to Ljubljana in 1991. "Voilà! At the intersection of the two diagonals lies Slovenia." Independent Slovenia indeed sits at the very center of Europe; legions of visitors and writers have described it as Europe in miniature. They are undoubtedly referring to Europe's moderate, Continental climate, its great geographic diversity, and the attractions that this diversity makes possible: spotless medieval towns in gently rolling hills, breathtaking Alpine peaks summoning skiers in winter and hikers in summer, pristine lakes and rivers, mineral springs, plunging valleys, a lovely coastline. But Europe's geography has not been an unmitigated blessing: it has left the continent vulnerable to armed conquests from the east and south, numerous internecine conflicts and two world wars. The Slovenian experience is no exception. Since 1991, the state has played host to an annual invasion of skiers and vacationers, helping to fill the state's coffers with tourist dollars. In prior years, it experienced incursions and disruptions of a less sanguine character, as the geopolitical landscape constantly attests.

Slovenia has three regions typical of the continent: its central and eastern plains, its alpine area, and its Adriatic coast. Its capital city, Ljubljana, is the center of the country at the heart of Europe, standing at the crossroads of three major regions of the country: the eastern Alps, the Pannonian plain, and the Adriatic Sea. All roads lead here. Like Slovenia itself, Ljubljana has occupied a place of importance from Roman times. Fond of strategic crossroads, the Roman legions established a regional outpost at the site and named it Emona. Ljubljana's fate after the Romans remains a subject of contention, but the Habsburg monarchy recognized the value of its location, making it a center for crafts and trade with Hungary, Croatia, and Italy. As the occupant of the highest place in the surrounding area, the Ljubljana castle had great value as a lookout tower during the many Turkish incursions into the Habsburg monarchy.

Known as Laibach under the Habsburgs, Ljubljana's fortunes began to rise after it attracted the attention of Napoleon in 1809. Napoleon made the city the capital of his Illyrian Provinces, because it offered the best chance of blocking Habsburg access to the Adriatic. Although the Illyrian Provinces went the way of Napoleon after 1815, the city maintained a higher profile in the Habsburg lands than previously. It played host to the heads of Europe's conservative courts at the 1821 Congress of Laibach, where the parties pledged to uphold the post-Napoleon status quo in Europe. When that arrangement crumbled in the revolutionary years of 1848–1849, Ljubljana became the headquarters of the Slovenian national movement. The first Slovene cultural institutions were founded here in the 1880s and 1890s,

Ljubljana City. (Janez Skok/Corbis

including the Slovenian national theater and museum; it has continued to serve as the country's cultural headquarters into the twenty-first century. In the first as well as the second Yugoslavia, Ljubljana was the natural choice to become the first city of the Slovene republic. In July 1991 it became the official capital of independent Slovenia.

Although Alpine peaks dominate Ljubljana's skyline, it is surrounded by what the authors of the *Atlas of Slovenia* term "the rolling hills and dreamy streams" of the region known as Dolenjska. Dolenjska forms part of the vast plain known as Upper Pannonia and has always enjoyed cultural as well as physical proximity with Ljubljana. Dolenjska is the Slovenian approximation of France's Loire Valley, heavily populated with castles and monasteries located along meandering rivers. Among the most famous monasteries is the Abbey at Stična, the oldest in all of Slovenia. Founded in 1136, this institution produced the Stična manuscript, one of the earliest surviving Slovene manuscripts. Nearby Bogenšperk Castle housed the library of Slovenia's legendary renaissance man, Janez Valvasor. A scientist, geographer, soldier, and writer, Valvasor enjoyed an eventful career in the Slovene lands. He authored one of the first physical descriptions of the Carniolian region, *The Glory of the Duchy of Carniola,* a sourcebook that continues to yield valuable information today. He was the first to write down the story of the Slovenian Robin Hood, Erazem Lueger, and catalog other folk tales and legends from the region. Another Valvasor discovery came in the identification of the *Proteus anguinus,* a remarkable fish that inhabits the dark, moist limestone caves of the Soča valley, where it is capable of walking as well as swimming. In his time away from scientific investigations, Valvasor traveled widely and wrote with Jeffersonian range on subjects from numismatics to beekeeping. He also managed to find time to team with the Hungarian nobleman, Miklós Zrinyi, to fight the Ottoman Turks. The Valvasor library now resides in the national museum at Ljubljana, but his legend lives on in Dolenjska.

The Dolenjska countryside is dotted with vineyards, underscoring yet another of its distinctive features. As part of the Sava/Bela Krajina area, it joins the eastern Posavje and western Primorska regions as a major producer of fine wines. Among its signature offerings are so-called blended wines, such as the appropriately named Dolenjsko belo (Dolenjska white), the product of some five different wine varieties.

The unhappier aspects of Slovenia's geopolitical past, never far from even the casual visitor, are also on display in Dolenjska, at Kočevski Rog. Here Josip Broz Tito's Partisans took shelter in the darkest days of World War II, in some of the karst caves that can be found in almost every region of Slovenia. These caves were a place of pilgrimage for true-believing Yugoslavs in the Tito years; Slovenes have modified the commemoration, but have managed to avoid controversy by dedicating them to the victims of World War II. The neighboring Posavje region also has a dark past. German forces ethnically cleansed this area, taking some Slovenes against their will to Germany and deporting others south, to occupied Croatia and Serbia.

Traveling south from Ljubljana, the British journalist Zoë Brân was struck by the dark woods around the approaches to Notranjska province. "I wonder what lies beyond those trees," she wrote. "This is a region rife with legend and folk fears. The Church pursued witches here later than anywhere else in Slovenia, and as the passenger fades into the forest, Notranjska appears much like a combined film set of *Seventh Seal* and *Deliverance*." Notranjska might aptly be described as Slovenia's Transylvania, shrouded in thick forest and mystery and peopled by folk heroes. One of its best-known landmarks is a local variant of Castle Dracula, a structure built straight into the side of a mountain. Although Predjama Castle dates to the thirteenth century, it is most often associated with Erazem Lueger, a beloved fifteenth-century outlaw who stole from the rich and gave to the poor. Five centuries later, the castle remains a perfect redoubt, rising 37.5 meters up on a vertical cliff and boasting such classic features as a moat, drawbridge, and numerous hidden entrances and exits. It even has its own underground cave. Lueger eventually attracted the ire of the Habsburg authorities, who obliterated him with a well-timed cannonball as he sat in the castle lavatory. But his favored Predjama Castle continues to loom large in Slovene lore and legend.

Slovenia is famous for its karst, the product of the dissolution of large concentrations of limestone by water. Over half of the country has significant amounts of it, and Notranjska offers one of the best examples of karst formations in the Postojna jama (cave). Carved out some 2 million years ago by the Pivka River, Postojna Cave was discovered in the seventeenth century and has been an object of continuing fascination. The British sculptor Henry Moore deemed it "the best exhibit of nature's sculpture I have seen." The cave is indeed imposing—it measures over 20 kilometers in length and is spacious enough to be a conference hall; Slovenes and Germans flocked there for holiday dances in the nineteenth century, and it still serves as a concert hall, hosting a parade of visiting orchestras, chamber groups, and singers, and an audience of up to 10,000 people each year. Thanks to the plethora of unique flora, fauna, and animal life thriving within, Postojna became the birthplace of a special science—speleobiology—whose adherents are devoted to the study of caves and their inhabitants. The world's first speleobiological station is headquartered near the cave there.

ALPINE SLOVENIA

The Slovenia of picture postcard fame, the land of awe-inspiring mountains and deep blue lakes, begins northwest of Ljubljana, in Gorenjska province. The jewel in the crown, Bled, is located in the northeast corner of the province. A creation of the famous Bohinj glacier, Bled is known worldwide for its emerald-colored lake and small island where there has been a church continuously since the ninth century. The baroque Church of the Assumption now dominates the island. Lake Bled attracts thousands of vacationers each year with its stunning setting and thermal waters; the Karadjordjevićs, rulers of the first Yugoslavia, favored it as a summer residence. A few miles south of Bled sits a second stunning glacial lake, Bohinj. Bohinj is a pilgrimage spot for cultural tourists, because the beloved Slovene poet France Prešeren set his epic *Baptism on the Savica* at the nearby Savica waterfall, the source of the Sava River. The Sava and the nearby Soča rivers carry water from over half of Slovenia's territory to the coast.

Bled and Bohinj form the backdrop for the entire Slovene Julian Alps, dominated by the imposing Mount Triglav (Three-Heads). Like the lakes, Triglav is at once a geographical and cultural institution. It is the tallest mountain in the country, the anchor of the Slovene Alps. As such, it is perhaps the most popular peak, and the most storied. According to legend, the mountain was home to a three-headed deity—"triglav" means "three headed"—who ruled all the realms of the mortal world: the earth, the sky, and the netherworld. In more recent times, it mystified would-be explorers until one of Slovenia's leading families, the Zois clan, financed an expedition that reached the summit in 1778. Other intrepid Slovene adventurers followed, in time giving way to large numbers of German alpine enthusiasts. By the nineteenth century, Triglav became a battleground in the Slovene-German language and culture wars. In response to what they perceived as German domination of the mountain, as in so many other aspects of life in Slovene-German areas, Slovene enthusiasts organized their own Slovene Mountain Society in 1893. Initially a tourist organization, it evolved into a cultural and political association that eventually played an important role in the Slovene national movement. Members of the society publicized their expeditions to Triglav and invested the mountain with great significance, so that a pilgrimage to the mountain became a demonstration of pride in one's nationality. To this day, it is widely believed that every Slovene should climb Triglav at least once in his or her life.

THE ADRIATIC LITTORAL AND ENVIRONS

The region that links the Slovenian inland with the country's narrow coastline is called Primorska (near the sea). It comes into view on the descent from the Julian Alps, through the scenic Vršič Pass, where visitors encounter, in the unlikeliest of sites, a Russian Orthodox chapel. Dedicated to St. Nicholas, the church commemorates the 1916 death of some four hundred Russian prisoners of war in an avalanche, as they worked on a road in the vicinity. The chapel is emblematic of both the beauty and the treachery of the descent from the Alps into the Soča Valley, which leads directly to the Slovene coast.

The Soča Valley has witnessed some of the most significant episodes in Slovene geopolitical history. Napoleon began his invasion of Austria in 1809 from the town of Bovec, an operation that culminated in the establishment of

Mount Triglav, Slovenia. (Corel Corporation)

the Illyrian Provinces, a key moment in Slovene cultural history. In World War I, Kobarid (then Caporetto) witnessed one of the few decisive battles of that four-year conflict, when Austrian and German forces punched through the Italian lines and broke the back of the Italian army. The Central Powers won that battle but went on to lose the war, paving the way for the assignment of Adriatic territory to the first Yugoslav state, the Kingdom of Serbs, Croats, and Slovenes. This did not sit well with the postwar Italian state, which ignored the verdict of the Paris peacemakers and took the region by force in the chaos attending the end of the war. Thousands of Slovenes thus became residents of Italy and endured a campaign of Italianization at the hands of Benito Mussolini's government. The second Yugoslavia regained part of the Soča valley at the conclusion of World War II, and the government of independent Slovenia took it in turn on Slovenia's exit from Yugoslavia in 1991.

The city of Nova Gorica bears especially vivid witness to the years of Italian-Slovene conflict. By the terms of the postwar Paris accord, the Italian-Slovene border split the Italian city of Gorizia in half. The new Yugoslav government responded by building up its part of Gorizia into an entity it subsequently christened Nova (New) Gorica. For more than a decade after the settlement, the border crossings were closed, but by the 1970s, the two governments had taken steps to facilitate the development of normal relations between the twin towns. In February 2004 a metal fence that had physically divided the two towns came down, thanks to the efforts of the towns' mayors. Three months later, on 1 May, residents marked the formal dissolution of barriers in Slovenia's official entry into the European Union with a public celebration and concert.

Toward the south along the brief coastline, one encounters the Karst region, which links north with south Primorska and the coast with the Vipava Valley to the east. This region got its name, not coincidentally spelled with a capital *K,* from its heavy concentration of karst—it is the primary karstic region of Slovenia. As one would expect, Karst has a surfeit of caves, nearly 6,000. The most celebrated are the Škocjan caves, which speleologists describe as the largest and most extensive system of caves on the continent. Like their Postojna counterpart, the Škocjan caves have been a mecca for biologists, mountaineers, tourists, and spelunkers since the early nineteenth century. They resemble large aboveground buildings, with anterooms, concert halls, and similar features. They are also the habitat for over 250 unique examples of both Alpine and Mediterranean flora and fauna and at least five different species of bats. In acknowledgment of their size and biodiversity, the United Nations designated the Škocjan caves a World Heritage site in 1986.

The Karst region's moderate climate ensured that caves would not remain its only attraction. In the sixteenth century, Slovenia's Habsburg rulers determined that it would be the best place for the stud farm they hoped would guarantee a steady supply of the best riding horses. In 1580 they established the farm at Lipizza and began the breeding program that produced the legendary Lipizzaner stallions of the Spanish Riding School in Vienna. The product of crossing Andalusian horses with a local breed, the Lipizzaners belonged to the Habsburgs until the collapse of the monarchy in 1918, their residence in Lipizza interrupted only by an evacuation to Hungary during the Napoleonic invasion. After World War I, their ownership was contested among Italy, Yugoslavia, and the new independent states of Hungary and Austria. The chaos surrounding the end of World War II drove the horses to Czechoslovakia, from which American soldiers herded them away from the advancing Soviet forces, to Bavaria. The postwar peace treaty assigned Lipizza to the new Yugoslavia, which promptly renamed it Lipica. At that time, fewer than twenty stallions remained and prospects looked dim for the reconstitution of the operation, since the new socialist government tended to view horsebreeding as a bourgeois pursuit. Slovenia's independence in 1991 meant a renaissance for the stud operation, even as it complicated the issue of ownership. The Slovene government now owns the territory of the farm and the horses, while the Austrian government insists that it owns the name "Lipizzaner." Lipizza, now Lipica, has become yet another symbol of Slovenia's turbulent geopolitical history during the last century.

The Slovenian coast begins just south of Karst, at the village of Ankoran. The coastline is notably short—from Ankaran to Portorož, just 40 kilometers in length—but proves long on controversy as well as historical interest. The city of Koper has always been an important part of the Adriatic economy. Known during its tenure in the Venetian republic as Capodistria, it became a major port and administrative center. Under the Habsburgs, it lost some of its importance after its northern neighbor, Trieste, became a major railway link with the mainland. In recent years, however, Capodistria/Koper has regained its former position of prominence. As Slovenia's only port, it services much of Slovenia's import-export trade and has attracted high-profile European clients such as Volkswagen, which has used Koper to get its vehicles to eastern Mediterranean countries such as Greece and Turkey. Koper is also the closest available outlet to the sea for landlocked neighbors Austria, Hungary, and the Czech Republic. In a recent year Austria accounted for nearly 30 percent of the total volume of cargo.

An Italian city until the mid-twentieth century, Koper has lost little of its past. In the 1954 settlement of the Adriatic territories, the city of Trieste and its Italian population went to Italy, but Yugoslavia retained Koper and a significant Italian minority. Now those Italian residents are citizens of Slovenia, and Koper remains a center of Italian language and culture in Adriatic Europe. A Koper municipal administrator summed up the eventful past of this key metropolis for a *Financial Times* reporter in the early 1990s. "My grandfather was born an Austrian," the official said. " My father was born Italian. I was born in Zone B (part of the disputed Trieste region administered by the allies of the Yugoslavs after the second world war). My daughter was born in Yugoslavia, and when she has children, they will be born in Slovenia. And my family has never left Koper."

Koper's neighbor to the south, Piran, has a well-deserved reputation as the region's loveliest seacoast area. A city with Roman origins that flourished under Venetian rule, Piran has retained its medieval and Italian character through the centuries, in part because of its high, thick walls erected in the 1600s to guard against Turkish invaders. Like Koper, it became part of the former Yugoslavia in 1954, after the London agreement, and so retains a large Italian population. Having had a long relationship with the Venetian republic, both Piran and Koper have played prominent roles in the drama ofYugoslav/Slovene/Italian relations in the twentieth century and house substantial Italian minority populations.

Slovenian relations with Italy appeared normalized by the 1990s, but the breakup of Yugoslavia brought fresh conflict, this time with neighboring Croatia. In the post-Yugoslav era, the Adriatic coast and waters appeared destined to be shared by the newly independent entities of Slovenia and Croatia. As it happened, the conventional method of fixing sea borders requires drawing a line equidistant from the shore of each country, which effectively denied Slovenia access to international waters. The two states attempted to remedy this obvious inequity by agreeing that Slovenia would have the lion's share of the bay of Piran, while Croatia compensated itself with Slovenian mainland territory. To date, this agreement has not proved satisfactory to either nation and has resulted in some memorable anomalies. To cite one example, patrons of one of the region's most popular restaurants, Kalin, wash their hands in Slovenian territory, order and eat their meals in Croatia, then return to Slovenia to pay their bill. Despite the obvious absurdity of this dispute, it is no laughing matter and its outcome remains in doubt.

One constant in the turbulent annals of the coastal region is its temperate climate, which has made it one of the three major wine-producing areas in the country. Primorska is a leading, even dominant, producer of red wines, of which those made from Karst Refošk grapes seem to enjoy the greatest renown among connoisseurs.

THE EASTERN PLAINS: CARINTHIA, STYRIA, PREKMURJE

In geopolitical terms, the east-central and eastern regions of Slovenia have much in common with the coast: they have been a bone of contention among Yugoslavia, Slovenia, and their often covetous neighbors. Carinthia (Koroška) has special significance for Slovenes, since the cradle of Slovene civilization, the Duchy of Karantania, was headquartered here. However, Karantania eventually fell to the first Habsburgs in the thirteenth century, and the region was intermittently attacked by Turks and Hungarians in the two centuries that followed. Carinthia remained Austrian until the fall of the Habsburg monarchy in 1918, after which it was plunged into postwar turmoil as a region disputed between the Austrian successor state and the new Kingdom of Serbs, Croats, and Slovenes. In the plebiscite

What's in a Name?

Visitors to Slovenia have much to look forward to: postcard-perfect European towns and villages, stunning mountains and lakes, pristine Adriatic beaches, fine wines. Those with an incomplete knowledge of recent political geography might get even more than they bargained for, thanks to Slovenia's shifting frontiers in the past century.

Europe-bound history enthusiasts will certainly want to visit Caporetto, site of the famous two-year Italian-Austrian stalemate that ended in the stirring Austrian victory of October 1917. Caporetto represented one of the few decisive victories of World War I. It was a fateful and fatal moment for the Italian army, which never recovered from it, and marked the beginning of Erwin Rommel's distinguished service in the German army. A young American volunteer ambulance driver named Hemingway later immortalized his experiences on the Caporetto battlefield in his novel *A Farewell to Arms.*

The Caporetto engagement took place on the Isonzo front, which belonged to Italy in 1917. History texts still refer to the area as Italian, but history itself has moved on: the area was transferred to the second Yugoslav state after World War II and passed into the hands of the new, independent Slovene state in 1991. After decades of conflict with Italy, Slovene citizens understandably wished to rename their new acquisitions. Caporetto is now Kobarid, and the valley in which it is found has become the Soča Valley. Notwithstanding the confusion over the new names, Caporetto/Kobarid will not disappoint those diligent enough to find it. In 1990 the Slovene government established the Kobarid Museum, an institution dedicated to the Caporetto battle and the ordeal of World War I. It is already famous, having received the 1993 Council of Europe award as the best museum on the Continent. Visitors can supplement their museum review with an historic walking tour, of which a notable highlight is the elaborate memorial to the Italian dead in the war. Slovene-Italian relations have been far from cordial in this century, yet Slovene citizens have always tended the memorial with attention, a rare acknowledgment of common humanity.

Another perennially popular attraction for visitors to Central Europe is Lipizza, home of the stallions favored by the famous Spanish riding school of the Habsburg monarchs in Vienna. Like Caporetto, Lipizza tends to retain its previous affiliation in print and on film, but let the visitor beware. Upon the 1918 demise of Austria's longtime rulers, the Habsburgs, Lipizza was transferred to Italy. The new regime in Italy, headed by Benito Mussolini, took possession of most of Lipizza's prized equines. World War II transformed the region's borders once again, as Tito's Yugoslavia claimed Lipizza, rechristening it "Lipica." In 1991, after Slovenia's recognition as an independent state, Lipica became a Slovene town. Since then, the stud farm has enjoyed a renaissance.

The Slovenes' repossession of Lipica did not end the controversy that has followed it and its equine residents through the twentieth century. On joining the European Union (EU), the Austrian government successfully asserted its claim to the Lipizzaner stud book, on the grounds that Austria was the historic home of the Lipizzaners. Since it now had possession of the farm, the Slovene government objected—to no avail since it was not yet a member of the EU. Undaunted, Slovene authorities turned to the World Trade Organization in 1999 in order to register the Lipizzaner name there, since EU intellectual property protections did not extend to animals. Ultimately, both the European Union and World Trade Organization demanded that the two sides settle the matter between themselves. Discussions are proceeding.

Meanwhile, visitors to Slovenia—indeed, anywhere in that neighborhood—are advised to consult the latest maps of Europe before plotting their journey. The volatile geopolitics of Central Europe can confound the savviest of travelers.

arranged to settle the dispute, the Slovene citizens of Yugoslavia lost some 90,000 of their countrymen to Austria, though they retained access to economically crucial mining areas nearby, in the Karavanke region. Relations between the Austrian state and its Slovene minority have often proved tense, occasionally erupting into open conflict even into the 1970s. In recent years Austria has mostly respected the rights of its Slovene citizens, guaranteeing them access to bilingual schools and making possible important cultural initiatives such as the publication of Slovene-language journals. However, on the eve of Slovenia's accession into the European Union, Austrian state broadcasting indicated plans to end a Slovene-language radio broadcast, which prompted staffers to make plans for a hunger strike in protest. It remains to be seen how Austrian-Slovene minority rights disputes will be arbitrated, now that the border between the two countries has disappeared with Slovenia's entry into the European Union.

A quick glance at the map reveals much about the Prekmurje region. Prekmurje's residents lived in the Hungarian half of the Habsburg monarchy from 1867 until the Habsburgs' demise in October 1918, after which its Slovene and Hungarian residents became citizens of the new Kingdom of Serbs, Croats, and Slovenes by terms of the 1920 Treaty of Trianon. As an ally of the Axis powers on the outbreak of World War II, the Hungarian state took back Prekmurje and pursued an aggressive policy of Magyarization there. At the conclusion of the war, the region returned to Yugoslav control. In the communist years the situation in Prekmurje was often tense because of Yugoslavia's volatile relations with Hungary and the rest of the Soviet Bloc. With the end of communism in both states, Hungarian-Slovene relations have improved on every level. In the constitution of independent Slovenia, the Hungarian population of Prekmurje is guaranteed special rights, including the use of the Hungarian language, bilingual classes in schools, and the use of Hungarian national symbols.

South of Prekmurje, Styria (Štajerska) has faced many of the same challenges as its neighbors. One of its regional cities, Celje, constituted one of the last bastions of independence in the Slovene lands. Having built a magnificent medieval town, Celje's celebrated dukes surrendered only to the overwhelming force and resources of the Habsburg Empire. Ptuj remains the oldest town in Slovenia, dating to the first century before Christ. It has experienced the tenure of Roman, Hungarian, Austrian, and Yugoslav rulers through the centuries. The country's second largest city, Maribor, became a regional headquarters for Nazi invaders in World War II and suffered bomb damage severe enough to require a significant reconstruction.

For all their travails through the centuries, the Slovene east and southeast enjoy geographical advantages that residents can exploit fully with the promise of long-term political stability. Prekmurje attracts thousands of European vacationers each year with its mineral and thermal waters and sulfurous mud deposits, which have transformed once sleepy border towns into popular spa resorts. Like their nineteenth-century predecessors, contemporary Europeans are fond of "taking the waters" at Moravske Toplice and Radenci. Prekmurje also boasts a share of the burgeoning Slovenian wine sector, growing a grape essential to sweet wines called Šipon.

Styria has always been home to legions of small farmers growing everything from hops to barley, but it is now best known as ground zero for Slovenian viticulture. This is headquarters of the Podravje, or Drava-region wine region, which is divided into several small subdistricts. The Ljutomer-Ormož area is widely regarded as the richest producer in the country, thanks to its exceptional location. It sits between the Mura and Drava Rivers and receives shelter from the Pannonian heat from the hills to its northwest, making its climate ideal for the cultivation of the famous whites Beli Pinot and Šipon. The Haloze district enjoys similar renown, beginning to the south of the Drava river plain and extending to the lower Pohorje hills. It produces rieslings that have recently received high marks from international wine connoisseurs, particularly Renski Rizling and Šipon. These areas have earned Slovenia a place on the international wine map and made it an attractive destination for wine and gourmet tourists.

"We have only traveled some 200 kilometres as the crow flies from the Mediterranean," writes a Slovene journalist, "and have experienced the most varied type of landscape, from the stone severity of the classical Karst and the limestone Alps to the flower of the Pannonian plain." It seems reasonable to conclude that Slovenes through the centuries have found the remarkable diversity of their landscape both a blessing and a curse. With Slovenia's accession to the European Union, it is to be hoped that blessings will predominate in the future.

HISTORY

It was once taken for granted that people living in small nations, such as the Slovene people, could not live on their own in Central Europe. They had all the liabilities associated with perennial subject peoples: they were too few in number, too lacking in natural frontiers, too dispersed geographically and politically to aspire to an independent existence. In postcommunist Europe, these assumptions have changed dramatically. Since the beginning of the Yugoslav wars of the 1990s, the Slovenes have lived in their own state in an area once dominated by empires or successor states. Their journey is compelling and perhaps instructive for other peoples emerging from turmoil, since Slovenes themselves admit they remain a work in progress more than a decade following their unlikely independence.

A South Slavic people related to the Croats, Serbs, and Bulgarians, the Slovenes arrived in South Central Europe in the middle of the sixth century. Details of their early years are sketchy. It is generally agreed that for some decades they were part of a loose organization of Slavs under the jurisdiction of the prince Samo, whose origins remain obscure. In the century following their arrival the Slovenes and their Czech, Moravian, and Slovak neighbors repulsed attacks from invading rivals, such as the Avars and Franks. Following the death of Samo in 658, the Slovenes began to live under their own local ruler in an independent duchy called Karantania, headquartered near the modern Austrian city of Klagenfurt (in Slovene, Celovec). In the eighth century the Slovenes came under the domination of the Bavarians, from whom they received the Roman Catholic Church and a cultural orientation toward the west. Both Bavarians and Slovenes eventually submitted to the rule of the Franks, who in turn fell to the perennial rulers of Central Europe, the Habsburgs. There was also a short-lived Slovene kingdom located at Lake Balaton in modern Hungary; it too eventually became part of the Habsburg lands. Having become Habsburg subjects in the year 1278, Slovenes were to be associated with them until the collapse of their empire in 1918.

Gradually, a small contingent of educated individuals emerged to explore ways in which Slovenes differed from those around them—beginning with their native tongue. Slovenes have always stood apart from their neighbors by virtue of their distinctive language, which shares a foundation with other South Slavic languages yet cannot be

The Slovene Language

The pride of the Slovene people, Slovene is the official language of independent Slovenia. It is the native language of most of the state's nearly 2 million people. An estimated 500,000 individuals of Slovene origin, mostly living in the United States, Canada, South America, and Australia, also count Slovene as their first language.

Reflecting the location of its first speakers, the Slovene language belongs to the South Slavic division of the Indo-European language family. The Slavic group includes the East Slavic languages, Russian, Ukrainian, and Belorussian. Polish, Slovak, and Czech are considered West Slavic languages, while Slovene joins Croatian, Serbian, Macedonian, and Bulgarian in the South Slavic classification. Among the latter languages, Slovene and Croatian use the Roman alphabet. Bulgarian, Macedonian, and Serbian, like Russian, Belorussian, and Ukrainian, are written in the Cyrillic alphabet, named for the Greek monk who created an alphabet for the Slavs in the ninth century.

These languages share a basic grammatical structure that differs significantly from that of English. All of them have grammatical gender, which means that each noun is classified as feminine, masculine, or neuter and requires appropriate adjectival forms and verb endings. Where English has multiple verb tenses (i.e., I am reading, I read, I was reading, I have read, I will read, I will have read), Slovene and the other Slavic languages feature only three: past, present, and future. Slavic languages express relationships between words through changes in form (pronouns) and endings (nouns and adjectives). There are six sets of forms and endings, or cases: nominative, dative, locative, accusative, genitive, and instrumental. For example, where English speakers say, "I write with a pencil," Slavic languages simply add an instrumental case ending to the word "pencil," rather than using the preposition "with." All related adjectives and pronouns either change forms altogether or use endings reflective of that "instrumental" meaning. The English language retains some evidence of cases—for example, English speakers say, "I see him," not "I see he"—but for the most part, cases have disappeared. Another characteristic of Slavic languages that often surprises nonspeakers is the absence of definite and indefinite articles. Native speakers of Slovene or related languages often give themselves away by using articles incorrectly in English or failing to use them, as in "I have house outside city."

Each Slavic language has distinctive features, and Slovene is no exception. Only Slovene retains the dual, a special set of endings used to denote two of something. One table is *miza.* The plural marker *e* denotes more than one table, *mize.* If you refer specifically to two tables, you must add the special dual marker *i,* hence *mizi,* two tables. In addition, dialects are a bigger issue in Slovene than in other Slavic languages because so many Slovenes have lived in areas where their language was heavily influenced by German, Italian, or Hungarian. Specialists have identified seven major linguistic districts in the Slovene lands—Pannonia (Hungarian border area), Primorska (Adriatic), Dolenjska (Carniola), Gorenjska (Upper Carniola), the Rovte, Styria (Štajerska), and eastern Styria (Vzhodna Štajerska)—in which forty or more dialects can be found. It is widely believed that the best Slovene is spoken in Dolenjska and Gorenjska (Carniola) provinces. Fittingly, Gorenjska province is the birthplace of France Prešeren, the father of modern Slovene.

With respect to the spoken language, Slovene consonants are pronounced basically as in English, with a few exceptions. Vowels can be tricky because their pronunciation changes depending on whether they are stressed or unstressed, and stress is not intuitive or predictable in Slovene. Vowels sometimes disappear altogether, as in words like *trg,* square, although there is a hint of a short *e* sound between the *t* and *r.*

mistaken for them. Ironically, the first man to recognize the distinctive features of the Slovene language had to abandon another pillar of Slovene culture—the Roman Catholic Church—in order to make available his native tongue in written form. During the Reformation, when the use of the vernacular was promoted over the universal Latin, the Slovene priest Primož Trubar came into contact with Protestant reformers determined to spread the gospel in local languages. He did his part to further their efforts, leaving the Catholic faith in the process, and produced the first catechism, New Testament translation, and primer in the Slovene language. Jurij Dalmatin, a native of Carniola and a disciple of Trubar's, devoted ten years of his life to translating the entire Bible into Slovene. Slovene scholars note with wonder that Dalmatin's translation served Slovene worshippers from its publication at Wittenberg in 1584 until the end of the nineteenth century. The sixteenth century also produced the Counter-Reformation, which guaranteed that Protestantism would remain a minority faith in the Slovene

lands. But Slovenes could now learn about God in their own language, a key advantage for the future.

The eighteenth century was crucial for the evolving Slovene national consciousness. In the 1760s the Habsburg rulers Maria Theresa and Joseph II attempted to streamline the monarchy with a series of reforms designed to modernize state administration. Maria Theresa decreed that all Habsburg subjects should receive primary education wherever they lived. Joseph II's Edict of Tolerance permitted the reorganization of Catholic dioceses to correspond with administrative boundaries, so that Slovene Catholics were bound together for purposes of worship. This was an important step for a people whose national consciousness was almost nonexistent. But another part of Joseph's reform program seemed certain to impede the further development of that consciousness. In line with his quest for an efficient administration in his multilingual empire, the emperor subsequently decided to make German the official imperial language.

This appeared to be a rational and necessary step, but the law of unintended consequences soon took effect. The decision outraged some key groups within the empire, notably the Hungarians. Protestant Eastern Hungarians excepted, they had used mostly Latin among themselves. Surely, if anything replaced Latin as the language of administration in Hungary, it should be Hungarian. Before long, the imposition of German inspired other subject peoples to explore and promote the virtues of their own languages.

Slovene writers and linguists embraced this trend. In the late eighteenth century the monk Marco Pohlin wrote a grammar of the Slovene language, entitled *Krajnska grammatika* (Carniolan Grammar), which emphasized that Carniola was home to a large number of Slovenes as well as Germans. The linguist Jernej Kopitar, who was to become one of the most prominent men of letters in Slovene history, broadened Pohlin's focus in composing his *Gramatik der slavischen Sprache in Krain, Kärnten und Steyermark* (Grammar of Spoken Slavic in Carniola, Carinthia, and Styria). Anton Linhart published the first attempt to tell the story of the Slavic peoples in the Habsburg Empire, *Versuch einer Geschichte von Krain und der übrigen südlichen Slawen Osterreiches* (History of Carniola and Other Austrian South Slavic Peoples). For the first time, readers learned that the Slovenes had not just a distinctive language but also a record of achievements that set them apart from the Germans with whom they had long lived.

In the first years of the nineteenth century, the French Revolution helped to shape Slovenia's cultural development. Having taken Carniola, Carinthia, Istria, and parts of Croatia from Austria in the 1809 Treaty of Schönbrunn, Napoleon Bonaparte organized these areas into an administrative unit that became known as the Illyrian Provinces. This arrangement was strictly pragmatic, the main motives being the weakening of Austria and establishment of French power on the Adriatic. However, this interlude saw developments in the Slovene lands whose effects would survive the end of Napoleon. The city of Ljubljana (in German, Laibach) became the capital of the Illyrian Provinces, signaling the beginning of its rise as an important regional and national center. Even as French replaced German as the language of administration, Slovene was introduced in Slovene primary schools, to the delight of their appointed administrator, the celebrated poet Valentin Vodnik. Vodnik enthusiastically set about writing a Slovene primer and produced a brief Slovene-French-German dictionary. It should be remembered also that the French administrators grouped together South Slavic peoples into one administrative unit for the first time, a point of emphasis for proponents of a South Slavic state later in the century.

In the post-Napoleonic era, Ljubljana achieved brief notoriety when it played host to a meeting of representatives of the conservative European courts associated with the Holy Alliance: Russia, Prussia, and Austria. Known in its Habsburg incarnation as the Congress of Laibach, this meeting produced pledges to crush any challenges to the post-Napoleon status quo. Under these circumstances, political activity was out of the question; Austrian chancellor Clemens von Metternich was determined to maintain the post-Napoleon status quo on the continent. Yet Slovene writers and thinkers quietly pursued aspects of the Illyrian legacy, emphasizing as always the advancement of their language. The former inspector of schools, Vodnik, continued his work on behalf of Slovene culture, writing and publishing a newspaper in Slovene, *Lublanske novice* (Ljubljana News). As the rector of the Ljubljana gymnasium, he also continued to promote the study of Slovene and authored a longer French-Slovene dictionary as well as a text on Slovene history. Vodnik's contemporary, Fr. Anton Martin Slomšek, worked tirelessly to bring the Slovene language to as many Slovenes as possible, whether or not schooling in the language was readily available. His primer on Slovene language and culture, *Blaže and Nežica in Sunday School,* became the first Slovene encyclopedia, providing practice in Slovene language and readable lectures on a wide range of subjects for parents and children alike. The man considered the father of modern Slovenian literature, France Prešeren, worked throughout the 1830s and 1840s, producing his magnum opus, "Zdravljica" (The Toast), in 1844. He could not have known that this poem would eventually become the national anthem of the independent Slovene state in the late twentieth century.

Perhaps the most important development in this period was the outcome of a dispute between Prešeren and his fellow writer Stanko Vraz. In the 1830s the Croatian scholar Ljudevit Gaj and other linguists were searching for common features among the three South Slavic languages of the Habsburg monarchy: Serbian, Croatian, and Slovene. Greater linguistic unity, it was reasoned, would pave the way for a South Slavic political union, perhaps the best defense against assimilationist tendencies in the Habsburg monarchy. Vraz shared Gaj's vision and advocated the adoption of the *štokavian* dialect that would bring the Slovene language closer to its linguistic neighbors, Croatian and Serbian. Prešeren strongly disagreed, maintaining that abandoning the traditional *kajkavian* could endanger the existence of Slovene. "It seems as if Dr. Gaj and other Slavonic men of letters were seriously in favor of uniting Slovene and Illyrian languages in a new language or even of abolishing the

Slovene dialect as a standard language," he wrote. Language was always of critical importance for Slovenes. Unlike Croats or Serbs, who tended to live in majority Croatian and Serbian regions, only about half of Slovenes resided in areas where Slovene was a majority language. Forty percent lived in Carinthia or Styria, where the population was predominantly Italian or German and unfriendly to attempts to introduce Slovene. Prešeren believed that the cause of Slovenes' cultural unity would be best served by preserving their distinct language and insisting that it be taught anywhere they resided.

The national awakening of the Slovenes and other Habsburg subjects began with the exploration of language and literature. The next phase, more pragmatic and political, was born in the revolutions of 1848–1849. The momentous events of February 1848 in Paris caused disturbances in Vienna sufficient to drive the Habsburg court into hiding. In regional capitals such as Prague, they produced agitation about reforming the empire; in Hungary, the March Laws laid the foundation for autonomy, even independence. In Ljubljana, enthusiastic crowds gathered in the main square to celebrate the shakeup in the Austrian capital. But Slovene goals for the revolutionary year were notably modest. Acknowledging the primacy of language, the authors of the Slovene action program called for the use of the Slovene language in schools in Slovene regions. In case more ambitious schemes became possible, they also stipulated the union of all Slovene-inhabited territories within the Habsburg monarchy. Slovenes living in Carniola, Styria, Carinthia, and along the Adriatic should be grouped and administered as one territorial unit. Eventually, if the empire underwent substantial change, the Slovene lands could be joined to those of other Slavic peoples within the empire. Slovenes would pledge allegiance to Vienna in matters of national import while retaining substantial control over their own local affairs.

Habsburg military victories over breakaway Italian provinces and independence-minded Hungarians finally ended the 1848 "springtime of nations." The new emperor, eighteen-year-old Franz Joseph, began his reign with a regime of centralization and strict control from Vienna. However, this interval of calm would prove short-lived. In 1854 the Austrian government entered the Crimean War, in order to prevent Russia from toppling the Ottoman Empire and taking a commanding position near the empire's South Slavic possessions. In so doing, it damaged its relationship with the Russians, who believed that Austria was indebted to them since Tsar Nicholas I had sent the Russian army to help crush the 1849 Hungarian uprising. Emboldened by Austria's apparent isolation and inspired by the flamboyant leader Count Camillo de Cavour, the Habsburg Italian provinces of Lombardy and Venetia broke away in the wars of Italian unification in 1859–1860. In 1866 Prussian troops defeated the Austrian army at Sadowa, effectively excluding Austria from Otto von Bismarck's unified Germany. Thus ended a string of reversals that was to force fundamental changes in the monarchy after 1867.

In all of these unsuccessful campaigns, Franz Joseph had to reckon with the possibility of agitation in Hungary. The empire could not continue as a great power if it could not assume the loyalty of its second-largest national group. Accordingly, Franz Joseph agreed with Hungarian leaders on a reorganization of the monarchy. The ensuing *Ausgleich* (Compromise) of 1867 divided the monarchy into two halves, Austria and Hungary. Hungarians gained substantial control over their own domestic affairs while retaining ties with the monarchy in the person of the emperor and a common parliament and foreign policy. In acknowledgment of the changes, the Habsburg monarchy thereafter became known as Austria-Hungary.

The reorganization had a seismic effect on the non-Hungarian groups in Austria-Hungary. The other groups now began agitating for a similar arrangement. The Croats renegotiated their special relationship with the Hungarians, signing a Hungarian-Croat Ausgleich, the *Nagodba,* which ensured Croats' rights to make their own decisions on local matters. For their part, Romanians in the Hungarian lands contemplated various schemes for a formal liaison with neighboring independent Romania. The 1860s and 1870s also saw the reemergence of pro-Yugoslav polemicists such as Bishop Juraj Strossmayer, who emphasized the possibilities of South Slavic unity in attempts to combat culturally objectionable initiatives from Vienna and Budapest. Their efforts in turn galvanized nationalists, who began to form their own movements celebrating the virtues of separatism.

In the Austrian half of the monarchy, the Czechs allied with Prime Minister Eduard Taafe, who formed an "Iron Ring" with them and other Slavs in Austria as a counterbalance to his pro-German opponents in the Austrian Parliament. Working with Taafe, Czech politicians achieved noteworthy gains. Beginning in the early 1880s, the language of administration in the Czech lands became the language of the petitioner, so that if a Czech spoke to an official in Czech, the official in question would be obliged to respond in Czech rather than German. This constituted a huge advantage, since Czechs knew both Czech and German, while the Germans generally did not know Czech. Taafe also helped the Czechs obtain a Czech division in Prague University, previously an all-German institution. If the Czechs could not aspire to an arrangement like the Ausgleich, they certainly had improved their position by the turn of the century.

Slovene leaders had looked on with dismay as some 40,000 of their conationals came under Hungarian rule as part of the Ausgleich. However, they swallowed their disappointment and hastened to do what they could in Austrian politics by joining the Iron Ring. Like the Czechs, they had no hope of a special relationship with Vienna, but they could win key concessions. The Slovene language, once dismissed as "baby talk" by an Austrian government official, made headway during the Taafe years. It became the language of instruction in elementary schools in the Slovenes' unofficial capital, Ljubljana. In 1872 the Styrian regional capital, Klagenfurt, was decreed a "mixed city," mandating the use of both Slovene and German in official situations. There occurred a flowering of Slovene culture in Ljubljana. Between 1870 and 1914, the city witnessed the construction of a Slovene national museum and the establishment of

a national theater and opera. In 1888 a Slovene candidate triumphed in the elections for Ljubljana mayor.

Slovene politicians took pride in these achievements. However, they knew that their gains came at the expense of Germans in the monarchy, and those Germans were certain to reassert themselves. Slovene representatives accordingly raised their profile in the Austrian Parliament, putting forth numerous plans to defend Slovenes' progress and ensure their future. The Slovene Clerical Party and its leaders, Ivan Šušteršič and Anton Korošec, strongly supported certain strategic reforms within the monarchy. In 1912 they became cosponsors of the Vienna Resolution, which urged the Austrian government to create a Slovene and Croat administrative unit in the Austrian half of the monarchy. Others argued that Slovene interests might be best served in an Austro-Slav-Hungarian federation, a three-cornered arrangement in which all three groups would function as one unit on national issues but administer their own local affairs. The National Progressive Party, home to professionals and businesspeople, advocated federalizing the Austrian half of the monarchy, while leaving the Hungarian side unchanged. They believed that this scheme would most effectively safeguard Slovenes' language and culture. A Slovene Socialist Party also came into existence at this time. In the Tivoli document of 1909, members identified as their goal the complete national unification of all Yugoslavs, irrespective of name, religion, alphabet, and dialect or language.

All these proposals for change notwithstanding, it should be stressed that no mainstream Slovene politician envisioned a future outside the Habsburg monarchy. The Slovenes were always among the strongest supporters of the Habsburgs in the nineteenth century, and life without the monarchy was unthinkable. The Habsburgs were justly regarded as the best guarantor of their smaller peoples' future.

WORLD WAR I AND THE BEGINNINGS OF A SOUTH SLAV STATE (1914–1918)

The world the Slovenes had known changed forever in the summer of 1914. In late June the heir to the Habsburg throne, Franz Ferdinand, announced that he would visit the monarchy's newest acquisition, Bosnia-Hercegovina. On 28 June, the royal party was to tour the Bosnian capital city, Sarajevo. As the archduke and his wife, Sophie, greeted cheering crowds from an open car, a young Serb affiliated with the nationalist underground shot and killed them both. The murder inspired no outpouring of grief, because the heir was widely disliked. Nonetheless, because some Serbian citizens had waged a cold war against the Habsburg monarchy since its annexation of Bosnia-Hercegovina. In 1908 Serbia was deemed complicit in the murder. In early July Franz Joseph issued an ultimatum to the Serbian leadership, a list of demands no sovereign government could accept. The German government, which counted Austria-Hungary as its only ally in Europe, assured Franz Joseph of its unconditional backing. The stage appeared set for a limited, punitive war between Austria and Serbia, until Tsar Nicholas II of Russia declared partial mobilization. In so doing, he set in motion a series of events that transformed a local conflict into a world war.

In the first months of the war, Slovenes joined other Habsburg subjects in rallying around the monarchy. Slovene troops fought loyally alongside their Slavic, Romanian, and German compatriots in the Habsburg army, especially in the long Austrian-Italian stalemate on the Isonzo front that culminated in the victory at Caporetto in October 1917. On the home front, Šušteršič and Korošec maintained an active Slovene presence in the Austrian Parliament. Inevitably, however, political consensus began to break down under the pressure of a savage continental struggle. In hopes of gaining any advantage, the leaders of both the Central Powers and the Entente tried to bring neutral Italy into the war on their side. Each side put forth territorial inducements to the imperial-minded Italian government, the Habsburg foreign ministry proffering parts of the south Tyrol and Adriatic territories—which were largely populated by Croats and Slovenes. The rumor that their government might bargain away ethnic and historic South Slavic areas outraged two Croat politicians, who decided that the South Slavs' future lay in the creation of an independent South Slav state, possibly to include Serbia. The Dalmatian-born lawyer Ante Trumbić and Franjo Supilo left Austria-Hungary in early 1915 to form the Yugoslav Committee, a two-man lobby on behalf of a "Yugo-slavia," a land by and for South Slavs from Serbia and the Habsburg monarchy.

In 1915 these plans seemed fanciful. The monarchy showed no signs of collapse, a certain prerequisite for a South Slav breakaway. The vast majority of South Slavic leaders continued to support the empire. They responded to the rumors surrounding territorial concessions to Italy in a joint declaration issued in May 1917. Read in the Austrian parliament by Korošec, the May Declaration called for a postwar arrangement that included a third administrative unit for the South Slavic peoples. The monarchy would become a "trialist" entity, consisting of an Austrian, Hungarian, and Slavic division, each enjoying local autonomy. It was felt that this arrangement would prevent future trespasses on the interests of the monarchy's Slovene, Croat, and Serb subjects. Some of the signatories believed that a unified South Slavic bloc could also join with Serbia if the future of the monarchy were to be called into question. After all, one empire—Russia—had already cracked and broken under the strain only two months earlier, in March 1917.

One month after the May declaration, the Yugoslav Committee advanced in its campaign for an independent South Slav state. The Committee's president, Trumbić, met with Serbian prime minister Nikola Pašić on the island of Corfu in June 1917 for talks regarding a possible union of Habsburg South Slavs and Serbia after the war. The Serbian government had shown little previous interest in this, because its major objective had always been the return of historic Serbian territories, especially Bosnia-Hercegovina. By 1917, with their Russian ally in the throes of revolution, Serbian leaders saw a South Slav union as an option and agreed to meet with Trumbić. Trumbić and Pašić emerged from their talks with a blueprint for a future South Slavic state. The Corfu Declaration said nothing about boundaries

King Alexander of Yugoslavia with his eldest son and heir Prince Peter, during the celebrations of the tenth anniversary of the King's accession. Prince Peter, the official head of the Yugoslav Sokols, wears the Sokol uniform. (Hulton-Deutsch Collection/Corbis)

or the organization of the future state. It did, however, stipulate the equality of the three major groups, Serbs, Croats, and Slovenes, of the Catholic and Orthodox faiths, of the Cyrillic and Roman alphabets, and of the Croat, Slovene, and Serbian flags. It put both Habsburg South Slavs and Serbian government officials on record as favoring the creation of a South Slavic entity, or "Yugo-slavia."

There followed months of stalemate on the battlefield, growing war weariness, and major changes in the balance of forces. The Russian provisional government fell in November 1917 to the revolutionary Bolsheviks, who promptly withdrew from the war. With the U.S. entry into the war, President Woodrow Wilson took an active role in bringing the conflict to a conclusion, issuing his Fourteen Points for the postwar peace in January 1918. This document appeared to dash hopes for an independent South Slav state, since it anticipated the survival of the Habsburg monarchy. No one wanted to contemplate multiple national groups cut adrift from an imperial structure in the aftermath of a world war. But the Habsburg Empire was reeling from the 1916 death of Franz Joseph, as well as battlefield losses and their economic and political consequences. The new emperor, Karl, floated several proposals for reorganizing the empire, as many of the subject groups had wished, but his efforts proved unavailing. The Czechs, Slovaks, Poles, and South Slavs now contemplated citizenship in newly independent and/or resurrected states. Acting in concert as a National Council under Korošec's direction, Habsburg Slovenes, Croats, and Serbs voted in late October to join Serbia in the creation of a new multinational entity. On 1 December 1918, the future king, Alexander, made it official in his proclamation of the Kingdom of Serbs, Croats, and Slovenes.

SLOVENES IN THE FIRST YUGOSLAVIA

High hopes attended the creation of the first independent South Slav state, despite the upheaval attending the end of the war and the difficult amalgamation of several disparate groups. The Serbs claimed the leading role by virtue of their existing state apparatus, the new capital in Belgrade, and the Serbian monarch, King Peter Karadjordjević, who would preside over the state. While the Corfu Declaration had said nothing about the organization of the future South Slav entity, Serbian politicians assumed that they would administer domestic as well as national affairs from Belgrade. In their view this arrangement only made sense. Serbia had a long history as an independent state, it had contributed significantly to the Entente victory, and its officials were experienced administrators in a dangerous neighborhood. They had recently fought three wars with neighbors large and small and prevailed in all of them.

The new citizens from the Habsburg lands could not agree to this arrangement. Prior to the collapse of the monarchy, most Croat and Slovene leaders had backed the idea of a federal state, an arrangement that would let them administer their own local affairs rather than take orders from Budapest or Vienna. Now it appeared that they would be taking orders from Belgrade. The Croats, led by Croat Peasant Party leader Stjepan Radić, were immediately and vehemently unhappy. Regardless of the political arrangements in which they lived, they had always managed to maintain their local autonomy and parliament (Sabor). For centuries prior to 1918, Croats had dealt with Croatian-speaking officials, sent their children to schools staffed by Croatian teachers, even answered to Croatian police officers. After the dreadful ordeal of the war, they hoped at least to regain what they had enjoyed previously. Life under Serbian domination certainly did not meet that standard.

Slovene leaders took a more nuanced view. True, they had failed to achieve their longstanding political goal, the union of all Slovene territories. Parts of Carinthia had elected via plebiscite to become citizens of the postwar Austrian state rather than join the new South Slavic entity. Thousands of Slovenes in the former Austrian port of Trieste (in Slovene, Trst) suddenly found themselves living in Italy, a fate forced on them by advancing Italian forces unwilling to accept the verdict of the Paris peacemakers on the status of Adriatic territories. Yet those in the kingdom saw clear advantages in the union with Serbia. They had official acknowledgment in the name of the new state, the Kingdom of Serbs, Croats, and Slovenes, a definite improvement on centuries of anonymity. Their language and flag enjoyed automatic equality with those of the Serbs and Croats. They advanced their cultural agenda in the construction of Slovene schools throughout Slovenia and the founding of the University of Ljubljana in 1919. In contrast to Croatia, where Serbs predominated at every level of government, Slovenes staffed Slovenian schools and other local administrative institutions. All of these gains came with the active support of the Belgrade government. The Slovene leader-to-be in the new state, Korošec, summed up the attitude of many when he told his disgruntled colleague, Croat Peasant Party stalwart Vladko Maček, that unlike the Croats, the Slovenes had gained in the new entity, from schools and language to administration.

Throughout the short life of the first Yugoslavia, Korošec led Slovenes in such a way as to remain on the sidelines, hoping to extract timely advantages, as the Serb-Croat dispute monopolized politics. In the voting on the state's Vidovdan Constitution, which legalized the centralist system of administration, the Slovene representatives opposed or abstained. True to his Habsburg background, Korošec wanted to see the new state divided into six provinces, each of which would have its own parliament and substantial powers to run its own local affairs. When the Serbs prevailed in the final vote, Korošec and his colleagues briefly joined the Croats in active opposition. Eventually, however, they concluded that they had little to gain by supporting the Croats in their feud with Belgrade. It helped that Slovenes received continual reminders of their relative good fortune from their compatriots in the Italian city of Trieste, where Benito Mussolini's regime had embarked on an Italianization campaign in Slovene areas.

In fact, Korošec was summoned as a mediator when the Serb-Croat conflict turned violent. In June 1928 a Montenegrin deputy to the Yugoslav Parliament became enraged at Radić, whom he viewed as an obstructionist. In full view of those attending the session, the deputy shot the Croat leader, who died of his wounds two months later. At that point, all Croatian deputies vowed unyielding opposition to the government. Hoping to defuse the crisis, King Alexander named Korošec to serve as interim prime minister and charged him with finding a way out of the impasse. The Slovene leader responded by reiterating his belief in a decentralized state. Yugoslavia, he maintained, should be reorganized into three units: Serbia, including Vojvodina and Bosnia, Croatia, and Slovenia. In this way, everybody won: Serbs would maintain control over much of their historic territory, while Croatia and Slovenia gained control over their own domestic affairs.

This solution proved unacceptable to the king, who shelved all suggestions for reform in favor of a royal dictatorship in January 1929. Alexander suspended the parliament, forbade the display of national paraphernalia, and redrew the state's administrative boundaries, hoping to obliterate, or at least blunt nationalist sentiment. The new regions, or *banovine,* were named for nearby rivers, Slovenia becoming known as Dravska Banovina. Like other residents of Yugoslavia, Slovenes also acquired new citizenship. Henceforth, Alexander declared, there were to be no national differences in his realm. His subjects would be known as Yugoslavs in a country called Yugoslavia.

Slovenes and Croats felt the impact of these changes acutely. Unlike the Serbs, who retained a tangible symbol of their nationality in King Alexander, they had lost their flags, their national regalia, and their ability to effect change in a legislature. They soon made known their discontent. The Croat cofounder of the Yugoslav state, Ante Trumbić, rallied opponents with his *Punctacije* (Declaration), in which he reiterated that a federal arrangement would be the only acceptable means of administering Yugoslavia. Korošec prepared his own version, the so-called Korošec Points, which stipulated wide autonomy for Slovenes and other Yugoslavs, a resumption of parliamentary politics, and the return of national symbols. "To achieve this," the Points read, "it is necessary for Slovenes, Croats, and Serbs to create by free agreement and on a democratic basis a state of self-ruling units, of which one would be Slovenia."

King Alexander responded to these nonviolent measures by ordering the arrest of many protesters. This was too much for some Croats, who went underground and founded the Ustaša (Uprising) movement, dedicated to the violent overthrow of the Yugoslav leadership and the creation of a Croatian state. Between 1930 and 1934, the country was periodically rocked by Ustaša bomb attacks and assassination attempts, in which there was evidence of foreign complicity. Eventually, the king's enemies found their mark. On 29 October 1934, King Alexander was murdered in Marseilles, at the beginning of an official visit to France.

The king's murder shook the country. Acting as regent for the ten-year-old king, Peter, Alexander's cousin Paul soon lifted the dictatorship, returning to Slovenia and the other republics a voice in the administration of the state. Meanwhile, the rise of revisionist powers Germany and Italy signaled danger for Yugoslavia and other small states that owed their existence to the Paris treaties. Under these circumstances, Slovene leaders allied themselves closely with the Belgrade government; the best guarantee of Slovenia's existence was in a Yugoslavia that kept covetous neighbors at bay. Nonetheless, Slovene Communists, particularly the young theoretician Edward Kardelj, joined mainstream Croat leaders in demanding a state system that guaranteed equality to all the state's nationalities. In 1939 it appeared that the looming threat of war might actually produce substantive change. After months of negotiations, the Croat Peasant Party leader, Maček, and Yugoslav Prime Minister Dragiša Cvetković announced the conclusion of a *Sporazum* (Agreement), which granted the Croats their longtime demand: formal autonomy within Yugoslavia. Since the agreement made no special provision for the 700,000 Serbs living in Croatia, or any of the other nationalities in Yugoslavia, it was bound to cause controversy. However, foreign events soon overshadowed domestic affairs. On 1 September 1939, Hitler's attack on Poland began the second major European war in two decades.

SLOVENES, PARTISANS, AND THE WAR FOR A NEW YUGOSLAVIA

A determined diplomacy of neutrality delayed the day of reckoning for Yugoslavia until the spring of 1941. On 27 March, a group of Serbian officers, disturbed by the country's apparent capitulations before the Croats at home and the Axis powers abroad, overthrew the government of Prince Paul and installed their own representatives. This act of defiance brought on an invasion by the German and Italian armies in early April and the dismemberment of the state. German forces took control of Serbia, installing the former Yugoslav general Milan Nedić as their representative. Croatia was handed over to the leaders of the Croatian revolutionary Ustaše, with Ante Pavelić installed as *poglavnik,* or leader, of the new "independent" state. Other lands were parceled out among the invaders or allied neighboring states. Hungary reclaimed parts of the Vojvodina, which it had lost in 1918; Bulgaria claimed Macedonia; and Italy much of the Dalmatian coast, Bosnia-Hercegovina, and Montenegro. The Italians and Germans divided the Slovene lands between them, Germany taking the northern two-thirds of its territory and the Italians the southern third. Hungary claimed Prekmurje, a tiny slice of eastern Slovenia it had ruled prior to 1914.

From the beginning of the occupation, the invaders took harsh measures against the local population. The Slovene lands witnessed a campaign of denationalization. On 26 April 1941, Hitler came to Maribor and exhorted those attending a rally in the main square, "Make this area German again." Nazi authorities began obliging him on 7 June 1941, deporting some 60,000 Slovene citizens and making plans to resettle the vacated areas with German citizens. Some "expellees" ended up in Germany; others made their way south to Serbia and Bosnia, while others were taken to a west Hungarian concentration camp. In the Hungarian-majority Vojvodina, Hungarians and Germans were encouraged to murder Serbs, as were Albanians in the Kosovo region. The Croatian Ustaše initiated a campaign of pogroms against Serbs and Jews as well as forced conversion to Catholicism.

These outrages led to the formation of opposition groups, long a tradition in Balkan history. In the Serbian lands, Draža Mihailović formed a group called the Četniks, after the Cheta, Serbian anti-Turkish bands of the nineteenth century. In June 1941 the Partisans, an organization founded by Yugoslav communists, raised their standard. Consistent with the international Communist Party position, this group and its leader, Josip Broz Tito, called on all Yugoslavs regardless of nationality to join the fight to expel the invaders. These two groups both opposed the invaders but soon parted ways over tactics. The Četniks had an overtly Serbian and anticommunist character, while the Communist-led Partisans appealed to all nationalities. Tito urged all-out war at all times on the invaders, while Mihailović feared the impact of massive reprisals on the Serb population, which had suffered heavy losses in three previous wars. Although no one said so explicitly, the two groups were also competing for the leadership of a postwar Yugoslavia. The Četniks represented the prewar centralist Yugoslavia, ruled primarily by Serbs; at a key organizational meeting in November 1941, Tito outlined the possibility of a new country in the Partisan motto, "brotherhood and unity."

In the Slovene lands, Kardelj and his revolutionary colleague Boris Kidrić emerged as the leaders of a broad coalition of forces known as the OF, Osvobodilna Fronta (Liberation Front). Even though some might have distrusted the overtly communist orientation of their leaders, all OF members seemed to feel that long-standing Slovene demands—territorial integrity, Slovene language in Slovene schools, autonomy—might best be realized in Tito's promises of "brotherhood and unity" for postwar Yugoslavia. They were opposed by the Domobranci (Home Defenders), an anticommunist group that formed in Italian-occupied areas and collaborated with the Germans after Mussolini's fall (in hopes of preventing a Partisan victory). They could not compete with the OF, which had apparently won the hearts and minds of most Slovenes. In November 1943, at a key Partisan organizational meeting in Jajce, the OF became formally affiliated with the Partisans, who were winning the war on the ground and in the conference rooms of the Allied Powers. By May 1945, the Partisan army had entered Ljubljana, the Slovene capital, and was poised to become the nucleus for a postwar Yugoslav government. The Partisan leadership promised the new state would be infused with the spirit of brotherhood and unity, but the remnants of the Domobranci got neither. Sent back to Yugoslavia after fleeing to Austria, some 10,000 faced summary execution by the new government.

SLOVENIA IN COMMUNIST YUGOSLAVIA (1945–1980)

The first postwar years were relatively good ones for Tito and the citizens of the new Yugoslavia, notwithstanding the devastation visited on the country by four years of total war. Unlike their neighbors, whose Communist rulers gained their positions through their connections with and wartime residence in the Soviet Union, the Yugoslav leaders had solid popular support based on their personal participation and sacrifice in the war. The major difficulty in prewar Yugoslavia, Serbian centralist rule, was resolved, at least in theory. The 1946 constitution, drafted by Kardelj, organized the country along federal lines, with each of the six constituent republics guaranteed local autonomy and the right to secede. The makeup of the country's leadership seemed to confirm that all nationalities would share in the running of the new state: Tito was part Slovene, part Croat, and Slovenia was well-represented in Kardelj and Kidrić, the principal architects of Yugoslavia's foreign and domestic policies. There was some disappointment in Slovenia over Tito's failure to secure the city of Trieste and its Slovene residents in the peace settlement. Just as in the first Yugoslavia, however, it was felt that Slovenia had improved its fortunes.

As postwar reconstruction proceeded, the country was confronted with an unanticipated crisis in foreign affairs. As a communist state, Yugoslavia naturally enjoyed close ties with the Soviet Union. Most of the leadership had spent at least some time there—though not as much as their comrades in neighboring countries—and viewed it as the model to which all states should aspire. Yugoslavia's early economic and agricultural policies mirrored those of the USSR: extensive construction of heavy industry and the elimination of private farming in favor of collectivized enterprises. But the Soviet-Yugoslav relationship had developed strains dating to the end of the war, when Soviet troops passed through Yugoslavia and indulged in a decidedly nonfraternal spree of looting and rape.

In the immediate postwar period, Yugoslav leaders came to believe that the Soviet leader, Joseph Stalin, saw his East European allies not as equal partners but as subordinates expected to take orders, cogs in a giant wheel. It was clear that Yugoslavia would be expected to serve as a supplier of raw materials for the industrial machine of the socialist countries, foregoing the necessary measures to develop a diversified economy. While the equality of socialist countries everywhere was loudly proclaimed, the Soviet leaders continually implied that their country was superior to all others. They expressed these sentiments most obviously in cultural exchange, flooding Yugoslavia with Soviet books, art, and music, while accepting virtually nothing from Yugoslavia. Perhaps most disturbing was the active and constant Soviet surveillance of Yugoslav leaders, in Belgrade and Moscow, to enforce ideological conformity and compliance with all directives. The USSR's imperiousness produced disbelief in the Yugoslav leadership. Its members did not believe that they had achieved their heroic victory to become the obedient servant of a great power.

The crisis reached a climax in early 1948. Tito had begun negotiations with the Bulgarian leader, Georgi Dimitrov, on a customs union between Yugoslavia and Bulgaria. The USSR promptly demanded that the proposal be abandoned and reserved for itself the right to rule on any future Yugoslav foreign policy initiatives. Kardelj and Djilas went to Moscow to remonstrate with Stalin, pointing out that customs unions made good sense and enumerating the numerous previous issues on which the Yugoslavs had consulted with Moscow first. Their efforts only made Stalin angrier. Tito responded by summoning Yugoslav Party leaders in March to an emergency meeting, where they announced a reevaluation of their relationship with the USSR. This decision proved fateful, as it resulted in Yugoslavia's expulsion from the Soviet orbit. Stalin attempted to frighten the Yugoslavs into submission, flooding the communist media with violent rhetoric and calling on Yugoslavia's neighbors to overthrow "Judas Tito." But the Soviet leadership stopped short of using military force, mindful of Partisan success against the German army. It was clear that the Yugoslavs would not abandon their position, so they faced the task of forging a future without the familiar economic and political structures of the Soviet Union.

Life in geopolitical limbo promised to be precarious and difficult. Yet the Yugoslav leadership, in which Slovene representatives Kidrić and Kardelj continued to play key roles, met the challenge. They combined some creative retooling of fundamental principles with timely help from former adversaries. The latter came within months after the break, in the form of diplomatic recognition and a generous financial package from the United States, whose leaders were eager to exploit this tear in the iron curtain. Henceforth, it would be a priority to "keep Tito afloat." New policies, many of which were created by Kardelj, emerged in due time. The general approach was to do the opposite of what the Soviet leaders did; if the latter existed only to issue orders to subordinates at home and abroad, the Yugoslav leaders would dramatize their willingness to share power with, and be responsive to, the citizenry. In the words of the Slovene economist Janez Stanovnik, it was not sufficient for a socialist system to "declare that it stands *for* the working people. It has to bring into being a system of management both *of* and *for* the working people." In industrial enterprises, the concept of workers' self-management, in which factory collectives were personally involved in the running of their workplaces, made its debut. On 27 June 1950, the Law on Management of State Economic Associations by Work Collectives was formally adopted, after which the Soviet-style Central Planning Commission was abolished. The unpopular policy of collectivization was eventually abandoned after the break with the USSR in favor of private agriculture, though farmers faced limits on land holdings. In relations with the Soviet Union and the other socialist countries, the concept of "separate roads" emerged. The Yugoslav leaders asserted their right to follow a course appropriate to their own circumstances rather than march in lockstep with the Soviet Union.

During the late 1950s and 1960s, it seemed that Tito, Kardelj, and their comrades had made all the right calls. After the death of Stalin, Soviet leader Nikita Khrushchev admitted that the USSR had wronged the Yugoslavs and acknowledged that there could indeed be roads to socialism that departed from the Soviet model. While this gesture did not end the Soviet-Yugoslav conflict, it signaled the end of active hostility. Afterwards, Yugoslavia enjoyed the best of all possible worlds: mostly friendly relations with both camps and formal alliance with neither. As before, Kardelj provided the theoretical basis for this policy, which eventually became known as nonalignment. Other states, notably India, Burma, Egypt, and Indonesia, adopted a similar stand refusing to ally with East or West. In March 1961 Belgrade hosted the first meeting of the non-aligned states. Yugoslavia was to be a mainstay of this movement until the end of the Cold War in 1989.

The general decentralizing trend in both domestic and foreign affairs meant that Yugoslavs enjoyed all the advantages of Soviet-style socialism—low rents, guaranteed employment, free health care, paid vacations—while retaining advantages denied their Hungarian, Romanian, and Bulgarian neighbors. Yugoslav citizens traveled abroad freely, and foreigners could visit Yugoslavia without visas, ensuring a steady stream of European tourists in search of affordable holidays. There was considerably more cultural freedom in Yugoslavia than in its neighbors, which made the country's public face an object of wonder for Western observers familiar with the dreary conformity of other socialist capitals. "Identify the country or countries which recently a) sentenced a poet to two weeks in prison for penning 'a mockery of the Holy Family and Jesus Christ;' b) promoted

Pepsi-Cola in full-page newspaper ads; c) gave away choice seashore plots of land to Sophia Loren, Gene Kelly, Kirk Douglas, Doris Day, and Frank Sinatra," *Time* magazine challenged its readers in 1971. Of course, the correct answer was "Yugoslavia." The only serious restriction, it seemed, involved discussion of incendiary, nationalist-oriented issues and pointed criticism of the leadership. Everyone remembered the example made of Milovan Djilas, a longtime Tito insider who condemned in his book *The New Class* his comrades' appetite for luxury living. Djilas was expelled from the inner circle and sentenced to prison.

For all the acclaim these innovations generated, they ultimately set in motion the law of unintended consequences. Yugoslavia had refused to become a colony of the Soviet Union, yet the decentralizing/diversification trend caused contradictions that awakened old antagonisms and violated some cherished socialist principles. It became obvious over time, for example, that Croatia and Slovenia were the most consistently prosperous republics in the country. Each had advanced industrial capabilities, historically industrious populations, and the advantages of desirable vacation spots such as the Lake Bled area and the Dalmatian coast. It came as no surprise that they contributed significantly more to the national economy than other republics, and that their citizens had a higher standard of living. Slovenia's per capita income was three times higher than that of the Kosovo region in 1960, and five times higher a decade later. At the same time, the Serbian republic always seemed to consume far more than it contributed, a perception exacerbated by the fact that Belgrade was the capital of the federal bureaucracy and home to the federal economic council and Investment Bank. Complaints began to circulate that Serbs were monopolizing economic resources and wielding administrative power disproportionate to their contributions. It was difficult to argue with statistics, which indicated that Slovenia alone accounted for some 25 percent of the country's export revenue year after year.

At the same time, the related issue of "political" factories came under scrutiny. Because the prosperity of Slovenia and Croatia was certain to cause resentment in the poorer southern parts of the country, Tito had to provide for economic initiatives that would lead to a measure of equality among the republics. In line with this goal, the federal government had financed large industrial enterprises and showcase projects such as soccer stadiums in Bosnia-Hercegovina, Macedonia, and Kosovo. Considerable sums of money from Slovenia and Croatia flowed into these projects, which often appeared at the behest of local officials regardless of need or profitability. Making use of the freedom of expression they enjoyed, Slovenian and Croat journalists questioned the viability of these enterprises. They charged that Croatia and Slovenia had become cash cows for the less industrious regions, which were only too happy to milk them. These complaints caused headaches in Belgrade. Yugoslavia's leaders had committed the country to a decentralized system of administration, yet found themselves bound to maintain the socialist ethos of brotherhood and unity, which frayed in the face of increasing inequalities of development. This problem would defy all attempts at solution, since it was the practical equivalent of squaring a circle.

In response, the authorities reflexively tried to emphasize their commitment to devolving power to the republics. In 1966 Serbian Communist leader Aleksandar Ranković, a consistent critic of decentralizing tendencies in the state, was dismissed from his post. Known as a Serbian nationalist and a consistent advocate of greater central control in Yugoslavia, Ranković was alleged to have been spying on Tito and those in the leadership who disagreed with his ideas. His dismissal was interpreted as an admission that other republics had suffered abuse at the hands of the federal government. This did not squelch the discontent, however; Croat leaders decided to take advantage of the circumstances to press for more favorable concessions. Beginning in 1967, they responded by voicing a host of complaints about what they saw as Serbia's disproportionate influence in the country. Some were cultural in nature, such as the purported Serbian dominance of a Serbo-Croatian dictionary, wherein the Serbian variant of idiomatic expressions allegedly appeared more often than the Croatian. Others pointedly addressed the difficulties of reconciling decentralized economics with "brotherhood and unity."

Croats protested against the concentration in Belgrade of key financial and administrative institutions, a sore point dating to the first Yugoslavia, when Belgrade bureaucrats made all the decisions about economic policy. Now, they claimed, bureaucrats and institutions in Belgrade took valuable Croatian-earned resources and distributed them to less industrious and less deserving individuals, including, of course, Serbs. A season of discontent became a national crisis when some began advocating measures that came close to secession.

Here was a clear illustration that the conflicting demands of regional economic autonomy and maintaining "brotherhood and unity" had no apparent solution. Thus it was incumbent on Tito to play his trump card. In the manner of a strict father, he summoned querulous Croats and reminded them where ethnic conflict could lead. "In some villages, because of nervousness, Serbs are drilling and arming themselves . . . do you want to have 1941 again?" he asked rhetorically. Then he used his authority as the leader of the Yugoslav Communists and founder of the state to purge the state apparatus of the offending individuals. It was understood that Tito had the last word in any contentious dispute.

Slovenes kept their usual low profile during these charged Serb-Croat episodes. The Slovenian republic's president in the late 1960s, Stane Kavčič, understood Croat complaints and even allowed discussion of similar issues in the journal *Perspektive.* Mostly, however, he concentrated on improving the republic's fortunes in a nonconfrontational manner, perhaps recalling Korešec's observation that "Croats debate, Slovenes work." He consistently supported the continued decentralization of the country's economic life. He explored the possibility of Slovenia's negotiating aid and development agreements individually with the less developed republics rather than leaving all such decisions to the Investment Bank and its bureaucrats in Belgrade. He was particularly interested in economic initiatives that played to Slovenia's unique strengths while appearing to benefit the rest of the country as well. To that end, Slovene representatives worked hard to promote projects involving close cooperation with neighboring European states. In 1969 they applied for, and secured, World Bank funding for extensive road improvements in the republic. Routes into and out of Slovenia were heavily used by truck traffic from Europe and free-spending vacationers in Slovenia and Croatia, so it made good sense to keep them in the best shape possible.

Unfortunately, this understated approach met the same end as the Croats' dramatic protest. As was customary, the funding for the road improvements went to the capital, Belgrade, for dispersal. When it arrived, however, Slovenia saw only a tiny fraction, as the Belgrade authorities used their prerogatives and designated most of the money for improvements in other republics. Kavčič protested vigorously, to no avail. In fact, his term as the chief executive of the Slovene republic was cut short by his refusal to endorse the leadership's decision on the funds. Slovenes in turn received an unsubtle reminder that even though they were free to work as hard at their many enterprises as they could, Tito and the federal government would decide who benefited from their hard work.

STRAINS WITHIN YUGOSLAVIA AND RISING RESENTMENT IN SLOVENIA

The difficulties of the late 1960s caused no major upheavals in Yugoslavia. All Yugoslavs received a vivid reminder of their good fortune when they witnessed the Soviet invasion of Czechoslovakia in August 1968. Their quality of life remained high by comparison to that of their neighbors. However, as one Slovene writer later noted, Yugoslavia looked good only when things were going significantly worse elsewhere. In the late 1970s and early 1980s things began to look worse in Yugoslavia, as the economy fell victim to a series of crises, causing a decline in the country's standard of living. Because the republics had the right to determine their own economic priorities, local bosses often opted for big steel and chemical plants, without regard to whether these duplicated similar enterprises next door. The workers' self-management experiment, once hailed as an attractive alternative to central planning, broke down under the strain of bad management and unrealistic expectations. Government spending began to exceed the rate of economic growth, and the country was wracked by serious inflation that cut purchasing power in half. "We used to buy clothes in Italy or travel to Vienna for a weekend at the opera," a Slovenian businessman complained to a Western reporter. "Now we can't even afford to go skiing here at home." As before, regional economic imbalances, exacerbated by unilateral federal decision making, continued to cause resentment in Slovenia and Croatia.

Tito and other members of the leadership sought to solve, or at least mitigate, these problems by drafting a new constitution in 1974. No matter what they did, however, they encountered the same difficulties, born of numerous attempts to reconcile socialist theory with the realities of Yugoslavia. In socialist countries, national distinctions were to disappear with the realization that citizens were all members of one large working class. Kardelj and others realized that this was unlikely to happen spontaneously in fractious Yugoslavia, so their solution was to allow each republic wide latitude to make its own political and economic decisions. At the same time, Tito and the leadership were obliged repeatedly to attempt to maintain some semblance of economic equality among the republics—because socialist theory permitted no inequalities in the working class, and because resentment was typically expressed in nationalist rhetoric and demonstrations. Furthermore, the Communist Party had the leading role, in fact the only role, in all key decisions in a socialist state. Thus they felt confident in retaining for themselves the right to decide how revenues would be distributed in the state. It might have behooved them to consider the introduction of market forces in certain sectors, or to negotiate more acceptable economic arrangements with Slovenia and Croatia. Instead, they decided on more of the same in the 1974 Yugoslav constitution. They offered a bit more devolution of power, in carving two autonomous republics out of the Serbian republic, while declining to make changes in federal economic policy. As always, Tito retained the right to the last word on any question.

The Western press marveled at Yugoslavia's ability to weather these storms and maintain its peculiar "socialism, of a sort." Longtime observers knew there was no secret to its longevity: the key was Tito and Kardelj, two old warriors who had founded the state and made it work despite steep odds. Tito in particular had become an iconic figure. He was the general who had led the nation to an improbable victory in 1945, the Yugoslav David who defied the Soviet Goliath, the final arbiter of and respected last word on the country's most contentious disputes. Only time would tell if Titoism, that improbable balancing act, would survive without Tito and a steadily rising standard of living.

THE SLOVENES AND YUGOSLAVIA AFTER TITO (1980–1987)

The deaths of Kardelj in 1979 and Tito in 1980 meant that Yugoslavia at last faced a real test of its long-term viability. In order to avoid the impression that some republics had more power than others, Tito's replacement would be a rotating presidency. Each republic would take turns contributing a leader, chosen by his parliament. In this way, it was hoped, the spirit of brotherhood and unity would survive the loss of its inspiration. However, early indications did not look promising. The country's deepening economic woes, which were now manifested in a ballooning federal debt, exacerbated the growing differences among the republics. In 1983 federal authorities finally recognized the emergency and took steps to try to address it, including an edict that all republics should share equally in the repayment of the debt, regardless of the percentage for which they might be responsible. This meant that Slovenia and Croatia, whose leaders already believed that their contributions kept the state viable, would have to bail out their less prosperous countrymen in the south. The citizens of both republics were already weary of this state of affairs and did not wish to see it continue.

Slovenes were at a crossroads after Tito. In the first Yugoslavia and the early decades of the second they had shown considerable satisfaction with their lot because they believed that their lives had significantly improved. In the years after Tito, though, they no longer seemed so certain. In the mid-1980s Slovenia experienced a remarkable period of cultural and political ferment that presaged a reevaluation of its status within Yugoslavia. Younger Slovenes led the way in creating this "Slovenian spring." They embraced trends seen elsewhere among European youth, advocating conscientious objection as an alternative to military service, campaigning for gay rights, and raising awareness of ecological issues. In 1986 they spearheaded a campaign to defeat a proposed increase in an environmental protection tax in Slovenia and won a promise from Slovene leaders to reevaluate ecological policy in the republic instead. But they broke some new ground as well, founding a new school of artistic expression called Neue Slowenische Kunst (New Slovenian Art). Adherents attracted much attention through their embrace of Nazi apparel and subject matter. The rock group Laibach, which eventually gained a following beyond Slovenia, devoted many of its songs to explorations of Hitler and other totalitarian leaders and concepts. It was widely supposed that these artists sought to use shock value in order to solidify support among their young followers, but many observers perceived that there was something more at work in their performances. They consistently mocked the traditions and ethos of Tito's Yugoslavia.

Portrait of Milan Kučan, president of Slovenia (1990–). (Government of Slovenia)

As a rule, officialdom in Europe viewed youth movements with skepticism. By contrast, the adults joined in the searching and probing in Slovenia. As Laibach broadcast its convictions about Slovenia's recent past, the respected cultural journal *Nova revija* urged a similar evaluation on its more mature readers. Its now famous issue 57 (1987), "Contributions to a Slovene National Program," was devoted entirely to the question of Slovenia's place in Yugoslavia. Contributors pulled no punches. As the most productive and industrious of all the republics, they argued, Slovenia should at least enjoy proportional political influence. They questioned the legal basis of Communist rule in Yugoslavia and outlined strategies that would distance Slovenia from the federal government. Far from attempting to choke off these sentiments, Slovene Communists in the post-Kardelj period often echoed them. Accordingly, younger leaders such as Milan Kučan contemplated a variety of solutions to the country's mounting economic ills, including such uncommunist measures as applying the laws of supply and demand and creating more open markets. At this point, no one was thinking about independence; the emphasis was on creating a more advantageous position for Slovenia within Yugoslavia.

Events in Serbia soon altered these assumptions. Like their fellow citizens in the other republics, Serbs were discussing changes they wished to see in post-Tito Yugoslavia. Their proposals differed in that they invoked the past rather than the future. Where Slovenia and Croatia were talking about greater pluralism and alternative solutions to pressing difficulties, Serbs seemed to be moving back toward the familiar confines of centralism and Serb dominance. In the mid-1980s some writers were proposing that Serbo-Croatian become the official language of Yugoslavia, a measure that would disenfranchise citizens who spoke Slovenian, Macedonian, and Albanian. There was more to come. In 1986 the Serbian Academy of Sciences issued a memorandum in which members outlined the numerous ways in which the Serbian republic had suffered unjust treatment in Tito's Yugoslavia. Serbs, the authors alleged, had seen the power of their republic deliberately diminished in the creation of autonomous Vojvodina and Kosovo. They had watched helplessly as Serbia became a mere supplier of raw materials to other republics, impoverishing itself in the process. They had endured the one-sided, public persecution of major representatives in the national leadership (Ranković) and the harassment and injury of their conationals at the hands of Albanians in Kosovo, once the cradle of Serbian statehood. It was strongly implied that these injustices should be remedied through an improved status for Serbs within Yugoslavia.

THE ROAD TO SLOVENE INDEPENDENCE (1987–1991)

The election of Slobodan Milošević to the presidency of the Serbian republic made the perception of a Serbian resurgence a reality. Milošević's first move as president was a personal visit to Priština, the capital of the Kosovo autonomous region. This area, site of Serbia's landmark defeat at the hands of the Turks in 1389, had a mixed Serb-Albanian population that often found itself embroiled in ethnic conflict. Once part of the Serbian republic, Kosovo had received autonomous status in Tito's 1974 revision of the Yugoslav constitution, a development that rankled in Belgrade since it meant that Albanian Yugoslavs would rule their fellow Serbs. In early 1987 Kosovo had witnessed periodic Serb-Albanian rioting, prompting Milošević to schedule a fact-finding trip for April. After one contentious meeting with local citizens on 24 April 1987, he abandoned all pretense at investigation and became a partisan. He appeared in the midst of a Serb-Albanian street fight in Priština to declare his determination that Serbs "will never be beaten again." This event, broadcast nationwide on the evening news, caused many outside Serbia to wonder whether Milošević intended to champion a Serbian ascendancy in Yugoslavia.

The Serbian president did nothing to discourage this impression. Soon after Kosovo, he began a purge of the Serbian Communist Party in order to rid himself of opposition. At the same time, he sent large crowds, later described as a Milošević "rent-a-crowd," of thugs and enforcers, to demand the reincorporation of the autonomous republics of Kosovo and Hungarian-majority Vojvodina back into Serbia. Frightened by the menacing demeanor of these crowds, the leaders of both republics had little choice but to yield to their demands. Leaders in other republics reacted strongly. Slovenia's representative to the federal presidency, the respected economist and diplomat Janez Stanovik, declared that Milošević's behavior smacked of Stalinism. His colleague Milan Kučan was more concerned with the immediate political impact. "By abolishing the autonomy of both provinces of Vojvodina and Kosovo," Kučan said later, "Serbia would directly control three of eight votes, in comparison with the other republics that had one vote each." Since Montenegro always voted with Serbia, Milošević would actually have four votes in the federal council—a commanding advantage. This could make possible the transformation of post-Tito Yugoslavia into "Serboslavia," an updated version of the type of Serbian centralist rule that had helped destroy the first Yugoslavia.

The events of the next year proved to be a chilling demonstration for Slovenes of Milošević's values. After Tito's death, the Slovene youth magazine *Mladina* had become a cutting-edge publication, enjoying ever increasing popularity among all age groups for probing the limits of self-expression in Yugoslavia. Like Slovenian rockers and artists, its journalists delighted in baiting the nation's leaders. They published caricatures of Slobodan Milošević in medieval armor in Kosovo, the Serbian avenger on a demented crusade. They helped to arrange the scheduling of a conference of homosexuals in Ljubljana on 25 May 1987, Tito's birthday, causing panicked federal authorities to ban this obvious show of disrespect on the pretext of fighting AIDS. But *Mladina* had serious investigative ambitions, too. In a particularly explosive series, their journalists were the first to expose and detail in print the execution of thousands of anticommunist Slovenes, the Domobranci, by Tito's regime in the aftermath of World War II.

Milošević and the federal authorities in Belgrade did not take such impertinence lightly. In late 1987 they began plotting a response they believed would put a stop to it altogether. In February 1988 Slovenian police arrested a young army recruit, Ivan Borstner, and three *Mladina* staffers, Janez Janša, David Tasić, and Franci Zavrl. They were imprisoned and charged with possession and copying of a classified document outlining contingency plans for the imposition of martial law in Slovenia.

It was widely believed that the Yugoslav army, whose Serb-dominated officer corps took great exception to *Mladina,* had ordered the arrest. No one believed the charges, as became abundantly clear in the spontaneous gathering of 20,000 Slovenes in Ljubljana's town square, the largest since World War II. They demanded the immediate release of the "Ljubljana Four" and condemned the army's attempts to suppress a bold, hard-hitting periodical. The Slovene Communist leaders went farther, accusing the Yugoslav military of attempting to interfere with the right of Slovenes to administer their own affairs. All Slovenes were shocked when the trial was conducted behind closed doors in Serbo-Croatian rather than Slovene, a direct assault on Slovene national identity. They were positively outraged by the convictions and prison terms that the trial produced in July 1988. If Slovenia could expect Serbian bureaucrats to continue running roughshod over Slovene sensibilities in the future, perhaps it was time to consider other options.

The *Mladina* affair convinced many Slovenes that Milošević wanted not just to promote Serbia at Slovenia's expense, but also to compel Slovenia to remain in Yugoslavia by force. Subsequent events only strengthened these convictions. On 28 June 1989, Milošević made a well-publicized return visit to Kosovo. The date he chose was no coincidence; it marked the historic six-hundredth anniversary of the battle of Kosovo, which Prince Lazar and his Serbian army lost to the Ottoman Turks. In a dramatic appearance near the site of the battle, Milošević unsheathed his rhetorical sword, proclaiming his intent to "avenge Kosovo." By this he meant that Serbs would not be defeated again. They would repel all assaults on their nation and culture and take their deserved leading role in post-Tito Yugoslavia. The Kosovo speech, and the Serb-Albanian clashes it fueled, produced great consternation in Slovenia. Both *Mladina* and *Nova revija* had devoted extensive coverage to human rights abuses around the world. A prominent Slovene politician had already resigned from the League of Communists executive council over this issue, condemning Serbian mindlessness in Kosovo. Kučan called it "the worst human rights problem in all of Europe" and condemned its corrosive impact on Yugoslavia's political life as well as its image abroad.

After Slovenia declares independence from Yugoslavia on June 25, the Slovenian territorial army takes up a defensive position in the capital, 2 July 1991. (Jacques Langevin/Corbis Sygma)

In February 1989 Slovene leaders held a public meeting to denounce Serbian ham-handedness in dealing with an Albanian miners' strike in Kosovo. As the meeting was broadcast nationwide, Serbs had the opportunity to witness this barrage of criticism. Although Slovene leaders had broken no laws, Milošević could not abide their show of disrespect and decided to send his Serb "supporters" to demonstrate in Ljubljana. The group was to set the Slovene public straight about Kosovo and rumored Slovene plans to redefine their republic's relationship with Yugoslavia. It was understood that the Milošević crowd would repeat the drill its members had perfected elsewhere: menacing the Slovene leadership to the point where they would flee for their lives. Slovenia's president, Janez Stanovnik, opted to ban the demonstration and turn back the crowd; they had nixed a chance for a town meeting, he said, and some of the prospective "truth tellers" had less than peaceful intentions since they were armed. Having failed to intimidate the Slovenian leadership, Milošević slapped economic sanctions on the rebellious republic. This was an absurd situation, comparable in American terms to Massachusetts boycotting Maine, but Milošević was adamant that the Slovenes learn they could not defy him.

In any case, it was not clear that the Slovenes cared what Milošević thought any more. Their leaders had already concluded that Slovenia could share the fate of the Kosovars and were preparing exit strategies. They began by amending the republic's constitution to alter Slovenia's relationship with the other republics of Yugoslavia. Specifically, they claimed authority to impose martial law in the republic, command Yugoslav army units in the country, regulate expenditures of Slovene revenues, and permit the formation of opposition political parties. Opposition parties in particular violated a key tenet of communist ideology, which reserved for the Communist Party a monopoly on political power. More important still, the Slovene leadership allowed for the official appearance of opposition in full awareness that many would-be candidates actively supported Slovenian sovereignty, or even outright independence.

In April 1990 the Communist leadership of Slovenia and Croatia formally separated from the League of Communists of Yugoslavia and held the first multiparty elections in Yugoslav history. The winners in both cases were mostly avowed anti-Communists. Slovenes gave the DEMOS a substantial victory, but voted in their longtime Communist Party leader, Milan Kučan, for president. As many observers noted, Kučan may have been the first Communist presidential candidate ever to prevail in a free election. Though they still talked of a future within Yugoslavia, Kučan and other Slovene leaders insisted on the reorganization of the country into a confederation of sovereign states bound together for purposes of deciding strictly national issues such as foreign and defense policy. Subsequent events showed they had the support of their constituents. In September 1990 a referendum on the country's future was announced. In December Slovene voters went to the polls to make their wishes known. An astonishing 80 percent expressed support for sovereignty. The leadership then reiterated its demands for a confederated Yugoslavia and declared Slovenia would secede in the absence of such an arrangement.

By early 1991, it was clear that Yugoslavia was headed for a breakup. In January it was disclosed that the Serbian Parliament had made an illegal midnight raid on the federal bank, withdrawing several billion dinars, with which they intended to pay wages and pensions in Serbia exclusively. Outraged by this "Great Serbian Bank Robbery," both Slovenia and Croatia promptly announced that they would no longer be bound by any federal economic laws. Milošević countered by ordering the immediate disarmament of territorial militias in Slovenia and Croatia, a process he had initiated secretly the previous fall. This move was particularly shocking, since Tito had created the militias in all six republics following the 1968 Soviet invasion of Czechoslovakia. He wanted to see "every man a soldier" so as to be able to wage Partisan-style guerrilla warfare against large invading forces, such as the Red Army. It was absolutely clear now that Milošević would hear nothing of confederation. He was preparing to send the Yugoslav army to prevent the exit of the rebellious republics and clearly hoped to decapitate any opposition in advance. Leaders of both nations drew the appropriate conclusion and indicated that they would declare formal independence in June.

As expected, Milošević and the Yugoslav army brass prepared countermeasures. In Croatia, the bid for independence ran into opposition from the republic's 700,000-strong Serbian majority, which was receiving covert armed assistance from Belgrade. Thus a small-scale civil conflict was under way in eastern Croatia by February. The Slovenes' situation was not as serious, because there were virtually no Serbs living in Slovenia, but officials knew they would face armed attempts to prevent their exit from Yugoslavia. Indeed, the federal authorities sent troops north in late June in order to bring Slovenia to heel. Those in charge of the operation did not believe that Slovenes would fight, especially since they had not yet received any formal support from abroad. No western government had recognized Slovenia, fearing that to do so would precipitate the disintegration of Yugoslavia and encourage separatist-minded groups elsewhere in Europe. A small show of force, it was reasoned, would suffice to convince Slovenia that resistance was folly.

But the Yugoslav army leadership had not reckoned with the determination of the new Slovene defense minister, an old antagonist. Newly installed in his post, former *Mladina* staffer Janez Janša organized a spirited defense based on the classic skills of the weak: speed and cunning. President Kučan did his part by proclaiming Slovene independence one day earlier than planned, 24 June, so that Slovene border guards could replace their federal counterparts and offer resistance at the frontier. Elsewhere, militia and ordinary citizens worked hard to slow and frustrate the invaders.

Ljubljana overnight became a city barricaded for its defense, with roads and railways blocked and soldiers and heavily armed forces seemingly everywhere. Electricity in the Yugoslav army barracks mysteriously shut off, and cars jammed the highways from all directions, trapping the oncoming tank convoys. It helped that federal troops did not know the terrain well and had made no provision for resupply; some units went through all their food and water in a day. The Slovenes' fortitude impressed the Yugoslav commanders, who were trained to fight back but proved mindful of their young recruits and their parents, many of whom did not want their sons involved in what they viewed as a discretionary war. "We will not yield," Janša had warned as he contemplated facing his former accusers. The Yugoslav army found the Slovene people fully deserving of his confidence.

On 2 July, a cease-fire was brokered; on 7 July, after hours and hours of negotiation, the Yugoslav federal government reached tentative consensus with Slovenian and Croatian leaders in the Brioni agreement. The declarations of independence both nations had issued were temporarily suspended in exchange for the withdrawal of Yugoslav army troops. However, to all intents and purposes Slovenia was now on its own. Milošević had decided to concentrate his fire on Croatia and Bosnia, where the presence of sizable Serb minorities guaranteed him a chance to reconquer ethnic and historic Serbian territory. At the country's first celebration of independence, President Kučan stressed that Slovenia's new status represented a major break with the past. "Probably in different conditions, we could mature further and link our destiny with that of others," he said, "but even so, we have managed by ourselves. We are a mature nation that knows what it wants. Indeed a new chapter is beginning in our life." Fourteen centuries of communal living behind them, Slovenes now contemplated an independent existence for the first time.

POLITICAL DEVELOPMENTS

Most of the former socialist states in Europe have experienced a combination of continuity and change in their political life since their independence over a decade ago. In Slovenia, the dynamic is slightly different: a high degree of continuity, and consensus, in a time of significant change. The politicians who plotted the Slovene republic's successful exit from Yugoslavia—mainly Milan Kučan, Janez Drnovšek, Janez Janša, Dmitrij Rupel—have stayed on as the leaders of the first independent Slovenia. During the state's first decade, they achieved substantial agreement in securing recognition of Slovene independence, creating essential institutions, solving problems associated with the Yugoslav wars, and determining the direction of the state in the twenty first century.

CLEARING THE WAY FOR INDEPENDENCE

By the late 1980s, the team that would preside over the first independent Slovene state was assembling. Many of its members were avowed anticommunists, intent on bringing

Special Ks

Aficionados of historical trivia are fond of pointing out that political leaders of various nations have shared some outstanding commonality in modern history. In the United States, for example, a disproportionate number of presidents hail from the states of Virginia or Massachusetts. In Slovenia, it is all in a name, or more accurately a letter: its most celebrated politicians all seem to have family names beginning in the letter *K*.

Anton Korošec shaped Slovene politics from the turn of the century until his death on the eve of World War II in 1939. Born in the Maribor region in 1872, Korošec began his professional life as a Roman Catholic priest. During his service as a parish priest in villages in Styria, he observed the difficulties his parishioners encountered with their German neighbors, who tried to deny them the use of their native language. He wanted to become a better advocate for them and won election to the Austrian Parliament on his second try. As a leader of the Slovene Clerical Party, Korošec was a strong supporter of the Habsburg monarchy. Like virtually all of his South Slavic colleagues, he pressed for strategic changes in its administrative structure but felt that it was the best arrangement for small nations like his own.

After World War I cast a shadow over all empires, he began to prepare for other possible outcomes. He was a founding member of the Yugoslav Club, a group of South Slav representatives in the parliament. In 1917 he delivered the May Declaration, which called for a reorganization of the Habsburg monarchy, to answer rising national aspirations among its South Slavic peoples. When all looked hopeless in 1918, Korošec faced the inevitable without flinching. According to legend, it was he who broke the news to Franz Joseph's successor, Karl, that there was no hope of salvaging the centuries-old monarchy.

Upon the collapse of the Austro-Hungarian Empire in October 1918, Korošec presided over the National Council, the institution that represented the monarchy's South Slavic peoples in the immediate postwar period. In this capacity, he helped negotiate Slovenia's entry into the Kingdom of Serbs, Croats, and Slovenes, later known as Yugoslavia. Because he knew that life in Yugoslavia represented a great improvement for Slovenes, who now had language guarantees, schools, and institutions of their own, he mostly supported the Serb-dominated leadership even as the Croats vehemently opposed it. At the time of his death, which nearly coincided with that of the first Yugoslavia, Korošec could justly claim to be a politician in the truest sense of the word. He had mastered the art of the possible for his people.

Edward Kardelj succeeded Korošec as unofficial leader of the Slovenes, though he would have disputed that title since his communist orientation held that national distinctions belonged to the dustbin of history. As a young revolutionary in the first Yugoslavia, which banned the Communist Party early in its existence, Kardelj spent much of his time in clandestine agitation. Like many of his comrades elsewhere, he eventually ended up in prison, where he wrote his first book, appropriately titled *Struggle*.

Kardelj and the Yugoslav Communists suddenly became relevant when the German army invaded Yugoslavia in April and then the Soviet Union two months later. Following Moscow's exhortations to wage all-out war on fascism, Kardelj rallied representatives of prewar Slovenian political parties to fight the invaders. His fortunes rose dramatically following his affiliation with Tito and the Partisan movement, the nationwide resistance, which eventually won the war with Germany and the right to form a communist Yugoslavia in May 1945. Kardelj emerged from the war as Tito's top thinker and policymaker in the second Yugoslavia, only to have his theoretical foundation rocked in the 1948 break with the Soviet Union. Like Tito, he met the challenge of reinventing the state. Since the Soviet model was no longer tenable, Kardelj created a new theoretical framework that emphasized local control of economic and social policy, declared the national question dead, and advocated a cultivated neutrality in foreign affairs:

(continues)

democracy and independence to Slovenia in an era when communism appeared headed for the dustbin of history. Others, notably Milan Kučan and Janez Drnovšek, were high-ranking Communists unhappy with the perceived economic exploitation of Slovenia and alarmed at the resurgence of nationalist/hegemonist sentiment in the Serbian republic. Following the 1988 trial of three *Mladina* journalists who exposed a Yugoslav army plot to "destabilize" Slovenia, both Communists and anti-Communists had seen enough of Slobodan Milošević's Yugoslavia to conclude that they should join forces to try to escape. Together, they prepared the citizenry for this throughout 1990 and 1991. They

(continued)

nonalignment with either the eastern or the western camps in the Cold War. In his lifetime, he was hailed for his unconventional thinking. However, following his death in 1979, it became clear that in creating a decentralized communist state, he had unwittingly made possible the resurgence of national feeling he fervently hoped would wither away. A committed socialist to the end of his life, Kardelj would undoubtedly be shocked and dismayed to discover that part of his legacy is an independent, capitalist Slovenia.

Stane Kavčič, the Communist Party leader of Slovenia in the 1970s, had a comparatively brief tenure by comparison with his compatriots. However, he had an influence well beyond his tenure in office; in a real sense, he is the author of Slovenia's successful transition from socialism to economic democracy and free markets. He consistently advocated the expansion of Slovene economic activity beyond Yugoslavia into Europe and urged Slovenian businesspeople to concentrate on areas likely to be both important and profitable in the future, such as electronics and home appliances. Firms specializing in those areas have made the most successful transitions in the period since independence and are fueling Slovenian prosperity today.

The fourth K, Milan Kučan, became the most prominent Slovene in the wake of Kardelj's departure. A native of Prekmurje, the Slovenian region closest to Hungary, he rose quickly through the Yugoslav Communist youth organization and entered the top ranks of the Slovene leadership in the 1970s. Kučan's star rose sharply in the difficult and confusing years following the deaths of Yugoslavia's founding fathers, Tito and Kardelj. Sensing that Slovenes were contemplating a different relationship with Yugoslavia, Kučan helped them decide how they wished to proceed. In the 1980s he winced at the youth culture that mocked Tito, yet read between the provocative lines and urged people to pay closer attention. When Slobodan Milošević came to power in Serbia on a platform of aggressive nationalism, Kučan saw danger ahead for Slovenes. He took the lead in distancing Slovenia from Yugoslavia, perhaps before its citizens were ready to take such a step. He was the first Communist leader to commit the heresy of allowing multiparty elections, breaking the monopoly of Communist rule in Slovenia. In 1990, when Slovene voters rewarded his leadership and elected him president, Kučan made history as perhaps the first Communist ever to triumph in a free election. Assisted ably by his deputies Dmitrij Rupel and Janez Janša, Kučan helped pave the way for Slovenia's exit from Yugoslavia. He helped deflect criticism away from Slovenia for precipitating a crisis in Yugoslavia by repeatedly stressing his willingness to remain in a confederated arrangement. When that proved to be a nonstarter, Kučan helped plan Slovenia's defense during the ten-day war with the Yugoslav army and lobbied hard for international recognition of Slovene independence, which came late in 1991.

After independence, Kučan had perhaps the most difficult task in postcommunist Europe: leading a people who had never lived independently in the creation of its own nation state. The challenges were legion: securing international recognition, creating financial, legislative, and judicial institutions from scratch, determining the size and character of national defense, and negotiating Slovenia's formal entry into organizations that would guarantee a secure future for Slovenes. Despite many difficulties, especially the unexpected rejection of Slovenia's application to enter NATO in 1997, Slovenes gave him over 55 percent of the vote in each of his two campaigns. Kučan left office in 2002, having seen the nation through the challenging first years and helping it celebrate ten years of independence and rising prosperity. Among his last achievements was Slovenia's successful application for NATO membership on its second try in November 2002.

For his leadership during the transition to independent statehood alone, Kučan may prove to be the most popular and successful Slovene statesman ever.

wrote and agitated in *Mladina* and *Nova revija,* held the country's first free elections, and carried through the referendum on sovereignty in December 1990. As conflict with Milošević sharpened, Kučan made a show of presenting various reorganization plans for Yugoslavia that would afford protection against further economic exploitation and attempts at political domination by Serbia. He doubtless knew that they would be rejected, but he hoped to inoculate Slovenia against charges that it initiated the breakup of Yugoslavia.

With their formal declaration of independence in June 1991, Kučan and his DEMOS—Demokratična Opozicija Slovenije, Democratic Opposition of Slovenia—colleagues braced for Milošević's attempt to prevent Slovenia from leaving and joined their fellow citizens in defeating a Yugoslav army force after ten days of fighting. In July 1991 they found themselves the leaders of a Slovenia in transition, an entity no longer a republic of Yugoslavia but not yet an independent state. Their first task was therefore to clear away the detritus of war and persuade the European Community and other key institutions to recognize the new state.

The process of securing recognition did not go smoothly. As then Foreign Minister Dmitrij Rupel remembers, there were no objections in principle to the idea of an independent Slovenia, but this necessarily brought with it the possibility that the Yugoslav state would collapse. The European Community (EC), which had the authority to extend recognition, was wary about the consequences of that eventuality—correctly, as subsequent events in Croatia and Bosnia demonstrated. All parties in the Brioni Agreement of 7 July agreed to delay action for three months, which would allow more time to assess the changing situation in Yugoslavia. Meanwhile, Kučan, Rupel, and others worked to secure the withdrawal of the Yugoslav army from Slovene territory. At first, they encountered resistance, even threats of renewed action from the Yugoslav government, but the problem largely solved itself with a mass exodus of Slovene soldiers from the ranks. There seemed little reason for the rest of the army to remain under those circumstances. That fall, there was lingering skepticism among EC nations as well as the United States about the wisdom of recognizing Slovenian (and Croatian) independence. By December, however, European Community representatives had decided to ratify the fait accompli and extend recognition to the two states. Recognition from the United States, which finally acknowledged the inevitable, came in April 1992.

THE FIRST CONSTITUTION

With recognition forthcoming, the architects who had made the new Slovenia could proceed with building an infrastructure for their state. As always, the first task was to draft a constitution. Ljubljana University law professor Miro Cerar chaired a commission of some one hundred experts, government officials, and interested citizens charged with studying constitutions of other European states and making appropriate recommendations to the Slovene leadership. Members of the commission looked at the Austrian, Italian, and German constitutions in order to acquire basic familiarity with a democratic document. They reviewed the constitution of Hungary, since that country had emerged from circumstances similar to Slovenia's. The Spanish and Greek constitutions also came under review, since those countries had once been dictatorships. Finally, the commission pondered the advantages and disadvantages of two prevailing models for the conduct of state business: the presidential system, anchored by a strong executive, and the parliamentary model, in which the national legislature had more power.

The inaugural Slovene constitution, ratified in December 1991, reflected the Cerar commission's findings, the experience of the recent past, and Slovenes' hopes for the future. The document had sixty-five articles, showcasing a strong belief in the rule of law, individual rights, and separation of powers, all characteristics of democratic constitutions. In a nod to European constitutional tradition, Slovene citizens were guaranteed a social safety net, to include pension benefits and health care. Slovenes' prized possession, the Slovene language, was enshrined as the country's official language. Slovenia's Italian and Hungarian minorities received the right to use their native language for official purposes in their local areas. In addition, they were each guaranteed one deputy to the Slovene legislature and the right of veto over any legislation directly affecting them. Memories of life under Tito and Milošević ruled out a strong executive, so the constitution provided for a powerful legislative branch. The president, who may serve two consecutive five-year terms, can appoint the prime minister; otherwise, his duties are largely ceremonial. Provisions for the rights of trade unions, workers' right to strike, and worker-management consultation demonstrated that the framers of the constitution did not regard their Yugoslav experience as entirely unworthy of emulation.

As political scientists have emphasized, there were only two points of serious disagreement in the writing of the constitution. One concerned the question of abortion, a contentious issue in all Catholic countries. Those on the right in the country's evolving political dynamic wanted it banned, while those leaning left campaigned for guarantees of abortion rights. Abortion rights proponents carried the day on that issue. Additionally, there was conflict regarding the nature of the National Assembly, whether it should have two houses or one. Opponents reached a compromise here. Slovenia would have a unicameral legislature, featuring a *državni zbor,* a national assembly composed of ninety representatives elected for four-year terms from throughout the country. This body was given primary responsibility for writing legislation. A *državni svet,* state council, to include regional interests and workers, managers, and cultural affairs representatives, would play an advisory role, though its forty members would have the right to introduce legislation. Taken together with the responsibilities accorded the president and the judiciary, this arrangement guaranteed a separation of powers and enfranchised citizens representing a variety of backgrounds, an important concession for a democracy in its infancy.

THE FIRST GOVERNMENT: TURMOIL AND TRANSITION

The constitution having been written and ratified, it was time to govern. The first nationwide elections, held in December 1992, saw the reelection of Milan Kučan as president. A coalition of like-minded parties, led by the perennially successful Liberal Democrats, won a majority of seats in the National Assembly and tapped Kučan's former Slovene Communist Party colleague, Janez Drnovšek, to serve as prime minister. This was an experienced team, and its members would need every ounce of that experience to meet the immediate challenges they faced. Some of these were fundamental, such as appointing members of the judiciary, assembling a Slovene foreign service, and dealing with

Janez Drnovšek. (Courtesy of the Embassy of the Republic of Slovenia)

hangover issues from Yugoslavia, such as restitution of land and property taken by the Communists from blacklisted institutions like the Catholic Church. Discussion about the structure and composition of the Slovenian army also commenced at this time.

The most pressing issue was extraordinary and dangerous. The Yugoslav-Croatian conflict had escalated into a full-scale war over Bosnia-Hercegovina. Some 30 percent of the population there were Serbs, another 30 percent were Croats, and both governments claimed these populations. But there were many Bosnian Muslims living in Serb and Croat areas. Neither Milošević nor Croatian President Franjo Tudjman wanted to see a "West Bank situation," with Muslims protesting their treatment before crowds of international journalists. Thus Serb and Croat forces began a campaign of intimidation and ethnic cleansing intended to rid the desired areas of non-Serb and non-Croat citizens.

The Bosnian war had immediate and serious consequences in Slovenia. Slovene manufacturers and businessmen had counted on continued trade with the Yugoslav republics that remained, because they had always constituted a major market for Slovene products. But war-related United Nations sanctions made this impossible, and the losses hit hard in Slovenia, with businesses struggling to retain their employees and remain viable. In the midst of this economic turmoil, thousands of desperate Bosnian Muslims, driven from their homes by ethnic cleansing, sought refuge in Slovenia.

The Drnovšek government fashioned pragmatic solutions to these twin emergencies. It attempted to mitigate the economic crisis by encouraging beleaguered businesses to take maximum advantage of established contacts abroad and initiating debate on the process of privatizing state enterprises. The National Assembly addressed the refugees' plight by allocating some $250 million to provide emergency food and shelter. Lawmakers were able to enlist the help of volunteer groups, who provided essential services and lobbied for donations from sympathetic foreign governments. In the United States, the Maryland state government paid for heating and medical care in some refugee centers.

Unfortunately, the war showed no signs of abating as 1992 wore on. Meanwhile the country's unemployment rate climbed into double digits, and Slovene citizens became anxious and fearful about the newcomers, who kept coming. Opinion polls showed rising anti-immigrant sentiment; over 90 percent of respondents in one poll favored restrictions on citizenship and organized political action among immigrants. Obliged now to take public opinion into account, the Slovene leadership toughened its stance. In January 1993 it closed the country's borders to refugees and tried to discourage those who remained from making Slovenia their permanent home. It housed them in camps away from major population centers, in dingy, makeshift buildings that reminded *Boston Globe* reporter James Carroll of a concentration camp. Residents faced restrictions on their movements, educational opportunities, and access to employment. In spite of criticism from the United Nations High Commission on Refugees, which felt that Slovenia should be more receptive to the refugees' plight, the leadership declined to open the state's borders immediately. Like other nascent democrats in Central Europe, Kučan, Drnovšek, and their allies found it necessary to take care of their own first, even if the decision did not play well abroad.

By 1995, the government's efforts had brought an improvement in the overall condition of the country. The most ambitious and successful businesses, such as Belinka chemical products, had retooled and reoriented themselves toward Western European markets after the loss of clients in Yugoslavia. After two years of contentious debate, in which individuals mistrustful of private enterprise sparred with those who saw privatization as the sine qua non of a prosperous Slovenia, a law on privatization had gained approval in the legislature in 1994. The foundation for an independent judiciary had been established, and discussions about the transformation of the Slovene military continued. The war in Bosnia was not over, but peace proposals were being floated, and the refugee tide had ebbed. The Kučan-Drnovšek government thus was able to shift out of crisis management into long-term planning.

Kučan and Drnovšek saw membership in the European Union as the major long-term goal for Slovenia. This was just the latest step in a steady progression. Far-sighted Slovene politicians had established close relationships with

EU member nations in the 1960s and 1970s, and a desire for unfettered contacts with Europe had played its role in the decision to seek separation from Yugoslavia. Now, four years after Slovene independence, the state met the basic criteria for membership. It had established a stable democracy and provided guarantees for its national minorities. It had a good, if not perfect, human rights record. Additionally, it had the beginnings of a functioning market economy and the potential to fulfill and implement the numerous European Union laws governing transport, social policy, and property rights. In 1993 the Slovene government became a member of the Council of Europe, an important first step toward EU membership.

The first government also asserted that membership in the North Atlantic Treaty Organization (NATO) would bring advantages for Slovenia. Since Slovenes had unpleasant memories of the Yugoslav army from their brief war for independence and saw few threats abroad, there was some reluctance to discuss military or defense matters. However, this changed in view of recurring friction between Slovenia and Croatia over access to the Adriatic and the volatile situation next door in the former Yugoslavia. The criteria for NATO membership were the same as for the European Union—stable democracy, human rights guarantees, and a functioning market economy. It was believed that Slovenia had an additional advantage in its position as a bridge between Italy and Hungary, another prospective NATO member, and as a buffer between the European democracies and the Balkans. Accordingly, in early 1994 the National Assembly took the first step toward membership by joining the NATO preparatory program, the Partnership for Peace. In 1995 Slovene soldiers participated in a joint exercise with the United States. Observers noted that NATO membership was not universally popular among lawmakers. Some worried about the loss of control that membership in a large military alliance would require. However, President Kučan, the leading parties in the National Assembly, and the business community actively supported NATO membership, terming it an "insurance policy for foreign investment and tourism." NATO membership represented the best guarantees of the security of small nations for the foreseeable future.

In 1996 Kučan and Drnovšek faced the voters in the second national election. They made their case for another term by citing their role in righting the state in the tumultuous first years and their promotion of Slovenia's membership in NATO and the European Union. Some of their colleagues in the National Assembly criticized what they perceived as the slow pace of economic reform and privatization, but the voters felt otherwise. They strongly endorsed the country's direction, returning Drnovšek and the Liberal Party to an advantageous position in the legislature and Kučan to the presidency with a healthy majority the following year. Consensus and continuity prevailed in a time of change.

THE SECOND NATIONAL GOVERNMENT: FOCUS ON THE FUTURE

All during the election year of 1996, the Slovene government kept its focus on the future. The country's EU application had run into unanticipated trouble in 1994–1995, when the Italian government raised the issue of compensation for property confiscated by the Tito government after World War II. The 1975 Treaty of Osimo was supposed to have made restitution a dead issue, but Italian representatives insisted that the breakup of Yugoslavia made possible a revision of that agreement. Hoping to avoid reopening a contentious issue, the Slovene side insisted that the treaty was still in force. After a few months of wrangling, in which the Slovene government demanded a review of the Slovene minority's status in Italy, the two sides agreed that Slovenia would amend its constitution to allow Italians or any other foreigners to buy property in the country. This move was, in any case, required to come into compliance with European Union property law, so it was not regarded as a surrender to Italian demands.

The resolution of this issue paved the way for Prime Minister Drnovšek to sign an Associate Membership agreement with the European Union on 10 June 1996. This implied acceptance into the EU after the completion of all the preliminary steps, including complying with the body of existing laws and regulations—the *acquis communautaire*—already in effect in EU member countries. Slovenia was considered to be on the fast track because its GDP already exceeded that of Greece and Portugal, which had already gained full membership.

NATO membership appeared to be a certainty as well by 1997. Visiting Ljubljana in the late summer of 1996, U.S. Defense Secretary William Perry sang Slovenia's praises, declaring that in areas important to NATO, "Slovenia is as advanced as any of the countries of Central and Eastern Europe." However, when the formal announcement of new NATO members came in the summer of 1997, Slovenia was not included. There were various reasons given for the exclusion, including Slovenia's alleged slow progress in adapting its military to NATO standards, disagreement among members about which new members would most benefit from membership, and reluctance to include a former Yugoslav republic while the situation in the former Yugoslavia remained unsettled. In any case, the Slovene leadership made clear its intention to press for acceptance in the next round of NATO expansion. It endeavored to make itself useful to the alliance, allowing the use of its airspace during NATO operations in Kosovo in 1999 and touting the special expertise it could offer the alliance. Foreign Minister Dmitrij Rupel frequently reminded audiences in important member nations about Slovenia's expert knowledge of the Balkans, its geographic advantage, and its ability to field units of Alpine troops.

As the national election of 2000 neared, the Kučan-Drnovšek administration appeared to be making steady progress in moving the state closer to EU membership. Formal negotiations on accession began in March 1998. Although Slovenia received some criticism regarding the pace of economic reform and adaptation of EU law, it was clear that membership would come sooner rather than later. Meanwhile, the benefits of EU membership began to come into focus with the influx of preaccession funds. Under the auspices of ISPA, the EU's Instrument for Structural Policies

Slovenia's Undead

By any standard, Slovenia is a bright star in the constellation of ex-Communist states, blessed with favorable climate, an industrious, sober citizenry, and enlightened political leadership. Like many of its former Communist neighbors, however, it has a dark past, as becomes clear with the reemergence of the *Domobranci*. They are the Slovene "undead," ghosts of World War II who haunt the country's political life even today.

The Domobranci (Home Defenders) were born in the blood-soaked crucible of the Yugoslav war-within-a war, the conflict that paralleled the wider war against the Nazis and the Italians between 1941 and 1945. Beleaguered Yugoslavs were fighting not just against the invaders, but also against each other for the future. A group with close ties to the Nazi regime, the Domobranci envisioned a Catholic, nationalist, and exclusivist future for Slovenia. Their countrymen in the rival group, the OF (Osvobodilna Fronta), considered themselves a popular front organization, hoping to join with other progressive forces on behalf of a broad-based and just postwar order. They found common cause with Tito's Partisans, whose postwar objective was a new Yugoslavia based on Communist principles and the Partisan ethos, "brotherhood and unity." The Partisans went on to expel the invaders and win the war, establishing a Communist Yugoslavia in May 1945.

Slovenes who ended the war on the Partisan side got the full benefits of victory: their own republic, language and culture guarantees, even the right to secede. They were brothers in unity with the Serbs, Croats, Bosnians, Albanians, and other constituent groups. However, brotherhood and unity were not extended to the Domobranci, who had fought against the Partisans. About 8,000 escaped to Austria, fearing the consequences of capture by the Partisans, only to be forcibly repatriated by British forces. In October 1945 they were shot without trial by Partisan forces in Slovenian territory at Kočevski Rog, their bodies buried in a mass grave.

But the Domobranci did not remain dead and buried. They have been continually disinterred and used to advantage through the years. Tito invoked them to discredit his Partisan comrade Edvard Kocbek, who offended the Partisan leadership by questioning their summary executions. How could any decent Partisan take up for Nazi collaborators and fascists? In the 1980s Slovene anti-Communists, including journalists Janez Janša and Dmitrij Rupel, exhumed them as part of a campaign to shake the foundations of Communist Yugoslavia. They used the bones in investigative exposés to beat the drums of agitation, demanding to know why Slovenes should remain in a state founded on bloody murder and lawlessness. The revelations proved explosive and effective.

After the birth of independent Slovenia, the Domobranci seemed destined to be reburied. In July 1990 Slovene politicians officially acknowledged them in a public ceremony of reconciliation. But the reburial was brief. Ambitious Slovene politicians such as Andrej Bajuk have disinterred them in attempts to break the hold of Milan Kučan and the Liberal Democrats on the country's leadership. An investment banker raised in Argentina, Bajuk promoted his family ties with the Domobranci as a leading member of the new center right party, Nova Slovenska Zaveza (New Slovene Union). Using this forum, he has called attention to Kučan and Drnovšek's Communist Party backgrounds, implying that the heirs of those who murdered the Domobranci are still running the country, holding back the pace of economic reform, and controlling elections. Meanwhile, unofficial commemorations of the Domobranci keep the issue alive, outraging those who still consider them the embodiment of fascist evil. The Domobranci continue to cast a long shadow on the country's political life.

Kučan and Drnovšek have always maintained that the Domobranci are a dead issue, a diversion from the essential tasks of the future. Still, the leadership has recognized the emotional resonance of the issue and attempted to find some common ground between those who defend and those who condemn the Domobranci. In the summer of 2003 the National Assembly passed legislation allowing for the acknowledgment of Domobranci monuments and graves in neutral language: "Victims of war and postwar killings, Republic of Slovenia." This gesture only inflamed both sides. Defenders decried a perceived refusal to admit mass murder and detractors vehemently protested a "revaluation" of people they believe to be quislings and fascists. Realistically, therefore, the Domobranci are likely to remain Slovenia's undead, unable to rest in peace until all Communist-era politicians pass from the scene.

for Preaccession, Slovenia received some $20 million for environmental improvements and transport projects. SAPARD, the Special Accession Program for Agricultural and Rural Development, also began to function in the country at this time. Prospects for NATO membership in the next expansion looked increasingly favorable as well, after a well-publicized visit to Slovenia by U.S. President Bill Clinton in 1999.

Consensus and continuity prevailed once again in the 2000 elections, as the Liberal Democrats and their allies saw their efforts rewarded with another majority in the National Assembly. In 2002 their dream of Slovenian EU and NATO membership was finally realized in the country's formal acceptance into both organizations on 1 May 2004. The third consecutive victory for the makers of independent Slovenia did not, of course, imply an absence of conflict in Slovene political life. Indeed, there were and are vocal elements in the country demanding a greater role for religion and morality in public life, including a ban on abortion and religious instruction in public schools. Others, mostly in the center-right parties, assert that the Kučan-Drnovšek leadership has too many ties to the communist past and should yield to a new generation. It is significant, though, that none of these individuals or groups opposed the basic direction of the country. There was, and continues to be, solid support for European Union and NATO membership among all responsible political parties and individuals.

SLOVENIA IN THE TWENTY-FIRST CENTURY

In 2001 the Slovene state celebrated its first ten years. Milan Kučan and like-minded colleagues who had shepherded the independent state through its first decade had compiled an enviable record of achievement. They had negotiated the tricky passage out of a rapidly disintegrating Yugoslavia and secured recognition of Slovene independence. They had helped produce a constitution worthy of the oldest European states, laying the time-tested foundations of successful democracies: the rule of law, the separation of powers, and guarantees of minority rights. They had made adjustments and taken tough decisions in the face of economic and human fallout from the Bosnian war. Finally, they had continued to look far into the future for the best guarantees of Slovenia's security and prosperity in the new Europe, preparing the country to join the European Union and the North Atlantic Treaty Organization. Briefly put, Slovenia's first generation of leaders continually demonstrated that there is great advantage in continuity and that politics can indeed be the art of the possible.

CULTURAL DEVELOPMENT

Slovene culture, like the Slovenian state, has an image problem: it has existed independently for only twelve years. No one seems to know what or where it is, and if someone takes a guess, he is more than likely to confuse it with something that sounds like Slovakia. Now that Slovenia has finally made its formal debut as a member of the European Union (EU), the world may come to appreciate both the country's distinct identity and its remarkably rich and diversified cultural life.

The fundamental concern of the Slovenes, a small people in the center of Europe whose lands have been administered by at least five different states over the centuries, has been their language. As that is the one element that has united them across physical borders and political divisions, the influence of the written word takes first place in any review of Slovene culture. Prior to the twentieth century, the Slovene language was spoken only in the countryside. It had no official recognition, and Slovenes with aspirations to education or work beyond the farm had to learn and function in German. Nonetheless, some Slovenes recognized the value of their native language. In the sixteenth century a Slovene priest, Primož Trubar, came to agree with Protestant reformers, who believed that the gospel should be made available in local languages. Trubar joined their campaign and acted on his convictions. He wrote a catechism and translated the New Testament into Slovene, a milestone in Slovene culture, and wrote an accompanying catechism. Jurij Dalmatin furthered his friend's cause and produced the entire Bible in Slovene translation. Trubar and Dalmatin's efforts guaranteed that Slovenes could learn about God in their own language. They also raised the profile of the Slovene language, sending a signal that it was a worthwhile pursuit.

The seventeenth century saw the debut of Slovenia's most famous intellectual, Janez Vajkard Valvasor. Born into a wealthy Ljubljana family in 1641, Valvasor had many opportunities to see the world but chose to devote his life to the study of the Slovene lands, especially Carniola. A tireless and wide-ranging researcher, Valvasor drew some of the first detailed maps of the region, based on his extensive travels there. He was intrigued by the proliferation of karst and the many natural curiosities it produced, such as disappearing rivers and lakes. Valvasor delighted in the many stories and legends of the Slovene peasantry, notably those associated with the local Robin Hood, Erazem Lueger. These invariably found their way into his notebooks, as did detailed descriptions of beekeeping, one of the Slovenes' most important agricultural endeavors. He laid out his life's work in a hymn of praise to Slovenia entitled *The Glory of the Duchy of Carniola*. While this book was published in German, it was clear that Valvasor's knowledge of the Slovene language made it possible. Its publication also demonstrated that the Slovene lands and its people had unique attractions and therefore deserved further study.

In the next century, more Slovenes picked up the Valvasor standard and promoted the study of Slovenia and the Slovene language. Following in the footsteps of Trubar, the monk Marco Pohlin wrote a grammar of the Slovene language, entitled *Krajnska grammatika* (Carniolan Grammar), which had the additional benefit of emphasizing that Carniola was home not just to Germans, but to a large concentration of Slovenes as well. The linguist Jernej Kopitar, who was to become one of the most prominent men of letters in Slovene history, followed up with his *Gramatik der slavischen Sprache in Krain, Kärnten und Steyermark* (Grammar of Spoken Slavic in Carniola, Carinthia, and Styria). At the same time, Anton Linhart published the first attempt to tell the story of the Slavic peoples in the Habsburg Empire, *Versuch einer Geschichte von Krain und der übrigen südlichen Slawen Osterreiche* (History of Carniola and Other Austrian South Slavic Peoples). Trubar, Dalmatin, Pohlin, and Kopitar had established that the Slovenes had an interesting and distinctive language. Echoing Valvasor, Linhart emphasized that they had a record of achievements that distinguished them from the Germans, in whose shadow they had long lived.

The Napoleonic invasion of Central Europe further advanced the cause of Slovenia and the Slovene language. Having vanquished Austria, Napoleon took parts of the Slovene and Croatian lands and grouped them for administrative purposes in an arrangement known as the Illyrian Provinces. He naturally took these measures in his own interest, hoping to block Austrian access to the Adriatic Sea. Even so, the Illyrian interlude, which began in 1809 and ended in 1813, brought meaningful long-term benefits for Slovenes. The city of Ljubljana (in German, Laibach) became the capital of the Illyrian Provinces and thereafter an unofficial Slovene capital. Slovene language instruction was introduced in Slovene primary schools, whose administrator was the celebrated poet Valentin Vodnik. Vodnik sought to assist his students by writing a Slovene language primer and a brief Slovene-French-German dictionary, the first such reference work in Slovene history.

The French interlude ended with the defeat of Napoleon, but some of the innovations and the possibilities it showcased lived on. Even in the barren period of absolutism and censorship that followed the Napoleonic era in the Habsburg empire, Slovene writers and thinkers pursued aspects of the Illyrian legacy, again with emphasis on the Slovene language. Vodnik dabbled in publishing, launching a Slovene-language newspaper, *Lublanske novice* (Ljubljana News). As the rector of the Ljubljana gymnasium, he also continued to promote the study of Slovene and authored a longer French-Slovene dictionary, as well as a text on Slovene history. Vodnik had a dedicated collaborator in Fr. Anton Martin Slomšek, who mostly worked in the countryside as a parish priest and bishop. His primer on Slovene language and culture, *Blaže and Nežica in Sunday School,* became the first all-purpose Slovene reader, providing practice in Slovene language and readable lectures on a wide range of subjects for parents and children alike. He went on to found the Society of St. Hermagor, the Slovene lands' first publishing house. Dr. Janez Bleiweis, a veternarian from Carniola, had a similar role in the evolution of Slovene culture. He published a journal entitled *News of Manufacturing and the Countryside,* in which he and a variety of specialists published a wide range of useful and interesting materials, from agricultural news to articles on linguistics and poetry.

Monument to poet France Prešeren and the Franciscan Church in Ljubljana. The poet France Prešeren (1800–1849) was known for his lyric poems, which incorporated Slovenian folk rhythms. (Bojan Brecelj/Corbis)

He continually emphasized the vitality and relevance of Slovene endeavors, asserting that "everyone should do his part to help our people emerge from the darkness of ignorance to the light of culture."

The post-Napoleonic period is perhaps best known for the debut of the man who would eventually be considered the father of Slovene literature. France Prešeren was born to a farming family in the town of Vrba in 1800. A gifted student, Prešeren demonstrated an interest in poetry early in his life, devouring everything from Homer through the early poets. As a young man, he gravitated toward Vienna and the study of law, because poetry did not hold out the promise of a viable profession. But poetry was his true passion—poetry in the Slovene language. He did not live long, and his life was not happy personally or professionally. His contributions to the Slovene language and culture are, however, legion. He was the first to write poetry in the Slovene language, poetry that soon earned him comparisons with the great romantic poets of his generation, like Alexander Pushkin and Adam Mickiewicz. Prešeren played Pygmalion to the Slovene language, winning it an entrée into the most respected circles in Europe.

He had the gift of all great national poets: he could address issues at once common to all humans and peculiar to his own people. His longest and best-known work, the epic *Krst pri Savica* (Baptism on the Savica), is set near the fabled Savica waterfall near Bohinj in Dolenjska province. It concerns the fate of Črtomir, the pagan leader of an early Slavic warrior force. Črtomir loses in battle to an invading Christian force and in the process loses his beloved Bogomila, who has meanwhile converted to Christianity in exchange for guarantees that Črtomir's life will be spared. The vagaries of fate, regrets from the past, and hope for the future despite defeat, all universal sentiments, figure prominently in this saga. Likewise, Prešeren's brief yet eloquent wish for better times, "Zdravljica" (The Toast), expresses a universal yearning for peace and freedom from a people who had known only turmoil and subjugation at the hands of their neighbors:

> God's blessing on all nations
> Who long and work for that bright day,
> When o'er earth's habitation
> No war, no strife shall hold its sway;
> Who long to see
> That all men free
> No more shall foes, but neighbours be.

These verses became the basis for the national anthem of the independent Slovene state after 1991.

In addition to producing the first widely acclaimed poetry in Slovene, Prešeren and his close friend Matija Čop founded the first Slovene literary magazine, the *Krajnska čbelica* (Carniola Bee). This periodical provided a showcase for Prešeren's work and brought poetry and prose written in Slovene to a wider audience in the Habsburg monarchy for the first time. The *Bee* began publication in 1830, whereas the bulk of Prešeren's work did not appear until 1847 in the anthology *Poezije*.

Prešeren's most important contribution may not be his poems, as legendary as they have become since his death. He foresaw as few people did the necessity of preserving the distinctiveness of the Slovene language. In the 1830s and 1840s South Slavic linguists and historians understandably sought commonality among the three South Slavic languages of the Habsburg monarchy: Serbian, Croatian, and Slovene. It was believed that linguistic unity would become the intellectual foundation for political union, in a period when the Habsburg imperial authorities were deliberately promoting centralization and Germanization. Some felt that the Slovene language should adopt the štokavian dialect shared by Serbian and Croatian, making them virtually interchangeable, at least in spoken form (Serbian is written in the Cyrillic alphabet, the consequence of having adopted Eastern rather than Western Christianity). Prešeren strongly disagreed. He argued that while Croats and Serbs tended to live in homogeneous areas, almost half of Slovenes lived in Carinthia or Styria, where the population was predominantly Italian or German and unfriendly to attempts to introduce Slovene. If they were to have any hope of maintaining their Slovene identity and culture, Prešeren believed, they needed to keep their language as distinct as possible. That meant rejecting the concept of linguistic unity, however attractive that seemed at first glance, and keeping Slovene close to the less popular kajkavian.

In honor of Prešeren's singular contributions, the Slovene state celebrates the anniversary of his death, 8 February, as a national holiday. The day is intended to demonstrate Slovenia's gratitude to Prešeren, their greatest poet, and also Slovenes' commitment to the arts and humanities. Offices and businesses are closed nationwide, would-be poets stage impromptu recitals of Prešeren's poems near his statue at the center of the city, and there are numerous readings and events in Ljubljana bookstores. The Slovene government honors its most talented men and women of culture as part of the festivities in the annual Prešeren award and Prešeren fund awards. In 2000 Prešeren Day marked the beginning of the bicentennial of the poet's birth, a yearlong series of celebrations.

Prešeren's death at the age of forty-nine immediately followed the revolutions of 1848, in which some of his compatriots proclaimed a plan for Slovene cultural and political union in Zedinjena Slovenija (United Slovenia). Prešeren, Čop, Kopitar, and others had helped lay the intellectual foundations. The revolutions did not have any immediate effects, but they did mark a point of no return: from that time, it was clear that Slovene intellectual and political leaders would work to advance the cause of Slovene language and culture in the Habsburg monarchy. The campaign was conducted in local, then national politics, concentrating on contesting German officials over the use of the Slovene language in local administrative matters and schools. Political efforts had a cultural corollary in associations like Matica Slovenska, a literary society dedicated to the dissemination of fiction and relevant nonfiction materials in the Slovene lands, and Južni Sokol, a club for Slovene sports lovers. These organizations furthered the work done in the previous era by Prešeren and

Slomšek, making available material to help Slovenes become acquainted with their language and heritage.

Prešeren had settled the dialect debate and achieved for Slovene language and literature a place in the intellectual life of the country. It fell to the next generation of writers to augment their influence and assist Slovene politicians in their struggles against Germans and Germanization.

Ivan Cankar began his career as a poet, exploring the decadent side of the Austrian fin de siècle in a collection of poems titled *Erotika*. For this he incurred the ire of the Catholic church leadership, achieving the rare distinction of seeing his work condemned. From poetry, Cankar moved on to drama, writing several plays about life in middle-class Slovenia circa 1900 that remain an important part of the Slovene theater repertoire today. But Cankar did not concentrate exclusively on art for art's sake. He contributed to the campaign for Slovenia's political and cultural future with his novel, *Bailiff Jernej*. Jernej is a kind of Slovene everyman, who serves his employer, Sitar, with devotion for many years. When Sitar dies, change comes to the house, and Jernej is marginalized, then dismissed. Convinced that his shabby treatment must somehow be illegal, Jernej travels to Ljubljana, then all the way to Vienna in search of justice. He finds instead scorn, contempt, and even arrest in the capital, at the hands of men who address him in German, a language he does not know.

Jernej is often read as a meditation on the status of Slovenes within the Habsburg monarchy at the end of the nineteenth century: willing servants for many years who find only opposition and disrespect when they finally assert themselves. In a recent essay on Slovene culture in the volume *Independent Slovenia,* Cathie Carmichael and James Gow argued that the novel anticipated some of the key issues Slovenes would face in the future, that is "the responsibilities to be faced once rights have been attained through independence, both regarding others in the self-standing house and on questions of a further condominium that might be considered." Cankar subsequently proved to be vitally interested in these questions. He gave a lecture in 1912 in which he cautioned Slovene advocates of a Yugoslav arrangement that they should be mindful of important cultural differences between Slovenes and their fellow Slavs. In fact those differences were acknowledged in the foundation of the Kingdom of Serbs, Croats, and Slovenes, leaving the Slovene contingent perhaps the only satisfied group in that ill-fated institution.

Like Prešeren, Cankar occupies a prominent place in Slovenia's pantheon of heroes. He does not have a national holiday, but the country's largest cultural center bears his name. The Cankarjev dom (Cankar Center) is an imposing, multiuse venue housing several art galleries, stages, and auditoriums, as well as an elaborate conference center. The Center pays fitting tribute to Cankar's range of literary activities and also recalls his focus on the future. It enlists both the public and private sector in its financing, receiving about 50 percent of its support from the Slovene government and requiring directors and patrons to raise the rest of the funds needed for operations.

After World War I, the Slovenes joined the Serbs, Croats, and other South Slavs in forming a new South Slavic state, the Kingdom of Serbs, Croats, and Slovenes (later renamed Yugoslavia). This was a great triumph for the Slovene people, their language, and culture. For the first time, Slovenes had their own administrative unit, their own regional officials, their own flag. More importantly, they were able to send their children to Slovene-language elementary and high schools without a fight, the Belgrade-based federal government having made this a priority. Even higher education for Slovenes in Slovenia became possible in the foundation of the University of Ljubljana in 1919, a development that seemed inconceivable before World War I.

Now that the Slovene language and culture were the equal of others in the state, it seemed that there were no major cultural or political battles to be fought in Slovenia. That was exclusively the province of Croats, who had seen no improvement and actually experienced a decline in their political standing in the first Yugoslavia. In fact, Serb-Croat conflict plagued the new state until 1939, when the Serb-dominated Belgrade government finally granted the Croatian areas administrative autonomy. Under these circumstances, it was difficult for Slovene writers to make themselves heard above the charges, countercharges, and recriminations.

In Tito's Yugoslavia, issues of greatest importance to Slovene culture again appeared settled. Slovenes could use their own language in local administration, educate their children in Slovene-language schools, and even attend their own Slovene university. In the state's constitution, Slovenes even had the theoretical right to secede if things went badly for them. It seemed that Slovene writers, who had often used their writing as a sword with which to defend Slovene culture, would find little to defend against and much to be thankful for. This was especially true after 1948. Although the Yugoslav leadership under Tito called itself "Communist," its break with the Soviet Union moved it to reject the rigid doctrine of socialist realism that artists and writers in the other communist states had to embrace. This meant that while comrades in other states had to write about issues their governments deemed important and structure their works to showcase communist values and heroes, Slovene and other Yugoslav writers enjoyed a relatively long leash. They had only to avoid explicitly nationalist subjects or direct criticism of Tito and the regime.

Despite these advantages, Slovenia's leading writer of the communist period, Edvard Kocbek, was anything but complacent. Kocbek was a poet who had made his mark shortly before the end of the first Yugoslav state by attempting to forge a third way between what he perceived as extreme nationalism in the Yugoslav government and extreme anticommunism in the Slovene Catholic Church leadership. According to John Cox, who has written extensively about Kocbek, he was vitally interested in questions of social justice and economic democracy and advocated for both in a journal he founded, *Dejanje* (Action).

Kocbek called himself a Christian Socialist, so he gravitated toward Tito and the Partisans in the crucible of World War II because they represented the best hope for a more just postwar world. In fact, he was close enough to the inner circle to become minister for Slovenia in Tito's interim postwar government. Yet he soon alienated his wartime comrades. He wrote eloquently of his wartime experiences in his first postwar poetry collection, *Strah in pogum* (Fear and Courage), but his depictions of Partisan opponents proved too dispassionate. Neutrality was never an option in discussing World War II, since the struggle and victory represented the source of the leadership's power and credibility. For this trespass on Partisan sensibilities, Kocbek was sentenced to obscurity, forbidden to publish for more than a decade.

Even after his intellectual exile ended, Kocbek was always living on the fringes of respectability. He had a persistent contrarian streak that did not play well with a leadership that preferred applause to admonition. In *On Freedom of Mind,* for example, he celebrated his free spirit, his refusal to fall into line with the rest of society:

> Even when I am tired
> I can still say the word: no,
> and when everyone is saying: yes,
> I guffaw that little word: no.
> With this word I control the situation,
> it's my form of affirmation, it makes me clear-headed and cruel.

Kocbek kept his distance from political action, refusing to be a cheerleader. He preferred to explore universal values such as love and free will, commenting that he valued poetry for its ability to reveal "the means by which man becomes reconciled to the world, secures himself against it, and mystically rises above it." At the same time, he felt compelled to probe the dark side of the regime he had helped to establish. In 1974 he gave a controversial interview to a Trieste newspaper condemning the draconian treatment meted out to the Slovene Domobranci, the anticommunist resistance group that contested the Partisans for the allegiance of Slovenes during World War II. These transgressions guaranteed that the full body of Kocbek's work would never appear in Tito's Yugoslavia.

Twenty years after his death, Kocbek's writing and fate are instructive. Perhaps it was no longer sufficient for Slovenes to be able to speak, educate their children, and write in the Slovene language. Kocbek hinted that Slovenes should aim higher, for the right to say and write whatever they wished without censure.

In the 1980s Kocbek's successors did aim higher, using Slovene language and literature to agitate for change in Slovenia's relationship with the Yugoslav state. The Slovenes had many complaints about their life in Yugoslavia by the 1980s, mostly concerning the federal government's misappropriation of their hard-earned revenues. But some observers were surprised to see the language issue surface again. Many Slovenes apparently felt that their language was endangered, that Serbo-Croatian was destined to become the official language of the state. They saw confirmation of this fear in the resurgence of Serbian nationalism after the Serbian Academy of Science's Memorandum of 1986 and the rise to power of Slobodan Milošević. Then came the 1988 arrest of the *Mladina* journalists over their controversial discoveries about the Yugoslav army. Citizens of Slovenia were shocked when Yugoslav army officials insisted on conducting the proceedings in Serbo-Croatian rather than Slovene. Perhaps the demise of the Slovene language might actually come to pass in Slobodan Milošević's Yugoslavia.

Concern for the future of the language was acute in Slovenia by the mid-1980s. Slovene writers now put that language to work in presenting other issues relevant to Slovenia's future. Two journals, *Mladina* and *Nova revija,* did their part in this process. Both produced controversial and hard-hitting material beginning in the mid-1980s, slaughtering sacred cows from the past and exposing corruption and deviousness in the present. *Nova revija* answered the Serbian Academy's Memorandum with a draft of a national program, which left open the possibility of sovereignty or even an independent Slovenia. *Mladina* produced the material that might have done the most to turn Slovene opinion against remaining in Yugoslavia, exposing plans by the Yugoslav army to "destabilize" Slovenia and justify an occupation by the Yugoslav army in order to silence criticism of Milošević. If the facts of that article did not convince everyone that the federal government bore active ill will toward Slovenia, the subsequent trial of the staffers and editor left no doubt. Once again, Slovene language and writing, and those who use it to maximum advantage, played a crucial role in shaping Slovenia's destiny.

VISUALS: ARCHITECTURE, PAINTING, FOLK ART

Slovene literature and language are decidedly parochial, developed and defended in reaction to outside influences. By contrast, the country's architecture is chronologically and nationally diversified—perfectly reflective of those outside influences. Venetian Gothic is on display in formerly Italian areas of the Adriatic. Austrian baroque is a fixture of such well-known attractions as the Church of the Assumption at Lake Bled. Neoclassicism, art nouveau, and socialist realism can all be found in Ljubljana, a reliable guide to the values and sensibilities of the regimes that built the structures through the centuries.

Despite the parade of foreign architects that built its cities, Slovenia eventually made its own unique contribution to the architectural world. Born in Ljubljana in 1872, Jože Plečnik was expected to follow his father into carpentry, but the younger man had other ideas. He studied briefly at the College of Handicrafts in Graz, where he first showed aptitude for design in helping a professor there with plans to redesign the Graz Ringstrasse. Following the death of his father, Plečnik went to Vienna, where he eventually gained admission to Otto Wagner's courses at the Vienna Academy of Arts. During his tenure there, the aspiring architect assisted with the design of several suburban railway stations and rubbed shoulders with some of the leading architects and designers of his day. At the end of his studies, Plečnik received the prestigious Prix de Rome and set off for a year of work and observation in France and Italy.

Venetian House, Piran, Slovenia. (Massimo Mastrorillo/Corbis)

Following his postgraduate year, Plečnik returned to Vienna and launched his career with a commission to build a new headquarters for the Zacherl Company. The finished product won him both fame and notoriety for its spare and austere appearance in Vienna's baroque center. While the Zacherl building was under construction, Plečnik made architectural history in designing the Church of the Holy Ghost, the first church in Central Europe to be constructed entirely in reinforced concrete. Prior to the outbreak of World War I, Plečnik's increasing interest in the expression of Slavic culture and traditions in architecture led him to accept the invitation of a Czech colleague to lecture at the Prague Academy of Fine Arts.

Shortly after the end of World War I, Plečnik's colleague, Professor Thomas Masaryk—by now the president of the new state of Czechoslovakia—offered him his most important assignment to date: the restoration of the fabled Hradčany Castle, headquarters of the new Czechoslovak government. Masaryk wanted the castle to reflect the character of the new state, which combined the novelty of democracy with Czech traditions. Plečnik did his best to fulfill the new president's charge. He constructed new passages within the castle that rendered it more accessible to the world outside and overhauled the network of garden paths to highlight the oldest trees on the grounds. In a nod to the new president's disdain for ostentation and formality, Plečnik worked to make points of transition from the palace grounds into public space as smooth as possible. At all times, the architect preserved as much as he could of the old building, as a mark of respect to its Czech builders.

The Hradčany restoration took almost fifteen years, because Plečnik did much of his work in Prague on weekends and vacations. By 1921, he had gone home to begin work at Slovenia's first institution of higher education, the University of Ljubljana. From there, he trained several generations of architects in his thirty-seven-year career and managed to change the face of the capital. Plečnik did numerous individual building projects, including the University and National Library, the distinctive, arched Central Market complex, St. Michael's Church, and the elaborate network of mortuary chapels at the city's Zale cemetery. While all of these have become treasured features of the city's landscape, the Zale chapels receive particular attention from art historians because they are regarded as a synthesis of the myriad influences that inform Plečnik's work: classical, Mediterranean, Egyptian, Byzantine. It might be most accurate to term Plečnik an enthusiast of the eclectic in his work there.

Beyond buildings and complexes, Plečnik overhauled the Ljubljana city plan and gave the city its contemporary look.

In this endeavor, he favored an intriguing mix of the classical, the populist, and the pragmatic. Classical touches—pyramids, obelisks, and pillars—are numerous on Ljubljana streets. Wide stairways and broad public thoroughfares dominate major attractions. The city's major playground, the Tivoli Park, features a signature Plečnik creation, the Jakopič Promenade, where Ljubljana residents like to stroll. Plečnik pragmatism is especially evident in the Tromostoje (Three Bridges), where a pedestrian thoroughfare appears alongside two bridges serving traffic, thereby making Ljubljana a friendly city for walkers. At one end of the Tromostoje stands Prešeren trg (square), with its monument to the immortal poet. This juxtaposition forges a link across the centuries between Slovenia's principal architect and the father of Slovene culture. A visiting journalist perceptively noted that "most vistas lead back to Prešeren trg" in the Slovenian capital.

Plečnik completed his body of work with structures and complexes in several other localities in Slovenia. Guidebooks most often direct attention to the chapel he designed for the Church of St. James in the town of Kamnik and embellishments to the Sava River embankment in Kranj, both in Gorenjska province. The architect did not succeed in his most controversial undertaking, an outsize parliament building that was to crown Castle Hill in Ljubljana. Tito supposedly vetoed it on the grounds that it focused excessive attention on Slovenia in an era in which "brotherhood and unity" was paramount. However, that unrealized vision took nothing away from Plečnik, who can justly be regarded as the Christopher Wren of Slovenia, especially its capital. If one wishes to see his monument in Ljuibljana, one only has to look around.

Generally speaking, Slovene painting tended to adhere to developments elsewhere in Europe, artists becoming identified with prevailing schools and movements in the world of art, depending on the era in which they worked. Some of the most celebrated are on permanent exhibition all day, every day thanks to the efforts of the Slovene National Gallery, which has built a magnificent virtual exhibit space for Internet visitors worldwide. There those unable to visit in person can avail themselves of a guided tour through Slovene art through the centuries, from the baroque era through contemporary artists. The talent level is invariably high there, but Ivan Grohar has a place of special honor. An exhibit of his work inaugurated the Tito era in the National Gallery in 1951, after which Grohar became the anchor of the Slovene collection there. Described as a modernist, Grohar painted classic scenes of life in the Slovene countryside, such as *Snow in Škofja Loka,* a picturesque town in Gorenjska province. He is also credited with raising the profile of the *kozolec,* the elaborate double-roofed hayracks that dot the landscape in the oldest Slovene regions, having incorporated them into several paintings. Few people recognized their quintessentially Slovene character, their value as examples of unique folk art, before they became a fixture of Grohar's work.

Although she is not yet a member of the online gallery, the realist painter Ivana Kobilica is a name that everyone should know. If Grohar is the best known and loved painter in Slovenia proper, Kobilica has achieved the highest degree of international recognition among Slovene painters. During her lifetime, she worked in Florence, Berlin, and Paris, where her talents won her membership in the prestigious Société Nationale des Beaux Arts. Her works, of which *Grandmother's Chest* and *Children in the Grass* enjoy the greatest renown, mark her as Slovenia's most accomplished exponent of realism. The first independent Slovene government paid tribute to Kobilica's achievements when it put her image on the national currency, the tolar.

Every nation seems to produce an aspect of culture it can call its own. In Slovenia, that honor goes to an art form associated with a once crucial element of farm life: beekeeping. The occupation of beekeeping has been known in Slovenia at least since the sixteenth century, when buckwheat was first planted in Carniola province. Buckwheat attracts bees, on whose presence Slovene farmers quickly capitalized. Wax was an essential element in the making of candles, and honey was the only sweetener for cooks until the refinement of sugar became possible in the eighteenth century. Keeping bees thus became a necessity, as the man who became the founder of scientific beekeeping knew well. Once headed for a career as an artist, Anton Janša acquired a reputation around Vienna for his knowledge of bees, which he had tended as a child on a farm near Bled in the 1740s and 1750s. The Austrian empress, Maria Theresa, tapped him to head the Imperial Beekeeping School, where he analyzed and chronicled the relationships in the beehive. He also wrote extensively about the medicinal uses of bee-related substances such as propolis, a staple of contemporary alternative medicine. These achievements made him the father of scientific beekeeping.

While Janša conducted advanced research in Vienna, the countryside had a more practical concern: how best to confine its bees. It seemed natural to use hollowed-out logs, but removing the honeycomb from them often proved difficult. By the middle of the eighteenth century, enterprising farmers had found a better way, producing the first so-called *kraj-nič* hives. These structures resembled small houses with individual "rooms," removable boxes containing individual hives. Bees were accessible from the front or the back, and keepers could remove honeycombs intact. These hives represented an invaluable innovation, a great step forward in the keeping of bees. In 1758 they acquired another dimension when someone painted a Madonna and Child on the front of a hive in Carniola Province.

That Madonna and Child represented the beginning of a folk art phenomenon known in Slovene as *panjske končnice*—the painting of beehive fronts. After 1758, beehive painting became commonplace, a typical feature of the Slovenian countryside, particularly in the regions of Carniola, Dolenjska, and Styria. There is no one explanation for its appearance. Since the first painting depicted the Virgin Mary and infant Jesus, experts believe that keepers may have sought divine protection for their bees. Janša and his successors repeatedly emphasized that bees could recognize colors, so that some farmers probably hoped to orient their bees with colorful panels. As time went on, the expanding range of subjects on the panels suggested other motives. In

An elaborate beehive in a valley in Slovenia. (Hans Georg Roth/Corbis)

an interview with *Slovenia News* in July 2003, Professor Janez Bogataj emphasized their use as a means of visual communication among people who often could not read; the panels acquainted people with folk tales and legends, told of successes and failures, and sometimes conveyed simple humor. One well-known motif has the hunted turning the tables on a hunter, animals packing away their traditional antagonist and licking their chops in anticipation of a tasty meal. By the nineteenth century, the most elaborately decorated fronts, which in one case included an intricate carving of a Turkish soldier and Napoleon, seemed intended to make a statement. The owner hoped to demonstrate to the neighbors that he had attained sufficient prosperity to indulge in something beyond life's essentials, perhaps even the luxury of hiring an artist to produce something extraordinary for his home.

By the twentieth century, further advances in beekeeping technology had consigned beehive covers to the realm of folk art. Ironically, these structures are probably more important to today's Slovenes than to their predecessors because they constitute an art form found only in Slovenia, something of transcendent value for a small people whose culture has always been influenced by its overlords. Experts have catalogued some 50,000 examples, identifying approximately 600 motifs in which festivals, religious beliefs, holidays, and human vices and virtues figure most prominently. The largest collection resides at the Beekeeping Museum in the town of Radovljica (in Gorenjska province), an institution dedicated exclusively to the history of beekeeping in Slovenia. There they represent an obligatory stop for thousands of traveling Slovene beekeeping enthusiasts, whose influence beyond Slovenia was sufficient to land the 2003 World Beekeeping Congress for the Cankarjev Center in Ljubljana.

Kozolci (singular, *kozolec*), "hayracks," represent a second uniquely Slovene contribution to world culture. Like beehive fronts, hayracks were originally a practical aid in the countryside. Slovene farmers needed a means to dry freshly cut hay, so they built simple, fencelike structures, vertical poles intersected by horizontal bars. In places where corn and wheat were cultivated, cover was essential, so roofed kozolci became a fixture there. These could be modest structures, resembling a small farmhouse. More prosperous farmers favored larger, double-roofed, intricately decorated models. According to Ljubljana University professor Dr. Borut Juvanec, who has traced the evolution of these structures, the kozolec front identifies the structure with a particular region. Those found above the Sava River are slender, while kozolci to the south of the Sava invariably are more robust. In areas such as Lake Bohinj, where many visitors have made note of these structures, the roofs have overhangs and slant patterns in order to protect more effectively against the heavy annual rainfall. In addition to communicating information about financial status and location, kozolci also speak to the passage of time. They became larger as farm implements became more numerous and complex; these required protection against the elements. As families acquired more conveniences, moreover, the kozolci saw additional duty as storage sheds. Today, the requirements of modern farming have rendered kozolci technologically obsolete, so they have joined beehive fronts in the country's ethnographic museums and gift shops.

MUSIC AND FILM

To date, music might be among the best-kept secrets of Slovene culture. Classical music has a long history in the Slovene lands, beginning in the sixteenth century with the composer Jakob Gallus. Gallus began as a tenor in the Imperial Chapel at Vienna, later becoming choirmaster to the Bishop of Olomouc in the modern-day Czech Republic. In the last years of his life, he composed a significant body of liturgical works as well, sixteen Masses, two Passions, and a cycle of music for the entire church year, some of which remains an active part of the repertory in Catholic churches in Europe and America. Of course, Gallus was considered Austrian, because there was no Slovenian political entity in the sixteenth century, but he acknowledged his Slovene roots by calling himself Jacobus Gallus Carniolus. Gallus Hall in Ljubljana's Cankarjev Center recently became the home of the Slovene Philharmonic, which debuted in 1701 as the Academica Philharmonicorum in Ljubljana. In its Austrian incarnation, it was one of the premier musical groups in the Habsburg Empire, well known for its talent and repertory, which included Schubert, Beethoven, Haydn, and Mozart. Gustav Mahler spent a memorable year as guest conductor in 1881–1882. Since its reconstitution in 1947 as the Slovene Philharmonic, the orchestra has maintained a busy recording schedule and showcased the talents of foreign and native artists, notably Slovenia's own piano virtuoso, Dubravka Tomšič and the classically trained avant-garde trombonist, Vinko Globokar. Globokar may be the only performer in Slovenia—or anywhere else—ever to incorporate into one of his compositions the playing of a trombone underwater.

In recent years, the end of the Philharmonic year has marked the beginning of two summer classics, the Summer Festival in Ljubljana and the Early Music Festival in Radovljica, whose reputation and participation grow yearly. An endangered species in some countries, classical music has retained an enthusiastic following in Slovenia.

Like their counterparts elsewhere in the former Yugoslav states, Slovene filmmakers have played mostly to home crowds since they made their debut after 1945. In the early years they focused on issues of strictly domestic interest, such as the Yugoslav experience in World War II. However, Slovenia's most prolific director, France Stiglic, has managed to do what Prešeren did for language and literature, appealing to audiences beyond Slovenia. His 1956 *Dolina miru* (The Valley of Peace), which played at the 1957 Cannes film festival, has become a minor world classic. In the film, two children, one German, one Slovene, escape from an orphanage in 1944 and encounter an African American pilot shot down in the area. Together, they search for the boy's uncle, who lives near what the children hope will be a "valley of peace," a refuge from unrelenting war. That the ending is unhappy is irrelevant; the bonds forged across racial and national divides between the children and the pilot reaffirm their common humanity in terrible circumstances. This film has found a following in America under the title, *Sergeant Jim,* spotlighting the African American airman.

In independent Slovenia, filmmaking has experienced many of the difficulties common to other ex-socialist states, namely a decline in state funding and temporary loss of audiences due to an influx of cheap offerings from Hollywood. These problems have not deterred the most talented and determined practitioners of the art, who have helped make possible new projects in the creation of the Slovene Film Fund, a joint government and private financing mechanism. In addition, Slovenia has become a member of Euroimages, a coproduction company for the continent, through which filmmakers will ideally be able to access more funding and theaters. This development coincided with Slovene collaboration on the 2001 hit film, *No Man's Land,* which augurs well for the future of the Slovene cinema.

FUSION: ART, MUSIC, ARCHITECTURE, POLITICS

In nearly all the socialist states, young journalists and artists took advantage of changing political winds in the 1980s to advance the cause of reform. In the Soviet Union, for example, Artyom Borovik went to Afghanistan in 1987 to report firsthand on Red Army troops fighting there. His searing portrait of a war gone disastrously bad, serialized in the weekly magazine *Ogonek,* created a sensation at home and helped convince Mikhail Gorbachev to declare victory and bring the troops home. In the Slovene republic, the forces driving change came not just from journalism, where *Mladina* and *Nova revija* hammered away at Milošević's Yugoslavia, but from art, rock music, drama, architecture, and art. The group known as Neue Slowenische Kunst (New Slovene Art) debuted four years after Tito's death, in 1984. Its members hoped to force their fellow citizens to think differently about the future, using outrageous images and devices. For example, its artists submitted a design of a poster commemorating Tito's birthday in the mid-1980s. Officials initially liked the design, only to recoil in horror when they discovered that the artists had deliberately copied a Nazi-era poster and put Tito in Hitler's place. The artists just laughed, because they saw communism and Nazism as sharing a common totalitarian origin.

The musical component—the rock group Laibach, the German name for the Slovene capital, Ljubljana—wore clothing reminiscent of Nazi uniforms in their concert appearances and used imagery from Nazi cinema in album covers and stage sets. Meanwhile, NSK member architects and city planners resurrected Plečnik's 1950s-era proposal for a grand Slovene parliament, rejected because it drew inordinate attention to Slovenia at the expense of other republics. The so-called Graditelji strongly implied that Slovenia deserved that building as a symbol of its contributions to Yugoslavia, which far exceeded its size and population. All NSK activities, of which the latter constitute only a small part, posed a simple question. If Slovenes constituted the most important and prosperous part of an entity that shared ideological origins with Nazism, should they not contemplate making other arrangements in an era replete with new possibilities? Politicians would be charged with determining and acting on the answer, but as usual, the question had its origins in Slovene culture.

PROSPECTS

A high-ranking Catholic Church leader once wondered aloud whether Slovene culture remained largely unknown because the Slovene people were a small group only recently constituted as a political entity, or whether the quality of cultural offerings was simply insufficient to win the attention of the wider world. As Slovenia prepares to become an official member of postmillennium Europe, that issue is about to get a hearing. Given the combination of distinctiveness and diversity so evident in Slovenia's cultural life, the verdict is likely to cheer and inspire from Ljubljana to Lipica.

ECONOMIC DEVELOPMENT

"As goes Slovenia, so goes the economy." This is perhaps the best description of the development of Slovene economic life over the past century. Slovenia's economy was born in Slovenia's tenure in the Habsburg Empire, occupying a place of disproportionate importance in the first and second Yugoslavia, and achieved independence in Slovenia's breakaway from the second Yugoslavia in 1991. It has faced daunting challenges resulting from its removal from the well-integrated Yugoslav market. Its success in overcoming these difficulties and obstacles has impressed outside observers, who describe it as one of the most dynamic economies in the new Europe. It eventually becomes apparent that the development of the Slovene economy parallels that of the Slovene state itself.

For most of its existence prior to the nineteenth century, the Slovene economy was based on agriculture. The coming of the industrial age in the Habsburg monarchy inevitably brought changes. The various Slovene regions experienced considerable diversification of economic activity during this period: Carinthia became known for mining and flax, Styria for livestock production and processing, areas near the Adriatic for silk and wine production. The contours of an Austrian general market, and Slovenia's role in it, were also becoming clear. For example, Slovene regions depended on wheat grown in the Croatian lands, Backa, and Banat. Carinthian raw materials were routinely shipped off to Croatia, Banat, and other regions.

By the dawn of the twentieth century, the expansion of railway links among Vienna, Ljubljana, and Trieste and an influx of German and French capital resulted in the development of manufacturing industries. Mining and metallurgical enterprises appeared, followed by chemical, food, and paper-processing plants and shipbuilding in the Trieste area. Imperial authorities built a large railway enterprise in Maribor that employed some twelve hundred people in its heyday. The foundations for the textile industry were established as well, a development that was to prove crucial in coming decades, Growth rates were impressive, averaging 40 percent over the period from 1890 to 1914.

Concentrated mainly in Carinthia, Styria, and Carniola, agriculture continued to employ the majority of Slovenes to 1914. The mainstays of the agricultural economy, then as now, were maize, hops, poultry, pig and dairy farming, beekeeping, and viticulture. A favorable combination of temperate climate and varied terrain—lots of heat in summer and moisture in winter, shielded from the worst excesses by its mountain ranges—has made wine a staple of the Slovene economy for many centuries. The Roman historian Tacitus spoke highly of the vintage he encountered near the modern-day city of Ptujin the first century. Viticulture was well established in Styria and Prekmurje regions in the ninth century, according to recent archeological discoveries. By the twelfth century, forests had been cleared to make way for vineyards, and would-be producers were even attempting to cultivate grapes in relatively inhospitable locales such as Ljubljana. From that time, the wine industry in the Slovenian lands underwent more or less continuous growth. By the mid-nineteenth century, some 125,000 acres were under cultivation.

The last decades of the nineteenth century were not kind to Slovenian winemakers. An invasion of the phylloxera aphid in the 1880s nearly destroyed vineyards throughout the region. Elsewhere, the countryside experienced some predictable hardships owing to industrialization. In fact, between 1850 and 1914, the Slovene lands produced an unexpected export: Slovenes themselves. About 300,000 left to seek work or a new life outside the Habsburg monarchy, many to America, where Cleveland became a permanent outpost of Slovenia abroad.

RAPID STRIDES AND FOUNDATIONS FOR THE FUTURE (1918–1941)

The Slovene economy underwent a major transformation the moment it became part of the Kingdom of Serbs, Croats, and Slovenes (later renamed Yugoslavia) in 1918. Where it had once been one of the least developed in the Habsburg monarchy, it was now by far the most diversified and industrialized in the new kingdom. This meant that while the Slovene economy faced the challenge of reorienting itself from the previous capital, Vienna, to the new one at Belgrade, it began its new life with significant advantages. For example, only Slovenia was equipped to produce the range and quantity of consumer goods that citizens of the kingdom would demand. Accordingly, great progress came quickly in key consumer industries such as construction materials, furniture manufacturing, and textiles. A milestone in the development of the latter came in the 1925 founding of two sewing shops in Murska Sobota, in southeast Slovenia. These eventually merged to become Slovenia's largest clothing maker, Mura.

Agriculture presented a more mixed picture. Producers suffered all the familiar consequences associated with the breakup of the Habsburg Empire, such as the closing of traditional markets followed by prohibitive trade barriers established in the new neighboring successor states. Their lot worsened with the economic downturn of the 1930s, as those countries, which had promoted themselves as dependable markets for export, turned inward and refused to buy surplus from the kingdom. Ironically, the only European power in a position to import foodstuffs after 1933 was Nazi Germany. Accordingly, it exercised increasing economic as well as political leverage over Yugoslavia and other Southeast European states in the late 1930s, a development that ultimately played a crucial role in the destruction of the postwar order in Europe.

Perhaps the most significant development for the future was the new accessibility of education in Slovenia. In the Habsburg monarchy, there were few schools and almost no instruction in the Slovene language. The Belgrade-based administration of the Kingdom of Serbs, Croats, and Slovenes took care to provide for education at all levels in Slovenia. The first Slovene university opened in Ljubljana in 1919; its first offerings were courses in economics. A technical high school soon began accepting students, and a system of primary schools was under way early in the 1920s. In addition, there were courses for farmers in winter, focusing on basic education as well as new techniques and machinery. The Slovene economy of the 1990s was the ultimate beneficiary of these institutions, since the citizens who made it successful had acquired their expertise in these institutions.

Despite the great hardships that the world financial crisis inflicted on Slovenia, indeed all of Yugoslavia's regions, Slovenia's economic contributions far exceeded its population and size vis-à-vis the other republics. It accounted for just 8–10 percent of the population of the state, yet it was responsible for 25 percent of the national product, a trend that would only become more pronounced in the future.

THE PRIMACY OF POLITICS: THE SLOVENIAN ECONOMY IN COMMUNIST YUGOSLAVIA

The foundation of the second Yugoslav state after 1945 initially presaged big changes in the economies of all the constituent republics. Communist theory, which Josip Broz Tito and the other founding fathers embraced with fervor, dictated that socialism be built on the foundations of heavy industry and collectivized agriculture. As it happened, the country's chief ideologue and economist—Edward Kardelj and Boris Kidrić, respectively—both hailed from Slovenia, so the campaign for industrialization seemed destined to have a major impact on the Slovenian economy.

Priorities changed abruptly after Tito's famous confrontation and break with Joseph Stalin and the Soviet Union in 1948. It had gradually become clear that the price of following Stalin faithfully would be economic and political subservience, a state of affairs that Tito was unwilling to accept. He and his comrades had not won a four-year war against internal and external enemies in order to become a colony to a great power. They intended to preside over a socialist country with a diversified economy, capable of existing on its own. Accordingly, while the central government at Belgrade retained veto power over economic planning, industrialization and collectivization were deemphasized in favor of a more rational approach to the country's capabilities. The highly touted policy of workers' self-management, in which the staff of individual enterprises helped to determine wages, priorities, and marketing strategies, debuted in the 1950 Law on the Management of State Economic Association by Work Collectives. As before, the manufacturing sector had a high priority in Slovenia, because that was an area of advantage for the whole country. Not only Slovenes required high-quality clothing, furniture, and pharmaceuticals.

In the 1960s strategic reforms opened Yugoslavia's borders and economy. Mindful of Slovenia's status as the most economically advanced of all the republics, a new generation of Slovene leaders hastened to take advantage of new opportunities. The leader of the Slovene republic, Stane Kavčič, encouraged efforts to establish economic relationships abroad and urged firms to focus on profitable, growth-oriented industries such as electronics and appliances. He believed that these priorities would be essential to Slovenia's retaining its economic viability in the future. Ambitious businesspeople responded enthusiastically to Kavčič's appeals. The home appliances giant Gorenje, once a manufacturer of heavy agricultural machinery, shifted its focus to slow cookers and then stoves, refrigerators, and other home appliances. After the change of orientation, company leaders expanded their reach within Yugoslavia and then forged contacts with neighboring European states, which produced significant sales there. Meanwhile, the Yugoslav automaker Revoz negotiated a contract with its French counterpart, Renault, in September 1972. The next year, the chemical firm Belinka negotiated joint venture investment and technology transfer agreements with similar firms in Belgium and Great Britain. These efforts helped Slovenia maintain the enviable position it had long had among the Yugoslav republics. As before, it had less than 10 percent of the population, yet contributed over 30 percent of Yugoslavia's exports, most in the areas Kavčič had identified as crucial.

As bright as the future looked in the 1960s, one nonnegotiable fact of Yugoslav political life was bound to cause difficulty for the Slovene economy. Yugoslav leaders always had a delicate balance to maintain in the state; they had to allow wide latitude in the individual republics so as to avoid the familiar charge that Belgrade—with its implied Serb dominance—was dominating the country. Besides, they were committed to the concept of workers' self-management in individual enterprises, since that constituted a legitimate innovation that set them apart from other socialist leaders. Yet they also knew that there was great economic imbalance among the republics, the northern, ex-Habsburg republics of Croatia and Slovenia surging ahead while the southern republics lagged behind. Since economic grievances tended to fuel nationalist sentiment, Yugoslav leaders expropriated funds from Croatia and Slovenia to finance development projects in the southern republics. If Macedonia and Kosovo had more and better economic opportunities, the reasoning went, workers there would perceive themselves equal to their fellow citizens in Croatia and Slovenia and endorse the state's ethos of "brotherhood and unity." This strategy was codified in the establishment of the General Investment Fund in the 1950s, which was administered by a special Yugoslav Investment Bank in Belgrade beginning in 1956.

This fund inevitably created resentment in both Slovenia and Croatia, the most economically advanced among the republics. While there was acknowledgment that measures to aid the poorer regions were necessary, it often seemed that the funds taken from Slovene coffers were not well spent. It was hard to see, for example, the value in a refrigerator plant located in a remote southern region that was inaccessible most of the year, or in a large soccer stadium in one of the least populated capitals. At the same time, the federal government sometimes proved unwilling to support projects that promised improvements specific to the Slovene economy, which continued to contribute more than its share to the country. In 1969 the republic applied for, and received, financial assistance from the World Bank for an overhaul of roads connecting Slovenia to Austria and Italy. This made sense, since Slovene exports reached European markets mostly through truck traffic. But because the funds went first to the central government at Belgrade, the bureaucrats there could distribute it as they wished. They decided that the money would be better spent elsewhere.

The predominance of politics in decisions affecting the Slovene economy remained an irritant while the country remained generally prosperous. By the 1980s, however, it was becoming a crisis for Slovenia and the rest of Yugoslavia. Early in the decade, Tito and Kardelj, the men who had founded Yugoslavia and made it work, passed from the scene. At the same time, the national economy buckled under the burden of a huge federal debt, the result of poor planning, overspending, and low growth. The post-Tito arrangement for political leadership, a presidency that rotated among leaders of all six republics, attempted to remedy these difficulties in part by requiring all republics to share equally in the servicing of the debt. This meant that Slovenia, which already contributed disproportionately to the national economy, would receive the same treatment as its less prosperous neighbors. A Slovene journalist opined that, once again, Slovenes were victims of overbearing political interference combined with an utter lack of economic perspective.

Consternation about Slovenia's political and economic role in Yugoslavia only grew after a series of provocative events that culminated in the coming to power of Slobodan Milošević as president of the Serbian republic in 1987. Milošević began his tenure by staging a public intervention on behalf of Serbs in a dispute with Albanians in Kosovo, appearing in the midst of a melée to proclaim before Yugoslav television cameras that Serbs "would not be beaten again." In the next few months Milošević masterminded the incorporation of two formerly autonomous republics into Serbia, thereby increasing the Serbian republic's political influence. These demarches caused concern in Slovenia and other republics, since the perception that Milošević was creating—that Serbs wished to dominate the other groups—had already destroyed one Yugoslav state. Concern became open alarm in Slovenia when officials from the Belgrade-based federal army arrested several journalists associated with the popular Slovene weekly *Mladina* and then tried them for antistate activity behind closed doors and in the Serbo-Croatian language. This episode had a fateful effect on Slovene attitudes toward their future in Yugoslavia. If Milošević's rule in Yugoslavia meant Serb bureaucrats taking liberties with Slovene sensibilities, perhaps Slovenes would have to seek other arrangements.

In fact, they did exactly that. Between 1989 and 1991, the Slovene leadership sought various means of altering Slovenia's position within Yugoslavia, with economic issues playing a key role. On several occasions, Slovene President Milan Kučan proposed that Slovenia and Croatia make their own financial assistance arrangements with the less developed republics rather than leaving such decisions to the federal government. Slovenes amended their constitution in 1990, pointedly reserving for themselves the right to manage their own revenues. Afterward, Kučan and his advisers insisted that the future viability of Yugoslavia depended on its becoming a confederation of sovereign states, so as to prevent what he saw as the exploitation of Slovenia and Croatia. When Milošević rejected and contested all these proposals, the Slovene leadership decided to ask its constituents to rule on their future in Yugoslavia. They answered with a resounding yes to the idea of sovereignty for Slovenia in December 1990.

This decision appeared inspired early in 1991, when Serb bureaucrats staged an illegal midnight raid on the Yugoslav federal treasury in order to pay pensions for Serbs exclusively at a time of great financial hardship for everyone. This outrage, known to history as the Great Serbian Bank Robbery, led directly to Slovenia's declaration of independence from Yugoslavia a few months later. After a brief, but difficult ten-day war with the Yugoslav army in June 1991, Slovenes won their independence. They would now have the opportunity to prove that a small, well-educated, and industrious people could stand on its own in postcommunist Central Europe.

THE SLOVENE ECONOMY IN TRANSITION (1991–1997)

The Slovenes began their new life with some clear advantages, even though they had never had their own state. Thanks to the educational foundations laid in the first Yugoslavia, Slovenia had a well-educated, multilingual workforce. Beginning with the Kavčič era, the Slovene republic always exported far more products to Europe than its neighbors and attracted the most direct foreign investment. Newly independent Slovenia therefore had good relationships with the wealthiest nations in Europe, especially Germany. In contrast to some of their former communist neighbors, struggling to manage the transition to a market economy, the new Slovene citizens could call on their experiences with workers' self-management. Despite frequent interference from Belgrade bureaucrats, workers in all the Yugoslav republics had been responsible for making their own business plan, setting their own targets, and devising marketing strategies. The Slovenes already had these skills, and their products had competed successfully with those of other republics in a functioning market within Yugoslavia. Simply put, Slovenes knew how to do business.

Still, though, laying the foundations for the country's economy seemed a daunting task in the first months after independence. For one thing, the bill from the war for independence was quite high, well beyond the estimated $2 billion in physical damage done by the Yugoslav army during the ten-day war. This was in part because of the circumstances surrounding Slovenia's exit from Yugoslavia. If the separation had taken place amicably, if Yugoslavia had not been engulfed in conflict, Slovenia might have maintained its contacts with the Yugoslav republics. But the outbreak of war in Croatia and Bosnia-Hercegovina disrupted existing political and economic relationships, after which United Nations sanctions suspended them indefinitely by imposing sanctions on Serbia. For Slovenes, this meant the loss of 30–40 percent of their existing market. At the same time, Slovene leaders urgently sought international recognition of their new state. This did not come immediately, because of disagreements in Europe and the United States over sanctioning the breakup of Yugoslavia. Until that was achieved, there could be no question of building a new economic infrastructure or forging new agreements with European partners.

In accordance with new European Community guidelines, Slovenian independence was recognized by most European states in January 1992. Two months later, Slovenia became a member of the Council for Security and Cooperation in Europe and the United Nations. Now Slovenes could concentrate on laying the foundations for a market economy. Restructuring the banking and financial systems was an obvious priority, as demonstrated in the creation of a Bank Rehabilitation Agency in 1991. Next came the establishment of new banks, in addition to the diversification of existing institutions. Today, a number of foreign banks also have representation in Ljubljana and other major cities.

Another key task was determining ownership of existing enterprises, or privatization. This process was obligatory for all states making the transition from socialism to a market economy, since the central government had owned and controlled all essential economic activities. This was a difficult process everywhere, but especially in Slovenia, where Slovene workers themselves had owned and administered their enterprises since the implementation of workers' self-management in the 1960s. Not surprisingly, it took the new Slovene government many months, and several draft proposals, to come to an agreement on a strategy. The final Law on Ownership Transformation of 1992 required 40 percent of stock to be transferred. Beyond that, as the *Economist* magazine explained, a number of means would be possible: public sale of shares, internal distribution of shares exchanged for ownership certificates, shares sold at a discount for cash. It was hoped that this arrangement would strike a balance between the interests of workers and management and provide for a speedy transformation of the socialist economic landscape. By 1998, privatization was well under way, although critics have pointed to slow implementation in large national enterprises such as public utilities and banks.

Meanwhile, Slovene employers and employees struggled to master this and other challenges in their new universe. Accustomed to socialist-era largesse, such as subsidized meals, paid vacations at desirable destinations, and full health benefits, workers faced the reality of competition outside a protected market, which brought lower wages, cuts in services, and the previously unthinkable—unemployment. Presumably, these measures would make it easier to compete in new venues and find new clients. It was anything but easy in the first months; as production fell, unemployment—anathema in socialist Yugoslavia—exceeded 10 percent, and inflation soared on the introduction of the Slovene currency, the tolar. Gradually, however, firms with good management adjusted and held their own. The experience of the Belinka chemical enterprise, which had established a reputation in Yugoslavia as a future-oriented company, was an instructive case in point. "The transition from the ex-Yugoslavia has caused us very big problems, because Slovenia was very much oriented to the former Yugoslav market," director Marjan Cerar told a *Boston Globe* correspondent in the summer of 1993. "The Bosnian market, due to the war there, doesn't exist, and the Serbian market, due to the United Nations sanctions, doesn't exist either. So, we must export wherever possible." Drawing on past experiences in self-management, Belinka took an ag-

Slovenian vineyard. (Bojan Brecelj/Corbis)

gressive approach to reinventing itself. It introduced immediate austerity measures, putting a freeze on hiring and liquidating the advantages its workers had known for decades, such as the resort hotel on the Adriatic for summer vacations. At the same time, it established joint-venture arrangements with firms in Russia and Italy and negotiated new contracts. Belinka products now were bound for Austria, labels on the packaging printed in German. Although profits initially disappointed, the company has remained viable in the new economy. Its goals for the twenty-first century, according to its Web page, include product diversification with a focus on environmentally friendly technologies.

"We know that everything won't be okay at the moment of independence," Slovene finance minister Marko Krajnec said shortly before the 1991 war. "In fact, it will be worse. But people understand that there will be a temporary lowering of living standards. After a transition period of three to five years, after we have improved the banking and economic system, we will be able to do business with the rest of Europe." Firms like Belinka made Krajnec's words a reality. By 1997, the Slovene economy had begun to recover from the first difficult years of transition, showing signs of steady, albeit slow, growth. In 1994 the Slovenian GDP registered a 3 percent rise; by 1997, it was growing at an annual rate of 5 percent. Reorientation of trade toward European markets had proceeded to the point that some 70 percent of the country's output now went to Germany, Austria, and other European states. Slovenia was also attracting foreign investment, as evidenced by the presence of Siemens, Renault, and the Austrian Creditinstalt bank in Slovenia. One sure—and ironic—indicator of this trend was the new career of Franci Zavrl, sentenced to an eighteen-month prison term by a Yugoslav military court in the infamous *Mladina* scandal of 1988. The sometime felon had founded an advertising and public relations agency—Pristop—that assisted Slovene and foreign businesspeople and government officials in learning to use the local media to their advantage. By 1997, this enterprise had made Zavrl one of independent Slovenia's wealthiest men.

By the end of 1995, Slovenia had achieved sufficient progress to begin preparations to enter the European Union, the holy grail for Central and Eastern European states emerging from communism. Its representatives were able to open negotiations by pointing out that almost three-fourths of the country's trade was conducted with European Union (EU) countries. Slovenia had met the preliminary criteria for candidate members, having established a stable political regime, restructured the economy sufficiently to permit successful competition in a larger market, and indicated its readiness to assume administrative responsibilities. In June 1996 Prime Minister Janez Drnovšek signed an agreement granting Slovenia associate membership in the

Bled Lake and Julian Alps. (Janez Skok/Corbis)

EU. This permitted the country's elected officials to begin to bring their financial and diplomatic policies in line with the numerous requirements for full members of the Union. One key task in this process was the passage of more than a thousand laws, bylaws, and sundry regulations approximating those of existing EU members. The date of Slovenia's accession to the EU was finally fixed for May 2004, following a formal vote of confidence from the citizenry, which enthusiastically voted in March 2003 for entry into the European Union. On 1 May 2004, Slovene citizens celebrated, as the nation formally joined the EU.

PREPARING TO JOIN EUROPE: THE SLOVENE ECONOMY AT THE MILLENNIUM

As Slovenia emerges from the difficulties of its first few years and contemplates the advantages and challenges of European Union membership, the contours of its independent economic life are coming into focus. Some long-established industries, such as mining, have gone into eclipse, probably not to return. Others, notably textiles, are experiencing tough times and may face radical restructuring or relocation. Employees of the well-established clothing company Mura, for example, now wonder whether their jobs will be outsourced to cheaper labor markets as their company struggles to survive in a tough market. On the other hand, the requirements of the new economy have spurred the creation of new fields of endeavor. One of the most prominent examples is Franci Zavrl's firm Pristop, whose fortunes have only risen since its establishment in the early 1990s. In 2003 Slovenia's premier advertising and public relations firm had representatives working in five countries and reported revenues of millions of euros.

One mainstay of the Slovene economy in the twentieth century, the manufacturing sector, is again proving to be a strong performer, especially in pharmaceuticals, appliances, and auto production/parts. In the first decade of independent Slovenia the drug companies Krka and Lek, the automobile manufacturer Revoz, and the Gorenje group, manufacturers of home appliances, have maintained the highest profile. Moreover, dedicated outdoors enthusiasts in Europe and North America have all come to know the ski, bike, and boat manufacturer Élan. In retail sales, another sector that has flourished in the transition period, Mercator has established itself as a major player in the competitive world of food markets. One also encounters the oil trader firm, Petrol, and the home entertainment company, BoFex, in discussions of successful new retailers in Slovenia.

As noted, Slovene manufacturers and retailers were forced to find new markets following the outbreak of war in Yugoslavia. Most concentrated on Western Europe, while Krka pharmaceuticals went east to revive old contacts in Warsaw and Moscow, successfully marketing dozens of drugs on the Russian market and making plans to open a production facility near the Russian capital. By the late 1990s, however, the Yugoslav markets were reviving, and Slovene firms were able to capitalize immediately. In a recent country profile, the *Economist* noted that by 2000, "almost every major Slovene company had either made some sort of investment in the rest of the region or was planning to do so." The Ljubljana-based Lek was among the first to take advantage of the improved circumstances, announcing plans in 1998 to build a greenfield plant in Macedonia in order to serve the emerging Balkan region. One of Slovenia's largest breweries, Pivovarna Union, expressed confidence in the recovery of Bosnia-Hercegovina by establishing a presence in Sarajevo. Meanwhile, Mercator and Petrol hastened to build markets and gas stations in Bosnia and Croatia when conditions made this possible. Mercator's CEO, Zoran Jankovič, declared his intention to become the largest retailer in Bosnia and the second largest in Croatia in the coming years. Significantly, he also mentioned plans to expand into Serbia, now generally acknowledged as the next frontier for Slovene economic activity in the post-Milošević era. Slovenia did a great volume of business with Serbia when both were republics of Yugoslavia.

Now as then, agriculture presents a mixed picture. Recent surveys indicate that even though Slovenes revere the traditions associated with rural life and highly value their homegrown agricultural products, this has not resulted in boom times for producers. About 5 percent of the country's workforce farms full-time, and Slovenia has long been an importer of foodstuffs. Slovene agriculture received a boost in the early 1990s with the outbreak of war in Yugoslavia, as farmers there were unable to market their products, and several successful cooperatives have formed in the past decade. Still, the outlook for domestic agriculture is unclear because of the uncertain impact of Slovenia's membership in the European Union, which will bring regional development funds to farmers at the same time it floods the Slovene market with competitors of all sizes.

One indisputably bright spot for the agricultural sector is wine production, which is making a remarkable comeback. While a revival was under way after the phylloxera invasion, the dislocations associated with World War I, Slovenia's entry into the Kingdom of Serbs, Croats, and Slovenes, and World War II meant that full recovery remained elusive. Most producers were able to resume their activities in Tito's Yugoslavia but were forced to accommodate the wishes of state authorities, who tended to prefer quantity to quality.

In these first years of independent Slovenia, the industry has taken full advantage of the century's territorial additions, with producers working successfully in three distinct regions. The oldest and most established of these is Podravje, which encompasses the Prekmurje and Styria regions. The area's climate and soil composition have determined the local specialty: sweet, aromatic white wines, similar to those found in the Saar and Rhine areas of Germany. In recent years wine journalists have sung the praises of the Renski riesling and the Šipon, which got its name from enthusiastic soldiers of Napoleon, who exclaimed *si bon* on sampling it for the first time. Šipon is the Slovenian equivalent of the Hungarian Tokaj, a yellowish, mellow sweet wine often served with desserts.

At the opposite end of the country, the Primorska region is chronologically the newest among Slovenia's producers, and also the most renowned in the new era. This region compares favorably to its neighbors in the production of white wines, particularly the well-balanced, mild Rebula. But it is the country's undisputed leader in the production of red wines—reds such as the Koper Refosk and the Vipava Valley Merlot account for over 50 percent of its yearly output, in contrast to the two other regions, where whites dominate. The Brda subdistrict, so named for its location amid low hills near the Italian border, has won a greater share of medals and awards in wine competitions than any other area of the country in recent years. One of its signature products is the Modri Pinot, "the noblest red of the cooler parts of Europe, the Riesling of Reds." Brda is home to two of the most celebrated among the country's wineries. One is Movia, the pride of the Kristančič family since the early nineteenth century. In the neighboring Vipava Valley, the Vipava 1894 winery is home to the popular Vipavski merlot and is now reviving two legendary Adriatic whites, Zelen and Pinela. In addition, the country's largest wine cooperative, the Dobrovo winery, processes the output of some eight hundred small vintners.

The third region, Posavje, lies between Primorje and Podravje, covering much of the territory known as Dolenjska. This is the geographical center of the country, where vineyards dot the low hills near the Krka and Sava Rivers. This region is often described as closest to central and south central France, in terms both of climate and fondness for blended wines. Most of Slovenia's wine producers are dedicated to the concept of a single grape, and many in Dolenjska devote all their efforts to producing high quality whites such as Beli Pinot and Renski Riesling. However, Posavje's winegrowers, like their French counterparts in the Champagne and Bordeaux regions, appear to relish the challenge of marrying different varieties in order to produce something more flavorful than the sum of its parts. Accordingly, the Posavje specialties include Cvicek, a blend of at least two prominent reds and one white, and Metliška Črnina, the result of the best reds from both Posavje and Podravlje regions. The region is similarly well known for *ledeno vino,* or ice wines, the product of grapes left exposed to freezing temperatures for a period of consecutive days. Ledeno vino seems to be a Central European classic, a frequent accompaniment to the Slovenian sweet cake, potica.

The revival of the wine industry will likely further improve the fortunes of tourism in Slovenia. Already, gourmet and "slow food" tours of Slovenia can be arranged. In the early 1990s the country had understandable difficulty in attracting tourists and conventions because of lingering anxiety about the war in Croatia and Bosnia-Hercegovina. By the mid-1990s, the regional situation had improved significantly, so that it made sense to begin a formal campaign to bring visitors to Slovenia. Established in 1996, the Slovene tourist board has actively promoted tourism in the country, assisted by the global reach of the Internet. It has received assistance from wealthy companies like the oil and gas concern Istrabenz, which has invested in tourist infrastructure in attractive vacation spots like the Postojna cave area. Considerable unsolicited help has also come from foreign journalists, who have discovered Slovenia and begun singing the country's praises in magazines and newspaper travel sections. In 1997 Marie Harris of the *New York Times* hailed the "spirited, independent Slovenia" she had encountered while vacationing in Europe. A few years later, her colleague Frank Bruni found "the full beauty of Europe packed into a succinct swath of mountains, lakes, and Adriatic coastline, topped off by the gorgeous and entirely cosmopolitan capital of Ljubljana." If Americans did not immediately book tours, Europeans did, especially Italians and Germans taking advantage of cheaper Slovene Adriatic holidays. As of 2003, tourism was officially a billion-dollar yearly enterprise.

Most observers familiar with Slovenia agree that the Slovene economy has emerged from its time of trial showing strength, flexibility, and potential. Personal income is the highest of all the postcommunist states, at nearly $10,000 annually, a figure double that of neighboring Hungary and the Czech Republic and exceeding that of such well-established European nations as Greece and Portugal. This translates into a standard of living that has won Slovenes the coveted right to visit the United States without a visa—a privilege not granted to Czechs, Slovaks, Hungarians, or Poles—because it is assumed that they will return to their prosperous Alpine home. Of course, there remain areas of concern, caused by global economic phenomena as well as problems specific to emerging democracies. Foreign investment has lagged behind expectations, in part because of the slow pace of privatization. Unemployment persists at a relatively high level and may increase, since the process of liquidating unstable or unprofitable industries will continue for the foreseeable future. Ultimately, the long-term health of the economy will depend on Slovenes' ability to negotiate the tricky passage into the European Union, which holds out the promise of help for the victims of the new economy while presenting formidable challenges for its erstwhile winners. If Slovenes can manage this, then their country will certainly be viewed as a model for other small states emerging from similar circumstances. As goes the Slovene economy, so goes Slovenia in the eyes of the world.

CONTEMPORARY CHALLENGES

The citizens of Slovenia, whose numbers barely exceed 2 million, have managed a series of outsized feats in the past two decades. Convinced that they could no longer tolerate life in Yugoslavia, where they had lived for seven decades, they carefully planned an escape. A resolutely peaceful and industrious group, they gathered themselves to fight and win a war against those who would prevent their departure, using speed and cunning. Appealing to a Europe fearful of chaos, they secured recognition and launched their ship of state in the midst of a dangerous storm in Croatia and Bosnia. In May 2004, just thirteen years after their declaration of independence, they joined the most powerful nations on the continent in the European Union and North Atlantic Treaty Organization. Understated self-confidence, resourcefulness, and adaptability have undergirded these remarkable successes. These assets will continue to be essential as Slovenes face the challenges and opportunities that life in the new Europe promises to bring.

The Wine-Making Mavens of Movia

If there is a recipe for maintaining a successful enterprise in a volatile geopolitical region like Slovenia's, its major ingredients would surely include a passion for quality, visionary leadership, adaptability, and luck. No one knows this better than the Kristančičs, the mavens of the renowned Movia Vineyard, an enduring symbol of Slovenia's economic fortunes.

The Kristančič family acquired the Movia estate in Goriska Brda at the beginning of the nineteenth century, dedicating themselves to wine production. The family weathered the geopolitical storms that roiled the eastern Adriatic, beginning as French citizens, then acquiring Italian, Austrian, and finally Slovene citizenship in the twentieth century. Regardless of which country ruled them, the Kristančičs kept their focus on making the richest, highest-quality red and white wines. By 1945, in addition to multiple citizenship changes, they had managed to survive the deadly phylloxera virus and the destruction and devastation of two world wars. The coming of communist Yugoslavia and its animus toward "bourgeois" enterprises such as wine making constituted perhaps the most serious threat yet to Movia and the Slovene wine-making tradition.

But the Kristančičs got lucky. Providentially Ales Kristančič's grandfather had joined Tito's Partisan resistance during World War II and rendered distinguished service. After the war, the Partisan leadership offered the elder Kristančič a ministerial-level appointment in the new government, but he declined and returned home to his vineyards. The family was wondering how to cope with Yugoslavia's new postwar border with Italy, which had inconveniently separated the estate house and cellars from some of the vineyards, when the authorities decreed that all properties exceeding ten hectares would be nationalized. Incredibly, the new border guaranteed that Movia would remain intact—its vineyards now in Italy did not count in the total. The next shadow to fall on Movia came in the campaign for collectivized enterprises in the countryside, a development that the Kristančičs categorically rejected on the grounds that it would be fatal to Movia's tradition. There might have been a price to pay for such impertinence, had Tito not visited Movia and sampled its signature product. Apparently even future-obsessed communist leaders could appreciate the value of fine old wines. Movia not only escaped unharmed, but soon became the official vintner to the president of Yugoslavia.

Movia was not exactly prosperous in socialist Yugoslavia. Yet there were significant advantages beyond the prestige associated with its status as the court winery. Time and resources for production were virtually unlimited; the Kristančičs had only to inform the Agriculture Ministry of their needs each year. And when the Yugoslav government sanctioned economic activity beyond Yugoslavia, Movia took advantage of the new opportunities offered. As Movia's current chief, Ales Kristančič, recently recalled, they went first to Slovenia's former rulers, where people remembered what kind of wine came from Movia. After winning acclaim in Vienna and Venice, Movia products attracted the attention of famed chef Alain Ducasse, who put them on the menu of his Monaco restaurant.

(continues)

THE ECONOMY IN A NEW ERA

There is challenge and opportunity for the Slovene economy as it becomes integrated with Europe's. Manufacturers and retailers will have the chance to market their products freely throughout Europe, where they have already forged solid relationships. New strategies will be required for those who hope to succeed there. For example, winemakers aiming to compete in European markets can focus their efforts on producing wines unique to Slovenia, like zelen whites, and tailor advertising campaigns to make those products known to the broader European public. At the same time, there will a reciprocal influx of products into Slovenia from larger EU members. Slovene wine lovers will now have more choices in their supermarkets. These consumers were mostly responsible for the comeback of Slovene wine making in the 1990s, and they value Slovene products, but they will certainly be tempted by the sudden availability of inexpensive offerings from wine powerhouses like France, Germany, and Italy. Slovene winemakers who concentrate on the domestic market will have to redouble their efforts to ensure that their products are competitive, in terms of both quality and price. They might also benefit from targeted advertising campaigns extolling the virtues of Slovenian viticulture, thereby creating more jobs in a new sector. Public and media relations are undoubtedly a growth industry for Slovenia, a nation seeking to make itself known.

Slovene tourism faces a similar dynamic in the new Europe. Tourists from EU states will now enjoy seamless travel to Slovenia. On the other hand, EU regulations on gas pricing will diminish the attractions of Slovenia for legions of day tourists from Italy and Austria, who have apparently made a habit of short car trips there for a meal and cheap petrol.

(continued)

Like the Slovene economy itself, the Kristančičs and Movia were relatively well-prepared for independence. They had established contacts well beyond Yugoslavia, so the loss of that market was not catastrophic; by the mid-1990s, exports accounted for over 50 percent of Movia's output. It quickly became apparent that Slovenes valued their home-grown wines, and Movia retained its exalted status as the official wine of the Slovenian government. But the Kristančičs continued to aim higher, concentrating on producing distinctive and high-quality wines for export. This decision proved to be a combination of the personal and prophetic. Ales Kristančič obviously wanted Movia mentioned in the same breath as the finest German, French, and Italian winemakers. But he also knew that the survival of high-quality wine making in Slovenia depended on it. Slovenia's European Union accession meant that cheap imports from France, Germany, and Italy would flood the Slovene market, making sales more a function of marketing than of quality or skill. Only those vintners willing to invest the time and resources to the production of artisanal wines for the international market would be able to continue functioning on the highest level. "It is crucial that a winemaker have the ability to create a wine that has an international style, and thereby prove to customers that they can be trusted," Ales Kristančič told an interviewer in 2003. "Yet many experts also wish for our wines to reflect the unique nature of the environment they are grown in. This is where our future lies," he concluded. "Our wine is a testament to our uniqueness" (Prešeren 2003).

Movia signature wines—Rebula, a dry white, Chardonnay, Veliko Rocce, or Big Red—are now a fixture of the best restaurants and wine distributors in France, Germany, Italy, and the United States, so Movia's future seems assured. Meanwhile, Ales Kristančič has taken his passion for time and quality to an even larger stage. He has become Slovenia's unofficial representative in the Slow Food group, a worldwide movement born of outrage at the construction of a McDonald's in central Rome. This group of chefs, restaurateurs, and rank-and-file food and wine lovers has dedicated itself to combating eat-and-run meals, fast food, and the influence of corporate farming on good eating. Thus, even as Slovenia joins the world of integrated, standardized nations that is the European Union—some would say McEurope—Kristančič and Movia continue to hold high the Slovene standard of quality and distinctiveness.

Tourist industry representatives now must extend their focus to include tourists from beyond driving distance. This should not be difficult if they can negotiate arrangements with discount air carriers such as Ryanair, which delivers thousands of holidaymakers to all the European states on a weekly basis. It will also be important to promote the port of Koper as an attractive alternative for cruise ships that now stop at Trieste. Slovenia has year-round appeal, from skiing and spelunking to city adventures, sun and fun on the coast, World War I sites, and horseback riding at Lipica. It also has huge potential as a wine destination. Slovene officials would do well to enlist Ales Kristančič to tout Slovenian cuisine and vineyards to the growing ranks of food and wine tourists worldwide. They are likely to be intrigued at the idea of exploring the terra incognita of the Slovenian wine landscape.

Other sectors have challenges of a different nature in the new conditions. In the latter part of the 1990s many prominent Slovene companies, such as the supermarket giant Mercator, returned to Yugoslav markets temporarily lost because of UN sanctions during the Bosnian war. The contracts they have negotiated may run into problems, because Slovenia's interstate commerce will soon be subject to EU customs regulations. The heads of these firms can work toward a transitional agreement with the EU, perhaps emphasizing Slovenia's role in the Southeast European Stability Pact. Meanwhile, many Slovenes employed in agriculture and manufacturing will be eligible for financial and technical assistance from the EU, enabling them to modernize, diversify, and restructure their operations in order to compete successfully with their counterparts elsewhere in Europe. Others, however, will certainly find themselves victims of technological obsolescence and will have to seek retraining or employment possibilities elsewhere.

GEOPOLITICS

The Slovene government spent the early 1990s shoring up relations with its neighbors Hungary and Italy, opening a new border crossing with the former in 1992 and settling a difficult property restitution case with the latter in 1994–1995. In the mid-1990s Slovene officials looked beyond their immediate environs. They sought an active role in the United Nations, achieving election as a nonpermanent member for the year 1998–1999. There, its representatives chaired the Security Council Sanctions Committee for Libya and put forth proposals for suspending sanctions on Iraq. In addition, Slovenes participated in UN peacekeeping missions in East Timor, the Golan Heights, and Cyprus. At the same time, Slovenia made itself useful to the NATO nations in key ways before winning approval from those nations for NATO membership in 2002.

The greatest geopolitical challenges and opportunities are next door, in Southeastern Europe. Slovenia and Croatia continue to dispute the fate of Piran Bay and coastline, the two sides trading accusations and recalling ministers as recently as the summer of 2003. It is unclear how the conflict will be resolved, but Slovenia's EU membership will likely bring a favorable result since Slovene officials will have some influence on Croatia's application to the EU. Beyond that, the Slovene government is uniquely positioned—geographically and politically—to help bring peace and stability to Southeastern Europe, which has known neither since Slovenia's escape from Yugoslavia in 1991. It has already acknowledged this by taking the lead in the implementation of the EU's Southeast Europe Stability Pact, which was launched in 1999. Slovene representatives participate actively in all three of the Pact's working groups: Democratization and Human Rights, Economic Reconstruction, and Security Issues. As managers of the International Trust Fund for Demining and Mine Victims' Assistance, an initiative partially funded by the United Nations, they have helped to clear the regions of war detritus and provide over $100 million in financial assistance to local victims of land mines. The region's future depends on a steady supply of well-trained, responsible administrators. Slovenia accordingly has been instrumental in the planning for new pact-related educational institutions too, such as the Regional Center for Excellence in Public Expenditure Management and the International Postgraduate School of Economics. Reviewing ten years of Slovene foreign policy in a speech before the United Nations, Dmitrij Rupel emphasized that his country was aiming high. He expressed the hope that Slovenia's efforts in Southeastern Europe will enable the countries of the former Yugoslavia to be reunited with Slovenia in the European Union. "Our activity in this area is not only necessary," he said, "but also beneficial."

SLOVENE CULTURE AND THE PASSAGE INTO EUROPE

It is indisputable that Slovenia has achieved a lifelong objective in entering the European Union; it is now officially classified as part of Europe rather than the Balkans.

In Slovenia, the Smart Money's on Culture—and Vice Versa

Although it is usually taken for granted in numerous daily transactions, a nation's currency can be a reliable clue to its core values. In the United States, citizens revere the men who made the American political system and saw it through its greatest crises—Jefferson, Washington, Franklin, Lincoln. Their images appropriately crown the nation's banknotes. Hungary's enduring obsession through the centuries was liberation from foreign rule. The Hungarian forint features those who did the most to further that cause, such as Ferenc Deak, the author of the Austrian-Hungarian Compromise of 1867. Who appears on Slovenia's currency, and what does it reveal about Slovenes?

The basic unit of Slovene currency is the tolar, soon to be replaced by the euro. The smallest denomination is the 10 tolar note, on which is found the visage of Primož Trubar, the father of the Slovene language, the man who gave Slovenes a version of the New Testament they could read. Janez Vajkard Valvasor, perhaps the most prolific intellect in the history of the Slovene lands, greets those who examine the 20 tolar note. He traveled the world yet preferred to focus his research in his native Carniola, where he investigated everything from hidden lakes to beekeeping. The 50 tolar note features the distinguished mathematician Jurij Vega, who fought in the artillery for Austria during the Napoleonic wars and later wrote three important scholarly works on logarithms. The best student mathematicians in Slovenia now compete yearly for the Vega Prize.

The painter Rihard Jakopič, a contemporary of Ivan Grohar's and a prolific impressionist himself, is honored on 100 tolar bills. He is credited with founding the Slovene Academy of Arts in Ljubljana, which explains why the most accomplished painter in Slovenia each year receives the Jakopič Prize. Jacob Gallus Carniolus reminds citizens of their musical heritage on the 200. The author of contemporary Ljubljana, Jože Plečnik, appears on the 500 note, while the father of Slovene literature, France Prešeren, greets those conducting transactions of 1,000 tolars. Slovenia's most international painter, Ivana Kobilica, and her contemporary, the writer Ivan Cankar, animate the 5,000 and 10,000 notes, respectively.

The Slovene government could have honored the makers of Slovenia's remarkable prosperity, its hardworking businessmen and entrepreneurs. If not for a courageous and far-sighted political class, Slovenes' passage into post-communist Europe might have proved divisive and costly. Yet the stars of the country's banknotes are invariably men and women of arts, letters, and sciences, people who did the most through the centuries to educate and equip their fellow citizens to assume the responsibilities essential to making a successful nation. It is clear that culture remains the real currency of the realm in Slovenia.

The opportunities for Slovenes in this arrangement are great: they can travel more freely, make their own work arrangements at home or in another EU country, and enjoy the best of cosmopolitan Europe, while continuing to live in one of its smallest, most livable corners. On the other hand, becoming part of a large union with a formidable body of standardizing regulations implies the forfeiture of some characteristics that make individual peoples unique. Since language and culture are among Slovenes' most prized possessions, many citizens now ask the old

Anton Martin Slomšek

One of Slovenes' recurring anxieties on the eve of their entry to the European Union is how to be proud of their language and culture *and* be a good citizen of Europe. There seems to be concern in some quarters about appearing to be too parochial, too attached to everything Slovene. In 1994 an American journalist was surprised to learn of controversy over needed improvements to the nation's Ethnographic Museum. It was evidently felt that the museum's focus on things unique to Slovenia could be interpreted as overly nationalist. On the other end of the spectrum, some Slovene youth have indulged in chauvinism, loudly proclaiming the superiority of Slovene culture over others. How should Slovenes carry the Slovene standard, so to speak, when they become part of a large conglomeration of European states? For inspiration, they might look to the man who will be Slovenia's first saint, Fr. Anton Martin Slomšek.

Anton Martin Slomšek was born in Slom, Styria (Štajerska), in November 1800. Early in his life, he knew that he loved God and his native language, so he decided to become a priest. Dismayed that so many of his parishioners and fellow priests were ignorant of their heritage and sometimes even the Slovene language, he took it upon himself to teach as many of them as possible. In the 1840s he made the totality of the Slovene lands his classroom. He preached regular sermons in Slovene, making an indelible impression on his listeners with his simple, yet vigorous language. "Our mother tongue is the greatest legacy we receive from our parents," Fr. Slomšek would say. "We must conserve it scrupulously and pass it on to our children." For those he could not reach from the pulpit, he wrote numerous books and pamphlets designed to amuse as well as instruct. *Blaže and Nežica in Sunday School,* a kind of mini-encyclopedia in Slovene, is one notable example. In order to ensure that Slovenes would always have access to good books in their language, Fr. Slomšek founded the Society of St. Hermagor in 1853, Slovenia's first publishing house. The Society was responsible for the publication of hundreds of Slovene language books and pamphlets in the mid-nineteenth century. It maintains an active presence today in Slovenia proper (Celje) and in Slovene areas of Austria (Klagenfurt) and Italy (Gorizia), so that citizens there will not lose touch with their heritage.

Fr. Slomšek was an active evangelist for Slovene language and culture whose deeds matched and even exceeded his words. Even more important, perhaps, was his worldview. He spent many years as Bishop of Maribor, in modern-day Styria province—an area of mixed Slovene and German population in his day. Although he sometimes encountered anti-Slovene sentiment among Germans there, he never responded in kind. In fact, he did the opposite, actively teaching and promoting his language while taking great care to be respectful and tolerant in his dealings with non-Slovenes. To do otherwise was unbecoming to a Christian, also dangerous in a multiethnic state like Austria-Hungary. "Extreme nationalism," Fr. Slomšek once said, "will be the cause of a terrible conflict which will make people turn on one another like savages." Subsequent events demonstrated that he was prescient as well as wise.

In 1999, almost seventy-five years after supporters opened a case for sainthood, Pope John Paul II announced that he would visit Slovenia to celebrate the beatification of Fr. Slomšek. The Pope almost certainly intended to send a message to the parties then at war in Kosovo by highlighting the life of an apostle of tolerance. "I would like to show the testament of the Blessed Slomšek," John Paul said in Maribor on 19 September 1999. "His example bears witness to the fact that it is possible to be a sincere patriot, and with the same sincerity live and cooperate with people of other nationalities, cultures and faiths." But Slovenes anxious about their culture and nationality in the new Europe can follow Fr. Slomšek's example, too. His personal motto was, "speak little, work a lot, support everything" that is positive about Slovenia and Slovenes. In fact, that is the special contribution Slovenes can make in Europe: speaking little, working a lot, and promoting their culture and language proudly and enthusiastically, without a hint of superiority or pridefulness. The recent history of nationalist-inspired violence on the continent shows clearly what a unique—and valuable—gift this will be.

question: how to preserve and advance them in the wider world?

The new era has already provided equal parts opportunity and challenge for Slovene literature. As books and analyses of the Balkan wars flooded the world's book markets, American and European scholars discovered Edvard Kocbek. His poetry has won acclaim in a variety of forums and attracted the interest of talented translators such as Michael Scammell. As collections of his work are published, a new generation of students and poetry lovers gets crucial exposure to Slovene letters. Responding to recent events, Slovene scholars have successfully resurrected the works of writers from earlier periods, such as Vladimir Bartol. Bartol's 1938 novel, *Alamut,* which chronicled a holy war waged by Persian Muslims against Turkish invaders, suddenly resonated in the wake of the events of 11 September 2001 and has appeared in fifteen languages, including Arabic. *Alamut* introduced thousands of Europeans to Slovene literature and made its publisher very happy. Contemporary writers have had no such breakthrough. They have traditionally been at their best when issues of national destiny loom large in public consciousness. Since the major issues associated with Slovenia's future seem to have been solved, they will have to find new questions to answer, new windmills at which to tilt. They also must reckon with the easy availability of popular fiction from Europe and America, published in translation. Their challenge, therefore, is to find an acceptable niche in a huge, profit-driven market.

Slovene musicians, artists, and filmmakers have a wider audience now, as members of the European Union. Like their compatriots in business, their principal task is to market themselves outside Slovenia, to find a way to make themselves known to the European public and beyond. They will benefit from their ability to access Ljubljana's well-known cultural infrastructure, which includes the Cankarjev center and the Ljubljana Summer Festival, which attract many international visitors. They can also compete for EU Culture 2000 resources, which provide funding for general and specific cultural projects. The future of Slovene folk art depends on the success of Slovene tourism and museum staffers' skill at winning EU funds in various categories and negotiating successful corporate partnerships. The days of government largesse for the arts having given way to market forces and individual initiative, Slovene cultural officials will draw on their ability to adapt.

The Slovene language does not appear to be endangered by EU membership. However, efforts to promote it could make good things happen. The Slovene Ministry of Culture would do well to emulate programs like the Summer School of Hungarian Language and Culture, held several times each year in Debrecen and Budapest, Hungary. Founded to raise awareness of Hungarian culture in the unfortunate aftermath of the Trianon Treaty of 1920 (which saw Hungary lose two-thirds of its territory), these intensive language and culture courses have attracted thousands of students from Europe, Asia, and America. These individuals tend to become unofficial ambassadors for Hungary, singing its praises at home, returning to work there, and even launching Hungarian-related business ventures both in Hungary and their home countries. A similar institution, perhaps based in Ljubljana and a prominent regional city, could serve as a means of extending the reach of the Slovene language. It could also pay dividends in tourism and foreign investment as it continually introduces Slovenia to the world.

POLITICS

Slovene political leaders have their own list of challenges and opportunities for the twenty-first century. They will help shape the destiny of Europe as deliberations on the European Union constitution continue. They also stand to emerge as a regional leader within the EU because of their involvement with the Slovene populations remaining in Austria and Italy and their unique history as both a European and Balkan country. Closer to home, they are deeply invested in the successful reconstruction of the war-torn Balkan area as leaders of the Southeast European Stability pact. Domestically, their principal responsibility in the near future is managing change, especially the country's entry into the European Union. This includes a variety of official tasks, such as arranging for the euro to replace the tolar as the country's currency, proceeding with other essential economic reforms, and bringing its border crossings with Croatia and Italy up to EU standards. It also means presiding over and planning for the distribution of EU funds for the restructuring of key economic sectors. Slovenia's politicians have a lot at stake as they tackle the latter task; many citizens are likely to lose their livelihoods in the process and face the necessity of finding other employment or retraining. How well their representatives help them cope with these changes will determine the shape of the political landscape in the next few years.

There is a hint of self-congratulation in the Slovene government's Web site celebrating the country's tenth anniversary. Slovenia's successes, the authors assert, have made it the envy of all countries emerging from socialism, "a champion that cannot be ignored, for it stands out above the others in every field." As the old saying goes, however, it is not bragging if one can back it up. By any reasonable measurement, Slovenia has had an extraordinarily successful first decade of independence. The most formidable challenge for the fathers of that independence will be to follow this remarkable first act.

SELECTIVE BIBLIOGRAPHY

Apicultural Museum. "Gallery of Painted Front Boards," http://rcul.uni-lj.si/~bfbee/muzej/muzej.html (accessed 5 August 2004).

Banac, Ivo. *The National Question in Yugoslavia.* New Haven: Yale University Press, 1984.

Bank of Slovenia. "Banknotes and Coins," http://www.bsi.si/html/eng/banknotes_coins/banknotes/index.html (accessed 5 August 2004).

Barbalic, Fran. "The Jugoslavs of Italy." *Slavonic Review* 15, no. 43 (July 1936): 177–190.

Barber, Tony. "Welcome to Slovenia." *Independent,* 31 March 1991.

Benderley, Jill, and Evan Kraft. *Independent Slovenia.* New York: St. Martin's, 1994.

Berk, Edi, and Janez Bogataj, eds. *Traditional Arts and Crafts in Slovenia.* Ljubljana: Domus, 1993.

Bernard, Antonia. *Petite histoire de la Slovénie.* Paris: Institut d'études slaves, 1996.

Brân, Zoë. *After Yugoslavia.* Melbourne: Lonely Planet, 2001.

Bruni, Frank. "Unheralded Gem on the Adriatic." *New York Times,* 5 August 2001.

Burkhardt, Francois, ed. *Jože Plečnik Architect, 1872–1957.* Cambridge: MIT Press, 1989.

Caparetto Museum Site and Virtual Tour. http://www.kobariski-muzej.si (accessed 5 August 2004).

Carroll, James. "We Are Not Guilty of Anything." *Boston Globe,* 5 April 1994.

Chamber of Commerce and Industry of Slovenia. *Slovenia Business Week,* http://www.gzs.si/eng/news/sbw (accessed 5 August 2004).

Cooper, Henry. *France Prešeren.* Boston: Twayne, 1981.

Delegation of the European Commission to the United States. "European Union in the US," www.eurunion.org (accessed 5 August 2004).

Djilas, Milovan. *Conversations with Stalin.* New York: Harcourt Brace, 1985.

Dolenc, Milan. *Lipizzaner: The Story of the Horses of Lipica: Commemorating the 400th Anniversary of the Lipizzaner.* St. Paul, MN: Control Data Arts, 1981.

Dyer, Richard. "Everything's Up to Date in Slovenia." *Boston Globe,* 15 October 1995.

Economist Intelligence Unit. *Slovenia: Country Profile 2001.* New York: Economist Intelligence Unit, 2001.

Fink-Haftner, Danica, and John R. Robbins. *Making a New Nation: The Formation of Slovenia.* Aldershot, UK: Dartmouth, 1997.

Gostisa, Lojze, ed. *Arhitekt Jože Plečnik.* Ljubljana: Mladska knjiga, 1968.

Government of the Republic of Slovenia, Public Relations and Media Office. *Slovenia: Ten Years of Independence,* http://www.uvi.si/10years/independence (accessed 5 August 2004).

Government PR and Media Office. *Republic of Slovenia,* http://www.uvi.si/eng (accessed 5 August 2004).

Gow, James, and Cathie Carmichael. *Slovenia and the Slovenes. A Small State and the New Europe.* Bloomington: Indiana University Press, 2000.

Harris, Marie. "Spirited, Independent Slovenia." *New York Times,* 11 May 1997.

Jelavich, Barbara. *The Habsburg Empire in European Affairs, 1814–1918.* Chicago: Rand McNally, 1968.

Jelavich, Charles. *South Slav Nationalisms: Textbooks and Yugoslav Unions before 1914.* Columbus: Ohio State University Press, 1990.

Juvanec, Borut. "Slovene Architecture: Kozolec," www.ijs.si/kozolci (accessed 5 August 2004).

Keegan, John. *World War I.* New York: Knopf, 1999.

Kirk, Tim. "Limits to Germandom: Resistance to the Nazi Annexation of Slovenia." *Slavonic and East European Review* 69, no.4 (October 1993): 646–647.

Klopčič, Vera, and Janez Stergar, ed. *Ethnic Minorities in Slovenia.* Ljubljana: Institute for Ethnic Studies, 1994.

Ladika, Susan. "Slovenia Surges Ahead of Its Neighbors." *San Francisco Chronicle,* 14 April 1997.

Lampe, John. *Yugoslavia as History: Twice There Was a Country.* Cambridge: Cambridge University Press, 1996.

May, Arthur J. *The Habsburg Empire, 1867–1914.* New York: Norton, 1968.

McNeil, Donald G. "Lipizzaner Stallions Dance into Trade Brawl." *New York Times,* 11 March 2000.

Nacionalni Atlas Slovenije. Ljubljana: Rokus Publishing House, 2001.

Natek, Karl, ed. *Discover Slovenia.* Ljubljana zalozba, 1992.

National Gallery, http://www.ng-slo.si/ngeng (accessed 5 August 2004).

NATO. "Issues: Enlargement," www.nato.int/issues/enlargement/index.html (accessed 5 August 2004).

Novak, Boris A. "Poetry in the Slovene Language," www.leftcurve.org/LC22WebPages/slovene.html (accessed 5 August 2004).

Prešeren, Polona. "Wine—Testament to Our Uniqueness." *Slovenia News* 14 (8 April 2003), http://slonews.sta.si (accessed 5 August 2004).

Puhar, Alenka, ed. *The Case of Slovenia.* Ljubljana: Nova Revija, 1991.

Ramet, Sabrina Petra. *Nationalism and Federalism in Yugoslavia, 1962–91.* 2d ed. Bloomington: Indiana University Press, 1992.

———. "The Slovenian Success Story." *Current History* 97, no. 617 (1998): 113–118.

———. "Slovenia's Road to Democracy." *Europe-Asia Studies* 45, no. 5 (1993): 869–886.

Rocks, David. "Slovenia Company Surviving after Loss of Yugoslavia." *Boston Globe,* 5 July 1993.

Rogel, Carole. "The Education of a Slovene Marxist: Edward Kardelj, 1924–1934." *Slovene Studies* 11, no. 1–2 (1989): 177–184.

———. *The Slovenes and Yugoslavism, 1890–1914.* New York: Columbia University Press, 1977.

———. "Slovenia's Independence: A Reversal of History." *Problems of Communism* 40 (July–August 1991): 34–40.

Rusinow, Denison. *The Yugoslav Experiment, 1948–74.* Berkeley: University of California Press, 1977.

Silber, Laura, and Alan Little. *Yugoslavia: Death of a Nation.* New York: Binyon, 1997.

Slovenia News, http://slonews.sta.si/index.php (accessed 5 August 2004).

Slovenian Film Fund, http://www.film-sklad.si/eng (accessed 5 August 2004).

Souda, Claude. "Le Domaine Movia." *Le Nouvel Observateur,* 14 August 2003.

Special Coordinator of the Stability Pact for South Eastern Europe. "Stability Pact for South Eastern Europe," http://www.stabilitypact.org (accessed 5 August 2004).

Spolar, Christine. "Bosnian War Refugees Languish in Slovenia." *Boston Globe,* 9 January 1993.

Stanovnik, Janez. "Planning through the Market: The Jugoslav Experience." *Foreign Affairs* 40, no. 2 (January 1962): 252–263.
Steichen, Girard C. "Slovenia's Next Test Is Economic." *Christian Science Monitor,* 11 July 1991.
"Survey of Slovenia." *Financial Times,* 28 April 1997.
Toš, Niko, and Vlado Meheljak. *Slovenia between Continuity and Change, 1990–1997: Analysis, Documents, Data*. Berlin: Editions Signal, 2002.
Virtual Slovenia, www.matkurja.com/eng (accessed 5 August 2004).
Williams, Carol J. "Slovenia Abuzz over Its Unique Beehive Art." *Los Angeles Times,* 2 February 1994.
Wilson, Neil. *Lonely Planet Slovenia*. Victoria, Australia: Lonely Planet, 2001.

CHRONOLOGY

149 B.C.E.	Ptuj is mentioned in Roman chronicles, making it the oldest known Slovene town.
Seventh century	Slavic peoples arrive in the eastern Alps of Central Europe.
623	Prince Samo leads Slovenes in the overthrow of the Avars.
745	Duke of Karantania accepts Christianity.
1144	Ljubljana first appears in chronicles as Laibach.
1146	Stična Monastery founded, oldest in Slovene lands.
Thirteenth century	Slovenes come under the jurisdiction of the Habsburg monarchy.
1550	Primož Trubar's Slovene primer and translation of the New Testament become the first books published in the Slovene language.
1584	Jurij Dalmatin makes available the entire Bible in Slovene.
1701	Ljubljana Philharmonic founded.
1740–1790	Reign of Maria-Theresa and Joseph II of Austria, a crucial period of reform for Slovenes and other Habsburg subjects.
1758	First appearance of thematic painting on a beehive front—Madonna and Child on a hive in Carniola province.
1768	Marco Pohlin's *Carniolan Grammar* appears in print.
1790	Anton Linhart publishes the first history of the South Slavic peoples, including the Slovenes.
1797	Inaugural issue of first Slovene-language newspaper ever published, *Lublanske novice* (Ljubljana News).
1809	Illyrian Provinces created by Napoleon; large parts of Slovene territories included; Slovene introduced as language of instruction in primary schools.
1813	Illyrian Provinces end with Napoleon's defeat and retreat.
1844	France Prešeren's "Zdravljica" (The Toast) published; becomes the anthem of independent Slovenia 150 years later.
1848	Year of revolution in Habsburg monarchy; Slovenia's national program enunciated, including provisions for use of the Slovene language and calls for possible administrative unity for Slovene lands in the monarchy.
1864	Matica slovenska society founded.
1867	*Ausgleich* (Compromise) concluded between Austria and Hungary; divides monarchy into two halves, united only in person of the emperor and for certain national issues. Some 40,000 Slovenes assigned to Hungarian half of the empire.
28 June 1914	Archduke Franz Ferdinand assassinated in Sarajevo, Bosnia; Austria's decision to punish Serbian government backed by Germany, triggering World War I.
26 April 1915	Treaty of London concluded; part of Slovene territory promised to Italians, on condition that they enter the war on Allied side.
29 May 1917	Anton Korošec reads the May Declaration in the Austrian Parliament, calling for the reorganization of the Habsburg monarchy into three parts, one of which would be for the monarchy's Slovenes, Croats, and Serbs.
20 June 1917	Yugoslav Committee head Ante Trumbić meets Serbian prime minister Nikola Pašić. Their talks produce the Corfu Declaration, a blueprint for an independent South Slavic state composed of Serbs, Croats, and Slovenes.
October 1917	The Habsburg monarchy wins the battle of Caporetto. Caporetto subsequently passes into Italian and later Slovene hands. Known today as Kobarid.
6 October 1918	The Narodno Vijeće, the National Council of the Habsburg South Slavic peoples, is formed. It will unite with Serbia to form a South Slav state.
1 December 1918	Kingdom of Serbs, Croats, and Slovenes proclaimed.
1919	University of Ljubljana founded.
June 1920	Treaty of Trianon signed, transferring the Prekmurje area and its Hungarian and Slovene residents to the new Kingdom of Serbs, Croats, and Slovenes.
28 June 1920	The first constitution of the Kingdom of Serbs, Croats, and Slovenes is ratified in Belgrade, codifying Serb centralist rule in the state.
10 October 1920	Austria is declared the winner of the Carinthia plebiscite; thousands of Slovenes become citizens of Austria.

1921	Treaty of Rapallo signed. Former Austrian Adriatic lands transferred to Italy; some 300,000 Slovenes go with them.
6 January 1929	King Alexander suspends the parliamentary life of the Kingdom of Serbs, Croats, and Slovenes and renames the state "Yugoslavia."
30 October 1934	King Alexander assassinated in Marseilles, France; Prince Paul becomes regent and lifts the dictatorship.
1938	Slovene Academy of Sciences founded in Ljubljana.
14 December 1940	Anton Korošec, de facto Slovene leader since 1914, dies.
27 March 1941	Serbian officers overthrow the government of Prince Paul, reject Yugoslavia's participation in the Tripartite Pact, and install their own representative.
6 April 1941	The German army invades Yugoslavia; Slovene lands are expropriated by Italy, Germany, and Hungary.
April 1941	Edward Kardelj leads Slovene resistance fighters in the foundation of the Osvobodilna fronta (OF, Liberation Front).
1943	The journal *Mladina,* Slovene youth magazine, founded.
November 1943	OF formally unites with Tito's Partisan organization under the rubric of "brotherhood and unity."
May 1945	Tito, Kardelj, and the Partisans emerge victorious from both the Yugoslav and world wars and prepare for a new Yugoslavia. Slovenes become one of six republics in the new state.
Summer 1945	Thousands of Domobranci, Slovene anticommunist resistance fighters, executed by the new Yugoslav leadership.
28 June 1948	Stalin expels Yugoslavia from the Cominform. Edward Kardelj emerges as a major architect of the new theoretical foundation for the state.
June 1950	Kardelj's Law on Workers' Self-Management announced.
1954	London Agreement settles Yugoslav-Italian territorial disputes. Yugoslavia receives Adriatic littoral, including Koper (Capodistria) and Piran (Pirano); Italy is given jurisdiction over Trieste.
May 1955	Austrian state treaty signed, guaranteeing minority rights for Slovenes in Austria.
1956	Yugoslav Investment Bank founded at Belgrade, designed to help remedy economic imbalances among the Yugoslav republics.
June 1961	First meeting in Belgrade of the nonaligned movement, a gathering of states formally aligned with neither east nor west.
1962	Gorenje enterprises shift focus from agricultural machinery to home appliances, "everything for the home." Emblematic of new Slovene economic priorities.
1979	Kardelj, the leading Slovene of Communist Yugoslavia and one of its founding fathers, dies.
May 1980	Tito, founder of Yugoslavia and Kardelj's close colleague, dies.
February 1987	The Slovene journal *Nova revija* publishes issue 57, "On the Realization of a Slovene National Program."
24 April 1987	Slobodan Milošević makes incendiary appearance amid Kosovo Serb-Albanian rioting; declares Serbs "will not be beaten again."
February 1988	Staffers of provocative youth magazine *Mladina* arrested for possession and copying of a classified document; Yugoslav army presumed behind the arrest and subsequent trial in July 1988.
September 1989	Slobodan Milošević announces a Serb economic boycott of Slovenia over Kosovo criticism, amendments to Slovene constitution.
January 1990	Slovenian Communist leaders quit the Yugoslav League of Communists.
April 1990	First multiparty elections held in Slovenia; anticommunist DEMOS coalition and longtime Communist leader Milan Kučan emerge victorious.
December 1990	Slovenes vote overwhelmingly for sovereignty.
February 1991	Slovenia announces it will declare independence in June unless Yugoslav government agrees to a confederated arrangement.
25 June 1991	Milan Kučan makes formal declaration of independence.
26 June 1991	Yugoslav army troops cross into Slovenia in attempt to stop Slovenes' breakaway; ten-day war ensues, in which sixty-six people lose their lives.
7 July 1991	Brioni agreement imposes three-month delay in granting Slovene independence.
15 January 1992	European Community formally recognizes the independent Slovene state.
May 1992	Slovenia becomes a member of the United Nations.
January–December 1992	Thousands of Bosnian refugees seek refuge in Slovenia.
November 1992	First general election in independent Slovenia. Voters elect Milan Kučan as president of Slovenia and return a majority of Liberal Democrats to the legislature, making Janez Drnovšek prime minister.

May 1993	Slovenia becomes a member of the Council of Europe.
30 March 1994	Slovenia joins the Partnership for Peace, a group for states preparing for NATO membership.
1996	Slovenia accepted as an associate member of the European Union.
November 1997	Kučan elected to a second term as president with 55 percent of the vote.
March 1998	Slovenia begins negotiations leading to full EU membership.
November 2000	Liberal Democrats and likeminded parties returned to power in the country's third national elections.
25 June 2001	Slovenia marks ten years of independence.
November 2002	Kučan completes his second and final term as Slovene president. Longtime colleague Janez Drnovšek replaces him.
November 2002	Slovenia's formal acceptance in NATO and the European Union confirmed, effective mid-2004.
March 2003	Slovenes vote decisively in favor of entry into the EU.
April 2004	Slovenia enters NATO.
1 May 2004	Slovenia becomes a member of the EU.